OPERATING SYSTEM FORENSICS

OPERATING SYSTEM FORENSICS

Ric Messier

Kevin Mackay, Technical Editor

AMSTERDAM • BOSTON • HEIDELBERG • LONDON
NEW YORK • OXFORD • PARIS • SAN DIEGO
SAN FRANCISCO • SINGAPORE • SYDNEY • TOKYO

Syngress is an imprint of Elsevier

Acquiring Editor: Chris Katsaropoulos
Editorial Project Manager: Anna Valutkevich
Project Manager: Punithavathy Govindaradjane
Designer: Mark Rogers

Syngress is an imprint of Elsevier
225 Wyman Street, Waltham, MA 02451, USA

ISBN: 978-0-12-801949-8

British Library Cataloguing-in-Publication Data
A catalogue record for this book is available from the British Library

Library of Congress Cataloging-in-Publication Data
A catalog record for this book is available from the Library of Congress

For information on all Syngress publications visit
our website at http://store.elsevier.com/Syngress

This book is dedicated to Harold and his purple crayon.
And Opus. I may not have gotten here without them.

Contents

8. Log Files

9. Executable Programs

10. Malware

11. Mobile Operating Systems

12. Newer Technologies

13. Reporting

Foreword

For the past few years, there seems to have been regular overhauls in the operating systems used by everyday people. Microsoft and Apple have both begun to release new versions of their operating systems with increasing regularity, now having low or no cost upgrades available. While this can be exciting for users, it can create headaches for the Digital Forensic analyst trying to keep up with the evidence that is coming across their desk. Each operating system, be it an Apple OS X version, Windows, or Linux distribution, has sources of evidence specific to it. All this plus the fact that mobile versions of operating systems are generally at least as regular their desktop brethren. Until now, there has been no single definitive resource on modern operating systems and all the aspects of investigations that go along with these operating systems.

Not too long ago, I was a student of Ric Messier in an undergraduate program for Digital Forensics. In this program, we were using the latest books available as the textbooks for our courses. That meant that there was a book for Windows, a book for OS X, and a book for Linux, not to mention the books specifically for iOS and Android, as well as each File System. While all of these resources were no doubt well written and informative, they were very specific, and sadly, they were a few generations behind the times. This book will be very helpful to begin to fill in the gaps. This will mean having one book as a resource for all of the major operating systems that an examiner will come into contact with during the regular course of their job. In addition, this contains information about newer versions of the operating systems. With new sources of evidence seemingly being introduced with each new operating system, having an updated resource with details on these latest sources can mean the difference between winning and losing a case.

As if that were not enough, Ric adds even more value by going into detail on various File Systems and their structures, as well as covering topics that have not been covered in any of the previous Operating Systems books that I have seen. Specific coverage on topics such as Mobile Forensics, Cloud Artifacts, Memory Analysis, and reporting just continue to make this book a must have for a forensic examiner. This ensures that this book will provide "soup to nuts" coverage of the entire subject matter. Topics as basic as "What is an operating system?" to as complex as "What does a file entry look like in HFS+?" will be covered in this one resource. One often overlooked topic that should get far more attention than it does, forensic reporting, will also be covered and completed with examples. While this is commonly the least favorite part of most examiner's jobs, a good report can make all the difference in everyday life as an examiner. With sample reports included in the book, you no longer have an excuse not to get reporting right.

Coming from a family of lawyers, as well as having experience working with various law enforcement agencies, I am well aware of some of the struggles faced by these professionals when faced with very technical subject matter. As with all forensic examiners who try to keep current, I am accustomed needing to buy books regularly to keep up to date with each of the various topics that are covered within this book. Having the information condensed makes it more readily available those who do not specialize in forensics and do not have the time to read all of the books that litter my desk and bookshelves. Lawyers trying to prosecute cases with digital evidence involved still need to have some background information so they will know what Alternate Data Streams are and how someone was trying to be sneaky using one. With digital evidence being part of nearly every court case, not to mention the entire topic of cyber warfare, these topics should be more common and more available for the masses.

This book covers nearly every aspect of a Digital Forensic case, and thus should be required reading for all examiners and students alike. As a Consultant at FireEye's Mandiant, this book will be kept handy as a resource for any of the less common items that come across my desk during my investigations, as well as for helping to keep everything fresh in my head. This one book will be replacing a shelf full of older resources as my new go-to manual. When Ric first mentioned to me that he was considering writing a book on Operating Systems, I was immediately excited. I knew that he would be able to condense all the information that used to take a handful of books into one book that covered far more than just operating systems. I can say with certainty that I wish this book were around a few years earlier, not just so that I would have had a more updated and helpful book to learn from, but to save me from carrying so many books around as a student going from class to class.

D.J. Palombo
Consultant, Global Security
Consulting Services
Mandiant, a FireEye Company

Preface

The writing of this book took about a year and a half. This was a time period that saw me through the break-up of or conscious uncoupling from a long-term relationship, a job change, the loss of my sister to cancer, seeing the last stages of my father's heart failure, and a lot of the usual ups and downs and bumps and bruises of life. I am thankful to have gotten to the end of this project. Thanks to my friend and technical editor, Kevin Mackay, for sanity checks and making sure I was still on the track and covering important concepts. Also, thanks to my friends Erin Maslon (nee Gruene), Allan Konar, and D.J. Palombo for being around to bounce ideas off and sanity check what I was writing.

I am also grateful to the dean, Dr Mika Nash, and assistant dean, Bob Green, of the Division of Continuing Professional Studies at Champlain College for giving me a place to be and a purpose for the last year and change. Also, for the hope that I am contributing and making a difference.

Ric Messier

My thanks to Ric Messier for allowing me to be a part of this fun project, John Revel, who helped me regain my inner peace by explaining that God has a plan, my daughter Lexi, who is an inspiration to me, keep up the hard work champ, I am so proud of you. And finally, my beautiful wife Tama, you are my rock and always push me to succeed. I love you and would be lost without you. Thank you for everything.

From *Kevin Mackay*, who is a sworn law enforcement officer in Fairfield County Connecticut where he has worked as a computer forensic investigator and assistant IT administrator. He is a state certified law enforcement instructor and teaches digital forensics at Champlain College, where he is an adjunct professor. He provides beta testing for Blackbag Technology.

Kevin Mackay

CHAPTER

1

Forensics and Operating Systems

INFORMATION INCLUDED IN THIS CHAPTER:

- A definition of forensics
- Description of some relevant laws
- A definition of operating systems
- A description of operating environments and shells

INTRODUCTION

While my most interesting experience in the field of forensics was trying to determine whether a coworker had been viewing and making use of pornography at his desk. My first experience with forensics was about 15 years ago, when I was working at a company that offered web hosting for customers. Certainly the pornography makes a more interesting story. At the time of my first experience, though, there was not a lot of information about how to perform a forensic analysis, though Wietse Venema and Dan Farmer had put together a course about that time and they had posted some notes to a website. That and the software they wrote, The Coroner's Toolkit, was what was available. As a result, I had to rely on what I knew about the underlying details of the operating system and the applications that were running on it. It is one thing to take one of the commercial software tools that will automate a lot of the forensic analysis for you. However, I find it useful to know what is happening under the hood, so I can not only interpret the results correctly, but also, I can see if they make sense based on the input that has been provided.

While there are several things that have changed over the years since I was first an undergraduate, one thing that really stands out for me is how technology is abstracting the user experience from the underlying system, both software and hardware. This is also true for developers. Where you used to know a lot about the system architecture to be successful as a programmer because resources were limited and you needed to make the best use of the resources you have, now resources like memory and disk are very cheap. Additionally, there are more than enough programming libraries that take care of a lot of the low level details. Programming languages such as Java and Python also take away a lot of the need to understand what is going on underneath.

The reason for bringing this up is that educating information technology students has changed along with the times. There is no longer the need to teach some of the deeper concepts of operating systems and system architecture to the majority of students and practitioners because they just do not need to know them. All of the details are being handled for them so it is better to let them focus on the aspects of technology that they will be impacted by in their day-to-day professional lives.

However, when a forensic investigator gets handed a system that has been involved in a crime, it is helpful for the investigator to know more than just how to run an application that is going to generate a report. The investigator needs to know what makes sense and where to follow up more deeply. In this regard, they should know more about operating systems and where critical information is stored, not to mention where a user may hide information. Every operating system has nooks and crannies along with various quirks. Understanding these nuances will allow an investigator to validate his results by examining the actual location of items that were parsed out with an automated process. This can provide evidence that the tools are working correctly.

And we now rejoin our regularly scheduled program already in progress. Knowing the details of each of the operating systems is helpful. That is where this book comes in. The idea behind this book is to talk about the details of the Windows, Linux, and Mac OS X operating systems in the context of a forensic analysis. Having said that, it is worth talking about what forensics and operating systems are before we jump into the deep end.

FORENSICS

You may be aware of how computer forensics works from watching shows like NCIS where the law enforcement investigators quickly and easily break into systems, through firewalls and around encryption to obtain information. In the real world, it does not work like that. First of all, we have legal issues to contend with. In fact, the word forensics itself comes from the Latin *forensis*, meaning public. It is related to the word forum, which meant a marketplace or public square in a Roman city. The word forensics, specifically, is about public debate or discussion, though it is commonly used to refer to things that relate to a court or legal proceeding. Our legal proceedings are a form of public discourse or debate, so the word forensics came to relate to legal matters and in the case of the topic for this book, it is about evidence that is prepared to present at trial.

Because of this, while there is an enormous technical aspect to forensics, there is also at its foundation, an understanding of the legal aspects of the tasks at hand. We often talk about performing a forensic investigation even when there isn't anything legal involved. You may be asked to perform an investigation on a corporate system because of a policy violation. This was the case when I was asked to take a look at the system of the employee who was looking at pornography at his desktop. He was likely going to be fired just based on the evidence of his manager, a woman, who was walking by his desk and witnessed the activity. However, they were looking for some amount of corroboration, so I was asked to take a look.

This was a case of a policy violation and a firing. However, there is always something to be taken into consideration when performing an investigation. At some point, there may be a need to go to court. If there were child pornography on the computer, for instance, it would need to be referred to law enforcement for appropriate prosecution. Anything I do to the system might compromise a prosecution of the employee, so I have to be very careful about what I do. I always need to be concerned with the handling of the evidence. It may also not be a case of a prosecution of the employee. The employee may make a case for wrongful termination, arguing something like malware on his system displaying pornographic images. Of course, if he was caught hat in hand, so to speak, that would be a different story, but it may not change the fact that he may sue the company. Once again, how I handle the evidence is incredibly important.

Along these lines, one of the most important concepts to talk about is the chain of custody. A chain of custody is the documentation of everywhere a piece of evidence has been as well as who the evidence has been handed off to. When someone hands the evidence off to someone else, both parties need to be documented. Additionally, there should be a way to verify that nothing has been changed. As a result, it is good to indicate what was done with the evidence and how it was validated as not having been tampered with along the way. With digital evidence, this is easily handled. Other types of evidence are less easily validated.

Evidence Inclusion and Exclusion

Regarding the handling of evidence; as it turns out, we have rules for that. Lawyers write them and they take some getting used to. They are also open to interpretation. It is worth mentioning at this point that there are three kinds of legal systems in the world currently. The following are the three different legal systems you will run across in different countries around the world.

- Civil law: Civil law originated in Europe and in terms of geography, it is the most predominant legal system you will find. Civil law countries define a set of laws and those laws are used to base legal decisions on. This may seem like something that is intuitive. After all, if we didn't base legal decisions on laws, what do we base them on? The difference here is that each individual judge is allowed to make his or her own interpretation of the law as it is written.
- Common law: Like civil law, common law makes use of a set of laws but assumes those laws need to be interpreted by judges. Those interpretations build into what is called case law, where the set of rulings made by previous judges can be used as a precedent to base new rulings on. While the legal system is founded on laws and statutes, the rulings take precedence over the plain details of the law. Civil law systems put the written laws over previous rulings, which is the major difference between the two systems.
- Sharia (Islamic law): Sharia is used in Islamic countries. Countries that use Islamic law use the Qu'ran as the basis for a moral code and a set of laws. These codes and laws are used to hold the citizens of the country accountable. Where legislatures commonly develop laws in other countries, there is no such process in countries bound by Islamic law. There are also no lawyers or juries. Defendants and plaintiffs are expected to represent themselves. The ruling of the judge is final. There are no statutes to rely on and the ruling of the judge does not bind any subsequent judges to a particular ruling.

The United States is a common law country, as is Canada, Australia, and a small handful of other countries. In the United States, the interpretation of the laws by judges builds up case law, which is what is used for subsequent judges to base decisions and rulings on. This is why it is relevant to talk about the types of legal systems when we talk about federal rules of evidence, since there is a set of case law built up around these rules. We base all of our evidence handling processes and procedures around this case law, so it is useful to know and understand it.

One of the first things to know about these rules is that they are bound up with the constitutional idea that everyone has the right to face those who provide evidence against them. This is in the sixth amendment, which also specifies that you have the right to a speedy trial. This is a challenge in the case of computer-based evidence since you cannot confront, challenge or question a computer. As a result, computer evidence has a challenge inherent in it. Any time you have evidence that is introduced in court by a person who is not called to provide the evidence or testimony directly, you are introducing hearsay and because everyone on trial has the right to question those providing evidence, it is not admissible as a way to establish a set of facts. Hearsay is a statement that took place out of court used to prove the truth. It is worth keeping in mind that the goal of any trial or court case is to find the truth of any particular matter. The court, meaning the judge or jury, is the trier of facts and the goal of anyone involved is to introduce facts and evidence to help the court come to the truth.

The truth is something of a lofty goal, of course, considering that in many cases the strategy will be to obfuscate information and in many other cases, there simply is not enough information to come to a conclusive truth. So, the goal is to come to enough of the truth to make the right decision. The purpose of introducing evidence is to help arrive at the truth in a fair way. Introducing evidence that cannot be appropriately questioned or examined is not considered to be fair. As a result, it is excluded. You might think that if I find a file on a computer, it must belong to the owner of the computer, and so why does this file need to be questioned? Even if a file is found on a computer it does not guarantee that the file belongs to the computer's owner. If you are connected to a network, someone could have placed it there. You may have acquired some malicious software that put it there. There is nothing about the file being on the computer that necessarily makes it the property of the computer's owner. It is important to place the suspect behind the keyboard, meaning put them at the scene of the crime when it happened. When a system has multiple users, this can be more challenging.

This does not mean that all digital evidence is excluded. There are circumstances where digital evidence can be admitted in court. A common exclusion to the hearsay rule is the allowance of business records. Records kept in the ordinary course of operating the business are exempt from the hearsay rule. Any activity that does not involve a human, meaning that it is something a computer program generates on its own, is not subject to the hearsay rule. For example, this might include system or application logs. Perhaps, a more specific example would be your Internet usage history since your browser keeps that without any human involvement. It is part of the normal operation of the browser. Instant messaging programs that keep records of conversations would also be considered an exception to the hearsay rule, in spite of the fact that it is the record of a conversation. Since a computer program recorded it, it is considered acceptable.

Of course, there are a number of other exceptions to the hearsay rule in the United States. Other countries have different rules regarding hearsay and not all countries place digital evidence in the hearsay category. This results in different standards for handling digital evidence in different countries. It is always worth checking on the regulations in whatever country you are working in.

Federal Rules of Evidence

The Federal Rules of Evidence (FRE) started life in 1965 when Supreme Court Chief Justice, Earl Warren appointed an advisory board to draft rules related to evidence handling. There was a desire to have a unified set of rules written down to make sure courts were handling the introduction of evidence in the same way. When they were eventually adopted as federal law in 1975, the legislation enacting them left open the possibility that states would introduce their own rules of evidence. Different states and local jurisdictions do have their own rules of evidence. Since this is not a legal text, I will not go into a lengthy discussion over the different sets of rules and while digital evidence can be used in a lot of cases, the major computer-based crimes themselves are based on federal law. As a result, we can somewhat arbitrarily decide, for the purpose of expedience, that we will have a brief discussion of the FRE.

The rules are reasonably comprehensive, including a lot of background and guidance on how to handle different types of evidence in different circumstances. One of my favorites, and also to give you an example for how comprehensive the rules are, is rule 403, Excluding Relevant Evidence for Prejudice, Confusion, Waste of Time, or Other Reasons. A judge can exclude evidence from trial if it appears to be prejudicial, meaning that it could lend itself to an interpretation that would not be fair to one party or another. The judge may also exclude evidence, if it appears to simply be a waste of time. Of course, the judge is also going to exclude evidence, if it is irrelevant to the case at hand but in this particular rule, the evidence is considered to be relevant.

Article VIII is about hearsay, including exceptions to the admissibility of something that may be considered to be hearsay. This is where, we are most concerned since computer records are essentially statements made out of court. The most important exception to be concerned with, as mentioned previously, is the exception for records of a regularly conducted activity. Since computer records are considered to fall into the category of regularly conducted activities, digital evidence like we will be discussing is considered admissible.

The thing about digital evidence is that it requires someone to explain it in simple terms to a jury and to the court. Forensic investigators may be called as expert witnesses to provide that explanation. Expert witness testimony is a very different skill than the technical skills needed to be a good forensic investigator, so not every investigator will be called as a witness. Because it is technical and requires an expert witness to explain it, it is considered to be scientific evidence. There are rules for the admissibility of scientific evidence. Generally, there are two ways that expert testimony is admitted and different states use different standards or tests to make that determination.

Frye Versus Daubert

In 1923, there was a case (Frye vs. United States) that began as a result of a conviction of a man named Frye for second-degree murder. His conviction came as a result of a polygraph test. The polygraph test was still very new at the time, particularly, when it came to being the foundation for a legal case. Frye appealed the conviction and the resulting ruling set the standard for decades for the admissibility of scientific evidence. What the ruling said was that any scientific evidence had to be commonly accepted within the field. This was to ensure that all of the proper vetting for the process or procedure had been done by the experts and that it was considered reliable. You may, after all, be basing a life in prison on something that is still experimental. That would not be fair to the defendant in the case. There is a lot of scientific evidence that cannot be admitted, in spite of how good and reliable it may be, simply because the professional community has not coalesced around its reliability as yet.

I am reminded of the case of Charlie Chaplin, who was brought into court in a paternity case, expecting him to pay child support for the baby of a woman he had a brief affair with. At the time, they did a blood test that demonstrated that he was not the child's father. However, blood testing was still new at the time and the evidence was not admissible so the ruling went against Chaplin. Ten years later, the California legislature passed a law allowing blood testing to be used as evidence in court cases and overturned the ruling against Chaplin. Technology continues to change and it takes some time for the world to catch up.

The Frye ruling created a standard test for the admissibility of evidence that ensured that the methods used were reliable and considered to be standard procedure. However, the Frye ruling is more than 90 years old and most states have moved away from using it as the standard. Instead, they use the more recent Daubert standard, which actually refers to the FRE.

In 1993, the Supreme Court ruled in Daubert versus Merrell Dow Pharmaceuticals that the FRE superseded the Frye test. In the FRE, section 702 states that expert testimony can be introduced if the expert's evidence can help the trier of fact come to the truth of a matter and if the testimony is based on sufficient facts. Also, the testimony must be based on reliable methods and procedures. This is different from the previous Frye test in that Frye expected there to be a consensus within the professional community regarding the method or procedure. Daubert suggests this not to be required, which opens the door to more scientific testimony than Frye would.

The Supreme Court ruling set Daubert, or the FRE, as the standard for all federal courts but states still are free to use their own standards for the admissibility of evidence. There are still more than a dozen states that have rejected Daubert and there are other states that neither accept nor reject Daubert. It is worth knowing, which is the prevailing standard in whatever jurisdiction you are working in. While most of the methods used in digital forensics are considered to be well-understood, operating systems are constantly changing and evolving and there may be new methods of data acquisition based on new ways of storing data. When file systems change, for example, there will be new methods for accessing the information from the file system. These new methods may not be admissible in a state where Frye is the standard but they may be admissible in a state where Daubert is the prevailing rule.

Evidence Handling

An important aspect of evidence rules is the requirement that you introduce the best possible evidence and also introduce originals. While all copies of digital evidence are considered to be original for the purposes of the court, you have to be very careful about how you handle it. Obviously, you want to do an investigation and you will need to get access to the evidence but you have to ensure that you do not alter it in anyway. The good news is that digital evidence is generally easily copied. Before you do anything, though, you need to get an idea of where you started. The typical, well-accepted way of doing that is to get a cryptographic hash of the evidence. This could be a Message Digest (MD) 5 hash, although the current preferred hash function is Secure Hash Algorithm (SHA) 1. This will generate a value that can be used to compare any subsequent copy against to ensure that it is identical. If we get the same hash value back from two different sets of evidence, we can be sure with a high degree of confidence that the evidence is identical.

Keeping evidence intact involves making identical copies, documenting every time you touch the evidence, including transporting it from one location to another or handing it off to another investigator. This would be where you would add to your documentation by noting all of this activity in a chain of custody record. It means using a write blocker, which is either a hardware device or a piece of software that prevents any write requests from going to a disk under investigation. This ensures that nothing is tampered with or altered during the course of the investigation.

While there will be expert testimony, there will also be evidence that will be introduced in court. This evidence needs to be in a state where it can be safely admitted. Without the ability to admit the evidence, you cannot put an expert witness on the stand to discuss and explain the evidence. Since the FRE was written before there was such a thing as digital evidence, they do not take digital evidence into account. Digital evidence has to be treated, more or less, like all other evidence except that it can be tampered with more easily, so we have to be especially careful with digital evidence so as not to put a court case at risk.

OPERATING SYSTEMS

First, let us get through some definitions. When you hear the term operating system, you likely envision something like in Figure 1.1. What you are looking at is the shell. The shell is the component that you see, also called the user interface. The operating system, in technical terms, is the software that interfaces with the hardware and controls the pieces of your computer system such as the processor, memory, hard disk, and other components. The shell can be changed or altered and you would still have the operating system that would allow you to do useful things with your computer. If you are used to Linux or Unix-like operating systems, you may be familiar with the term kernel. The kernel and the operating system can be considered synonymous. Sun Microsystems made the distinction by referring to the operating system as SunOS and the operating environment, which includes all of the programs that the users would use, including the shell as well as the graphical user interface.

Why make the distinction here? Because some operating systems allow you to change out the shell or the interface. In Windows, the shell is Windows Explorer. There have been third-party tools that change the shell from Windows Explorer to another interface. In Linux, you might see Gnome or KDE as your user interface but you can just as easily boot into a command line shell. In Mac OS, you can boot into single-user mode and get just a command line interface. No matter what the interface you are using for the operating environment, you still have the operating system. The operating system allows us to do the forensic analysis because it is responsible for memory management and file management as well as user management, logging, and other important details you will be looking for when you are performing an investigation on a system.

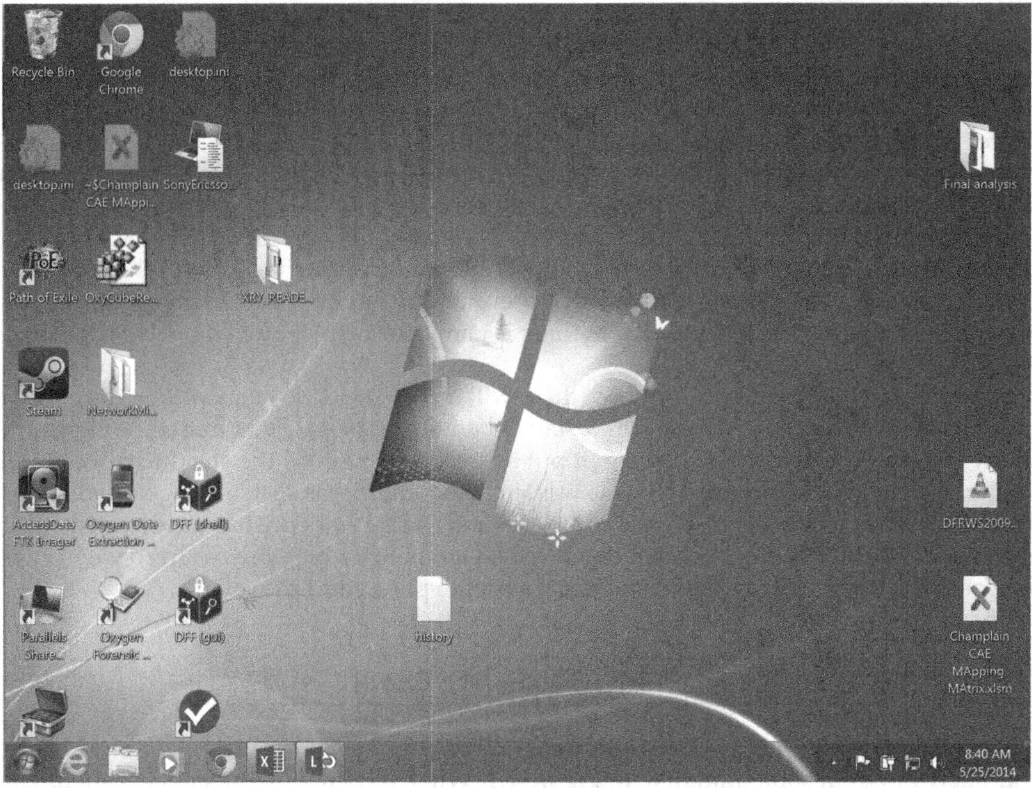

FIGURE 1.1 **Printed with permission from Microsoft.**

Another reason for making the distinction is because when we talk about Linux, there are a lot of different distributions that come with a lot of different software packages, including the user interface. Some people make a point to refer to the entire operating environment as GNU/Linux because a good portion of the software that a user will be interacting with comes from the GNU project. The one thing that is common across all of them is the kernel, which is called Linux. That is the operating system and the piece that provides the majority of relevant evidence that we will be looking for even if we would normally get to the information, or even create it, using the programs provided by the GNU project.

While at the technical level, there is a difference between the operating system and the operating environment. Most people are used to referring to the operating environment and not making much of a distinction between it and the underlying kernel. As a result, we will be using the term operating system to describe the entire collection of system software to avoid any confusion. If we have to refer to the system software component that actually interfaces with the hardware, we will use the term kernel or driver depending on what is more relevant.

We will be looking at three different operating systems over the course of this book. Microsoft Windows will be the most common operating system that a forensic investigator will run across including both desktop and server versions. In a large corporate environment, you will be likely to run across various distributions of Linux and while the names of the distributions may change, the fundamentals of the information we will be looking for are the same across all of the platforms. The biggest difference we will run across will be the file system, how files are written to and accessed on the storage devices. Finally, we will take a look at the Mac OS X system. According to NetMarketShare, adding up all of the versions of Mac OS X in use, about 7% of the desktops tracked are using Mac OS X.

Microsoft Windows

Microsoft was initially known as a company that provided interpreters for the BASIC programming language. When IBM introduced their personal computer (PC), they needed an operating system for it so they turned to Microsoft to provide it. Microsoft had no experience with operating systems so they, in turn, went to Seattle Computer Products, who had an operating system called 86-DOS. 86-DOS was developed to be similar to CP/M, which was an operating system popular with the Intel microprocessors. Microsoft took 86-DOS, renamed it to be MS-DOS and provided it to IBM to be packaged with their PCs. When you got DOS from IBM, it was called PC-DOS, rather than MS-DOS.

In 1982, Microsoft began work on the next generation operating system, though in fact it was really just a new user interface that sat on top of DOS, a model that would continue for the next 20 years. They called it Interface Manager initially, though eventually the name became Windows. Windows 1.0 was released in 1985 and you can see what it looked like in Figure 1.2. Windows, like DOS, came on floppy disks and the operating system was designed to read from and write to floppy disks. This would have an impact on the file system design and this would also continue to influence the file system for decades.

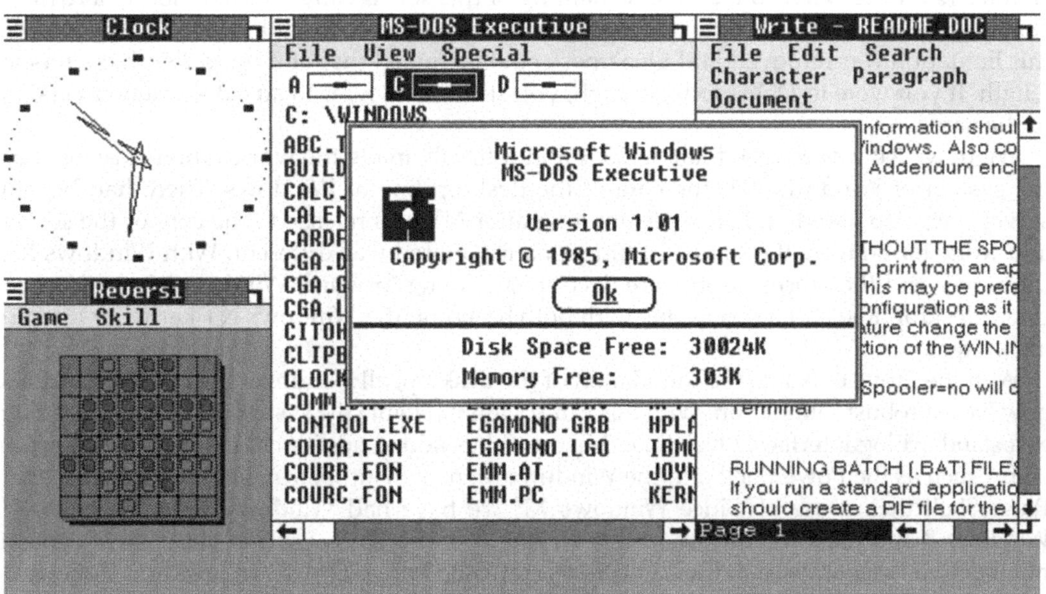

FIGURE 1.2 **Printed with permission from Microsoft.**

While Windows 3.0 was a pretty big release, 3.11 was one of the most transformative releases, since it came bundled with a networking stack. Finally, people could build a local network quickly and easily without a lot of networking experience. Previously, introducing networking was complicated and generally involved introducing a server, where all of the individual desktop systems could get access to file shares or printers. When you bought the server software, you got the client software that could be installed on desktops, allowing them to connect to the network, assuming they had the appropriate network interface cards. With Windows 3.11, also called Windows for Workgroups, you could install the software and your desktop system would just be on the network and it would allow you to communicate with all of the other systems.

Windows for Workgroups was released in the early 1990s and at about the same time, Windows NT was released. Windows NT was designed to be more robust with a very different operating system or kernel. The interface was essentially the same as the existing Windows 3.x interface. NT, or New Technology, continued to be more of a professional workstation operating system for about a decade. In the intervening time, Microsoft released Windows 95 that completely changed the look of the interface away from a big container where windows resided. Instead, you had a desktop where you could stick icons and Microsoft introduced a menu system to get to applications and settings. This style of launching programs had not been seen previously on personal computers. You can see an example of the Windows 95 desktop in Figure 1.3.

Even with Windows 95, DOS was still under the hood, though it was the first release to do a better job of hiding DOS 7. You booted up to the Windows interface rather than booting to DOS and launching Windows. At the same time, Microsoft changed the file system by increasing the size of files, filenames and partitions. This was a significant change. Previously, files were restricted to 8 uppercase characters for the name and 3 upper case characters for the extension. Old-style naming of this sort is called 8.3 notation where the 8 character name and the 3 character extension are separated by a dot (.). With Windows 95, this limitation was removed and filenames could be mixed case and up to 255 characters in length. If you were in DOS mode, though, you still had to refer to an 8.3 shortened version of the name.

Windows XP was released late in 2001 and it finally made the workstation-class operating system of Windows NT, the core of the desktop line of Windows. There had been a server line, also based on NT, since not long after NT was released. The core of the server and workstation were the same but functionality offered was different. With Windows XP, the server and the workstation were decoupled. Going forward, Windows was separated into a desktop line and a server line with both based on the Windows NT kernel or operating system.

With the move to NT as the foundation of the desktop, all Windows systems on desktops now have a robust foundation. With this came a more reliable file system (NTFS) and logging to a standard log interface. Over time, Microsoft has added additional management mechanisms such as the PowerShell and the Windows Management Instrumentation interface that PowerShell makes use of. Since Windows XP, we have had Windows Vista, Windows 7, Windows 8 and most recently, as of this writing, Windows 8.1. Each of these has a version number that is separate from the name that you would know it by. The names and associated version numbers are in Table 1.1.

TABLE 1.1 Windows Versions

Name	Version number
Windows NT 3.1	3.1
Windows NT 3.5	3.5
Windows NT 4.0	4.0
Windows 2000	5.0
Windows XP	5.1
Windows Vista	6.0
Windows 7	6.1
Windows 8	6.2
Windows 8.1	6.3

The server versions are not represented in the table, though they do slot in where appropriate in chronological order. Typically, the server release will have the same version number as the desktop release that is out about the same time. As an example, Windows 7 and Windows Server 2008 were released in the same rough timeframe and as a result, they have the same version number. In most cases, the underlying components of the server release match those from the desktop. This is not true with Windows Server 2012, as it uses a completely new and proprietary file system called ReFS (Resilient File System). There will be more on this as we talk about file systems later on.

Linux

While we could probably trace this one back even further, the best starting point to use when talking about Linux is 1964. That does not mean that Linux itself began in 1964, which is five years before Linus Torvalds, the creator of Linux, was born. The Multics project was started in 1964, though. Multics stood for Multiplexed Information and Computing Service, and it was a project developed by Bell Labs, MIT, and General Electric, as a way to develop a multiuser, multiprocessing operating system to hopefully make more efficient use of what were then multimillion dollar personal computers, since typically only one user could use each computer at a time. Multics had a number of lofty goals but eventually, Bell Labs pulled out of the project and a couple of the team members went off and created a different operating system in response to their work on Multics. As a joke, they referred to it as Unics.

Unics was a scaled-down version of Multics and development of Unics resulted in the development of the C programming as well. Eventually, the entire operating system was written in C. At some point, the name became Unix and it was appropriately trademarked by Bell Labs. However, the computing community at the time was reasonably small and well connected and Unix began to be used on a number of places outside of Bell Labs. By the late 1970s, Unix had spawned a variation that behaved just like Unix did, but was written from scratch without any of the Unix source code. This version was called the Berkeley Systems Distribution (BSD), managed and largely written by a man named Bill Joy. BSD became a popular academic release, in part because it could be run on less expensive minicomputers like the Digital Equipment Corporation's VAX and PDP systems without the licensing costs of Digital's operating systems.

By the mid-1980s, Unix had become a popular operating system in computer science curricula because it was much smaller than other operating systems and it was also portable, meaning it could be compiled and run on any system architecture that could support a C compiler. The fact that it was widely available and could be reimplemented without licensing costs, as long as there were not any trademark or copyright infringements with either the name Unix or any of the Bell Labs source code, meant that it worked well to be included in textbooks that taught operating system design. One of those books, written by Andrew Tannenbaum, was based on an implementation of Unix called Minix. Minix was short for mini-Unix and it was published along with a textbook on operating system design. The source code for the operating system was freely available and that is how it ended up in the hands of college student Linus Torvalds.

Torvalds used Minix as a starting point and wrote the kernel of a Unix-like operating system that he eventually called Linux. Since the kernel was just the core of the system, it needed a lot of other components to go along with it, including what are commonly called userland utilities. These userland utilities came from the GNU Project. GNU is what is referred to as a recursive acronym and it stands for GNU's Not Unix. Programmers can have a peculiar sense of humor.

The GNU project was the brainchild of MIT graduate and former programmer at MIT's legendary Artificial Intelligence Lab Richard Stallman. Stallman believed that software should be free. In Stallman's parlance, free should be thought of in the same terms as free speech rather than free beer. He formed the GNU Project out of frustration that source code that had formerly been readily available (free) was no longer available and felt that stifled the computing culture as well as innovation. The GNU project provided compilers that Torvalds used to build his operating system, as well as userland utilities, including all of the common Unix utilities like ls, cat, ps, and so on.

The combination of the Linux kernel with the GNU utilities was enough to create a working system so users could have a Unix-like operating system of their own. Interestingly, while Stallman and his supporters have long complained about the common name for the collection of kernel and system software being Linux when they feel it should be called, GNU/Linux, the GNU Project has been working on their own kernel for roughly 30 years but have yet to get a distribution together based on their software and kernel. It is this combination of software, though, that we will be looking at and, without intending to get into lengthy debates, we will use the word Linux to talk about the whole collection of software for simplicity's sake.

Linux does predominantly follow the Unix standards for file system layout as well as facilities like logging, networking, process management, and system management. As a result, while we will be talking about Linux, we could just as easily be talking about almost any other Unix-like operating system.

Graphical User Interface

The one thing that neither Linux nor the GNU Project provided was a graphical user interface when Linux was created. In fact, generally Unix-like systems relied on an MIT project called X that provided the foundation for a graphical interface, though did not actually provide much in the way of an interface itself. In fact, if you were to run X all by itself, you would get a gray, crosshatch pattern on your screen and nothing else. X was developed in 1984 using a client-server model, though it is not quite client and server the way you may expect it to be. If you are running an X application from a remote system but displayed on your monitor, you are the server and the remote system is the client. The reason for this is because you are serving up the keyboard, monitor, and mouse.

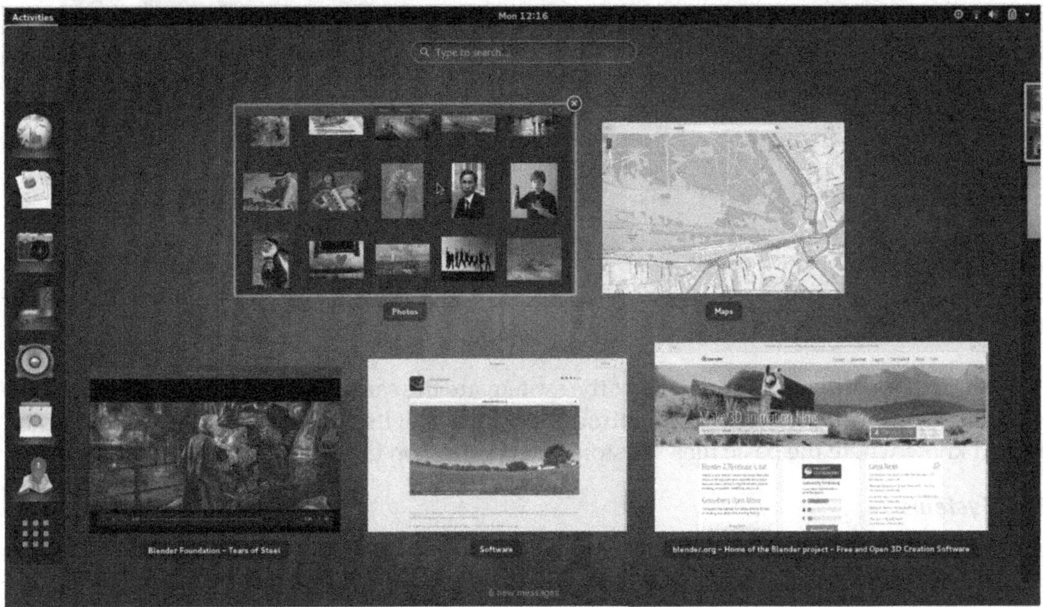

FIGURE 1.3

X has a fairly lengthy history of not being a very well liked system but perhaps some of that has to do with not completely understanding what X is and what the design goals were. X was designed to be simple and extensible. It was also designed to provide graphics primitives and a set of protocols that could be used to build on top of when creating actual graphical user interfaces. Simplicity was preferred over functionality in some of the early design goals. In the thirty years since X was first conceived, there have been other systems developed but X is the one that continues to be used. You will likely never see X itself, though, which is currently developed by the Xorg Foundation, but instead, you will see one of the interfaces that sits on top of X. Two of the most predominant ones today are Gnome and KDE. You can see the latest release of Gnome, which has undergone several stylistic changes across versions, in Figure 1.3. KDE, which has always more or less modeled its visual design on Windows, can be seen in Figure 1.4.

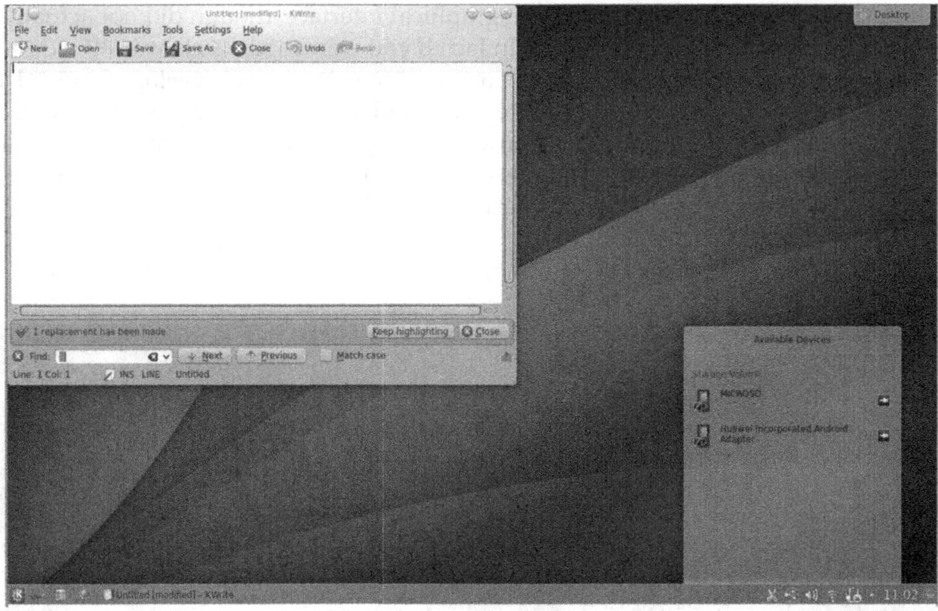

FIGURE 1.4

While the majority of components of the system are the same, regardless of what user interface is used, each graphical interface introduces artifacts of its own, and a forensic investigator should know where the basic files are stored depending on the interface used on the system.

File Systems

Unlike the other operating systems we will cover, Linux has a large number of file systems, though most Linux-based distributions generally default to one of the ext family of file systems. Because of some limitations with the file system that was part of the Minix operating system, developers on the early Linux kernel created a new file system called ext for extended file system. There were some limitations with the ext file system as well, though, so they quickly developed the second extended file system or ext2. This has been the foundational file system for Linux since the early 1990s. The rest of the ext family of file systems (ext3 and ext4) are based on adding features to the base ext2 file system.

One feature the ext2 file system did not include was journaling, which is a feature designed to protect data on the file system from corruption or loss in the case of some sort of catastrophic failure. In 2001, ReiserFS was introduced as an alternate file system that did support journaling. Ext3 was introduced in the same year as an extension to ext2 that also supported journaling. In 1999, the IBM file system, JFS that was first developed for AIX in 1990 was ported to Linux. Any one of these file systems may have been used, as well as a small number of other possibilities, to install Linux on.

Mac OS X

In the 1970s, there was one company that was really pushing out the boundaries when it comes to computer desktop technology. The laser printer, graphical user interface, a user interface using a desktop as a model, object-oriented programming, bitmapped graphics, What You See Is What You Get (WYSIWYG) editors, and local area networking were all developed at the Xerox Palo Alto Research Center (PARC). Just as Microsoft did when they decided to develop a graphical user interface, Apple took a trip to PARC to see their technology in 1979. As a result of that trip, Steve Jobs decided that the GUI with a desktop paradigm was the way to go and it resulted, in time, with the Apple Macintosh after a stop at the failed Lisa business computer.

The Macintosh computer was introduced in 1984. Just as with Microsoft Windows, the Apple operating system, called System, was on a floppy though in the case of System, it was on a 3½ in. floppy, where DOS was originally on a 5¼ in. floppy. The bigger disk had less capacity giving Apple more space to put the operating system on, though the hardware itself only had 128 KB originally. Just to put that into perspective, that is about 8000 times less memory than a low-end computer today and probably about 8000 times less memory than your smart phone has in it. Eventually of course, they added more memory to the hardware.

You may have noticed that I have been talking about the hardware. Unlike the other operating systems we have been talking about, Mac OS has always been tied to specific hardware. System ran on a Macintosh computer, which was designed specifically to support the sorts of things the operating system was going to do. A couple of things set it apart from the PC compatible systems that were prevalent at the time. One was that it used a Motorola 68,000 processor, unlike the Intel processors that the IBM systems were using. On top of that, it had a built in monitor that could support the type of graphics the operating system was using, which can be seen in Figure 1.5.

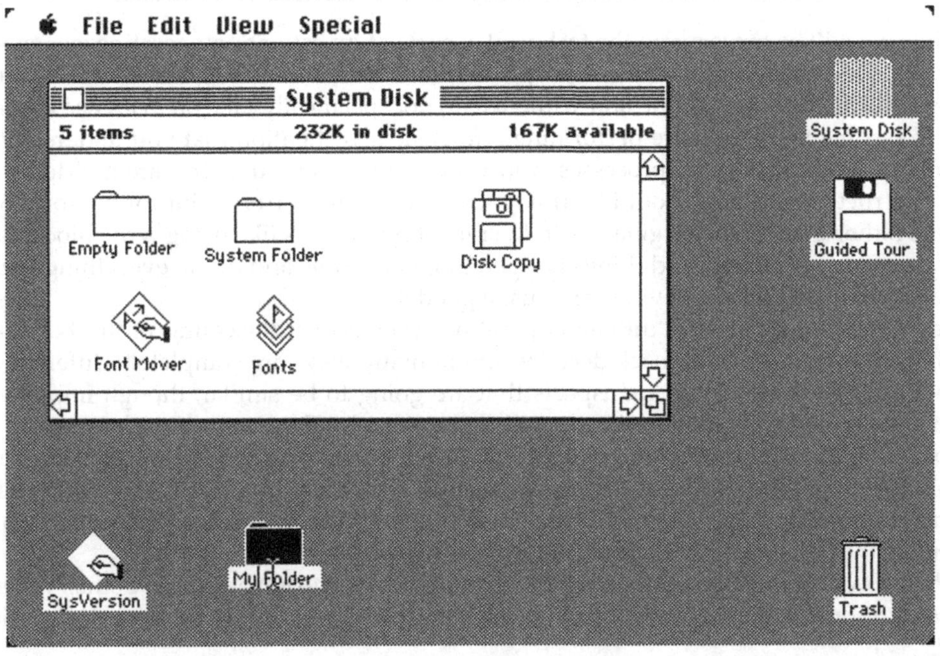

FIGURE 1.5

Eventually, Steve Jobs was forced out of Apple and he went on to start a new company called NeXT Computers. Normally, this would be irrelevant because we are talking about forensics on Mac OS X. However, it is all related. By the early and mid-1990s, System, the Macintosh operating system, was well behind the times. For a long time, System lacked protected memory and pre-emptive multitasking as well as support for multiple users. At the same time, Jobs' company was not doing very well itself, having transitioned from a hardware company to simply a software company. When Jobs came back to Apple, he brought the NeXTStep operating system with him.

Today, we have the Mac OS X operating system, which is effectively a merging of the look of the older System/Mac OS with the foundation and some of the concepts from NeXTStep. NeXTStep is a UNIX operating system with a Mach kernel and components from BSD. When you are running a Mac OS X system, you have a Unix-like operating system underneath. You can always drop to a shell and access your system with common Unix utilities. However, not everything is based on Unix. The file system in use with Mac OS X is HFS+, which is an extension of the much older Hierarchical File System (HFS) that Apple developed in the mid-80s.

When we are investigating a Mac OS X system, it is a hybrid operating system. We get some of the file system layout from UNIX along with some of the logging but when it comes down to looking at system configuration, we will be looking at property lists (plists) rather than the more traditional plaintext-based configuration files that come from Unix-like operating systems.

CONCLUSIONS

While we will be focusing on the technical aspects of investigating operating systems and those skills are useful for a range of people and jobs, you should remember that a forensic process is ultimately a legal one and while we do not specifically take on evidence handling, we will assume that if you are performing a forensic investigation that you understand appropriate evidence handling processes. You want to make sure that you are not doing anything destructive and you should be doing any investigation from a bit-for-bit copy of the original rather than on the original itself. In spite of best efforts like using write blockers and other protective measures, bad things happen to good people and doing everything you can to protect yourself and your evidence is just a good idea.

We will be looking at three different operating systems over the course of this book, all of which have histories that go back decades and in many ways are completely different from one another. However, there are aspects that are going to be similar, though implementation details will vary. For example, they all make use of a file system in order to store data to storage media. They all handle memory management and provide a way to get access to information about the processes that are in memory. Basic features that you would expect to see in a useful operating system of course exist in all of them. What we will need to do is to determine the details for each of the operating systems.

While we cover three operating systems in this book, we do get an added bonus. When we go through some of the methods for Linux and Mac OS X, we can use those same techniques on other Unix-like operating systems like FreeBSD, NetBSD, OpenBSD, Solaris, HP-UX, or AIX. All of these are Unix-based and so many of the techniques and tools will be available for those operating systems as well.

SUMMARY

These are some ideas that are worth remembering from this chapter:

- Forensics comes from the Latin meaning public and it relates to court cases so forensic investigations are about providing evidence in a court case.
- The goal of a legal trial is to find the truth of the case and anyone providing evidence has the job of assisting the trier of fact (generally the judge).
- You should always document your chain of custody as you move evidence from one investigator to another.
- Windows originated as an add-on on top of DOS, which was strongly influenced by CP/M.
- Windows NT began development in the late 1980s and all current versions of Windows are based on the original NT foundation.
- Linux is based on a Unix-like operating system and is actually just the kernel of the whole operating environment.
- Linux supports a large number of file systems and any of them could have the operating system installed on them.
- Mac OS X is based on the foundation of System/Mac OS and the operating system NeXTStep.
- Mac OS X is a Unix-like operating system that includes a lot of tools and systems that you would find in other Unix-like operating systems.

EXERCISES

1. Investigate the laws and processes in your state or locality related to the introduction of technical evidence.
2. Compare the logging features available in Windows XP with those available in Windows 8.
3. Describe the differences in logging capabilities between Linux and Mac OS X.
4. Outline a set of best practices for handling digital evidence.

Bibliography

Federal Evidence Review, 2014. Federal rules of evidence. Available from: http://federalevidence.com/rules-of-evidence (accessed 22.05.2014.).

Frye v. U.S | Casebriefs, n.d. Casebriefs. Available from: http://www.casebriefs.com/blog/law/evidence/evidence-keyed-to-fisher/lay-opinions-and-expert-testimony/frye-v-u-s/ (accessed 24.05.2014.).

CHAPTER

2

File Systems

INFORMATION INCLUDED IN THIS CHAPTER:

- Windows File Systems–FAT, FAT32, NTFS, ReFS
- Linux File Systems–ext2/3/4, ReiserFS
- Mac OS X File Systems–HFS+

INTRODUCTION

When operating systems such as Windows/DOS and Mac OS/System were created, floppy disks were the dominant storage media on personal computers. You couldn't store a lot of information on them. Because of the lack of storage capacity, files could be stored in a flat manner, means without directories, to help organize them in a way that was manageable for most people. You could look at a listing of files on your floppy and be able to fairly quickly see, what was on there simply because the floppy could not store all that much information. Some of the needs of file systems in the 1970s and into the early 1980s were different than they are today. The concept of multigigabyte files and multiterabyte or larger devices would have been difficult to conceive.

There are other considerations that file systems did not have to be concerned with on single-user systems. This means there is a lot of information about files that we make use of regularly today that wasn't being stored then because it wasn't necessary. For a start, the owner of the file is important information that was not stored then. If there is one and only one user of the computer, there is no reason to store information about the owner because there can only be one owner. Similarly, granting permissions to other users would not have been required. As a result, there was nothing in the early versions of FAT or HFS that would have kept that sort of information. Earlier versions of Linux file systems would have had that information because they were based around an operating system that had been multi-user for a couple of decades. And, of course, Linux file systems were quite a bit older than the file systems being used on Microsoft or Apple operating systems.

What sort of information does a file system need to keep track of, then? With a file system, you are looking for a way for the computer to store information that the users are going to care about and make use of. In addition to the file contents, obviously, users need to be able to get access to a file, so the file system needs to know where all of the relevant data bits that go with a file are stored. They may also want some very rudimentary version control, so information about dates associated with the file will be useful–created, accessed, and modified. Accessed is different from modified because I may simply open a file to look at it without writing any changes to the disk. That would be an access but the only thing I would have modified would be the accessed date in the metadata for the file. None of the contents of the file would have been altered so the modified date would remain the same. You could have a file that was created and written on the same day but then never modified again over a period of many years. As a result, you would have the accessed date being changed a lot, but the modified date would be left as it was. The created date, for obvious reasons, never changes.

There is a difference between copy and move. In the case of moving a file from one location to another, you are not changing anything other than where the file inserts into the directory structure. In the case of a copy, you are creating a complete new file, so the create time will reflect a create date of when the file was copied.

What sort of data do we want to keep track of in a file system, then? Here is a list of information that may be maintained about the file, though this list would vary from one file system to another, means, it may be incomplete in some cases and have too much in other cases.

- File name
- File owner
- Location of file data on the disk
- File creation, accessed, and modified dates
- Access control information–who is allowed to access the file
- Permissions–may be more basic than access control
- System-specific information like executable, setUID, setGID
- Type of entry–regular file, special file, directory
- Size of file–actual as well as on-disk
- Special attributes–hidden, backed up

There is a mix of purposes going on here. Some of the information is required for the file system to maintain itself. Other information is there to make life easier for users. No matter what the purpose is, as forensic investigators, we want to be able to get all of it. Because of that, we want to be able to understand not only the file system itself, its data structures and locations, where data is stored but also, we need to know, how to get information about what file systems are on the hard disk and where they are. There are currently two ways of storing that information.

DISK GEOMETRY

Historically, disks have been divided up into cylinders, heads and sectors. This way of describing access to the disk has largely been superseded but you will still see disk access referred to in this way. The problem with this method is that it essentially ties addressing to a physical layout of the device and assumes that the device is a set of rotating disks. The partitions on a disk are still described in terms of the cylinder, head, and sector address. Since these disks are a stack of double-sided circles, we need a way to get to the data that is stored on them. This would be unlike a square that could be broken up into a lot of small boxes where data could be stored.

Figure 2.1 shows what a disk layout would look like. You will see a series of concentric circles. These concentric circles are the tracks and you can think of them as continuing through all of the disks across both sides. When you stack all of those tracks up, you end up with a cylinder, a three-dimensional object, created from all of the two-dimensional tracks. Across the tracks, you will see lines that cut the rings into pie-shapes. The pie shapes are called track sectors. When you cut the track sectors along the lines of the track, creating what is basically a quadrilateral with a couple of curved edges, you have a sector. The sector is a basic building block from a storage perspective. Sectors are sometimes referred to as blocks and when we talk about personal computers, a sector or block is 512-bytes. The very first sector on a disk is called the master boot record.

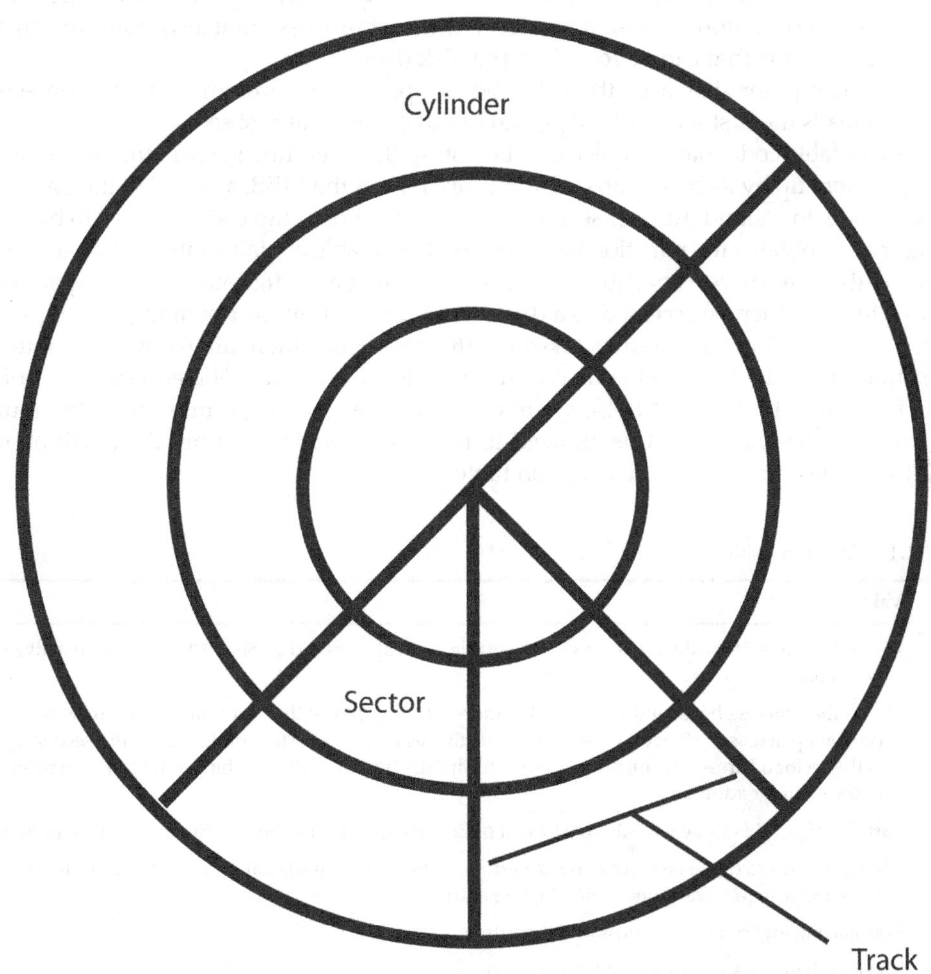

FIGURE 2.1

CHS addresses allow us to address 1024 (2^10) cylinders, 64 (2^6) heads, and 256 (2^8) sectors. The total number of locations in that case is 16,777,216 addresses (1024 × 64 × 256). This is limiting so disks are now commonly accessed using logical block addressing (LBA), which provides a set of contiguous addresses that can be used regardless of what the physical disk looks like. The disk drive itself would be expected to translate from the logical block address to a physical location on the disk. This allows the operating system to access disk drives without having to know exactly how the drive is constructed.

MASTER BOOT RECORD

The master boot record (MBR) serves a couple of functions and has served those functions for decades now and while, it is slowly being replaced by the newer and more functional unified extensible firmware interface (UEFI), it continues to be an important data structure on disk drives. It not only stores information about the boot process but it also stores information about the file systems that can be found on the disk drive.

When the computer that uses the MBR boots up, it goes through its power-on self-test (POST) then reads the first sector of the primary hard drive. That first sector, which is 512 bytes, contains executable code that is expected to bootstrap the operating system, that is, pulling the operating system up by its bootstraps. A significant part of the MBR, also called the boot sector, is the boot code. In a standard boot sector, the size of the bootstrap code area is 446 bytes. The boot sector also contains the partition table. The partition table contains information about each partition on the hard drive. A partition is a way of defining a contiguous chunk of space on the hard drive that can then be accessed as a drive or volume within the operating system.

Each of the partition table entries takes up 16 bytes. Since there are 64 bytes allocated for the partition table, the partition table can store up to four entries. The entries may point to extended partition tables stored elsewhere on the disk allowing for more than the four basic partition entries that would be allowed in the space available within the partition table. Table 2.1 lists the entries from the partition table.

TABLE 2.1 Partition Table

Length	Value
1 byte	Bootable/active. If the device is active or bootable, the value would be 80h. 00h would be inactive or nonbootable.
3 bytes	This is the cylinder, head, and sector (CHS) address of the start of the partition. This address is broken up across the 3 bytes – the first byte is the head address. The first six bits of the second byte is the sector address. The high two bits of the middle byte and all eight bits of the last byte belong to the cylinder address.
1 byte	Partition type. This value indicates the format or filesystem that could be expected to be on the partition.
3 bytes	The CHS address of the last sector in the partition. The address is allocated across the three bytes in the same way that was done in the starting address.
4 bytes	The starting logical block address of the partition
4 bytes	The length in blocks or sectors of the partition.

While the CHS address remains in the partition table entry, the more relevant ones are the LBA addresses for the start and length of the partition. Since each partition is a set of contiguous sectors, we do not need to make note of the ending sector. All we need to know is the length of the partition. That will give us the size as well as the ending sector. You can see the results of the Linux utility fdisk below. You will see the start and end addresses are in LBA. In the case of the first partition on the drive, which is a FAT32 partition, the size is 2,100,000–2048 or 2,097,952 sectors. Each sector is 512 bytes so we can multiply 512 bytes times 2,097,952 to get the number of bytes in the partition.

```
Disk /dev/sdb: 2147 MB, 2147483648 bytes
255 heads, 63 sectors/track, 261 cylinders, total 4194304 sectors
Units = sectors of 1 * 512 = 512 bytes
Sector size (logical/physical): 512 bytes / 4096 bytes
I/O size (minimum/optimal): 4096 bytes / 4096 bytes
Disk identifier: 0x9a7af307

   Device Boot      Start         End      Blocks   Id  System
/dev/sdb1            2048     2100000     1048976+   c  W95 FAT32
(LBA)
/dev/sdb2         2101248     4194303     1046528    7
HPFS/NTFS/exFAT
```

On current Windows systems, fdisk is no longer supported, since fdisk, as it used to exist on Windows does not support the NTFS file system. Instead, you can use the logical disk manager to look at the partitions on a disk. You can also use the diskpart utility, as seen in Figure 2.2. With diskpart, you can manipulate the disks on your system including creating and formatting partitions.

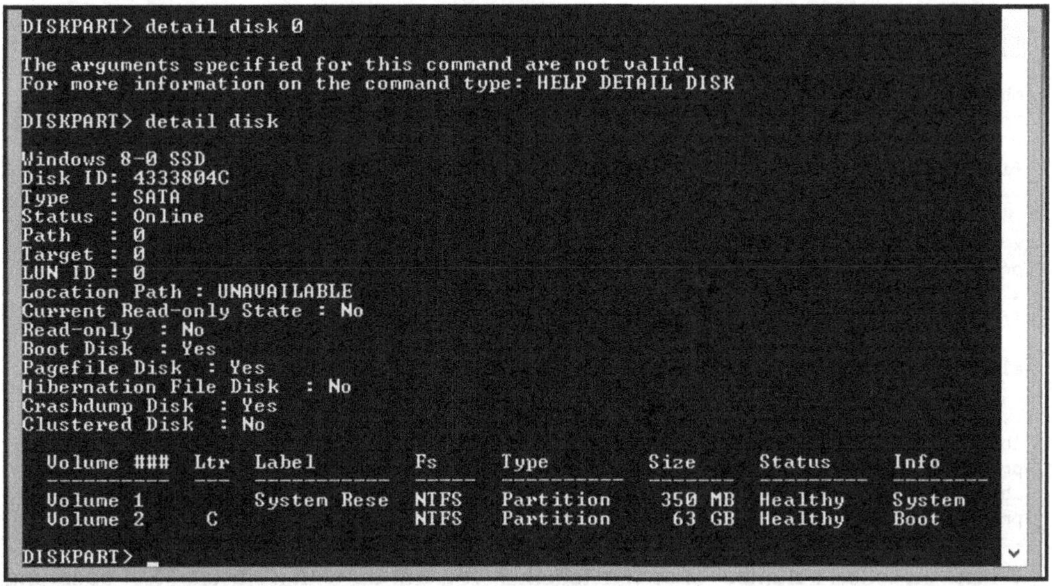

```
DISKPART> detail disk 0

The arguments specified for this command are not valid.
For more information on the command type: HELP DETAIL DISK

DISKPART> detail disk

Windows 8-0 SSD
Disk ID: 4333804C
Type   : SATA
Status : Online
Path   : 0
Target : 0
LUN ID : 0
Location Path : UNAVAILABLE
Current Read-only State : No
Read-only  : No
Boot Disk  : Yes
Pagefile Disk  : Yes
Hibernation File Disk  : No
Crashdump Disk  : Yes
Clustered Disk  : No

  Volume ###  Ltr  Label        Fs     Type        Size     Status     Info
  ----------  ---  -----------  -----  ----------  -------  ---------  --------
  Volume 1         System Rese  NTFS   Partition    350 MB  Healthy    System
  Volume 2     C                NTFS   Partition     63 GB  Healthy    Boot

DISKPART> _
```

FIGURE 2.2

While the partition table is the piece of the master boot record that you are going to be most interested, the boot loader is a critical component of the master boot record. The boot code is operating system specific, which means that every operating system have its own code to load the operating system. In the case of Linux, you may find several different boot loaders, each with their own boot code. The boot code has to locate the actual operating system to be loaded from disk and read it into memory, transferring control over to it, once the system is loaded.

We can quickly grab the master boot record to take a look at it. There are several tools that we can use for this task and we will continue to use these tools as we grab data from the file system. While there are a number of commercial tools you can use to pull data from drives, there are also free and open source tools that can be used as well. One of the easiest tools that is usable across multiple platforms is a tool from the set of common Unix utilities, dd. dd is a utility designed to perform a bit for bit copy of a source media into a destination. We can use it to grab the first sector of the disk.

```
dd if=/dev/sda of=mbr.dd bs=512 count=1
```

Using dd, we set the input file as the device of the primary hard drive. In this case, the primary hard drive is /dev/sda so that is our input file. The output file could be another disk device but in this case, we just want to dump the contents out to a file. Since we don't want to copy the entire device, we need to set the block size to 512 bytes and then copy only one block of 512 bytes. Once we have the file with the master boot record contents, we can move that file to another location and investigate the file. We might use a number of tools like a hexadecimal editor to investigate the contents of the MBR or we could also use programmatic tools to look at the contents, including writing custom scripts like the one below.

```
#!/usr/bin/python3
import struct

f = open("mbr.dd", "rb")

mbr = bytearray()
try:
    mbr = f.read(512)
finally:
    f.close()

x = struct.unpack("<i", mbr[0x1B8:0x1BC])
print("Disk signature: ", x[0])
x = mbr[0x1BE]
if x == 0x80:
    print("Active flag: Active")
else:
    print("Active flag: Not active")

lbastart = struct.unpack("<i", mbr[0x1C6:0x1CA])
print("Partition Start (LBA): ", lbastart[0])
lbaend = struct.unpack("<i", mbr[0x1C9:0x1CD])
print("Partition End (LBA): ", lbaend[0])
```

When you collect a number of sectors together, you end up with a cluster. Most operating systems do not use sectors as the minimum allocation size. Instead, they gather up a number of contiguous sectors into a larger cluster and that becomes the allocation unit used, when they are writing data out to the disk. The advantage is that it limits the number of storage units, you need to keep track of. In some file systems, every cluster gets an entry in the file table and the fewer clusters you have, the less overhead your file system takes up on the disk. Deciding the cluster size is always a trade-off of efficiency of the file system and lost storage space. When you are using a cluster size of 8096 bytes, for example, you are using 16 contiguous sectors to store your data into. For the sake of scale, let us say that you are storing a number of small files, all in the 150–300 byte range. You end up with more than 7000 bytes that will not get used for every file you store. The same is true for large files. At some point, you run into the case where the last cluster you use will have a number of bytes, up to 8095, that will not be used.

UNIFIED EXTENSIBLE FIRMWARE INTERFACE

The Unified Extensible Firmware Interface (UEFI) was created in part, to solve the problem of large hard drives. This has been a challenge since, the initial master boot record and partition table were created. With the old master boot record partition table, we had slots for four partitions. We got over that by allowing extended partitions and storing additional partition tables elsewhere on the hard drive. In reality, UEFI is a replacement for the basic input/output system (BIOS) of a computer but since, it modifies the way the computer boots and the way the system interacts with hard drives, we need to cover it here. In Figure 2.3, you can see that the UEFI sits between the operating system and the firmware. This provides the operating system a consistent interface to the firmware of the system, which then communicates with the hardware. The layer of abstraction simplifies the operating system, reducing the potential number of ways it needs to communicate, depending on the hardware that sits below it. As noted, this was previously a function of the BIOS. While there were number of advantages to UEFI over BIOS, the one we are most interested in at this time is the support for booting from larger hard drives, which was not possible from BIOS. As a result, Intel began to develop UEFI to support that feature, as well as, several others that would benefit larger systems that may be in use in enterprises.

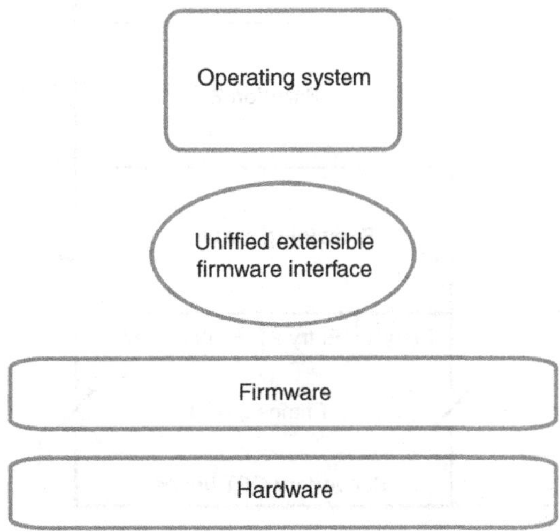

FIGURE 2.3

The really important part of UEFI, though, is the introduction of the globally unique identifier (GUID) partition table (GPT), since we are not going to be working with the firmware or the interface with the underlying hardware. The part we care about is how we can take a look at the partitions that are available on the hard drive. The GUID partition table was introduced with UEFI and removed the limitations on the number of partitions on a hard drive, as well as, the size of the partitions. As a result, the number of sectors or blocks taken up on the disk to support the description of the partitions has increased. A disk with a GPT still has an MBR, but it is used in a way that would prevent utilities that did not recognize the GPT from overwriting or corrupting the drive.

The first sector on the drive is still the master boot record, though it is now called the protective MBR. The next sector is the primary GPT header, which includes identifying information about the disk like the GUID, which, as its name suggests, is a globally unique identifier. No other disk in the world should ever have the same identifier. The GPT header also indicates the number of partitions, as well as, the location of the partition table. This is because with a UEFI drive using a GUID partition table, you have backups to the partition tables. You can see the way all of this comes together on the disk in Figure 2.4.

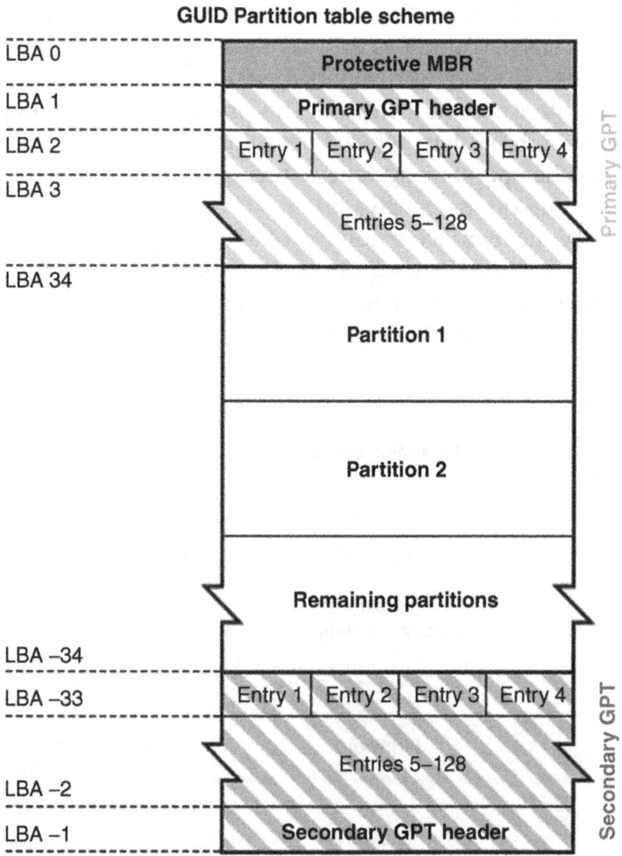

FIGURE 2.4

You can see the GPT header in the hex dump in Figure 2.5. The first eight bytes are the signature, which will read EFI PART, as you can see in the Figure 2.5. At 40th byte, which is the 41st byte since we start counting at 0, you will get the first usable LBA on the disk. 56th byte is the starting byte for the 16 bytes for the GUID for the disk. The GPT header also has the future in mind. While current partition entries in the GUID partition table are 128 bytes, there is no guarantee that will continue to be the case. At some point, we may get such large disks that we need to make the partition table entries bigger. To support that, at position 84, there are 4 bytes indicating how big a partition table entry is.

```
  0 28732AC1 1FF8D211 BA4B00A0 C93EC93B CCFF5891 5CDEB24C A3FA1D7E 6F8FE6E1 (s*¡ ˘“ ∫K †…>_;Ă˙Xë\ﬁ≤L£˙ ~oèÊ·
 32 28000000 00000000 27400600 00000000 00000000 00000000 45004600 49002000 (      '@                E F I
 64 53007900 73007400 65006D00 20005000 61007200 74006900 74006900 6F006E00 S y s t e m   P a r t i t i o n
 96 00000000 00000000 00000000 00000000 00000000 00000000 00000000 00000000
128 00534648 0000AA11 AA110030 6543ECAC 5F5D4C06 5B0E594D 94E3527D 9C396DB8  SFH  ™ ™  0eCÏ¨_]L [ YMî„R}ú9m∏
160 28400600 00000000 5F112A3A 00000000 00000000 00000000 43007500 73007400 (@       _ *:             C u s t
192 6F006D00 65007200 00000000 00000000 00000000 00000000 00000000 00000000 o m e r
224 00000000 00000000 00000000 00000000 00000000 00000000 00000000 00000000
256 746F6F42 0000AA11 AA110030 6543ECAC 38D789A1 E2D14E44 9AADB8F0 D8615A1F tooB  ™ ™  0eCÏ¨8◊â°,-NDö≠∏•ÿaZ
288 60112A3A 00000000 7F703D3A 00000000 00000000 00000200 52006500 63006F00 ` *:     p=:              R e c o
320 76006500 72007900 20004800 44000000 00000000 00000000 00000000 00000000 v e r y   H D
352 00000000 00000000 00000000 00000000 00000000 00000000 00000000 00000000
384 00000000 00000000 00000000 00000000 00000000 00000000 00000000 00000000
416 00000000 00000000 00000000 00000000 00000000 00000000 00000000 00000000
448 00000000 00000000 00000000 00000000 00000000 00000000 00000000 00000000
480 00000000 00000000 00000000 00000000 00000000 00000000 00000000 00000000
512
```

FIGURE 2.5

We can extract the values out of the GPT header easily enough to be able to analyze the disk. This could be done using the hex editor like the one I used in Figure 2.5. This requires doing a lot of conversion from hexadecimal to either decimal or some other format. In most cases, we would be converting the hexadecimal value into a decimal value, as in the case where, we are taking the four bytes that represents the starting logical block address and we need to convert it to decimal. The other thing we need to take into consideration is the values that are written out from an Intel-based system are going to be backwards from the way you expect it to be. Intel uses what we call little-endian format because the little end of a set of data is going to be the first one you see. The least significant value in a multibyte value is going to be the first one you encounter so if you were to see 1234, as an example, what it really represents is four thousand, three hundred twenty-one because the least significant value, 1, is the one that was written first. When you are converting data from a hex dump, you need to keep that in mind and reverse the byte values before doing the conversion.

Big-endian versus little-endian is an important concept. You are used to big-endian because of the way we usually write numbers. Keep in mind that if you are working with data from an Intel-based system, as all personal computers today are, you are working with little-endian and the byte order needs to be reversed, but only within the values. You do not reverse the entire data structure, just each individual value.

Another way of doing the conversion is programmatically. I have a simple Python script below that will take a file as input. The file should be the sector containing the GPT header. It would be easy enough to alter this simple program to actually pull the data from the disk itself, but in this case, to keep it simple, I assume that you have used dd or some other disk dump utility to grab the header information. While there is more information available in the GPT header, the program only extracts the following data from the GPT header.

```
Signature:  EFI PART
GPT Header Size:  92
Current Header Address:  1
Backup GPT Address:  977105059
First usable address:  34
Last usable address:  977105026
Start of partition entries:  2
Number of partitions:  128
```

The program listing follows. Again, this is a very simple program that can easily be extended to show additional information from the GPT header. You will note the use of struct.unpack from most of the print statements. This is because of the little-endian format. The function struct.unpack takes care of the little-endian issue and will convert a set of bytes into another value, like a decimal integer.

```
import argparse, struct, uuid
from sys import exit

args = argparse.ArgumentParser()
args.add_argument("-i", type=str, help="The source of the GPT
header", required=True)

passedArgs = vars(args.parse_args())
fileName = passedArgs['i']

gptBytes = bytearray()
try:
    f = open(fileName, "rb")
    # read the contents of the GPT header into a byte array
    gptBytes = f.read(512)
    f.close()
except:
    print("file error")
    exit(0)

sig = gptBytes[0:8].decode("utf-8")
print("Signature: ", sig)
print("GPT Header Size: ", struct.unpack("<i",
gptBytes[12:16])[0])
print("Current Header Address: ", struct.unpack("<q",
gptBytes[24:32])[0])
print("Backup GPT Address: ", struct.unpack("<q",
gptBytes[32:40])[0])
print("First usable address: ", struct.unpack("<q",
gptBytes[40:48])[0])
```

```
print("Last usable address: ", struct.unpack("<q",
gptBytes[48:56])[0])
print("Start of partition entries: ", struct.unpack("<q",
gptBytes[72:80])[0])
print("Number of partitions: ", struct.unpack("<i",
gptBytes[80:84])[0])
```

Partition entries follow the GPT header. Each partition table entry is 128 bytes, which means that you can put four partition table entries into each block or sector on the disk. Since a UEFI/GPT disk supports 128 partitions, there are 32 blocks that are allocated for partition entries, with four partitions in each block. Out of the 128 bytes for the partition entry, 16 bytes are used to describe the partition's physical properties, namely the starting and ending addresses on the disk (Table 2.2).

The partition type GUIDs defines what the partition contains. Each operating system has a number of GUIDs that define whether it is a system partition, a boot partition, swap partition, or some other type of partition. Windows, Mac OS, and Linux, all have different partition types with different GUIDs defined. Figure 2.6 shows a hex dump of a GUID partition table (GPT). This particular table has three partitions defined. The partition name is multi-byte, so each character takes up two bytes. As a result, when you look at the decoded values on the right hand side of the hex dump, you will see a space between each of the characters in the partition name. This particular disk has partitions named System Partition, Customer, and Recovery HD. The customer partition starts at sector 42 and ends at sector 409639. We get those values by reversing the eight bytes in the two address sections of the GPT and then converting the hexadecimal to decimal.

Using the information in the GPT, we can figure out where all of the data on the disk is and what each partition will be used for. What we do not necessarily get out of this is the file system for each partition, though we can make some good guesses in most cases based on the GUID partition type. In the case of Windows, for example, some of the partition types will be FAT32 and others will be NTFS. Mac OS partitions are generally going to be HFS+. The place we will run into issues is from Linux systems, where the partitions can be formatted for any file system that Linux supports.

TABLE 2.2 The Layout of a Partition Entry in a GUID Partition Table

Offset	Length	Value
0	16	Partition type in GUID format
16	16	Unique partition GUID
32	8	Logical block address of partition start (little endian)
40	8	Logical block address of partition end (little endian)
48	8	Attribute flags
56	72	Partition name

WINDOWS FILE SYSTEMS

Windows file systems inherit their capabilities from a couple of sources. The first and most obvious one is DOS. We are still, in some cases, using a file system that was created in the 1970s. Some changes have been made to support larger files on larger file systems but the basic design and functionality of the file system is the same, as it was deployed on DOS systems in the early 1980s. Windows also makes use of the New Technology File System that takes many of its cues from the Digital Equipment Corporation's (DEC) VAX/VMS, an operating system designed to run on DEC's VAX minicomputer. The reason for the lineage is because the chief architect for Windows NT was one of the software engineers on the project to develop VAX/VMS at DEC. A lot of the learning that came as a result of building that operating system translated into the design of Windows NT, including the file system.

While the File Allocation Table (FAT) file system and the New Technology File System (NTFS) are the common file systems in use on Windows systems. Microsoft has introduced a new file system to go along with Windows Server 2012 called Resilient File System (ReFS). If you are working with server operating systems from Microsoft, you may run into this file system and it is not clear whether Microsoft will eventually supplant the now standard NTFS with ReFS on their desktop systems at some point in the future. Both NTFS and ReFS are proprietary to Microsoft and there is not as much documentation available for the underlying technical details.

File Allocation Table (FAT)

The File Allocation Table (FAT) file system is a very simple design. It can afford to be since, it does not contain much in the way of information about the files other than a very basic set of metadata in addition to the contents of the file. There are actually three versions of the FAT at the moment because of the need to support larger partition sizes. Initially, FAT supported 12 bit entries for addresses but that was not big enough so that was changed to be 16 bit entries, creating what is called FAT16. Now, you will commonly see FAT32, which has 32 bit entries for addresses.

While we talk about FAT as being a file system, it is also a data structure that resides in the partition. This may appear to be confusing at times, since it has two separate meanings. In fact, one refers to the other. The format or file system is actually named after the table that gets created, when the file system is formatted. In order to avoid as much confusion as possible, I will refer to the file table itself as the file table or as a table and the file system itself as either FAT or the File Allocation Table.

Because of the simplicity of FAT, it ends up being implemented in a lot of different places. Devices like digital cameras, digital recorders, or other basic, digital consumer devices often implement FAT as the file system to store data on. When you pull a storage card out of one of those devices, it will be formatted in a version of FAT. Another place, where you will often find FAT implemented is the boot partition of a computer. Since FAT is such a simple file system, most operating systems can read and write to it. Additionally, it is easy for the boot code to be implemented to get data off it. EFI systems may use FAT in the boot partition. The boot partition would then be used to store files that would boot the actual operating system. Using FAT in the boot partition can also help in cases where you are booting more than one operating system from the same hard drive. Since it is FAT, you do not have to worry about whether any of the operating systems can read or write to the boot partition.

Partition Boot Sector

The partition boot sector is the first sector in the partition and it describes the location of all the important data structures on disk, such as, where the table resides physically, as well as, where the backup table is. It has instructions for where to find the actual operating system by way of a jump instruction in the first three bytes. The BIOS Parameter Block (BPB) is a section of the partition boot sector. Different file systems store different data in the BPB. It has information that describes the partition. It also indicates how big the cluster size on the disk is. FAT supports a number of cluster sizes up to 32 k. A cluster size of 32 k would be 64 contiguous sectors. The following table specifies the information that is stored in the BPB on a FAT partition. Different versions of FAT have slightly different parameters, so we will look at the Extended BIOS Parameter Block that describes a FAT32 partition (Table 2.3).

TABLE 2.3 The Information that is Stored in the BPB on a FAT Partition

Starting byte	Length	Description
0x0B	2 bytes	Bytes per sector. This is the size of the hardware sector. This is generally 512.
0x0D	1 byte	Sectors per cluster. This is the number of contiguous sectors that make up a single cluster.
0x0E	2 bytes	Reserved sectors. A number of sectors may be reserved after the BPB before the first allocation table starts. This indicates how many sectors have been reserved.
0x10	1 byte	Number of file allocation tables.
0x11	2 bytes	The number of entries in the root directory. The number of entries in the root directory is limited and this value indicates how many entries exist in the root, or top level, directory. On FAT32 volumes, this value will be 0.
0x13	2 bytes	The number of sectors on the hard drive if that number can be put into 16 bits. Otherwise, this field is 0 and the large sectors field is used instead.
0x15	1 byte	This is the type of media where the partition exists. This will commonly be 0xF8 for a hard disk
0x16	2 bytes	The number of sectors that a FAT consumes.
0x18	2 bytes	The number of sectors per track.
0x1A	2 bytes	The number of heads.
0x1C	4 bytes	The number of hidden sectors.
0x20	4 bytes	This is the large sectors field and has 4 bytes where the small sectors field only has 2. This is the number of sectors on the hard drive.
0x24	4 bytes	The number of sectors that each FAT consumes
0x28	2 bytes	Not used by Windows Server 2003
0x2A	2 bytes	File system version where the most significant byte is the major version number and the least significant byte is the minor version number.

(Continued)

TABLE 2.3 The Information that is Stored in the BPB on a FAT Partition *(cont.)*

Starting byte	Length	Description
0x2C	4 bytes	Root cluster number. This is the cluster number where the root directory is located on the drive. Typically, this may be 2.
0x30	2 bytes	File system information sector number. The file system has a number of reserved sectors. This is the sector number within those sectors, where the FSINFO structure is located.
0x32	2 bytes	Backup boot sector.
0x34	12 bytes	Reserved
0x40	1 byte	Physical drive number. Hard drives would typically start numbering at 0x80.
0x41	1 byte	Reserved
0x42	1 byte	Extended boot signature
0x43	4 bytes	Volume signature number. This is a random value used to distinguish between drives.
0x47	11 bytes	Volume name or label.
0x52	8 bytes	System identifier. This should be FAT32 on a FAT32 system

The BPB carries some information about the physical disk, like the number of heads and the size of the tracks on the drive, but the majority of the information describes the file system, including the name of the volume. With the information in the BPB, we can locate the file table on the hard drive, since it is the first cluster after the reserved sectors that follow the BPB itself. In other words, starting with the master boot record, the organizational data structures on a FAT filesystem are laid out in the order shown in Figure 2.6. The diagram assumes a single partition on the hard drive. Any additional partitions would not include the master boot record but would have the BPB start in the first sector belonging to those partitions.

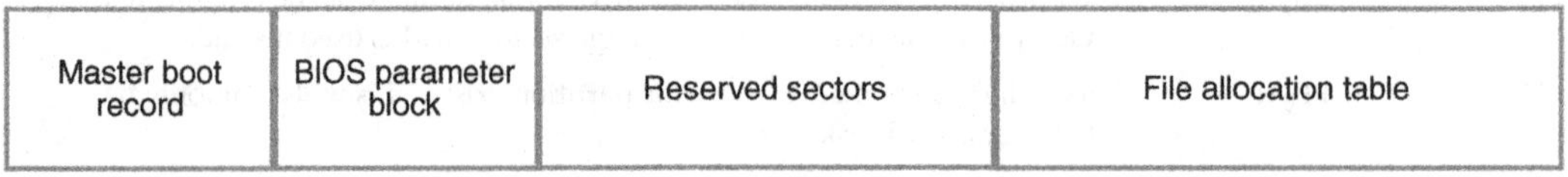

Master boot record	BIOS parameter block	Reserved sectors	File allocation table

FIGURE 2.6

In cases, where a disk has multiple partitions, each partition would have its own BIOS parameter block and data structures that would be placed on the disk where appropriate to that file system.

File Table

Each cluster within the partition has an entry in the file table. On large disks, this makes the file tables very large, taking up a lot of space for the overhead of the file system. This is not at all to say that every cluster takes up entire sectors. Each entry within the file table takes a different amount of space, based on the version of FAT in use, in part because the cluster address is larger from one version of FAT to another. In FAT32, we use 32 bits to address a cluster and each cluster is composed of some number of contiguous sectors. So, each entry in the file table is really just a 32-bit number indicating the next cluster to look at. You can see a simple example in Figure 2.7. This shows an array of entries in the table, where the value in the table indicates the next cluster for the file.

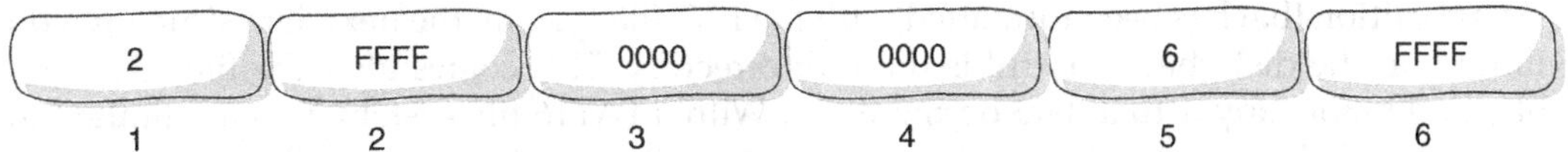

FIGURE 2.7

There are a couple of values that are special, however, and you can see them. When we get to the end of the file, we need to know that. If a particular cluster is the last one that belongs to a file, the cluster gets the value of FFFF in our example. In real life, the value in those fields would commonly be FFFFFFFF, which is the maximum value that can be stored in the table entry. If a file only took up one cluster, the value in that cluster would be FFFFFFFF. A cluster that is not in use gets the value 00000000 indicating that there is nothing there. It does not belong to a file and is therefore free to use.

When we need to allocate space for a file, we just read down through the file allocation table, until we find one of those entries indicating that it is empty. If the operating system wants to allocate multiple clusters and ensure that those clusters are contiguous, it can keep scanning until, it finds a number of entries in the table that are free and contiguous, then it can allocate those clusters to the file. In some cases, having all of the clusters in a file one after another on the drive can help performance. In other cases, the operating system may want to allocate the clusters in a file differently to get a different performance factor, depending on how the underlying drive works.

Solid State Drives (SSDs) are special cases. Since SSDs use storage technology that can wear out, the drive uses something called wear leveling. This means that logical addresses may not always refer to the same spot on the disk over time, as the drive firmware moves some physical addresses out of current use to give them a break and maintain the overall longevity of the drive. In practical terms, an SSD will have more actual storage space than is advertised to the operating system. Not all of that storage will actually be in use at any given time.

We have the list of clusters that are in use but that is not very helpful, when we want to get access to actual files rather than simply allocating space on the drive. In order to figure out, how we go about chasing down the files out of a FAT file system, there is one other thing we need to go over. We need to talk about the root directory.

Root Directory

You may notice that each entry in the file table says nothing at all about file names or any other attributes. You may be wondering where that information is stored. We cannot simply live with just knowing how to get to the next cluster in a file. When someone gets a listing of all the files, it is nice to print useful information like the name, for instance. Without the name, knowing how all the clusters relate to one another is not really helpful to the user. The user wants to get to the data on the drive by the name of the file, rather than the cluster location. As a result, we need a way to store information about the name, as well as, time-related information and then specific details like whether it is a directory or a hidden file.

In a partition that has been formatted with the FAT file system, the next data structure you will find on the disk that is useful is the root directory. This comes after the file allocation tables and before any actual data on the drive. With a FAT16 file system, you are limited in the number of files you can store in the root directory, though that is generally okay, since the limit is 512 files, which is often a pretty substantial directory. This has changed in FAT32, though, where the root directory no longer has limitations on its size. A directory, like the root directory, consumes clusters on the drive but rather than having file data, it has data structures that describe each directory entry. This would be a collection of files or directories. Table 2.4 shows the data that is stored in each directory entry.

The root directory gives us the ability to locate files on the partition. In order to locate files, you have to start with the BPB to locate the root directly. From there, you will find a list of files and directories that you can use to chase through the directories. Each directory structure entry points to a cluster on the drive. In the case of directories, that cluster will contain another set of directory entries. In the case of files, the clusters contain the file data. The process for finding a file on a FAT file system is locating the file by starting at the root directory. Once you find the right directory entry, you get the cluster associated with the file. You then need to look up the cluster in the file table, in order to determine if the file only takes up one cluster. At the same time, you need to read the data out of the cluster. If the file table indicates there is another cluster, you go to that cluster in the file table while also reading the data out of the cluster. You continue this process until you reach the end of the file.

TABLE 2.4 Information Contained in a Directory Entry

Name	Size	Description
Name	11 bytes	The name of the entry in short name format, commonly referred to as 8.3 since it is an 8-character name with a 3-character file extension.
Attribute byte	1 byte	A byte with flags indicating specific attributes for the entry like whether it is a directory, hidden file, operating system file, or if it needs to be backed up (archived).
Creation time and date	5 bytes	The date and time the file was created.
Last access date	2 bytes	The day the file was last accessed
Last modification time and date	4 bytes	The last date and time that the file was changed on disk.
First cluster	4 bytes	The beginning cluster address of the file data
File size	4 bytes	The size of the file

File Analysis

One tool that can help a lot is The Sleuth Kit (TSK), which is really a set of command line tools that can be used to get access to information on a raw disk or image. TSK is a follow-on to a set of tools called The Coroner's Toolkit (TCT), which was written by Wietse Venema and Dan Farmer in the late 1990s. TCT was one of the very first open source forensics tools. TCT has not been updated but TSK has been. The first place we want to start when it comes to performing file analysis is getting the partition table. Certainly this could be done using a standard tool like fdisk but TSK includes mmls, which is a tool used to extract the partition table. You can see the use of mmls on a disk with a single FAT32 partition in Figure 2.8.

```
kilroy@dallas ~ $ sudo mmls /dev/sdb
DOS Partition Table
Offset Sector: 0
Units are in 512-byte sectors

     Slot    Start        End          Length       Description
00:  Meta    0000000000   0000000000   0000000001   Primary Table (#0)
01:  -----   0000000000   0000002047   0000002048   Unallocated
02:  00:00   0000002048   0004194303   0004192256   Win95 FAT32 (0x0C)
```

FIGURE 2.8

Once I know where the partition is, I can get access to it using the tool fls from TSK. fls provides a listing of the files in the root of the partition. This is done by simply specifying the partition or image and, if necessary, the type of the partition, though fls is often very good at determining the partition type on its own, so you do not need to tell it. This is particularly true in the case of FAT32 partitions. Since it is such a common partition type, plus the fact that you can determine which partition type it is by reading the structures on the disk, it is easy to determine the right partition. You can see a listing of files in Figure 2.9.

```
kilroy@dallas ~ $ sudo fls /dev/sdb1
r/r 4:  parsedisk.py
r/r 6:  pc.py
r/r 8:  pst.py
r/r 10: readdisk.py
r/r 12: scapytest.py
d/d 13: SPIKE
d/d 15: Pictures
d/d 17: sulley
v/v 66944771:   $MBR
v/v 66944772:   $FAT1
v/v 66944773:   $FAT2
d/d 66944774:   $OrphanFiles
```

FIGURE 2.9

Once we get the list of files, we can take a look at each entry. Let us pick one and take a closer look at it. The fourth one down is a file named readdisk.py. You will see, based on the r/r, that this is a regular file as opposed to d/d, which would be a directory. There are two letters because the first relates to the file name data and the second refers to the metadata. This would be irrelevant in the case of a FAT file system, since there is no difference between the file name data and the metadata on a FAT filesystem. Other filesystems do make the distinction, which is why fls includes both. You will also see v in the list which are virtual files that TSK makes reference to, but do not exist as real files on the disk. The next thing you will see after the entry type indicator is the location. Using this piece of data, we can retrieve the contents from the file using another TSK tool. This particular tool, icat, will grab the information based on an inode number. This is a remnant of the history of the tool, which was designed to look at inodes. Inodes are information sectors in a UNIX file system, akin to directory entries in the FAT file system. In this case, we are going to use the address to grab data from the file system. You can see the use of this tool in Figure 2.10.

```
kilroy@dallas ~ $ sudo icat /dev/sdb1 10
#!/usr/bin/python3
import struct

f = open("mbr.dd", "rb")

mbr = bytearray()
try:
    mbr = f.read(512)
finally:
    f.close()

x = struct.unpack("<i", mbr[0x1B8:0x1BC])
print("Disk signature: ", x[0])
x = mbr[0x1BE]
if x == 0x80:
        print("Active flag: Active")
else:
        print("Active flag: Not active")

lbastart = struct.unpack("<i", mbr[0x1C6:0x1CA])
print("Partition Start (LBA): ", lbastart[0])
lbaend = struct.unpack("<i", mbr[0x1C9:0x1CD])
print("Partition End (LBA): ", lbaend[0])
```

FIGURE 2.10

The one thing that we are missing from all of this information is metadata like time stamps, as well as, the location on the disk. In order to get that information, we have to use another tool altogether. The tool we will be using is istat and it retrieves all of the information out of the directory entry, including the file name and the time stamps. Figure 2.11 shows an example of the use of istat. The examples, I am providing here were performed on a Linux system, though TSK runs on multiple operating systems. There are a few Linux distributions that include TSK installed right out of the box. These distributions are commonly used by forensic analysts.

```
kilroy@dallas ~ $ sudo istat /dev/sdbl 10
Directory Entry: 10
Allocated
File Attributes: File, Archive
Size: 488
Name: READDISK.PY

Directory Entry Times:
Written:        Tue Jun 24 15:11:44 2014
Accessed:       Tue Jun 24 00:00:00 2014
Created:        Tue Jun 24 15:11:44 2014

Sectors:
8240 0 0 0 0 0 0 0
```

FIGURE 2.11

You will notice the time stamps on the files. These times indicate the apparent time that the file was created, changed, and accessed. However, all of these times are stored in the directory entry for the file and those directory entries are easy to get access to. They can easily be modified to another value. Using the Linux command touch, I was able to change the time on the file readdisk.py, as you can see here:

```
-rwxr-xr-x 1 root root 488 Jun  1  1985 /mnt/readdisk.py
```

It now looks like the date on the file has been changed to June 1, 1985, even though this particular file was just created in the last couple of weeks and not nearly thirty years ago. Of course, the interesting thing is that if you look a little bit closer, you will see that the written time and the accessed time have changed, but the created date and time has remained the same. This is due to a limitation with the touch utility. There are other tools that are capable of making changes to all of the dates and times and you could certainly make alterations yourself using a hex editor. In order to get the complete picture, we just check istat again on the file after the changes made to the date and time.

```
Directory Entry Times:
Written:   Sat Jun  1 14:51:00 1985
Accessed:  Sat Jun  1 00:00:00 1985
Created:   Tue Jun 24 19:48:48 2014
```

The changes that we see, make it obvious that something has happened to this file, since the written and accessed dates and times are before the create date and time. In the real world, you cannot make a change to a file that has not been created yet. That would be like me trying to go and edit the text in this chapter before I had actually written it. Well, maybe it is not quite the same. Without any way to verify the data in the file system and protect it from outside changes, this sort of thing is always possible and FAT is not the only file system affected due to this problem.

New Technology File System (NTFS)

The New Technology File System (NTFS) was developed by Microsoft to be part of the NT operating system, which Microsoft was intending to be a head up competitor of OS/2, the operating system Microsoft was developing with IBM. OS/2 was everything that DOS/Windows was not. It was stable, robust, and reliable. NT was supposed to be all those things as well, while still being wholly Microsoft's. NT was developed by a team of people led by Dave Cutler who came from Digital Equipment Corporation. Cutler had a lot of experience with solid, reliable operating systems. Unlike FAT, which was the file system of DOS/Windows, NTFS needed to be resilient, reliable, and be able to support larger drives than those supported by FAT at the time. Additionally, it needed to support security mechanisms like the ability to prevent some users from getting access to the files, while still allowing other users to get that access.

One major difference between NTFS and FAT is that when you format a FAT partition, you are creating all of the data structures on the disk. This means that you are creating a file table, where all of the clusters have an entry. This is all done at the time the disk is formatted. In the case of NTFS, the effect of formatting is the same – the data structures get written out to the disk but unlike FAT, only the minimal amount of information is written. This means that the master file table is created with just the bare bones entries in the table. The table continues to grow as more files are added to it. In the case of FAT, the table has a fixed size based on the number of clusters on the file system. With NTFS, the table is only as large as it needs to be based on the files that are being stored.

NTFS makes use of a journal, which is a transaction log. The journal is used to recover the file system in case of a system failure.

The data structures on disk are completely different for NTFS than they were for FAT, not surprisingly. The way it was designed was based on entirely different requirements with more system capacity allowing for more complexity in the file system structure. One big difference between NTFS and FAT is that NTFS is a proprietary file system and so details are not always available, which means support within other operating systems is not always there. Even in cases, where another operating system may implement support for NTFS, they do not always implement write support for the file system to prevent corruption of any data or files. Access to NTFS is handled by drivers and it is up to the author of the driver to know how NTFS works, so, it can make all the appropriate changes in order to implement writing.

Just as in the FAT file system, NTFS makes use of the BPB to store values related to the location of critical file system data structures. Rather than looking over the entire BPB again, we will take a look at the values in the BPB that are specifically related to NTFS. Table 2.5 shows the list of values including their offset within the BPB and the description of their purpose. You will notice, if you do the arithmetic on the hexadecimal, that there are gaps. These gaps are entries in the BPB that either don not relate to NTFS and so are not checked or else they are reserved.

At offset, 0x30 is the location of the address of the Master File Table (MFT). MFT is the location of the information for all of the files and directories in the entire file system. Every file or directory will have an entry in the MFT and everything on the disk is considered a file, including all of the metainformation about the file system. It is such an important data structure, considering that it is essentially the NTFS itself, that it has a backup. The backup is located at the address in

TABLE 2.5 The List of Values Including their Offset Within the BPB and the Description of their Purpose

Offset	Length	Description
0x0B	2 bytes	Bytes per sector
0x0D	1 byte	Sectors per cluster
0x15	1 byte	Media descriptor. This will generally be F8 for a hard drive.
0x28	8 bytes	Total number of sectors
0x30	8 bytes	Cluster number for the Master File Table. This file is called $MFT in the file table.
0x38	8 bytes	Cluster number for the Master File Table mirror. This file is called $MFTMirr in the file table.
0x40	1 byte	Clusters per MFT record. Each MFT record contains information relating to a file or directory in the file system.
0x44	1 byte	Clusters per index buffer.
0x48	8 bytes	Volume serial number

0x38 and it is called the MFT Mirror. Actually, both the MFT and the MFT Mirror have their own entries in the Master File Table. Since they are special files, they have special names. The name of the MFT is $MFT and the mirror is $MFTMirr. There are a number of other special files in the MFT that contain information about the file system and the volume. Since the information has to be stored somewhere, NTFS implements all of the information as files in the file system, so it does not have to be outside of the file system and require a separate structure to keep track of it. Table 2.6 shows the list of all of the special files that are also in the MFT.

Where the FAT was a list of clusters indicating whether the cluster was in use or not, and if it was, what the next cluster in the file is, the MFT holds considerably more information.

TABLE 2.6 The List of all of the Special Files that are also in the MFT

File name	MFT record	Description
$Mft	0	Every file or folder has an entry in the MFT. These are stored in this file.
$MftMirr	1	This is the mirror of the MFT
$LogFile	2	The transaction log. This allows the file system to recover in case of a failure.
$Volume	3	This is information about the volume including the label and version.
$AttrDef	4	A table of attribute names, numbers, and descriptions.
$	5	The root folder.
$Bitmap	6	A representation of the clusters that are in use.
$Boot	7	This is the BPB from the volume and includes boot code.
$BadClus	8	Includes any bad clusters from the volume.
$Secure	9	This is the security descriptors for the files on the volume.
$Upcase	10	Converts lowercase to uppercase characters in Unicode.
$Extend	11	Information about optional extensions for quotas, object identifiers, and other extensions.

In fact, in some cases where the file is very small, the entire contents of the file may be contained within the entry in the MFT. You can see a diagram of an MFT entry for a small file where the standard information, file name, security descriptors, and the data are all contained within the MFT entry (Figure 2.12).

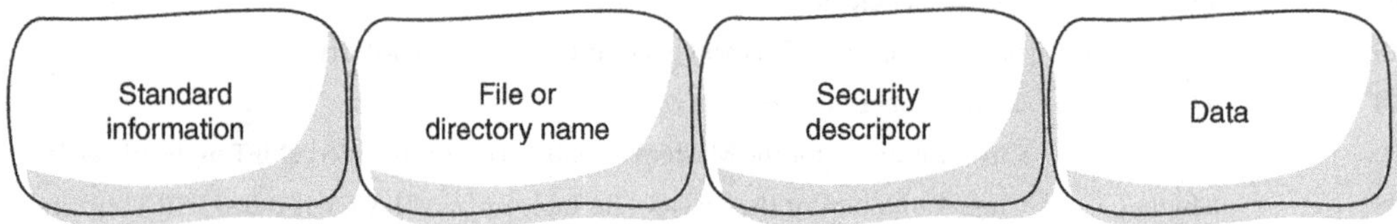

FIGURE 2.12

Each file or folder in the file system is represented as a set of attributes. The attributes are clearly defined and every file has a different set of attributes that may be used to describe them, since every file is different. Each attribute record is 1024 bytes and you can find out from the extended BPB, how many clusters each MFT entry consumes. From there, you can determine how many attributes each MFT entry can handle and whether additional MFT entries may be required to store all of the information for a particular file.

NTFS attributes can be either resident, where the information related to the attribute is stored in the MFT, or non-resident where it is stored external to the MFT. A non-resident attribute would be the $DATA attribute that points to clusters on the disk for the location of the file content data.

As an example, let us say that you have a cluster size of 8 sectors. This means that each cluster is 4096 bytes (512 × 8). If your clusters per MFT record had a value of 1, you could have a total of 4 attributes in each MFT record because each attribute is going to be 1024 bytes and you have a total of 4096 bytes, you can store your attributes into. If you need additional clusters for a file in the MFT, you can link to them and many files may need several clusters in order to contain all of the attributes. The list of attributes that can be associated with a file is well defined and can be found in Table 2.7.

TABLE 2.7 MFT Attribute List

Attribute type	Description
Standard information	This would have time stamp information as well as other details about the file.
Attribute list	Has the location of the attributes that do not fit into this record.
File name	You may have multiple entries for this attribute – one for the 8.3 short name and one for the long name as well as any other names or links as required. The long name can be up to 255 Unicode characters.
Security descriptor	This has information about the access control list.
Data	This would contain file data.
Object ID	A unique identifier, though not all files will have object IDs.
Logged tool stream	This would be used by the encrypting file system and is similar to the data attribute.

TABLE 2.7 MFT Attribute List *(cont.)*

Attribute type	Description
Reparse point	If the entry were used as a mount point or a directory junction, this attribute would be needed.
Index root	If the entry were a folder, this attribute would be used.
Index allocation	If the entry were a folder, this attribute would be used.
Bitmap	If the entry were a folder, this attribute would be used.
Volume information	A special attribute that would only be used for the $Volume file. This would contain the volume version.
Volume name	A special attribute that would only be used for the $Volume file. This would contain the volume name.

Attribute type 0x10 - Standard information

Create time	2014/03/12, 14:32:59.747
Modified time	2014/06/16, 15:51:35.856
MFT changed time	2014/06/27, 17:49:45.496
Last access time	2014/03/12, 14:32:59.747
Flags	00002020
Max versions	0
Version number	0
Class ID	0

Attribute type 0x30 - File name

Parent directory ref	000100000000E656
Create time	2014/03/12, 14:32:59.747
Modified time	2014/03/12, 14:32:59.747
MFT changed time	2014/03/12, 14:32:59.747
Last access time	2014/03/12, 14:32:59.747
Allocated size	0
Actual size	0
Flags	00002020 (A no-index)
Reparse	00000000
Name namespace	Win32 & DOS
Name	AgRobust.db

FIGURE 2.13

Figure 2.13 shows the details from two attributes from a file on an NTFS partition. This was captured from the utility NTFSWalker. The two attributes shown here are the standard information attribute and the file name attribute. You may have noticed that the standard information has a set of timestamps and the file name attribute also has a set of time stamps and the two do not really match up. That is because the file system keeps track of when the file name was changed, since you can change the file name separately from accessing the file itself. I do not have to open the file, which would be considered an access of the file, in order to change the file name, which can be done using the Windows File Explorer.

Standard information is always resident. The contents of the standard information attribute will always be found in the MFT itself. The standard information attribute has the value of 0x10.

Alternate Data Streams

The alternate data stream is a peculiarity of NTFS, resulted from a need to support the resource forks that were used in Apple's file system. Additionally, Netware had support for additional streams associated with files. The result of the need to support multiple data streams in files, which turned into what we know as alternate data streams. While long ago, Microsoft has dropped support of third party file systems like Apple's, the functionality remained within the file system. In the case of NTFS, the alternate data stream was implemented as an attribute. You can see an example of this in Figure 2.14, where it shows up as another DATA attribute with a different name from the primary name of the file.

Over time, Microsoft found uses for the alternate data stream, including storing icons, just as Apple had done. One of the important things to keep in mind about an alternate data stream is that it cannot be seen when you look at a directory listing. It does not show up as a file, because it is not one. You would no more see an alternate data stream in a file listing in Windows Explorer than you would see the access control list, which is another attribute of a file. You need to dig deeper in order to see the access control list, just as you need to dig deeper to see the alternate data stream. In order to see the list of alternate data streams, you need to either get an external utility including streams from the Windows Sys-Internals tool set or you need to add a special switch to the dir command in the command processor (cmd.exe). This is a directory listing with the /R switch that displays alternate data streams.

```
E:\>dir /R
 Volume in drive E is MyVolume
 Volume Serial Number is 4879-7D0B

 Directory of E:\

06/27/2014  06:14 PM       270,314,496 autopsy-3.0.10-64bit.msi
                                    26 autopsy-3.0.10-
64bit.msi:Zone.Identifier:$DATA
               1 File(s)    270,314,496 bytes
               0 Dir(s)  3,938,492,416 bytes free
```

Attribute type 0x30 - File name	
Parent directory ref	0005000000000005
Create time	2014/06/27, 19:00:11.932
Modified time	2014/06/27, 19:00:11.932
MFT changed time	2014/06/27, 19:00:11.932
Last access time	2014/06/27, 19:00:11.932
Allocated size	270315520
Actual size	0
Flags	00000020 (A)
Reparse	00000000
Name namespace	Win32
Name	autopsy-3.0.10-64bit.msi
Attribute type 0x80 - Data	
Type	01
Length	72
ID	0001
Flags	0000
Data runs	45:65995
Attribute type 0x80 - Data	
Type	04
Name	Zone.Identifier
Length	88
ID	0004
Flags	0000
Length of contents	26
Contents as ANSI	[ZoneTransfer]ZoneId=3
Contents as Unicode	?????????????

FIGURE 2.14

The alternate data stream in this case is called Zone.Identifier and it shows up with the file name followed by a colon then the name of the alternate data stream. This is another use that Microsoft has found for the alternate data stream. The contents of this alternate data stream indicate the zone that the file came from. This is how Microsoft protects you from downloaded content. The file in the listing was downloaded from a web site. The contents of the alternate data stream indicate the file came from zone 3, the Internet zone. When you try to open the file, you will get an alert indicating that the source was untrusted and do you really want to open it. If you were to remove or alter the alternate data stream to indicate a trusted zone, you would no longer get that message.

Not every application supports alternate data streams. Even if you feed the entire path to the alternate data stream as a file name to some programs, the program will generate an error that it cannot find the file. Certainly you will not be able to open them from the file open dialog by attempting to browse to it, since the alternate data stream will not show up in the file open dialog, just as it will not show up in Windows Explorer. Much of what you do to manipulate or view alternate data streams from the user perspective is done at the command line. It is also easy to create alternate data streams using the command line. In order to embed one file into the alternate data stream of another file, we can use a simple command.

```
E:\>dir
 Volume in drive E is MyVolume
 Volume Serial Number is 4879-7D0B

 Directory of E:\

06/27/2014  06:14 PM       270,314,496 autopsy-3.0.10-64bit.msi
06/27/2014  06:08 PM           601,656 ntfswalker.zip
03/26/2014  08:53 AM        10,021,892 volatility.exe
               3 File(s)    280,938,044 bytes
               0 Dir(s)   3,927,867,392 bytes free

E:\>type volatility.exe > ntfswalker.zip:volatility.exe

E:\>dir /R
 Volume in drive E is MyVolume
 Volume Serial Number is 4879-7D0B

 Directory of E:\

06/27/2014  06:14 PM       270,314,496 autopsy-3.0.10-64bit.msi
                                    26 autopsy-3.0.10-
64bit.msi:Zone.Identifier:$DATA
06/28/2014  09:08 AM           601,656 ntfswalker.zip
                            10,021,892
ntfswalker.zip:volatility.exe:$DATA
                                    26
ntfswalker.zip:Zone.Identifier:$DATA
03/26/2014  08:53 AM        10,021,892 volatility.exe
                                    26
volatility.exe:Zone.Identifier:$DATA
               3 File(s)    280,938,044 bytes
               0 Dir(s)   3,917,844,480 bytes free
```

Using the type command, which is usually used to output a file to the screen at the command line, we redirect the output into the alternate data stream. Since the command processor understands the alternate data stream, we end up with one file embedded into an attribute of another file. This is highly useful for hiding information, since users will not see the alternate data stream without doing some looking for it, though it is trivial for a forensic tool to locate this information. This has been used in the past to hide malware, so Microsoft has made it harder to run programs straight out of the alternate data stream. Where you used to be able to launch the alternate data stream as a program using the start command, which does not work any longer as a way to protect users from malicious software. This does not mean that it is impossible to launch executables out of alternate data streams. Microsoft has the Windows Management Instrumentation (WMI), which is fundamental to tools like Power Shell. Using the console implementation of WMI, you can launch the program stored as an alternate data stream. In the case of volatility.exe stored as an attribute of ntfswalker.zip as seen before, you would run the command *wmic process call create ntfswalker.zip:volatility.exe*.

Fortunately, you do not need big, expensive forensic tools to detect these alternate data streams. First, you have the dir command, but you have to run that in each directory, which can be very tedious. Another tool you can use is the streams utility available from Microsoft's SysInternals suite. Both dir and streams are command line utilities. If you are looking for a graphical interface to perform this function, you can use ADS Locator. Figure 2.15 shows the use of ADS Locator scanning my home directory on a Windows 7 system.

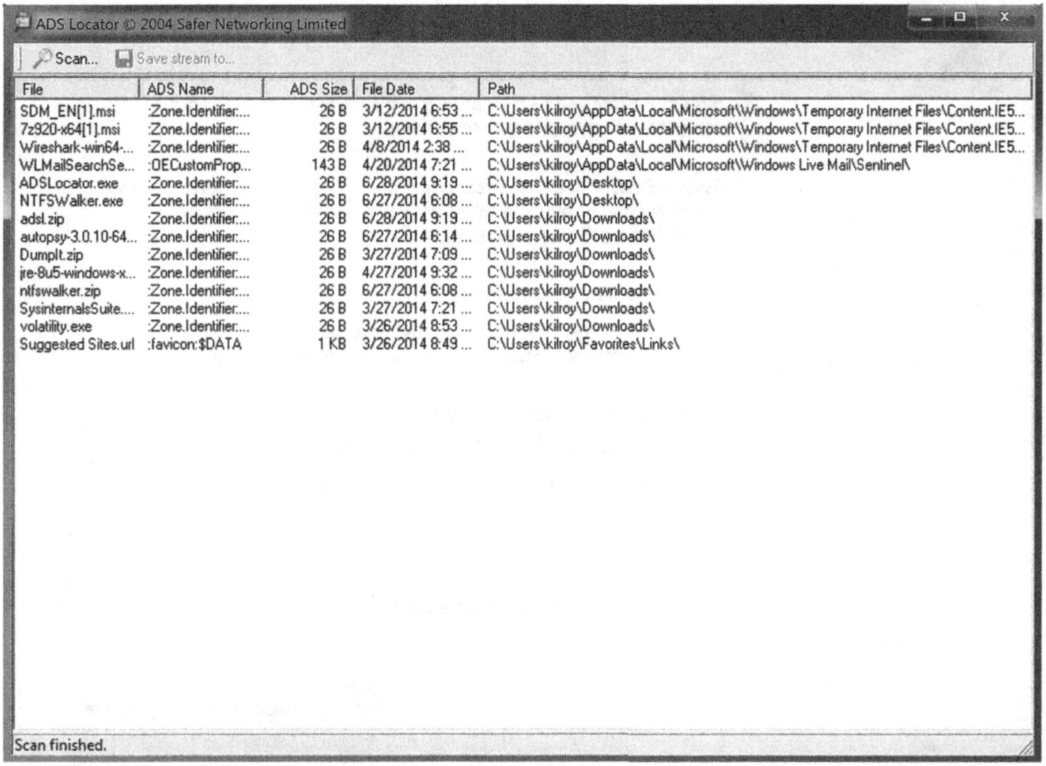

ADS Locator © 2004 Safer Networking Limited

Scan... Save stream to...

File	ADS Name	ADS Size	File Date	Path
SDM_EN[1].msi	:Zone.Identifier:...	26 B	3/12/2014 6:53 ...	C:\Users\kilroy\AppData\Local\Microsoft\Windows\Temporary Internet Files\Content.IE5...
7z920-x64[1].msi	:Zone.Identifier:...	26 B	3/12/2014 6:55 ...	C:\Users\kilroy\AppData\Local\Microsoft\Windows\Temporary Internet Files\Content.IE5...
Wireshark-win64-...	:Zone.Identifier:...	26 B	4/8/2014 2:38 ...	C:\Users\kilroy\AppData\Local\Microsoft\Windows\Temporary Internet Files\Content.IE5...
WLMailSearchSe...	:OECustomProp...	143 B	4/20/2014 7:21 ...	C:\Users\kilroy\AppData\Local\Microsoft\Windows Live Mail\Sentinel\
ADSLocator.exe	:Zone.Identifier:...	26 B	6/28/2014 9:19 ...	C:\Users\kilroy\Desktop\
NTFSWalker.exe	:Zone.Identifier:...	26 B	6/27/2014 6:08 ...	C:\Users\kilroy\Desktop\
adsl.zip	:Zone.Identifier:...	26 B	6/28/2014 9:19 ...	C:\Users\kilroy\Downloads\
autopsy-3.0.10-64...	:Zone.Identifier:...	26 B	6/27/2014 6:14 ...	C:\Users\kilroy\Downloads\
DumpIt.zip	:Zone.Identifier:...	26 B	3/27/2014 7:09 ...	C:\Users\kilroy\Downloads\
jre-8u5-windows-x...	:Zone.Identifier:...	26 B	4/27/2014 9:32 ...	C:\Users\kilroy\Downloads\
ntfswalker.zip	:Zone.Identifier:...	26 B	6/27/2014 6:08 ...	C:\Users\kilroy\Downloads\
SysinternalsSuite....	:Zone.Identifier:...	26 B	3/27/2014 7:21 ...	C:\Users\kilroy\Downloads\
volatility.exe	:Zone.Identifier:...	26 B	3/26/2014 8:53 ...	C:\Users\kilroy\Downloads\
Suggested Sites.url	:favicon:$DATA	1 KB	3/26/2014 8:49 ...	C:\Users\kilroy\Favorites\Links\

Scan finished.

FIGURE 2.15

This capture was taken from a virtual machine that is not used much, so there are not a lot of entries. If you were to run this on a system that was used a lot and especially a system that uses Internet Explorer, you would see a lot of entries here. The only reason I call out Internet Explorer is because it stores temporary files that are cached from the Internet as plain files on the file system. Every one of them will get that zone identifier as an alternate data stream associated with the file. Other browsers stuff those files into a database so they do not get the zone identifier, though you also cannot get to them directly.

Volume Shadow Copy

When you install a program or perform a system update, you may see a message indicating that the installer is setting a restore point. We use this in order to return to a known good condition of the system. This functionality was introduced in Windows XP. The system manages these snapshots and they create something like a versioning system for files. In Figure 2.16, we have the ability to restore from a restore point and you can see that the last restore point, which is the one selected, was created as a result of installing the Autopsy program.

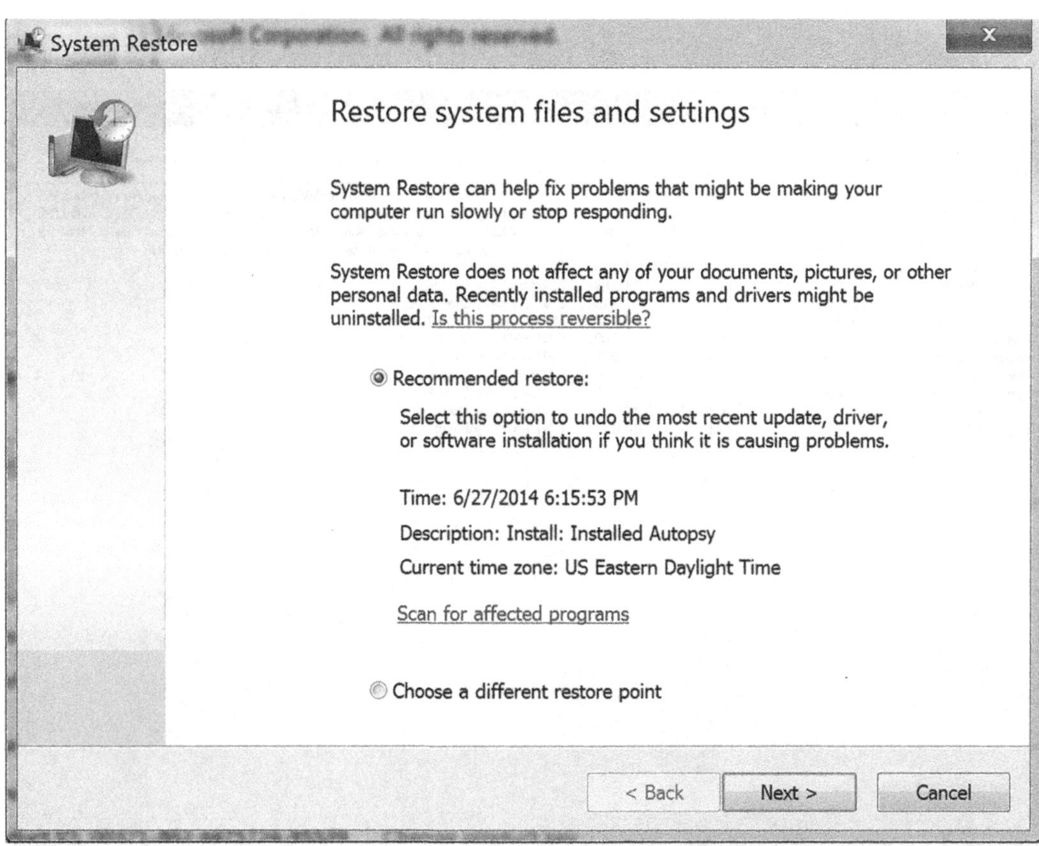

FIGURE 2.16

While the volume shadow copy is associated with NTFS, it can be used to recover data and we will go into it in more detail in the next chapter where we cover data recovery strategies.

Sparse Files

In most cases, file space gets allocated as the space is needed. As a file grows, more space on the hard drive will be requested. As an example, when I started this chapter, it was a small file so it probably took up a cluster. As I continued to write, more clusters have been added. In the case of sparse files, you allocate a large amount of space all at once and it is empty until you fill it with something. This may be commonly used by an application like a database program. The application would then be responsible for re-allocating the space within the file for whatever purpose necessary for the application. In the meantime, the file is full of 0s. This is not the ASCII character zero but instead the value of 0. In order to create the file, Windows provides a utility. You can create a 1M file using the command fsutil file createnew test.txt 1000000. Once the file is created, you can see that there are zeros in it using as hex editor, as in Figure 2.17.

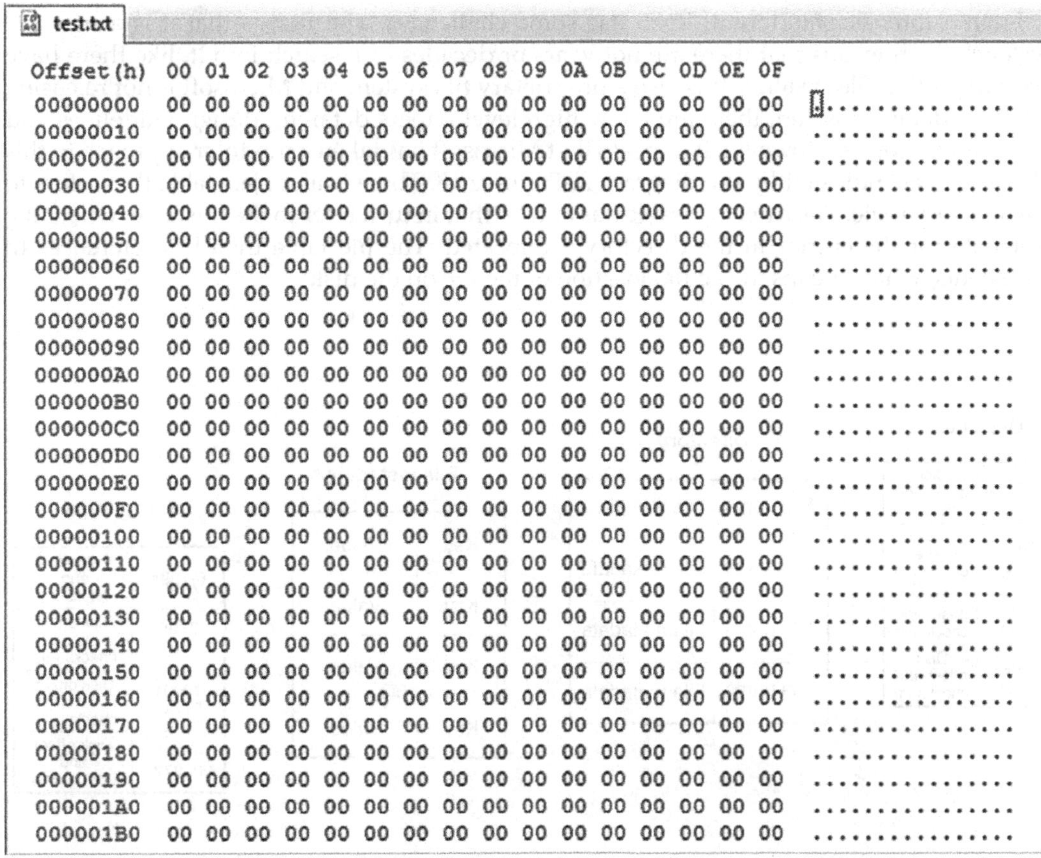

FIGURE 2.17

If you were to check a directory listing, you would find that the size of the file was the size you requested. Further, checking properties on the file shows that the size of the file is what you requested and the size on disk is the size taken up by the clusters required to store a file of that size. This type of file may be useful for storing information inside, since it could be buried deep in the middle of a lot of empty space or garbage. A sparse file will also compress well since it is primarily 0s.

Resilient File System (ReFS)

The Resilient File System (ReFS) is a new file system designed by Microsoft, initially only available on their server operating system, starting with Windows Server 2012. It has since been made available on the consumer/desktop operating system starting with Windows 8.1. ReFS is a completely different file system than NTFS. Where NTFS stores metadata for the files (the master file table with all the attributes) in a single location on the partition, ReFS stores metadata across the volume. ReFS is not considered a drop-in replacement for NTFS since it offers different functionality. As an example, ReFS does not support encrypted files or compression within the file system.

From a forensic standpoint, ReFS has some challenges. The first is that it is a new file system, which means that there are not years or decades of research into it, like there have been with other file systems. It is also a proprietary file system and Microsoft is not releasing technical details. Instead, there are a few high level papers detailing design guidelines and other similar topics. However, it appears that Microsoft has taken a modular approach to this file system, as indicated by the diagram in Figure 2.18. There is an object table that refers to the directory table. The directory table has entries that in turn refer to the file table, where the metadata for the entries in the directory are located. The file table then has references to the extents, which means the actual location of the file on the disk.

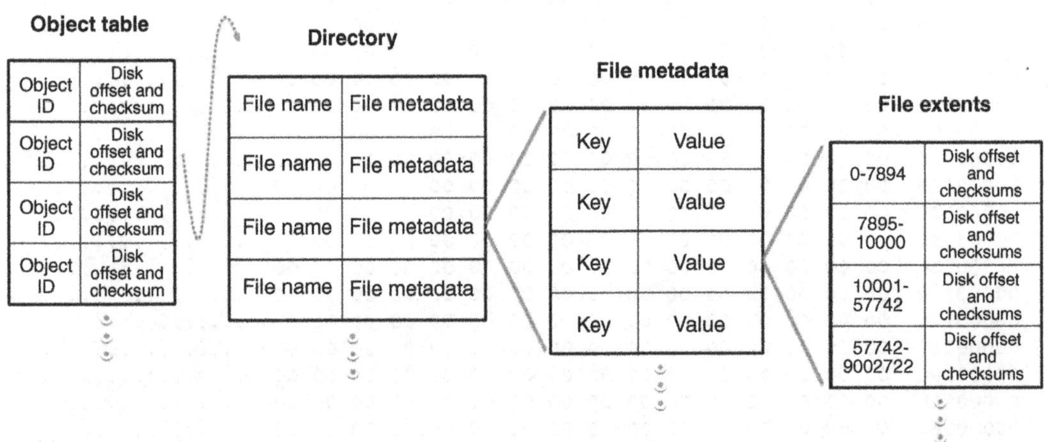

FIGURE 2.18

Existing utilities no longer work with ReFS, unless they have been specifically re-written to support ReFS. This should not be much of a surprise. Actually, some utilities simply no longer work at all and are not expected to. The utility chkdsk, used to check a disk's health and the sanity of the metadata, will not work with ReFS. The file system maintains internal consistency, so there is no longer a need for an external utility to check that. Microsoft has published application programming interfaces (APIs), which they expect developers to use to interact with ReFS. Until the APIs have been reverse engineered to run on other platforms, tools developed to interface with the file system would have to run on Windows. This rules out, for the time being, Linux-based forensic boot CDs.

Checking the sanity of a file system means that the metadata needs to be valid. The metadata also needs to match up to, what is on the disk.

LINUX FILE SYSTEMS

Linux got started from a textbook-based distribution called Minux. Minux was written in the 1980s, when personal computers were taking off. Minux would have been used regularly on personal computers by students. The point here is that in the 1980s on personal computers, we were often using small floppy disks and even in cases where we had hard disks, they were not very large. As a result, the design of the file system used in Minix was not very robust for the needs of a large number of users, especially for larger volumes. The file system designed for Minix was capable of supporting a volume size of 64 megabytes. The Minix file system was replaced in the early versions of Linux with the Extended File System (ext) file system, which was more capable than the Minix file system in many regards, including being able to support a volume that was 2 gigabytes. Even the ext file system was not adequate however, and it quickly gave way to the Second Extended File System (ext2) file system that had more capabilities than the ext file system.

The implementation of Minix and the ext series of file systems, all owe their heritage to some basic concepts that came from UNIX. When the developers of UNIX put their file system together, they used a set of inodes, which are data structures designed to store information about the file. This would include dates and times associated with the file as well as ownership privileges and location of the data associated with the file. Directories are implemented as files listing the files in the directory. It is worth saying that again in a different way to make it very clear. Directories are stored in the file system just like a file.

Where we had BIOS parameter blocks with the Windows-based file systems, in Unix-like systems, we use superblocks. A superblock contains information regarding the configuration of the file system. The file system is laid out using blocks, which are the same as the clusters discussed earlier in which they were contiguous sectors. While Windows-based file systems use clusters, Linux file systems like the ext family use blocks and block groups. Block groups are contiguous clusters of blocks and they are used to increase the performance of the file system. Wherever possible, the file system will keep a file within the same block group to keep down the amount of moving around the disk as the mechanical components have to do in order to read or write to the file.

ext2

As with other file systems, we have to start with the place that has all of the information about the structure of the volume and the location of important data structures. In the case of ext2, this is the superblock. The superblock is similar to the BIOS parameter block in the FAT and NTFS file systems, though since the file system is different, it has a different set of information. The superblock contains the location of the important data structures on the disk as well as sizes of structures like blocks and block groups. The superblock will have multiple copies, with each block group getting a copy of the superblock. Table 2.8 shows the entries in the superblock.

TABLE 2.8 Superblock Entry Fields

Offset	Size	Description
0	4 bytes	Number of inodes
4	4 bytes	Number of blocks
8	4 bytes	Number of blocks reserved for use by the superuser
12	4 bytes	Total number of free blocks
16	4 bytes	Total number of free inodes
20	4 bytes	The first data block
24	4 bytes	The size of each block
28	4 bytes	The size of a fragment, which is smaller than a block but still a multiple of 2 times the size of the sector. Fragments can be used to reduce unused disk space from slack.
32	4 bytes	The number of blocks in a block group.
36	4 bytes	The number of fragments per block group.
40	4 bytes	The number of inodes per block group.
44	4 bytes	The modified time.
48	4 bytes	The write time.
52	2 bytes	The number of times the file system has been mounted since the last time it was verified
54	2 bytes	The maximum number of times the file system can be mounted before it has to be verified.
56	2 bytes	The magic number indicating that the file system is ext2.
58	2 bytes	Indicates whether the file system was unmounted cleanly or if it may have errors.
60	2 bytes	Indicates what to do if errors are detected.
62	2 bytes	This is the minor revision level.
64	4 bytes	The last time the file system was checked for errors.
68	4 bytes	The maximum time, in Unix time, that the file system can go without being checked
84	4 bytes	The first inode
88	2 bytes	The size of an inode
90	2 bytes	The block group number where this copy of the superblock is being stored.

The disk is organized into block groups. Each block group is self-contained and includes its own copy of the super block as well as a group descriptor, block bitmap, inode bitmap, inode table, and the associated data blocks. Figure 2.19 is a visual representation of the organization of the file system. Each block group in the upper row contains all of the metadata blocks and the data blocks depicted in the lower row. While there is some inefficiency here in terms of replicating metadata across the file system, it can make access to data faster by using what is effectively a tree in order to get to the data rather than one very long linked list, as in the case of the FAT file system.

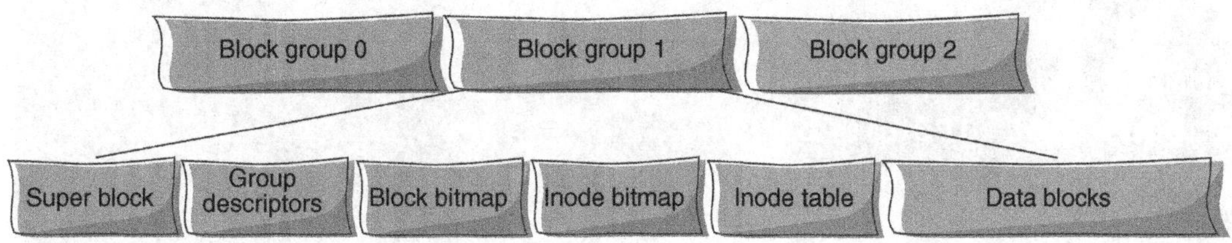

FIGURE 2.19

Bitmaps are used in the ext2 file system. A bitmap is a representation of something in the form of the bits in a block. The blocks allocation bitmap, for example, would be a way to determine whether an individual block was in use or not by checking the status of the bit that relates to that block. The same is true of the inode bitmap. Each block has a number of inodes. In order to determine whether there are free inodes, you would check the inode bitmap. The group descriptor block includes the block numbers for the blocks bitmap, the inode bitmap and the inode table, as well as, the free counts for the blocks and inodes. This tells you how full this particular block group is.

TSK has a set of tools that will help us to deconstruct the data structures on the ext file system. Figure 2.20 shows the output from the command fsstat that was run on an ext2 file system. The first set of information is about the entire file system, indicating the number of block groups, the size of each block, the number of inodes in each block group and the number of free blocks. Below that is a description of the first block. The data bitmap of the first block takes up a single block and based on the information in the superblock, each block is 4096 bytes. Based on the fact that our data blocks go from block 1569 to block 32767, we have 31198 blocks available for data.

You may notice that while there are 31198 blocks available for data, there are only 8192 inodes available. Since you need to have an inode for each file, you could end up in a situation where you have a large number of blocks that are free but you can no longer store any information in the block group because you have run out of inodes. This would mean a large number of small files, of course, but it is possible. In the case we are looking at, a full block group would assume something more than four blocks consumed by each file. This would allow the group to fill up with data while still having enough inodes available.

Since we have been talking about inodes, we should talk about what is in an inode. The inode includes 2 bytes indicating the mode, which includes the permissions for the file the inode is associated with. It also includes the user ID for the owner, the group ID, the size, and the time values. The inode stores the create time, the accessed time, the modification time, and

```
CONTENT INFORMATION
--------------------------------------------
Block Range: 0 - 15728383
Block Size: 4096
Free Blocks: 13058302

BLOCK GROUP INFORMATION
--------------------------------------------
Number of Block Groups: 480
Inodes per group: 8192
Blocks per group: 32768

Group: 0:
  Inode Range: 1 - 8192
  Block Range: 0 - 32767
  Layout:
    Super Block: 0 - 0
    Group Descriptor Table: 1 - 4
    Data bitmap: 1025 - 1025
    Inode bitmap: 1041 - 1041
    Inode Table: 1057 - 1568
    Data Blocks: 1569 - 32767
  Free Inodes: 4449 (54%)
  Free Blocks: 22781 (69%)
  Total Directories: 734
```

FIGURE 2.20

the deleted time. All time values are stored in UNIX time, which is represented as the number of seconds since January 1, 1970. Of course, this value is 1/1/1970 00:00 but it is in UTC, which means you may see date and time from December 31, 1969 if your time zone is behind UTC. For example, if I were to set the access time on a file to the very beginning of UNIX time in my time zone, it would show up as 19:00 on 12/31/1969 because my time zone is –0500.

While the term is Universal Coordinated Time or sometimes Coordinated Universal Time, it is abbreviated UTC because of a compromise between English and French.

The inode structure also includes three levels of references to data blocks. The first level is a direct reference to the data blocks associated with the file. There are a limited number of direct links out of the inode, though, so if more data blocks are required, the file system would make use of the next level, which are indirect references. These indirect references point to another inode, which would then have direct references to data blocks. Finally, there is a third level of indirection. This would be a reference to an inode that would refer to another inode, which would in turn have direct references to the blocks where the data is actually stored. Figure 2.21 has a visual representation of this tiered model. Using a tiered model like this allows for large file sizes without too much performance loss trying to find all of the blocks.

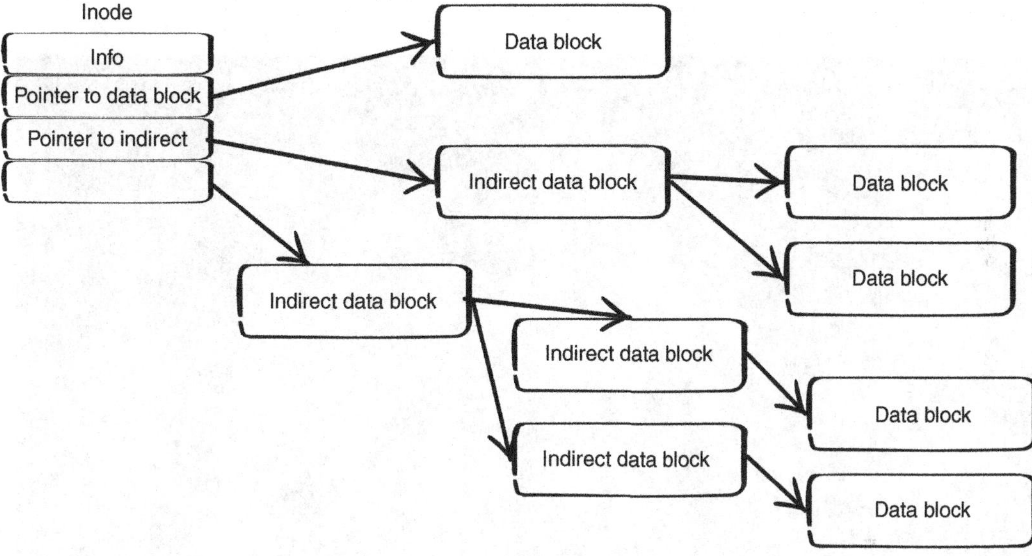

FIGURE 2.21

The last piece of the ext2 puzzle is a directory entry. A directory is a specialized file that contains a list of all the files or additional directories in the directory. Each directory entry includes the values in Table 2.9. The type indicator referred to in the table indicates whether it is a regular file, a directory, a character device, block device, or another special file.

TABLE 2.9 Directory Entry Values

Starting byte	Ending byte	Description
0	3	Inode
4	5	Total size of this entry
6	6	Name length
7	7	Type indicator
8	8 + n–1	Name characters where n is the length of the name

When it comes to finding all of the data related to a particular file, you start with the root directory, which will be in inode 2. After reading through the values in inode 2, you will have a list of the files and directories in the root directory. Figure 2.22 shows the details for inode 2 on a partition that has the ext2 file system on it. You can see that it is owned by the root user and group and has a single direct block. That direct block would be the "file" for the root directory. You would find the data by getting the block number, then calculating the sector value by multiplying the block number times the size of the block. Once you have that, you know where you can start reading on the disk to get the contents of the directory. In order to read through the file system, you would then read through the directory entries, identified in each directory as an entry with the directory flag set.

```
kilroy@dallas ~ $ sudo istat /dev/sda1 2
inode: 2
Allocated
Group: 0
Generation Id: 0
uid / gid: 0 / 0
mode: drwxr-xr-x
Flags:
size: 4096
num of links: 26

Inode Times:
Accessed:       Sat Jul  5 14:25:37 2014
File Modified:  Sun Apr 20 19:40:39 2014
Inode Modified: Sun Apr 20 19:40:39 2014

Direct Blocks:
127754
```

FIGURE 2.22

You can use additional tools from TSK in order to get more details from the file system. The tool ils will list all of the inodes from the file system, providing the details from each of those inodes. You could also use fls to get a listing of files from the file system. In order to get the contents from a particular entry in the file system, you would use icat. When you run icat, you will get the raw contents from the disk. If this is a text file, you will get the contents of the text file. If it is something other than a text file, you will just get the raw bytes, which means you may need to dump it out to a file and then open it with a hex editor.

ext3/4

ext is a family of file systems, though the foundation is ext2. The ext3 file system, for example, is built on top of ext2, which means that all of the data structures that we went over for ext2 still apply. The difference between an ext2 file system and an ext3 file system is the presence of a journal. A journal is used to recover data in case of a system failure. It stores transactions that can then be checked against the file system to ensure that the change is still in place. If it cannot be found, the transaction can then be applied to the file system in order to restore a sane state to the volume. The details about the journal are included in the superblock. The UUID for the journal is 16 bytes and begins at offset 208 in the superblock. The journal inode is stored at offset 228, followed by the journal device at offset 232.

ext4 builds on top of ext3 with some changes. First, ext4 supports a larger file system than the previous versions. You can now have a volume of size 1 exabyte, which is 2^60 bytes. Additionally, ext4 replaces the use of blocks with the use of extents. An extent is a range of contiguous physical blocks. This change will support better performance with large files. An extent can be up to 128 megabytes of contiguous space with a 4 KB block size. ext4 is backwards compatible with previous versions, which means that the data structures we covered for ext2 still apply.

APPLE FILE SYSTEMS

As with the file systems associated with Microsoft operating systems, Apple has gone through some iterations as technology has improved. The very first file system created for the Macintosh was the Macintosh File System (MFS), created for storing information on 3.5 in. floppy disks. When Apple started to support hard drives attached to the Macintosh, they developed the Hierarchical File System (HFS), which improved performance on larger, faster storage devices, since MFS was designed to run on small, slow storage. HFS underwent changes in 1998 as part of the integration with the NeXT software. NeXT used BSD underneath and Mac OS X now also uses BSD for the underlying components to the operating system. However, Mac OS X does not use a file system from the BSD or UNIX world. Instead, it uses an altered version of HFS called HFS+.

Structurally, HFS and HFS+ are very similar but HFS+ includes some important differences, including support for larger files and larger volumes. Additionally, it adds data structures that improve performance over the older HFS file system. These additional data structures take the form of binary trees or B-trees. The original HFS stored information about the contents of the file system in B-trees. HFS+ continues that but it adds additional B-trees for storing catalog data. This allows for indexing, overflow extents to support larger files, and attributes to support extensions to the file system.

HFS made use of data forks, which were continued in HFS+ and, as noted earlier, the resource forks drove the implementation of alternate data streams in NTFS. The data forks were implemented as a way to store graphical data associated with a program and they initially served, in part, as a way to avoid implementing virtual memory within the Macintosh operating system. Storing graphics and text associated with a program also made translating a program to a different market, which might include the need to use another language.

Typically, a user would not directly see the contents of a resource fork. It would not show up in the Finder as a separate entry, for example. The operating system would take care of displaying the contents as appropriate. One example of this would be showing the icon for the program in the Finder. The contents of the resource fork would generally be set at the time the program was built. The resource fork may also be used to store a piece of information indicating the program that would be used to open a particular file, which would mean the system would not have to rely on a file extension to determine file associations.

Modern Macintosh systems use the GPT format to store information about the partitions in use because they use UEFI, rather than a BIOS. Figure 2.23 shows the output of the diskutil list command, showing the partitions on this Macintosh system. Mac OS X uses the BSD concept of disk slices, which is why each entry in the partition table is named ending in s0, s1, s2, and so on. Those indicate the slice number, which is equivalent to a partition that you may be more used to seeing, if you come from the Windows or Linux world.

```
kilroy@opus:~$ diskutil list
/dev/disk0
   #:                       TYPE NAME                    SIZE       IDENTIFIER
   0:      GUID_partition_scheme                        *500.3 GB   disk0
   1:                        EFI EFI                     209.7 MB   disk0s1
   2:                  Apple_HFS Macintosh HD            499.4 GB   disk0s2
   3:                 Apple_Boot Recovery HD             650.0 MB   disk0s3
/dev/disk1
   #:                       TYPE NAME                    SIZE       IDENTIFIER
   0:     Apple_partition_scheme                        *16.7 MB    disk1
   1:        Apple_partition_map                         32.3 KB    disk1s1
   2:                  Apple_HFS Flash Player            16.7 MB    disk1s2
```

FIGURE 2.23

You will also notice that the disk in this Macintosh has an EFI slice, where the boot data would be stored, as well as a recovery slice. The recovery slice is used to boot up the system in case of a failure of the primary operating system. The recovery boot could be used to repair any issues with the primary operating system to restore it to fully functional status before rebooting.

HFS+

HFS+ uses sectors as a fundamental storage unit, which is 512 bytes. Where FAT has clusters, which are contiguous sectors, and ext has blocks, HFS+ has allocation blocks. These, just as with clusters and blocks, are contiguous sectors that are used to allocate to files. Where a sector size is commonly 512 bytes on a hard drive, the default size of an allocation block is 8 sectors or 4 KB. When you group a number of contiguous allocation blocks together, you get an extent. There is no set size for an extent. In order to determine the size of an extent, you would need to look at the extent descriptor, which would include information about the starting allocation block and the ending allocation block. This would give you the size of the extent.

In place of a BPB or a superblock, HFS+ uses a volume header. The volume header is located 1024 bytes from the beginning of the volume. The first two sectors are reserved space and the third sector is the volume header, which takes up that single sector. A copy of the volume is stored in the next to last sector on the drive. The copy is used by disk repair utilities, in case there is a problem with the drive. Table 2.10 shows the structure of the volume header.

TABLE 2.10 The Structure of the Volume Header

Offset	Size	Description
0x00	2 bytes	Signature
0x02	2 bytes	Version
0x04	4 bytes	Attributes for the volume, which includes indications about whether the volume was cleanly unmounted, and whether the volume has a journal.
0x08	4 bytes	The version that was last mounted.
0x0C	4 bytes	The location of the journal info block. This is only used, if the volume contains a journal.
0x10	4 bytes	The date of creation for the volume.
0x14	4 bytes	The date the volume was modified.
0x18	4 bytes	The date the volume was backed up.
0x1C	4 bytes	The date the volume was last checked to ensure it was consistent.
0x20	4 bytes	The total number of files on the volume.
0x24	4 bytes	The total number of folders on the volume.
0x28	4 bytes	The size of the block on the volume.
0x2C	4 bytes	The total number of blocks on the volume.
0x30	4 bytes	The number of allocation blocks that are not being used on the volume.
0x34	4 bytes	A hint to the operating system about where to start search for free blocks.
0x38	4 bytes	The default clump size for resource forks.
0x3C	4 bytes	The default clump size for data forks.
0x40	4 bytes	The next ID value for the catalog.
0x44	4 bytes	This is incremented each time the volume is mounted. In the case of a system volume, this would get incremented each time the system is booted.
0x48	8 bytes	The encodings bitmap, used to keep track of text encodings used for file and folder names.
0x50	32 bytes	This contains information that Finder uses. It also includes information used by the boot process, including the directory of the bootable system.
0x70	80 bytes	This includes information about the allocation file.
0xC0	80 bytes	This contains information about the extents.
0x110	80 bytes	This contains information about the attributes.
0x1B0	80 bytes	This contains information about the startup file

The allocation file contains information about blocks that are free and blocks that are not free. The allocation file is stored as a regular file but contains a bitmap for blocks that are in use. The catalog file is a binary tree (B-tree) representation of all of the files and folders on the system. The catalog is stored as a B-tree to make it easier to locate the information. A file record in the catalog file is capable of storing information about 8 extents. If a file takes up more than 8 extents, the extras are stored in the extents overflow file. The attributes file is new to HFS+ plus, since there was not anything similar in HFS. The attributes file is used to store attributes from files and directories. One of the common uses for attributes is to maintain access control lists.

Each entry in the catalog file has a set of information placing the entry within the file system, as well as, locating the data associated with the file. Each catalog node, referred to as a node, since it is stored in a tree structure, might contain directory records, file records, directory thread records, or file thread records. Depending on the entry type, the record may include the directory ID, directory flags, as well as date information, or it may include the file ID, the first allocation block of the data fork, the first allocation block of the resource fork, the clump size, and date information. There are also different data records for the thread information types. While the details about the HFS+ file system can be difficult to come by, except those at a high level, you can go digging within Apple's developer documents to get C program headers defining the data structures used within HFS+.

Navigating the file catalog uses the name of the file or directory, as well as, the directory ID of the parent directory. Each key record consists of the key length, the parent ID, and the catalog node name. There are two types of nodes that you would find within the B-tree structure of the HFS+ catalog, which would be common in a B-tree implementation and those are index nodes and leaf nodes. A leaf node is simply a node in the tree that has no children.

The HFS+ file system stores a lot of metadata about the file. Some of that information is stored in attributes in the file system, while some of the information is stored in the catalog file. You can use the built-in utility mdls to get a listing of all of the metadata attributes for a particular file. You can see the list of attributes for a small Python script in Figure 2.24.

SLACK SPACE

In every file system, there will be slack space and that slack space can be very important to a forensic investigator. We have spent some time talking about the file systems and where data is stored but there are also a lot of places where data is not stored and, in reality, that can have data as well. When files are deleted from a file system, what really happens in most cases is that the metadata is removed from the directories and the clusters or blocks are returned to being marked as free. Most of the time, the data that was written to the blocks remains there on the disk. If the file system does not reallocate the space, the data is still there to be read from the disk. Even if the file system reallocates the blocks or clusters, there is a chance that some of the data still exists on the drive.

Let us say, you have a cluster size of 4 KB. If you have a file that is 12843 bytes, the file system will allocate 4 clusters to the file but only a small portion of the last cluster will actually

```
kilroy@opus:~$ mdls httpattack.py
kMDItemContentCreationDate     = 2014-03-26 22:46:20 +0000
kMDItemContentModificationDate = 2014-03-26 23:31:43 +0000
kMDItemContentType             = "public.python-script"
kMDItemContentTypeTree         = (
    "public.python-script",
    "public.shell-script",
    "public.script",
    "public.source-code",
    "public.plain-text",
    "public.text",
    "public.data",
    "public.item",
    "public.content"
)
kMDItemDateAdded               = 2014-03-26 22:46:20 +0000
kMDItemDisplayName             = "httpattack.py"
kMDItemFSContentChangeDate     = 2014-03-26 23:31:43 +0000
kMDItemFSCreationDate          = 2014-03-26 22:46:20 +0000
kMDItemFSCreatorCode           = ""
kMDItemFSFinderFlags           = 0
kMDItemFSHasCustomIcon         = (null)
kMDItemFSInvisible             = 0
kMDItemFSIsExtensionHidden     = 0
kMDItemFSIsStationery          = (null)
kMDItemFSLabel                 = 0
kMDItemFSName                  = "httpattack.py"
kMDItemFSNodeCount             = (null)
kMDItemFSOwnerGroupID          = 20
kMDItemFSOwnerUserID           = 501
kMDItemFSSize                  = 1061
kMDItemFSTypeCode              = ""
kMDItemKind                    = "Python Source"
kMDItemLogicalSize             = 1061
kMDItemPhysicalSize            = 4096
```

FIGURE 2.24

be used by the data in the file. The disk space allocated for the file is 16384 bytes, leaving 3541 bytes that are not being used by the file but the operating system has not cleared out whatever may have been there from a file that previously occupied that space. It is like moving into a rental house where the previous tenant left a small pile of boxes in the basement. You occupy the house but there is still something left over from the previous tenant, which is not yours but is still in the house. You can, of course, remove it and take up the space yourself or, if you do not need the space, you may leave it. The same is true with the space at the end of the cluster that is unused by the file. You can see a visual representation of this in Figure 2.25. The unused space in the cluster is commonly called slack space.

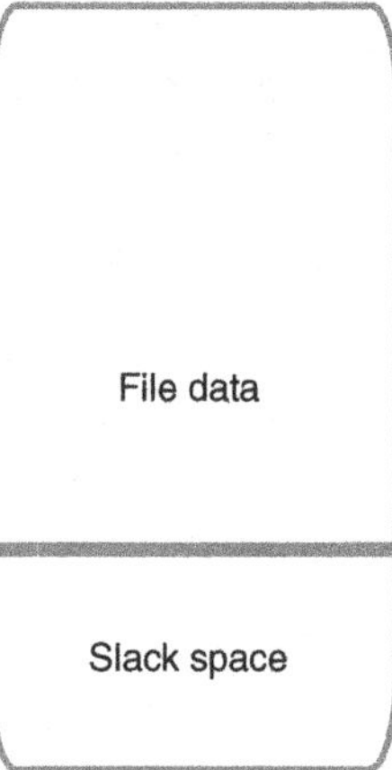

FIGURE 2.25

All of the unused space, where files have not been allocated may have data in it as well. This may be a result of long-deleted files or it may be a result of some processes deliberately bypassing the file system in order to write data out to the disk. While this takes some effort, it is possible, and a way to store information without the operating system knowing anything about it. Of course, if you are not careful, you might end up having the data overwritten by the file system unless you ensure to take the blocks out of circulation by marking them as bad, for example.

There is one more place that data may be hidden. You may have a case where you have space between, before, or after partitions on the hard drive. This space could store a lot of information, though it could be difficult to get information into that space and out of it from inside of a running operating system. This might require access from outside of the operating system by using a boot CD to dump data out to the disk just as a way to hide it.

In order to reclaim data from the hard drive and slack space, we can again take advantage of TSK utilities, as well as some common Linux/UNIX utilities. Assuming, we have a disk image and we know what we are looking for, we can use the following technique to grab data out of slack space on the drive. I should say, there are a large number of ways to accomplish this task, but this is one that takes advantage of tools that are easy to get hold of and it also demonstrates some of the things we have been talking about. First, we would perform a search through the disk image but we need to have the byte offset, where we locate the search term. I have created a file on the disk that will be in the disk image with the word "wubble" in it. The reason for this is because I want to have a search term that will be easy to narrow down for the purposes of this demonstration. If I were to search for the word "for" as an example, I would get a lot of hits back and it would take a long time to find, what I was looking for. So, in order to find the file with the word wubble in it, I will use the grep command as follows.

```
grep -oba wubble image.dd
91551:wubble
```

The parameters I passed in, -oba, tells grep that I need the byte offset and I want to search the entire file rather than just stopping at the first location. The result we get, 91551, is the byte number where the word wubble has been found. I need to determine the cluster that the word has been found in, so I need to divide 91551 by whatever the cluster size is. In our case here, the size is 4096 bytes. We end up with cluster number 22, though the result I got was 22 and some change because the alignment is going to be off a little since I am not looking for the word that starts at the first byte of the file. I can use the blkcat command from TSK to get the contents of block 22.

```
blkcat image.dd 22
```

Depending on what file system I am looking at and the size of the file, I may find either an entry in the master file table on an NTFS partition, or I may find the cluster or block, where the file itself resides. If it is a small file, you will find the MFT entry where the file contents are just another attribute in the file. You will also find the type of file and the file name as well as other attributes, if you are looking at a hex dump of the output. If the file is large, you can also check the blocks close to the one you identified to get additional contents. You can also trace back to the entry in the file table to get any additional blocks to find more of the contents.

CONCLUSIONS

Disk storage is at the heart of most modern computer systems so when performing a forensic investigation, you will spend a lot of time digging through the file system for data. In some cases, you may use application tools to get information like log data but you will also spend a lot of time working in the details of the file system. While there are certainly a number of tools that can help this process, including several tools that will completely automate file system investigations, I believe it is necessary to understand the file system internals in order to make sense of the results from the tools. Because of that, you need to know what the different data structures for each file system are, as well as, what would be found within those data structures.

There is a move toward even more complex data structures, in order to make file systems more efficient as they grow in size. The move toward structures like B-trees on file systems like Apple's HFS+ is likely to be more common. The reason is simply because as file systems become larger, the overhead on file systems like FAT is just too high and a serial list of file table entries is just too time consuming to search. The fastest way to locate information on an extraordinarily large file system is going to be by using more complex data structures.

There are a number of tools that can be used to search file systems once you have acquired an image and once you understand the structure, you can even develop your own tools that can search data you specifically are looking for.

SUMMARY

These are some ideas that are worth remembering from this chapter:

- The smallest allocation unit within most file systems is the 512-byte sector.
- Most of the file systems, we discussed, use a single sector to describe the file system within, including providing pointers to other important data structures on the volume.

- Different file systems use different aggregation names, but all aggregate sectors into larger units, whether they are called clusters, blocks, or allocation blocks.
- Each file system uses a different data structure to describe the information on the file system, including the file allocation table, the master file table, the catalog file, and the inode table.
- The ext file systems use a tree-like structure to refer to all of the blocks used by a file.
- The HFS+ file system uses an extents overflow file to store information about large files.
- The NTFS file system may store the entire contents of the file within the master file table if the contents do not consume more than 1024 bytes.

EXERCISES

1. Use dd to extract a copy of a file system from your system. You can use a Linux boot disk like SIFT, DEFT or Kali or you can get a copy of dd for Windows. Make sure to get an MD5 or SHA1 cryptographic sum of the file.
2. Obtain a copy of The Sleuth Kit from http://www.sleuthkit.org and install it on your system. Use the image you have obtained and the utilities from the Sleuth Kit to get a listing of all of the files on the image.
3. Delete a file from your file system and use utilities from the Sleuth Kit to locate the data from an image you acquire.

Bibliography

Brokken, F.B., 1995. Proceedings to The First Dutch International Symposium On Linux, Amsterdam, December 8th and 9th, 1994. Groningen: State University of Groningen, Print.

File Systems, n.d. Microsoft TechNet. Available from: http://technet.microsoft.com/en-us/library/cc938949.aspx (accessed 25.06.2014.).

How FAT Works, 2003. Local File Systems. Available from: http://technet.microsoft.com/en-us/library/cc776720(v=ws.10).aspx (accessed 24.06.2014.).

Legacy Document, 1996. Catalog Files (IM: F). Available from: https://developer.apple.com/legacy/library/documentation/mac/Files/Files-105.html (accessed 13.07.2014.).

Lucas, M., 2013. Windows Server 2012: Does ReFS replace NTFS? When should I use it?. – Ask Premier Field Engineering (PFE) Platforms. Available from: http://blogs.technet.com/b/askpfeplat/archive/2013/01/02/windows-server-2012-does-refs-replace-ntfs-when-should-i-use-it.aspx (accessed 29.06.2014.).

Sinofsky, S., n.d. Building the next generation file system for Windows: ReFS. – Building Windows 8. Available from: https://blogs.msdn.com/b/b8/archive/2012/01/16/building-the-next-generation-file-system-for-windows-refs.aspx (accessed 29.06.2014.).

Stoffregen, P., 2005. Understanding FAT32 Filesystems. Paul's 8051 Code Library: Understanding the FAT32 Filesystem. Available from: https://www.pjrc.com/tech/8051/ide/fat32.html (accessed 23.06.2014.).

http://www.win.tue.nl/~aeb/linux/fs/fat/fat-1.html

CHAPTER

3

Data and File Recovery

INFORMATION INCLUDED IN THIS CHAPTER:

- Data carving
- Slack space
- Searching for data
- Data hiding

INTRODUCTION

Once you understand the layout of the file systems you are working on, you can better understand how to go about retrieving information from the disk. There are a number of reasons you may need to go digging. One of the reasons is because someone may have deleted a file and it may not clearly show up in the primary file tables but the data may still live on the drive. There may also be file contents in the slack space after the end of a file. There may be file contents sitting in a sparse file on the file system and grabbing the contents of the file out of the clusters or blocks directly may be easier than trying to read through the sparse file trying to figure out how the contents of that file are organized. Data recovery is founded on understanding where to find the important data structures within a file system. Of course, you also need to know what data you are looking for.

There are a number of places where data or evidence could be hiding, depending on the file system. There are so many different ways to stuff data into a hard drive and so many places where data can continue to hide out. The user may have even lost track of that data. In some cases, you cannot rely on the contents of the directory because it is trivial to put data in places where you may not expect it to be, including simply changing the name. I can rename a JPEG file and make it slightly harder to locate, depending on how you are going about searching for it. Fortunately, there are easy ways to resolve this.

Disk drives can be enormous expanses of digital real estate and in cases where file systems support sparse files, you cannot rely on the directory information to locate data. There is also compression to be taken into consideration, both file compression as well as file system compression, where the file system itself performs the compression before storing the bits to the drive.

DATA CARVING

Data carving is simply locating the boundaries of a file using a known file signature and pulling the data off of the drive that exists within those boundaries. You can do this without relying on the file system itself since you may be trying to extract a deleted file that no longer has an entry in the file tables or the file name could have been renamed to disguise what the file actually is. It could also be the case that the data has been stuffed into another file so it may look like one thing, even if you open the file, and actually it could be two things altogether. In cases, where you have forked data like an alternate data stream or a resource fork, you could potentially have data that is simply stored outside of the ability of many common operating system utilities to locate or display.

As a result, we perform data carving. While it is helpful to understand the process and be able to do it manually, if necessary, there are also a number of utilities that will perform the tasks for us. Personally, I think it is fun to get down in the mud and start pulling the bytes out of the disk by hand, putting the file back together, though that is not always the most appealing to some practitioners. So, we will take a look at doing all of this in a couple of different ways – both manually and using some automated tools.

In order to carve data out of a hard drive, though, we need to know first what we are looking for and then how far we have to look. In cases where the data has been deleted, there may not be file table entries indicating all of the clusters or blocks that belong to a file. If we had those file table entries, we likely would not be carving data, since we would know where all of the file data was. However, there may be cases where we find one particular file type that does have a file table entry, so we would need to go backward to locate the other relevant clusters.

In order to determine the beginning and the ending point, we need to know what the file should look like. In the case of text files, you will not have anything other than the text. With binary files, like videos or pictures, we need to have an idea of what those files look like. Typically, you will be looking for specific bytes that are referred to as header bytes. This will give you an idea of where the start of the file is. Once you have the starting point in the file, you need to know when to stop reading. In most cases, the file type will not have the length of the file located in the header or the data of the file so ideally, there will be a footer or a set of defined ending bytes that will signal to you when the file is at an end. This is not the same as performing a read on a file, as in a program, since the operating system knows when the file is at an end because it knows how big the file is. In our case, we are looking at this at the byte level, so we need to know when to stop.

Table 3.1 shows a list of common file types that you may be particularly interested in locating. In this table, you will find the header byte pattern as well as the footer byte pattern, if it exists. If it does not exist, you have to just keep reading until you think you have enough. Without some guidance in the file table, if we are really looking at an orphaned file, which is a file that no longer has an entry in the file tables, we will need to assume that the data is stored in contiguous clusters rather than scattered around the file system. If the file is really scattered around the disk and there is no file table entry to tell us where to find all the associated clusters, we may be able to recover some of the data but not all of it.

This is obviously just a small number of files, though they are the ones you will commonly run across. In some cases, you will have a footer to know where the file ends, though as you can see above, that is not that common. In most cases, the header information will describe the contents of the file and in some cases, the file will be broken up into chunks with its own

TABLE 3.1 A Sample of File Signatures

Header bytes	Footer bytes	File type
0xffd8ffe	0xffd9	JPEG image file (jpg, jpeg)
0x1f9d		Compressed file (zip, z) using Lempel-Ziv-Welch algorithm
0x1fa0		Compressed file (zip, z) using LZH algorithm
0x425a68		Bzip2 compressed file (bz2)
0x0000001466747970 71742020		QuickTime movie file (MOV)
0x89504e470d0a1a	Multiple chunks in each file. Each chunk ends with IEND	Portable network graphics (PNG) file
0x424d		BMP file
0xfffb 0x494433		MPEG-1 Layer 3 (MP3) file without an ID3 tag MP3 file with an ID3 tag
0xd0cf11e0		Microsoft Word document (doc)
0x664c6143		Free Lossless Audio Codec (flac)
0x52494646		Waveform audio (wav)
0x4344303031		ISO9660 CD-ROM image file (iso)
0x25504446		Portable Document Format (PDF)
0x474946383761	0x003b	GIF

header and footer sections, as in the case of the Portable Network Graphics (PNG) file. With a WAV file, the header section includes all of the metadata and the end of the file is simply all of the data itself. You will notice that a Word document is in the table, though the current version of Word does not use the same format.

When we are talking about a Word document, we are actually looking at a ZIP file that contains a well-defined folder structure, including a number of XML files to describe all of the contents of the Word document. These XML files not only include the text of the document but also the properties and the formatting. In Figure 3.1, you can see a hex dump of the top of a Word .docx file. This is a different set of header bytes than a ZIP file or the former .doc

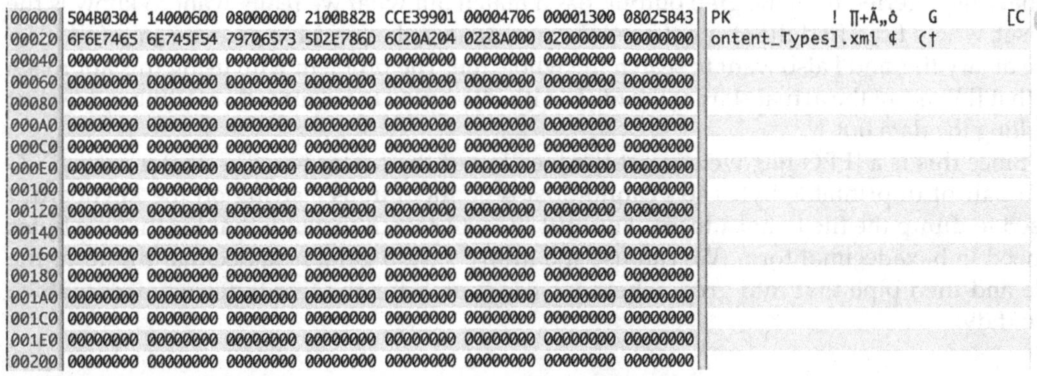

FIGURE 3.1

file. You may often find that header bytes can change in application files like this if there are significant version changes.

Data carving differs from file recovery because data carving does not care about the file system. As far as, we are concerned when it comes to data carving, all we are looking at is a set of bytes on a drive. What it comes down to is locating the header bytes on the drive and then just extracting data from subsequent bytes. While there are automated ways to carve data out of a hard drive, we will take a look at how to do it the old-fashioned way first. We are going to use some tried and true UNIX utilities to get the data that we want. For our purposes here, I created a small NTFS partition and put some files on it, then copied a JPEG image to the partition. First, I am going to create an image that I can perform my searches on rather than using the raw partition. Once I have the image, I can search for the pattern, JFIF, since that would be what I would find at the beginning of a JPEG file. You can see the steps in Figure 3.2.

```
kilroy@dallas ~ $ sudo dd if=/dev/sdb1 of=ntfs.dd
204800+0 records in
204800+0 records out
104857600 bytes (105 MB) copied, 0.388808 s, 270 MB/s
kilroy@dallas ~ $ grep JFIF ntfs.dd
Binary file ntfs.dd matches
kilroy@dallas ~ $ grep -oba JFIF ntfs.dd
54525958:JFIF
```

FIGURE 3.2

The first step you can see is to get the image using the utility dd. Once I have the image in a file, I want to search for the string JFIF. There are a few ways to do this but the easiest is just to use grep. You can see that grep returns the information that the b disk dump, which is the binary file referred to in the grep output, has a match but what we really want to know is the offset, where I can find the string. I need the parameters oba for dd to give me an offset from the binary file, and I also want to search the whole file. The problem with using this approach is that JFIF is not the actual start of the file but it will give us the right sector for when we start pulling the data out.

Since this is a JPEG file, we can get the location of the footer too. The footer for a JPEG is a pair of unprintable bytes so I cannot just type them in as a string on the keyboard. I need to dump the file to hexadecimal output so I can search through that for the two bytes I need in hexadecimal form. We can use the utility xxd to get a hexadecimal dump of the file and then pipe that into grep, where we can search for the two bytes we need, which are ff d9.

```
kilroy@dallas ~ $ xxd ntfs.dd | grep 'd9 ff'

0ce43f0: f8d9 f9d9 fad9 fbd9 fcd9 fdd9 fed9 ffd9

................

340b620: 36d9 ff00 bf6a 2ba4 a280 0acf f107 87b4

6....j+.........

34104f0: 2803 f7d9 ff00 e0aa 1fb3 32f4 f883 70ff

(.........2...p.

3410a90: 5007 e1d9 ff00 823a 7c7e 1d24 f029 fa6a

P......:|~.$.).j

34112c0: 65d9 ff00 cfa5 b7fd fb5f f0a3 fb32 cffe

e........_...2..

341e130: afd9 ff00 e155 dcb6 5e20 f88b a55f ea11  .....U..^

..._..

3423380: 26ff 00ff 0045 57d9 ff00 b7ef edaf f183

&....EW.........

3425d10: 0978 987d 74d9 ff00 f89a 00fe 99a3 f1d7

.x.}t...........
```

You may be wondering why I searched for d9 ff rather than ff d9, since, ff d9 is the footer for the file. The reason is that we are dealing with an Intel system and Intel systems use little-endian form so with a multi-byte value, it is actually going to appear to be backwards to us. Since xxd dumps the output into lines where the first column in the line is the address of the first byte in the line, we do not need to have grep tell us the offset. The first column and then counting over gives us the offset. The one issue we have is that the address is in binary and the byte offset we had from grep is in decimal. The address we have from grep is 54525958 bytes from the start of the file. We have multiple potential hits using xxd and grep and after doing a little math, let us assume that the best one is the last one because it gives us about 154,000 bytes.

We need to figure out which sector we need to start grabbing data out of. Divide the number of bytes, 54525958, by 512, which is the number of bytes per sector. That gives us 106496 as the starting sector. When we do the same to the ending sector, after converting 3425d10 to decimal first, we get 106798. That is 302 sectors. I can grab those 302 blocks out of the disk image using dd as follows:

```
kilroy@dallas ~ $ dd if=ntfs.dd of=captured.jpg bs=512

skip=106496 count=302

302+0 records in

302+0 records out

154624 bytes (155 kB) copied, 0.000803993 s, 192 MB/s
```

Once I have extracted the data, I can use any image viewer to check and see whether it is really an image file or not. This could be a Web browser or any other image viewer. I ended up getting the image I was looking for, but if I had stopped using one of the other addresses for that particular byte pattern, I would only get a partial image. In the case of this file, I happen to have a pattern to look for to tell me where the end of the file may be, but that is not the case with all file types. We can also check in this case, since the file used is in the master file table and we can check all of the data blocks associated with the file to make sure we got the right ones. First, we have to convert our addresses to clusters. Our file system has a cluster size of 4096, so we take our byte location and divide by 4096 to get the right cluster. Our starting cluster is 13312, based on our byte count. In Figure 3.3, you can see the first data cluster associated with the file is 13312, according to the attributes in the master file table.

```
$FILE_NAME Attribute Values:
Flags: Archive
Name: NetNeutrality.jpg
Parent MFT Entry: 5     Sequence: 5
Allocated Size: 167936          Actual Size: 0
Created:        Sat Jul 26 20:21:46 2014
File Modified:  Sat Jul 26 20:21:46 2014
MFT Modified:   Sat Jul 26 20:21:46 2014
Accessed:       Sat Jul 26 20:21:46 2014

Attributes:
Type: $STANDARD_INFORMATION (16-0)   Name: N/A   Resident   size: 48
Type: $FILE_NAME (48-3)   Name: N/A   Resident   size: 100
Type: $SECURITY_DESCRIPTOR (80-1)   Name: N/A   Resident   size: 80
Type: $DATA (128-2)   Name: N/A   Non-Resident   size: 166302  init_size: 166302
13312 13313 13314 13315 13316 13317 13318 13319
13320 13321 13322 13323 13324 13325 13326 13327
13328 13329 13330 13331 13332 13333 13334 13335
13336 13337 13338 13339 13340 13341 13342 13343
13344 13345 13346 13347 13348 13349 13350 13351
13352
```

FIGURE 3.3

If the file was not listed in the file table or it did not appear to be a JPEG, which is what we were looking for, we would have to resort to performing this data carving rather than simply copying the file out of the file system. We do not have to do things the hard way, though, since it can be time consuming and requires a lot of knowledge about the byte patterns, we are looking for. So, we can use a tool like scalpel to handle all of the known different file types and how to find them. Figure 3.4 shows some of the output from scalpel as it checks through the file system image.

```
kilroy@dallas ~ $ scalpel ntfs.dd
Scalpel version 1.60
Written by Golden G. Richard III, based on Foremost 0.69.

Opening target "/home/kilroy/ntfs.dd"

Image file pass 1/2.
ntfs.dd: 100.0% |*************************************|  100.0 MB    00:00 ETA
Allocating work queues...
Work queues allocation complete. Building carve lists...
Carve lists built.  Workload:
gif with header "\x47\x49\x46\x38\x37\x61" and footer "\x00\x3b" --> 0 files
gif with header "\x47\x49\x46\x38\x39\x61" and footer "\x00\x3b" --> 0 files
jpg with header "\xff\xd8\xff\xe0\x00\x10" and footer "\xff\xd9" --> 1 files
png with header "\x50\x4e\x47\x3f" and footer "\xff\xfc\xfd\xfe" --> 0 files
tif with header "\x49\x49\x2a\x00" and footer "" --> 0 files
tif with header "\x4d\x4d\x00\x2a" and footer "" --> 1 files
avi with header "\x52\x49\x46\x46\x3f\x3f\x3f\x3f\x41\x56\x49" and footer "" -->
 0 files
mov with header "\x3f\x3f\x3f\x3f\x6d\x6f\x6f\x76" and footer "" --> 0 files
mov with header "\x3f\x3f\x3f\x3f\x6d\x64\x61\x74" and footer "" --> 0 files
mov with header "\x3f\x3f\x3f\x3f\x77\x69\x64\x65\x76" and footer "" --> 0 files
mov with header "\x3f\x3f\x3f\x3f\x73\x6b\x69\x70" and footer "" --> 2 files
mov with header "\x3f\x3f\x3f\x3f\x66\x72\x65\x65" and footer "" --> 23 files
```

FIGURE 3.4

One of the challenges with using a data carving approach is that we are relying on byte patterns on the drive. Byte patterns like ff d9 cannot be guaranteed to only appear in the files, we are looking for. We saw that in the case of trying to carve out the JPEG, where the pattern we were looking for that, indicated the end of the file was found several times inside the JPEG image itself. In the case of running scalpel against the image I have here, scalpel believes, it found a number of MOV files because it found the right byte patterns. You can see a portion of the number of MOV files found from the audit log scalpel generates in Figure 3.5. There were also some Pretty Good Privacy (PGP) files on the disk, according to scalpel. The problem is that none of that is true.

File	Start	Chop	Length	Extracted From
00000032.pgp	13483007	YES	100000	ntfs.dd
00000031.pgp	13406506	YES	100000	ntfs.dd
00000030.pgp	13482497	YES	100000	ntfs.dd
00000028.pgp	13485055	YES	100000	ntfs.dd
00000027.pgp	13406514	YES	100000	ntfs.dd
00000000.jpg	54525952	NO	166302	ntfs.dd
00000029.pgp	54647312	YES	100000	ntfs.dd
00000033.pgp	54559623	YES	100000	ntfs.dd
00000008.mov	71315876	YES	10000000	ntfs.dd
00000007.mov	71315797	YES	10000000	ntfs.dd
00000006.mov	71315755	YES	10000000	ntfs.dd
00000005.mov	71315536	YES	10000000	ntfs.dd
00000004.mov	71303926	YES	10000000	ntfs.dd
00000003.mov	71312168	YES	10000000	ntfs.dd
00000002.mov	71312124	YES	10000000	ntfs.dd
00000026.mov	88094230	YES	10000000	ntfs.dd
00000025.mov	88094192	YES	10000000	ntfs.dd
00000024.mov	88093880	YES	10000000	ntfs.dd
00000023.mov	88092122	YES	10000000	ntfs.dd
00000022.mov	88091455	YES	10000000	ntfs.dd
00000021.mov	88083169	YES	10000000	ntfs.dd
00000020.mov	88082984	YES	10000000	ntfs.dd
00000019.mov	88082871	YES	10000000	ntfs.dd
00000018.mov	88082611	YES	10000000	ntfs.dd
00000017.mov	88081688	YES	10000000	ntfs.dd

FIGURE 3.5

Compare the number of MOV files in Figure 3.5 against the file listing in Figure 3.6. You will see that there are no PGP files and no MOV files. You cannot just blindly trust the output from a tool like scalpel, so you have to go through each file scalpel finds and make sure that the file actually contains what you expect it to contain. Scalpel found 33 files that it believes to be some sort of media file or PGP file. Only one of those files is actually real. The rest of the files are clusters of bytes that are just found in the random noise on the disk. These byte clusters may occur naturally in a file that isn't actually the file type identified by Scalpel. In some cases, what you may be looking at are the remnants of old files that were never wiped, but in this case, this is a virtual hard drive that was created for the purposes of this exercise.

Of course, we are looking at open source utilities. There are commercial programs as well that will allow you to carve data out of a disk or disk image. A couple of common commercial programs are FTK and EnCase, both considered standards in the world of digital forensics. FTK and EnCase have long been considered standards in the industry but newer products like Blacklight are entering the market. These new products are finding homes and are considered just as acceptable as the older programs. As with a lot of complex tools of this nature, there is not nearly as much work involved in locating files from a disk image. After going through the steps to import the disk image, FTK will display all of the files available and also break them out into categories. You can see in Figure 3.6 that there are tabs on the top of the window, including a tab for graphics. Clicking this tab, I get a list of the graphics that FTK found in the disk and when I select the image that we were working with before, FTK was able to render it for me.

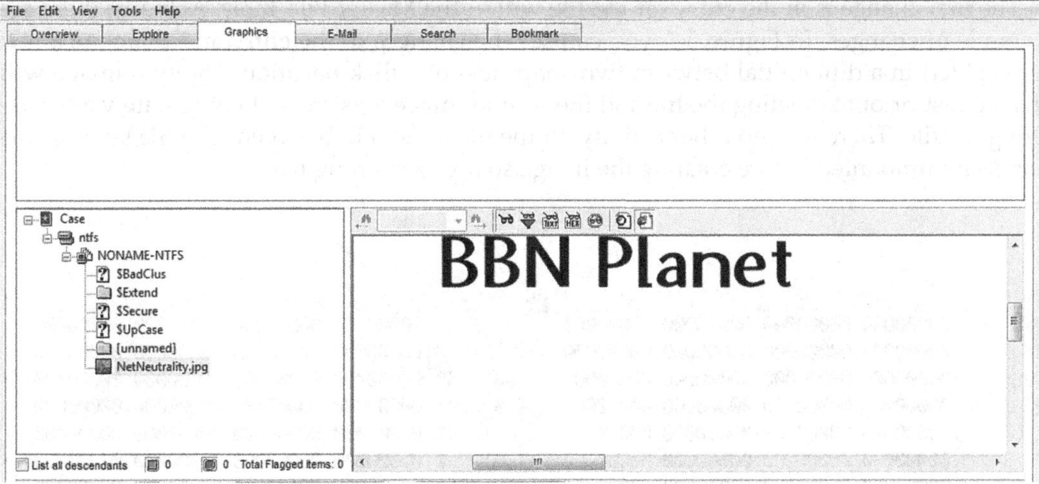

FIGURE 3.6

Using a program like FTK demonstrates how easy it can be to locate data using high-end commercial tools as compared with doing it manually or even using an open-source, automated tool like Scalpel.

SEARCHING AND DELETED FILES

Every operating and file system handles deleted files differently. In fact, with modern operating systems, there are really a couple of levels of file deletion. The first level, that we are probably all used to, is the Recycle Bin or the Trash, depending on the operating system you are using. When a file is moved to the Recycle Bin, it is still on the file system but it is no longer linked into the directory in the same place. When you empty the recycle bin, the file becomes deleted and there are a couple of changes that happen within the file system when that happens.

Starting with Windows Vista, Microsoft changed the way they handled the recycle bin. Inside the recycle bin directory, named $Recycle.Bin at the root of the drive, you will find directories named for the security identifier of the user. If you have a multi-user system, you will have multiple directories underneath the $Recycle.Bin directory. Inside these directories, you will find two types of files. The first type of files starts with $I and contains the metadata for the deleted files. Each of these files is 544 bytes. The other file has a name that starts with $R and contains the actual data from the deleted files. The remainder of each of these names is a set of random values. The $I file includes the information about the original file name, path, length and deleted date/time stamp.

The first change is in the entry for the file within the Master File Table. Actually, there are a couple of changes. In Figure 3.7, you can see the changes to the entry and there are a few highlighted in a differential between two snapshots of a disk partition. The first image was created just prior to deleting the file and the second image was created immediately after deleting the file. There was no other activity on the file system in between. The file system was not even unmounted before creating the image so it was running live.

```
ntfs-del.dd vs ntfs.dd
0017F60 00000000 00000000 00000000 00000000   0017F60 00000000 00000000 00000000 00000000
0017F70 00000000 00000000 00000000 00000000   0017F70 00000000 00000000 00000000 00000000
0017F80 00000000 00000000 00000000 00000000   0017F80 00000000 00000000 00000000 00000000
0017F90 00000000 00000000 00000000 00000000   0017F90 00000000 00000000 00000000 00000000
0017FA0 00000000 00000000 00000000 00000000   0017FA0 00000000 00000000 00000000 00000000
0017FB0 00000000 00000000 00000000 00000000   0017FB0 00000000 00000000 00000000 00000000
0017FC0 00000000 00000000 00000000 00000000   0017FC0 00000000 00000000 00000000 00000000
0017FD0 00000000 00000000 00000000 00000000   0017FD0 00000000 00000000 00000000 00000000
0017FE0 00000000 00000000 00000000 00000000   0017FE0 00000000 00000000 00000000 00000000
0017FF0 00000000 00000000 00000000 00000D00   0017FF0 00000000 00000000 00000000 00000D00
0018000 46494C45 30000300 00000000 00000000   0018000 46494C45 30000300 00000000 00000000
0018010 02000000 38000000 C0010000 00040000   0018010 01000100 38000100 C0010000 00040000
0018020 00000000 00000000 04000000 50000000   0018020 00000000 00000000 04000000 50000000
0018030 0E000000 00000000 10000000 48000000   0018030 0D000000 00000000 10000000 48000000
0018040 00000000 00000000 30000000 18000000   0018040 00000000 00000000 30000000 18000000
0018050 1F547661 4EACCF01 485E7661 4EACCF01   0018050 1F547661 4EACCF01 485E7661 4EACCF01
0018060 485E7661 4EACCF01 1F547661 4EACCF01   0018060 485E7661 4EACCF01 1F547661 4EACCF01
0018070 20000000 00000000 00000000 00000000   0018070 20000000 00000000 00000000 00000000
0018080 30000000 88000000 00000000 00000300   0018080 30000000 88000000 00000000 00000300
0018090 70000000 18000100 05000000 00000500   0018090 70000000 18000100 05000000 00000500

4: Replace 12 bytes at offset 0x5460 with 4 bytes
5: Insert 8 bytes at offset 0x5465
6: Replace 1 byte at offset 0x55fe with 1 byte
7: Replace 1 byte at offset 0x57fe with 1 byte
8: Replace 2 bytes at offset 0x18010 with 1 byte
9: Insert 1 byte at offset 0x18012
10: Delete 1 byte at offset 0x18015
11: Insert 1 byte at offset 0x18016
12: Replace 1 byte at offset 0x18030 with 1 byte
```

FIGURE 3.7

Out of the list of changes highlighted by our hex editor, the first one you can see is the sequence number for the file. This number has increased from 01 to 02 in the image taken after the file was deleted. This indicates that there was a change to the file between images. One of the changes made is two bytes away from the 0200 (remember, this is little endian so that is really a 0002) and that is where we go from 01 in the image on the right, which is the entry before the file was deleted to 00 on the left. That value is the link count. Figure 3.8

shows the entry after the file was deleted with the bytes outlined in red. The 00 at the right end of the three bytes outlined indicates that there are no entries that link to this entry, meaning that this entry is not used. That is an indicator to us that the entry in the file table has been deleted.

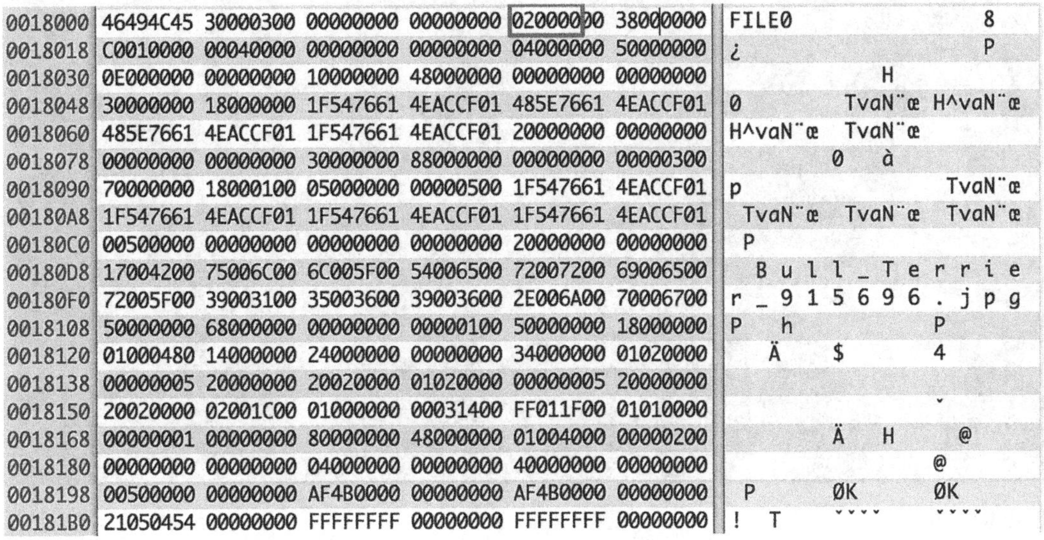

```
0018000 46494C45 30000300 00000000 00000000 02000000 38000000  FILE0            8
0018018 C0010000 00040000 00000000 00000000 04000000 50000000  ¿                P
0018030 0E000000 00000000 10000000 48000000 00000000 00000000            H
0018048 30000000 18000000 1F547661 4EACCF01 485E7661 4EACCF01  0       TvaN¨œ H^vaN¨œ
0018060 485E7661 4EACCF01 1F547661 4EACCF01 20000000 00000000  H^vaN¨œ TvaN¨œ
0018078 00000000 00000000 30000000 88000000 00000000 00000300          0  à
0018090 70000000 18000100 05000000 00000500 1F547661 4EACCF01  p               TvaN¨œ
00180A8 1F547661 4EACCF01 1F547661 4EACCF01 1F547661 4EACCF01   TvaN¨œ TvaN¨œ TvaN¨œ
00180C0 00500000 00000000 00000000 00000000 20000000 00000000   P
00180D8 17004200 75006C00 6C005F00 54006500 72007200 69006500   B u l l _ T e r r i e
00180F0 72005F00 39003100 35003600 39003600 2E006A00 70006700  r _ 9 1 5 6 9 6 . j p g
0018108 50000000 68000000 00000000 00000100 50000000 18000000  P  h           P
0018120 01000480 14000000 24000000 00000000 34000000 01020000     Ä     $      4
0018138 00000005 20000000 20020000 01020000 00000005 20000000
0018150 20020000 02001C00 01000000 00031400 FF011F00 01010000                  ˇ
0018168 00000001 00000000 80000000 48000000 01004000 00000200           Ä  H    @
0018180 00000000 00000000 04000000 00000000 40000000 00000000                  @
0018198 00500000 00000000 AF4B0000 00000000 AF4B0000 00000000   P      ØK      ØK
00181B0 21050454 00000000 FFFFFFFF 00000000 FFFFFFFF 00000000  !  T     ˇˇˇˇ    ˇˇˇˇ
```

FIGURE 3.8

Other portions of the entry for this file have been altered as well but the other thing we are really concerned with, aside from the indication that the entry is not being used, is the update to the $Bitmap file, which is a special file in the master file table that shows clusters, which are in use and not in use. All of the clusters that had been allocated to this file have been released back and are now flagged as available in the $Bitmap, so when the operating system needs to get storage for a new file, those clusters could be used.

This does not mean, though, that the references to the clusters have been removed from the entry in the master file table. It also does not mean, as we have seen above, that the entry from the master file table has been removed. If we were to use the utility fls from The Sleuth Kit, we can see the listing for the file, as seen in Figure 3.9. The listing does not look like the listings for other files, however. You can see that the entry is -/r rather than r/r, which it would be if it were a regular file. The first entry is the file type from the file name structure and the second entry after the / is the file type as indicated in the metadata structure. The -/r, we get for our deleted file, Bull_Terrier_915696.jpg, indicates that there is no file type in the file name structure. There is also an asterisk after the file type indicator but before the metadata address. The -128-1 is an indicator that this is an NTFS file system and we are pointing to the $Data attribute for the file. Finally, we can see that while the data has a size, the actual size or the size that has been allocated to the file is 0. This is because all of the disk space has been deallocated from the file entry.

```
r/r 78-128-2:   unit_test.py
r/r 79-128-2:   vmcontrol.py
-/r * 80-128-2: Bull_Terrier_915696.jpg
d/d 81: $OrphanFiles
kilroy@dallas ~ $ istat ntfs-del.dd 80
MFT Entry Header Values:
Entry: 80        Sequence: 2
$LogFile Sequence Number: 0
Not Allocated File
Links: 0

$STANDARD_INFORMATION Attribute Values:
Flags: Archive
Owner ID: 0
Security ID: 0  ()
Created:        Wed Jul 30 19:31:25 2014
File Modified:  Wed Jul 30 19:31:25 2014
MFT Modified:   Wed Jul 30 19:31:25 2014
Accessed:       Wed Jul 30 19:31:25 2014

$FILE_NAME Attribute Values:
Flags: Archive
Name: Bull_Terrier_915696.jpg
Parent MFT Entry: 5     Sequence: 5
Allocated Size: 20480          Actual Size: 0
```

FIGURE 3.9

Beneath the output from fls, you can see that I have run istat on the metadata entry in the master file table. It clearly indicates that this is not an allocated file and also shows that there are 0 links to this particular entry. All of the date entries are up to date and accurate and there are also references to five clusters used for the file in the $Data attribute for the file. There is also an indicator of where the file lived in the directory structure. As a result, you can still determine everything you need to about deleted files by looking at the directory information because it is not purged just because the file is deleted. While the $Bitmap entry has been updated to free up the used clusters, the actual data in the clusters is still intact until the operating system has chosen those clusters to overwrite.

In order to retrieve the data, we can use the methods described above for data carving or recovering information from the file system. In this case, it is pretty easy, since we still have a directory entry for the file and we can find the clusters that were used. From there, it is simple math to determine where in the disk image, we need to go looking to extract the information. Or, of course, you could use tools like Autopsy, FTK or EnCase to retrieve the deleted file.

The process on an ext file system is similar in terms of how the operating system handles, deleting the file or flagging that it has been deleted. Again, I had a small volume that I had formatted ext3, where I copied a number of files then created an image of the partition before deleting one of the files. Once I deleted the file, I created another image of the partition for comparison to the file system without the file deleted. You can see in Figure 3.10, that there are a number of places in the file system, where information has changed when I do a comparison on the raw hexadecimal values from the two images.

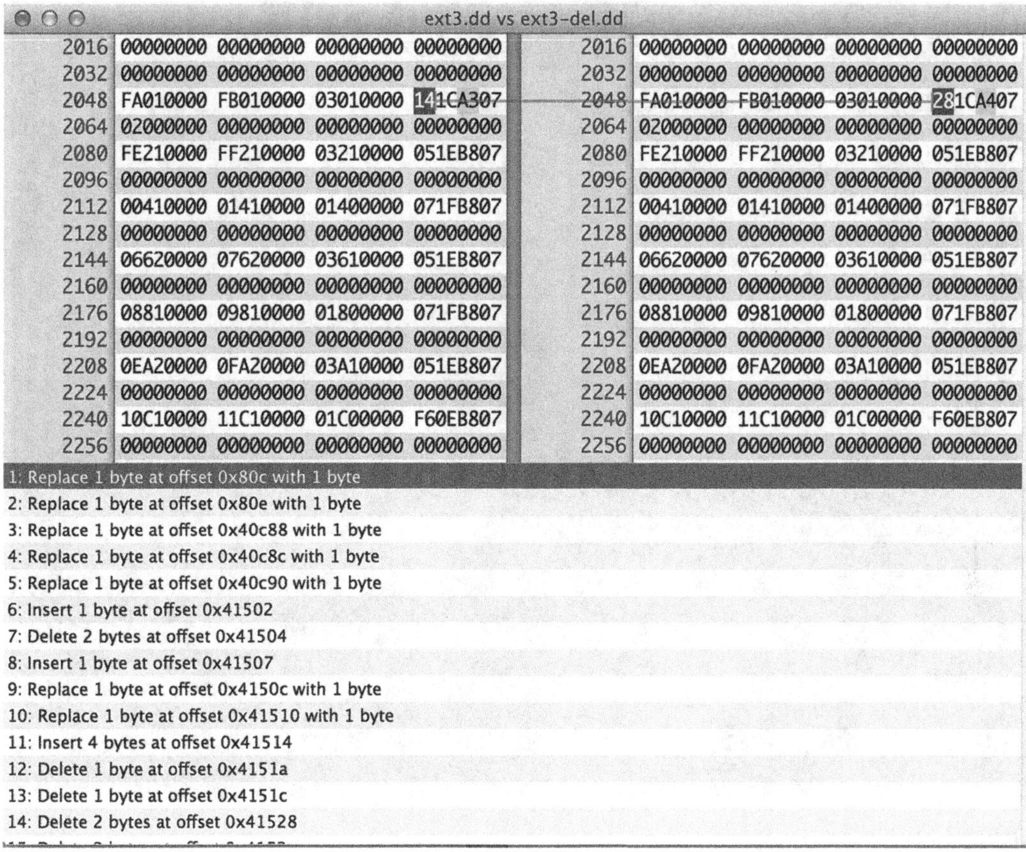

```
ext3.dd vs ext3-del.dd
2016 00000000 00000000 00000000 00000000   2016 00000000 00000000 00000000 00000000
2032 00000000 00000000 00000000 00000000   2032 00000000 00000000 00000000 00000000
2048 FA010000 FB010000 03010000 141CA307   2048 FA010000 FB010000 03010000 281CA407
2064 02000000 00000000 00000000 00000000   2064 02000000 00000000 00000000 00000000
2080 FE210000 FF210000 03210000 051EB807   2080 FE210000 FF210000 03210000 051EB807
2096 00000000 00000000 00000000 00000000   2096 00000000 00000000 00000000 00000000
2112 00410000 01410000 01400000 071FB807   2112 00410000 01410000 01400000 071FB807
2128 00000000 00000000 00000000 00000000   2128 00000000 00000000 00000000 00000000
2144 06620000 07620000 03610000 051EB807   2144 06620000 07620000 03610000 051EB807
2160 00000000 00000000 00000000 00000000   2160 00000000 00000000 00000000 00000000
2176 08810000 09810000 01800000 071FB807   2176 08810000 09810000 01800000 071FB807
2192 00000000 00000000 00000000 00000000   2192 00000000 00000000 00000000 00000000
2208 0EA20000 0FA20000 03A10000 051EB807   2208 0EA20000 0FA20000 03A10000 051EB807
2224 00000000 00000000 00000000 00000000   2224 00000000 00000000 00000000 00000000
2240 10C10000 11C10000 01C00000 F60EB807   2240 10C10000 11C10000 01C00000 F60EB807
2256 00000000 00000000 00000000 00000000   2256 00000000 00000000 00000000 00000000
1: Replace 1 byte at offset 0x80c with 1 byte
2: Replace 1 byte at offset 0x80e with 1 byte
3: Replace 1 byte at offset 0x40c88 with 1 byte
4: Replace 1 byte at offset 0x40c8c with 1 byte
5: Replace 1 byte at offset 0x40c90 with 1 byte
6: Insert 1 byte at offset 0x41502
7: Delete 2 bytes at offset 0x41504
8: Insert 1 byte at offset 0x41507
9: Replace 1 byte at offset 0x4150c with 1 byte
10: Replace 1 byte at offset 0x41510 with 1 byte
11: Insert 4 bytes at offset 0x41514
12: Delete 1 byte at offset 0x4151a
13: Delete 1 byte at offset 0x4151c
14: Delete 2 bytes at offset 0x41528
```

FIGURE 3.10

Additionally, when we take a look at the file listing from the volume and then check the inode, where the JPG we deleted has its information stored, we see something very similar to what we saw under NTFS. First, we can see in Figure 3.11 that there is an * after the file type. This is a reflection of what we find in the inode for the file, which indicates that there are no links to this inode entry, meaning that there is no directory entry that refers to this particular inode. In effect, the inode is dead. You can also see, the same as with NTFS that the actual size is set to 0, because all of the space has been deallocated so the space can be used by other files. You can also see an entry called Direct Blocks, which would be the file blocks where the data is stored. While it does not clearly show it here, there are no direct blocks listed, so the inode still has data about the file but it no longer refers to the data on the disk.

Resources can be allocated, which means that they are reserved and cannot be used by someone else. When the resources are no longer needed, those resources are deallocated, meaning that the resources are returned to the pool of what is available.

```
kilroy@dallas ~ $ fls ext3-del.dd
d/d 11: lost+found
r/r 12: 0308Capture.py
r/r 13: cap.py
r/r 14: parsedisk.py
r/r 15: pc.py
r/r 16: pst.py
r/r 17: readdisk.py
r/r 18: scapytest.py
r/r * 19:       Bull_Terrier_915696.jpg
r/r 20: captured.jpg
r/r 21: collected.jpg
d/d 25689:      $OrphanFiles
kilroy@dallas ~ $ istat ext3-del.dd 19
inode: 19
Not Allocated
Group: 0
Generation Id: 3862195867
uid / gid: 0 / 0
mode: rrw-r--r--
size: 0
num of links: 0

Inode Times:
Accessed:       Fri Aug  1 13:56:05 2014
File Modified:  Fri Aug  1 13:56:30 2014
Inode Modified: Fri Aug  1 13:56:30 2014
Deleted:        Fri Aug  1 13:56:30 2014

Direct Blocks:
```

FIGURE 3.11

While the inode is no longer linked into any directories, which we can see, is the case with the link count being set to 0, the data is still on the disk and while we cannot find the direct blocks that the file uses, we can still use the other recovery techniques discussed earlier to retrieve the file contents. This is a JPEG file, so we can look for the header and the footer and recover the contents of the file from the disk.

SLACK SPACE AND SPARSE FILES

Slack space is actually a pretty simple concept but it is also an important one to a forensic examiner. Slack space is commonly considered to be the space after the end of a file but before the end of the cluster or block. You may be wondering why this is important. Imagine that you have been using your disk for several months to several years. You have added and deleted countless files over that period of time. Likely, the spaces where you have created and deleted files have been overwritten several times over that period of time. When you delete a file, as we saw previously, the file contents do not get removed from the disk. When the disk head passes over, assuming that there is a disk head, it reads electromagnetic charges on the disk. When disks are manufactured, there are charges on the disk. Not everything is a 0 or a

1 uniformly. The same is true with solid-state hard drives that use flash storage. As a result, even disks that have never been written to will look like there is data on them.

When you have some amount of space that has been allocated to a file but you do not use all that space, there may still be information in the space between the end of the file and the end of the cluster or block. You can see file properties in Figure 3.12 demonstrating the difference. While the size is 1819 bytes, the size on disk is 4096 bytes because that 1819 byte file takes up a single cluster and the cluster size on the drive is 4096 bytes. This leaves 2277 bytes that are not being taken up by the file but also cannot be used for anything else.

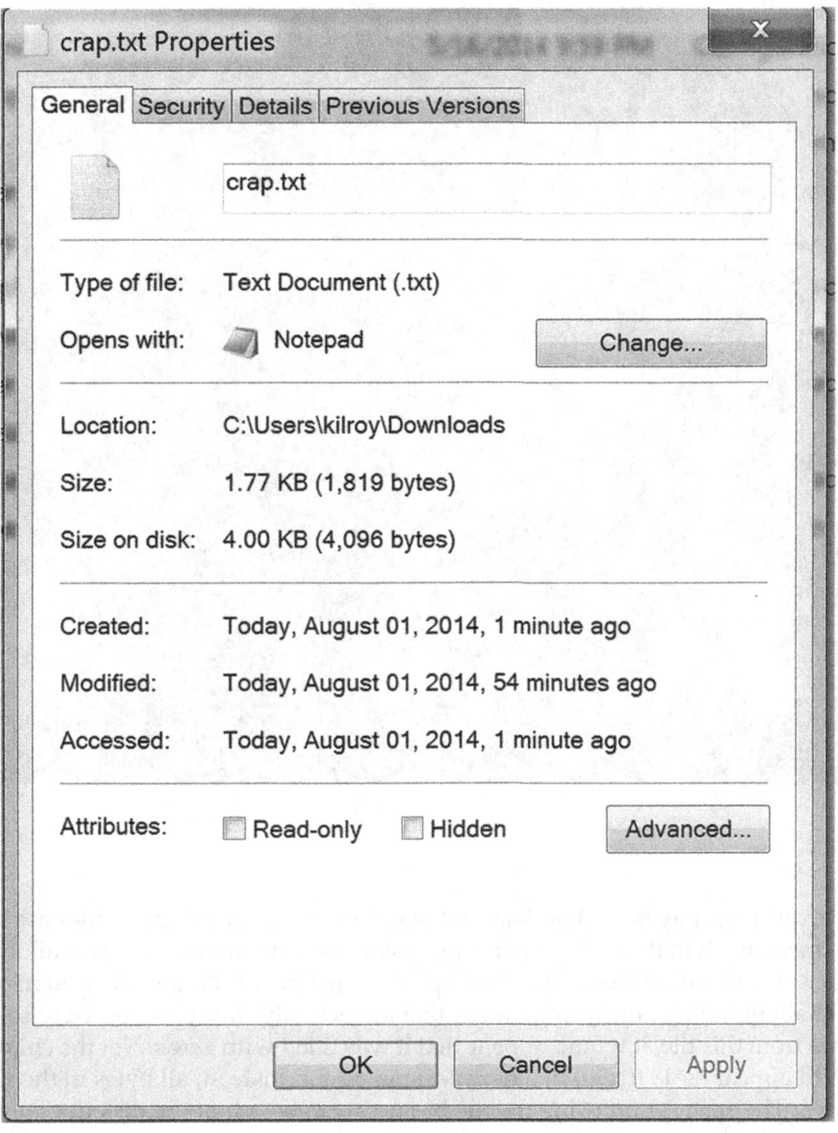

FIGURE 3.12

It is not necessarily the case, though, that there will be data stored in slack space. In some cases, the file system may actually be zeroed out. This may be especially true in cases where you are using a virtual hard drive. Since, there is no physical hard drive that may have electromagnetic residue that appears to be data, the slack space on the virtual hard drive may appear to be actually empty or full of zeros. You can see that in Figure 3.13, where there are zeros filling the remainder of the sector after the end of the file being displayed in the hex editor. This was similarly true using a flash drive with a freshly formatted partition. In that case, there were also zeros between the end of the file and the end of the cluster.

```
inode: 12
Allocated
Group: 0
Generation Id: 894991231
uid / gid: 0 / 0
mode: rrw-r--r--
size: 5242880
num of links: 1

Inode Times:
Accessed:       Mon Aug  4 17:42:11 2014
File Modified:  Mon Aug  4 17:42:11 2014
Inode Modified: Mon Aug  4 17:42:11 2014

Direct Blocks:
0 0 0 0 0 0 0 0
0 0 0 0 0 0 0 0
0 0 0 0 0 0 0 0
0 0 0 0 0 0 0 0
0 0 0 0 0 0 0 0
0 0 0 0 0 0 0 0
0 0 0 0 0 0 0 0
0 0 0 0 0 0 0 0
0 0 0 0 0 0 0 0
0 0 0 0 0 0 0 0
0 0 0 0 0 0 0 0
0 0 0 0 0 0 0 0
:
```

FIGURE 3.13

While hard drives may be full of data that was there previously, sparse files are large files that do not have much in them. The operating system is aware that the file was allocated with a particular size but rather than taking up space on the partition, the file system will carry information about the file, including blocks that are actually in use. If you were to try to access the data from this file, it would appear that it was filled with zeros. Not the character "0", which would appear as 48 (0x30) in a hexadecimal editor. Instead, all bytes in the file would contain zeros. The application using the file has no awareness that the disk does not actually contain those zeros.

There are several reasons why you may want to use a sparse file rather than a regular file. You might want to create a sparse file for a database, for example. You expect the file to grow and you want to be able to manage the location and organization of the pages within the database. The database application or server is best able to determine where in the file it wants to write the data. Log files may also use sparse files. In this case, you allocate the size of your log file and then you may want to manage how you write the data out to the sparse file. You may want to do this if, rather than growing the file as you continue to write log messages out, you want to maintain a consistent size for your log files and just overwrite older log entries.

Some file systems have native support for sparse files. NTFS, for example, has a setting within the file attributes indicating whether a file is sparse. On a Linux system, you can easily create a sparse file using dd. The command below will create a sparse file and you can see that while the file was created, no data was written out. The command works because we have asked dd to skip 5120 blocks before writing anything out. Each block is 1 k, which we set with bs, or block size. Saying count = 0 means that we are not actually going to write any data out, so we skip 5120 1 k blocks and then do nothing. This allocates all of that space without filling it with anything.

```
dd of=sparsefile bs=1k seek=5120 count=0

0+0 records in

0+0 records out

0 bytes (0 B) copied, 0.000144669 s, 0.0 kB/s
```

We can take a look at what that file looks like in the data system using the tools from The Sleuth Kit. That will provide you an indication of how the file is stored within the file system. Using fls once I have created the sparse file, I can get the inode for the file, which will provide me with the information about the file, including the date of creation, the size, the owner, and permissions. Additionally, it will provide me with the list of data blocks associated with the file. In Figure 3.13, you can see that the file is 5,242,880 bytes in size, but when you go down to look at the data blocks associated with the file, you can see they are all set to 0. This is because the file has been created but no data blocks have been allocated to it as yet. This means, it has an entry in the root directory and also has an inode carrying the metadata, but there is no place to go to look for the data because at this point there is not any. Once data has been written to the file, the data blocks will be populated with the actually blocks in the file system where the data can be found.

On the Windows side, you would use fsutil to manage the creation of sparse files from the command line. This can also be done programmatically, of course. The first thing we are going to do is create the file. Once we have created the file, we are going to set the flag to indicate to the file system that the file is sparse. Finally, we need to set the range within the file so that the file system knows how much of the file is sparse. We want the whole file to be sparse for this exercise so I am going to set the range to be 0 through the size of the file.

```
C:\Users\kilroy>fsutil file createnew sparsefile 100000
File C:\Users\kilroy\sparsefile is created

C:\Users\kilroy>fsutil sparse setflag sparsefile

C:\Users\kilroy>fsutil sparse setrange sparsefile 0 100000
```

Once we have a sparse file on an NTFS partition, we can extract that partition, so we can perform some analysis on it. We have used the Linux dd tool previously to grab data from hard drives and certainly there are commercial tools that will do this, but there is also a Windows version of dd and it is worth taking a look because of the syntax used to refer to the drives. Since, your device path depends on the order in which the operating system finds the volumes, we need to get a list of the volumes from the operating system along with the mapping for how each volume is mounted. You can see the list below, indicating that \\?\Device\HarddiskVolume4 of = windows.dd is mounted as the drive e: so, we will use that as the input file for dd so that we can get our capture.

```
C:\Users\kilroy\Documents>dd --list
rawwrite dd for windows version 0.6beta3.
Written by John Newbigin <jn@it.swin.edu.au>
This program is covered by terms of the GPL Version 2.

Win32 Available Volume Information
\\.\Volume{9e0b5583-aa2d-11e3-9eb8-806e6f6e6963}\
  link to \\?\Device\HarddiskVolume1
  fixed media
  Not mounted

\\.\Volume{79434c96-a6bb-4a44-bd00-4a92e4220aa4}\
  link to \\?\Device\HarddiskVolume4
  fixed media
  Mounted on \\.\e:

\\.\Volume{9e0b5584-aa2d-11e3-9eb8-806e6f6e6963}\
  link to \\?\Device\HarddiskVolume2
  fixed media
  Mounted on \\.\c:

\\.\Volume{9e0b5588-aa2d-11e3-9eb8-806e6f6e6963}\
  link to \\?\Device\Floppy0
  removeable media
  Mounted on \\.\a:

\\.\Volume{9e0b5587-aa2d-11e3-9eb8-806e6f6e6963}\
  link to \\?\Device\CdRom0
  CD-ROM
  Mounted on \\.\d:

C:\Users\kilroy\Documents>dd if=\\?\Device\HarddiskVolume4
of=windows.dd
rawwrite dd for windows version 0.6beta3.
Written by John Newbigin <jn@it.swin.edu.au>
This program is covered by terms of the GPL Version 2.

204792+0 records in
204792+0 records out
```

Once we have the image, we can use the same process as we used above to see what the file system thinks about that particular file. If it is truly sparse, it will be flagged as sparse and, since it is empty, it will not have any data clusters associated with it. I can use fls to get the list of files and the associated entry in the master file table. Once I have the right entry, I can use istat on the entry in the master file table to see what the metadata for the file says, as well as, getting a list of all of the data blocks. Figure 3.14 shows the output from istat on the master file table entry for the sparse file that was created.

```
$STANDARD_INFORMATION Attribute Values:
Flags: Archive, Sparse
Owner ID: 0
Security ID: 268  ()
Created:          Mon Aug  4 18:05:18 2014
File Modified:    Mon Aug  4 18:05:34 2014
MFT Modified:     Mon Aug  4 18:05:34 2014
Accessed:         Mon Aug  4 18:05:18 2014

$FILE_NAME Attribute Values:
Flags: Archive
Name: sparsefile
Parent MFT Entry: 5     Sequence: 5
Allocated Size: 0       Actual Size: 0
Created:          Mon Aug  4 18:05:18 2014
File Modified:    Mon Aug  4 18:05:18 2014
MFT Modified:     Mon Aug  4 18:05:18 2014
Accessed:         Mon Aug  4 18:05:18 2014

Attributes:
Type: $STANDARD_INFORMATION (16-0)   Name: N/A   Resident   size: 72
Type: $FILE_NAME (48-3)   Name: N/A   Resident   size: 82
Type: $FILE_NAME (48-2)   Name: N/A   Resident   size: 86
Type: $DATA (128-4)   Name: N/A   Non-Resident, Sparse   size: 100000  init_size
: 0
0 0 0 0 0 0 0 0
0 0 0 0 0 0 0 0
0 0 0 0 0 0 0 0
0 0 0 0 0 0 0 0
```

FIGURE 3.14

You can see from the entry that the file is considered sparse, since it shows up that way under the flags field. You can also see that the allocated file size is 0 and the actual file size is 0. Interestingly, we created the file to have a size of 100,000 bytes. That shows up in the list of attributes, where the $DATA attribute says that the size is 100,000 bytes, and you can also see that there is a list of blocks that have been placed into the $DATA attribute, but they all have a value of 0. This means that the entry in the file table has already allocated space for the blocks in an attribute but since those blocks have not actually been allocated on the volume, they have no values. Once the application starts to place data into the file, those block entries will get real values that can be used to pull data from.

DATA HIDING

There are a lot of places to hide data and we have already talked about slack space within a file system. There is one very common place that data is hidden on Windows systems and that is in alternate data streams. While we talked about alternate data streams, we did not talk about what they look like within the file system and how you would pull the data out of them on a raw disk image. The first thing we need to do is to get the file list from the image. Using fls from The Sleuth Kit against an NTFS image with an alternate data stream, I can see the file and the alternate data stream that are attached to the same entry within the master file table. From there, I can use istat to get the information about where all of the data associated with the file is located on the drive. In Figure 3.15, you can see the two $DATA entries for the single entry in the master file table.

```
$FILE_NAME Attribute Values:
Flags: Archive
Name: Ch02_Messier.docx
Parent MFT Entry: 5     Sequence: 5
Allocated Size: 90112           Actual Size: 0
Created:         Fri Aug  1 17:43:54 2014
File Modified:   Fri Aug  1 17:43:54 2014
MFT Modified:    Fri Aug  1 17:43:54 2014
Accessed:        Fri Aug  1 17:43:54 2014

Attributes:
Type: $STANDARD_INFORMATION (16-0)   Name: N/A   Resident   size: 72
Type: $FILE_NAME (48-3)   Name: N/A   Resident   size: 90
Type: $FILE_NAME (48-2)   Name: N/A   Resident   size: 100
Type: $DATA (128-1)   Name: N/A   Non-Resident   size: 88296  init_size: 88296
8359 8360 8361 8362 8363 8364 8365 8366
8367 8368 8369 8370 8371 8372 8373 8374
8375 8376 8377 8378 8379 8380
Type: $DATA (128-5)   Name: cmd.exe   Non-Resident   size: 345088  init_size: 34
5088
40 41 42 43 8381 8382 8383 8384
8385 8386 8387 8388 8389 8390 8391 8392
8393 8394 8395 8396 8397 8398 8399 8400
8401 8402 8403 8404 8405 8406 8407 8408
8409 8410 8411 8412 8413 8414 8415 8416
8417 8418 8419 8420 8421 8422 8423 8424
8425 8426 8427 8428 8429 8430 8431 8432
8433 8434 8435 8436 8437 8438 8439 8440
8441 8442 8443 8444 8445 8446 8447 8448
8449 8450 8451 8452 8453 8454 8455 8456
8457 8458 8459 8460 8461
kilroy@dallas ~ $
```

FIGURE 3.15

You can see from the istat output that there are two $DATA entries for the file. The first $DATA entry has no name associated with it. The reason for this is that the name is attached to the $FILE_NAME attribute. The second $DATA entry is the alternate data stream and you can see that it has a name associated with it and it is the cmd.exe file that was stored as an alternate data stream associated with the .docx file. Each $DATA entry has a list of blocks associated with it, where the actual data is stored on the disk. In order to get it out manually, we can use dd or we could also use blkcat. Since the data is not stored contiguously, you would have to concatenate whatever you get in order to create the file in the end. Using blkcat would require pulling each block one at a time and then concatenating the results. You can see in Figure 3.16 that the first block of the file, as extracted by blkcat and displayed by xxd, shows the start of an executable. You can see this from the text "This program cannot be run in DOS mode" which indicates a program designed to run under Windows.

```
kilroy@dallas ~ $ blkcat windows.dd 40 | xxd
0000000: 4d5a 9000 0300 0000 0400 0000 ffff 0000  MZ..............
0000010: b800 0000 0000 0000 4000 0000 0000 0000  ........@.......
0000020: 0000 0000 0000 0000 0000 0000 0000 0000  ................
0000030: 0000 0000 0000 0000 0000 0000 f000 0000  ................
0000040: 0e1f ba0e 00b4 09cd 21b8 014c cd21 5468  ........!..L.!Th
0000050: 6973 2070 726f 6772 616d 2063 616e 6e6f  is program canno
0000060: 7420 6265 2072 756e 2069 6e20 444f 5320  t be run in DOS 
0000070: 6d6f 6465 2e0d 0d0a 2400 0000 0000 0000  mode....$.......
0000080: 4d7c a48a 091d cad9 091d cad9 091d cad9  M|..............
```

FIGURE 3.16

xxd is a Linux program that is used to convert binary information to hexadecimal values. It formats these values into columns so the address of each value can be easily located.

We could also use dd to pull the blocks 40–43 together and then pull the blocks 8381–8461. Once you have all of the data, you can put it back together and get the alternate data stream out of the file system. With a smaller file, you would likely not have to pull your data from multiple locations on the hard drive. There is another interesting thing about the entry in the master file table. You can see the four time entries in the master file table entry, all set to be the same time. Interestingly, the alternate data stream was added several days after the file was created. This means that even though an additional $DATA attribute was added to the entry, the MFT modified date was not changed.

TIME STAMPS/STOMPS

Time, to paraphrase Douglas Adams, is an illusion and file times doubly so. You could see above, though you will have to take my word for some of it, that the file times in the MFT were not updated, when a new $DATA entry was created. The thing about time stamps on files is that they are just pieces of data associated with a file. In fact, they are typically stored as a large integer value that represents an offset of time from a particular source time. In the case of what is often called UNIX time, the source time is January 1, 1970 at midnight, or 00:00:00. We count the amount of time since that date in order to get the current time and date, so when you look at the value in the metadata structures, you will see just a large integer value.

In the case of Windows systems, time and date is stored as a 64-bit value that is the number of 100 ns since January 1, 1601, Universal Coordinated Time (UTC). Times are stored as UTC and the system is then responsible for adjusting based on local time when the time and date are displayed. Other operating systems rely on 1 s granularity, so you cannot get a time value on any file at a time that is more detailed than on second boundaries. Older operating systems also did not use as much storage to keep track of the time and date. Instead of 64-bit, they used 32-bit values, which restricted the useful life of those values since at some point, you have to either reset your starting point, making all the previous values ambiguous, or you have to just stop using them after a certain point. The 32-bit values used to store date and time information has generally been superseded by 64-bit values in modern operating systems because, even though the common 2038 date seems quite far away, 2000 also seemed a long way off when programmers started using 2-digit values to indicate a year.

Time can be altered. Not in the sense of taking your friend's watch and resetting it to be an hour or two earlier or later. You would think that would be pretty obvious, just by comparing the apparent time with the daylight for a start. When suddenly the sun is rising at 3 am, which would suggest something is not quite right. When it comes to files, since the time and date are stored as integer values within the metadata of the file table, the time and date can be changed. There is nothing that prevents someone from going in and making those changes. There are a number of tools that will do that. One of those is called timestomp.exe and there is also a graphical user interface (GUI) available to interface with it. You can see the GUI in Figure 3.17.

Using a tool like timestomp gives you the ability to change the different timestamps that are associated with the file. Depending on the file system, you might have three or four timestamps on each file or directory. When you first write the file to the disk, the metadata in the file table is created and you set a file creation time. Any time you make changes to the file, you are changing the modified time. Any time you read from or write to the file, you are changing the accessed time. In the case of NTFS, as we saw earlier, there is also a timestamp associated with, when the metadata or MFT entry was changed. Theoretically, all of those timestamps are reliable and can show when the file was created, accessed or modified. There are plenty of ways to change the date of a file, though, including a standard UNIX/Linux utility, touch. Using touch, you can set the date on the file to whatever date you want it to be. Additionally, touch will allow you to free-form the date you add to it. In Figure 3.18, you can see a couple

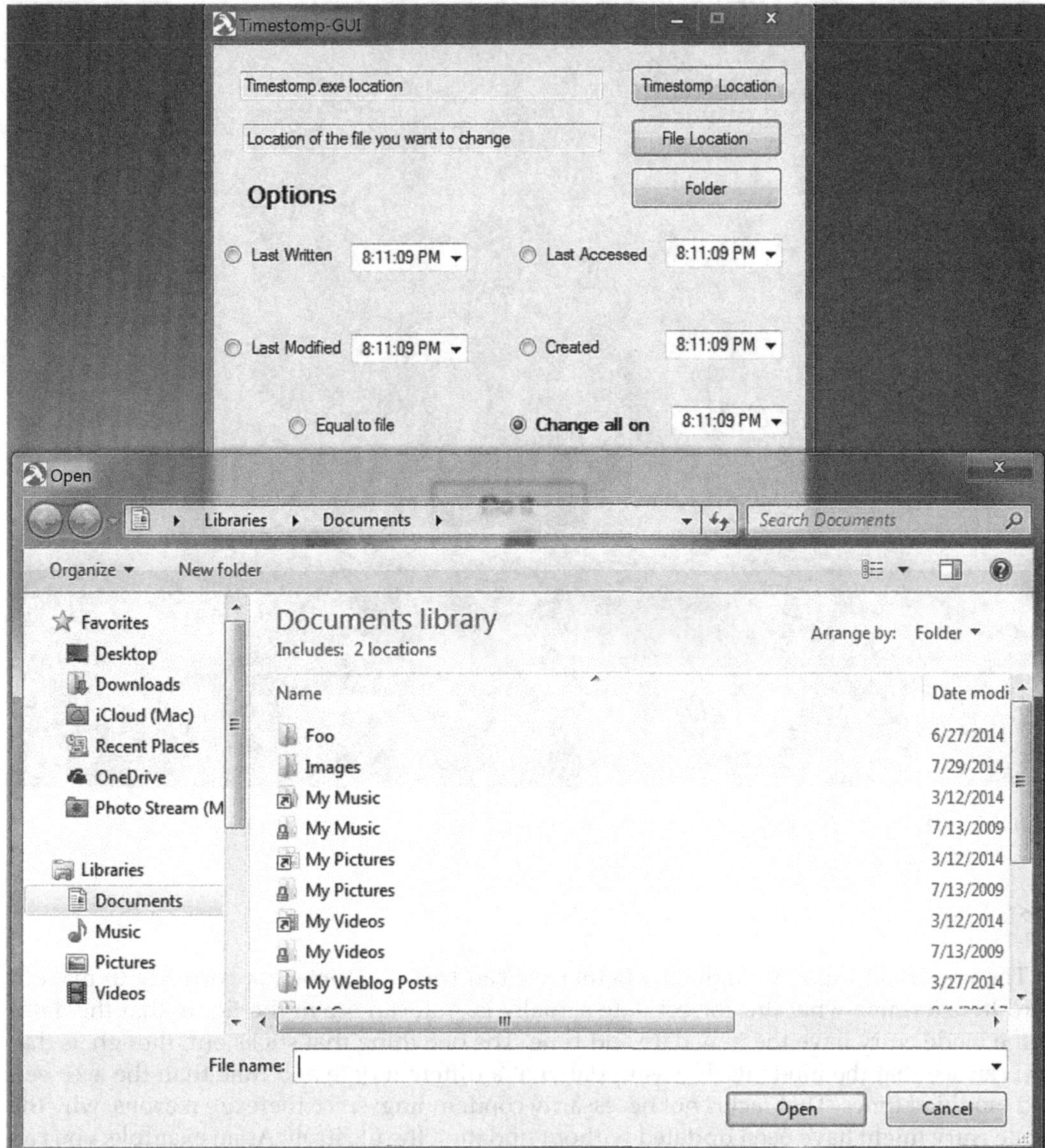

FIGURE 3.17

of different ways to change the date of a file. The first uses a traditional date and time and the output of l s clearly shows the new date and time on the file. The second uses a text-based approach, where I set the date to be "last Monday." You can see from the output that touch determined the correct date based on that input and the date is set correctly but the time just gets set to midnight.

```
kilroy@dallas /mnt $ touch foo
kilroy@dallas /mnt $ ls -la foo
-rw-r--r-- 1 kilroy kilroy 0 Aug  9 16:38 foo
kilroy@dallas /mnt $ touch --date "6/20/1965 04:19" foo
kilroy@dallas /mnt $ ls -la foo
-rw-r--r-- 1 kilroy kilroy 0 Jun 20  1965 foo
kilroy@dallas /mnt $ touch --date "last Monday" foo
kilroy@dallas /mnt $ ls -la foo
-rw-r--r-- 1 kilroy kilroy 0 Aug  4 00:00 foo
kilroy@dallas /mnt $ sudo istat /dev/sdb1 12
inode: 12
Allocated
Group: 0
Generation Id: 633796345
uid / gid: 1000 / 1000
mode: rrw-r--r--
size: 0
num of links: 1

Inode Times:
Accessed:       Mon Aug  4 00:00:00 2014
File Modified:  Mon Aug  4 00:00:00 2014
Inode Modified: Sat Aug  9 16:38:54 2014

Direct Blocks:
```

FIGURE 3.18

The important thing, though, is whether we can trick the metadata correctly to make it hard to determine what the correct date actually is. You can see in the figure that the dates in the inode entry have the new date and time. The one thing that sticks out, though, is that you can see that the inode itself was updated at a different date and time than the accessed and modified times. That fact is not necessarily condemning, since there are reasons, why the inode entry might have been updated without updating the file itself. As an example, you can see in Figure 3.19, adding a hard link to the file updates the link count and the inode table but does not touch the file times.

Just because the file times and the inode times do not match, it is not conclusive that the times on the file have been altered. The important thing is that there are many reasons, why time stamps on files change. You cannot always rely on the file times in the file system, since there is nothing to prevent you from making those changes. One thing you can do to keep an eye on the file system and give you that additional information, you need to verify what happened with the file times is to use auditing on your particular file system. We will cover auditing in a subsequent chapter.

```
kilroy@dallas /mnt $ ln foo fool
kilroy@dallas /mnt $ sudo istat /dev/sdb1 12
inode: 12
Allocated
Group: 0
Generation Id: 633796345
uid / gid: 1000 / 1000
mode: rrw-r--r--
size: 0
num of links: 2

Inode Times:
Accessed:        Mon Aug  4 00:00:00 2014
File Modified:   Mon Aug  4 00:00:00 2014
Inode Modified:  Sat Aug  9 16:51:30 2014
```

FIGURE 3.19

There are a number of utilities that can be used to make adjustments to file times. In fact, the Metasploit exploit framework includes a module named timestomp to make adjustments to file times.

TIME LINES

Time lines will be a recurring topic but since we were talking about times, it is a good opportunity to talk about them in the context of the information from the file systems that we have been talking about. Since we have been spending so much time on the utilities that come with The Sleuth Kit (TSK), we can take another look at them to generate a timeline. Other programs like Internet Evidence Finder and Blacklight are also capable of generating good timelines, of course.

What would be great, as we are recovering data from the file system, is to get a listing of all of the files from an image or volume, but in order based on the time stamp on the file. We can easily do this using the same fls utility, we have used before. Using the following commands, we can get a listing of files that includes the timestamp information and then use another TSK utility, mactime, to present the file listing in date and time order. The utility mactime was one of those that was first written to be part of The Coroner's Toolkit that later ended up in TSK. Figure 3.20 shows the listing of the files in the correct order.

```
fls -m /mnt /dev/sdb1 > body.txt

mactime -b body.txt
```

```
Mon Aug 04 2014 00:00:00        0 ma.. r/rrw-r--r-- 1000    1000    12      /mnt/foo
                                0 ma.. r/rrw-r--r-- 1000    1000    12      /mnt/foo1
Fri Aug 08 2014 15:17:24    12288 mac. d/drwx------ 0       0       11      /mnt/lost+found
Sat Aug 09 2014 16:51:30        0 ..c. r/rrw-r--r-- 1000    1000    12      /mnt/foo
                                0 ..c. r/rrw-r--r-- 1000    1000    12      /mnt/foo1
Sun Aug 10 2014 14:35:33      120 mac. r/rrw-r--r-- 1000    1000    13      /mnt/0308Capture.py
                              483 mac. r/rrw-r--r-- 1000    1000    14      /mnt/cap.py
                               99 mac. r/rrw-r--r-- 1000    1000    15      /mnt/createfile.py
                              338 mac. r/rrw-r--r-- 1000    1000    16      /mnt/parsedisk.py
                              120 mac. r/rrw-r--r-- 1000    1000    17      /mnt/pc.py
                               70 mac. r/rrw-r--r-- 1000    1000    18      /mnt/pst.py
                              525 mac. r/rrwxr-xr-x 1000    1000    19      /mnt/readdisk.py
                              148 mac. r/rrw-r--r-- 1000    1000    20      /mnt/scapytest.py
Sun Aug 10 2014 14:35:37 10318788 mac. r/rrw-r--r-- 1000    1000    21      /mnt/rekall-forensic_1.
0.2_amd64.deb
                         10222356 mac. r/rrwxr-xr-x 1000    1000    22      /mnt/rekall-forensic_1.
0.3_amd64.deb
Sun Aug 10 2014 14:35:45     1819 mac. r/rrw-r--r-- 1000    1000    23      /mnt/crap.txt
```

FIGURE 3.20

What we are saying with the first command is that we want the modified, accessed, created times, as well as the mount point, so that mactime can present the entire path to the file including the mount point. This will give the output some context rather than simply a list of files and directories. We also have to provide an image and then we are going to redirect the output to a file called body.txt. We use that body.txt file as input to mactime and you can see a portion of the output in the figure. The output includes dates and times as well as access control information like permissions, owner, and group. You can also see the location of the metadata in the column before the filename. This is an ext3 filesystem, so this is the inode, where the information about the file is stored.

VOLUME SHADOW COPIES

Let us say that you cannot find the file you are looking for on the volume you are working with. It is possible, it was deleted at some point. On Windows systems, there may be another place where you can find the file. You may have seen at some point, when your system was performing an update, a system restore point being created. This system restore point has been around for more than a decade, since Windows XP, and it uses the volume shadow copy feature. The volume shadow copy is a way to store copies of files in a location that is not part of the primary file system but can still be accessed without resorting to off-system backup files. This is primarily useful from a system perspective when applications are being installed, so critical files that may be changed are backed up in case something goes wrong.

If an installation of an application or a system update does go wrong, the update can be rolled back by removing the new files and putting back any files that were removed or modified. The system gets those older files from the volume shadow copy storage location. It is not only the system that can use this location, however. Not only that but as a user, you can modify settings related to this feature. If you go into properties of your computer, or more specifically, go to My Computer or Computer, right click and select properties, you can then go to the System Protection tab and find the settings. One thing we can do from there is to determine, how much storage space we want to use for the storage of these volume shadow copies (Figure 3.21).

System Protection for Local Disk (C:)
Restore Settings
System Protection can keep copies of system settings and previous versions of files. Select what you would like to be able to restore:
Restore system settings and previous versions of files
Only restore previous versions of files
Turn off system protection
Disk Space Usage
You can adjust the maximum disk space used for system protection. As space fills up, older restore points will be deleted to make room for new ones.
Current Usage: 650.23 MB
Max Usage:
2% (1.26 GB)
Delete all restore points (this includes system settings and previous versions of files).
Delete
OK
Cancel
Apply

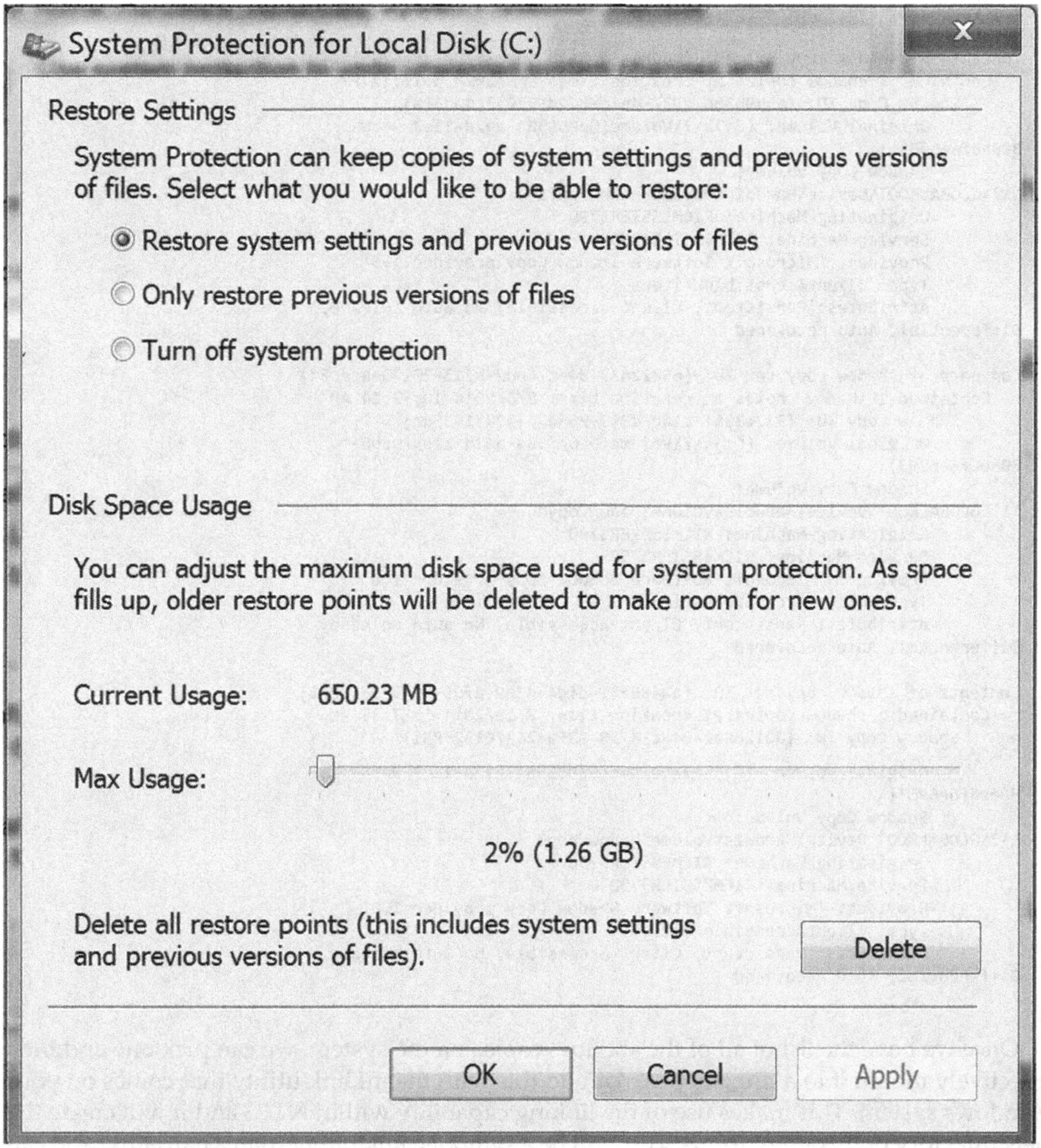

FIGURE 3.21

In order to really get at the volume shadow copies, however, we need to use the vssadmin tool that comes with Windows. With vssadmin, we can get a list of providers, volumes and storage locations. We can also get a list of the current shadow copies that exist on our system, as you can see below.

```
C:\Windows\system32>vssadmin list shadows
vssadmin 1.1 - Volume Shadow Copy Service administrative command-line
tool
(C) Copyright 2001-2005 Microsoft Corp.

Contents of shadow copy set ID: {b66e5c34-0e28-4dec-b2b8-a8f4799f8a40}
   Contained 1 shadow copies at creation time: 8/3/2014 5:15:12 PM
      Shadow Copy ID: {ebb0b306-ad37-4efd-8d4d-9c037c4aa3fa}
         Original Volume: (C:)\\?\Volume{9e0b5584-aa2d-11e3-9eb8-
806e6f6e6963}\
         Shadow Copy Volume:
\\?\GLOBALROOT\Device\HarddiskVolumeShadowCopy1
         Originating Machine: RICMESSIER379D
         Service Machine: RICMESSIER379D
         Provider: 'Microsoft Software Shadow Copy provider 1.0'
         Type: ClientAccessibleWriters
         Attributes: Persistent, Client-accessible, No auto release,
Differential, Auto recovered

Contents of shadow copy set ID: {65822433-04ec-4bd2-b713-20173eacec34}
   Contained 1 shadow copies at creation time: 8/6/2014 10:53:14 AM
      Shadow Copy ID: {332c359f-c16e-43f9-965e-8aa9831935dc}
         Original Volume: (C:)\\?\Volume{9e0b5584-aa2d-11e3-9eb8-
806e6f6e6963}\
         Shadow Copy Volume:
\\?\GLOBALROOT\Device\HarddiskVolumeShadowCopy2
         Originating Machine: RICMESSIER379D
         Service Machine: RICMESSIER379D
         Provider: 'Microsoft Software Shadow Copy provider 1.0'
         Type: ClientAccessibleWriters
         Attributes: Persistent, Client-accessible, No auto release,
Differential, Auto recovered

Contents of shadow copy set ID: {aa489861-dfd4-43d9-af93-8943e5623011}
   Contained 1 shadow copies at creation time: 8/10/2014 1:27:35 PM
      Shadow Copy ID: {dd1208a2-048c-4778-88fa-24370132f861}

         Original Volume: (C:)\\?\Volume{9e0b5584-aa2d-11e3-9eb8-
806e6f6e6963}\
         Shadow Copy Volume:
\\?\GLOBALROOT\Device\HarddiskVolumeShadowCopy3
         Originating Machine: RICMESSIER379D
         Service Machine: RICMESSIER379D
         Provider: 'Microsoft Software Shadow Copy provider 1.0'
         Type: ClientAccessibleWriters
         Attributes: Persistent, Client-accessible, No auto release,
Differential, Auto recovered
```

Once we have the list of all of the shadow copies on the system, we can pick one and then effectively mount it to a directory. We can do this with the mklink utility that comes on your Windows system. This makes use of the linking capability within NTFS and it will create the new directory or link point for us. This will be a symbolic link rather than a hard link. You can see how it works below. We use mklink and specify that we want to create a directory rather than a file by using the /D flag. Then we just specify the link location and the location of the volume shadow copy.

```
C:\Windows\system32>mklink /D c:\vss
\\?\GLOBALROOT\Device\HarddiskVolumeShadowCopy3\
symbolic link created for c:\vss <<===>>
\\?\GLOBALROOT\Device\HarddiskVolumeShadowCopy3\

C:\Windows\system32>dir \vss
 Volume in drive C has no label.
 Volume Serial Number is AC13-C61F

 Directory of C:\vss

07/13/2009  11:20 PM    <DIR>          PerfLogs
08/06/2014  03:17 PM    <DIR>          Program Files
07/24/2014  08:04 PM    <DIR>          Program Files (x86)
04/01/2014  09:54 PM    <DIR>          Python27
03/27/2014  07:22 PM    <DIR>          Tools
03/12/2014  01:33 PM    <DIR>          Users
07/29/2014  08:14 PM    <DIR>          Windows
               0 File(s)              0 bytes
               7 Dir(s)  21,957,378,048 bytes free
```

We use the device path in order to specify the location of the volume shadow copy. Once we have effectively mounted the volume shadow copy by creating the link, we can search through the volume shadow copy for the file. We can also copy files to and from the volume shadow copy. Copying files into the volume shadow copy can be dangerous, though, if you expect the file to remain there. The system manages the storage used for the volume shadow copies, which might mean that where you hoped that file would stay hidden for a while and also accessible when you needed it, the system might delete the whole shadow copy out from under you and that file will be gone. So, while this is a powerful forensic and anti-forensic tool, it is not always predictable, since, it is not entirely under your control.

Once you are done working with the volume shadow copy, you can remove the link. It is, after all, just a soft link, which means you can safely remove the link directory, you created and leave the volume shadow copy in place, still managed by the system. You can see below how I removed the link using rmdir, then showed how the link was gone. You can also see the list of shadow copies is still intact, including the one that I linked to.

```
C:\Windows\system32>rmdir \vss

C:\Windows\system32>dir \vss
 Volume in drive C has no label.
 Volume Serial Number is AC13-C61F

 Directory of C:\

File Not Found

C:\Windows\system32>vssadmin list shadows
```

```
vssadmin 1.1 - Volume Shadow Copy Service administrative command-
line tool
(C) Copyright 2001-2005 Microsoft Corp.

Contents of shadow copy set ID: {b66e5c34-0e28-4dec-b2b8-
a8f4799f8a40}
   Contained 1 shadow copies at creation time: 8/3/2014 5:15:12
PM
      Shadow Copy ID: {ebb0b306-ad37-4efd-8d4d-9c037c4aa3fa}
         Original Volume: (C:)\\?\Volume{9e0b5584-aa2d-11e3-9eb8-
806e6f6e6963}\
         Shadow Copy Volume:
\\?\GLOBALROOT\Device\HarddiskVolumeShadowCopy1
         Originating Machine: RICMESSIER379D
         Service Machine: RICMESSIER379D
         Provider: 'Microsoft Software Shadow Copy provider 1.0'
         Type: ClientAccessibleWriters
         Attributes: Persistent, Client-accessible, No auto
release, Differential, Auto recovered

Contents of shadow copy set ID: {65822433-04ec-4bd2-b713-
20173eacec34}
   Contained 1 shadow copies at creation time: 8/6/2014 10:53:14
AM
      Shadow Copy ID: {332c359f-c16e-43f9-965e-8aa9831935dc}
         Original Volume: (C:)\\?\Volume{9e0b5584-aa2d-11e3-9eb8-
806e6f6e6963}\
         Shadow Copy Volume:
\\?\GLOBALROOT\Device\HarddiskVolumeShadowCopy2
         Originating Machine: RICMESSIER379D
         Service Machine: RICMESSIER379D
         Provider: 'Microsoft Software Shadow Copy provider 1.0'
         Type: ClientAccessibleWriters
         Attributes: Persistent, Client-accessible, No auto
release, Differential, Auto recovered

Contents of shadow copy set ID: {aa489861-dfd4-43d9-af93-
8943e5623011}
   Contained 1 shadow copies at creation time: 8/10/2014 1:27:35
PM
      Shadow Copy ID: {dd1208a2-048c-4778-88fa-24370132f861}
         Original Volume: (C:)\\?\Volume{9e0b5584-aa2d-11e3-9eb8-
806e6f6e6963}\
         Shadow Copy Volume:
\\?\GLOBALROOT\Device\HarddiskVolumeShadowCopy3
         Originating Machine: RICMESSIER379D
         Service Machine: RICMESSIER379D
         Provider: 'Microsoft Software Shadow Copy provider 1.0'
         Type: ClientAccessibleWriters
         Attributes: Persistent, Client-accessible, No auto
release, Differential, Auto recovered
```

Each drive in a Windows system will have its own volume shadow copy storage to maintain files and directories from that drive or volume. You may have several volumes on your system that contain system-related information about applications, and each one of those would need to house its own volume shadow copy information. For every volume that is protected by the system, there will be a System Volume Information directory at the root of the volume. This is where the volume shadow copy information is stored.

SUMMARY

There are a lot of different ways for a file system to retain information and that information and data can be there long after the user believes that it is gone. This is important for a forensics practitioner because a suspect may attempt to remove incriminating evidence and you will need to know not only where it may still be located but also how to get to it. This is why skills like data carving are important. It is also, why you need to know about the metadata structures within the file system and some of the different capabilities of operating systems like Windows, which protects the system through the use of volume shadow copies.

You will note that we are continuing to use open source tools to investigate our file systems and images. One reason for this is that it does not constrain us to expensive commercial tools, since you will always have the ability to get these tools, but more importantly, it demonstrates the underlying concepts associated with these techniques. You are not relying on an automated tool to perform the work for you without explaining exactly what was going on. When processes are hidden like this, it might obscure bugs within the application. There have been cases where commercial tools have become unreliable as a result of bugs. This is not to say that open source tools are bug free because they are not. If you understand what is going on, you can find another tool to check your results against to ensure they are consistent.

EXERCISES

1. Get a list of the volume shadow copies on your system using vssadmin and then create a link to one of them in order to explore the files and directories that are there. Can you tell from the files and directories, what may have triggered this particular copy?
2. Store an image on an external volume like a USB stick or a secondary virtual drive, if you are in a virtual machine. Using the techniques described in this chapter, locate and extract the image file.
3. Delete the file and write some additional files out to the volume. Are you still able to recover the image file?

Bibliography

Drinkwater, R., 2010. Forensics from the sausage factory: Volume shadow copy forensics cannot see the wood for the trees? Available from http://forensicsfromthesausagefactory.blogspot.com/2010/02/volume-shadow-copy-forensics-cannot-see.html (accessed 10.08.2014.).

File Times, n.d. Windows. Available from http://msdn.microsoft.com/en-us/library/windows/desktop/ms724290(v=vs.85) (accessed 07.08.2014.).

CHAPTER

4

Memory Forensics

INFORMATION INCLUDED IN THIS CHAPTER:

- Virtual memory
- Windows, Linux, Mac OS memory
- Memory extraction
- Swap space

INTRODUCTION

Data is permanently stored on what is called secondary storage, which is what we have been talking about so far – disk drives, USB flash drives, and other forms of permanent storage. However, when a computer is running and programs are using the data that has been retrieved from the disk, the programs and data are placed into primary storage or main memory. Well, it is used to be called as main memory. Over the years, of course, memory has become significantly faster and quite a bit larger. When I was getting started in the early 1980s on an IBM mainframe, the system had 16 M of real memory in it, and it was considered a fairly large system, capable of supporting hundreds of simultaneous users. This has considerable more memory than the TI-99/4A, which was the first personal computer I have ever used and it had something like 16 k of memory. Not only that, but if you wanted to store something, you had to write it out on a cassette tape. Today, of course, we measure memory in gigabytes, an order of magnitude or two larger than memory that was used 30 years ago in even extremely large systems.

It is disk storage that has managed to increase exponentially, since we collect memory, we need a place to put it and terabyte, petabyte, or exabyte storage devices are easily capable of taking a memory dump from even large enterprise systems with multiple gigabytes of memory. While we can analyze memory statically, it is better to get a snapshot of the contents of memory, so that it can be analyzed at your leisure later. One of the reasons is that memory is constantly changing as programs continue to run. When you collect information from system memory then check again a moment later that information may be different. As an example, I could grab the list of network connections to a particular system and then a couple of minutes later, check those network connections again. They may have changed in that time as different programs have either concluded their business over the network or as, perhaps, other programs begin to engage in other business.

When we collect a snapshot of memory, we alleviate those concerns because we will be analyzing the contents of memory, as they were when we took the snapshot not as they are at this moment in time and then at another moment in time, when they have changed. We have consistency in this way. However, there is a problem in doing this. The problem is that we cannot acquire all multiple gigabytes at the same instant in time. It takes several seconds to acquire all of the contents of memory and in that time, the operating system is continuing to run, moving information around in memory. Additionally, when you acquire memory, you are likely to introduce a new program into memory for reading the contents of memory. In order to run a program, it has to be read into memory, so just the process of acquiring a memory image means that the memory image has been altered.

One way around that is to make use of a hardware capture device, which will interface directly with the memory bus inside the system and extract the contents from there. Since most of these hardware devices cannot be inserted into a running system, you would need to install it before you need it, which would be incredibly prescient on your part. Certainly, you could install that device into all the systems that may be under your control, if you are in an enterprise environment but that is expensive and what if the device you are trying to look at is a personal computer for a suspect rather than something you are looking at for a corporate investigation?

Since memory is under the control of the operating system, just as the underlying device for a disk partition, it requires administrative privileges and, more than that, commonly a special device driver, in order to get access to the memory. While you could face corruption of a hard drive by allowing a program to get access to the information in a partition, accessing memory, and specifically writing directly to it could cause catastrophic issues for an operating system, including system crash as well as data corruption across the system. As a result, we have to be very careful when we directly access memory. Preferably, this is read-only rather than read-write.

REAL MEMORY AND ADDRESSING

Your system has a certain amount of memory in it. A long time ago, programs used to have exclusive access to memory, since on a DOS system, you ran one program at a time and it had access to everything. The operating system provided you the access to the disks but everything else was managed, as necessary, by the programs running on the system. Programs that needed more memory than was available physically, would have to manage that on their own. Some programs instituted the concept of overlays, where the program would be split into sections and the overlay would be read into memory, as it was needed.

Imagine a set of Lego blocks, one stacked on top of another, where each Lego had a little pocket inside, capable of storing a small amount of information. That is one way of thinking about memory. In reality, of course, memory is not lined up like a stack of blocks but it is often portrayed in that way, just as in Figure 4.1. Each block has an address associated with it, which you can see noted on the left-hand side next to the stack of blocks.

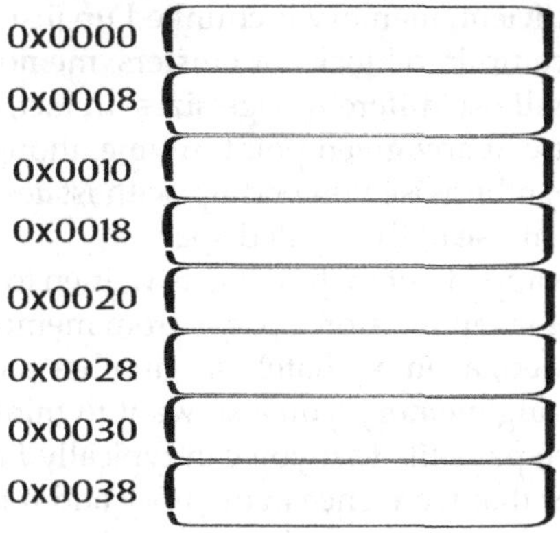

0x0000
0x0008
0x0010
0x0018
0x0020
0x0028
0x0030
0x0038

FIGURE 4.1

While you may not have realized it, you have probably been referring regularly to the size of the block. The blocks are based on the number of bits you can cram into the processor at the same time. This size is referred to as the bus width and you can think about it as the number of seats in a particular row on a bus, where each seat fits a single bit. Modern desktop and server systems use 64-bit addressing, means that you can send 64-bits of an address into the processor at one time. Since that is the size of an address, you can get access to 2^64 bytes of memory. This is 1.84467440737096E19 bytes, considerably larger than the 4,294,967,296 bytes available to a 32 bit system.

Processors since the 1980s have included two modes – one of them is real mode and the other is protected mode. In real mode, applications get access directly to memory, but real mode also offers only a limited memory space. In order to get complete access to the entire memory space, the processor needs to be in protected mode. Protected mode offers hardware support for virtual memory as well as a considerably larger memory space, up to the full bus size of the hardware provided. The idea behind protected mode was to give the processor the ability to run multiple processes at the same time in a way that the processes are protected from one another. Part of this protection comes from using virtual memory.

VIRTUAL MEMORY

Virtual memory has been around since around 1960 or so. The support for it in a PC came in the mid-1980s, but it took several more years for operating systems to catch up and support it. The idea behind virtual memory is to provide applications access to more memory than you have physically available. In order to make this possible, you have to be able to offload the excess memory somewhere. Commonly, that somewhere in the hard drive of your system. Primary storage, or memory, is fast but on comparison with hard drive space, it is considerably more expensive.

When you start running short of physical memory, the operating system will shuffle data out of primary storage off to secondary storage. This has performance issues, of course, but the trade-off is that you can be more productive by having more programs running, including services that help you, which even you may not be aware, are running. In order to make life easier and the system more efficient, memory is chunked up just like space on a hard disk is. When we break the disk space up into blocks or clusters, memory is broken up into pages. Different operating systems will use different page sizes. In fact, each operating system may have multiple page sizes in use at any given point in time, though each page size would be a multiple of a base page size, otherwise you end up with issues around fitting the different pages together to make efficient use of the limited space.

When a page needs to be swapped out to disk, it gets written to something called a page file or a swap file. The page file or swap file stores pages from memory that have been swapped out because they are not needed, as immediately as, another page set is. As a result, when you are thinking about capturing memory, you also want to think about the pages that have been swapped out to disk. The page file that you can typically find on a Windows system at C:\pagefile.sys contains pages that were once in memory and might be active.

When a program gets loaded into memory, it gets an address space that has no relation to the physical memory where the program is actually stored. This may be an address space that the program already knows about or the address space may be provided, means it is relocatable. In either case, it is up to the CPU itself to perform the translation between the address, the program believes it wants and the real address that it is actually referring to. Once the CPU has done this translation, it can retrieve the contents of memory but it has to do this every time the execution of a program refers to a location in memory. This is how virtual memory works and it does require additional hardware support to perform that address translation.

The other thing about virtual memory is that it provides a way to offer what appears to be a single, contiguous chunk of memory to a running process when in fact, the storage locations are spread across the whole range of physical memory. We can do this because the processor is doing all of the work, to make everything look seamless to the program but from a forensics standpoint, you need to have the list of memory addresses associated with the process or program in order to reconstruct the whole memory space to get all of the data out. You can see a simple example of how this might look in Figure 4.2. Processes A and B both have two separate memory segments in real memory but you can see from the addresses that the program sees, the two segments appear to be contiguous.

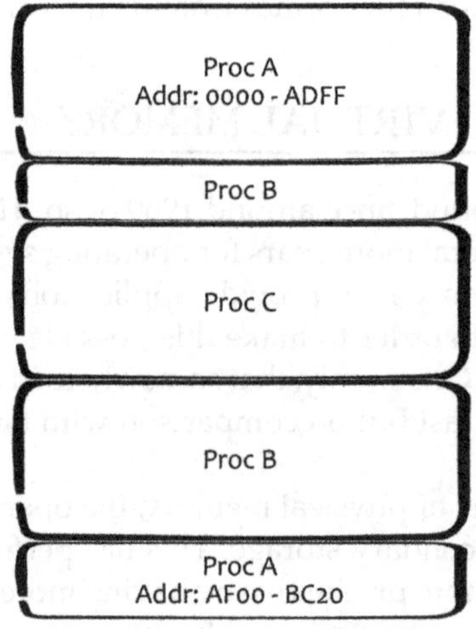

FIGURE 4.2

The term virtual memory might mean one of two things. The first is just the fact that the operating system allows applications to think there is more memory available than that which is physically in the machine. It may also refer to the swap or page file on the disk. The operating system keeps track of where each memory page is located through the use of a page table.

MEMORY LAYOUT

When you are analyzing memory, you need to know where all of the information is stored. This requires some information about the operating system and the sorts of information it stores, as well as, where it stores them. The common information you may want to know about, like the network connections and users that are logged in are stored in special data structures within the memory, which has been reserved for the operating system itself. This memory, since it is critical to the running of the overall system, may never be swapped out, depending on the sort of information present there. Certainly, there are components of the operating system that will never leave primary memory or else the system will stop operating. You cannot perform a swap if the routine that does the swap is out on the hard drive, for example.

As a result, there are really two types of memory in reality. Different operating systems may handle the allocation differently but you have kernel memory, owned by the operating system that will never leave physical memory and then you have user memory. User memory can be swapped in and out at any point unless, of course, the process is actually in the processor and executing at that point. However, even knowing where the memory is allocated is not enough. You need to know, how all of the kernel memory space is allocated.

Data Structures

No matter what operating system we are talking about, the data that is stored by the kernel, the core of the operating system, is stored in data structures. It is not stored randomly. A data structure is a way of collecting a number of different data types, like characters, strings, and integers, all together into the same place in memory. Let us say that I was collecting a lot of information about a program, for instance, I would want the process ID or the number the operating system identifies a process by, the path of the program, any parameters passed into the program, and a wide variety of other pieces of information, all stored together because they are related to the one process identified by the process ID. I do not want to store all of those pieces of data related to the one process in different parts of memory, if they are all related to each other. This chunk of data is structured in a particular way so that every piece can be quickly located within the chunk. This chunk is called a data structure because, it is data that has been structured in a particular way for easy retrieval later.

These data structures maintain a lot of information that is related to one particular object, like a process. However, when you have a collection of related objects, you need to collect them in a particular way. As a result, you need to use another data type to wrap your other data structure into. Commonly, you would use a list of data structures. The list collects all of the related information and then connects each individual object together, so the operating system can move easily from one to another. The operating system will keep track of all of the processes using the collection of process data structures. It needs to know where these data structures are located in memory in order to manage the processes they refer to. Rather than storing addresses to each storage location, the operating system will keep track of one object and then each object will carry a reference to the next object in the list. As an example, you can see a linked list in Figure 4.3.

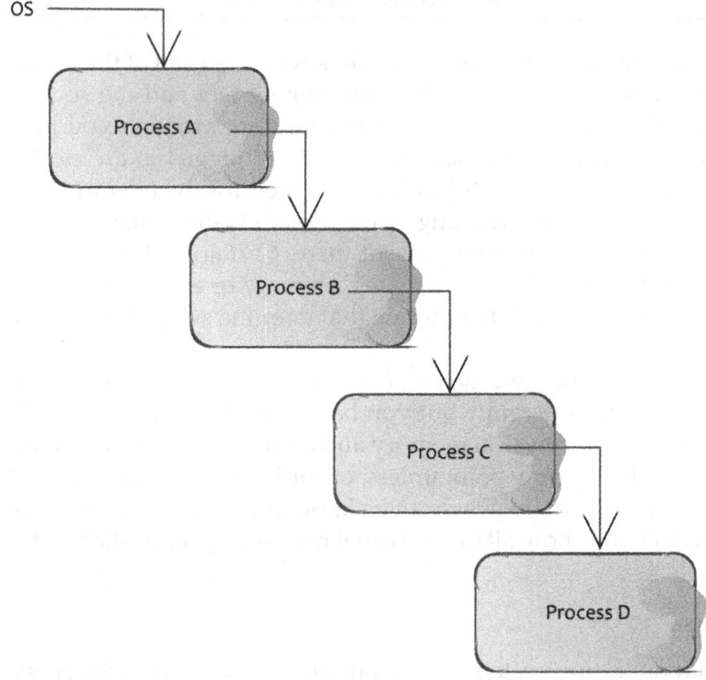

FIGURE 4.3

The point of a linked list is to allow a program to quickly and easily move from one item to another in the list. It is considered more space efficient than allocating a very large amount of space for an unknown number of items. What happens is that you start at the head of the list and then following along from item to item, until you either get to the end or find the one you are looking for. For example, in a modern system programs (called processes once they are in memory and executing) are constantly opening and closing based on the needs of the user. Each time a process starts, the kernel needs to create a data structure to carry the information about that process. When the operating system starts up, we have no idea how many processes are going to be needed over the time that the system is running and operational, so we use these dynamically allocated chunks of data.

Just because we have allocated the chunk of memory for the process data, it does not mean that we have a guaranteed place to put it because, again, we cannot tell how many of these processes we will need, so we allocate the memory for it as required. And then, to keep all of the processes together, we use a linked list. The nice thing about a linked list is that you can always add by tacking a new reference onto the end of the list. When a process in the middle of the list drops out of the list when the program execution stops, you just take the reference from the previous position in the list and point it at the position that comes after the process that's terminating. You can see an example of that in Figure 4.4, where process B is terminating, leaving process A and C now directly connected.

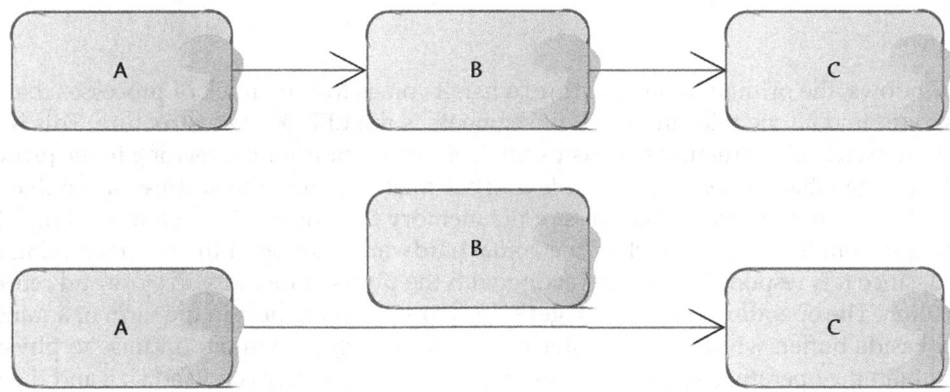

FIGURE 4.4

You can see in the lower sequence that B has dropped out and A now links directly to C. In some cases, it may make sense to have links in both directions. You can see by just Figure 4.4 that if I was pointing a C, I have no way to get back to B without starting over at A and seeking through to B. Obviously, this is not as big of a deal when you are dealing with three processes. If you are looking at several dozen, though, it can be much more timely to keep starting over, just to get to the process one or two before the one you are currently looking at. When you add links in both directions, it is called a doubly linked list because it has links in two directions.

Two other data structures that are important to understand are stacks and heaps. The reason for this is that they are types of memory allocations used in programs. When a program starts up, there are a number of memory segments that are created inside the memory space that belongs to the program. The first memory space is where all of the code resides. This is all of the actual executable statements that need to live in memory until they can be pulled into the processor. However, all of the data that the code acts on is stored somewhere else. There are places where storage is allocated when the program first runs. There is also a chunk of space that is allocated for something called a stack. Each time a function in a program runs, a new set of memory is added to the stack. This new set of memory that belongs to the function includes data used by the function as well as reminders of how to get back to the previous place in memory, where execution was happening before the program jumped into this function. Each chunk of memory that belongs to a particular function is called a stack frame. The stack is constantly growing and shrinking as functions run and then end. If function A makes a call to function B, which then calls function C, all of the memory used by function A is still on the stack, underneath the frames allocated to the functions B and then C.

A heap is just a large blob of memory, where data is stored temporarily in no particular order. The memory manager in the operating system makes the allocations on the heap as the program needs it. We will deal in more detail with stacks and heaps later in the book, when we really break down what programs look like and the types of data that has to be kept for each program. However, when we are talking about memory forensics, a lot of the data we will be pulling, will come out of the stacks and heaps from the running programs.

Windows

In Windows, the primary data structure, when it comes to keep track of processes that are necessary to find all the relevant memory segments is the EPROC data structure. This is the executive process data structure that keeps track of a lot of information relating to the process, including page table entries. A page table entry is a way to map the address space that the process is aware of the physical address of the memory that the hardware knows about. The operating system has to keep track of the actual hardware location of the memory being referenced, since it is responsible for interacting with the physical memory to store and retrieve information. The operating system may get some hardware help here in the form of a translation lookaside buffer, which does a faster lookup from virtual memory address to physical address than the operating system. However, the lookaside buffer is a fixed size and the operating system itself may need to keep track of some of this information on its own. In either case, the memory locations for each process are necessary in order to be able to retrieve it.

In the case of Windows, there are a number of ways to investigate information that is stored in memory. There are a number of pieces of information that will be useful to a forensic investigator. If you are looking at a live system, you can check the list of open network connections using a tool like netstat. The netstat utility, which is common across the operating systems that use TCP/IP for network protocols, will retrieve the list of listening ports as well as connections in a variety of states, including established and different states of the open and close handshakes. Below, you can see sample output from netstat using the switches –an. These switches say to show all connection information without doing any name lookups. If you leave off the n, netstat will perform name lookups on all of the IP addresses in the list.

```
C:\Users\kilroy>netstat -an

Active Connections

  Proto  Local Address          Foreign Address        State
  TCP    0.0.0.0:135            0.0.0.0:0              LISTENING
  TCP    0.0.0.0:445            0.0.0.0:0              LISTENING
  TCP    0.0.0.0:554            0.0.0.0:0              LISTENING
  TCP    0.0.0.0:2869           0.0.0.0:0              LISTENING
  TCP    0.0.0.0:3780           0.0.0.0:0              LISTENING
  TCP    0.0.0.0:5357           0.0.0.0:0              LISTENING
  TCP    0.0.0.0:10243          0.0.0.0:0              LISTENING
  TCP    0.0.0.0:49152          0.0.0.0:0              LISTENING
  TCP    0.0.0.0:49153          0.0.0.0:0              LISTENING
  TCP    0.0.0.0:49154          0.0.0.0:0              LISTENING
```

```
  TCP    0.0.0.0:49155          0.0.0.0:0              LISTENING
  TCP    0.0.0.0:49158          0.0.0.0:0              LISTENING
  TCP    127.0.0.1:2869         127.0.0.1:50461        TIME_WAIT
  TCP    127.0.0.1:2869         127.0.0.1:50462
ESTABLISHED
  TCP    127.0.0.1:5354         0.0.0.0:0              LISTENING
  TCP    127.0.0.1:5357         127.0.0.1:50492        TIME_WAIT
  TCP    127.0.0.1:5432         0.0.0.0:0              LISTENING
  TCP    127.0.0.1:5432         127.0.0.1:49163
ESTABLISHED
  TCP    127.0.0.1:5432         127.0.0.1:49176
ESTABLISHED
  TCP    127.0.0.1:5432         127.0.0.1:49177
ESTABLISHED
```

Another way to get a similar set of information but in a graphical form is the TCPView utility provided by Microsoft. This is part of the SysInternals suite of tools originally written by Mark Russinovich and Bryce Cogswell for the company Winternals Software LP beginning in 1996. The company and the software suite was eventually acquired by Microsoft in 2006 and all of the software tools are available for free as the SysInternals suite from the Microsoft site. This is a fairly large collection of programs that provide deep insight into what is going on inside the operating system and within the programs. The tool from SysInternals that allows us to look at network connections is TCPView, which you can see in Figure 4.5. Where netstat provides us with a static list, TCPView allows us to interact with each entry, as you can see from the context menu.

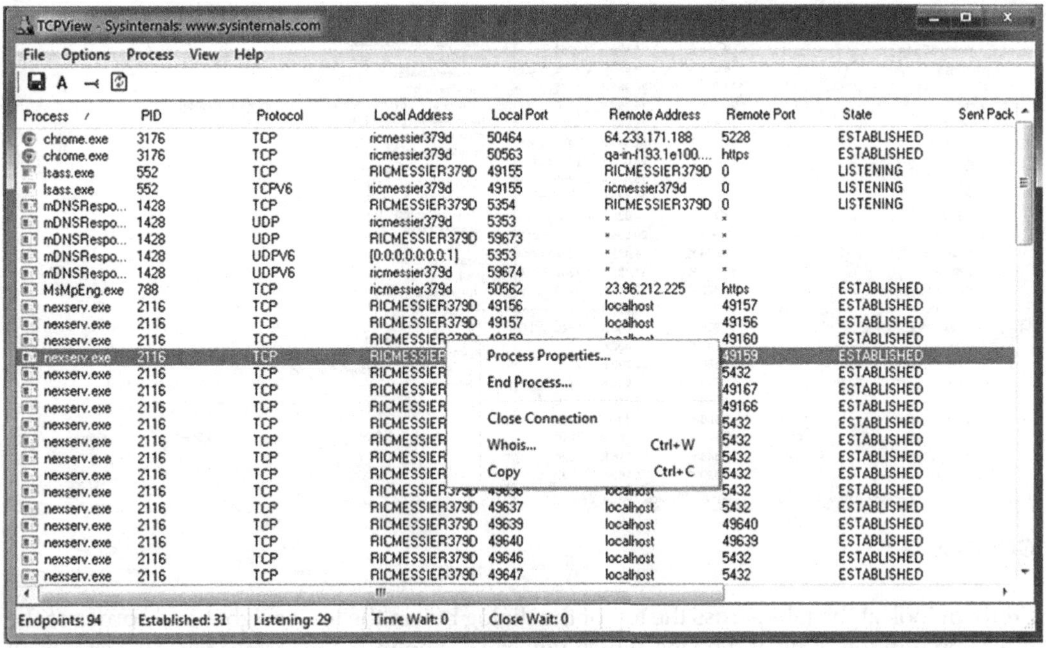

FIGURE 4.5

Also unlike netstat, TCPView is process oriented. The very first column is the process that owns the port entry. TCPView will also provide statistics about network usage, showing the amount of traffic that has passed through the port. While you can get netstat to provide you with process information, it is not provided by default and you do not get the data flow information like you can get with TCPView. The advantage to netstat, of course, is that it is bundled with the operating system and not a separate download, though the SysInternals suite of tools will run nicely from a USB stick and they are not very large.

When it comes to processes, there are a couple of utilities that can be used to look more closely at process internals. One of these included with SysInternals is ProcExp, seen in Figure 4.6. ProcExp shows a tree view of all the processes running on the system. The processes are ordered as a tree so you can see what parent spawned the various child processes. The master process, or super parent, if you prefer, is the system process, which shows up at the very root of the tree view. In addition to just a list of processes, you can open up the properties of each of the processes to look at different sets of information.

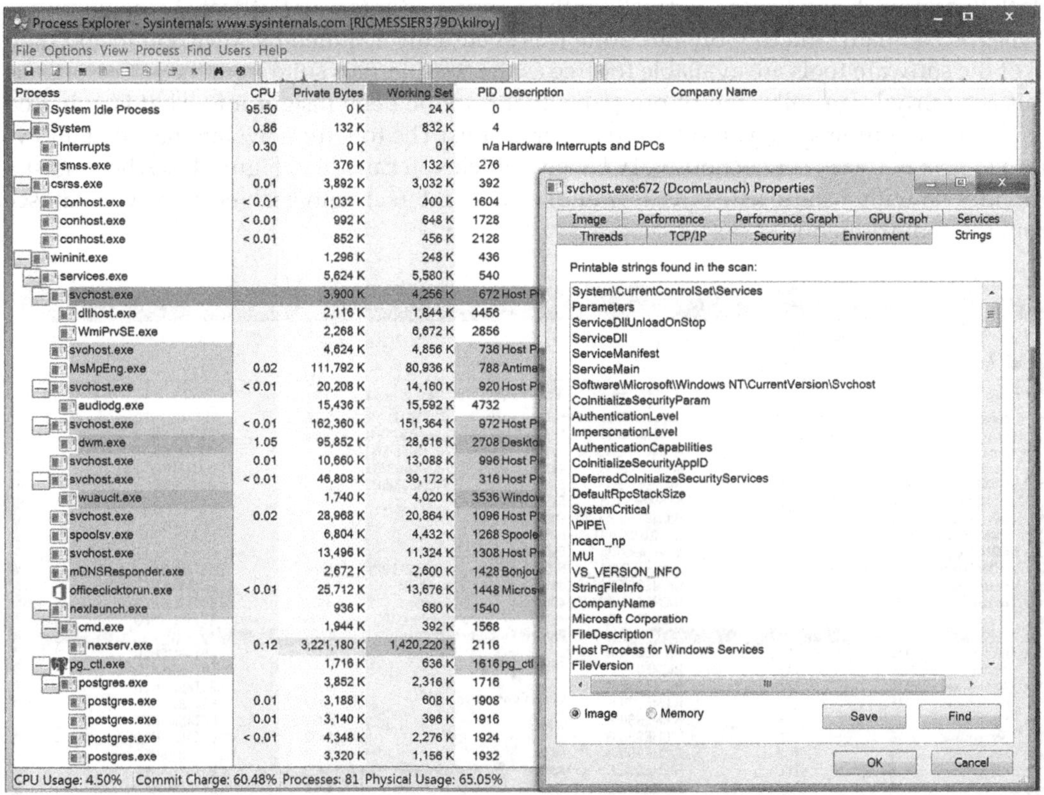

FIGURE 4.6

You can look at the tabs across the top of the dialog box in the lower right hand corner of the application window. One of the tabs, which you can see open, is the Strings tab. This shows all of the memory sections that look like they would be human readable strings. These strings can be very important pieces of information. All stored data within the program will show up here.

This might include text strings used for errors or warnings in the program, as well as, a list of libraries and external functions that are called from within the program. Additionally, you may get other important pieces of information that are in use including information that may have been provided by the user. Another tab showing information related to the program is the TCP/IP tab. This shows process specific information related to network communications. In Figure 4.7, you can see the list of network connections related to the process mDNSResponder.exe. This is the process that handles the Bonjour service, which is a local zero configuration service for connecting to devices like printers or media services on your local network.

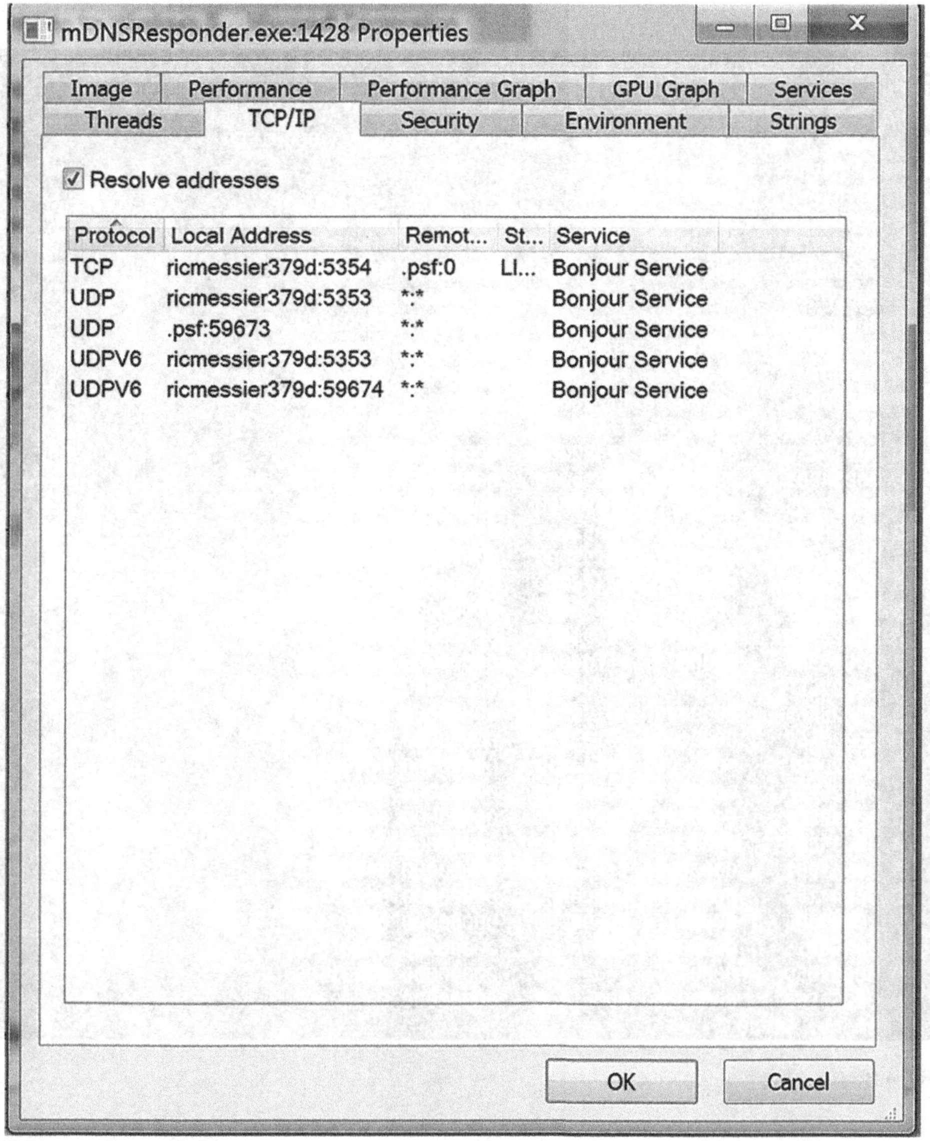

FIGURE 4.7

SysInternals also comes with a utility to create a mini dump of a process. The mini dump is useful for debugging purposes and it generates a .dump file that can be opened with a debugger or with the utility dumpchk from the Windows Software Development Kit. In Figure 4.7, you can see the output from running dumpchk against a mini dump created by procdump. This dump will provide specifics about memory segments that are used by the process. In this case, the dump was created from the Notepad application. You can see the list of memory segments used by Notepad. There is a lot of additional information available in the mini dump but it is primarily useful for developers and especially those who are looking to determine why a program may have crashed (Figure 4.8).

```
Stream 3: type TokenInformationStream (19), size 00000308, RVA 00000CEC
  1 Tokens
    Token 2b8 for 4556
Stream 4: type MemoryListStream (5), size 000001F4, RVA 00001FF9
  31 memory ranges
  range#    RVA       Address               Size
       0 000021ED    000007fe`fe059000    00000000`000025e8
       1 000047D5    00000000`77409dea    00000000`00000100
       2 000048D5    000007fe`ff5ff000    00000000`000019b4
       3 00006289    000007fe`feed9000    00000000`00002a90
       4 00008D19    00000000`775fa000    00000000`00001980
       5 0000A699    000007fe`fbe6c000    00000000`000030fc
       6 0000D795    000007fe`fd23b000    00000000`00000760
       7 0000DEF5    000007fe`ff2a8000    00000000`00004240
       8 00012135    000007fe`ff642000    00000000`00001028
       9 0001315D    00000000`77482000    00000000`00001a58
      10 00014BB5    000007fe`fbb3b000    00000000`00002d20
      11 000178D5    000007fe`ff4b5000    00000000`00006b28
      12 0001E3FD    000007fe`f7e52000    00000000`00001810
      13 0001FC0D    000007fe`fdf53000    00000000`00002a10
      14 0002261D    000007fe`fc478000    00000000`0000091a
      15 00022F37    000007fe`fd83a000    00000000`00000890
      16 000237C7    000007fe`fd691000    00000000`00001ba8
      17 0002536F    000007ff`fffdd000    00000000`00002380
      18 000276EF    000007fe`fefd0000    00000000`00004780
      19 0002BE6F    00000000`00131320    00000000`00002000
      20 0002DE6F    00000000`00133348    00000000`00000020
      21 0002DE8F    00000000`0014a410    00000000`00000410
      22 0002E29F    000007fe`fda83000    00000000`00002630
      23 000308CF    000007fe`fd8d1000    00000000`00005602
      24 00035ED1    00000000`77742000    00000000`0000bae0
      25 000419B1    00000000`fffc0000    00000000`00002844
      26 000441F5    000007fe`fb6ce000    00000000`000031e0
      27 000473D5    000007fe`fe590000    00000000`00009440
      28 00050815    000007fe`ff05c000    00000000`00001848
      29 0005205D    000007fe`feea7000    00000000`00001508
      30 00053565    00000000`000cfca8    00000000`00000358
  Total memory: 516d0
```

FIGURE 4.8

There are a number of other command line utilities provided by the SysInternals suite that can view a lot of information stored in memory. These utilities, though, require a running system, since they access the Windows application-programming interface (API) to retrieve information from the operating system. Rather than directly accessing memory, these utilities use the operating system itself to report back on what is happening inside the operating system. Fortunately, it is not necessary to have a running system in order to extract data but getting memory images and analyzing them comes later.

Mac OS X

Mac OS X inherits the current core of its operating system, the kernel, from research efforts at Carnegie Mellon in the 1980s. This kernel is based on the Mach kernel developed by Carnegie Mellon and it was designed to replace the kernel in the Berkeley Software Distribution (BSD) implementation of UNIX, except that it is designed to be very small and modular – a microkernel. In the Mac OS X kernel, core functions are inside the kernel proper while everything else is implemented as a kernel extension (KEXT). This means that access to some sections of memory is limited to the kernel itself. This helps to protect the kernel and the information it stores. This also means that there are two types of memory maps in Mac OS X. The first type is the kernel map, which is only available to the kernel itself and refers to memory allocated to the kernel. Kernel extensions (KEXTs) cannot get access to this memory. The other type of memory map relates to processes or programs that run in user space.

The memory map is a doubly linked list, where each entry holds information about pages of virtual memory attached to the task that the memory map belongs to. In addition to the memory maps, Mac OS X uses the universal page lists (UPLs) as data structures that are used to communicate with the virtual memory system. As with all modern operating systems, Mac OS X uses virtual memory. The virtual memory system is responsible for determining whether a page of memory is in physical RAM or in swap space on disk as well as handling the lookup of the physical address. In order to get access to the memory, there are a number of programmatic functions that are available but that requires writing programs. In order to get information about the memory space allocated to each program, you can use the vmmap utility from a terminal session to get a list of all of the memory allocations to a particular process. In Figure 4.9, you can see the output from that list. The problem with this list is that you would need a way to get into the memory space of the program in order to actually look at that memory.

Once you have a list of all of the addresses associated with the process, you can also make use of a debugger to view memory. This requires Xcode to be installed on the system. You can attach to running processes and potentially view the contents of memory associated with the process. This could be done from the Xcode GUI or also from the command line utility lldb, which is similar to the GNU debugger (gdb) that is used on Linux systems. Either way, this requires extensive intervention with the running operating system unless Xcode is already installed. Even then, Xcode is a development platform rather than a tool to do forensic investigations from. As a result, it is better to use the few command line utilities that are available like vmmap and, of course, netstat for network connections. When it comes to serious kilroy — bash — 80×43

```
kilroy@opus:~$ vmmap 33766
Process:         Google Chrome Helper [33766]
Path:            /Applications/Google Chrome.app/Contents/Versions/39.0.2171.71/
Google Chrome Helper.app/Contents/MacOS/Google Chrome Helper
Load Address:    0x109a43000
Identifier:      com.google.Chrome.helper
Version:         39.0.2171.71 (2171.71)
Code Type:       X86-64
Parent Process:  Google Chrome [59497]

Date/Time:       2014-12-14 20:46:25.961 -0500
OS Version:      Mac OS X 10.10.1 (14B25)
Report Version:  7
Analysis Tool:   /Applications/Xcode.app/Contents/Developer/usr/bin/vmmap
Analysis Tool Version:  Xcode 6.1.1 (6A2008a)
----

Virtual Memory Map of process 33766 (Google Chrome Helper)
Output report format:  2.3  -- 64-bit process

==== Non-writable regions for process 33766
REGION TYPE                      START - END             [ VSIZE] PRT/MAX SHRMOD
  REGION DETAIL
__TEXT                 0000000109a43000-0000000109a44000 [    4K] r-x/rwx SM=COW
  ...Chrome Helper
__LINKEDIT             0000000109a45000-0000000109a48000 [   12K] r--/rwx SM=COW
  ...Chrome Helper
__TEXT                 0000000109a48000-000000010ee2e000 [ 83.9M] r-x/rwx SM=COW
  ...ome Framework
__LINKEDIT             000000010f2d1000-000000010f3ea000 [ 1124K] r--/rwx SM=COW
  ...ome Framework
MALLOC (admin)         000000010f3eb000-000000010f3ec000 [    4K] r--/rwx SM=ZER

MALLOC (admin)         000000010f3ed000-000000010f3ee000 [    4K] r--/rwx SM=PRV

MALLOC (admin)         000000010f3ee000-000000010f3ef000 [    4K] r--/rwx SM=ZER

__TEXT                 000000010f3f0000-000000010f428000 [  224K] r-x/rwx SM=COW
  ...ns/A/CoreMIDI
__LINKEDIT             000000010f42d000-000000010f44e000 [  132K] r--/rwx SM=COW
  ...ns/A/CoreMIDI
MALLOC (admin)         000000010f44e000-000000010f44f000 [    4K] ---/rwx SM=NUL
```

FIGURE 4.9

investigation of memory, it is better to capture the RAM and use a tool to perform the analysis offline. If you are using virtual machines, simply suspending the virtual machine will give you a file that you can use to perform analysis on. In the case of VMWare, that file is the one with the extension .vmem.

Linux

One advantage to Linux when it comes to performing research into forensic analysis is the fact that it is open source. This means that all of the source code that goes into building the operating system is available, so we can really look at what all of the data structures within the kernel look like. There are other advantages to Linux. In addition to being open source, the operating system is very transparent. The reason for this is that it makes life much easier for system administrators and system programmers. Important information about the operation of the kernel is widely available to most users and especially those who have administrative rights on the system. This does not require a special build system or any unique or unusual configuration of the operating system. This is just the way Linux works.

One of the first places to get information about the operating system, the processes that are running and especially the memory that is in use by each program, is the proc file system. This pseudo file system is created when the operating system is running. When the system is down, you will not find anything in the /proc directory on the disk. This file system exists only in memory and it is created and mounted, when the operating system boots up. The listing below shows all of the file systems that have been mounted in a Linux system and you can see the second entry in the list is the proc mount. There is no source other than simply proc, because it is created and managed by the operating system.

```
root@quiche:~# mount
sysfs on /sys type sysfs (rw,nosuid,nodev,noexec,relatime)
proc on /proc type proc (rw,nosuid,nodev,noexec,relatime)
udev on /dev type devtmpfs
(rw,relatime,size=10240k,nr_inodes=255003,mode=755)
devpts on /dev/pts type devpts
(rw,nosuid,noexec,relatime,gid=5,mode=620,ptmxmode=000)
tmpfs on /run type tmpfs
(rw,nosuid,noexec,relatime,size=205748k,mode=755)
/dev/disk/by-uuid/314fd24a-9b5f-4c4f-b9e7-41e91b8d5c6e on / type
ext4 (rw,relatime,errors=remount-ro,data=ordered)
tmpfs on /run/lock type tmpfs
(rw,nosuid,nodev,noexec,relatime,size=5120k)
tmpfs on /run/shm type tmpfs
(rw,nosuid,nodev,noexec,relatime,size=964440k)
binfmt_misc on /proc/sys/fs/binfmt_misc type binfmt_misc
(rw,nosuid,nodev,noexec,relatime)
```

Inside the /proc directory is a directory entry for each of the processes running on the system. In addition to the process directories that we will look at shortly, the /proc directory has a lot of useful information about the operating system in entries that appear to be files. One example is the version file that has the version string for the kernel including the version number and the type of processor, the kernel was built for. In the case of the system from the mount listing above, the processor is 64-bit and it shows up referenced as amd64. The version entry also shows me the compiler that was used to build the kernel. In addition to version and processor information, there is an entry in the /proc file system showing the memory locations of all of the functions in shared libraries residing in the kernel. Basically, this is a list of all of the API functions that are available. You can see the list of those functions and the memory location where they can be found in the listing below.

```
ffffffff8100d047 t set_32bit_tls
ffffffff8100d077 t set_ti_thread_flag
ffffffff8100d07d t clear_ti_thread_flag
ffffffff8100d083 T set_personality_ia32
ffffffff8100d150 t start_thread_common.constprop.4
ffffffff8100d1c0 T __show_regs
ffffffff8100d402 T release_thread
ffffffff8100d438 T start_thread
ffffffff8100d445 T start_thread_ia32
ffffffff8100d477 T __switch_to
ffffffff8100d86f T set_personality_64bit
ffffffff8100d8df T get_wchan
ffffffff8100d95b T do_arch_prctl
ffffffff8100dbf9 T copy_thread
ffffffff8100de20 T sys_arch_prctl
ffffffff8100de35 T KSTK_ESP
ffffffff8100de58 t on_sig_stack
ffffffff8100de80 t xstate_sigframe_size
ffffffff8100de8c T restore_sigcontext
ffffffff8100dfaf T setup_sigcontext
ffffffff8100e0d3 t do_signal
ffffffff8100e561 T sys_sigaltstack
ffffffff8100e572 T do_notify_resume
```

This is only a small list of the functions that are available. The complete list is more than 32,000 entries long on this system. Primarily, though, the /proc file system is about all of the information about the processes that are running at the time the /proc file system is checked. Each process gets its own tree of information available. In Figure 4.10, you can see the list of entries in the directory for process 2511. On this particular system, that process is polkitd-no-debug, which is a message passing service for processes to communicate with one another.

The bottom part of the Figure 4.10 shows the memory map for the process. This is a list of all external libraries that are available in the process image and the memory location. You can also see the memory location of the heap, or the dynamic memory available to the program. What you do not see in this capture because it is closer to the end of the complete memory map is the location of the stack. The stack is where most function data is stored and this is a location of a lot of useful information. The address shown, 7fff48026000-7fff48047000, shows the entire size of the stack since it has a starting and ending point. Of course, the stack will grow and shrink as needed in order to accommodate additional function data as more functions are

```
root@quiche:/proc/2511# ls
attr         coredump_filter  io          mountstats     pagemap      stat
autogroup    cpuset           limits      net            personality  statm
auxv         cwd              loginuid    ns             root         status
cgroup       environ          maps        numa_maps      sched        syscall
clear_refs   exe              mem         oom_adj        sessionid    task
cmdline      fd               mountinfo   oom_score      smaps        wchan
comm         fdinfo           mounts      oom_score_adj  stack
root@quiche:/proc/2511# cat maps
00400000-00402000 r-xp 00000000 08:01 1575503                            /usr/li
b/policykit-1/polkitd
00602000-00603000 r--p 00002000 08:01 1575503                            /usr/li
b/policykit-1/polkitd
00603000-00604000 rw-p 00003000 08:01 1575503                            /usr/li
b/policykit-1/polkitd
01251000-013c0000 rw-p 00000000 00:00 0                                  [heap]
7f804758f000-7f804759a000 r-xp 00000000 08:01 3561890                    /lib/x8
6_64-linux-gnu/libnss_files-2.13.so (deleted)
7f804759a000-7f8047799000 ---p 0000b000 08:01 3561890                    /lib/x8
6_64-linux-gnu/libnss_files-2.13.so (deleted)
7f8047799000-7f804779a000 r--p 0000a000 08:01 3561890                    /lib/x8
6_64-linux-gnu/libnss_files-2.13.so (deleted)
7f804779a000-7f804779b000 rw-p 0000b000 08:01 3561890                    /lib/x8
6_64-linux-gnu/libnss_files-2.13.so (deleted)
7f804779b000-7f80477a5000 r-xp 00000000 08:01 3560582                    /lib/x8
6_64-linux-gnu/libnss_nis-2.13.so (deleted)
7f80477a5000-7f80479a4000 ---p 0000a000 08:01 3560582                    /lib/x8
6_64-linux-gnu/libnss_nis-2.13.so (deleted)
7f80479a4000-7f80479a5000 r--p 00009000 08:01 3560582                    /lib/x8
6_64-linux-gnu/libnss_nis-2.13.so (deleted)
7f80479a5000-7f80479a6000 rw-p 0000a000 08:01 3560582                    /lib/x8
6_64-linux-gnu/libnss_nis-2.13.so (deleted)
```

FIGURE 4.10

called. Again, think of the stack of plates in a cafeteria, fed with a spring. Diners will come in and take plates off the top and the dish washers will come by and add stacks. The size of the stack is constantly in flux.

While this is the location of the stack frame and the location of all of the process memory, it does not include the libraries, functions and any associated memory for the kernel. For that, we have to turn to another file altogether, and this file will become necessary when we start to perform a memory analysis. When you build a kernel, this file is created and resides on the system. It is typically called System.map, though it may also include another suffix indicating which kernel the map goes to. For example, the file the map section below came from is named System.map-3.7-trunk-amd64 on my system. What you see below is just a very small sample of the entries in the system map. On this system, there are a total of 54,299 entries.

```
0000000000000000 A VDSO32_PRELINK
0000000000000000 D __per_cpu_start
0000000000000000 D irq_stack_union
0000000000000000 A xen_irq_disable_direct_reloc
0000000000000000 A xen_save_fl_direct_reloc
0000000000000040 A VDSO32_vsyscall_eh_frame_size
00000000000001e9 A kexec_control_code_size
00000000000001f0 A VDSO32_NOTE_MASK
0000000000000400 A VDSO32_sigreturn
0000000000000410 A VDSO32_rt_sigreturn
0000000000000420 A VDSO32_vsyscall
0000000000000430 A VDSO32_SYSENTER_RETURN
0000000000004000 D gdt_page
0000000000005000 d exception_stacks
000000000000b000 D cpu_llc_shared_map
000000000000b040 D cpu_core_map
000000000000b080 D cpu_sibling_map
000000000000b0c0 D cpu_llc_id
000000000000b0c4 D cpu_number
000000000000b0c8 D x86_bios_cpu_apicid
000000000000b0ca D x86_cpu_to_apicid
000000000000b100 d cpu_loops_per_jiffy
000000000000b140 D xen_vcpu_info
000000000000b180 D xen_vcpu
000000000000b188 d idt_desc
000000000000b1a0 d shadow_tls_desc
000000000000b1b8 d xen_cr0_value
000000000000b1c0 D xen_mc_irq_flags
000000000000b1d0 d mc_buffer
000000000000bde0 D xen_current_cr3
000000000000bde8 D xen_cr3
000000000000be00 d xen_runstate
```

The system map is really a symbol table and a symbol is a variable or function so the symbol table is a mapping of the names of each symbol to its location in memory. Remember that the kernel memory does not ever get swapped out, so where these entries get loaded will stay there only. This is why, we can have a static symbol table for the kernel; because it loads the same way every time and never moves around, which makes it faster and more reliable. You will see a letter between the memory location and the symbol name. The letter indicates what type of entry it is. The d and D entries indicate that the symbol refers to an initialized variable – a location where data that has been given a value is stored. Other symbol types are for code sections (t,T), uninitialized data (b,B), absolute locations (A) or read-only data (r,R). There are other types of symbols but those are the primary ones, we are concerned with.

Of course, you may be interested in retrieving information from these data locations and there are certainly utilities that will provide a lot of information about a running system, just as with operating systems like Windows or Mac OS X. When it comes to getting a list of running process, like you might with the Windows task manager or the Mac OS X activity monitor, you can use either ps or top. ps will provide you with a static snapshot listing of the processes running when the utility is run. Just as with Windows and Mac OS X, we can use netstat to get a listing of all of the network connections that are open on the system.

Since UNIX, the predecessor of Linux, has a long history of command line use and it has always been an operating system geared toward programmer and system administrator usage, there are a large number of utilities that are available for checking things like memory usage (free) and disk usage (du, df). Linux is a multiuser operating system so you can also get a listing of all of the users who are logged in using the who command. Additionally, with Linux, you can get direct access to devices using another pseudo file system. The /dev file system includes devices like disk drives, serial input devices, sound devices and some system devices that are useful for specific purposes like generating zeros or random numbers. When it comes to acquiring disk drives, we use the /dev tree and one way of capturing memory on a Linux system, if we want all of RAM, involves the use of the /dev tree as well.

CAPTURING MEMORY

Older operating systems did not protect memory as well as modern operating systems do. As the need for forensic acquisitions has increased with more information being stored on computers and more crimes taking place that involve the use of computers, operating system manufacturers have shut down the access to physical memory. On a Linux system, for instance, there used to be a device for getting access to the system memory. This device, /dev/mem, would allow direct access for both reading and writing. While this is great for forensic purposes, allowing writing was a good way to cripple your operating system. The moment you write to a chunk of memory without the oversight of the operating system, you run the risk of writing over a critical section of memory. For example, you may write over the memory management functions or you might write over the functions that perform process management – getting processes into and out of the processor.

With Linux utilities like dd, you could pick the location you wanted to write to and the amount of data you wanted to write, so you could easily access a particular piece of memory and insert your own data or code. Several years ago, this function was removed in the 2.6 kernel line. Similarly, direct access to Windows memory has been removed since Windows 2003 Service Pack 1 and on the desktop side, it was removed in Windows Vista. The device used in Windows was \Device\Physicalmemory but that is no longer available for direct access. Previously, access control lists were in place to protect the device but now, there is no access to the device from user-mode. This means the device still exists but only the kernel itself can get access to it. This is different from Linux where the device simply no longer exists.

However, there are some other options when it comes to getting access to physical memory in order to get memory captures to analyze the contents later on another system. Depending on the operating system, there are utilities or even kernel-mode drivers that can be implemented to get access to the memory. These utilities and drivers are all run on the system where you are capturing memory. Running the program or installing the driver will alter the memory you are trying to capture. In order to run, the driver needs to be loaded into memory and the program will also need to be loaded into memory in order to execute. This has the potential for forcing a program out of memory and into swap space.

The memory has to be captured from a running system because once the system is powered off the memory is cleared. Dynamic random access memory (DRAM) requires an electrical signal to keep the bits in place. Once the power has been removed, the capacitors used to store the bits will quickly discharge, meaning there are no bits. You cannot even take the memory out, put it into another system and read stray bits off it as you would be able to with a device like a disk drive where files have been erased. What you may be able to do, though, is freeze the RAM while it is in the system. This may give you a small window, assuming you can keep it frozen, to get the memory to another system, where you can slot it in and capture it there. The capacitors will retain their charge for four seconds or more. This gives you a short window of time to freeze the sticks of RAM. This approach does require that you have the ability to freeze the RAM, keep it frozen and also have a RAM reader on another system, which you can use it to extract the contents, once you have slotted the frozen RAM in and it receives a charge again.

Windows

Not surprisingly, Windows has the most options when it comes to capturing RAM. Commercial forensics tools like EnCase and FTK have their own memory capture programs. In the case of FTK, the FTK Imager program will not only capture disk images, it will also capture memory. Figure 4.11 shows the dialog box prompting for details before capturing memory. In addition to physical memory, it will also capture the pagefile.sys file, the file where all memory that has been swapped out from physical RAM to disk is stored. This program runs, as it has to, as an administrator.

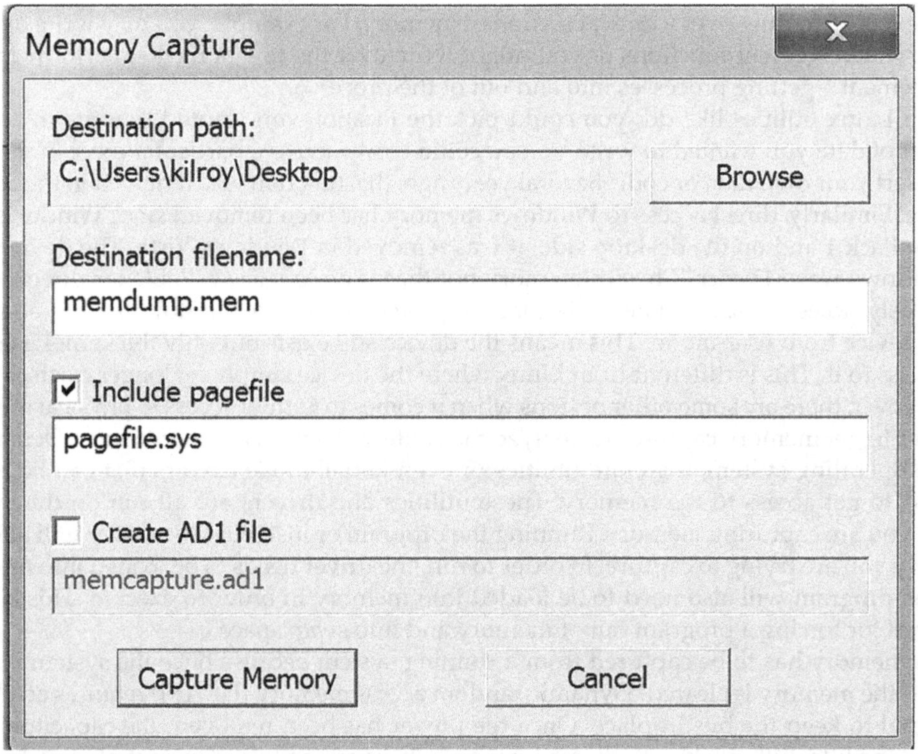

FIGURE 4.11

Programs like BelkaSoft's Live RAM Capturer run in kernel mode. This is necessary to bypass restrictions placed on memory to protect it. In order to get complete access to the physical memory on a system, the access has to be from the deepest level of access available. This is called kernel mode and sometimes ring 0 mode on a Windows system. Kernel mode permissions are not things an application can request and be granted. In order to run in kernel mode, the functionality has to be implemented as a device driver that inserts itself into the kernel space. In Figure 4.12, you can see that RAM Capturer is prepared to capture memory and it has loaded the device driver that comes with the application. Without this device driver, the program would not be able to get access to system memory in order to capture it. Windows does implement user account control (UAC), where applications needing administrative access, including installing a device driver even temporarily, will generate a prompt that the user has to accept. Capturing memory with this program once the device driver is loaded is as simple as clicking the Capture! button.

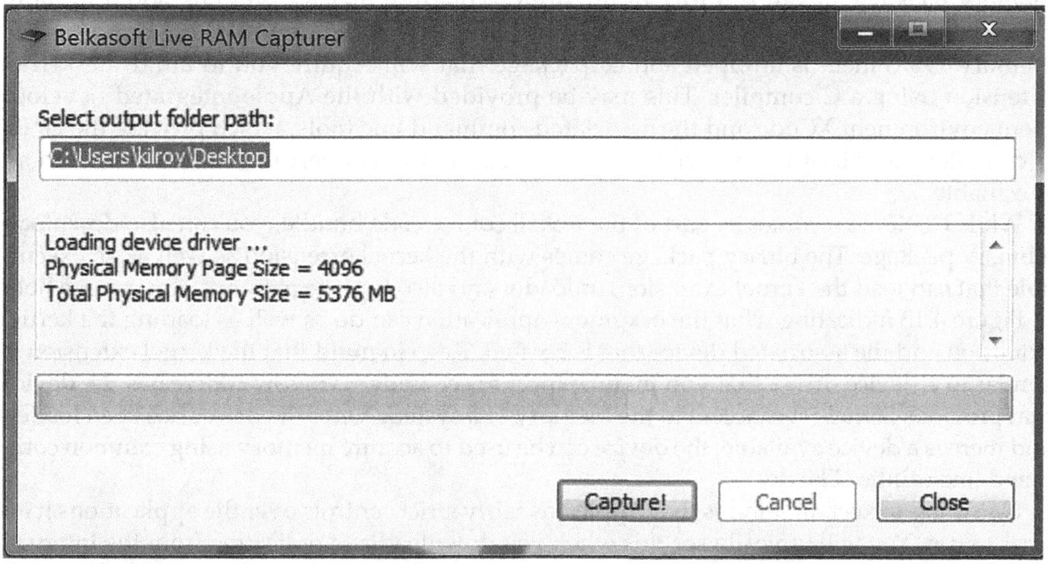

FIGURE 4.12

While those are two programs that are capable of capturing memory, there are a number of others. Some programs are commercial and others are free or open source. One thing to keep in mind is limiting the amount of involvement with the operating system. Some utilities will require installation, which impacts the running system. Other utilities will run standalone. A utility like Moonsols DumpIt will run well from a USB stick. As noted previously, any utility run on the system under investigation will have an impact on that system, so smaller utilities are better to minimize the impact, as long as you are able to capture the memory you need in a format you can use.

Any time you capture evidence like getting a memory dump, make sure you document the capture and get a cryptographic hash so you can verify it later.

Mac OS X

There are not as many options for acquisition of memory, when it comes to Mac OS X. Apple does a good job of restricting low level access to developers. However, it is possible to create a kernel extension, which is what you would need to get access to physical memory on a Mac OS X system. This will allow the program to run from the kernel space rather than attempting to look into the kernel from outside. From the commercial side, BlackBag Technologies has a product named MacQuisition that will perform Mac OS X forensics, including memory acquisition and analysis.

On the open source side, there is OSXPmem, which is now part of the Rekall forensics memory package. Rekall is a fork of the utility Volatility that we will talk about in more detail later. OSXPmem is a kernel extension that creates a device providing access to the memory. OSXPmem is an open source package that will require you to build the kernel extension using a C compiler. This may be provided with the Apple integrated development environment XCode and the associated command line tools, which provide the GNU C compiler and all of the associated utilities required to convert the source code into an executable.

While OSXPmem comes as part of the Rekall source code bundle, you can also download a binary package. The binary package comes with the kernel extension as well as an executable that can load the kernel extension, unload it and also capture memory. You can see help in Figure 4.13 indicating what the osxpmem application can do as well as loading the kernel extension and the associated device that is created. Keep in mind that the kernel extension is similar to a device driver that you might expect to see under Windows. It creates the device that provides kernel-level access to the memory of a system. Once the driver has been loaded and there is a device available, the device can be used to acquire memory using common command line utilities like dd.

One thing to keep in mind is that Apple has fairly strict controls over the applications it allows to run. You will typically see this when you download an application from the Internet. If it is not appropriately signed cryptographically using a digital signature, Mac OS X will prevent it from running unless you force the operating system to give you the option to run it anyway. In the case of installing kernel extensions, Mac OS X is similarly very reluctant to allow untrusted code from executing in the kernel space with top-level permissions. If you were to build the osxpmem package yourself, you would have to use an appropriate developer's signature from Apple, in order for the resulting executable to be able to run without warnings from the operating system about it being untrusted. It is likely that there will come a point where Apple will simply not allow kernel extensions to be loaded without the application being appropriately signed.

One of the reasons for this, of course, is the risk to the operating system from a poorly written or simply malicious extension. While the osxpmem binary package comes with

```
kilroy@opus:                    $ sudo ./osxpmem
Usage: ./osxpmem [OPTION...] FILE
Dump physical address space to FILE.

  -h, --help              display this help and exit
  -v, --verbose           enable verbose logging
  -l, --load-kext         load /dev/pmem driver and exit
  -u, --unload-kext       unload /dev/pmem driver and exit
  -d, --display-mmap      print physical memory map and exit
  -f, --format [FORMAT]   set the output format (default is elf)

 Output formats:
  elf                     64-bit ELF core dump with a program
                          header per physical memory section.

  mach                    64-bit MACH-O core dump with a
                          segment load command per physical
                          memory section.

  raw                     Flat binary file where physical pages
                          are written to their corresponding
                          offset in the file. Memory holes and
                          gaps in physical address space are
                          zero-padded.
kilroy@opus:                    $ sudo ./osxpmem -l
kilroy@opus:                    $ ls /dev/pmem
/dev/pmem
```

FIGURE 4.13

the programs being signed by an Apple-sanctioned developer, when running it on my MacBook Pro using Mac OS X 10.10 and 16 G of memory, the operating system crashed while trying to use the /dev/pmem device and dd to capture memory. When the driver causes a problem, it is not isolated to just the driver, since the driver has access to the kernel memory space. As a result, you do nott get an application crash if something goes wrong, you get a crash of the entire operating system. This is similar to what you may be familiar with on the Windows side as a so-called blue-screen of death. The same thing can and does happen with Mac OS as well, but it does not go to a blue screen. The system halts and you get a gray screen, just as you do when the system starts up. Instead of the bomb dialogs that were common in earlier versions of Mac OS, there is a message indicating that the system had a problem and it needs to be restarted. You can see what that screen looks like in Figure 4.14.

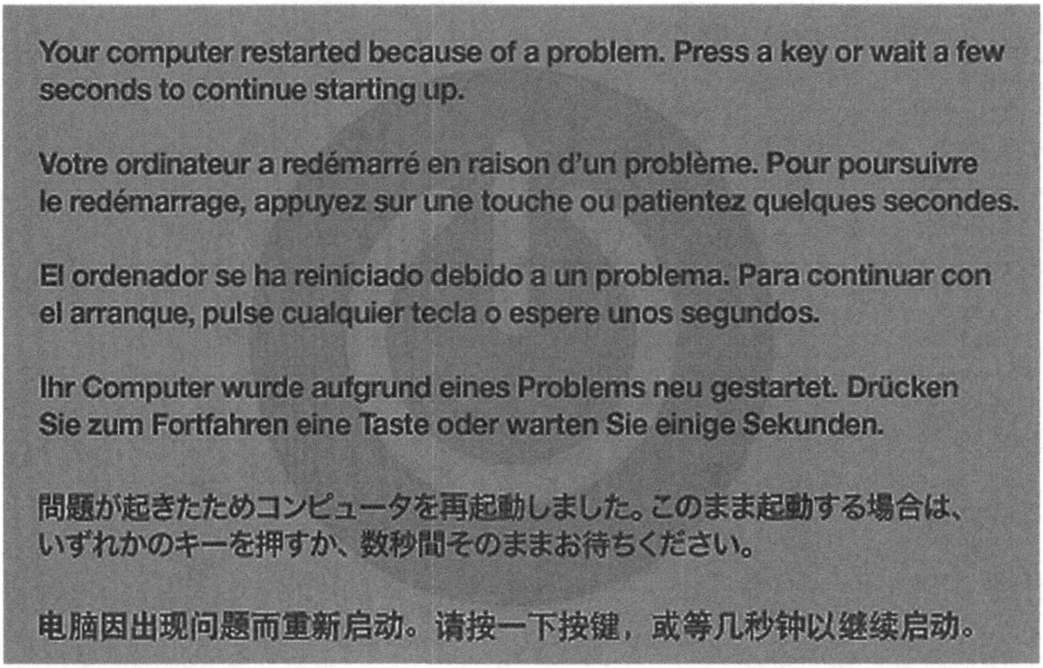

Your computer restarted because of a problem. Press a key or wait a few seconds to continue starting up.
Votre ordinateur a redémarré en raison d'un problème. Pour poursuivre le redémarrage, appuyez sur une touche ou patientez quelques secondes.
El ordenador se ha reiniciado debido a un problema. Para continuar con el arranque, pulse cualquier tecla o espere unos segundos.
Ihr Computer wurde aufgrund eines Problems neu gestartet. Drücken Sie zum Fortfahren eine Taste oder warten Sie einige Sekunden.
問題が起きたためコンピュータを再起動しました。このまま起動する場合は、いずれかのキーを押すか、数秒間そのままお待ちください。
电脑因出现问题而重新启动。请按一下按键，或等几秒钟以继续启动。

FIGURE 4.14

This is something to keep in mind as you are looking to acquire memory using any tool, actually. You want to make sure you have tested it thoroughly in a controlled environment to ensure it works reliably in a manner you expect. You do not want to get to a point where you are trying to acquire critical data in an investigation and have it all be wiped away by a system crash from an untested utility.

While we do not spend a lot of time on it, the importance of tool validation cannot be emphasized enough. You should always be testing your tools, especially when you perform updates, against known images to ensure you get expected results.

Linux

Linux, as you would expect, has open source solutions to the problem of memory capture. Where there used to be a /dev/mem device available, it was removed from the Linux kernel several versions back. The danger to providing a universal device to get access to memory is the potential for overwriting critical sections of memory that may lead to a system crash. Additionally, you might also open the door to malicious applications collecting the contents of memory simply by connecting to an exposed device. This does not mean, though, that you cannot get a memory device on your Linux system. Instead of being built into the kernel, it is now a separate package that you can build as a kernel module.

One of the kernel modules available is fmem, which you can build from source or it may be available in some of the package repositories depending on your Linux distribution. The thing about kernel modules is that in order to build them you need the kernel source code, so you can build the module for the right kernel. In some cases, the kernel and module version will have to match. As a result, Linux modules are not generally as portable as, say, Windows drivers. From the standpoint of being a forensic analyst, you may need to carry around modules for a wide variety of Linux distributions and relevant kernel versions. The other choice would be to build the driver from source, which may require that the kernel source be downloaded to the system, using up disk space and potentially altering drive contents. This is a case where forensic analysis has to skirt the border between collecting evidence and corrupting evidence.

Once you have the kernel source, you can build the module by running make against the source. This will leave you with a .ko file, which is the kernel object that can be loaded as a device driver. In order to load it, you run insmod, which will insert the module into kernel memory. As with any kernel module, no matter what the operating system, you will need to insert the module as an administrator. You can see the process of inserting the module in Figure 4.15. Once the module is loaded, you can use a tool like dd or dcfldd to capture the memory.

```
kilroy@dallas ~/Downloads/fmem_1.6-0 $ ls
AUTHORS    debug.h     fmem.mod.o  lkm.o           Module.symvers  TODO
ChangeLog  fmem.ko     fmem.o      Makefile        README
COPYING    fmem.mod.c  lkm.c       modules.order   run.sh
kilroy@dallas ~/Downloads/fmem_1.6-0 $ sudo insmod fmem.ko
kilroy@dallas ~/Downloads/fmem_1.6-0 $ ls /dev/fmem
/dev/fmem
```

FIGURE 4.15

In order to verify that the module is loaded, you can run the utility lsmod. You can see the output below. The output shows the name of the module as well as the size.

```
kilroy@dallas ~ $ lsmod
Module                  Size  Used by
fmem                   13201  0
```

There are other packages that can be used to capture memory on Linux systems but another one worth mention is LiME (Linux Memory Extractor) because it not only works on Linux systems but it is also targeted at performing memory forensics on Android smartphones. This is possible because under the hood, Android is running a modified Linux kernel, targeted at the processor architecture in use in Android smartphones. LiME requires that you build a module that can be inserted into the kernel, just as with fmem. One of the other really interesting features of LiME is that you can capture memory over a network. In Figure 4.16, you can see two sessions being used to capture memory. In the lower session, I have inserted the kernel module into memory, passing in the parameters necessary to have the kernel module listen for a connection on port 8990. Once there is a connection, the kernel module will dump the memory out to that connection and then the module will close, unloading itself from memory in the process.

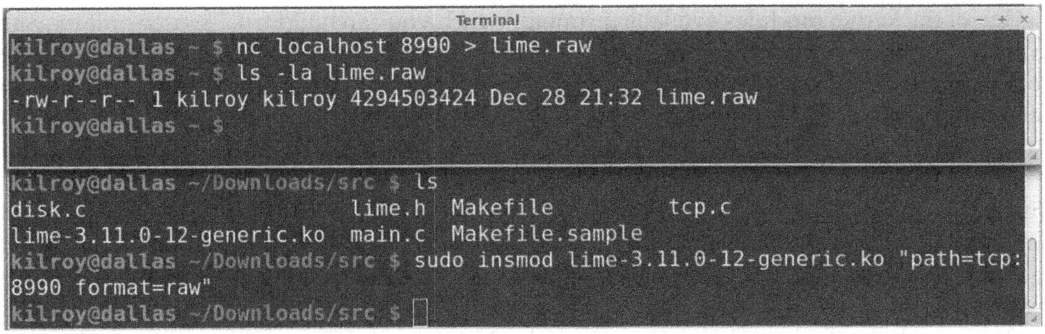

```
Terminal
kilroy@dallas ~ $ nc localhost 8990 > lime.raw
kilroy@dallas ~ $ ls -la lime.raw
-rw-r--r-- 1 kilroy kilroy 4294503424 Dec 28 21:32 lime.raw
kilroy@dallas ~ $

kilroy@dallas ~/Downloads/src $ ls
disk.c                      lime.h  Makefile          tcp.c
lime-3.11.0-12-generic.ko   main.c  Makefile.sample
kilroy@dallas ~/Downloads/src $ sudo insmod lime-3.11.0-12-generic.ko "path=tcp:
8990 format=raw"
kilroy@dallas ~/Downloads/src $
```

FIGURE 4.16

LiME also accepts parameters that will dump the capture to disk rather than to listen for a network connection. Instead of using a tcp:port parameter for the path, you would provide a path to a file. You can also specify different types of output instead of raw. The output type would commonly be determined by the tool you are using to analyze the capture. LiME supports padded captures, which uses 0s to pad out the sections of memory that have not been mapped. It also supports a LiME format that puts a header before all mapped memory segments.

ANALYZING MEMORY CAPTURES

Again, there are a number of commercial tools that can be used to perform analysis of a memory capture. In our case, we will be using an open source tool because it demonstrates some of the complications of analyzing memory as well as providing good insight into the details that are available. The open source tool we will be using is Volatility. Volatility is a tool written in Python that will run on multiple operating systems as long as Python is supported. It will also run on Windows as a standalone binary. It relies on profiles of the different operating systems in order to work. The profile specifies where all of the interesting pieces of information are stored in the memory dump. This is different for different versions of an operating system. Windows 7 will have a different profile than Windows 8. Even service packs may have a different mapping than the base operating system. These profiles will have to be created by someone and the different Windows versions have profiles already built in. Linux is more problematic because every kernel build is different, depending on the features that are turned on or built as modules. When a Linux kernel is built, the build process creates a map file. This map file can then be used to create a profile that can be used with Volatility.

In order to create the profile, you need to merge the system map – the file indicating the addresses where all the tokens are stored – with a DWARF file. DWARF is a debugging format originally designed for Linux systems, though now widely used in other places. Since the common executable file format on Linux systems is ELF, the debugging format was named

DWARF. The debugging file created on your system from the Volatility source tree, merged with the system map, will give you a profile that you can then use to analyze the memory capture.

Once you have the memory capture, it is easy to perform the analysis using Volatility. Since, commonly you would be performing an analysis on a Windows system, simply because of the comparative volume of Windows systems and users, the default commands used to extract information are designed to work on Windows systems. For example, in Figure 4.17, you can see the process list from a Windows 7 system. Above the process list, you can see the command used to acquire the list. We provide the profile name, in this case Win7SP1x64 indicates a Windows 7, Service Pack 1 system on a 64-bit processor, and the file name of the capture file, as well as the task we want to run against the memory dump.

```
kilroy@dallas ~ $ vol.py --profile=Win7SP1x64 -f windows7.mem pslist
Volatility Foundation Volatility Framework 2.4
Offset(V)          Name                    PID   PPID   Thds     Hnds   Sess  Wow64 Start                          Exit

0xfffffa80018929e0 System                    4      0     98      601     -1      0 2014-12-29 16:01:38 UTC+0000

0xfffffa8002b7f040 smss.exe                276      4      2       29     -1      0 2014-12-29 16:01:38 UTC+0000

0xfffffa80037f3550 csrss.exe               368    360      9      795      0      0 2014-12-29 16:01:42 UTC+0000

0xfffffa8003aaf060 wininit.exe             424    360      3       74      0      0 2014-12-29 16:01:42 UTC+0000

0xfffffa80039aa620 csrss.exe               436    416     11      368      1      0 2014-12-29 16:01:42 UTC+0000

0xfffffa8003b28730 winlogon.exe            492    416      4      110      1      0 2014-12-29 16:01:42 UTC+0000

0xfffffa8003b6c060 services.exe            528    424     14      271      0      0 2014-12-29 16:01:42 UTC+0000

0xfffffa8003bc8060 lsass.exe               540    424     10      777      0      0 2014-12-29 16:01:42 UTC+0000

0xfffffa8003b7e350 lsm.exe                 548    424     10      151      0      0 2014-12-29 16:01:42 UTC+0000

0xfffffa8003e27920 svchost.exe             664    528     12      367      0      0 2014-12-29 16:01:43 UTC+0000

0xfffffa8003e691e0 svchost.exe             732    528      7      316      0      0 2014-12-29 16:01:43 UTC+0000

0xfffffa8003e90730 MsMpEng.exe             780    528     40      581      0      0 2014-12-29 16:01:43 UTC+0000

0xfffffa8003f26060 svchost.exe             908    528     22      529      0      0 2014-12-29 16:01:44 UTC+0000
```

FIGURE 4.17

From the memory dump, we can acquire process information, user sessions, network connections, and indicators of malware. Since we are looking at a Windows system, one of the areas that we will be concerned about is the contents of the registry, since some of the registry only exists in memory. Fortunately, Volatility has all of the tools we need to be able to investigate the registry. First, we can get a list of the hives that are available. You can see the list of hives from a Windows 7 system in Figure 4.18. The list of hives can be obtained, as you can see, using the hivelist task.

```
kilroy@dallas ~ $ vol.py --profile=Win7SP1x64 -f windows7.mem hivelist
Volatility Foundation Volatility Framework 2.4
Virtual            Physical           Name
0xfffff8a0013a1010         0x6b426010 \??\C:\Users\kilroy\ntuser.dat
0xfffff8a001816010         0x548d4010 \??\C:\Users\kilroy\AppData\Local\Microsoft\Windows\UsrClass.dat
0xfffff8a0038f8010         0x4e82f010 \??\C:\System Volume Information\Syscache.hve
0xfffff8a007484010         0x7a4ae010 \Device\HarddiskVolume1\Boot\BCD
0xfffff8a00000f010          0x49c5010 [no name]
0xfffff8a00002e010          0x2dda010 \REGISTRY\MACHINE\SYSTEM
0xfffff8a000065410          0x4911410 \REGISTRY\MACHINE\HARDWARE
0xfffff8a0007ef010         0x7aa87010 \SystemRoot\System32\Config\DEFAULT
0xfffff8a000807010         0x64001010 \SystemRoot\System32\Config\SAM
0xfffff8a000930010         0x78a46010 \SystemRoot\System32\Config\SOFTWARE
0xfffff8a000932410         0x7914f410 \SystemRoot\System32\Config\SECURITY
0xfffff8a000f52010          0x2040010 \??\C:\Windows\ServiceProfiles\NetworkService\NTUSER.DAT
0xfffff8a0010bd010         0x723dc010 \??\C:\Windows\ServiceProfiles\LocalService\NTUSER.DAT
```

FIGURE 4.18

The hive list not only provides us the list of hives but where they can be found in memory, both virtual memory, as well as physical memory. You can also see where they exist on the drive. In some cases, they do not exist on the drive. Instead, they are created from the running system configuration, meaning they exist in memory as the system is booted and operating. We can use Volatility to extract the contents of a key out of the registry. As an example, we can get the list of USB storage devices that have been attached to the system. We can do this by looking for the key ControlSet001\Services\USBSTOR using the printkey task or command within Volatility (Figure 4.19).

```
kilroy@dallas ~ $ vol.py --profile=Win7SP1x64 -f windows7.mem printkey -K "ControlSet001\services\USBSTO
R"
Volatility Foundation Volatility Framework 2.4
Legend: (S) = Stable   (V) = Volatile

----------------------------
Registry: \REGISTRY\MACHINE\SYSTEM
Key name: USBSTOR (S)
Last updated: 2014-10-05 21:11:52 UTC+0000

Subkeys:

Values:
REG_DWORD      Start            : (S) 3
REG_DWORD      Type             : (S) 1
REG_DWORD      ErrorControl     : (S) 1
REG_EXPAND_SZ ImagePath         : (S) system32\DRIVERS\USBSTOR.SYS
REG_SZ         DisplayName      : (S) USB Mass Storage Driver
REG_SZ         DriverPackageId : (S) v_mscdsc.inf_amd64_neutral_8b1e6b55729c3283
REG_DWORD      BootFlags        : (S) 4
```

FIGURE 4.19

Windows is not the only operating system that Volatility supports, of course. The commands or tasks for the other operating systems may be less obvious, though, particularly, if you rely on the help by running vol.py –h. This will show you, all the tasks or commands that will work for a Windows system. In order to get the list of all the things you can do with Mac or Linux systems, you need to run vol.py –info. This will also give you a list of all the profiles that are supported. After copying the profile I created for my system into the right place – in my case it was /usr/local/lib/python2.7/dist-packages/volatility-2.4-py2.7.egg/volatility/plugins/overlays/

linux/ -- I found the name of the profile that Volatility uses to identify it, which is the operating system category (Linux), followed by the name of the file without the .zip extension and then the processor architecture. As you can see in Figure 4.20, the name of my profile is Linuxmintx64.

```
kilroy@dallas ~ $ sudo vol.py --info
Volatility Foundation Volatility Framework 2.4


Profiles
--------
Linuxmintx64      - A Profile for Linux mint x64
VistaSP0x64       - A Profile for Windows Vista SP0 x64
VistaSP0x86       - A Profile for Windows Vista SP0 x86
VistaSP1x64       - A Profile for Windows Vista SP1 x64
VistaSP1x86       - A Profile for Windows Vista SP1 x86
VistaSP2x64       - A Profile for Windows Vista SP2 x64
VistaSP2x86       - A Profile for Windows Vista SP2 x86
Win2003SP0x86     - A Profile for Windows 2003 SP0 x86
Win2003SP1x64     - A Profile for Windows 2003 SP1 x64
Win2003SP1x86     - A Profile for Windows 2003 SP1 x86
Win2003SP2x64     - A Profile for Windows 2003 SP2 x64
Win2003SP2x86     - A Profile for Windows 2003 SP2 x86
Win2008R2SP0x64   - A Profile for Windows 2008 R2 SP0 x64
Win2008R2SP1x64   - A Profile for Windows 2008 R2 SP1 x64
Win2008SP1x64     - A Profile for Windows 2008 SP1 x64
Win2008SP1x86     - A Profile for Windows 2008 SP1 x86
Win2008SP2x64     - A Profile for Windows 2008 SP2 x64
Win2008SP2x86     - A Profile for Windows 2008 SP2 x86
Win2012R2x64      - A Profile for Windows Server 2012 R2 x64
Win2012x64        - A Profile for Windows Server 2012 x64
Win7SP0x64        - A Profile for Windows 7 SP0 x64
```

FIGURE 4.20

While you can scroll up and down through the entire output from –info, you can also feed it into grep and look for specifically what you are looking for. In my case, I want to find all of the Linux plugins or commands that are available so I run vol.py –info | grep linux and I get the list of plugins that I can use against a Linux image. One thing I probably want to do is to get a list of processes that are running on the system. I can use a few plugins to be able to do that, depending on the information I may want to accompany the name of the process. I can get environment information, command line information, or just the list of processes with their process ID, which you can see in Figure 4.21.

The top of the list is mostly unremarkable, since all the processes are in order by process ID, which means that many of them are going to look the same across different systems, distributions, and versions of Linux. The first process is often going to be init, since it is the super parent on Linux systems that all other processes are spawned by somewhere down the road. This is starting to change with distributions that are using systemd as a different way to get a Linux system up and running, but init is still common. However, much further down the list

```
kilroy@dallas ~ $ sudo vol.py --profile=Linuxmintx64 -f mem.raw linux_pslist
Volatility Foundation Volatility Framework 2.4
Offset             Name                 Pid  Uid   Gid   DTB                StartTime
0xffff880149760000 init                   1 0     0            0x148860000 0
0xffff880149761770 kthreadd               2 0     0                   -0x1 0
0xffff880149762ee0 ksoftirqd/0            3 0     0                   -0x1 0
0xffff880149765dc0 kworker/0:0H           5 0     0                   -0x1 0
0xffff880149791770 migration/0            7 0     0                   -0x1 0
0xffff880149792ee0 rcu_bh                 8 0     0                   -0x1 0
0xffff880149794650 rcuob/0                9 0     0                   -0x1 0
0xffff880149795dc0 rcuob/1               10 0     0                   -0x1 0
0xffff8801497a0000 rcuob/2               11 0     0                   -0x1 0
0xffff8801497a1770 rcuob/3               12 0     0                   -0x1 0
0xffff8801497a2ee0 rcuob/4               13 0     0                   -0x1 0
0xffff8801497a4650 rcuob/5               14 0     0                   -0x1 0
0xffff8801497a5dc0 rcuob/6               15 0     0                   -0x1 0
0xffff8801497b0000 rcuob/7               16 0     0                   -0x1 0
0xffff8801497b1770 rcuob/8               17 0     0                   -0x1 0
0xffff8801497b2ee0 rcuob/9               18 0     0                   -0x1 0
0xffff8801497b4650 rcuob/10              19 0     0                   -0x1 0
0xffff8801497b5dc0 rcuob/11              20 0     0                   -0x1 0
0xffff8801497c8000 rcuob/12              21 0     0                   -0x1 0
0xffff8801497c9770 rcuob/13              22 0     0                   -0x1 0
0xffff8801497caee0 rcuob/14              23 0     0                   -0x1 0
0xffff8801497cc650 rcuob/15              24 0     0                   -0x1 0
0xffff8801497cddc0 rcuob/16              25 0     0                   -0x1 0
```

FIGURE 4.21

of processes are the ones that were most recently running, when we captured the memory. In fact, we can see the very last processes to start up in the short list below. You can see the sudo process that then creates the insmod process, which was used to insert the LiME module that captured the memory we are inspecting.

```
0xffff8801486dc650 kworker/0:0      8192 0     0                -0x1 0
0xffff88014622aee0 kworker/u64:1    8222 0     0                -0x1 0
0xffff88014622c650 sudo             8235 0     1000      0x146710000 0
0xffff880146634650 insmod           8236 0     0         0x144b25000 0
```

Volatility comes with a large number of plugins that are available for the Windows, Mac OS X and Linux operating systems. It can take a long time to work through all of the different plugins and what they do. Volatility is also under active development so new modules are being added regularly. It is worth noting that Rekall, which was forked out of Volatility, is also available for memory forensics work. One problem with Volatility as mentioned before is the profiles for the different systems. If you are using a Windows system, you are probably in good shape but if you are using a Linux system, you may have a hard time. Rekall is hosting a large quantity of profiles for different systems that makes it easier to perform forensics work on systems that are not Windows-based. Additionally, Rekall supports an interactiveeerr3qew5WEy mode to acquire data from a memory image, where Volatility expects that you will run one plugin after another to get the information that you need.

PAGE FILES AND SWAP SPACE

When systems that use virtual memory run out of physical memory, they need to offload chunks of that memory, called pages, somewhere else. That is typically either an actual file or it is a special partition. Pages are usually small chunks of data, whereas storing and retrieving those pages is the responsibility of the operating system. Each operating system will have memory pages that are of a consistent size, though most modern operating systems use a page size of 4096 bytes. All pages on the system are then 4096 bytes. This makes it much easier to both allocate and locate pages because you do not have to worry about trying to figure out where page boundaries are. Every 4096 bytes is a new page. When memory gets full, the operating system will swap pages of physical memory out to disk in order to make room for memory allocations from other programs.

On Windows, the operating system allocates a file to write those pages out into. This file is commonly called pagefile.sys and itis generally located in the root of the C: drive, though you can configure the pagefile on the other system hard drives. The contents of the pagefile will generally remain on the disk across reboots, which means that if there was memory that was swapped out to disk while a system was running, the pagefile.sys will have that information after the system has been shut down.

This is not always the case, though. It is possible to configure a Windows system to wipe its pagefile before shutting down in order to protect the memory. The pagefile.sys file is also locked while the operating system is running. The kernel can get access to the pagefile.sys while the operating system is running, but other programs cannot, including Windows Explorer, so while the system is running you cannot use Windows Explorer to copy pagefile.sys to another location. When you try that, you will get a file in use error, as seen in Figure 4.22.

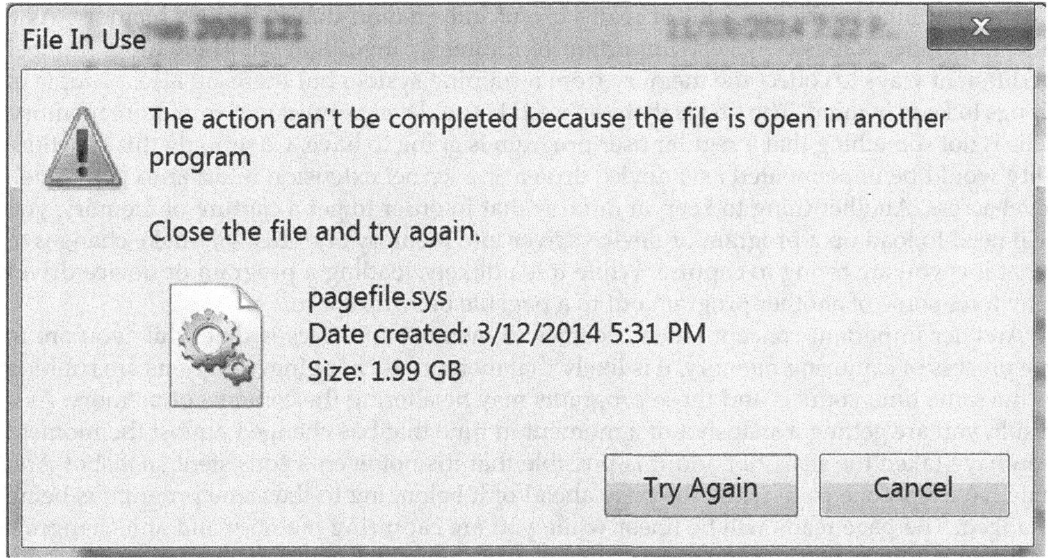

FIGURE 4.22

The problem with the pagefile is that the operating system keeps track of where everything is. The pagefile itself is just a collection of bytes in 4096 byte chunks. Yes, there may be data in there but it would be hard to say, where it came from. There is no context for anything found in the pagefile. One way of performing an analysis on a page file is to use either a strings utility to get human readable data out or to use a hex editor. The hex editor would show you all of the bytes, but since, the pagefile is likely several gigabytes of data with little in the way of form or structure, it may be hard to find anything that way.

One of the best ways to look for information in the pagefile is to look for patterns. There is a pattern matching language called YARA that is often used to look for malware. YARA uses C-like structures to create very powerful and flexible scripts to look for data. There is a utility written in Python called page_brute that can be used to search a Windows pagefile for various artifacts. The default rule set will search for Web and FTP communications, as well as administrative shares. Of course, if you have an idea what you are looking for, you can add rules. What page_brute does is chunk up pagefile.sys into 4096 byte blocks and then it uses the YARA rules to look for interesting data out of each block.

The biggest problem with the pagefile is that everything is typically stored in 4 k chunks and if you get complete documents stored in the pagefile, they are fragmented and the information about, what is stored, where is kept in the kernel memory space, while the operating system is running.

SUMMARY

The running system has a lot of really useful information that is kept in memory. As a result, memory forensics is very important to a forensic investigation. There are a number of different ways to collect the memory from a running system but there are also a couple of things to keep in mind. The first is that you need kernel-level permissions to acquire memory. This is not something that a regular user program is going to have. Commonly this functionality would be implemented as a device driver or a kernel extension in order to get kernel-level access. Another thing to keep in mind is that in order to get a capture of memory, you will need to load up a program or device driver into memory and this will make changes to what it is you are trying to capture. While it is unlikely, loading a program or device driver may force some of another program out to a pagefile or swap space.

Another important concept when it comes to memory forensics is that while you are in the process of capturing memory, it is likely that memory is changing. Programs are running at the same time yours is and those programs may be altering the contents of memory. As a result, you are getting a snapshot of a moment in time that has changed almost the moment you have taken the snapshot and it is possible that itis not even a consistent snapshot. You may have read one page while the page ahead of it belonging to the same program is being changed. The page reads will be linear while you are capturing memory and any changes a program makes to those changes may appear to be completely random by comparison with a linear reading process.

Fortunately, there are a number of forensics programs that will analyze memory dumps. This includes open source tools like Volatility and Rekall. The command-line oriented Volatility and Rekall provide a lot of control over what you look for, as well as offering the ability to extend the functionality for those who are capable of programming in Python. These tools are also in active development and there may be new plugins as well as new support for different operating systems.

Operating systems have long used secondary or hard disk storage to temporarily store the contents of primary storage (RAM). Unfortunately, there is not much in the way of structure to this storage outside of what the operating system keeps track of. The best way to analyze this storage is to use a form of pattern matching, whether itis through the use of a hexadecimal editor, YARA, grep or some other pattern matching utility. This, though, requires you to know what patterns you are looking for and what those patterns may look like. You may only get 4096 bytes, meaning that you may only get incomplete data sets back from your searches because the remainder of the data may be in memory rather than on disk.

EXERCISES

1. Use RAM capturer to acquire the memory from a Windows system. Once you have collected the memory, get an MD5 and a SHA1 hash of the resulting file.
2. Use FTK imager to acquire the memory from a Windows system. Get hashes of the resulting file.
3. Acquire the memory from a Linux system using LiME or fmem. Get hashes of the resulting file.
4. Use Volatility to get the process list from the Windows memory dump.
5. Use Volatility to get the process list from the Linux memory dump.
6. Use Volatility to get the list of network connections from the virtual memory from a snapshot of a virtual machine.

Bibliography

Ligh, M., Case, A., 2014. Art of Memory Forensics Detecting Malware and Threats in Windows, Linux, and Mac Memory. Wiley, Hoboken, NJ.

Russinovich, M., 2008. Blogs. Available from: http://blogs.technet.com/b/markrussinovich/archive/2008/07/21/3092070.aspx (accessed 29.12.2014.).

Russinovich, M., Solomon, D., 2012. Windows Internals, sixth ed. Microsoft Press, Redmond, Washington.

Walters, A., Petroni, N., Jr, 2007. Volatools: Integrating Volatile Memory Forensics into the Digital Investigation Process. Available from: http://www.blackhat.com/presentations/bh-dc-07/Walters/Paper/bh-dc-07-Walters-WP.pdf (accessed 29.12.2014.).

CHAPTER

5

System Configuration

INFORMATION INCLUDED IN THIS CHAPTER:

- Windows registry
- .inf files
- Linux /etc directory
- Mac OS plist files

INTRODUCTION

One advantage we are looking for now is the fact that system configuration has really settled down to some pretty specific areas. This has not always been the case. Windows, for example, generally has configuration details stored in the Windows registry. The registry, interestingly, was originally intended as a way to store specifics about component object model (COM) objects that were providing remote functionality to other systems. Over time, the registry has grown to include all of the system configuration details, as well as configuration storage for applications. Any program can get access to the registry and store information there and it is easy because Microsoft includes application programming interfaces (APIs) that allow any programmer to very quickly and easily get access to the registry.

The advantage here is that it provides us a single place to look for information rather than a lot of .ini files scattered all over the place, which is the way before the registry. In the case of other operating systems, like Linux and Mac OS, that are UNIX-based, there are still text-based configuration files. On Mac OS, there are property lists or plists, containing property-value pairs, where all of the preference settings can be stored. With Linux and other UNIX-based operating systems, it is a harder proposition since there is no consistent approach provided by the operating system or by APIs provided by the operating system vendor. Every application or system service has to provide a solution for themselves. You might have text-base configurations, which is commonly the case or you may have a parser that creates a configuration file for you, as is the case with Sendmail.

The real question is where all of the useful information is and how to get to it. Each operating system will be a different case so we can cover them in sequence, starting with Windows, since the registry is such a dense topic.

WINDOWS

Windows maintains a database of configuration settings. These settings are broken up into system-wide and user-specific. If there are multiple users on the system, each user will get their own set of user-specific settings. The registry is organized as a series of hives, which is a way the operating system separates out the type of content. These hives, for the information that remains persistent across reboots, are stored in C:\Windows\System32\config. With the breadth of information that is stored in the registry, you might imagine that it is accessed on a regular basis. You would be right, as it turns out. Between the operating system and the applications, there is a lot of activity in the registry. We can use the process monitor (procmon.exe) utility from the SysInternals team at Microsoft to see how much activity. You can see an example from just a few seconds on a Windows 7 system in Figure 5.1.

You will regularly see the short expressions HKLM and HKCU when it relates to the Windows registry. These terms mean HKEY Local Machine and HKEY Current User. Local Machine is any setting that is system wide, while Current User relates to the user that is logged in at the time you look at the registry.

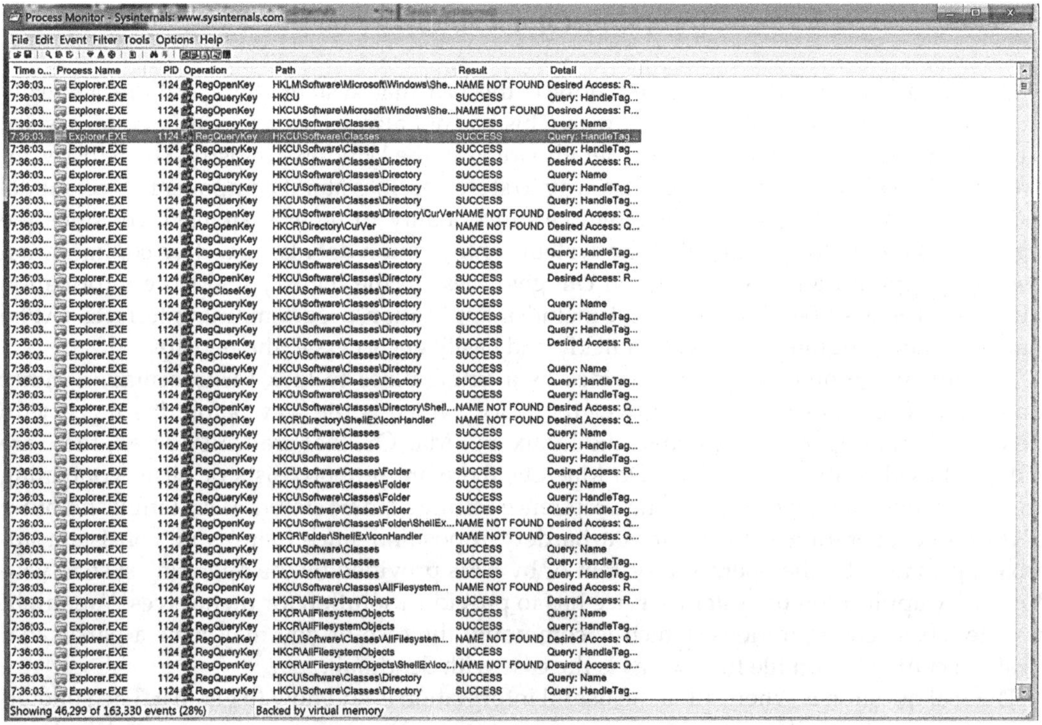

FIGURE 5.1

While it is referred to as a database, it does not look much like a traditional database when you try to interact with it. First, traditionally information retrieved from databases is presented in a table with rows and columns. While it may well be stored on disk in a similar fashion to a traditional database, it is commonly presented like a tree. The utility commonly used to look at and edit the registry is regedit.exe and you can see the tree presentation in Figure 5.2. You can also see the different hive files that you will find on disk presented in the left-hand pane. The files that you will find in C:\Windows\System32\config are DEFAULT, SAM, SECURITY, SOFTWARE and SYSTEM. The information in those keys are stored on the disk. Other information in the registry is in memory and is only available while the system is running.

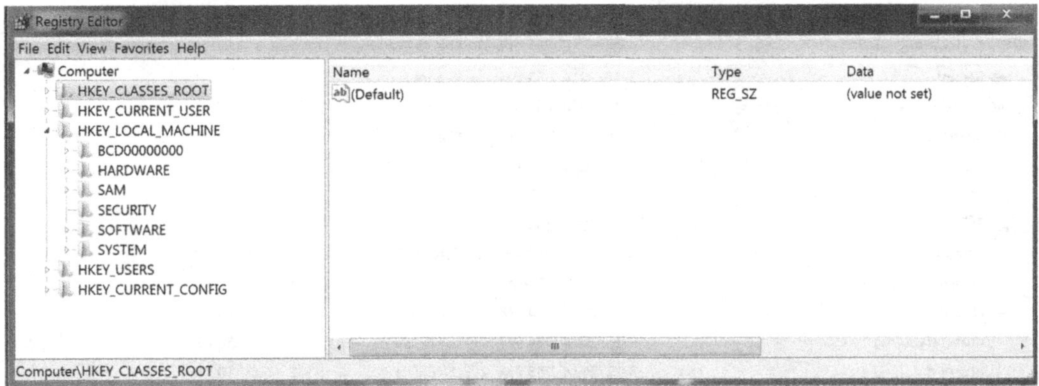

FIGURE 5.2

When the system starts up, it creates a set of default keys and begins populating them. You can also see those default keys in Figure 5.2. The default keys are HKEY_LOCAL_MACHINE, HKEY_CURRENT_USER, HKEY_USERS, HKEY_CLASSES_ROOT, and HKEY_CURRENT_CONFIG. The data under HKEY_LOCAL_MACHINE gets populated from the files in System32 while keys and values under HKEY_CURRENT_USER are found in the ntuser.dat file in your home directory. For example, my user on my Windows 7 system is kilroy, so the location of ntuser.dat for me would be C:\Users\kilroy. You can see the ntuser.dat file in my home directory along with the directories for documents, pictures, music, as well as all of the other files, and directories (Figure 5.3).

You will also note that there are .log files in the directory listing as well. Because the registry is really a database, it makes use of transaction logs. Changes to the registry, while the system is running, are written to the .log files, in case something happens to the system so transactions can be put back into the registry. While you can see them in my home directory, the log files also exist in the system32 directory for all of the system hives.

Underneath the keys you see are more keys. These are commonly called sub-keys. Each key can have a set of keys as well as values. The keys are like folders that hold more folders or files. You can think of the values as files in that contain specific data, while the keys might contain a combination of values and keys. Each value has a data type associated with it. You can have strings, multi-line strings, binary, and multiple sizes of integer values. This

Name	Date modified	Type	Size
Links	5/16/2014 9:59 PM	File folder	
Local Settings	3/12/2014 1:33 PM	File folder	
My Documents	9/13/2014 7:28 PM	File folder	
My Documents	3/12/2014 1:33 PM	File folder	
My Music	5/16/2014 9:59 PM	File folder	
My Pictures	5/16/2014 9:59 PM	File folder	
My Videos	5/16/2014 9:59 PM	File folder	
NetHood	3/12/2014 1:33 PM	File folder	
OneDrive	3/12/2014 2:52 PM	File folder	
Oxygen Forensic Suite	3/30/2014 4:09 PM	File folder	
pip	4/2/2014 3:14 PM	File folder	
PrintHood	3/12/2014 1:33 PM	File folder	
PycharmProjects	8/23/2014 12:17 PM	File folder	
Recent	3/12/2014 1:33 PM	File folder	
Saved Games	5/16/2014 9:59 PM	File folder	
Searches	5/16/2014 9:59 PM	File folder	
SendTo	3/12/2014 1:33 PM	File folder	
Start Menu	3/12/2014 1:33 PM	File folder	
Templates	3/12/2014 1:33 PM	File folder	
.gitconfig	4/1/2014 10:17 PM	GITCONFIG File	1 KB
.rekallrc	8/6/2014 3:17 PM	REKALLRC File	1 KB
NTUSER.DAT	9/15/2014 9:24 PM	DAT File	5,888 KB
ntuser.dat.LOG1	9/15/2014 9:24 PM	LOG1 File	256 KB
ntuser.dat.LOG2	3/12/2014 1:33 PM	LOG2 File	0 KB
NTUSER.DA	3/12/2014 2:36 PM	BLF File	64 KB
NTUSER.DA	3/12/2014 2:36 PM	REGTRANS-MS File	512 KB
NTUSER.DA	3/12/2014 2:36 PM	REGTRANS-MS File	512 KB
ntuser.ini	3/12/2014 1:33 PM	Configuration setti...	1 KB
sparsefile	8/5/2014 1:42 PM	File	98 KB

Type: LOG2 File
Size: 0 bytes
Date modified: 3/12/2014 1:33 PM

FIGURE 5.3

combination of data types provides a wide variety of information that the system or the application can store.

Rather than dwelling on all of the features and capabilities of the Windows registry, since there are entire books written about this topic, we can move along to the various artifacts that you may find stored away in the registry as well as different ways of getting access to that information. While commonly you would get access to the registry from a system that is booted up so you can work with the live registry, there are ways to access the registry offline.

Registry Access

There are a few ways to access the registry, whether you are talking about a live or a dead system. Starting with Windows-based tools, there is, of course RegEdit, which you may already be familiar with. It is a graphical tool that presents data in an easy to understand tree view and also provides you the ability to add or modify information in the registry. One advantage to use RegEdit is that you can quickly and easily search for specific values in the registry. You can see RegEdit in Figure 5.4, showing the find dialog box, which is what you would use to locate information in the registry. However, one of the drawbacks of using RegEdit is that it is really designed to be used on a live system. One thing you can do with RegEdit is to both import into the registry and export from the registry.

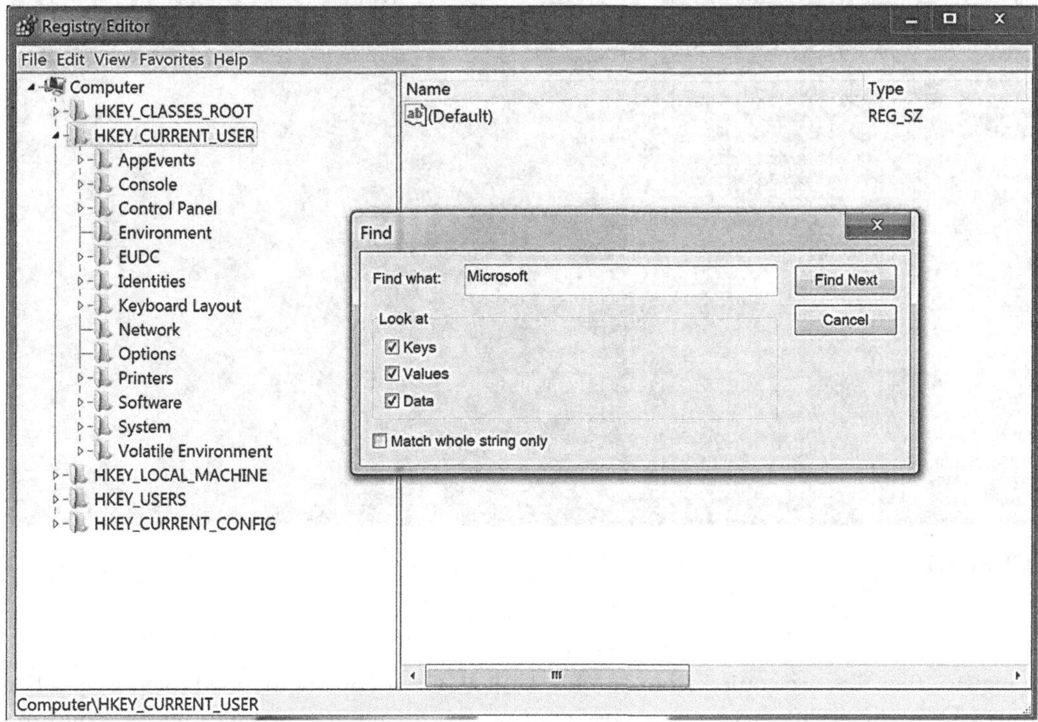

FIGURE 5.4

There is also a command line tool available on Windows systems that can be used to interface with the registry. The command reg is also designed to work with the registry on the local system and cannot be used to work with registry files from other systems. It does have a lot of power to extract information in a way that is easy to store. If you wanted a list of keys, for example, and you needed it in a text form, you could use the reg utility to run the query against the registry and then, since it is just text that you would get as output, you can do whatever you want with the text. A sample of output from a query with a list of keys underneath HKLM\Software\Microsoft can be seen in Figure 5.5.

You are not limited to using Windows, though, to work with registry files. You can also use the utility chntpw on a Linux system. While it was designed as a way to change the passwords on a Windows system in case you had accidentally locked yourself out, it can be used to do extensive querying of the registry files. Of course, since this is a Linux system, you have no way of opening the live registry on the system, as there is not one so, it will only work

```
C:\Windows\system32>reg query HKLM\Software\Microsoft

HKEY_LOCAL_MACHINE\Software\Microsoft\.NETFramework
HKEY_LOCAL_MACHINE\Software\Microsoft\Active Setup
HKEY_LOCAL_MACHINE\Software\Microsoft\ADs
HKEY_LOCAL_MACHINE\Software\Microsoft\Advanced INF Setup
HKEY_LOCAL_MACHINE\Software\Microsoft\ALG
HKEY_LOCAL_MACHINE\Software\Microsoft\AppVISV
HKEY_LOCAL_MACHINE\Software\Microsoft\ASP.NET
HKEY_LOCAL_MACHINE\Software\Microsoft\Assistance
HKEY_LOCAL_MACHINE\Software\Microsoft\BidInterface
HKEY_LOCAL_MACHINE\Software\Microsoft\COM3
HKEY_LOCAL_MACHINE\Software\Microsoft\Command Processor
HKEY_LOCAL_MACHINE\Software\Microsoft\Connect to a Network Projector
HKEY_LOCAL_MACHINE\Software\Microsoft\Cryptography
HKEY_LOCAL_MACHINE\Software\Microsoft\CTF
HKEY_LOCAL_MACHINE\Software\Microsoft\DataAccess
HKEY_LOCAL_MACHINE\Software\Microsoft\DataFactory
HKEY_LOCAL_MACHINE\Software\Microsoft\DevDiv
HKEY_LOCAL_MACHINE\Software\Microsoft\Dfrg
HKEY_LOCAL_MACHINE\Software\Microsoft\DFS
HKEY_LOCAL_MACHINE\Software\Microsoft\Direct3D
HKEY_LOCAL_MACHINE\Software\Microsoft\DirectDraw
HKEY_LOCAL_MACHINE\Software\Microsoft\DirectInput
HKEY_LOCAL_MACHINE\Software\Microsoft\DirectMusic
HKEY_LOCAL_MACHINE\Software\Microsoft\DirectPlay8
HKEY_LOCAL_MACHINE\Software\Microsoft\DirectPlayNATHelp
HKEY_LOCAL_MACHINE\Software\Microsoft\DirectShow
HKEY_LOCAL_MACHINE\Software\Microsoft\DirectX
HKEY_LOCAL_MACHINE\Software\Microsoft\DownloadManager
HKEY_LOCAL_MACHINE\Software\Microsoft\Driver Signing
HKEY_LOCAL_MACHINE\Software\Microsoft\DRM
HKEY_LOCAL_MACHINE\Software\Microsoft\DVR
```

FIGURE 5.5

on registry files that are copied from another system. Or, if you are inclined to boot up a live Linux CD that includes this, you can use chntpw against the registry files on the Windows hard disk in the system you have booted the CD on.

With chntpw, you can load up registry keys from the system, as well as the user specific file ntuser.dat that carries the HKEY_CURRENT_USER tree with all of the configuration settings that belong to the user that owns the file. Once they are loaded, you can query and edit any value that is in the registry. In Figure 5.6, you can see the list of functions, you can perform with chntpw and in Figure 5.7, you can see a listing of keys in the system hive under the policy key.

Another tool that is very useful for getting information from registry files is the RegRipper tool. RegRipper will extract data from hive files but it will not work on a live system. You need to have the hive files from either a captured disk image or obtained some other way. When the system is booted up, the hive files are not accessible, which is why, RegRipper needs the files from a capture or some other form of dead system. RegRipper targets specific aspects of the registry that are useful for a forensic analysis, which makes it really helpful to get directly to information you may need. You can see the interface for RegRipper in Figure 5.8.

RegRipper requires a set of plugins in order to operate and each plugin is written in Perl, which means that anyone can write a plugin for the tool. The plugins also provide profiles

```
> ?
Simple registry editor:
hive [<n>]              - list loaded hives or switch to hive numer n
cd <key>                - change current key
ls | dir [<key>]        - show subkeys & values,
cat | type <value>      - show key value
hex <value>             - hexdump of value data
ck [<keyname>]          - Show keys class data, if it has any
nk <keyname>            - add key
dk <keyname>            - delete key (must be empty)
ed <value>              - Edit value
nv <type#> <valuename>  - Add value
dv <valuename>          - Delete value
delallv                 - Delete all values in current key
rdel <keyname>          - Recursively delete key & subkeys
ek <filename> <prefix> <keyname>  - export key to <filename> (Windows .reg file
format)
debug                   - enter buffer hexeditor
st [<hexaddr>]          - debug function: show struct info
q                       - quit
```

FIGURE 5.6

```
> hive 2
Switching to hive #2, named <SECURITY>, size 262144 [0x40000]

> ls
Node has 2 subkeys and 0 values
  key name
  <Policy>
  <RXACT>

> ls Policy
Node has 17 subkeys and 1 values
  key name
  <Accounts>
  <DefQuota>
  <Domains>
  <PolAcDmN>
  <PolAcDmS>
  <PolAdtEv>
  <PolAdtLg>
  <PolDnDDN>
  <PolDnDmG>
  <PolDnTrN>
  <PolEKList>
  <PolOldSyskey>
  <PolPrDmN>
  <PolPrDmS>
  <PolRevision>
  <SecDesc>
  <Secrets>
```

FIGURE 5.7

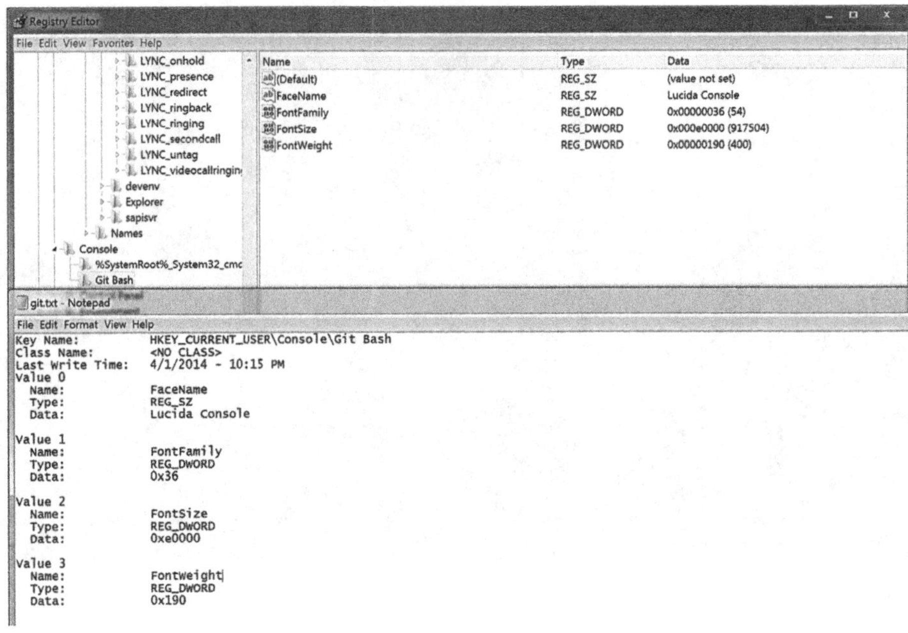

FIGURE 5.8

for RegRipper, so the tool will know, what to look for based on the hive file it has. There is, though, a lot of detail that is generated in the output and even that can be daunting. A sample of the output is below and while it is verbose about what keys it is looking at and what it is looking for, it will still take a lot of research and digging to find the information you need.

```
----------------------------------------
rdphint v.20090715
(NTUSER) Gets hosts logged onto via RDP and the Domain\Username

Software\Microsoft\Terminal Server Client\Servers not found.
----------------------------------------
realplayer6 v.20080324
(NTUSER.DAT) Gets user's RealPlayer v6 MostRecentClips(Default)
values

Software\RealNetworks\RealPlayer\6.0\Preferences not found.
----------------------------------------
realvnc v.20091125
(NTUSER.DAT) Gets user's RealVNC MRU listing

Software\RealVNC\VNCViewer4\MRU not found.
----------------------------------------
recentdocs v.20100405
(NTUSER.DAT) Gets contents of user's RecentDocs key

Software\Microsoft\Windows\CurrentVersion\Explorer\RecentDocs not
found.
----------------------------------------
rootkit_revealer v.20110204
(NTUSER.DAT) Extracts the EULA value for Sysinternals Rootkit
Revealer.

Software\Sysinternals\RootkitRevealer not found.
```

Registry Artifacts

There are a large number of artifacts that can be extracted from the Windows registry that would be of significance for a forensic investigation. You can track the actions of a user, discover software and its configuration, and get a lot of additional information, as we have already seen through the use of tools like RegRipper. Considering the variability of the registry from one system to another, there will be a lot of keys and values that may be specific to a system. This will be especially true when it comes to malware or user-hidden data. However, there are still a lot of places that are well-known.

One important consideration with registry keys is the time stamps associated with those keys. When you make changes to a key, there is a time stamp that gets updated to indicate the last time the key was written to. You cannot see the time stamp from inside of the registry editor, however. In order to see the time stamp, you export the key to a text file and then when you open the text file, you will see the last time the key was written to plainly indicated. You can see an example of this in Figure 5.9. It is easy to export out of the registry editor. You select the key you want to get information from and either right-click or go to the File menu and select Export. You will have a choice of export types. In order to get the date and time the key was last changed, you need to select text file. You can export to a registry file but you will not get the time the key was last changed that way, just the list of all of the subkeys and values, so the file could be re-imported into the registry.

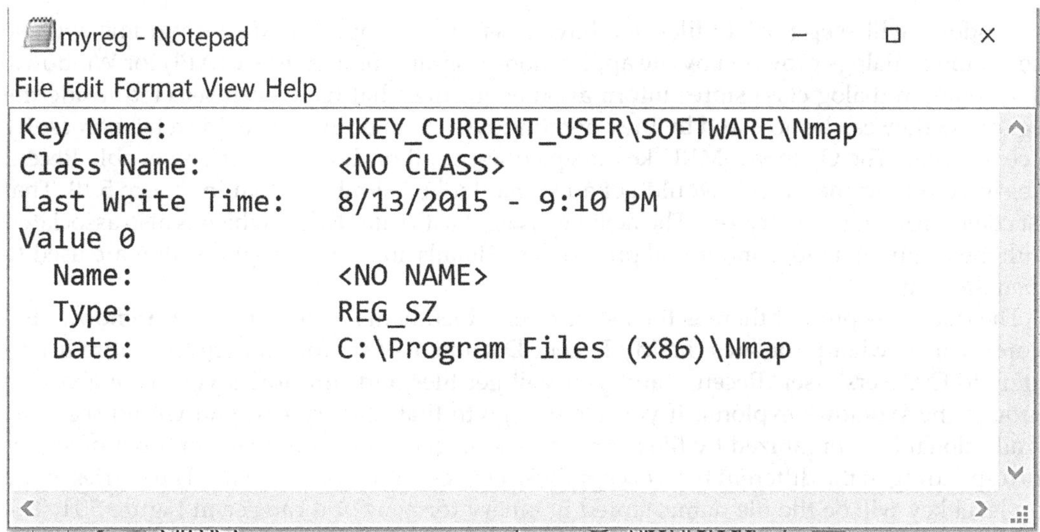

FIGURE 5.9

HKLM\Software\Microsoft\Windows\CurrentVersion\Run
HKCU\Software\Microsoft\Windows\CurrentVersion\Run
HKLM\Software\Microsoft\Windows\CurrentVersion\RunOnce
HKCU\Software\Microsoft\Windows\CurrentVersion\RunOnce

All of these registry keys perform the same function. The purpose of values in these keys is to have software run automatically. You will notice that there are four keys. Two of the keys are for software you want to start, when the computer starts up. Any value in the HKLM keys will execute when the computer starts. As you can see, one will run every time the computer starts while the other will only run once. The value will be deleted from the registry before the command line specified is executed. You can change this behavior by adding a ! at the beginning of the value. This will keep the value from being deleted until after the command executes. The reason for this is to ensure that the program executes. If the value is deleted but the program specified fails, the value will already have been deleted and so it will never run again.

The other two values have the same purpose except that they are based on individual users. Because of that, the values are not stored in the system hives. Instead, the values are stored for each user and you would get access to them by investigating the ntuser.dat file for each user. In order to install a value in the HKLM keys, you need to have administrative privileges but any user can install one of these values into the HKCU tree.

HKCU\Software\Microsoft\Windows\CurrentVersion\Explorer\ComDlg32\OpenSaveMRU
HKCU\Software\Microsoft\Windows\CurrentVersion\Explorer\ComDlg32\LastVisitedMRU
HKCU\Software\Microsoft\Windows\CurrentVersion\Explorer\RecentDocs

Windows will keep track of files that have recently been opened. Most programs will use the common dialogs provided by the application-programming interface (API) for Windows. That common dialog class stores information about files that have been selected inside the registry so they can be accessed by the operating system, in order to provide a list of recently accessed files. The OpenSaveMRU key keeps track of all of those files. If you enable Recent files in your Start menu, you would get a list that looked similar to that in Figure 5.10. That list comes from this registry key. The next key is the LastVisitedMRU, which is also associated with the common dialog, and it will provide you details about the programs that are used to open those files.

The last value present there is the list of recent documents opened through Windows Explorer. This is what populates the My Recent Documents list. You can see the entire list by going to C:\Users\user\Recent\ and you will get files and directories you have accessed through the Windows explorer. If you were to go to that registry key, you would see a list of additional keys organized by file extension and in each key would be a number of values corresponding to the different files, except those entries would be in binary. The entries in the top level key will be the file name, stored in binary form, as you can see in Figure 5.11. The entries in subkeys that correspond to the file extensions will also be the file name information in binary form.

HKEY_LOCAL_MACHINE\SYSTEM\ControlSet001\Control\Windows

There are a couple of things in this particular key that may be of some value. The first is the shutdown time. This is a binary value that keeps track of the time, the system was last shutdown. The binary value is a 64-bit number that represents the number of 100 ns that have elapsed since January 1, 1601. The number must be converted to a date to get a value, of course. The utility Dcode will perform the time conversion for you.

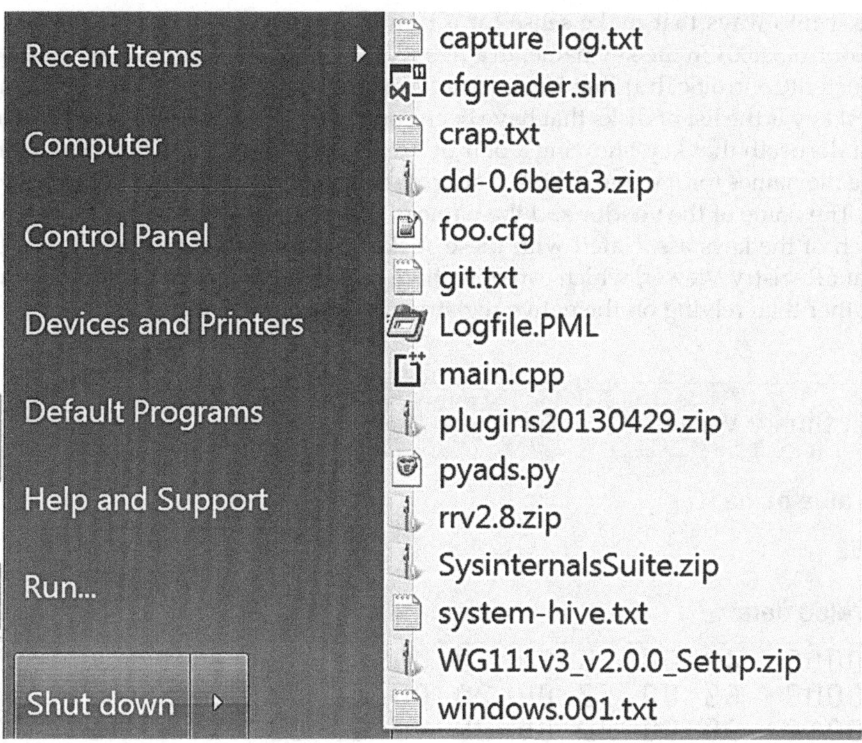

FIGURE 5.10

CurrentControlSet001 is the last set of configuration values that you booted with. There may be multiple control sets, including one that relates to the "last known good" set of configurations. Last known good is an expression you may see when you are provided a choice of settings to boot from, if you are experiencing problems booting.

HKEY_LOCAL_MACHINE\SYSTEM\ControlSet001\Control\ComputerName\ComputerName

This key is fairly self-explanatory. When you are working on a dead set of registry files, this key will make it clear, what is the name of the computer you working on. This will help tie the registry files to the specific computer that the registry files were removed from.

SYSTEM\ControlSet001\Control\DeviceClasses\{53f56307-b6bf-11d0-94f2-00a0c91efb8b}
SYSTEM\ControlSet001\Control\DeviceClasses\{53f5630d-b6bf-11d0-94f2-00a0c91efb8b}

This pair of keys relates to drives that have been connected to the system. The key names were also taken by looking at the SYSTEM hive file rather than looking at the live system. Keep in mind that the live registry will look a little different from just looking at the hive files. The operating system creates the registry in memory from the contents of those files but also organizes it into ways that make sense for a running system. As an example, you will see CurrentControlSet001 in the key name. In a live registry, the keys used by the running system will be CurrentControlSet but that key will not exist in the hive file. It is created in memory.

The first key is the list of disks that have been connected. In Figure 5.11, you can see the list of keys underneath that key, showing a pair of drives presented by the virtual machine. This shows the file names for the two drives. Underneath that, there appears to be four USB sticks attached. The name of the vendor and the name of the product are included in a string value under each of the keys associated with these sticks. The screen capture was taken from the AccessData Registry Viewer, which can open hive files that have been captured from a dead system rather than relying on the native registry viewer from a live system.

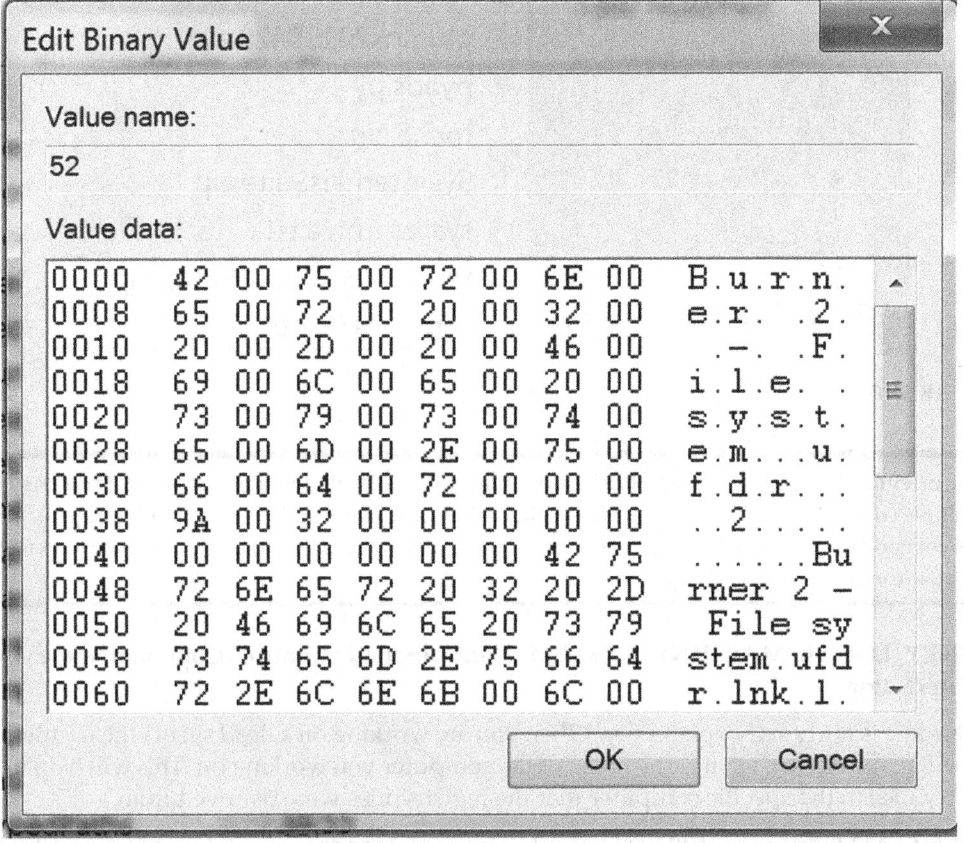

FIGURE 5.11

The other key shown is the list of volumes. A volume is different from a disk because a disk may have multiple volumes, although a volume may also contain multiple disks. This registry key will show you the volumes that have been connected to the system. If you check the properties of the keys, you will see the last time each key was written to. That will show you the last time the volume was mounted, since the key will not be written without the volume in place. The information included in the string value under one of these keys is below. You can see the complete device path as well as the vendor name and the product name.

```
\.\.?.\.S.T.O.R.A.G.E.#.V.o.l.u.m.e.#._.?.?._.U.S.B.S.T.O.R.#.D.i
.s.k.&.V.e.n._.K.i.n.g.s.t.o.n.&.P.r.o.d._.D.a.t.a.T.r.a.v.e.l.e.
r._.S.E.9.&.R.e.v._.P.M.A.P.#.0.0.1.9.E.0.6.B.4.A.0.7.E.D.2.0.7.7
.3.4.0.0.2.5.&.0.#.{.5.3.f.5.6.3.0.7.-.b.6.b.f.-.1.1.d.0.-
.9.4.f.2.-.0.0.a.0.c.9.1.e.f.b.8.b.}.#.{.5.3.f.5.6.3.0.d.-
.b.6.b.f.-.1.1.d.0.-.9.4.f.2.-.0.0.a.0.c.9.1.e.f.b.8.b.}...
```

HKEY_LOCAL_MACHINE\SYSTEM\CurrentControlSet\Enum\USBSTOR

This key relates to the two keys above. It shows the USB devices that have been connected to the operating system. Just as in the information available before, you will see the list of devices, including the vendor and product information. Additionally, you find keys including device parameters and properties. You can see the USBSTOR key with the associated subkeys in Figure 5.12.

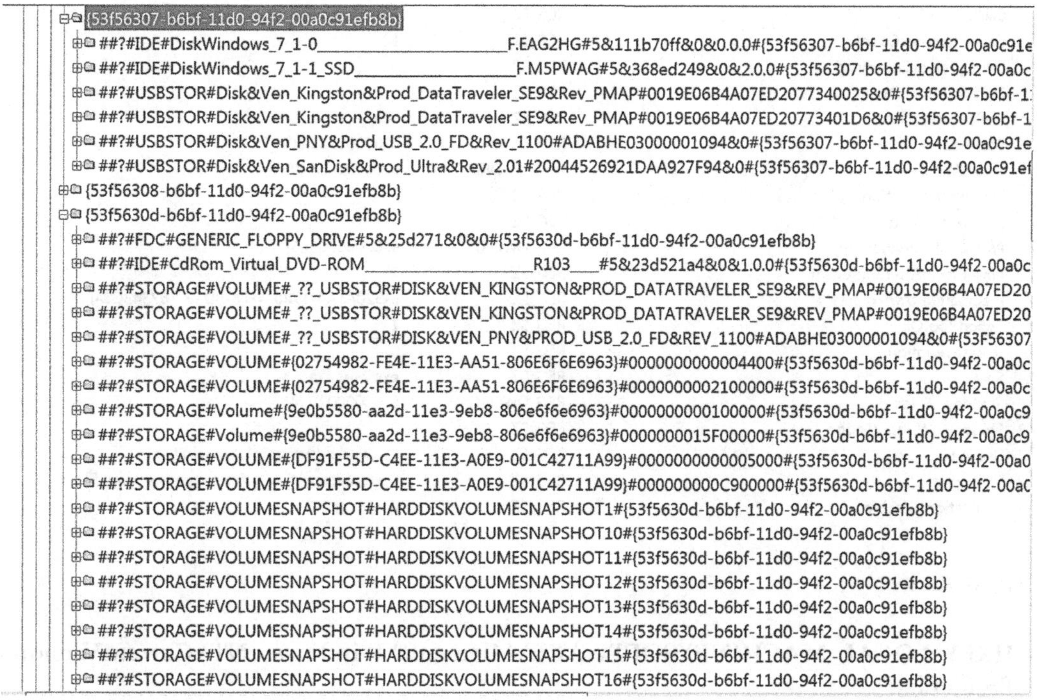

```
{53f56307-b6bf-11d0-94f2-00a0c91efb8b}
  ##?#IDE#DiskWindows_7_1-0________________________F.EAG2HG#5&111b70ff&0&0.0.0#{53f56307-b6bf-11d0-94f2-00a0c91e
  ##?#IDE#DiskWindows_7_1-1_SSD____________________F.M5PWAG#5&368ed249&0&2.0.0#{53f56307-b6bf-11d0-94f2-00a0c
  ##?#USBSTOR#Disk&Ven_Kingston&Prod_DataTraveler_SE9&Rev_PMAP#0019E06B4A07ED2077340025&0#{53f56307-b6bf-1
  ##?#USBSTOR#Disk&Ven_Kingston&Prod_DataTraveler_SE9&Rev_PMAP#0019E06B4A07ED20773401D6&0#{53f56307-b6bf-1
  ##?#USBSTOR#Disk&Ven_PNY&Prod_USB_2.0_FD&Rev_1100#ADABHE03000001094&0#{53f56307-b6bf-11d0-94f2-00a0c91e
  ##?#USBSTOR#Disk&Ven_SanDisk&Prod_Ultra&Rev_2.01#20044526921DAA927F94&0#{53f56307-b6bf-11d0-94f2-00a0c91ef
{53f56308-b6bf-11d0-94f2-00a0c91efb8b}
{53f5630d-b6bf-11d0-94f2-00a0c91efb8b}
  ##?#FDC#GENERIC_FLOPPY_DRIVE#5&25d271&0&0#{53f5630d-b6bf-11d0-94f2-00a0c91efb8b}
  ##?#IDE#CdRom_Virtual_DVD-ROM____________________R103___#5&23d521a4&0&1.0.0#{53f5630d-b6bf-11d0-94f2-00a0c
  ##?#STORAGE#VOLUME#_??_USBSTOR#DISK&VEN_KINGSTON&PROD_DATATRAVELER_SE9&REV_PMAP#0019E06B4A07ED20
  ##?#STORAGE#VOLUME#_??_USBSTOR#DISK&VEN_KINGSTON&PROD_DATATRAVELER_SE9&REV_PMAP#0019E06B4A07ED20
  ##?#STORAGE#VOLUME#_??_USBSTOR#DISK&VEN_PNY&PROD_USB_2.0_FD&REV_1100#ADABHE03000001094&0#{53F56307
  ##?#STORAGE#VOLUME#{02754982-FE4E-11E3-AA51-806E6F6E6963}#0000000000004400#{53f5630d-b6bf-11d0-94f2-00a0c
  ##?#STORAGE#VOLUME#{02754982-FE4E-11E3-AA51-806E6F6E6963}#0000000002100000#{53f5630d-b6bf-11d0-94f2-00a0c
  ##?#STORAGE#Volume#{9e0b5580-aa2d-11e3-9eb8-806e6f6e6963}#0000000000100000#{53f5630d-b6bf-11d0-94f2-00a0c9
  ##?#STORAGE#Volume#{9e0b5580-aa2d-11e3-9eb8-806e6f6e6963}#000000015F00000#{53f5630d-b6bf-11d0-94f2-00a0c9
  ##?#STORAGE#VOLUME#{DF91F55D-C4EE-11E3-A0E9-001C42711A99}#0000000000005000#{53f5630d-b6bf-11d0-94f2-00a0
  ##?#STORAGE#VOLUME#{DF91F55D-C4EE-11E3-A0E9-001C42711A99}#000000000C900000#{53f5630d-b6bf-11d0-94f2-00aC
  ##?#STORAGE#VOLUMESNAPSHOT#HARDDISKVOLUMESNAPSHOT1#{53f5630d-b6bf-11d0-94f2-00a0c91efb8b}
  ##?#STORAGE#VOLUMESNAPSHOT#HARDDISKVOLUMESNAPSHOT10#{53f5630d-b6bf-11d0-94f2-00a0c91efb8b}
  ##?#STORAGE#VOLUMESNAPSHOT#HARDDISKVOLUMESNAPSHOT11#{53f5630d-b6bf-11d0-94f2-00a0c91efb8b}
  ##?#STORAGE#VOLUMESNAPSHOT#HARDDISKVOLUMESNAPSHOT12#{53f5630d-b6bf-11d0-94f2-00a0c91efb8b}
  ##?#STORAGE#VOLUMESNAPSHOT#HARDDISKVOLUMESNAPSHOT13#{53f5630d-b6bf-11d0-94f2-00a0c91efb8b}
  ##?#STORAGE#VOLUMESNAPSHOT#HARDDISKVOLUMESNAPSHOT14#{53f5630d-b6bf-11d0-94f2-00a0c91efb8b}
  ##?#STORAGE#VOLUMESNAPSHOT#HARDDISKVOLUMESNAPSHOT15#{53f5630d-b6bf-11d0-94f2-00a0c91efb8b}
  ##?#STORAGE#VOLUMESNAPSHOT#HARDDISKVOLUMESNAPSHOT16#{53f5630d-b6bf-11d0-94f2-00a0c91efb8b}
```

FIGURE 5.12

HKEY_LOCAL_MACHINE\SOFTWARE\Microsoft\Windows NT\CurrentVersion

This key stores all of the information about the operating system parameters including the operating system product name, the build number, the version information that includes whether there is a service pack installed, the owner, the organization, and the location of the system root directory among other pieces of information.

HKEY_LOCAL_MACHINE\SOFTWARE\Microsoft\Windows NT\CurrentVersion\Winlogon

This key also hosts a wealth of information, as you can see in Figure 5.13. Among other values, you can see what the default username is. This is required if the system is set to automatically login without the user entering a username or password. The shell information is configured in this registry value. You may not be aware of this but the user interface you see with the start button, the task bar, a desktop, and so forth is really a shell over the top of the operating system. This shell can be replaced. By default, the value is explorer.exe and that is the value you can see here from this system. It would be uncommon for this value to change but if it has, it might mean that something malicious may have happened on the system. This key also stores any legal warnings that may be displayed on login. This is sometimes common with business systems so the business can warn users about acceptable use.

Name	Type	Data
(Default)	REG_SZ	(value not set)
AutoAdminLogon	REG_SZ	1
AutoRestartShell	REG_DWORD	0x00000001 (1)
Background	REG_SZ	0 0 0
CachedLogonsCount	REG_SZ	10
DebugServerCommand	REG_SZ	no
DefaultDomainName	REG_SZ	
DefaultUserName	REG_SZ	kilroy
DisableCAD	REG_DWORD	0x00000001 (1)
ForceUnlockLogon	REG_DWORD	0x00000000 (0)
LegalNoticeCaption	REG_SZ	
LegalNoticeText	REG_SZ	
PasswordExpiryWarning	REG_DWORD	0x00000005 (5)
PowerdownAfterShutdown	REG_SZ	0
PreCreateKnownFolders	REG_SZ	{A520A1A4-1780-4FF6-BD18-167343C5AF16}
ReportBootOk	REG_SZ	1
scremoveoption	REG_SZ	0
Shell	REG_SZ	explorer.exe
ShutdownFlags	REG_DWORD	0x0000002b (43)
ShutdownWithoutLogon	REG_SZ	0
Userinit	REG_SZ	C:\Windows\system32\userinit.exe,
VMApplet	REG_SZ	SystemPropertiesPerformance.exe /pagefile
WinStationsDisabled	REG_SZ	0

FIGURE 5.13

HKEY_LOCAL_MACHINE\SOFTWARE\Microsoft\Windows NT\CurrentVersion\ProfileList

This key carries the list of users that have been logged into this system at some point. The users are identified by security identifiers (SIDs) and each user has its own key underneath the ProfileList key. There are a number of built in user profiles that should have entries here. There are a number of well-known SIDs, where the value is always going to be the same, no matter what system you are on. One of those is S-1-5-18, the SID for Local System, the account used for services by the operating system. Another is S-1-5-19, the NT Authority account for local services. Another is S-1-5-20, the NT Authority account for network services. Among other things, the location of the home directory for each user can be found in the key for each profile.

HKEY_LOCAL_MACHINE\SOFTWARE\Microsoft\Windows\CurrentVersion\Explorer

The Explorer key carries a lot of subkeys that may have information of value. One of them may be a list of mount points, which would be a mapped network drive. This would be a remote file share that has been given a local designation like a drive letter. Additionally, you will find a list of shell folders where important storage locations are configured like common startup, common application data, common documents, or common administrative tools.

HKEY_LOCAL_MACHINE\SYSTEM\ControlSet001\services

There is a lot of information here and it is useful to have a utility to pull the information out rather than trying to look through it a key at a time. This key contains all of the services and drivers that are installed on the system. A service is an operating system controlled program that runs under the covers. You do not launch a service from the Windows Explorer. You run it from the Services control and each service can be configured to automatically run, start manually, or be disabled. A service that is configured to start manually may be started by another service, whether that service is started up by a user or if the service is started automatically, when the system starts up.

Each entry in this key provides information about the executable, the name, the type – whether it is a service or a driver – and how it is configured to start. You will notice, I said driver as well as service. The system drivers are listed here as well, since drivers may be installed on a system but may not run very often, depending on whether the device controlled by the driver is present or not. Drivers can also be used for malicious purposes and are often necessary for particular types of malware, if that malware requires low-level access to the system for things like a custom file system. This may be the case for malware that makes use of the master boot record to maintain control of the boot process.

HKEY_CURRENT_USER\Software\Microsoft\Windows\CurrentVersion\Explorer\Shell Folders

All of the well-known folders for each user such as documents, music, fonts, history, and other similar directories are configured in this key. If there have been any changes to these values to point them to locations that are not default, you will find the changes here.

HKEY_CLASSES_ROOT\Local Settings\Software\Microsoft\Windows\Shell

Shell bags are a little known feature of Windows outside of the forensics community and perhaps, some other technologists who are deeply familiar with how Windows works. A shell bag is a set of configuration information for file system folders that have been accessed through the Windows Explorer. There are two subkeys in this key. One of them is the list of all of the shell bags. The key is called Bags. The other one is called BagMRU and it is a list of folders that have been used most recently.

MRU is a set of initials you will see regularly in the Windows registry. It means Most Recently Used and is a list of values the user has used. This may be files or directories. Any MRU list will give you an indication of what the user has made use of or gained access to.

While you can find all of the information about the shell bags in the Windows registry by using RegEdit or another registry viewer like that available from AccessData, it is easiest to use a tool that is custom designed for the job of reading the shell bag information. One such tool is available from NirSoft and it is called ShellBagView. You can see the ShellBagView application in Figure 5.14. One important piece of information found in the shell bags is the last accessed time for a particular directory. Additionally, if a directory is in a shell bag, it means the user has accessed that directory at least once because there are view settings for explorer to use.

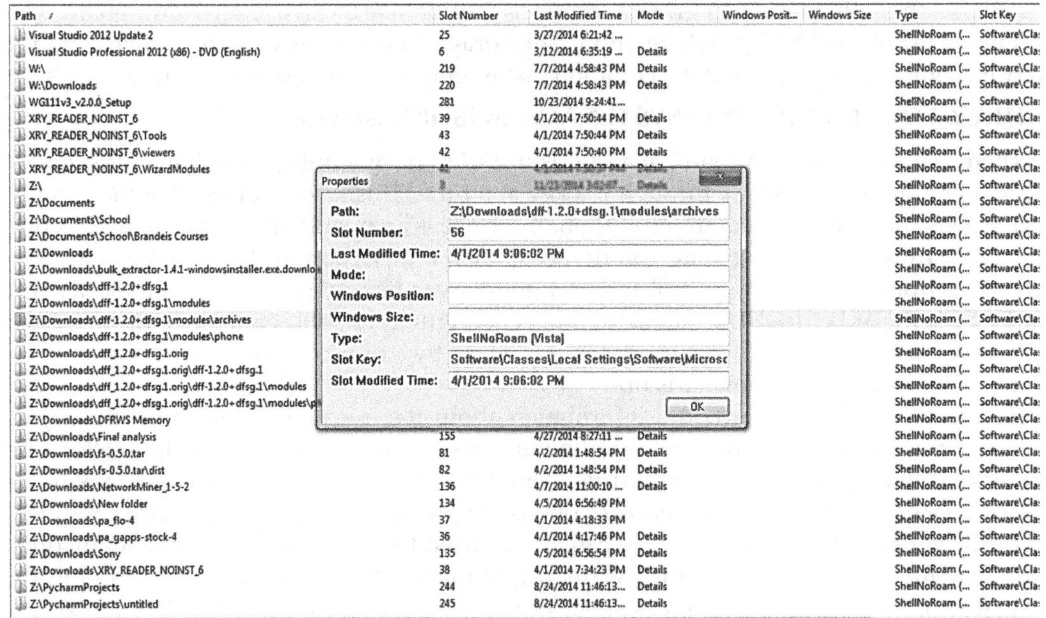

FIGURE 5.14

It is important to note that the registry values noted here changed in Windows 7. Before that, in Windows XP where shell bags first made their appearance, the registry key was HKEY_USERS\SID\Software\Microsoft\Windows\Shell and HKEY_USERS\SID\Software\Microsoft\Windows\ShellNoroam. The SID in both of those keys gets replaced by the Universally Unique Identifier (UUID) for the user you are looking at. As an example, the path to the user information for my user is HKEY_USERS\S-1-5-21-2381150070-693575941-1573647280-1000. The long string that starts with S is the security identifier for my user.

HKEY_CURRENT_USER\Software\Microsoft\Windows\CurrentVersion\Explorer\FileExts
HKEY_CLASSES_ROOT

Those registry keys provide an association between a file extension and a handler. The handler is the program associated with the particular file extension. This is another set of registry keys that can be useful when you are looking for malware. A malware author could hijack one of these keys to alter the behavior of a computer. Several years ago, I ran across a piece of malware that altered the handler for the .exe file extension. What happened at that point is that the malware got to run before any program to ensure that the program was not able to make any alterations to the operating system to remove the malware. While this was for the .exe file extension, the same thing could be done with any other file extension. When the .exe file extension gets hijacked poorly, it becomes obvious that the system has become infected. When you hijack other file extensions like mp3, html, wav, and other media-related file extensions, the malware can continue to ensure it maintains its infection while being less intrusive.

The Windows registry is a very rich set of information and while this is significant list, when it comes to checking for values that are important for forensic practitioners, there is always the potential for there to be a lot of additional registry keys that are important. Considering the fact that any user or program can potentially open the registry and write keys to it, there is a potential for a wide variety of data to be stored into a built-in database within the operating system.

Another set of values that is worth knowing about is the list of wireless networks that the system knows about. When your computer connects to a wireless network, the registry key HKLM\SOFTWARE\Microsoft\Windows NT\CurrentVersion\NetworkList\Profiles. Since this is a list of networks related to the system and not a particular user, it is stored in the LocalMachine keys.

MAC OS X

Mac OS X systems use files called property lists, commonly called plists, to store configuration settings. The use of property lists goes back to the days of NeXSTEP, which was the user interface designed for the NeXT computer. NeXT is the company Steve Jobs created after being ousted from Apple Computer in the mid-1980s. The property list was intended to store serialized objects like dictionaries. Serialization is the process of taking a data structure from memory and translating it into a form that can be written to disk and then later read back into memory, so the data structure form and contents are intact. A dictionary is a special data structure that is used to store a name, value pairs. This is sometimes called a map but it is often used to maintain configuration data. You have a configuration setting and the value associated with that configuration setting.

When Apple folded in the work of NeXT to create Mac OS X 10.0 in 2001, they changed the format of the property list file and began using an XML-based format. XML is very inefficient from a storage perspective, with all of the string tags and closing tags that are required for the XML format in addition to the data itself. Starting with 10.2 in 2002, Apple began to use a binary format that was still XML-based. The binary format, means that it was not stored as ASCII or Unicode strings, which would be human readable on disk, saved space but also required something other than a text editor to view the data in the property list. Fortunately, there are a small number of utilities that can read and display the property lists, including the developer toolkit, XCode that Apple provides for free. There are also some text editors for Mac OS X that will read and write the format necessary for property lists. This includes BBEdit and TextWrangler, which are popular text editors often used by programmers.

In 2011, Apple also added support for the JavaScript Object Notation (JSON), which is a way of representing complex datatypes and passing them back and forth between a Web server and its client. There are some incompatibilities between JSON and the property list format, however, including some of the supported data types. Table 5.1 indicates the data types that Apple supports in its property lists. These data types stem from the data types supported by the underlying libraries that Apple supplies to create programs. One of those libraries is the NeXTStep (NS) library set and another is the Core Foundation (CD) library set.

TABLE 5.1 Apple Property List Data Types

Data type	XML tag	Representation
String (NSString)	<string>	UTF-8 encoded string
Number (NSNumber)	<real>, <integer>	Decimal string (each number character is stored as a character)
Boolean (NSNumber)	<true/>, <false/>	No data stored, just the tag
Data (NSData)	<data>	Base64-encoded data
Array (NSArray)	<array>	Stored based on the contents of the array, storing any number of child elements
Dictionary (NSDict)	<dict>	<key> tags and plist element tags

One directory where you will find a number of plist files is in the /System/Library/CoreServices directory. In general, property lists will be stored underneath a Library directory, whether it is the System directory as in this case or under the user's own Library directory (~/Library). There is also a /Library directory in the root of the filesystem. SystemVersion.plist is a file you will find on a Mac OS X system that isn't a server and that will be found in the /System/Library/CoreServices directory. If you are looking at a Mac OS X Server installation, the file will be ServerVersion.plist. The following is an example of the SystemVersion.plist file, which is stored in plaintext.

```
<?xml version="1.0" encoding="UTF-8"?>
<!DOCTYPE plist PUBLIC "-//Apple//DTD PLIST 1.0//EN"
"http://www.apple.com/DTDs/PropertyList-1.0.dtd">
<plist version="1.0">
<dict>
      <key>ProductBuildVersion</key>
      <string>14B25</string>
      <key>ProductCopyright</key>
      <string>1983-2014 Apple Inc.</string>
      <key>ProductName</key>
      <string>Mac OS X</string>
      <key>ProductUserVisibleVersion</key>
      <string>10.10.1</string>
      <key>ProductVersion</key>
      <string>10.10.1</string>
</dict>
</plist>
```

You can see the format from that sample. This file consists of a property list (plist) that has a dictionary with six keys. This is really just a set of six named values: ProductBuildVersion, ProductCopyright, ProductName, ProductUserVisibleVersion, and ProductVersion. Each time the system is updated, the values here will update accordingly to new versions and a new build number. Two other plist files in the same directory are PlatformSupport.plist and InstallableMachines.plist. These two files indicate the different hardware platforms and systems, by model name, which are supported by this version of the operating system.

Each application installed on a system may have a number of plist files associated with it. In the /System/Library directory, there are 76 directories containing information about the different system applications as well as libraries for all of the different components necessary for the operating system. Out of those 76 directories, there are nearly 10000 (ten thousand!) plist files related to the different components. In addition, on my Mac OS X system, I have more than 3500 plist files in my own library directory that contains configuration information and applications that are specific to me. You can see the results of the searches for those plist files in Figure 5.15. I used the sudo command to obtain administrative access in order to find any file in the current directory that matched the form *.plist. I then used the wc (word count) command to count the number of lines, giving me the number of files that were found matching the format I was looking for.

```
kilroy@opus:/System/Library$ cd /System/Library
kilroy@opus:/System/Library$ sudo find . -name "*.plist" -print | wc -l
    9965
kilroy@opus:/System/Library$ cd ~/Library
kilroy@opus:~/Library$ sudo find . -name "*.plist" -print | wc -l
    3529
```

FIGURE 5.15

There are, though, some specific files that are worth looking at. First, all of the system preferences are stored in plist files in /Library/Preferences. One file in particular that is of interest is the file com.apple.SoftwareUpdate.plist. This file includes all of the information about system updates including the last date that updates were checked, the last date an update was successful, and the number of updates that are available. You can see this file opened in BBEdit in Figure 5.16.

Other important plist files on a Mac OS X system include:

- */Library/Preferences/com.apple.loginwindow.plist*: Includes the list of users that are automatically logged in as well as the user that was most recently logged in.
- */Library/Preferences/com.apple.preferences.accounts.plist*: Deleted users
- */Users/username/Library/Preferences/com.apple.sidebarlists.plist*: Media, volumes, and devices that are in the sidebar in the System Finder. An example of one of the entries, indicating my home directory, is in Figure 5.17.
- */Users/username/Library/Preferences/MobileMeAccounts.plist*: Information about iCloud accounts.

```
<?xml version="1.0" encoding="UTF-8"?>
<!DOCTYPE plist PUBLIC "-//Apple//DTD PLIST 1.0//EN" "http://www.apple.com/DTDs/PropertyList-1.0.dtd">
<plist version="1.0">
<dict>
    <key>LastAttemptSystemVersion</key>
    <string>10.10.1 (14B25)</string>
    <key>LastBackgroundCCDSuccessfulDate</key>
    <date>2014-11-29T19:51:12Z</date>
    <key>LastBackgroundSuccessfulDate</key>
    <date>2014-11-29T19:51:12Z</date>
    <key>LastFullSuccessfulDate</key>
    <date>2014-11-29T19:51:02Z</date>
    <key>LastRecommendedUpdatesAvailable</key>
    <integer>0</integer>
    <key>LastResultCode</key>
    <integer>2</integer>
    <key>LastSessionSuccessful</key>
    <true/>
    <key>LastSuccessfulDate</key>
    <date>2014-11-29T19:51:02Z</date>
    <key>LastUpdatesAvailable</key>
    <integer>0</integer>
    <key>PrimaryLanguages</key>
    <array>
        <string>en</string>
    </array>
    <key>RecommendedUpdates</key>
    <array/>
    <key>SkipLocalCDN</key>
    <false/>
</dict>
</plist>
```


FIGURE 5.16


```
<dict>
    <key>Alias</key>
    <data>
    AAAAAACSAAMAAQAAznXkgAAASCsAAAAAAAJkkQAG6rYA
    AM6wIr0AAAAACSD//gAAAAAAAAAA/////wABAAQAAmSR
    AA4ADgAGAGsAaQBsAHIAbwB5AA8AGgAMAE0AYQBjAGkA
    bgB0AG8AcwBoACAASABEABIADFVzZXJzL2tpbHJveQAT
    AAEvAAAVAAIADf//AAA=
    </data>
    <key>CustomItemProperties</key>
    <dict>
        <key>com.apple.LSSharedFileList.Binding</key>
        <data>
        ZG5pYgAAAABAAAAAAAAAAAAAAAAAAAAAAA
        AAAAAAAAAAAAZGxmdQIAAAAAAAAA
        </data>
        <key>com.apple.LSSharedFileList.TemplateSystemSelector</key>
        <integer>1935820909</integer>
    </dict>
    <key>Name</key>
    <string>kilroy</string>
</dict>
```


FIGURE 5.17

- */Users/username/Library/Preferences/loginwindow.plist*: Applications that are configured to automatically start when the user logs in. You can see an example of one of these entries in Figure 5.18.

```
<?xml version="1.0" encoding="UTF-8"?>
<!DOCTYPE plist PUBLIC "-//Apple//DTD PLIST 1.0//EN" "http://www.apple.com/DTDs/PropertyList-1.0.dtd">
<plist version="1.0">
<dict>
    <key>AutoLaunchedApplicationDictionary</key>
    <array>
        <dict>
            <key>Hide</key>
            <false/>
            <key>Path</key>
            <string>/Applications/Microsoft Office 2011/Office/Microsoft Database Daemon.app</string>
        </dict>
    </array>
    <key>BuildVersionStampAsNumber</key>
    <integer>29426464</integer>
    <key>BuildVersionStampAsString</key>
    <string>14B25</string>
    <key>SystemVersionStampAsNumber</key>
    <integer>168427776</integer>
    <key>SystemVersionStampAsString</key>
    <string>10.10.1</string>
</dict>
</plist>
```

FIGURE 5.18

- */Library/Preferences/com.apple.alf.plist*: Firewall settings
- */Library/Preferences/SystemConfiguration/com.apple.airport.preferences.plist*: WiFi settings, including all of the security set identifiers (SSIDs) that the system has connected to in the past. An example of one of the entries in this property list file is shown in Figure 5.19. It shows the configuration settings for the SSID Boingo Hotspot. You can see the Base64 encoded version of Boingo Hotspot in the setting SSID. The decoded string is in the setting SSIDString.
- */Library/Preferences/SystemConfiguration/com.apple.nat.plist*: Settings related to internet sharing
- */Library/Preferences/SystemConfiguration/com.apple.smb.server.plist*: If you are using server message block (SMB) or Windows file sharing, the settings for your server configuration are here, including the name you are sharing to the network with.
- */Library/Preferences/SystemConfiguration/com.apple.NetworkInterfaces.plist*: The list of network interfaces available on the system including their settings
- */Library/Preferences/SystemConfiguration/preferences.plist*: This includes a complete list of settings for different connection methods including bluetooth, modem and network interfaces. This includes settings like whether an interface is configured to use dynamic host configuration protocol (DHCP) to acquire Internet protocol (IP) settings. On my system, the complete file is 1200 lines long, but you can see a sample of the different settings in Figure 5.19.
- */Users/username/Library/Preferences/com.apple.finder.plist*: The preference settings for the system finder

```
<dict>
    <key>CurrentSet</key>
    <string>/Sets/17B12D43-4E34-4F72-9A7D-84A74AB40687</string>
    <key>Model</key>
    <string>iMac11,1</string>
    <key>NetworkServices</key>
    <dict>
        <key>29013F04-9963-4AFA-917A-9EB10F79BA38</key>
        <dict>
            <key>DNS</key>
            <dict/>
            <key>IPv4</key>
            <dict>
                <key>ConfigMethod</key>
                <string>DHCP</string>
            </dict>
            <key>IPv6</key>
            <dict>
                <key>ConfigMethod</key>
                <string>Automatic</string>
            </dict>
            <key>Interface</key>
            <dict>
                <key>DeviceName</key>
                <string>fw0</string>
                <key>Hardware</key>
                <string>FireWire</string>
                <key>Type</key>
                <string>FireWire</string>
                <key>UserDefinedName</key>
                <string>FireWire</string>
            </dict>
            <key>Proxies</key>
            <dict>
                <key>ExceptionsList</key>
                <array>
                    <string>*.local</string>
                    <string>169.254/16</string>
                </array>
                <key>FTPPassive</key>
                <integer>1</integer>
            </dict>
            <key>SMB</key>
            <dict/>
            <key>UserDefinedName</key>
            <string>FireWire</string>
```


FIGURE 5.19

- */Users/username/Library/Preferences/com.aol.aim.plist, com.adiumX.adiumX.plist, com.apple.iChat.AIM.plist, com.apple.iChat.plist, com.apple.SubNet.plist, com.skype.skype.plist, com.yahoo.messenger3.plist*: These are configuration files for various instant messaging client software including AOL Instant Messenger, iChat (lately called Messages), Yahoo Messenger, Skype and Adium (a multi-protocol client specifically for Mac OS X).

If you enable "system files" when you are searching in Finder, you can look for names, phone numbers and other information that was used in iMessage, or Messages.

- */Users/username/Library/Safari/Bookmarks.plist, Downloads.plist, History.plist, LastSession.plist*: These files contain the list of bookmarks, the contents of the download window, browsing history, and the contents of windows and tabs from the last browsing session in Apple's Web browser Safari.
- */Users/username/Library/Preferences/com.apple.LaunchServices.QuarantineEventsV2*: This file stores downloads that may have come from Safari or mail.

While this is a fairly broad set of configuration information, there is a lot more to be found in the plists on the system, especially when you start looking at application-specific plists. Plist files, as you can see, have stored not only configuration settings but also any other types of persistent data an application needs to store by simply serializing the objects application, keeps in memory.

LINUX

Linux inherits the bulk of its configuration specifics from UNIX and UNIX has generally used the /etc directory to store configuration settings. Of course, they also use dot files to hide files that should not be altered by normal users. When you do a normal file listing, you do not see all the files that start with a period or a dot, as in .vimrc, which is the file used to store the configuration settings for the vim file editor. Those are specifically hidden from display because it should be the program that manages those files rather than the user managing them directly. However, it is easy to "unhide" those files by simply changing the way you are looking at the files. If you are just getting a file listing, you can add –a as a flag and get all files, including the dot files.

Dot files, or configuration files, have a number of different formats depending on the program that is managing the configuration file. In most cases, you will see something like the listing below, which is a section of my configuration file from the vim file editor.

```
""""""""""""""""""""""""""""""""""""""""""""""""""""""""""""""""
" => General
""""""""""""""""""""""""""""""""""""""""""""""""""""""""""""""""
" Sets how many lines of history VIM has to remember
set history=700

" Enable filetype plugins
filetype plugin on
filetype indent on

" Set to auto read when a file is changed from the outside
```

```
set autoread

" With a map leader it's possible to do extra key combinations
" like <leader>w saves the current file
let mapleader = ","
let g:mapleader = ","

" Fast saving
nmap <leader>w :w!<cr>
```

There is an advantage to this type of configuration file. It is generally easy for people to read. You can see cases where we are setting configuration settings using the set directive. If I want to make changes to this file, I could without using anything other than a text editor. This is not the only style you can expect to see in configuration settings. You might see simply *variable=value* or even *variable value*. This last style might expect to have a tab in between the variable and the value. In any case, this is very easy to read. Some configuration files may use XML to set configuration variables and settings.

In addition to the configuration files that would show up as bare files in the home directory of any user, you may also have a series of files that are required for a specific application. In this case, you may need a directory. Again, this would commonly be put into a dot directory. Again, this would be hidden from a normal directory listing. One example of this, and a critical one at that, is the .ssh directory. ssh is secure shell, which is a replacement for a much older remote access protocol called telnet. ssh is commonly used for administrators or users to log into other systems on the network. The communication is encrypted in transmission.

ssh maintains a number of configuration settings that are important and worth looking at. There are in fact two places to look at the configuration settings. The first is in /etc/ssh and the second is in the directory ~/.ssh, which is the .ssh directory within the user's home directory. The system-wide configuration settings relate to all of the connections within the system. This may include whether the system will allow key-based authentication. A system allowing key-based authentication does not require a password. Just a key that has been shared ahead of time where the public key is stored in the right file on the server. When the client computer connects with the matching private key, the connection is just allowed. This will be true even if the private key is not protected by a password.

There are a number of other settings in the server configuration file, of course. In the configuration file for the client, you will find specific settings that the user wants including a list of hosts that the user regularly connected to. This allows the user to use short names rather than IP addresses or full hostnames. This may also include usernames for each of the hosts, as well as whether to forward X11 connections. X11 is a complete system providing the underpinnings of a graphical user interface, including the ability to use a keyboard, mouse and display on a remote host. The application runs on one end but the display is generated on the remote end. In X11 parlance, the end where the keyboard, mouse, and display are present is called the server.

In many systems, you will have /etc/network directory. This is dependent on the particular Linux distribution but many Linux distributions include this directory where all of the network interfaces are configured. The primary file that contains the interface configuration settings is interfaces. A sample interfaces file is below:

```
# loopback interface

auto lo

iface lo inet loopback

#  primary Ethernet interface with static address

iface eth0 inet static

address 192.168.1.5

netmask 255.255.255.0

gateway 192.168.1.254

#  secondary Ethernet interface with DHCP address

auto eth1

iface eth1 inet dhcp
```

Another configuration file related to networking is the /etc/resolv.conf file that is used to store the information regarding the domain name system (DNS). This file stores the domain name that would be used in cases where the full domain name is not supplied. If I just offer a hostname, my system will attach the configured search domains in order to get a fully qualified domain name to look up. The resolv.conf file has search parameters that specify the domains to search through as well as nameserver entries pointing to DNS servers that the client will use.

The /etc/pam.d directory stores a lot of configuration files related to login. This will provide specifics about user accounts, including password policies and where the user account information is stored. It also includes configuration settings for e-mail accounts, ssh accounts, and file share users, as well as other login types. The common-auth file and the login file are the primary files used to specify, how a normal user will login. PAM is pluggable authentication modules, which is a modular software architecture used to provide authentication services across the entire system.

On Linux systems, as on other systems, users are encouraged to login as a normal user. However, there are a lot of activities that require administrative access. On Linux systems, this is handled with the sudo command. This is a software package that is separate from a minimal Linux installation but sudo is generally included on most distributions simply because it is good security practice, even if it may get ignored. Not everyone can make use of the sudo command to get administrative access on a system. This is all configured in the /etc/sudoers file. Anyone who is a member of a group configured in the sudoers file, can get temporary administrative access. Normally, someone running sudo would have to enter their password in order to run a command as administrator. A sample section of a sudoers file is below. This particular file includes the NOPASSWD directive that says anyone who is part of the admin group does not need to enter their password to get administrative access.

```
# User privilege specification
root ALL=(ALL:ALL) ALL

# Members of the admin group may gain root privileges
%admin ALL= NOPASSWD: ALL

# Allow members of group sudo to execute any command
%sudo ALL=NOPASSWD: ALL
```

Linux systems have inherited the cron utility from its UNIX parents. cron is a utility designed to allow jobs or programs to run automatically on a particular schedule. There are sets of configuration files used for cron. First is /etc/crontab, which is a tabular file used to indicate what jobs to run and when to run them. Commonly, there will be a set of jobs already configured to run hourly, daily, weekly, and monthly. In order to add jobs to run at each of those intervals, you can add scripts to the directories /etc/cron.hourly, /etc/cron.daily, /etc/cron.weekly, /etc/cron.monthly.

Each distribution of Linux may have a different set of configuration files that are used to set up the system. In some Linux systems, for example, the /etc/inittab file is used to configure how the system comes up. It may come up in single user mode, multi-user mode, or graphical interface mode. There are other startup settings that are configured in the inittab file. Other Linux distributions may not use the older inittab file. They may use a system like Upstart, which is designed to replace the init system. Configuration files for Upstart are found in the /etc/init directory. There are a number of configuration files typically in that directory that will manage the way a system starts up.

Depending on the number of applications that are installed, you will find a different number of configuration settings on a Linux system. For example, if you had a Web server and a database server installed, you would find directories for those two applications in the /etc directory and each would have a number of configuration files that went along with them. Many applications, particularly those, which are larger and more complex, are moved to the conf.d style of configurations. Rather than a monolithic configuration file, the conf.d style is a directory that contains a number of smaller files. This style makes it easier to add or change configuration settings, though it can also add complexity by having a number of places where a configuration setting can be implemented.

Primarily, though, when you are looking for configuration settings on a Linux or other UNIX-like operating system, you will be looking in the /etc directory for system-wide settings and in the home directory of each user for user-specific configurations. In the user directory, you may be looking for files whose names end in rc or there may be a number of configuration files in a dot file.

SUMMARY

On Windows systems, the primary way of storing configuration settings is with the Windows Registry. The Registry is essentially a database used to store particular data types. The Registry consists of hives where the data is stored. The Registry is broken down into keys and values. Each key might be thought of as a folder where other keys or values can be stored. The values are where the data is actually stored. You might have strings, binary information, double words, or quad words (numerical values) that can be stored. One significant advantage of the Windows Registry is each key and value can have a set of properties, including access control lists as well as time and date information storing, when the key or value was last written. Typically, the registry is read with the Windows utility regedit but there are other utilities that will read registry files, including the AccessData utility Registry Viewer. There are also programming languages like any .NET language and also Python that have libraries for reading registry information.

With a Mac OS X system, the primary means of storing configuration information is in property list (plist) files. Currently, plist files are commonly in XML format but stored as binary in order to compress the space the files were taking, since XML is very space intensive. Fortunately, there are utilities like Apple's Xcode or the text editors BBEdit and TextWrangler that can read and write the binary format of the plist files. All operating system configuration information is stored in plist files. The locations you will commonly find these plist files are in /Library, /System/Library and ~/Library, the Library directory inside the user's home directory. The user's Library directory stores user-specific information related to applications that are installed.

While different Linux distributions may have different locations for storing specific configuration information, the system directory where the configuration files are located is /etc. Underneath /etc, there may be different directories or files depending on what applications are in use and which system initialization program is in use. For the most part, configuration files are text-based and often of the form name = value or name value. Some files may use tabs as delimiters between the name of the configuration variable and the value. When it comes to the user configuration, you may find configuration files in the user's home directory. These may be named ending in rc or they may be in specific application directories. Because these are configuration-related, they are not commonly expected to show up in a regular directory listing, since the application may manage the configuration file so it would be hidden from the average user. These directories, and configuration files themselves would start with a '.' and are commonly called dot files to indicate that they are hidden from the user.

EXERCISES

1. On a Windows system, locate all of the programs that are configured to run when the system starts up and when the user logs in based on the registry keys.
2. On a Windows system, find the list of security identifiers that are in the ProfileList on your system.

3. On a Linux system, determine how the network interfaces on the system get its network information.
4. On a Mac OS X system, locate all of the files that have been downloaded from the Safari browser.

Bibliography

Appleexaminer.com, 2014. Focus Files, Areas of Interest. Available from: http://www.appleexaminer.com/MacsAndOS/Analysis/InitialDataGathering/InitialDataGathering.html (accessed 30.11.2014.).

Ballenthin, W., 2014. Windows Shellbag Forensics. Available from: http://www.williballenthin.com/forensics/shellbag (accessed 24.11.2014.).

Registry, n.d. Windows. Available from: http://msdn.microsoft.com/en-us/library/windows/desktop/ms724871(v=vs.85).aspx (accessed 11.09.2014.).

Russinovich, M.E., Solomon, D.A., 2012. Windows Internals, sixth ed. Microsoft Press, Redmond, Washington.

CHAPTER

6

Web Browsing

INFORMATION INCLUDED IN THIS CHAPTER:

- Web browser artifacts
- E-mail artifacts
- Messaging artifacts

INTRODUCTION

Most of our lives are lived on the Internet these days. Between e-mail, social networking, YouTube, and a wide variety of other Web sites we visit regularly, our access to the network is very common. In addition, our lives living inside of digital artifacts such as browsing habits, bookmarks, histories, e-mail archives, and logs of who we message, there is no point in pretending that the Internet is not an enormous pathway for attacks. This may come in the form of malware inserted into Web sites or it may just be phishing attacks or other forms of spam that may or may not come with malware. It can be difficult to get actual numbers since the organizations are not required to provide vetted statements, but reliable estimates suggest that spam advertisement of just off-shore pharmacies generates tens of millions of dollars a year for the Russian business interests behind that spam. This is just the amount of money generated from the pharmacy businesses.

E-mail is also used to infect PCs around the world to create a collection of connected computers commonly called a botnet. Many of the worldwide network and system breaches have taken place because someone opened an e-mail message. While laws around the world are not generally on the same page, when it comes to whether these activities are illegal or not, countries such as the United States, Great Britain, and Germany to name just three are all generally on the same page with regards to attacking and compromising systems.

Understanding how to find e-mail messages and parse them correctly is an important skill. Of course, searching for browser artifacts has long been established as important. Almost fifteen years ago, I was asked to dig up some evidence that an employee at a company I was working for, had been using the work computer to look at pornographic Web sites at work.

There are so many other reasons to go looking for browsing history and any other pieces of information that may be available related to a user's Web browsing.

Web- or Internet-based communications have also been increasing over the years. Conference calls through services like WebEx, international calling using services like Skype, instant messaging through a variety of platforms – these are all in common usage and collectively are overtaking the use of traditional desk phones to communicate. There are ways to locate artifacts related to the use of those services and they are just as important as getting call detail records from a telephone company.

A PRIMER ON STRUCTURED QUERY LANGUAGE (SQL)

We are in the era of big data. In the early days of common Internet usage with Web browsers, when Mosaic was the common browser of choice and even after that with Internet Explorer and Netscape, a variety of text-based files were used to store information like history and bookmarks. In the case of Netscape, bookmarks were stored as HTML files, which are of course text-based, though with a well-known structure. Today, though, browsing usage has increased and strictly text-based storage of data is inefficient. Instead, many browsers have moved to using databases to store a lot of information. As a result, in order to perform forensic analysis of browsing activity, it is helpful to understand a little about how databases work.

The most common type of database in use at the moment is relational. Relational databases were first described in 1970 and they are based around the idea of a relation, which is really a set of data all belonging together in a collection. This collection, in practice, is called a table. Each database may consist of multiple tables that are connected in some way, even if it is loosely connected. The table consists of attributes and tuples, where the tuples are actually entries in the table. You can think of attributes as columns in the table and a tuple as a row. A visual representation may make more sense and you can see what each of these words means in context in Figure 6.1.

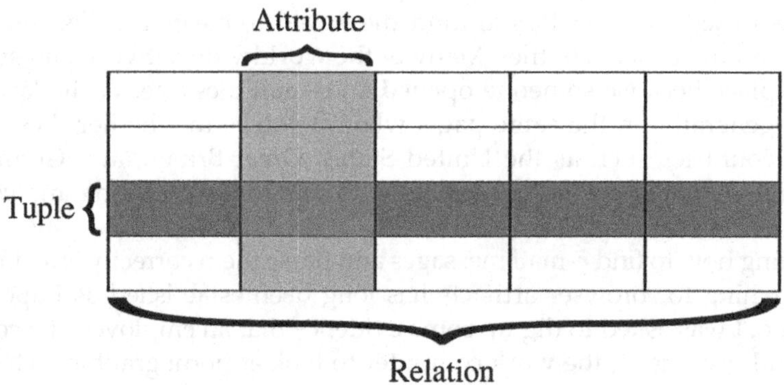

FIGURE 6.1

We need a programmatic way of getting data into the tables as well as getting it out again. One way of doing that is to use the structured query language (SQL), originally called the structured query English language and abbreviated SEQUEL. The language was developed in the early 1970s and the name had to be changed to avoid a trademark conflict, though the acronym SQL is commonly pronounced sequel[1]. As with any programming language, it can take ages to learn the intricacies and details to become an expert. However, there are some fundamentals, which we can use that are pretty easy to pick up and we can extract information from the databases, we are looking at using these SQL basics. Let us start with a very simple table, which you can see in Figure 6.2 and which looks a lot like a spreadsheet with the columns and rows.

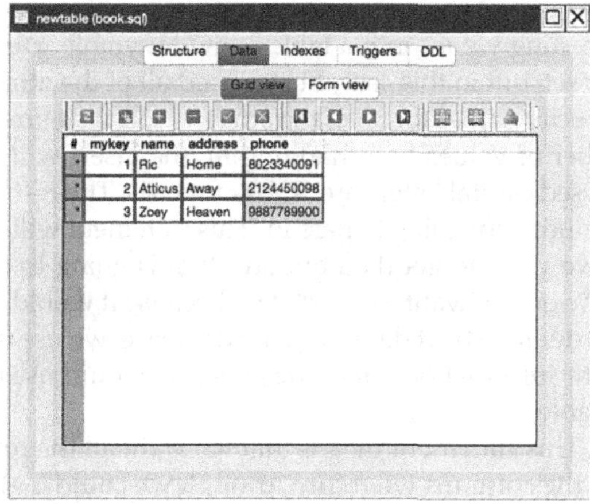

FIGURE 6.2

You will notice that each column has a name rather than a number. These are the attributes and they have names so we can refer to them. In order to create that table, we would use the following SQL.

```
CREATE TABLE mytable (
      mykey INTEGER PRIMARY KEY NOT NULL,
      name VARCHAR NOT NULL,
      addr VARCHAR NOT NULL,
      phone VARCHAR
);
```

You will notice that this looks an awful lot like English, which was really the point. We are going to create a table named mytable. The contents of the table are four attributes. The first attribute is called mykey and it is an integer, means that it is a whole number. This attribute cannot be blank, which means NOT NULL. If we were to try to insert a row without this value, the insert would fail. You will also note that it says PRIMARY KEY, which means, a

[1]The original specification for SQL clearly indicated that this was a set of initials, meaning it should properly be pronounced Ess-Queue-Ell. However, that is often ignored and, as noted, it is commonly pronounced sequel.

value that the row or tuple will be identified by. When you specify a value as being a primary key, each value must be unique. You cannot have multiple keys in a single table that all have the same value. Again, this would generate an error within the database. The other attributes within the table are all string values, referred to as a VARCHAR, which means a data type that has a variable number of characters. You can specify exactly how many characters the VARCHAR is constrained to, but in this case, the number of characters is unspecified.

We need to know the attribute names in order to do anything useful like putting data into the database. We do this with an INSERT statement. In order to insert a set of values into the database, the syntax for the INSERT statement would look like this:

```
INSERT INTO mytable (mykey, name, addr, phone) VALUES (4,
"Harold", "Colorado", "3034567765");
```

This means, we are inserting values into a table named mytable. We can limit the number of attributes we are going to set, but in this case, I have used all of the attribute names, which suggests that I am going to specify values for all of the attributes. If the number of attributes I specify does not match the number of values I am handing in, the insert will fail. The portions of the statements where I have used capital letters are SQL keywords. The rest is related to the structure of the database and the values I am going to pass in. This statement will add a row into our table. At some point, though, we want to get data out and that is going to be the common way we interact with databases. We do not want to insert data because it would corrupt the information, we are investigating. In order to extract data from the database, we use the SELECT statement. If we wanted to pull all of the information out of the table, we would use the following statement:

SELECT * FROM mytable;

It is really that simple. This statement means that we want all the rows and all the columns. We are not going to limit the columns we return, though we could. I also have not set a condition on the select statement, which means, we get all the rows that are available. If we wanted to limit the data we get back, we could alter the SELECT statement. Let us say, I wanted only the name and addr attributes where the key is bigger than 3. That query would look like this:

```
SELECT name, addr FROM mytable WHERE mykey > 3;
```

You may have noticed that I have a semi-colon at the end of each line. It is common to terminate SQL statements with a semi-colon. I can use a variety of matching conditions to indicate the data that I want to return from the table. Using different conditional clauses, we can get different results. You can use common conditionals like <, > or =, as well as some others that are geared toward specific data types like dates or strings.

You may think of databases as needing a server. The reality is that while databases do commonly use servers, meaning applications that manage the storage for a number of databases as well as the connections to the server from various clients. However, it is possible to use what is called an embedded database, which means that the storage management is embedded into the application and the databases are really just a collection of files on disk. This is commonly the case where browsers are concerned. One of the most popular embedded databases is called Sqlite and it is the one we will be using the most, since it is what Chrome and Firefox use to start with. There are a number of applications you can use to interact with these Sqlite databases depending on the operating system you use, including extensions for some browsers that you can use to open and query these database files, we are going to be working with. In terms of this chapter, I will be using a combination of tools, including the sqlite command line program.

WEB BROWSING

There are a number of Web browsers that are available across multiple operating systems. Many of these browsers work on multiple operating systems. We will be spending our time with four browsers and a little time on a fifth browser. First, we have to cover Internet Explorer. It is only used on the Windows operating system currently, though it used to be in development for other operating systems as well. Since, Windows is the predominant desktop operating system and Internet Explorer is still a significant player in the browser space, we have to cover it. Additionally, programs that use the underlying libraries that make Internet Explorer work may leave artifacts in the same places that Internet Explorer does.

The second browser that we need to cover is Chrome. Chrome runs on Windows, Linux and Mac OS X. There is also an open source version of Chrome called Chromium. Chromium will run on multiple operating systems and looks like Chrome, so the artifacts will look the same. Another open source-based browser is Firefox. Firefox uses the Gecko rendering engine (the component of the browser that takes the source code and makes it look like something) from the Mozilla Foundation. The same engine is in use by several other open source browsers. In addition, the primary browser used by Debian-based Linux distributions is Iceweasel, which is based on Firefox.

Finally, the last major browser to cover is Safari, developed by Apple for use on Mac OS X and Windows. Safari is included by default in Mac OS X, but it commonly comes in fourth in usage percentages Well below Safari in usage statistics is Opera, though it has long and a fairly loyal following. As a result, we will touch briefly on Opera over the course of this coverage.

Google Chrome

Google Chrome is a browser that runs on a wide variety of operating systems. Interestingly, many Web browsers have a shared history, when it comes to underlying components. Google took the WebKit engine from Apple, which created WebKit from a fork of an open source-rendering engine called KHTML. WebKit served as the foundation for Chrome until 2013, when Google began developing its own rendering engine that is based on a fork of WebKit. Google calls this new rendering engine Blink. In order to extend the functionality of Chrome, Google allows third party developers to create extensions, though it is far more controlled about what developers are allowed access to than Firefox, which began using add-ons before Chrome even existed.

In terms of configuration settings and user-related details, we will be looking at Sqlite3 databases. What I did not mention earlier is that in addition to being a Web browser, Chrome is an application delivery platform. Instead of having to develop standalone applications, you can develop applications to be displayed inside of Chrome. All installation, updating, and management is done inside of Chrome. The reason for mentioning this is because there are some applications that can be used to view Sqlite databases inside Chrome. One of them, TadpoleDB, uses Chrome to deliver an interface to the tadpoledb.com Web site. You can upload your Sqlite databases through the client interface displayed in Chrome and then browse the data, which includes executing queries. For our purposes, since this is potentially personal or sensitive information, I am going to stay local and use a native client rather than uploading a database to a remote website.

TABLE 6.1 Chrome Database Locations by Operating System

Operating system	Path
Windows XP	C:\Documents and Settings\username\Local Settings\Application Data\Google\Chrome\User Data\Default\Preferences
Windows Vista and above	C:\Users\username\AppData\Local\Google\Chrome\User Data\Default\Preferences
Mac OS X	/Users/username/Library/Application Support/Google/Chrome/Default/Preferences
Linux	/home/username/.config/google-chrome/Default/Preferences

Chrome stores the important information in different places depending on the operating system. Table 6.1 indicates the directory path you can look for the user-specific databases for each operating system.

The preferences file is a plain text file. It has a clear format that can be discerned by looking at it and fields are named in such a way that you may be able to either easily determine or at least guess what they mean. Below is a section from the preferences file on a Windows 7 system. This particular section refers to the login status with Google, including the username that was used to authenticate. One thing about Chrome is that once you are logged in with Google, you can sync various settings and preferences across different instances of Chrome on different systems, if you are logging in with the same Google credentials. Further down in the file, you can see the different capabilities that sync with Google including apps, bookmarks, passwords, preferences, and themes. This not only means that you have a consistent experience across different instances of Chrome on different systems, but also that you are storing all of this information with Google, so it can be pushed down to the different systems you are using Chrome on.

```
"google": {
   "services": {
      "signin": {
         "CLIENT_LOGIN_STATUS": {

      "time": "Wednesday, March 26, 2014",
      "value": "Successful"
   },
   "GET_USER_INFO_STATUS": {
      "time": "Wednesday, March 26, 2014",
      "value": "Successful"
   },
   "LSID": "",
   "OAUTH_LOGIN_STATUS": {
      "time": "Wednesday, March 26, 2014",
      "value": "Successful"
   },
   "SID": "",
   "SIGNIN_TYPE": {
      "time": "Wednesday, March 26, 2014",
      "value": "Signin with credentials"
   },
   "USERNAME": "ric@cloudroy.com"
},
```

There are a number of files in the default directory and some of them are actually databases, though it may not be immediately apparent that they are databases. When you open up the history file, you get to see how the database is constructed, including the schema. The schema, which you can see for the history database in Figure 6.3, is a description of the data carried in the database. This includes the tables in the database as well as the attributes or columns in each of the tables. While there are several tools we could use for this, I am using one called SqliteBrowser. It will open up local Sqlite databases and provide us a visual look at the database and its contents.

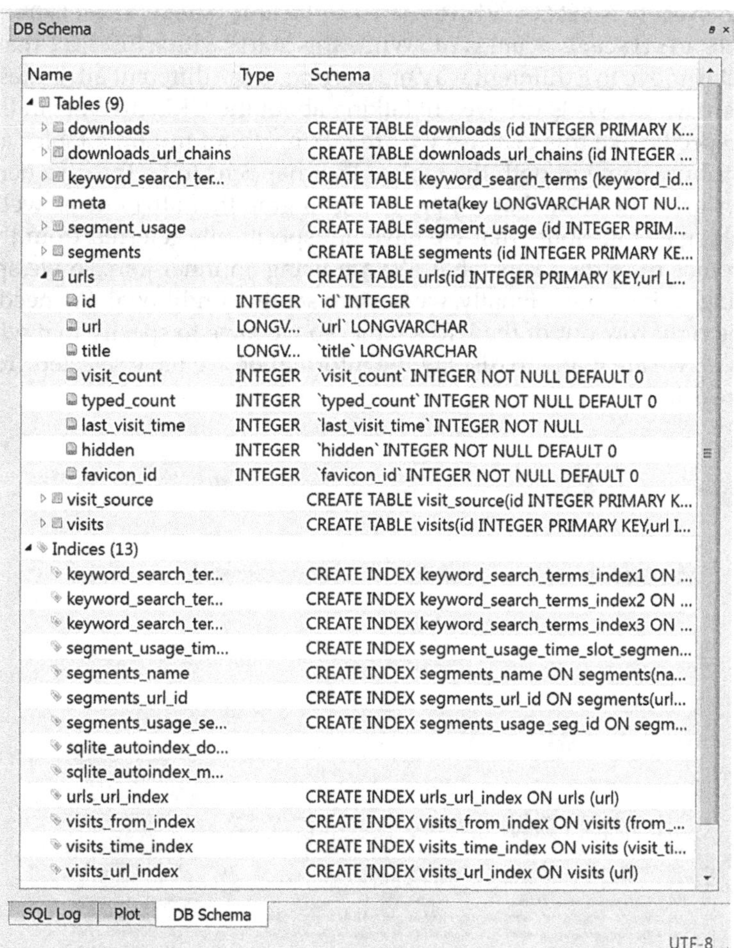

FIGURE 6.3

Using a visual browser like the one we are using, we can drill into the data. Using just the visual approach, though, will only get us so far. One of the ways that SQL databases are commonly used is having data from one table refer to data from another table. In Figure 6.4, we can see the visits table. The piece we are missing from this is the actual URL that has been visited. In place of the URL, we have a number. This number refers to a row in the URLs table that is also part of this particular database. We need a way to link those two values. This requires performing a SQL query, so we can join the two tables. There are a number of joins that are available, depending on how you want to pull the information together. What we are going to do is to use an inner join, which means that we are going to pull the information from both tables based on specific criteria because we need to know the actual URL from the URLs table, rather than just the URL ID that is available in the visits table.

This requires slightly some more complicated SQL syntax than we have seen before. What we are going to execute is `SELECT visits.url, urls.url, visit_time FROM visits INNER JOIN urls WHERE visits.url = urls.id`. While this starts with a SELECT that was covered earlier, we quickly move to a different way of referring to the different attributes in each table. In the case where we say visits.url, we are talking about the URL attribute in the visits table. We have to be specific like this because we are talking about multiple tables and there may be the same attribute name in both the tables. That happens to be the case here, so, we also have to say urls.url to be clear that we are going to grab that attribute as well. We indicate that we are pulling any attribute that we have not specifically referred from the visits table, so visit_time comes from the visits table. We are using an inner join, so we specifically say that we are doing an inner join. Finally, we have to set the conditional. We need to make sure that we pull the right row out of the URLs table, so we have to specify that where, visits.url is equal to urls.id, we are going to display the information we have selected. You can see the results in Figure 6.4.

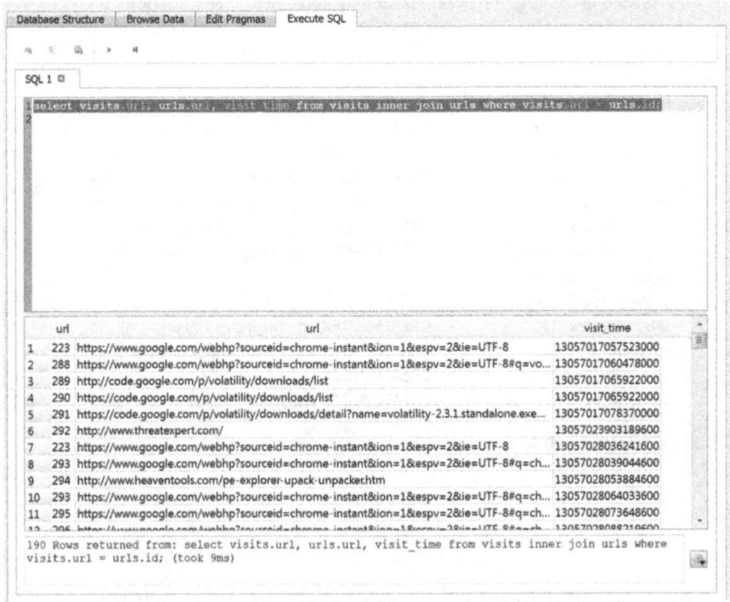

FIGURE 6.4

These sorts of SQL queries can be challenging, especially if you are not sure what fields across the two tables map together. Keep in mind that the key field is the unique identifier and that unique identifier is going to be the one used as an identifier in other tables. In the case that we looked before, the URL field in the visits table refers to the ID field in the URLs table. That ID field is the unique identifier that we can use to grab the text from the URLs table, since that is where we get the information that will actually make some sense to us. These joins are necessary to save space. Why use space to put the same information in multiple tables, when you can refer to information stored in one table.

The Structured Query Language was developed for relational databases. A relational database is used to relate pieces of information, so you can be more flexible in how you use the data you have. Being able to pull data from multiple tables and combine it through related information is the power of these databases. Well-structured databases allow you to make connections that would be harder to make just looking at the information in a flat manner.

One area we should talk about here because we saw it in the results of this query. We can see the time the URL was visited. The first URL visited in our results was visited at 13057017057523000. You may not recognize it but that is a time. There are a number of different time formats. A common one is the UNIX Epoch time, measured as the amount of time in seconds or milliseconds from January 1, 1970, which is considered to be beginning of the UNIX Epoch. There are a number of ways to perform that conversion including the Web site www.epochconverter.com. This particular timestamp, though, is not based on the UNIX epoch. Instead, it goes back much further. The timestamp is a 64-bit integer value that does not start with epoch time. It indicates the number of seconds since midnight on 1/1/1601 UTC.

The thing about SQL is that there are often a number of ways to execute queries to get the same sort of information. Where we did a specific join above, we can do a query that is not a specific join but still joins the tables. We can also have SQL to perform the date conversion for us. The following query will extract the information we need and simultaneously give us a human readable time.

```
SELECT datetime(((visits.visit_time/1000000)-11644473600),
"unixepoch"), visits.url, urls.url, urls.title FROM urls, visits
WHERE urls.id = visits.url;
```

The value 11644473600 is the number of seconds since January 1, 1601. We subtract that value off and we end up with the amount of time between UNIX epoch time and the real time, which can easily be converted using the datetime function. When we run this query, we end up with a list very similar to what we had before, but we have human readable dates. This query also throws in the title from the URL, which we had not pulled before. You can see the results of this query in Figure 6.5.

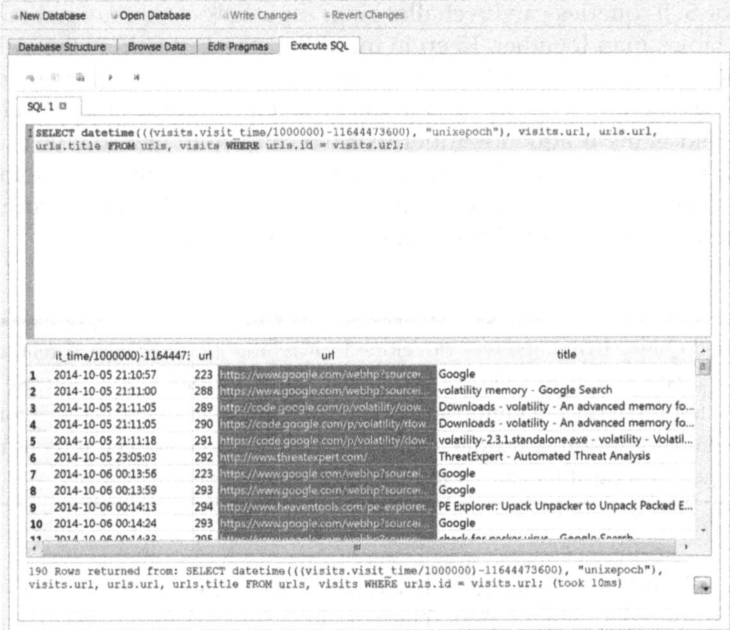

FIGURE 6.5

There are, of course, a number of databases that may be worth investigating. The following are database files that are stored within the same default directory that the history database is stored in (Table 6.2).

Internet Explorer

Internet Explorer is Microsoft's Web browser that is now only available with their Windows operating system, though it used to run on Mac OS, Solaris and other operating systems. Internet Explorer has evolved over time, especially as use of the Internet has changed and increased. We are now storing a lot more information about use and we need good ways to retrieve that information. Just as with Chrome, we have to keep track of cookies, history, and pages that have been visited. This requires several files and those file types have changed over time and certainly the locations of the files has changed with different versions of Windows.

Web Cache

The cache is the storage of files that have been retrieved from the Web. We cache the files primarily to speed up our browsing. Each page can set a cache control value indicating how long a life the page should have. This helps us determine which pages may be dynamic and which may be more static. In cases, where the cache control is set fairly high, we do not have

TABLE 6.2 Chrome Databases

File	Description
Cookies	Stores the cookie details from Web sessions
Favicons	Stores the icon associated with a Web site that shows up in the address bar after the connection with the site has been made.
History	Stores the browsing history
Logins	Stores login information from Web sites that have been visited
Network action predictor	Used to speed up rendering of pages
Origin bound certs	Stores information related to transport layer security (TLS) certificates
QuotaManager	Stores information related to the quota manager, that handles quota for various application programming interfaces (API)
Shortcuts	Provides hints about how to fill in the omni box when you start typing.
Top sites	Provides URLs for sites that have been visited a lot in order to populate the top sites page.
Web data	Stores information about data that has been put into Web forms for retrieval later.
Web RTC Identity Store	Stores information about communications services that make use of the Web real time communication API.

to bother wasting time with requests because we expect it will not be changing. Instead, we pull the content off our disk, which is considerably faster, we hope. Every browser maintains a cache of pages, images, and other files that have been downloaded from servers around the Internet. In the case of Internet Explorer, the Web cache changed in IE 10. Before that, Microsoft used the cache file format. With IE 10, Microsoft began using the extensible storage engine database file (EDB) format. This moved the cache into a database and away from more of a flat file model.

You can easily find the cache files themselves and search through them on the file system, or you can find the EDB file on the hard drive and analyze it to locate the specific files that you may find relevant, based on their URL and modification times. The database stores all of that information, as well as the location of the cache file. The cache file will have a different name than the file name that was stored on the server. If the file on the server was called aliishot.jpg, for example, that does not mean that the file in the Web cache will also be stored with that name, so we need a way of looking up the data based on the URL and then finding the file name on the file system. Fortunately, there are tools that are capable of doing that and you do not even need to figure out the structure and format of the EDB file on the disk. You can use a tool like Nirsoft's IECacheView to look at the cache on your system. You can see the results of running IECacheView in Figure 6.6.

The cache viewer shows the file name on our file system, as well as the modification time and date, which means that the time, the file was stored or was last touched. This may include updating the timeout value on the cache. This is also a value that is stored in the database, by the way. You can see when the cached file is expected to expire and needs to be refreshed.

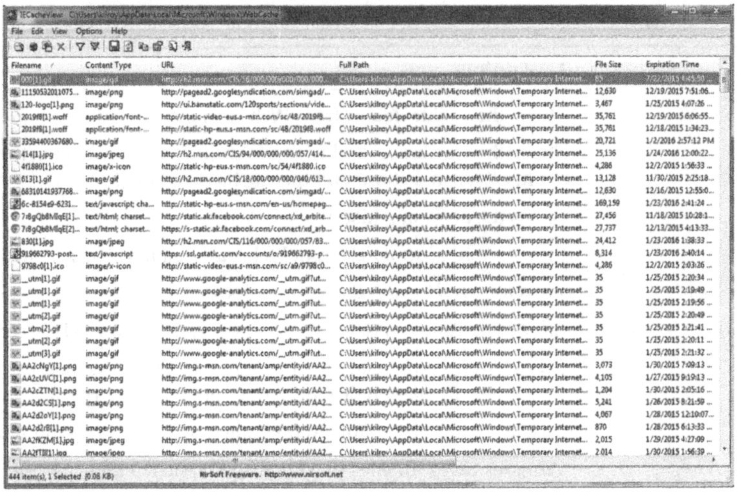

FIGURE 6.6

Of course, your system does not wait until the very last moment of that timeout value, before refreshing the file. Instead, it performs checks partway through the valid time.

The Web cache is stored in *C:\Users\%USER%\AppData\Local\Microsoft\Windows\WebCache* for IE 10. Replace %USER% with the actual name of the user in the file path. On older systems, you would use *C:\Documents and Settings\%username%\Local Settings\Temporary Internet Files\Content.ie5,* again replacing %username% with the name of the user you are trying to analyze. If you are using a version of IE prior to 10 but you are using Windows Vista or Windows 7, you would go to *C:\Users\%username%\AppData\Local Settings\Microsoft\Temporary Internet Files* to get to the Web cache. On a Windows 8 system, it would be located in C:\Users\%username%\AppData\Local\Microsoft\Windows\NetCache.

Cookies

Every time you visit a Web page, there are small pieces of data that are exchanged between your system and the Web server. This is a way of tracking you and making sure you get the experience, you want related to that Web site. As an example, if you go to weather.com and look up the weather for your location, you may well want to see that same weather each time you visit the page, so you do not have to keep looking it up every time. As a result, the Web server will ask your client to store a small piece of information, called a cookie, on your file system, so when the Web server asks again, your system can return it. These cookies have the potential to store a lot of information. At a minimum, it will store a reference to a website that a user had visited.

Again, we rely on Nirsoft for a tool that will open the cache file. They have a free tool called IECookieViewer that you can see in Figure 6.7. Each line in the upper pane shows you the various cookies that are available, including the site they have been generated from. Each cookie, though, can have several values with it so when you select one of the cookies, you can see the key/value pairs in the lower pane. Much of this information may not be very useful to us because it probably looks random. In the case of authentication cookies, where a user needs to indicate that they have actually authenticated to a server, they should be random so they cannot easily be predicted or duplicated.

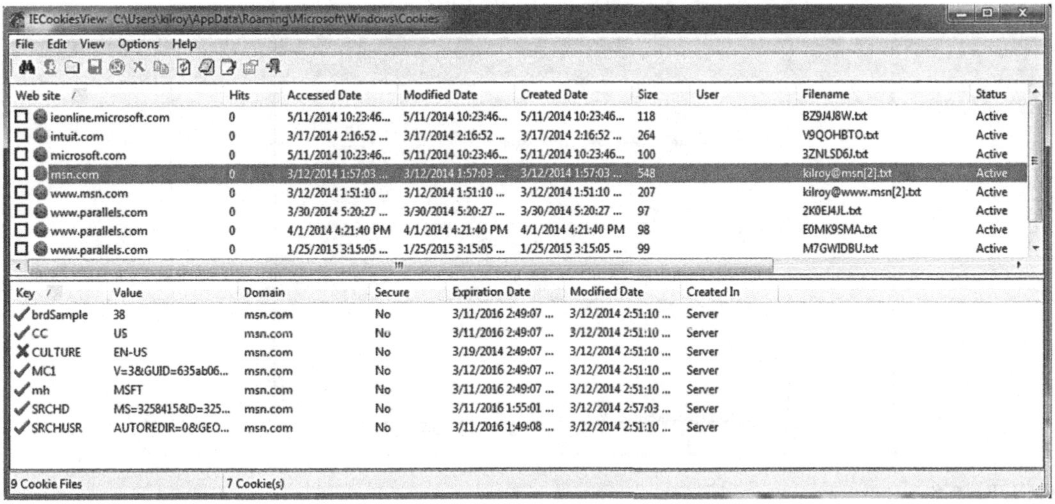

FIGURE 6.7

Having a utility like this to pull the cookies off the disk is very helpful, especially if, as in the case of this one, it can be run from an external USB stick. There are no external libraries that are required and no existing registry keys so there is no installer. It is a standalone executable file that can be stored on a USB stick and carried to any device you want to analyze. The same is true for the previous Nirsoft utility we analyzed.

With Windows 7, the cookie location is in

C:\Users\%username%\AppData\Roaming\Microsoft\Windows\Cookies. This is changed in Windows 8. With Windows 8 and 8.1, the location is now *C:\Users\%username%\AppData\Microsoft\Windows\INetCookies*. With Windows XP, they were stored with the temporary Internet files in *C:\Documents and Settings\%username%\Local Settings\Temporary Internet Files*.

History

Of course, knowing where a user has been visiting is important. Assuming the history has not been cleared, you can use a number of tools to get the history of the user from a system. Again, Nirsoft comes to the rescue for us. We can use BrowsingHistoryView to get the data from Internet Explorer, as well as other common Internet browsers. You can see the startup dialog in Figure 6.8, asking which browsers I want to check for history. Once you have selected your browsers, the tool will extract all the history and display it. The history will show locations as well as access times that can be used to generate a timeline of activities.

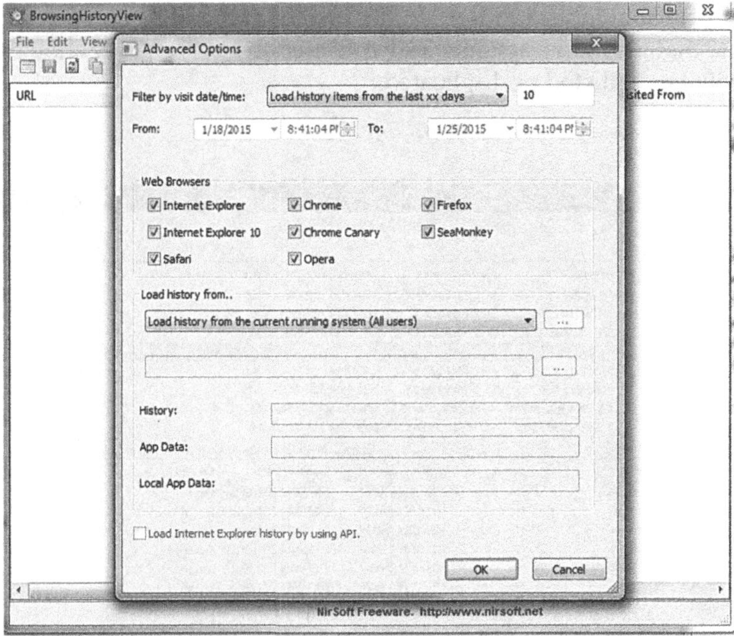

FIGURE 6.8

The location of the history has changed with different versions of Internet Explorer as well as with different versions of Windows. Under Windows XP, the history was stored in *C:\Documents and Settings\%username%\Local Settings\History*. With Windows Vista, the location of the history changed to

C:\Users\%username%\AppData\Local\Microsoft\Windows\History.

You will notice that the history location falls under the Windows directory and not the Internet Explorer directory. This is because Windows keeps track of all history including files and Web sites that have been visited.

Up until Internet Explorer, Microsoft used the index.dat file as a database of information related to browsing history. If you are investigating Internet Explorer 9 or earlier, you can use a variety of tools to read the index.dat.

Safari

Apple replaced the default browser in Mac OS X in 2003 with Safari, a browser developed internally at Apple. Prior to Safari, Apple was shipping Mac OS X with Netscape and, for a period of time, Internet Explorer. Safari does not only run on Mac OS X, however. It will also run on Windows systems. As with most applications under Mac OS X, the data for Safari is stored under an application-specific directory within the users library folder. Safari data is stored in /Users/username/Library/Safari. Just like other browsers, we have specific information that we want to track – history and cache for a start. Additionally, Safari keeps

TABLE 6.3 Safari Data Locations by Operating System

Artifact	Operating system	Location
Cache	Mac OS	/Users/$USER/Library/Caches/com.apple.Safari
Cache	Windows XP	C:\Documents and Settings\%USERNAME%\Local Settings\Application Data\Apple Computer\Safari\
Cache	Windows 7	C:\Users\%USERNAME%\AppData\Local\Apple Computer\Safari\
History	Mac OS X	/Users/$USER/Library/Safari/History.plist
History	Windows XP	C:\Documents and Settings\%USERNAME%\Application Data\Apple Computer\Safari\History.plist
History	Windows 7	C:\Users\%USERNAME%\ AppData\Roaming\Apple Computer\Safari\History.plist
Downloads	Mac OS X	/Users/$USER/Library/Safari/Downloads.plist
Downloads	Windows XP	C:\Documents and Settings\%USERNAME%\Application Data\Apple Computer\Safari\Downloads.plist
Downloads	Windows 7	C:\Users\%USERNAME%\ AppData\Roaming\Apple Computer\Safari\Downloads.plist

track of the last browsing session, which would be the list of tabs that were open and the sites they were open to. Safari will also have a list of files that had been downloaded. Table 6.3 shows the location of the different files that Safari maintains. The table lists the file locations by operating system.

The plist files are binary property lists. There are a number of tools that may be used to open those files, including Xcode, provided by Apple for Mac OS X as a development platform. Other tools like Plist Pad will run on Windows and work with XML plist files but do not support binary plists. Since this is the format for these files associated with Safari, this particular tool is not as helpful, so it is necessary to know whether the tool you are trying will support binary plists as well as XML plists.

The cache, however, is stored as a Sqlite database. You can read this using any Sqlite browser. You can see one of the tables in Figure 6.9. The database keeps track of all of the cache entries. The entries themselves are stored in the fsCachedData directory underneath the directory, where the Cache.db file is stored, depending on the operating system where the data is located.

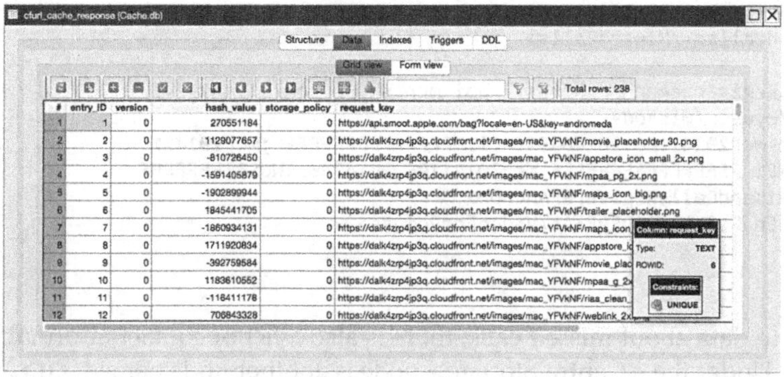

FIGURE 6.9

In the case of the history, the date and time of the access of the file is stored as the number of seconds since January 1, 2001 at 00:00:00 UTC. Outside of the typical browsing history, cache and downloads, there are also plist files for the last session in a file called LastSession.plist and the top sites, which is a small number of pages that are commonly accessed. This list of pages can be displayed on a new tab in Safari. The list of top sites is also stored in a binary plist file called TopSites.plist.

MESSAGING SERVICES

There are a large number of messaging services available and there are also a number of multi-protocol clients that will aggregate services connections into a single client. One significant messaging service is Google Hangouts that previously had some other names. Hangouts does not require a client, though. It runs completely through a Web browser, which means all of the content regarding friends lists and conversational content is stored with Google's servers.

Skype is also a messaging service that has additional features like video and audio communication. Skype has a long history but at the moment, it is owned by Microsoft and offers messaging as well as voice and video to clients. Because it can send messages and also has a list of contacts, it is worthwhile to take a look at the data that is being stored. On a Windows system, we would be looking at C:\Users\<username>\AppData\Roaming\Skype\<skypeuser> where you replace <username> and <skypeuser> with the actual user values you are looking for. Under Mac OS X, the information would be stored under /Users/<username>/Library/Application Support/Skype/<skypeuser>. The primary database is named main.db.

One of the first things, we will be looking for, is the list of contacts. In the case of Skype, data is stored in a couple of different formats. The first one, we will be looking at, is the XML configuration file named config.xml. In addition to configuration data, this file also stores information about missed calls as well as servers that the client will talk to. Here is a snippet from the config.xml file, showing the registrar server for missed calls.

```
    <Call>

<DPC>41030501410203027469 6D6B6176616E61676831000003A2DDD99B050501
```

In addition to data about missed calls, there is also a list of contact information within the config.xml file. Under the <CentralStorage> node is another node named <u>, where there is a list of contacts that the user has stored. There are also timestamps stored in the config.xml file indicating connection times. The timestamps in config.xml are stored in Unix timestamp format. There are a number of places to convert the timestamp into a human readable form. For example, the timestamp 1419731534 converts to Sun, 28 Dec 2014 01:52:14 GMT using the Web site www.onlineconverters.com. This particular value comes from the <ConnectivityTimestamp> node, indicating the last time this particular system connected to the Skype network.

Aside from the xml file, Skype uses Sqlite to store additional data. There are a handful of database files. The most interesting database is called main.db. Inside main.db, there are number of tables including tables for contacts and calls. You can see the complete list of the tables that are in the database in Figure 6.10.

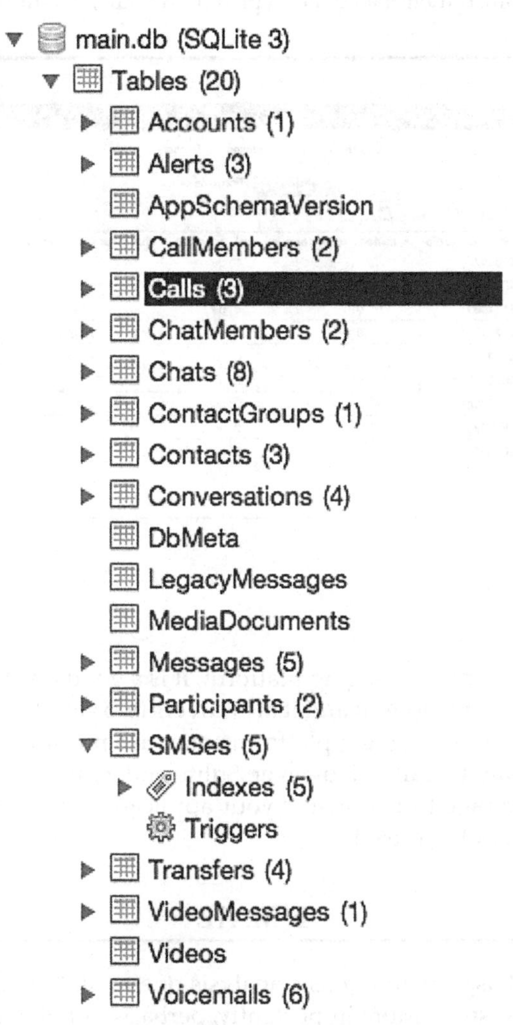

FIGURE 6.10

While there are other database files in the user's Skype directory, the one where you will get nearly all of the interesting information is this main.db database file. From here, we can also get the list of contacts that were cached in the config.xml file. We can also get a list of accounts associated with this particular installation. You can also get a list of calls and conversations. You can see a list of calls in Figure 6.11. This includes starting times, also stored in Unix timestamp format. The calls table also stores information about whether the call was a conference call and the other participants who were involved in the call. You can also get an indication of whether there were call quality problems.

One of the challenges moving forward in many aspects of forensics is the matter of encryption. If data is encrypted, particularly when it comes to databases, it will be difficult to retrieve. Fortunately, Skype has maintained their data unencrypted for a while, making it much easier to retrieve information.

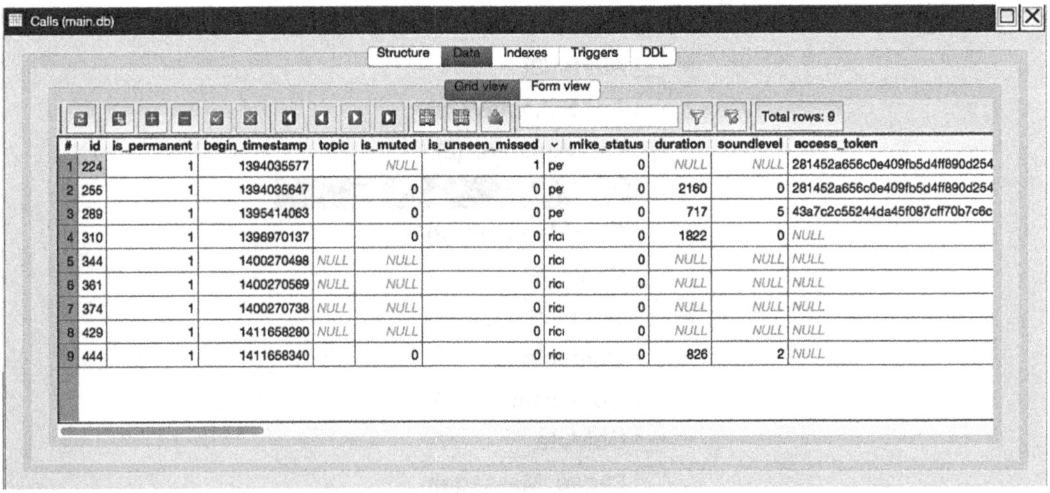

Calls (main.db)

Structure | Data | Indexes | Triggers | DDL

Grid view | Form view

Total rows: 9

#	id	is_permanent	begin_timestamp	topic	is_muted	is_unseen_missed	⌄	mike_status	duration	soundlevel	access_token
1	224	1	1394035577		NULL	1	pe	0	NULL	NULL	281452a656c0e409fb5d4ff890d254
2	255	1	1394035647		0	0	pe	0	2160	0	281452a656c0e409fb5d4ff890d254
3	289	1	1395414063		0	0	pe	0	717	5	43a7c2c55244da45f087cff70b7c6c
4	310	1	1396970137		0	0	rici	0	1822	0	NULL
5	344	1	1400270498	NULL	NULL	0	rici	0	NULL	NULL	NULL
6	361	1	1400270569	NULL	NULL	0	rici	0	NULL	NULL	NULL
7	374	1	1400270738	NULL	NULL	0	rici	0	NULL	NULL	NULL
8	429	1	1411658280	NULL	NULL	0	rici	0	NULL	NULL	NULL
9	444	1	1411658340		0	0	rici	0	826	2	NULL

FIGURE 6.11

While Skype is not the only messaging platform, it is a good one to cover the possible artifacts that may be interesting to look at and it also covers two significant data formats that may be commonly in use. Other messaging platforms may use proprietary storage techniques or they may simply use plain text files. However, Sqlite and XML are widely used because it is very easy to embed a storage format inside your application from existing libraries without having to put a lot of work in yourself.

E-MAIL

There are a couple of aspects to forensic analysis of e-mail. The first is simply finding the storage files on the file system. More importantly, perhaps, is being able to investigate the e-mail messages. The reason, this is more important because e-mail is easy to fake. Being able to read through the headers of an e-mail message is critical to be able to understand what is happening with an e-mail message. Where did it come from? What about the e-mail address and the source system? There are some things that can be faked and others that are impossible to fake because of the way the network works. I can pretend to be anything that I want but when it comes to tracking the Internet Protocol (IP) address the messages come from, that is up to the server and if one system makes a connection to another, the receiving system has to know the real IP address of the connecting system or else messages would not get back to the connecting system and the communication will simply fail.

There are different formats for mail files, depending on the client. Clients that have an older heritage may use what is called an mbox format. The mbox format was originated on UNIX systems and leaves messages intact. The mbox format is strictly text-based, where messages get appended to an existing file, including all of the headers, since the message is maintained in Internet message format. The very first header indicates that the start of a new message is a From: header. There are a number of viewers available for the mbox format, since it is been around for so long. In fact, a large number of e-mail clients are capable of reading in from the mbox format. Since it is a text format, it is also easy to read in any plain text viewer.

Once you have a message, you need to know how to read it, so let us take a look at a spam message that I have received recently and pull it apart. The following are headers from a message that showed up in my Junk folder that appears to come from one of my cousins. At least the name is correct, though the e-mail address is certainly not and many of the other headers simply make no sense and do not connect up well.

```
Received: from BLUPR05MB008.namprd05.prod.outlook.com
(10.255.210.155) by
 BL2PR05MB004.namprd05.prod.outlook.com (10.255.228.153) with
Microsoft SMTP
 Server (TLS) id 15.1.59.20 via Mailbox Transport; Mon, 19 Jan
2015 12:59:27
 +0000
Received: from CO2PR05CA011.namprd05.prod.outlook.com
(10.141.241.139) by
 BLUPR05MB008.namprd05.prod.outlook.com (10.255.210.155) with
Microsoft SMTP
 Server (TLS) id 15.1.59.20; Mon, 19 Jan 2015 12:59:26 +0000
Received: from BN1AFFO11FD017.protection.gbl
(2a01:111:f400:7c10::176) by
 CO2PR05CA011.outlook.office365.com (2a01:111:e400:1429::11) with
Microsoft
 SMTP Server (TLS) id 15.1.59.20 via Frontend Transport; Mon, 19
Jan 2015
 12:59:25 +0000
Received: from tucker.diecastwings.net (162.216.5.96) by
 BN1AFFO11FD017.mail.protection.outlook.com (10.58.52.77) with
Microsoft SMTP
 Server (TLS) id 15.1.59.14 via Frontend Transport; Mon, 19 Jan
2015 12:59:24
 +0000
Received: from [113.190.190.40] (port=1518
helo=hollandfarmcsa.com)
      by tucker.diecastwings.net with esmtpa (Exim 4.84)
      (envelope-from <marcy@hollandfarmcsa.com>)
      id 1YDBv2-00055f-0a; Mon, 19 Jan 2015 07:59:01 -0500
```

```
Subject: From  Peter Staubach
From: Peter Staubach <marcy@hollandfarmcsa.com>
     boundary="Apple-Mail-7447E604-0B4F-3580-F3CB-3386EB49A6D1"
X-Mailer: iPhone Mail (11D257)
Message-ID: <35af50299531$162a32fe$ebf9e5ec$@hollandfarmcsa.com>
Date: Fri, 19 Dec 2014 01:58:46 +0000
To: messages@redacted.com
MIME-Version: 1.0 (1.0)
X-AntiAbuse: This header was added to track abuse, please include
it with any abuse report
X-AntiAbuse: Primary Hostname - tucker.diecastwings.net
X-AntiAbuse: Original Domain - nothing.com
X-AntiAbuse: Originator/Caller UID/GID - [47 12] / [47 12]
X-AntiAbuse: Sender Address Domain - hollandfarmcsa.com
X-Get-Message-Sender-Via: tucker.diecastwings.net:
authenticated_id: marcy@hollandfarmcsa.com
X-Source:
X-Source-Args:
X-Source-Dir:
Return-Path: marcy@hollandfarmcsa.com
X-EOPAttributedMessage: 0
X-MS-Exchange-Organization-MessageDirectionality: Incoming
Received-SPF: None (protection.outlook.com: hollandfarmcsa.com
does not
 designate permitted sender hosts)
Authentication-Results: spf=none (sender IP is 162.216.5.96)
 smtp.mailfrom=marcy@hollandfarmcsa.com;
X-Forefront-Antispam-Report:
CIP:162.216.5.96;CTRY:;IPV:NLI;EFV:NLI;SFV:SPM;SFS:(428002)(19900
3)(189002)(46102003)(110306001)(16236675004)(46816001)(45086001)(
50986999)(19617315012)(33646002)(2441003)(93146003)(104016003)(15
975445007)(16799955002)(50226001)(106466001)(15188155005)(5643440
04)(107886001)(71366001)(229853001)(36756003)(6806004)(2171001)(8
7836001)(512954002)(2521001)(84326002)(101416001)(64706001)(10558
6002)(19580395003)(92566002)(450100001)(62966003)(86362001)(77156
002)(512874002)(99676004);DIR:INB;SFP:;SCL:5;SRVR:BLUPR05MB008;H:
tucker.diecastwings.net;FPR:;SPF:None;MLV:ovrspm;PTR:tucker.dieca
stwings.net;A:1;MX:1;LANG:en;
X-MS-Exchange-Organization-Network-Message-Id: 247bb865-2708-
4f29-b119-08d201fee3ab
X-DmarcAction-Test: None
X-Microsoft-Antispam: UriScan:;
X-Microsoft-Antispam:
BCL:0;PCL:0;RULEID:(3005004);SRVR:BLUPR05MB008;
X-MS-Exchange-Organization-AVStamp-Service: 1.0
X-Exchange-Antispam-Report-Test: UriScan:(120078557341701);
X-Exchange-Antispam-Report-CFA-Test:
BCL:0;PCL:0;RULEID:(601004)(2003001)(2001001);SRVR:BLUPR05MB008;
X-MS-Exchange-Organization-SCL: 5
X-Exchange-Antispam-Report-CFA-Test:
BCL:0;PCL:0;RULEID:;SRVR:BLUPR05MB008;
X-MS-Exchange-CrossTenant-OriginalArrivalTime: 19 Jan 2015
12:59:24.6183
 (UTC)
X-MS-Exchange-CrossTenant-Id: 16eac45c-b554-4ddd-ba6c-
8370ef247262
```

```
X-MS-Exchange-CrossTenant-FromEntityHeader: Internet
X-MS-Exchange-Transport-CrossTenantHeadersStamped: BLUPR05MB008
X-MS-Exchange-Organization-AuthSource:
BN1AFFO11FD017.protection.gbl
X-MS-Exchange-Organization-AuthAs: Anonymous
X-MS-Exchange-Transport-EndToEndLatency: 00:00:03.4412772
Content-type: multipart/alternative;
     boundary="B_3504974971_4322447"
```

The first thing to look at is the message path. This is indicated by the list of received headers. This shows you all of the simple message transfer protocol (SMTP) servers, the e-mail has come through. SMTP is the protocol used to send messages from the sender to the mail server where the recipient's mailbox is located. The mail server we are most interested in is the one at the very bottom of the stack. This is the very first server that was contacted by the sender, so itis the one closest to the people who sent the message. It will also indicate the address that contacted the SMTP server. According to this header, the message was received from the IP address 113.190.190.40. We can figure out where this IP address is in a number of different ways. The first is to use a whois lookup. If you have a Mac OS X system or a Linux system, you can use the whois utility that comes with your OS. You can also go to a Web site like Geek Tools (www.geektools.com) and use the whois link there. According to whois, the IP address belongs in Vietnam. This is a flag since I know my cousin does not live in, nor he has been to Vietnam.

If we want to know specifically where the IP address is located, we can use another Web site that will give us a geographic location. There are a number of Web sites that will do this and the locations are not always exact because they rely on metadata that would be provided by service providers. However, they are reasonably accurate so we can use the IP address we have and plug it in. According to geoiptool.com, the IP address in question is the city of Dung in the region of Thanh Hoa in Vietnam. Based on the whois information, we know that the IP address in question belongs to the Vietnam Post and Telecom Corporation. If this was a company that might respond to a subpoena or other legal document, we could contact the company and get further information about the IP address at the time of the e-mail message.

We do have some additional places we can look. First, we can check the SMTP server that was first to receive the message. It claims to be tucker.diecastwings.net and the IP address there is 162.216.5.96. I can do a lookup of the IP address and it does resolve to tucker.diecastwings.net so that matches and appears legitimate. Beyond that, we can check domain names that show up in the headers. The only one is hollandfarmcsa.com. This is not always the case in message headers like this but it happens to be here. In a legitimate set of message headers, you will get all legitimate information but sometimes, you need to dig a little. We can look up the domain name hollandfarmcsa.com by using whois. According to the information whois provides, it belongs to someone named Marcelyn in Deerfield, NH. This would make sense, considering the e-mail address this appears to be from is marcy@hollandfarmcsa.net.

What have we learned from this? We can determine where the message originated. If we wanted, we could look up all of the intermediate SMTP servers that have handled this message. In this case, it is a lot of different servers in the Microsoft infrastructure, as it gets passed through to the server where e-mail sent to me is stored. This is, in part, because of the spam filtering Microsoft does on messages hosted with them. If you pass through several anti-virus or spam filtering gateways, you will generally see those IP addresses show up in the received list.

So far, we have talked about text-based storage and investigation. Not all mail clients store their messages in text-based formats. In the case of Outlook, for example, local storage is in what Microsoft calls personal folders. These are commonly stored in .pst files in the directory of each user. There are also .ost files that are used for offline storage in the case of connections to an exchange server.

There are a number of tools that will read the .pst files and provide you with the contents. One of them is a utility that extracts the .pst file and puts them into an mbox format. You can see the process of using readpst in Figure 6.12. This is a Linux utility and the output is a set of mbox files stored in the directory that you specify. Once the messages are in mbox form, they are in plain text and can be read with any plain text viewer. If you are on Linux and are inclined to write programs, there is a library that will read PST files. This is the library that was used to create readpst. The output from the tool is here, though the e-mail messages we are looking at are nearly two decades old. You can see the boundaries indicating that libPST was used to create the file.

```
From "Gumby316@aol.com" Fri Aug 28 22:13:31 1998
Status: RO
From: Gumby316@aol.com <Gumby316@aol.com>
Subject: hi
To: rosie@washere.com
Date: Sat, 29 Aug 1998 02:13:31 +0000
Message-Id: <a190aa9.35e763cb@aol.com>>
MIME-Version: 1.0
Content-Type: multipart/mixed;
        boundary="--boundary-LibPST-iamunique-1582081564_-_-"


----boundary-LibPST-iamunique-1582081564_-_-
Content-Type: text/plain; charset="windows-1252"

are you the rosie that has here own show


----boundary-LibPST-iamunique-1582081564_-_---

From "Bayrdgmom@aol.com" Fri Aug 28 19:13:10 1998
Status: RO
From: Bayrdgmom@aol.com <Bayrdgmom@aol.com>
Subject: please respond to e-mail dated 8/27/98
To: rosie@washere.com
Date: Fri, 28 Aug 1998 23:13:10 +0000
Message-Id: <cabe9dd3.35e73986@aol.com>>
MIME-Version: 1.0
Content-Type: multipart/mixed;
        boundary="--boundary-LibPST-iamunique-127938372_-_-"
```

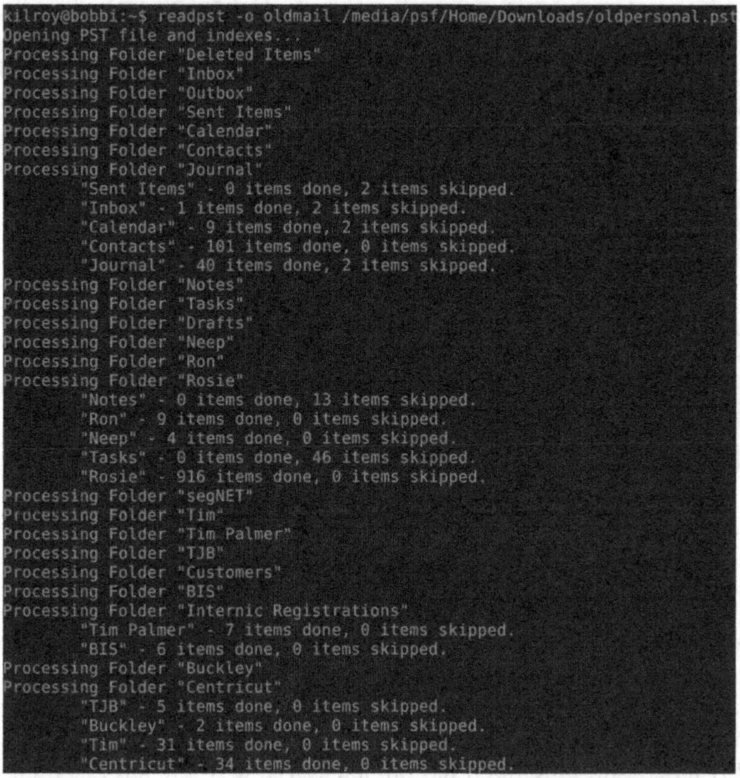

```
kilroy@bobbi:~$ readpst -o oldmail /media/psf/Home/Downloads/oldpersonal.pst
Opening PST file and indexes...
Processing Folder "Deleted Items"
Processing Folder "Inbox"
Processing Folder "Outbox"
Processing Folder "Sent Items"
Processing Folder "Calendar"
Processing Folder "Contacts"
Processing Folder "Journal"
        "Sent Items" - 0 items done, 2 items skipped.
        "Inbox" - 1 items done, 2 items skipped.
        "Calendar" - 9 items done, 2 items skipped.
        "Contacts" - 101 items done, 0 items skipped.
        "Journal" - 40 items done, 2 items skipped.
Processing Folder "Notes"
Processing Folder "Tasks"
Processing Folder "Drafts"
Processing Folder "Neep"
Processing Folder "Ron"
Processing Folder "Rosie"
        "Notes" - 0 items done, 13 items skipped.
        "Ron" - 9 items done, 0 items skipped.
        "Neep" - 4 items done, 0 items skipped.
        "Tasks" - 0 items done, 46 items skipped.
        "Rosie" - 916 items done, 0 items skipped.
Processing Folder "segNET"
Processing Folder "Tim"
Processing Folder "Tim Palmer"
Processing Folder "TJB"
Processing Folder "Customers"
Processing Folder "BIS"
Processing Folder "Internic Registrations"
        "Tim Palmer" - 7 items done, 0 items skipped.
        "BIS" - 6 items done, 0 items skipped.
Processing Folder "Buckley"
Processing Folder "Centricut"
        "TJB" - 5 items done, 0 items skipped.
        "Buckley" - 2 items done, 0 items skipped.
        "Tim" - 31 items done, 0 items skipped.
        "Centricut" - 34 items done, 0 items skipped.
```

FIGURE 6.12

Fortunately, you are not limited to command line tools under Linux. There are Windows programs as well. One of the utilities you can use to read PST files is Outlook PST Viewer, which you can see in Figure 6.13. One of the advantages is that it is very easy to use. You tell it where your .PST file is and it opens it up for you, displaying your messages just as you would if you were using Outlook itself. You can see the folder list in the left hand pane and the message list on top on the right and then the text of the message below that, if you have selected a message to view.

One of the downsides of it, though, is that you cannot extract individual e-mail messages into a separate file for closer analysis and you cannot see the complete set of headers, as you would be able to from Outlook itself. However, in addition to e-mail messages, Outlook stores a lot of information in its PST files. Outlook is, after all, more than just an e-mail client. It is a personal information manager, so it will store contacts and calendar in addition to the messages and notes. Older versions of Outlook also used something called a journal, allowing users to store notes that could be flagged as calls, appointments, or other specific types. Outlook PST Viewer will show all of these additional types of information in addition to just being able to show the messages.

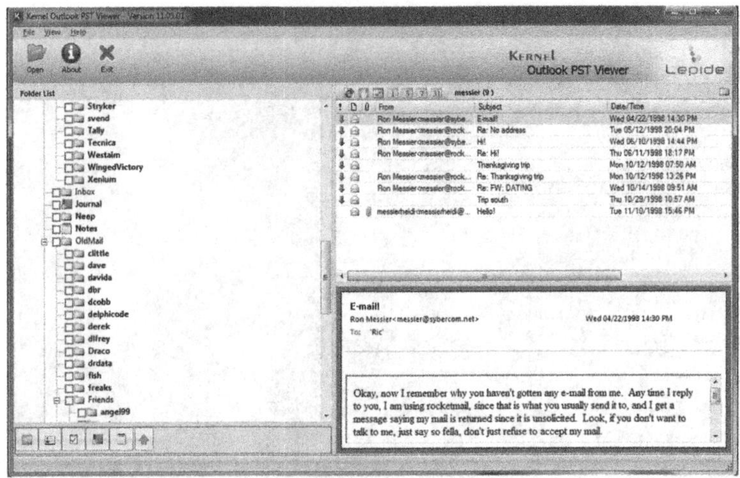

FIGURE 6.13

CONCLUSIONS

The Internet has become a very important communications medium over the past decade and a half or more. What this means is that there is a lot of Internet-related data on systems, including e-mail messages, Internet browsing history, and of course, various messaging platforms. With so much data in play, vendors want to be able to access it quickly and this means there is probably a need for an embedded database. While Microsoft has their own versions of embedded databases, including for storing messages on client devices, other software development companies have begun to really rely on Sqlite as the embedded database of choice.

A major advantage to using an established software platform like Sqlite is you do not have to spend a lot of time coming up with your own storage mechanisms. You just have to worry about including the Sqlite libraries and then develop to the Sqlite API. It saves a lot of time and provides a stable platform to store data and retrieve it quickly. The good thing about this from the forensics side is that you can learn a little SQL and how to use a Sqlite browser and you have a big jump on acquiring information across a wide variety of platforms.

EXERCISES

1. Extract the history from a Google Chrome installation. Get the very first entry in the database.
2. Find a message from your Junk mail folder and check to see whether the hostnames and IP addresses match. Is there anything out of order with it?
3. Get the cookies from Internet Explorer. How many cookies are stored on the system?

Bibliography

Krebs, B., 2012. Krebs on Security. Available from: http://krebsonsecurity.com/2012/06/pharmaleaks-rogue-pharmacy-economics-101/ (accessed 31.12.2014.).

CHAPTER

7

Tracking Artifacts

INFORMATION INCLUDED IN THIS CHAPTER:

- Location Information
- Document Artifacts
- Shortcuts and links

INTRODUCTION

Tracking information can give a lot away about users and they may not even realize that it is happening. There are a number of ways that users can be tracked, whether it is their activities on the system or their locations, when they are attached to networks. Applications also leave artifacts that can be tracked long after the document that was created by the application has left the system. Even after a document has left the system, there may still be shortcuts to get to it. These shortcuts can be used to deduce the previous existence of a document.

LOCATION INFORMATION

When you visit a Web site these days, you may be asked if the browser can get your current location. This may be especially true if you are on a mobile device but even stationary systems can give up their locations. While it was not always the case that you could obtain a location from a system, since there was no way for the system to know where it was located, there are now a number of reasons to keep track of this information. In order to understand how all of this happens, it is useful to get an understanding of how Internet Protocol (IP) addresses are handed out as well as the information that is stored about them.

The Internet is and always has stored information in a decentralized way. The more international the Internet became, the less centralized any information associated with the network was. While the Advanced Research Projects Agency was aware of all of the different hosts on the network, in the early days, all addressing to names were mapped via hosts files. Initially, there was one single hosts file that had to be replicated across all of the systems on the network. This file included the hostname and the IP address that belonged to it. This became unwieldy and eventually, the Domain Name System (DNS) was introduced. The problem with DNS is that it is still decentralized. There is no one system on the network that carries all of the information about the systems on the network.

It is even more complicated than that, though. The reason, we use domain names is a way of organizing hosts into collections, we can understand better. IP addresses are mostly meaningless to us. It is a lot easier to remember www.google.com than it is to remember 173.194.123.81, or even 173.194.123.80, or 173.194.123.84. Each name on the Internet has the potential to correspond to a number of actual addresses that the network will understand, making the problem even worse. Each domain name is registered with a regional Internet registry (RIR) and the information that is kept relates to the person or business including the address and phone number as well as e-mail address. The domain names are kept in root name servers. In order to get IP addresses, a system has to check the root server to get the actual name server that is associated with the domain and that name server will give up the IP address. In reality it is more complicated than that but that is a reasonable overview.

The RIRs also keep track of who owns particular IP addresses. Addresses are handed out in blocks, generally from the RIR to a service provider and there, if necessary, to businesses. This was not always the case, of course, and there are legacy allocations that go back decades to the days, when IP address blocks were first handed out. At the time, there were billions of addresses available and no idea that we would one day have more devices that needed addresses than we had people on the planet, so why not hand out addresses to businesses, who were first on the network in enormous quantities. Figure 7.1 shows one of those legacy allocations. This one was given to General Electric. You can lookup this information either using the whois command on a system or by going to a website like http://www.geektools.com.

GE's address associated with the allocation as their headquarters in Connecticut. The problem is that not all of the systems that are owned by GE are located in Connecticut. So, how do we determine where these systems are actually? First, why does it matter? One of the primary reasons for needing this functionality arose from the use of voice over IP (VoIP) for voice services to individuals. Once there was a legal requirement to support enhanced 911 (E911), each phone number needed to have a real address associated with it. Without that, the police or fire departments would not know where to go in the case of an emergency. Certainly, the phone service provider could use the billing address but that is not always reliable. First, I might buy my parents a Vonage service. I can buy the box, have it shipped to me and pay the bill and then take the box to my parents' house and install it there. There is nothing to prevent me from using the VoIP adapter anywhere I want to, so the billing address will be utterly useless if, that is, what conveyed to the public safety answering point (PSAP).

This is, of course, just one reason to want to know where IP addresses actually live in the world but it is a good one. How do we then make sure that we have addresses in case law enforcement needs to roll services to your location? We have to implement something that the existing infrastructure does not have. A way to track your location based on your IP address. This requires some cooperation from the various service providers, who are responsible for knowing who you are and what your IP address is. It is really the service providers that have all the information in this case because they are the ones, who know where the IP address is entering their network and where that is. They know this because they have to be able to move network communications to and from that location, a process called routing.

```
NetRange:       3.0.0.0 - 3.255.255.255
CIDR:           3.0.0.0/8
NetName:        GE-INTERNET
NetHandle:      NET-3-0-0-0-1
Parent:          ()
NetType:        Direct Assignment
OriginAS:
Organization:   General Electric Company (GENERA-9)
RegDate:        1988-02-23
Updated:        2008-03-28
Ref:            http://whois.arin.net/rest/net/NET-3-0-0-0-1

OrgName:        General Electric Company
OrgId:          GENERA-9
Address:        Internet Registrations
Address:        3135 Easton Turnpike
City:           Fairfield
StateProv:      CT
PostalCode:     06828-0001
Country:        US
RegDate:
Updated:        2011-09-24
Ref:            http://whois.arin.net/rest/org/GENERA-9

OrgAbuseHandle: GET2-ORG-ARIN
OrgAbuseName:   General Electric Company
OrgAbusePhone:  +1-203-373-2962
OrgAbuseEmail:  nic.admin@ge.com
OrgAbuseRef:    http://whois.arin.net/rest/poc/GET2-ORG-ARIN

OrgTechHandle: GET2-ORG-ARIN
OrgTechName:   General Electric Company
OrgTechPhone:  +1-203-373-2962
OrgTechEmail:  nic.admin@ge.com
OrgTechRef:    http://whois.arin.net/rest/poc/GET2-ORG-ARIN

RTechHandle: GET2-ORG-ARIN
RTechName:   General Electric Company
RTechPhone:  +1-203-373-2962
RTechEmail:  nic.admin@ge.com
RTechRef:    http://whois.arin.net/rest/poc/GET2-ORG-ARIN
```

FIGURE 7.1

There are a number of Web sites that an IP address can be tracked down to a location. One Web site is www.maxmind.com and since we have already been talking about General Electric, we can take a look at where their address is located. Using the MaxMind Web site, which you can use in demo mode without having to pay anything, we find what is in Figure 7.2. According to MaxMind, the IP address that is associated with GE's website is located at 42.3626, -71.0843, which is apparently in Cambridge, Massachusetts. In this case, the IP address belonging to GE's Web site does not belong to GE but instead to Akamai, so GE is likely making use of the load balancing/geocaching service. Since Akamai is located in Cambridge, the location provided is going to be that of Akamai's headquarters.

Other Web sites will not only provide the longitude and latitude but will also map it for you. One example is www.geoiptool.com and you can see the results of a lookup in Figure 7.3. This particular IP address was extracted from spam e-mail I received recently. You can see the text details in the box to the left and then a pinpointed location on the map on the right-hand side. Just simply going to that website will provide a map of your location. The site knows where you are coming from and performs the lookup for you. Any IP address you find on a system can be looked up.

Windows is capable of logging addresses that have been assigned. Most systems use the dynamic host configuration protocol (DHCP) to assign IP addresses. We can enable logging

GeoIP2 City Demo

IP Addresses

23.48.50.181

Enter up to 25 IP addresses separated by spaces or commas. You can also test your own IP address.

GeoIP2 City Results

IP Address	Country Code	Location	Postal Code	Coordinates	ISP	Organization	Domain	Metro Code
23.48.50.181	US	Cambridge, Massachusetts, United States, North America	02142	42.3626, -71.0843	Akamai Technologies	Akamai Technologies	akamaitechnologies.com	506

ISP and Organization data is included with the purchase of the GeoIP2 ISP database or with the purchase of the GeoIP2 Precision City or Insights services.

Domain data is included with the purchase of the GeoIP2 Domain Name database or with the purchase of the GeoIP2 Precision City or Insights services.

If you'd like to test multiple IP addresses, we offer a demo for up to 25 addresses per day.

FIGURE 7.2

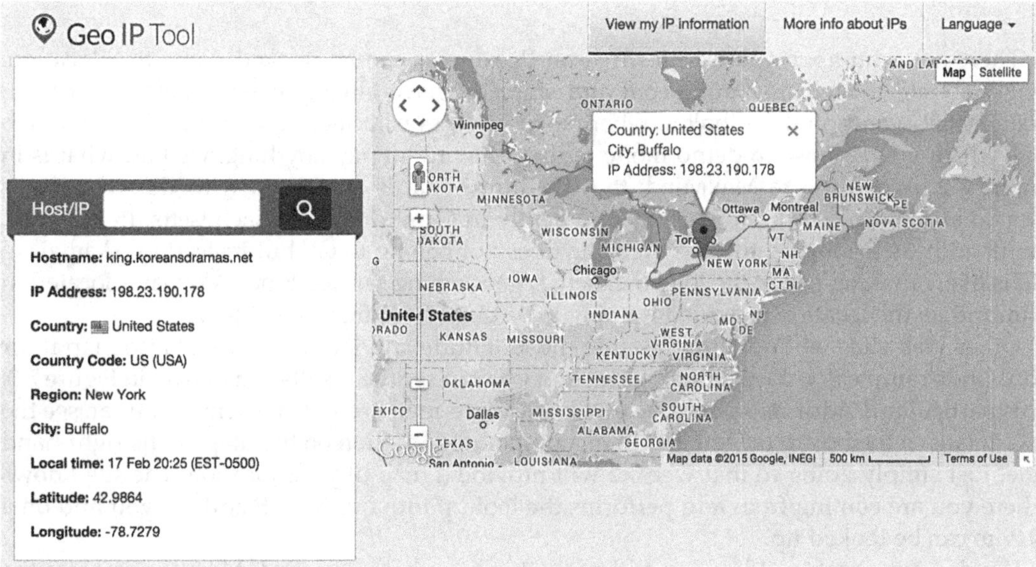

FIGURE 7.3

on Windows systems to log all of the addresses that have been assigned to a system. This is not the default state, though. In order to enable that logging you would have to open up the Event Viewer on a Windows system. Once the system has had logging enabled, you can find the events in the Event Viewer that will show the address that has been assigned. You can see one of these events in Figure 7.4. On any Windows system, you can get the last address that was assigned even without DHCP logging by opening up a command prompt and running ipconfig /all, which will show you the current IP addresses that are associated with the network interfaces on the system. If your system is not attached to a network in order to pick up a new address, the old address will remain in place.

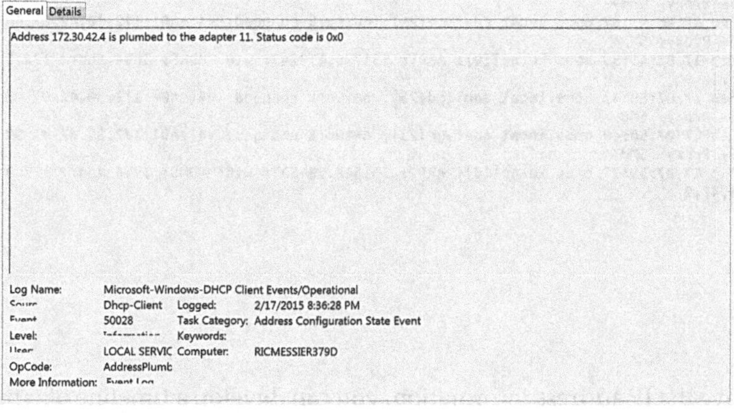

FIGURE 7.4

On Mac OS X and Linux systems, it is even easier since all IP address changes get logged by the system. On Mac OS X, there is a system service named configd that manages associating IP addresses with a network adapter. The file /var/log/system.log is where configd will log any address changes. All you have to do is check that file for entries by configd and you will see all of the times, when the system has either assigned a new address or just renewed the existing address. You can see the use of the grep tool on a Mac OS X system to locate configd entries in Figure 7.5. On Linux systems, you can do a similar thing, though there is also a file that keeps track of DHCP leases. Under Linux Mint, the file is located in the /var/lib/dhcp directory but no matter where it is located, it is likely to be called dhclient.leases.

If the dhclient.leases file only has a single lease in it or if you cannot find it, you can still check for entries the DHCP client daemon – either dhclient or dhcpcd most likely – made in the system log file. You can run grep dhclient /var/log/* to get the DHCP offers that the system gets from a DHCP server. On the Linux system I am running, the entries are found in the syslog file, though other Linux distributions may use other files to store them in. We will get in more detail about the log files in Chapter 8, but if you search through all of the files in /var/log, you will locate whatever file the information is stored in.

```
kilroy@opus:~$ sudo grep 172 /var/log/system.log
Feb 17 01:16:36 opus.local configd[25]: network changed: v4(en0-:172.30.42.9) DN
S- Proxy- SMB-
Feb 17 01:16:42 opus.local configd[25]: network changed: v4(en0!:172.30.42.9) DN
S+ Proxy+ SMB+
Feb 17 01:17:21 opus kernel[0]: ARPT: 131639.577198: wl0: MDNS: IPV4 Addr: 172.3
0.42.9
Feb 17 03:05:21 opus.local configd[25]: network changed: v4(en0-:172.30.42.9) DN
S- Proxy- SMB-
Feb 17 03:05:28 opus.local configd[25]: network changed: v4(en0!:172.30.42.9) DN
S+ Proxy+ SMB+
Feb 17 03:06:06 opus kernel[0]: ARPT: 131690.882326: wl0: MDNS: IPV4 Addr: 172.3
0.42.9
Feb 17 04:54:09 opus.local configd[25]: network changed: v4(en0-:172.30.42.9) DN
S- Proxy- SMB-
Feb 17 04:54:13 opus.local configd[25]: network changed: v4(en0!:172.30.42.9) DN
S+ Proxy+ SMB+
Feb 17 04:54:54 opus kernel[0]: ARPT: 131744.794031: wl0: MDNS: IPV4 Addr: 172.3
0.42.9
Feb 17 06:42:54 opus.local configd[25]: network changed: v4(en0-:172.30.42.9) DN
S- Proxy- SMB-
Feb 17 06:43:02 opus.local configd[25]: network changed: v4(en0!:172.30.42.9) DN
S+ Proxy+ SMB+
Feb 17 06:43:39 opus kernel[0]: ARPT: 131796.110243: wl0: MDNS: IPV4 Addr: 172.3
0.42.9
Feb 17 07:58:42 opus.local configd[25]: network changed: v4(en0-:172.30.42.9) DN
S- Proxy- SMB-
Feb 17 07:58:48 opus.local configd[25]: network changed: v4(en0!:172.30.42.9) DN
S+ Proxy+ SMB+
Feb 17 07:59:27 opus kernel[0]: ARPT: 131848.984537: wl0: MDNS: IPV4 Addr: 172.3
0.42.9
```

FIGURE 7.5

Once you have the IP address information, you can develop a timeline of where the system has been and when they have been there.

Networks and Location

Mobile devices can generally obtain their location from either global positioning system (GPS) or, barring that, from the cellular network. This assumes, though, that the device has GPS capability or a cellular modem in it, in order to make use of that information. This is not always the case but a number of Web applications make use of the location information so other means of obtaining location from the device itself is essential. In place of GPS, devices can make use of the WiFi positioning system (WPS), which should not be confused with WiFi protected setup (also WPS). WPS allows applications like a Web browser to acquire information about location. When you connect to a website that wants to get your location information, you will be presented with a dialog asking, if you want to allow the site to get your location, as you can see in Figure 7.6.

On some systems, you will get a notice indicating that location will improve location accuracy. This is because of the WiFi Positioning System (WPS). Mobile and nonmobile systems can make use of WPS to get location data.

---

http://www.bedbathandbeyond.com wants to use your computer's location. Block Allow

FIGURE 7.6

The browsers we use have application programming interfaces (APIs) that will provide information about the location to the Web site requesting it. Of course, you can turn this feature off but it is on by default in most browsers. One of the ways they can do this is to use WPS. There are a number of websites available that keep track of the location of WiFi networks. One of them is wigle.net and you can see the results of a lookup of attwifi in a city not far from me, in Figure 7.7. Some sites like Wigle.net work by collecting information provided by users. The data is effectively crowdsourced so anyone who is collecting WiFi data can submit their information and their location, and all of this goes into a database that can be used to locate WiFi networks.

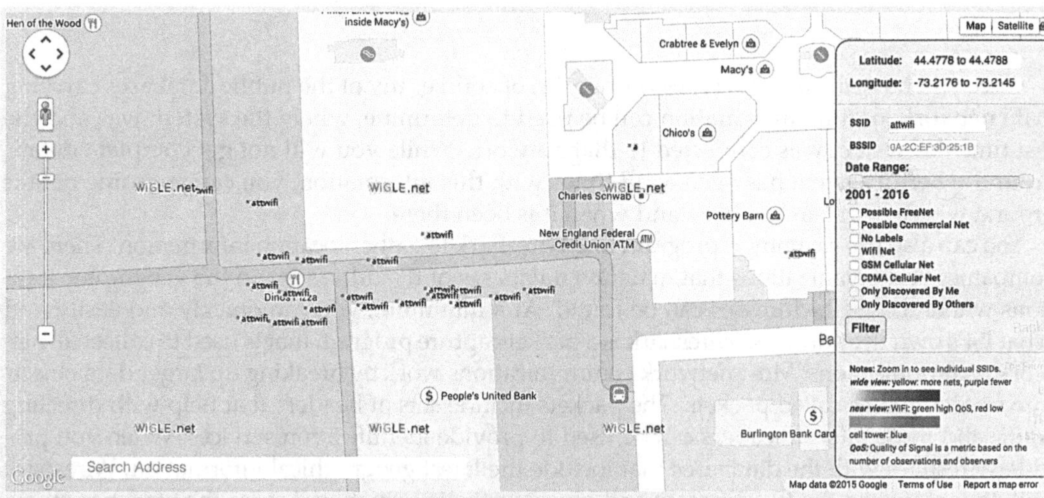

FIGURE 7.7

While your personal computer does not currently cache location information that can be investigated later, it does is keep track of wireless networks you have connected to over time. Those networks may be located, which can place the computer at that location.

In the case of Windows, you can look in the registry. The key you are looking for is HKEY_LOCAL_MACHINE\Software\Microsoft\Windows NT\CurrentVersion\NetworkList\Profiles. In there, you will find the list of all the profiles for networks you have connected to, including your wireless networks. You can also use the netsh wlan show profiles command. On Mac OS X, System Preferences will give you a list of the wireless networks you have connected to, as you can see in Figure 7.8. The file /Library/Preferences/SystemConfiguration/com.apple.airport.preferences.plist is an XML property list carrying the list of wireless networks that your system has connected to.

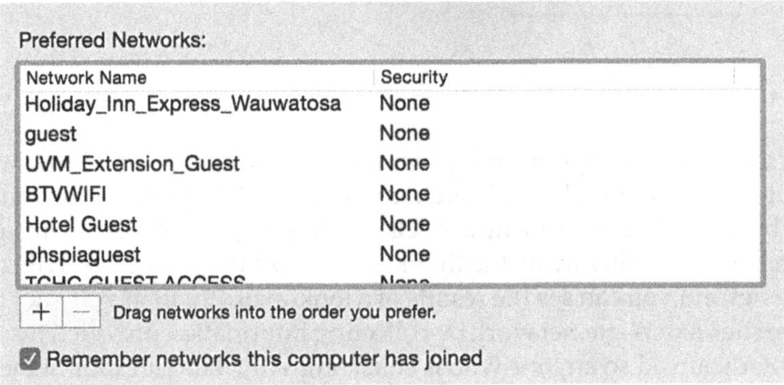

Preferred Networks:

Network Name	Security
Holiday_Inn_Express_Wauwatosa	None
guest	None
UVM_Extension_Guest	None
BTVWIFI	None
Hotel Guest	None
phspiaguest	None

Drag networks into the order you prefer.

Remember networks this computer has joined

FIGURE 7.8

Once you have the list of wireless networks, of course, any of the public databases carrying WiFi network location information can be used to determine, where the system was and the last time the system was connected to that network. While you will not get complete details around where a system has been at all times with this information, you can get some details around where a system has been and when it is been there.

You can also use a common program like Wireshark to gather location information. There are companies and organizations that maintain databases of IP addresses and the geographic locations where those IP addresses can be found. At a minimum, you can quickly and easily find what ISPs own IP addresses. Wireshark is a packet capture program that is used to collect all network communications. Most network communications work by breaking up larger data objects into smaller pieces called packets. The packets include sets of headers that help with directing traffic and those packet headers can be used to provide identification services. When you provide Wireshark with the databases that include the latest geographical information, Wireshark will do lookups on the IP addresses and give you the information. Under the Statistics menu, you can look up all the endpoints from your packet capture. You can see the results in Figure 7.9.

The AS number shown in the figure is autonomous system number that corresponds to the ISP, which owns the block of IP addresses that the endpoint address comes from. The database provides the owner to Wireshark. In some cases, you can get the longitude and latitude of the IP address, if it is in the database. The databases that were installed into Wireshark in this case were the GeoLite AS number, city and country databases from MaxMind.

DOCUMENT TRACKING

One of the issues with digital documents is that you can drop a document anywhere and it will just show up and you have no way of knowing where it came from. Just because you find a document on a system does not necessarily mean that the person who owns the system had anything to do with putting it there. There are a number of ways of getting files onto a system, including any file shares, Bluetooth devices or even malware that may be dropping files onto

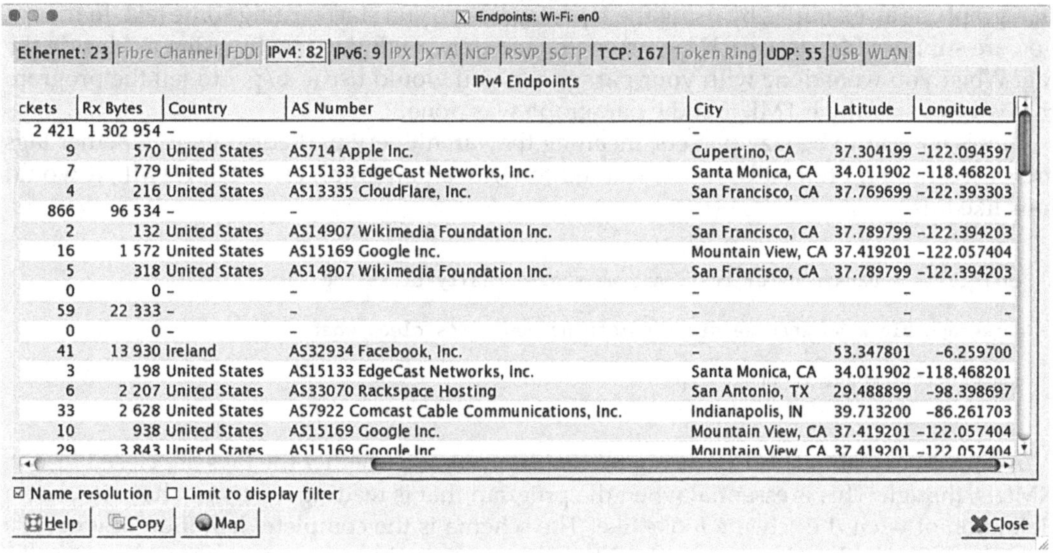

Endpoints: Wi-Fi: en0

Ethernet: 23 | Fibre Channel | FDDI | IPv4: 82 | IPv6: 9 | IPX | JXTA | NCP | RSVP | SCTP | TCP: 167 | Token Ring | UDP: 55 | USB | WLAN

IPv4 Endpoints

ckets	Rx Bytes	Country	AS Number	City	Latitude	Longitude
2 421	1 302 954	-	-	-	-	-
9	570	United States	AS714 Apple Inc.	Cupertino, CA	37.304199	-122.094597
7	779	United States	AS15133 EdgeCast Networks, Inc.	Santa Monica, CA	34.011902	-118.468201
4	216	United States	AS13335 CloudFlare, Inc.	San Francisco, CA	37.769699	-122.393303
866	96 534	-	-	-	-	-
2	132	United States	AS14907 Wikimedia Foundation Inc.	San Francisco, CA	37.789799	-122.394203
16	1 572	United States	AS15169 Google Inc.	Mountain View, CA	37.419201	-122.057404
5	318	United States	AS14907 Wikimedia Foundation Inc.	San Francisco, CA	37.789799	-122.394203
0	0	-	-	-	-	-
59	22 333	-	-	-	-	-
0	0	-	-	-	-	-
41	13 930	Ireland	AS32934 Facebook, Inc.	-	53.347801	-6.259700
3	198	United States	AS15133 EdgeCast Networks, Inc.	Santa Monica, CA	34.011902	-118.468201
6	2 207	United States	AS33070 Rackspace Hosting	San Antonio, TX	29.488899	-98.398697
33	2 628	United States	AS7922 Comcast Cable Communications, Inc.	Indianapolis, IN	39.713200	-86.261703
10	938	United States	AS15169 Google Inc.	Mountain View, CA	37.419201	-122.057404
29	3 843	United States	AS15169 Google Inc	Mountain View, CA	37.419201	-122.057404

☑ Name resolution ☐ Limit to display filter

Help Copy Map Close

FIGURE 7.9

a system. There are pieces of information that get created when a document is created and that can be left in the document, even though they may not be readily apparent at first glance. The Office documents generally use the same tracking structures, while other common document formats use different methods of storing information.

Metadata in a Word document was used as an evidence against Dennis Rader, the Bind, Torture Kill killer. A deleted Word document was found on a floppy disk and the metadata associated with the file indicated that it had been edited by the user Dennis. This evidence was used to help associate him with the crimes.

Where vendors used to use primarily proprietary document file formats, there has been a move in the last half dozen years or more toward

eXtensible Markup Language

The eXtensible Markup Language (XML) is related to the HyperText Markup Language (HTML) used to generate Web pages. It is a very good way to store data, while also storing the description of what the language is meant to be. Where HTML has defined tags to make it clear what each piece of data is, XML is meant to have the user create the tags in order to provide the description. A tag is the description of the data. You create a tag by inserting a word and then some parameters within a <> block. In the case of HTML, you would create a paragraph, as an example, by using the <p> tag before you start writing some text. In theory, you are supposed to close each tag when you are done with the data by using a / inside the tag. When you were done with your paragraph, you would use a </p> to tell the program that was parsing the HTML that the paragraph was done.

Browsers tend to be lazy parsers, meaning they aren't very particular about whether tags are closed or not. Preferably, if you wanted to write a paragraph of text in HTML, it would look like this.

```
<p>This is a paragraph of text. And we should really close the

paragraph block so when we start something new, it's clear what

context it's meant to be in.</p>
```

As mentioned above, HTML is not all that fussy about whether the tags are closed or not, XML is, though. This is essential when the program that is reading it may not have as clear a definition of what the schema looks like. The schema is the complete definition of what the data should look like. If you wanted to store information about a phone contact, for example, you would specify the schema to include name, phone, address, city, state, zip, and birthday. An XML record using a schema that included this might look like this.

<name>Ric</name>
<phone>303-465-4508</phone>
<address>My Address</address>
<city>My City</city>
<state>Normal(ish)</state>
<ZIP>90210</ZIP>

You may find a lot of data is stored in an XML format, including both Microsoft Office documents and sometimes, the Portable Document Format (PDF) file may store information in XML format. Because of the ease of use and the extensibility, XML has become a very popular format.

If you are working with Web sites, you may use the XML sitemap to determine the author of the site content. XML sitemaps are used to prove authorship of the content to avoid having your content be removed from search engines like Google in the case of duplication on other sites. Google will index the original content and the other sites will not.

Office Documents

The Microsoft Office documents moved to an eXtensible Markup Language (XML)-based document format with Office 2007. The file formats use Open XML to store most of the document data. While the use of XML in Office documents is fairly common knowledge, it is less knowledgeable that Office documents with the newer format, the ones where the file extension ends in 'x', are really just zip files. You can uncompress an Office document and you will get three directories: _rels, docProps, and word. You will also get an XML file named [Content Types].xml, including all of the MIME types that are included within the document. The word directory contains the actual document contents, in XML-based files. The directory we are most concerned with is the docProps directory.

Inside this directory, there is a set of files that includes a thumbnail, which is a small visual depiction of the file to be displayed in file listings if needed, as well as another XML file named core.xml, which contains the properties for the file. This includes statistics like the last time the file was modified, as well as, the creator. The creator will provide tracking information, identifying the person that originated the document. This can, of course, help to connect a particular user to any document, regardless of where it may be and who may be in possession. Of course, this value can be manipulated but commonly, the document is populated by the application based on information provided by the operating system.

Another way to track information within Office documents is by the help of comments as well as edits. Comments will get tracked with a user and date and time. Changing the review settings to only show Final without any of the markup, will hide this information. Even if the edits and comments are not being displayed in the document window when you are looking at it, they are still stored within the zip file/document structure. In a Word document, within the word directory, once you have unzipped it, you will see a file named Comments.xml. This stores all of the comments that are associated with the document. Deleting a comment will not retain the comment for historical purposes. Once the comment is deleted, it disappears from the Comments.xml file. The XML below is an example of a comment that was inserted within this particular chapter, as it was being written.

```
<w:comment w:id="0" w:author="Ric Messier" w:date="2015-03-07T15:50:00Z"
w:initials="RM"><w:p w14:paraId="5A8C4E38" w14:textId="3477368D"
w:rsidR="00907562" w:rsidRDefault="00907562"><w:pPr><w:pStyle
w:val="CommentText"/></w:pPr><w:r><w:rPr><w:rStyle
w:val="CommentReference"/></w:rPr><w:annotationRef/></w:r>
```

The XML keeps track of the author of the comment as well as the date and time it was created. This is based on the date and time of the system when the comment was created, of course, so any manipulation of that value will have an impact on the date and time of the comment. The XML also indicates where the comment should be placed within the document. It references the paragraph ID and the text ID to make sure the comment is positioned in the right place when the document is opened. This is necessary, of course, since the comment isn't stored with the text of the document.

Ultimately, there are a lot of pieces of information that will get stored with Office documents once you have extracted the zip file and dug into the XML itself. In many cases, you can simply open the document in the appropriate Office program but you are going to only see, what the Office program wants to show you. This can be the properties and the comments, if you enable viewing of the comments in the interface.

PDF

Adobe created the PDF in the early 1990s, as a way of describing documents in a way that was not bound to a particular program or platform. It was, however, a proprietary format until 2008, when Adobe released the specifications. PDF uses a particular language that describes the documents. This is another example of a document description language, similar to HTML. It also bears some resemblances to PostScript, in the sense that PostScript is another document description language designed by Adobe. PostScript, though, was designed as a way of telling a printer how to print the contents of a document, so it was about layout as much as anything else. PDF, however, could be used by any number of programs to describe the contents of the document. This could be used to store a document that could be edited rather than one that was intended to be static.

Much like the Word documents described earlier, PDF documents can be annotated with comments. These comments are stored in the document and the comments have names associated with them in most cases. The PDF editor will associate the username with the comment, so they can be referenced later with the correct person getting the attribution for what they said. In addition to the comments, each PDF will also include information about the creator of the document as well as date information. The PDF format supports compression of text that is stored but information like properties may be stored in plaintext in the file. As an example, you can see the Title object from the file below, as well as the entry in the file that references that particular object, associating it with a property.

```
76 0 obj
(Ch07_Messier)
endobj
77 0 obj

<< /Title 76 0 R /Author 78 0 R /Subject 79 0 R /Producer 77 0 R
/Creator
80 0 R /CreationDate 81 0 R /ModDate 81 0 R /Keywords 82 0 R
/AAPL:Keywords
83 0 R >>
```

The first number that you see, 76, is the object identifier. That first line indicates that the following block of information is an object. You will see that object number 76 relates to the title in the document properties. Of course, there are other ways you can view the properties without having to dig through the actual file contents. Getting the information from either a PDF editor or just from the operating system, you can get the essential properties. You can see them in Figure 7.10. These are the properties of a PDF file that was created using the print to PDF feature in Mac OS X.

The operating system extracted the relevant information from the document properties in Word, since that is the origin of the PDF, and placed all of those properties in the PDF. All of this assumes, though, that the generator of the PDF has placed the important details into the properties, but most commercial software that users are likely to make use of, will put those properties in. If those properties were not in place, it would be unusual and might suggest an unusual setup of the application or operating system. It might also suggest tampering with the PDF.

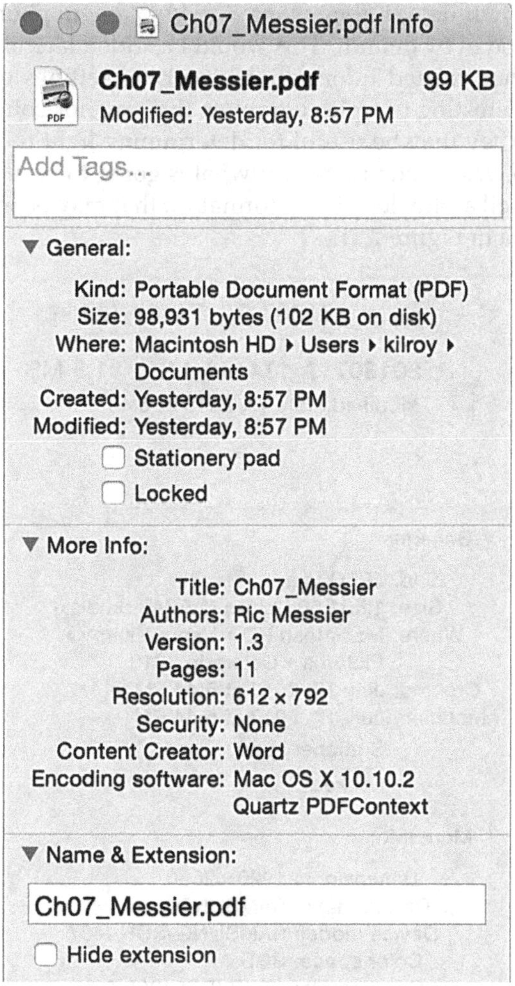

Ch07_Messier.pdf Info

Ch07_Messier.pdf 99 KB
Modified: Yesterday, 8:57 PM

Add Tags...

▼ General:

Kind: Portable Document Format (PDF)
Size: 98,931 bytes (102 KB on disk)
Where: Macintosh HD ▸ Users ▸ kilroy ▸ Documents
Created: Yesterday, 8:57 PM
Modified: Yesterday, 8:57 PM
Stationery pad
Locked

▼ More Info:

Title: Ch07_Messier
Authors: Ric Messier
Version: 1.3
Pages: 11
Resolution: 612 × 792
Security: None
Content Creator: Word
Encoding software: Mac OS X 10.10.2 Quartz PDFContext

▼ Name & Extension:

Ch07_Messier.pdf
Hide extension

FIGURE 7.10

Image files

Image files often store extensive information about where they were created, the program that created them, and the date and time they were created. In the mid-1990s, the Japan Electronics Industry Development Association specified formats for digital media storage. As part of that effort, they specified the exchangeable image file format (Exif) to define metadata that would be stored in these media files, as well as the format for the data files themselves. Formats like the Joint Photographic Experts Group (JPEG), Tagged Image File Format (TIFF), and the Waveform Audio File Format (WAV) use this Exif data. Other file formats, like the Moving Picture Experts Group (MPEG) formats, use different ways of storing metadata. In the case of Exif, you can extract a lot of information related to tracking users, though you will not get any information about usernames within the Exif because they are commonly captured on devices that do not have users associated with them. A photographer could, though, store information in the Exif data, if they wanted to but camera phones and digital cameras do not put the information in by default. This would be added later through post-processing.

While f-stops and other, related information about the settings of the camera when the picture was taken are interesting to a photographer, they are not going to be as interesting to a forensic investigator. They may be useful for determining light that may have been in the location when the photo was taken but mostly, what is going to be of interest in the Exif data is the date and time as well as any location information that may be in the file. You can see an example of Exif metadata in Figure 7.11.

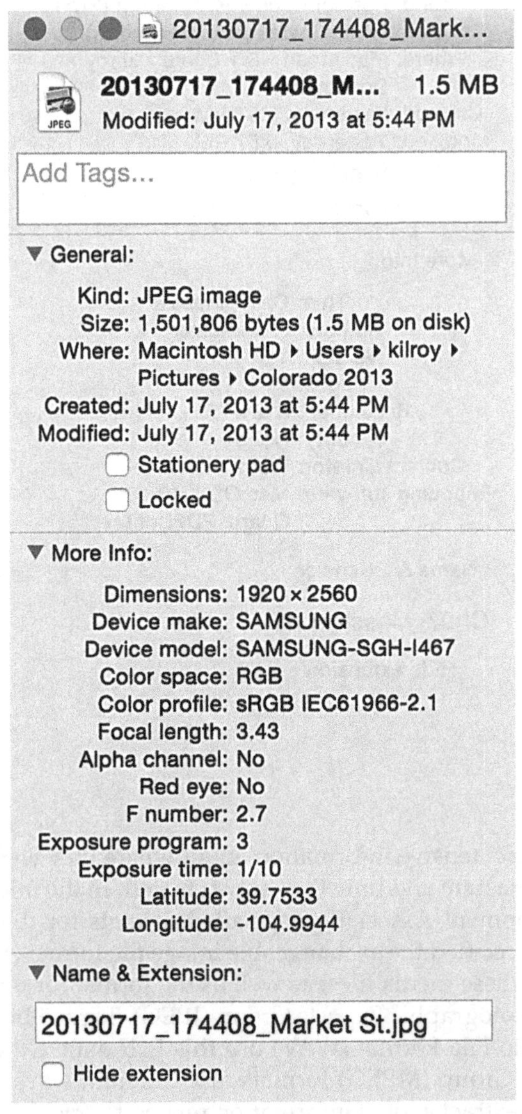

FIGURE 7.11

Many file formats will store a thumbnail that can be displayed quickly to provide an indication of the contents of the file. If a file has been modified in some way, the thumbnail image may not be updated and may present the original, unaltered image. You can see this thumbnail with an Exif viewer.

The image, this Exif data was taken from includes the latitude and longitude of the device that took the picture, when the picture was taken. You do not have to look it up. It will point to Cook Street on Market Street in Denver, Colorado. The picture in question was taken with my phone, as you can see from the manufacturer and device information. This is also useful data. The one thing that you do not get from this is the serial number of the device to tie the photo to a very specific instance of a Samsung Galaxy Note. Knowing the type of device that took the photo is very helpful, though.

One thing to note is that this information is considered to be private and social media Web sites may strip this information from photos that are stored with them. This is the case with Facebook, for instance. Facebook's rationale is that removing Exif data will protect the privacy of the user, though some users complain that it removes their copyright information. This is the compromise for protecting people from being located by someone trying to track them. It is not hard to think of a case, where this data might be used by an abusive ex-spouse trying to locate their victim. Of course, there is a lot of good that could be done by leaving the Exif data in, as might be the case in locating children who have been abducted.

While Facebook does strip the identifying information from images, so someone who sees the images cannot extract that data, they do retain all of the original data. If you obtain a warrant and issue it to Facebook, you can get the information that was in the original image.

This is such sensitive information, in fact, that I was once approached by a woman at a museum who could see I was taking photos. She wanted me to delete photos that I had taken and she was very upset. She was concerned her children may have been in the photo. This is not an unreasonable fear, if you are in a difficult domestic situation. You do not want your children to be identified and then located as having been to this particular museum, which may narrow searches for them. As a result, while Exif data is both useful and important from a forensics perspective, it may not always be available, depending on where the photo came from.

There are a number of ways to view Exif data, including through browser extensions. Some browsers, like Firefox, allow you to add functionality to the browser through these extensions or add-ons. Firefox supports add-ons like Exif 2.0 to view Exif data.

SHORTCUTS

Shortcuts are common across operating systems. A shortcut is a way to locate a file in a different place without having multiple copies around. I might, for instance, want to link to a file on my Windows desktop without actually placing the file there. For instance, the file may be located deep within a directory structure, where it is necessary for a particular program to run but you want it to be more accessible. You make a shortcut or a link to it and then place the link somewhere that is easy to get to. You will be able to easily access the file without disrupting the normal usage of the file. The most common use of shortcuts, in fact, is linking to programs. On a Windows system, when you go to the menu to locate a program to run it, you are making use of a shortcut. The program file itself is not installed in the menu. Instead, the menu is created by a number of shortcuts stored in a particular directory. You can see the properties of a shortcut in Figure 7.12.

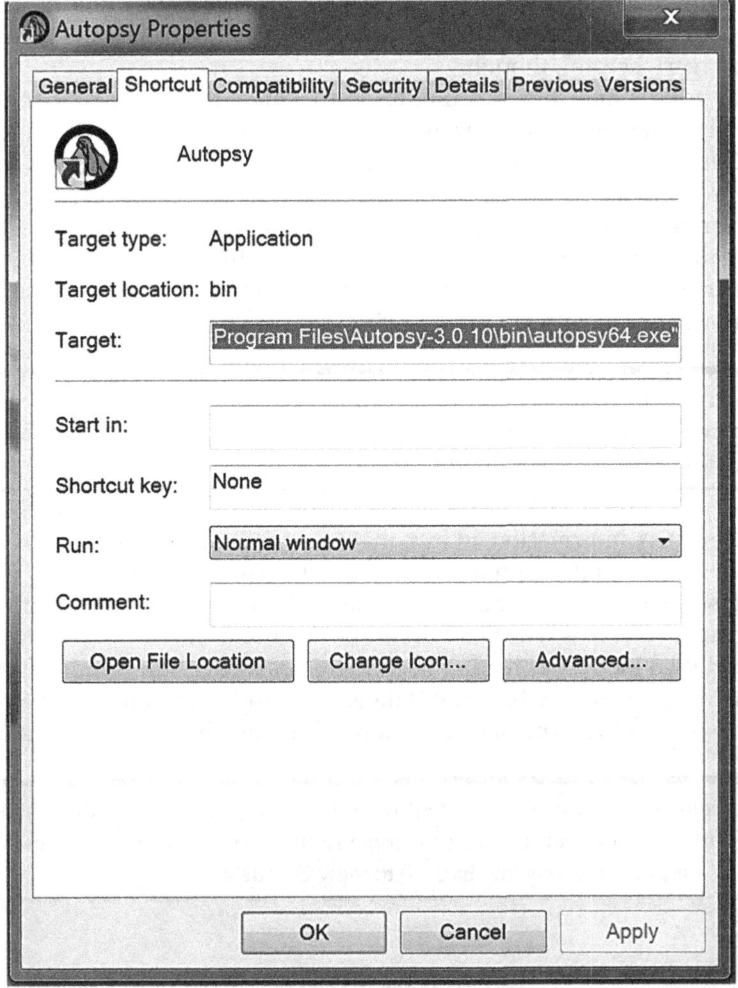

FIGURE 7.12

The properties give you the location that it points to. The problem with this is that the shortcut will still exist, even if the original file does not exist any longer. When you delete a source file that has a shortcut, the shortcut does not look any different. You will still have the properties indicating the location, where the original file is located. This may be one way to indicate that a file was once on a system. On Windows, you can similarly store shortcuts for files stored on a network as well as pages that are on a Web server. The link you store on your system will contain a reference to the location of the resource, wherever it happens to be. While you could create a false shortcut, it is more common that the shortcut exists because either the user went to the Web site and stored the shortcut as a reference for later, or because the file was once on the system or at least on a system that was accessible at one time. When you delete a source file, you may not automatically delete all of the shortcuts that may have been created, which will leave behind artifacts even if the source file is gone.

Microsoft will also use .lnk files to keep shortcuts. The .lnk file is a small binary file that includes metadata related to the target. This includes information about the directory that the target starts in, which is important in the case of links to programs. The Windows shell will indicate a .lnk file with an arrow over the top of the icon for the file. This is an indicator that the file is a shortcut and not the actual file.

On a Linux system or even on a Mac OS X system, the situation is slightly different because they are both based on Unix. With any Unix-like operating system, I can create a link. Of course, with a Unix-like operating system, I can create either a soft link or a hard link. Without complicating anything, we will focus on soft or symbolic links, since those would be more common. In Figure 7.13, you can see the creation of a symbolic link to a PDF file. Underneath the creation of the link, a file listing shows that the "file" foo.pdf is really just a symbolic link that points to Ch07_Messier.pdf.

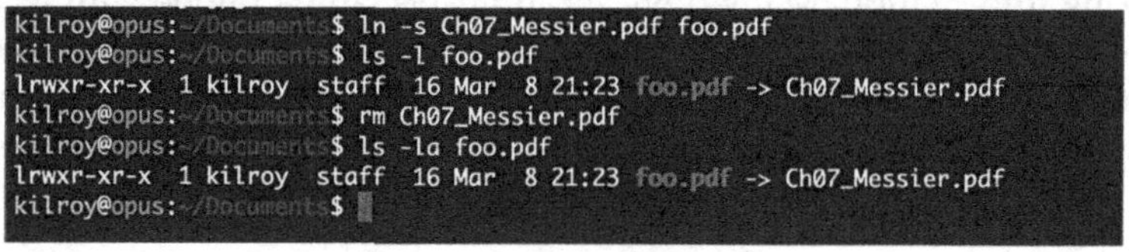

```
kilroy@opus:~/Documents$ ln -s Ch07_Messier.pdf foo.pdf
kilroy@opus:~/Documents$ ls -l foo.pdf
lrwxr-xr-x  1 kilroy  staff  16 Mar  8 21:23 foo.pdf -> Ch07_Messier.pdf
kilroy@opus:~/Documents$ rm Ch07_Messier.pdf
kilroy@opus:~/Documents$ ls -la foo.pdf
lrwxr-xr-x  1 kilroy  staff  16 Mar  8 21:23 foo.pdf -> Ch07_Messier.pdf
kilroy@opus:~/Documents$
```

FIGURE 7.13

Underneath that, I delete the source file and then show a file listing again. In some cases, a user environment will show the link is broken by coloring it differently. In this case, there is no difference between the link, where the source file is still there and the file having been deleted. This was done on a Mac OS X system. Some Linux systems using the right shell and flags to the ls command will show that the link is broken. On the Mac OS X system, I have to attempt to access the link. When I do that, I get an error indicating that the link does not exist when in fact, it is the source file that does not exist and not the link.

Just as with the Windows system, however, the link is evidence that the source file once existed. This may be common, again, in cases of program files where a shortcut was created to a specific version of a program with a different name in the link. I can create a link on a Unix-like system to a file that does not exist, just as it is possible on a Windows system. This would be unusual, however. At this point, it would be important to check file system information to see, if there is a reference to a file that may have been written at some point to corroborate the link that exists.

CONCLUSIONS

Tracking is an important feature. There are so many ways today to track us and often we welcome it. In the case of a lost phone or a lost car, I definitely want to be able to track it. In that case, tracking is useful. However, our operating systems leave behind artifacts of not only our existence but also the way we use them. This can be done by the addresses we get, when we plug into a network. This is becoming more and more common since we often want to have accurate information about what is near us. We are in the information age where more and more information is available. We are constantly connected. Why bother calling the phone company to find out restaurants that may be nearby when all we have to do is run a quick Web search and allow our Web browser or our mobile device to get our location?

In addition to network information, of course, there are artifacts from the documents we create and make use of on our systems that can leave behind indications of not only our presence but also our activities. I may leave comments in a Word document that would not only indicate I opened it up but also that I interacted with it. All I have to do is create one of these files and my name is automatically associated with it in most cases, assuming that my operating system has my name. This is, of course, not always the case, but it is pretty common for people to provide their names, when they are asked during the system setup.

All of this information, though, leaves behind evidence of where we have been and what we have been doing. Of course, the data that is stored in our media files may be the biggest source of tracking information. Many devices, and especially a phone with a camera in it as all smartphones have, will automatically tag photos that are taken with location information with a great deal of precision. Of course, there are ways to edit the Exif data but then the timestamps in the metadata may not match with the file timestamps. All of this is important information.

EXERCISES

1. Locate the metadata in a Word file by both unzipping the .docx file and reading the XML as well as looking at the properties on the file in Word.
2. Install Exifviewer 2.0 in Firefox or another Exif viewer and use it to view the Exif data from an image file
3. Download an image file from Facebook and Twitter. Compare the Exif data from the resulting downloads to see if you can locate any Exif data.

CHAPTER

8

Log Files

INFORMATION INCLUDED IN THIS CHAPTER:

- Windows event logs
- Unix Syslog
- Application logs
- Mac OS X logs
- Security logs
- Auditing

INTRODUCTION

System administrators rely on log files as part of their every day lives. Without log files, an administrator would be unable to determine what happened when something goes wrong. These are essential system files. However, they are not only essential for system administrators. They can also be very good sources of information for a forensics professional, no matter what platform the logs are on. Windows systems have a well-developed mechanism to acquire and store log information and there are a lot of subsystems of the operating system that generate logs. Logs can be used to track user actions including logging in and logging out. One of the major advantages of log files are they are typically time stamped, which means that you can use the actions you find in them to generate a timeline.

You can often enable accounting on a system, which will lead to more detailed logs. On Windows systems, for instance, you can enable success or failure logs on a number of actions including file access. Touching a file will lead to a log entry being generated. This has to be enabled before the action is performed. It cannot be enabled in retrospect. In addition to system logs of user actions, there may also be security logs from a host-based firewall, antivirus scanner or file integrity scanner. Any one of these security features can provide a lot of useful information. In the case of either a traditional forensic investigation or looking for artifacts as part of an incident response, log files can provide critical information.

WINDOWS EVENT LOGS

While Windows event logs are used extensively by the operating system, they can also be used by any application. With Windows 2000 and up through Windows Server 2003, including

Windows XP, there were typically three event log files on every system, Application, System, and Security. These files were stored in the C:\Windows\System32\config directory. Starting with Windows 2000, applications were able to create their own logs using the logging service within the operating system. In Windows, there is a logging service that applications can make use to send messages, so they can be managed and protected by the operating system. This alleviates the need for each application to have its own logging functionality. It also makes sure that all logs are stored in the same place. If applications were responsible for their own logs, they may be scattered all over.

Older event log files are binary in nature and can be parsed using the evtparse.pl Perl script written by Harlan Carvey, who is a well-known researcher in the field of Windows forensics. One advantage of using a tool like this is that it does not use any Windows libraries and you can present the event log files as untouched and any information obtained from it as being intact. The output from this tool is presented in a way that can be used to generate a timeline. Because the output is text-based, it is easier to sort and manipulate than it is from having to view the information in the Windows Event Viewer. A sample of the output from evtparse is below. This sample is from a Windows XP system that has been used for a lot of research over time. This is from the SecEvents.evt file, which contains security event log entries. These log entries appear to represent a login attack against this particular system.

```
1348517374|EVT|FORENSICS-C765F2|S-1-5-18|Security/529;Failure;billw,,3,NtLmSsp
,MICROSOFT_AUTHENTICATION_PACKAGE_V1_0,\\192.168.1.39
1348517374|EVT|FORENSICS-C765F2|S-1-5-18|Security/529;Failure;adam,,3,NtLmSsp
,MICROSOFT_AUTHENTICATION_PACKAGE_V1_0,\\192.168.1.39
1348517374|EVT|FORENSICS-C765F2|S-1-5-18|Security/529;Failure;adm,,3,NtLmSsp
,MICROSOFT_AUTHENTICATION_PACKAGE_V1_0,\\192.168.1.39
1348517374|EVT|FORENSICS-C765F2|S-1-5-18|Security/529;Failure;heythere,,3,NtLmSsp
,MICROSOFT_AUTHENTICATION_PACKAGE_V1_0,\\192.168.1.39
1348517374|EVT|FORENSICS-C765F2|S-1-5-18|Security/529;Failure;kendra,,3,NtLmSsp
,MICROSOFT_AUTHENTICATION_PACKAGE_V1_0,\\192.168.1.39
1348517374|EVT|FORENSICS-C765F2|S-1-5-18|Security/529;Failure;keel,,3,NtLmSsp
,MICROSOFT_AUTHENTICATION_PACKAGE_V1_0,\\192.168.1.39
1348517374|EVT|FORENSICS-C765F2|S-1-5-18|Security/529;Failure;plugh,,3,NtLmSsp
,MICROSOFT_AUTHENTICATION_PACKAGE_V1_0,\\192.168.1.39
1348517374|EVT|FORENSICS-C765F2|S-1-5-18|Security/529;Failure;xyzzy,,3,NtLmSsp
,MICROSOFT_AUTHENTICATION_PACKAGE_V1_0,\\192.168.1.39
1348517374|EVT|FORENSICS-C765F2|S-1-5-18|Security/529;Failure;kettle,,3,NtLmSsp
,MICROSOFT_AUTHENTICATION_PACKAGE_V1_0,\\192.168.1.39
```

There are a few things worth mentioning from these log entries. The first is FORENSICS-C765F2, which is the name of the system, this log came from. S-1-5-18 is a well-known security identifier, which Windows identifies accounts by internally. This particular security identifier is the one for LocalSystem. The notation Failure seems self-explanatory. This was a failure in an attempt to authenticate against the system. Security/529 indicates that this was a logon failure, even if the rest of it did not more or less scream a logon failure. The username that was attempted, appears to change in each of the log entries but in each one of the attempts, the request comes in over the network, based on the value 3, which is the logon type. The \\192.168.1.39 at the end of the log entry is the means by which the login attempt was made. Someone was trying to connect to the system to gather information like the user shares.

Using the system logging facility means that all the logs are formatted the same with a consistent set of information. With Windows Vista and Windows Server 2008, Microsoft began to store their logs in different formats and also present them differently. Since that time, the logs have been in an XML-based structure. This allows them to be well-structured in a self-documenting format. The following is an example of an event from a Windows 2012 server.

```
<Event xmlns="http://schemas.microsoft.com/win/2004/08/events/event">
<System>
  <Provider Name="Microsoft-Windows-Security-SPP" Guid="{E23B33B0-C8C9-472C-A5F9-
F2BDFEA0F156}" EventSourceName="Software Protection Platform Service" />
  <EventID Qualifiers="16384">903</EventID>
  <Version>0</Version>
  <Level>0</Level>
  <Task>0</Task>
  <Opcode>0</Opcode>
  <Keywords>0x80000000000000</Keywords>
  <TimeCreated SystemTime="2015-03-22T23:29:44.000000000Z" />
  <EventRecordID>287</EventRecordID>
  <Correlation />
  <Execution ProcessID="0" ThreadID="0" />
  <Channel>Application</Channel>
  <Computer>windowsserver12</Computer>
  <Security />
  </System>
  <EventData />
  </Event>
```

The Windows event logs uses different levels to indicate how critical an entry in the event log is. These levels are Error, Warning, Information, and Audit. There are a couple of challenges when it comes to Windows event logs. One of the first is the volume of messages that may be generated on any given system and the number of files they may be spread across.

Windows Server Services

Microsoft Windows Server comes with a number of services available that can be enabled as necessary. Why is this useful from a forensics standpoint? At least some of these services will generate logs. On an enterprise network, Windows servers will often be the placed where network services such as the Domain Name System (DNS) and Dynamic Host Configuration Protocol (DHCP) are run. You can see a list of the roles available to Windows Server 2012 in Figure 8.1. A number of services comes along with those roles. Each of the services may generate log entries (Table 8.1).

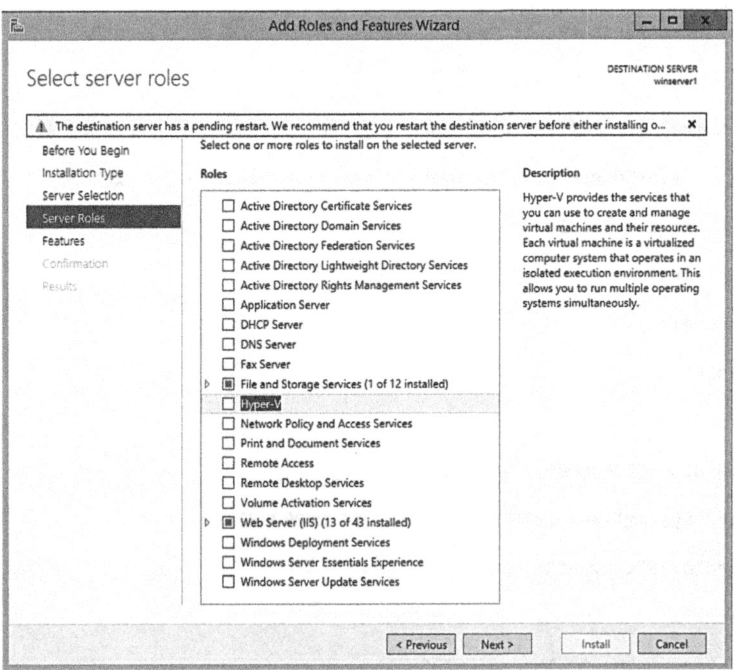

FIGURE 8.1

These Windows services may generate log entries into the standard Windows log categories but they may also generate their own log files. All of these logs should be available in the location of Windows event logs, which is C:\Windows\System32\Winevt on recent Windows systems. Since they will all use the standard Windows logging facilities, they will be stored in the same Windows event log format.

TABLE 8.1 Service Logs

Service	Description
Active directory services	Windows server has a number of services related to Active Directory that manage authentication, manage trust between different Active Directories and manage storing information about users.
Application server	An application server allows developers to write network-based services that can be consumed over the Internet, commonly through a Web browser.
DHCP server	DHCP allows a server to provide network configuration information to clients on the network. The server would log the association between an IP address and a client.
DNS server	DNS provides a way to resolve IP addresses from hostnames and vice versa. Additionally, it stores other network-related information like the mail server for a particular domain.
Fax server	This service provides a central location for fax reception and transmission. This can provide log information about those communications.
File and storage services	File sharing services are managed through this service. If you connect to a network server to store or retrieve documents, you are making use of this service.
Hyper-V	The Hyper-V service provides a hypervisor for hosting virtual machines on a Windows server.
Print and document services	The print server allows users to print to a queue stored on the server that manages printers either remotely or locally attached.
Remote access	The remote access service allows users to connect to this server, either using a dial-up or virtual private network (VPN). Connections to this service will be logged.
Remote desktop service	Allows users to connect remotely to this server to obtain a desktop.
Web server	This will install a Web server service onto the Windows server. Additionally, you can install a File Transfer Protocol (FTP) or a Simple Mail Transfer Protocol (SMTP) server. This is the Internet Information Service (IIS).
Windows Server Update Services	The Windows Server Update Services (WSUS) service provides a local system that clients can connect to in order to get Windows updates and hot fixes. This allows the local enterprise to test updates before they are deployed to desktops. It also saves Internet bandwidth by only having the update downloaded once. This will also maintain a record of clients who have updated.

Parsing XML-based Log Files

Microsoft offers a utility that can be used to parse through any sort of log file but one place where it can be useful is searching through the XML-based event files. The LogParser utility accepts Structured Query Language (SQL) queries to look for specifics from the log files. It will also allow you to extract details from the event logs and put them into a more useful format, like a comma separated values format. If you are on the system where the log files are stored, you can export the logs to either an event log file that is not opened by the operating system and can be worked on, or it can extract to an XML file. You can see in Figure 8.2, the export dialog and the different formats that you can send the log entries to.

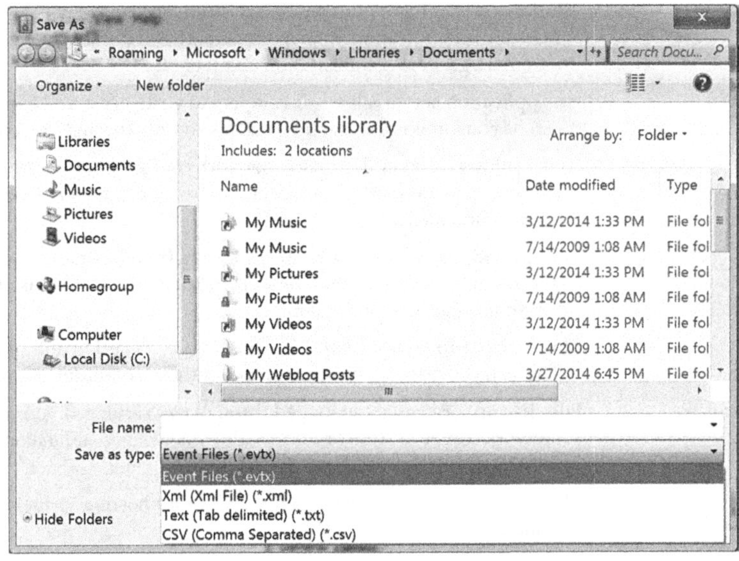

FIGURE 8.2

Once you have the file, you can start running queries against it. For example, if I wanted to extract the EventID and the strings from the events, I could run the following query:

```
C:\Program Files (x86)\LogParser 2.2>LogParser.exe -i:evt -o:csv "SELECT EventID,Strings

from \Users\kilroy\Documents\security1.extx"
```

This will leave you with a comma separated value (CSV) file with the EventID and associated strings. In this case, it was from the Security event log. If you wanted to extract all of the values from the file, you could use SELECT * instead of SELECT EventID,Strings. The resulting CSV file can then be sorted and searched using a spreadsheet program like Excel. It can also be imported into a database, if you would like to create reports from the data or do other searching and querying from the results. This can be useful if you are extracting information from a lot of different systems to aggregate into a single place.

While you can use the traditional command shell and the LogParser program is a great way to read through EventLogs, you can also use PowerShell. PowerShell has a number of features that make it a great tool for performing complex tasks like searching for strings from log files. PowerShell uses cmdlets to perform tasks and the select-string cmdlet is a great way to search for data out of a lot of log files.

UNIX SYSLOG

Syslog has become a standard log format on Unix-like operating systems over the last 30 years. Where it originally started as a logging mechanism for the mail server, Sendmail, it has grown to become a standard logging protocol that has multiple implementations. Syslog cannot only handle system and application logs for a single Unix system, it can also support log messages from remote systems. This central logging system is a very common scenario where all of the systems that support syslog send their messages to a central log server. This makes investigations considerably easier, since you can investigate log messages from all of the systems within an enterprise by looking at one log repository. Storing log messages away from the system, they were generated on also means they cannot be tampered with.

Syslog can be configured based on facility and severity. The facility determines which log file, a log message will be sent to. Syslog defines default facilities that are categories that log messages can be organized into. The severity of a log message determines whether a log message is actually written to a log file. All of this is configurable. You can see a standard configuration file below. On the left hand side, you can see the facility and the severity and on the right hand side, you can see the log file where the messages are stored. As an example, the line that says mail.* indicates that all messages for the mail facility will be stored in the file /var/log/mail.log. The * indicates everything. If you wanted to only log specific severities, you would need to indicate what severities you were to log. The facility will tell you what files to look in for specific messages.

```
#
# First some standard log files.  Log by facility.
#
auth,authpriv.*                 /var/log/auth.log
*.*;auth,authpriv.none          -/var/log/syslog
#cron.*                         /var/log/cron.log
#daemon.*                -/var/log/daemon.log
kern.*                   -/var/log/kern.log
#lpr.*                   -/var/log/lpr.log
mail.*                   -/var/log/mail.log
#user.*                  -/var/log/user.log
```

While in general, the facilities may be easily determined just based on their name, some of them may be harder to figure out. For example, the mail facility is pretty clearly about anything to do with mail. The auth facility is where you would store authorization messages.

TABLE 8.2 Syslog Facilities

Facility number	Keyword	Facility description
0	Kern	kernel messages
1	User	user-level messages
2	Mail	mail system
3	daemon	system daemons
4	Auth	security/authorization messages
5	syslog	messages generated internally by syslogd
6	Lpr	line printer subsystem
7	News	network news subsystem
8	Uucp	UUCP subsystem
9		clock daemon
10	authpriv	security/authorization messages
11	ftp	FTP daemon
12	–	NTP subsystem
13	–	log audit
14	–	log alert
15	cron	clock daemon
16	local0	local use 0 (local0)
17	local1	local use 1 (local1)
18	local2	local use 2 (local2)
19	local3	local use 3 (local3)
20	local4	local use 4 (local4)
21	local5	local use 5 (local5)
22	local6	local use 6 (local6)
23	local7	local use 7 (local7)

Others may be a little more obscure, like lpr. While it is still in use, the name is historic and it refers to line printers from the mainframe and mini computer days. Table 8.2 shows complete list of facilities.

There are eight severities available for syslog. The severities are referenced by number in order to save space but they also have specific meanings. In configuration files, you will generally see the short notation used. The short notation is also historic due to space limitations. The more bytes that could be saved, the more room there was for more important information (Table 8.3).

TABLE 8.3 Syslog Severity

Number	Severity	Short notation
0	Emergency	emerg (panic)
1	Alert	alert
2	Critical	crit
3	Error	err (error)
4	Warning	warning (warn)
5	Notice	notice
6	Informational	info
7	Debug	debug

The log messages you will find may end up looking very confusing, until you get used to reading them. You can see below a small sample of log messages out of the /var/log/auth.log from a Linux Mint system. The file names may be different but it is common for log files to be stored in the /var/log directory.

```
Apr  1 20:41:20 hodgepodge dbus[580]: [system] Rejected send message, 7 matched rules;
type="method_return", sender=":1.55" (uid=0 pid=8664 comm="/usr/sbin/dnsmasq --no-resolv -
-keep-in-foreground") interface="(unset)" member="(unset)" error name="(unset)"
requested_reply="0" destination=":1.51" (uid=0 pid=8520 comm="NetworkManager ")
Apr 19 20:39:43 hodgepodge sudo:   kilroy : TTY=unknown ; PWD=/home/kilroy ; USER=root
; COMMAND=/usr/lib/linuxmint/mintUpdate/checkAPT.py
Apr 19 20:39:43 hodgepodge sudo: pam_unix(sudo:session): session opened for user root by
(uid=0)
Apr 19 20:39:56 hodgepodge cinnamon-screensaver-dialog: gkr-pam: unlocked login keyring
Apr 19 20:40:12 hodgepodge sudo: pam_unix(sudo:session): session closed for user root
```

Since syslog is a standard, all syslog messages are going to have the same format. Let us pull one of these lines apart to see all of the individual components. The last line is a good one to look at. The first part of it is the date and time. April 19 at 8:40:12 PM. This is stored based on the local time zone of the system, though it is not noted here. In order to determine what time zone the system is in, you would have to check on the system using the date command or checking the contents of the /etc/localtime file, which is a binary file that stores the information about the time zone the system is configured to be in. Every computer system has to be told what time zone it is in, since times are stored as absolute values that are the difference between a known value and the current time. In the case of Unix, the time is January 1, 1970 at 00:00:00 but the reference point is always Greenwich Mean Time (GMT). In the case of logfiles, what is stored is not the time relative to January 1, 1970 at midnight, it is a string of characters indicating the date and time. As a result, any effort to reconcile times from the logs into a single coherent timeline with other time-based information has to know what the correct time zone for the system is.

Time zones are really important because time is not fixed across the world. There are number of terms that you may see when it comes to the first time zone. Historically, it was Greenwich Mean Time because it was the time zone where the Royal Observatory in Greenwich, England was located. The time zone has remained the same but you may see it referred to as UTC, which is a compromise acronym for Coordinated Universal Time. You may also hear the same time zone referred to as Zulu Time.

After the date and time is the name of the program or application that generated the log. The program in this case is sudo, which is a program that is used to temporarily escalate privileges to an administrative level. After that is the specific message that the program sudo wanted to log. This is application-specific and does not follow any particular format. In most cases, it will be human readable, at least assuming that the human has an understanding of Linux or the specific program or application in question. This particular message seems fairly straightforward. The first entry in the log sample above, though, is less straightforward. It would require someone who knew the internals of the dbus program to really understand what it is saying. In most cases, the entries you will be looking for will be much easier to understand. You will see entries in the auth file that users have logged in and logged out and that sessions have been created. Other log files will contain entries that will be relevant to the programs or applications that created the log entry.

APPLICATION LOGS

Not all programs use the Windows Event Viewer or syslog for their logging purposes. Different applications will use different logging mechanisms. One of the common applications that would generate log files is a Web server. Web servers on both Windows and Linux do not commonly use the built-in logging mechanisms. In the case of Apache, which is a cross-platform Web server that will run on Linux, Windows, and Mac OS X. Since it is cross platform, it makes more sense to develop a single logging mechanism rather than having to add logging functions for each of the platforms Apache runs on. Additionally, the first Web server was developed in 1990 before syslog had really become a standard, so the National Center for Supercomputing Applications (NCSA) developed a log format for their Web server. This log format remains in use today. The log format, called the Common Log Format, has the following format:

```
host identity userid date request status size
```

While the Common Log Format is used across many Web servers, it is not the only log format that is available. Perhaps more common is the W3C Extended Log Format. The extended log can be configured per server by providing a format to the server to indicate, what you want your log messages to look like. You can get the same information available in the common log format, as well as other pieces of data. An example of the W3C extended log format is below. The first part of this particular log entry has the same structure as a common log format log entry.

```
10.211.55.3 - - [21/Apr/2015:21:32:50 -0400] "GET / HTTP/1.1" 200 3594 "-" "Mozilla/5.0

(X11; Ubuntu; Linux x86_64; rv:36.0) Gecko/20100101 Firefox/36.0"
```

The host is the hostname or IP address of the requesting client. In the example, the IP address is 10.211.55.3. This is followed by a – indicating that there is no identity provided. This has to do with the ident protocol, used to identify network users. There is also no username provided. The second dash indicates that there is no authorized user. If a user were to authenticate over HTTP using an authentication mechanism, like basic or digest authentication, that username would be shown in place of the second dash. The next block of data is the address. You can see this is formatted as date and time. After the time, it indicates the offset from Greenwich Mean Time (GMT). The next section, in quotes here, is the request including the method (GET) and the identifier ("/"). After that is the response code. HTTP uses a number of response codes, depending on whether it was a successful request or whether there may have been an error condition, or other circumstances to convey to the requestor. This particular response code, 200, is the one you want to see, since it is the number equivalent of OK, meaning that the request was successful. The next value is the number of bytes that were transferred as part of this request. The next two may or may not be part of the log file you see because they are part of the extended format. The last one section, however, can be very valuable. This is the user agent string and it contains the name of the program or browser that was used to make the request, as well as the operating system the browser was running on. In this case, the request was made from Firefox running on a Linux system.

While Apache is certainly not the only Web browser available, it is a very common one. On Linux systems, you will commonly find the log files stored in /var/log/apache2 for the Apache version 2 series of Web servers. Other operating systems will store the Apache logs in other locations. On Mac OS, since it is a Unix-like operating system, the logs will be stored in the same directory as on Linux. On a Windows system, however, the log directory will likely be in \Program Files\Apache Software Foundation\Apache2.x, where x is the minor version number that is installed. Under that there should be a directory called logs, where the log files are stored.

Of course, if you are running a Windows system, you will likely be using Microsoft's Internet Information Server (IIS) rather than Apache, since it comes with the Windows Server family. The good news is that IIS can still use the same Common Log Format to write out logs in. It will also write using the W3C Extended Log Format and an IIS log format.

```
73.16.58.2, -, 4/27/2015, 23:16:26, W3SVC1, winserver1, 10.240.178.66, 1311, 354, 925, 200,
0, GET, /, -,
73.16.58.2, -, 4/27/2015, 23:16:26, W3SVC1, winserver1, 10.240.178.66, 484, 344, 99936, 200,
0, GET, /iis-85.png, -,
73.16.58.2, -, 4/27/2015, 23:16:26, W3SVC1, winserver1, 10.240.178.66, 62, 328, 1382, 404, 2,
GET, /favicon.ico, -,
73.16.58.2, -, 4/27/2015, 23:16:37, W3SVC1, winserver1, 10.240.178.66, 46, 362, 1382, 404, 2,
GET, /iisstart, -,
73.16.58.2, -, 4/27/2015, 23:16:46, W3SVC1, winserver1, 10.240.178.66, 1374, 362, 452078,
200, 0, GET, /logs.zip, -,
```

While much of the information captured is the same as that from the Apache log file we looked at earlier, Windows stores different information because of the integration with the operating system and associated service and user information. Table 8.4 has the fields and the information associated with them.

TABLE 8.4 Windows Log Data from IIS

Field	Information
IP address	73.16.58.2
User name	– (meaning there was no authenticated user)
Date and time	4/27/2015, 23:16:26
Service instance	W3SVC1 (IIS allows administrators to name the instance of the Web server based on IP address, port or application running)
Server name	winserver1 (the name of the system)
Server IP address	10.240.178.66 (the local IP address of the server that handled the request)
Time taken	1374 (in milliseconds)
Client bytes sent	354 (bytes sent from the client)
Server bytes sent	925 (bytes sent from the server)
Status code	200 (HTTP status code, 200 indicates a success)
Windows status code	0 (indicates a success)
Method	GET (the HTTP request method received from by the server)
Target	/ (this is the actual target requested)
Parameters	– (no parameters were sent)

Reading through log files like those from a Web server can be challenging. Fortunately, there are a number of programs that will take those logs and generate aggregated information, including graphs and charts. Some of the programs, such as analog, awstats, and webalyzer will take a number of log formats as input and generate the aggregated output. In Figure 8.3, you can see the value of using aggregated data rather than a series of comma separated lines. The chart shows the different IP addresses that came to visit this particular server. This particular chart came from the program AWStats.

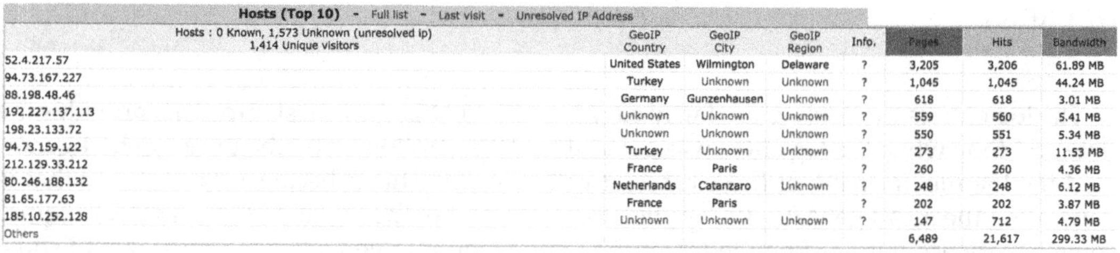

Hosts (Top 10) - Full list - Last visit - Unresolved IP Address

Hosts : 0 Known, 1,573 Unknown (unresolved ip) 1,414 Unique visitors	GeoIP Country	GeoIP City	GeoIP Region	Info.	Pages	Hits	Bandwidth
52.4.217.57	United States	Wilmington	Delaware	?	3,205	3,206	61.89 MB
94.73.167.227	Turkey	Unknown	Unknown	?	1,045	1,045	44.24 MB
88.198.48.46	Germany	Gunzenhausen	Unknown	?	618	618	3.01 MB
192.227.137.113	Unknown	Unknown	Unknown	?	559	560	5.41 MB
198.23.133.72	Unknown	Unknown	Unknown	?	550	551	5.34 MB
94.73.159.122	Turkey	Unknown	Unknown	?	273	273	11.53 MB
212.129.33.212	France	Paris		?	260	260	4.36 MB
80.246.188.132	Netherlands	Catanzaro	Unknown	?	248	248	6.12 MB
81.65.177.63	France	Paris		?	202	202	3.87 MB
185.10.252.128	Unknown	Unknown	Unknown	?	147	712	4.79 MB
Others					6,489	21,617	299.33 MB

FIGURE 8.3

The one downside to the aggregated data like this is that many log analysis programs do not provide breadcrumb trails through a Web site from a specific server. In some cases, this can be important. However, in some cases, the aggregated data is more important. This will provide good information of the usage of the server at specific periods of time. Searching through the log files for specific IP addresses may be able to provide the trail through the Web site, if that is necessary. A number of tools can be used for this purpose, though one of the best tools for this is grep that comes installed on Unix-like systems, like Linux and Mac OS X but can also be obtained for Windows systems. Using a tool like grep, you can extract all of the lines from a log file that contain a specific IP address.

MAC OS X LOGS

Mac OS X inherits much from Unix, including the syslog daemon used as a way to handle log requests. While there is a syslog daemon running on a Mac OS X system, its sole job is to forward any log messages to the Apple System Log manager. This is a separate daemon that is used to not only handle system log messages like syslog would, but also to handle log messages from programs written using the Apple application programming interfaces. Much like Microsoft, Apple supports application logging. Since Mac OS X inherits at least in part from Unix, it brings along syslog. As a result, Apple has their own logging service for their applications but they also forward all of the syslog messages for any legacy applications or any Unix applications to the Apple System Log manager. In order to view those logs, including all of the syslog messages, you can use Activity Manager. Figure 8.4 shows the Activity Manager with the log entries on the right hand side and the list of log files that are available in the pane on the left.

FIGURE 8.4

The log entries themselves are fairly easy to read. First is the timestamp. This provides the date and time when the log entry was generated. This is followed by the program that generated the log file. In many of these cases, it is the kernel. This is because it is a driver that is generating the message. After the application is the text of the log message. This does require some experience with or knowledge of the application that generates the message. In some cases, they are written in reasonably plain English. In other cases, they are more cryptic. This depends on the application, its developers and the needs of the application; what information is needed to be logged, so an experienced technician or engineer can resolve the underlying cause for the log message.

There are multiple locations for storing logs on an Apple system, depending on the types of logs they are. Of course, there is the common location of syslog messages in /var/log, though on the Mac OS X system, this is a link to the location /private/var/log. You will see some log files that may look familiar. For example, system.log and authd.log may be ones you would see on other Unix-like systems. You will see messages like the following:

```
Apr 28 21:18:59 portnoy.local sudo[3520]:   kilroy : TTY=ttys000 ; PWD=/private/var/log ;

USER=root ; COMMAND=/usr/bin/tail system.log
```

This is exactly the type of message that you will see on any Unix-like operating system, including Linux. This is a message from sudo, which is a utility used to temporarily elevate privileges for a user.

Another location for log files is /Library/Logs. This location is used to store application logs. The /Library/ location is where system level information is stored with preference settings and other support files for applications. Each user also has a Library directory to store user-specific preference settings and other support files for applications. This is the same sort of information as can be found in the /Library/ directory except that it is specific to each individual user. This is commonly referred to as ~/Library/Logs, where the ~ character indicates the home directory of the current user. In my case, the ~ translates to /Users/kilroy/ so the log directory for my user is /Users/kilroy/Library/Logs/. This is a list of the contents of the log file directory for my user.

```
kilroy@portnoy:/Library/Logs$ ls ~/Library/Logs
ACC.log                          NELog 04-04-2015 14-11-35.log
Adobe                            NELog 04-22-2015 10-38-57.log
AdobeDownload                    NELog.log
AdobeIPCBroker.log               PDApp.log
AdobeIPCBrokerCustomHook.log SMSMigrator
AndroidStudio                    SparkleUpdateLog.log
CSXS                             Ubiquity
DiagnosticReports                amt3.log
DiskUtility.log                  fsck_hfs.log
FaceTime                         oobelib.log
GoogleSoftwareUpdateAgent.log parallels.log
Handoff                          talagent.log
```

Some of these are just log files and others are directories that contain multiple log files. As an example, the parallels.log file contains log entries for the Parallels virtualization application. A log file like that will provide details of when different virtual machines were started and when they were shutdown. As well as other entries, of course. Each application may provide a lot of interesting detail that could be used to track the activities of each individual user. Since the log files are stored in the user's home directory and relate to that user, the logs would only be created in the case if the user was logged in and running applications.

SECURITY LOGS

Security logs are often useful things to have around. There are a number of types of security logs available. These can range from firewall logs to antivirus logs, as well as different types of intrusion detection logs. Firewall logs can be used to provide evidence of network connections. The amount of data available from these logs depends on settings for the firewall. Firewalls can be network-level as well as application-level. An application level firewall can provide details around attacks that have taken place and have been stopped. The details around the attack can be very useful.

When it comes to antivirus logs, presumably you are not going to get any evidence about a malware infestation. If you are running antivirus and you have a virus on your system, there was not a signature. As a result, what you can get from the log is when the signatures were or were not updated. Finally, intrusion detection programs can provide good evidence of attack attempts. There are a variety of those programs around. This can include network-based intrusion detection as well as host-based.

There are a wide variety of intrusion detection products on the market for both the network and host. One very common intrusion detection system is Snort, which is an open source network-based intrusion detection system. Snort will run on Linux, Windows, and Mac OS X. Snort has also spawned a number of associated products for management, updating rules, and viewing logs.

Firewall Logs

One type of security log is a firewall log. Linux systems use iptables for their firewall software. It is built into the kernel. The Linux firewall can be configured to log network communication and the resulting log file looks like this:

```
Apr 28 20:52:56 bobbi kernel: [ 2580.527149] IN=eth0 OUT=

MAC=00:1c:42:9b:c4:29:34:36:3b:c4:4e:d2:08:00 SRC=172.30.42.9 DST=172.30.42.20

LEN=44 TOS=0x00 PREC=0x00 TTL=59 ID=36102 PROTO=TCP SPT=43733 DPT=21

WINDOW=1024 RES=0x00 SYN URGP=0

Apr 28 20:52:56 bobbi kernel: [ 2580.527193] IN=eth0 OUT=

MAC=00:1c:42:9b:c4:29:34:36:3b:c4:4e:d2:08:00 SRC=172.30.42.9 DST=172.30.42.20

LEN=44 TOS=0x00 PREC=0x00 TTL=57 ID=44658 PROTO=TCP SPT=43733 DPT=53

WINDOW=1024 RES=0x00 SYN URGP=0

Apr 28 20:52:56 bobbi kernel: [ 2580.527807] IN=eth0 OUT=

MAC=00:1c:42:9b:c4:29:34:36:3b:c4:4e:d2:08:00 SRC=172.30.42.9 DST=172.30.42.20

LEN=44 TOS=0x00 PREC=0x00 TTL=57 ID=41888 PROTO=TCP SPT=43733 DPT=111

WINDOW=1024 RES=0x00 SYN URGP=0

Apr 28 20:52:56 bobbi kernel: [ 2580.527826] IN=eth0 OUT=

MAC=00:1c:42:9b:c4:29:34:36:3b:c4:4e:d2:08:00 SRC=172.30.42.9 DST=172.30.42.20

LEN=44 TOS=0x00 PREC=0x00 TTL=58 ID=26046 PROTO=TCP SPT=43733 DPT=25

WINDOW=1024 RES=0x00 SYN URGP=0
Apr 28 20:52:56 bobbi kernel: [ 2580.527832] IN=eth0 OUT=

MAC=00:1c:42:9b:c4:29:34:36:3b:c4:4e:d2:08:00 SRC=172.30.42.9 DST=172.30.42.20

LEN=44 TOS=0x00 PREC=0x00 TTL=37 ID=29575 PROTO=TCP SPT=43733 DPT=139

WINDOW=1024 RES=0x00 SYN URGP=0
Apr 28 20:52:56 bobbi kernel: [ 2580.527939] IN=eth0 OUT=

MAC=00:1c:42:9b:c4:29:34:36:3b:c4:4e:d2:08:00 SRC=172.30.42.9 DST=172.30.42.20

LEN=44 TOS=0x00 PREC=0x00 TTL=56 ID=36470 PROTO=TCP SPT=43733 DPT=1720

WINDOW=1024 RES=0x00 SYN URGP=0
```

In each of these entries, written out by syslog, you can see the details about each of the packets that were logged. It helps to understand networking protocols in some way. Each of these messages include the source and destination IP address, the length and the source and destination ports. Much of the rest of the information provided in these messages would primarily be relevant to security engineers who may be involved in responding to alerts.

Windows Firewall Logs

The Windows operating system has a firewall built into it. The Windows firewall will also generate logs and those logs can be found on most systems in the file C:\Windows\system32\logfiles\firewall\pfirewall.log. If the operating system files are stored in a different location from C:\Windows, then the rest of the directory structure would fall under that. In technical documentation, you will see this referred to as %systemdir%. This is a variable used in the operating system to indicate the root of the Windows system files. Since the vast majority of installations will use the default C:\Windows, it is generally easier to refer to the directory structure using that. The Windows firewall is not necessarily enabled by default on all installations and in cases, where it is enabled, the logging may not be enabled. In order to have logs to review, it is important to have log files. The settings for the Windows Firewall allow you to set both allowed and dropped packets to be logged, as shown in Figure 8.5.

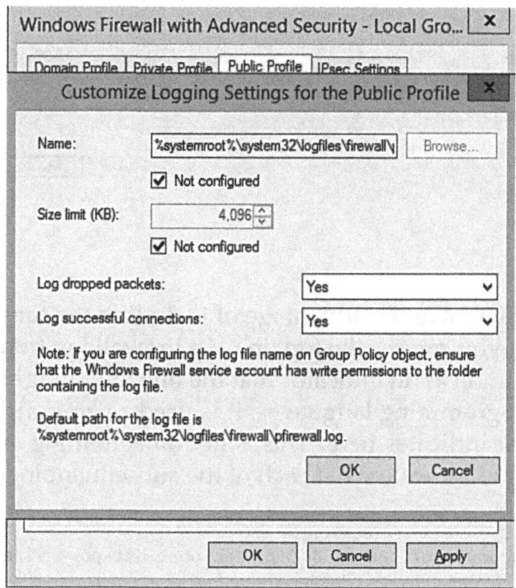

FIGURE 8.5

One of the nice things about the Windows firewall, though, is that you can block or allow, based on specific programs and not simply ports. This can be very helpful in the case of trying to chase down malicious programs and what they are doing. If you have a program, you believe to be malicious on your system, you can create a firewall rule based on the program, so you can watch everything it is doing. Creating a firewall rule on a Windows system uses a wizard, as many features do on a Windows Server system, which you can see in Figure 8.6. Once you have the rule, based on the program, you can monitor its behavior. While there are other ways of doing this, this is probably the most efficient, since other methods like packet capture programs do not always have the ability to filter based on the program that generates the network communication.

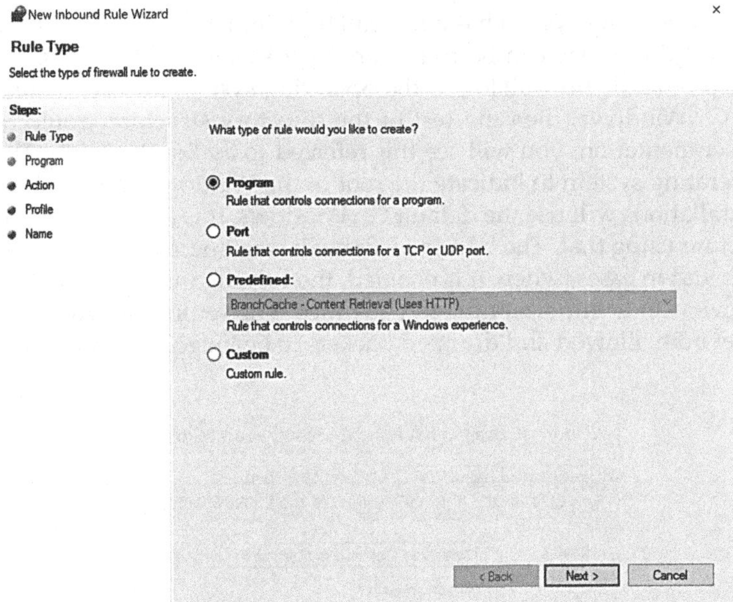

FIGURE 8.6

The Windows logs often have the advantage of including the format for the log file at the very top. As an example, you can see the top line of a firewall log from a Windows system below. The # symbol is common as an indicator that the line following should not be interpreted as anything. In some programming languages, it is used as an indication of a comment and that is essentially what it indicates here. This is not an actual log entry itself, but instead a little self-documentation to indicate what each of the subsequent log entries contain.

```
#Fields: date time action protocol src-ip dst-ip src-port dst-port size tcpflags tcpsyn tcpack

tcpwin icmptype icmpcode info path
```

The Windows firewall log shows similar information to that from the Linux firewall. The Windows firewall, though, is clearer about what the disposition of the packet is. In the iptables logs above, there is no indication whether it was dropped or allowed. This is because with an iptables firewall, you can log, drop, or accept. If you log, it just logs the packet without indicating that anything else happened to the packet. The log fragment below makes it clear, right after the date/time stamp, it shows that messages were allowed. If one had been dropped, the action entry would say DROP.

```
2015-05-03 18:30:24 ALLOW UDP fe80::b9fd:4b62:2788:ff21 ff02::1:3 56427 5355 0 - - - - - -
- SEND
2015-05-03 18:30:24 ALLOW UDP 172.30.42.31 224.0.0.252 60711 5355 0 - - - - - - - SEND
2015-05-03 18:30:25 ALLOW UDP 172.30.42.31 172.30.42.255 137 137 0 - - - - - - - SEND
2015-05-03 18:30:37 ALLOW 2 172.30.42.1 224.0.0.1 - - 0 - - - - - - - RECEIVE
2015-05-03 18:30:37 ALLOW 2 172.30.42.31 224.0.0.252 - - 0 - - - - - - - SEND
2015-05-03 18:30:38 ALLOW TCP 172.30.42.31 173.194.123.104 49221 443 0 - 0 0 0 - - -
SEND
2015-05-03 18:30:38 ALLOW TCP 172.30.42.31 173.194.123.63 49222 443 0 - 0 0 0 - - -
SEND
```

You can see from the log entry here that it logs both IP version 4 and IP version 6 packets. The first entry is from a system running IPv6, which explains the longer address. The other thing you will notice from these logs, that you may not get from the iptables logs is the direction of the packet. Of course, the amount of data you get in your log files is all configurable. The system this log fragment came from was configured to log accepted packets and it will log both directions. As a result, you can see both SENT and RECEIVE here in this log. You will also see the protocol that is being used and while TCP and UDP are both pretty easy to read, the entry that says 2 may be a little more obscure. The 2 indicates the IP protocol number. Both TCP and UDP have corresponding numbers, but since they are so common, they often just get translated by most tools that will read and display that. You may need to find a table of IP protocols. This particular protocol is the Internet Group Management Protocol (IGMP). IGMP may be used in streaming applications like video and gaming, but it can also be used for network management.

Antivirus Logs

Every antivirus program will have its own set of logs. All of the different operating systems have their own anti-virus programs. Mac OS X, Linux, and Windows are all susceptible to viruses and other forms of malware. Covering all of the different antivirus programs could be an entire book considering the large number of antivirus programs out there. On Windows systems, though, there is a malware detection program that has been common for the last couple of versions. Over the last few years, Windows Defender has taken on more and more, when it comes to malware. When it began, it was an antispyware program for Windows XP.

As of Windows 8, though, it is a full-fledged antivirus program that comes installed with the operating system. Since this is the only operating system vendor that bundles an antivirus program, it is worth looking at the log files. When you are on a Windows system, you can use a program that comes with Windows Defender to gather up all of the relevant log files. By running MpCmdRun -getfiles in the C:\Program Files\Windows Defender directory, you will gather up all of the logs into the C:\ProgramData\Microsoft\Windows Defender\Support directory. You will end up with eight log files. One of the important logs you will end up with is the WindowsUpdate.log file. This file is a log of, not surprisingly, all of the updates that have been downloaded and installed on the system. Antivirus programs require constant updates because malware signatures are constantly changing with millions and millions of new pieces of malware created each year. An example of a portion of that is below.

```
2015-05-03    18:28:23:502    996    cf0    DnldMgr      *************
2015-05-03    18:28:23:502    996    cf0    DnldMgr      ** START **   DnldMgr:
Downloading updates [CallerId = Microsoft Security Essentials (EDB4FA23-53B8-4AFA-
8C5D-99752CCA7094)]
2015-05-03    18:28:23:502    996    cf0    DnldMgr      *********
2015-05-03    18:28:23:502    996    cf0    DnldMgr        * Call ID = {DE003C6A-D2D6-
4833-9F14-682C590060BF}
2015-05-03    18:28:23:502    996    cf0    DnldMgr        * Priority = 2, Interactive = 1,
Owner is system = 1, Explicit proxy = 1, Proxy session id = -1, ServiceId = {7971F918-A848-
4430-9279-4A52D1EFE18D}
2015-05-03    18:28:23:502    996    cf0    DnldMgr        * Updates to download = 1
2015-05-03    18:28:23:502    996    cf0    Agent    *    Title = Definition Update for Microsoft
Security Essentials - KB2310138 (Definition 1.197.1372.0)
2015-05-03    18:28:23:502    996    cf0    Agent    *    UpdateId = {AA436F62-F164-4384-
BA98-DA9F58AB9C80}.201
2015-05-03    18:28:23:502    996    cf0    Agent    *     Bundles 4 updates:
2015-05-03    18:28:23:502    996    cf0    Agent    *       {142AB37F-2C98-48E0-BB68-
FD698C4A3266}.200
2015-05-03    18:28:23:502    996    cf0    Agent    *       {EEAD0CFA-23BF-4BCB-991C-
A32108B662BBC}.200
2015-05-03    18:28:23:502    996    cf0    Agent    *       {092F4313-298A-415D-A3D9-
77B14FA54157}.200
```

```
2015-05-03    18:28:23:502    996    cf0    Agent    *        {144AA08C-3CBA-4812-A8C1-
944C77229962}.201
2015-05-03    18:28:23:502    996    f10    AU    WARNING: AU ignoring update during
offline scan:
2015-05-03    18:28:23:502    996    f10    AU    #########
2015-05-03    18:28:23:502    996    f10    AU    ##  END  ##  AU: Search for updates
[CallId = {3DF8C77F-F155-4A96-A299-EBC9D0032911}]
2015-05-03    18:28:23:502    996    f10    AU    #############
```

From this log file, you can see the different updates that were added. They are identified by a globally unique identifier (GUID). As an example, {092F4313-298A-415D-A3D9-77B14FA54157} is one of the updates. Another log file is the MPLog-XXXXXXXX-XXXXXX.log file. The Xs in the filename will actually be a string of numbers generated by your computer. This log file will include service information. As an example, when the service has been disabled, which might be an indication that something bad has happened on the system, you might get something like the following:

```
34
34W34i34n34d34o34w34s34 34D34e34f34e34n34d34e34r34 34L34o34g34,34 34(34c34)34
34234034034634
34
34S34t34a34r34t34e34d34 34O34n34 34S34u34n34 34M34a34y34 34034334 34234034134534
34134834:34134334:34034934
34
34*34*34*34*34*34*34*34*34*34*34*34*34*34*34*34*34*34*34*34*34*34*34*34*34*
34*34*34*34*34*34*34*34*34*34*34*34*34*34*34*34*34*34*34*34*34*34*34*34*34*
34*34*34*34*34*34*34*34*34
34
34P34r34o34d34u34c34t34
34d34i34s34a34b34l34e34d34.34.34.34S34t34o34p34p34i34n34g34 34s34e34r34v34i34c34e34
34
34W34i34n34d34o34w34s34 34D34e34f34e34n34d34e34r34 34L34o34g34,34 34(34c34)34
34234034034634
```

```
34

34S34t34o34p34p34e34d34 34034n34 34S34u34n34 34M34a34y34 34034334

34234034134534 34134834:34134334:34034934 34(34E34x34i34t34 34C34o34d34e34 34=34

35035x35035)35

35

35*35*35*35*35*35*35*35*35*35*35*35*35*35*35*35*35*35*35*35*35*35*35*35*35*35*35*

35*35*35*35*35*35*35*35*35*35*35*35*35*35*35*35*35*35*35*35*35*35*35*35*35*35*35*

35*35*35*35*35*35*35*35*
```

The MpOperationalEvents.txt file is used to store information about the anti-malware service. There are other logs that will be gathered as part of the process but they relate to the program that is gathering the files and are less likely to be of much interest. The ones related to the different services will be of much more value, unless gathering the files has generated some sort of error, in which case you can use these log files to determine where the problem might be.

AUDITING

One of the ways by which you might gather a lot of useful information is by enabling auditing on a system. Auditing allows you to keep track of a variety of events including getting file access, Active Directory access, and changes to user accounts, as well as logon activities. You can see the different categories of audit events in Figure 8.7. On enterprise networks, you would do this using a group policy on your Windows Server. However, desktop systems can also generate audit events. On your desktop system, you would use the Local Security Policy to create an audit policy. Figure 8.7 shows the configuration of the audit policy. For each category, you have the option of enabling success or failure auditing. Of course, you can also do nothing and just get no audit events.

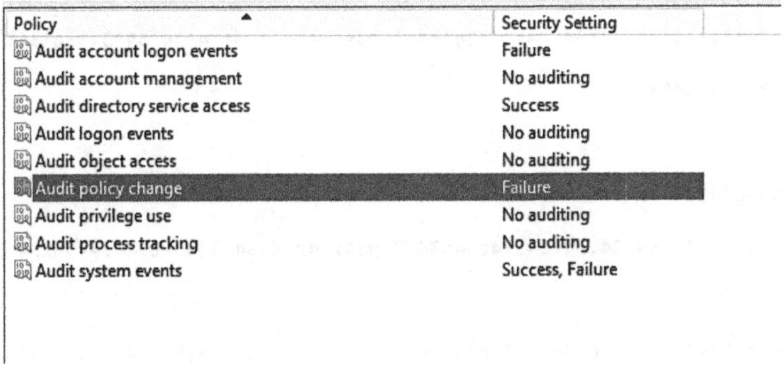

Policy	Security Setting
Audit account logon events	Failure
Audit account management	No auditing
Audit directory service access	Success
Audit logon events	No auditing
Audit object access	No auditing
Audit policy change	Failure
Audit privilege use	No auditing
Audit process tracking	No auditing
Audit system events	Success, Failure

FIGURE 8.7

When you are done, you get events in your event logs just as you would with other events. Once the logs are there, you can view them with the Event Viewer as well as querying them with the Log Parser to get a complete list of all of the audit events. Once you have the logs, you can do whatever you need with them. But you have to enable the auditing in order to have the data. There are a number of reasons why you might use auditing, both from a security as well as forensics perspective. If you enabled success auditing on file access, for example, you would have the operating system telling you when a particular file in the filesystem was accessed and who it was accessed by. While you cannot guarantee a particular person, you can get the username. Add this to login success or failure audit logs and you have some additional information that you can use.

Linux systems also have the ability to enable auditing. Linux comes with an auditing daemon called auditd that can be installed to do the auditing. The audit daemon in Linux allows for quite a bit more granularity than the audit function in Windows. In Linux, you have to create all the rules yourself rather than just enabling success or failure on individual categories. This can generate a lot of output, as seen below.

```
type=CWD msg=audit(1430701212.732:554):  cwd="/etc/audit"

type=PATH msg=audit(1430701212.732:554): item=0 name="/var/log/audit/" inode=1444910

dev=08:01 mode=040750 ouid=0 ogid=0 rdev=00:00 nametype=NORMAL

type=SYSCALL msg=audit(1430701212.736:555): arch=c000003e syscall=257 success=yes

exit=3 a0=ffffffffffffff9c a1=13959e8 a2=90800 a3=0 items=1 ppid=24114 pid=26659

auid=4294967295 uid=0 gid=0 euid=0 suid=0 fsuid=0 egid=0 sgid=0 fsgid=0 tty=pts4
ses=4294967295 comm="bash" exe="/bin/bash" key="LOG_audit"

type=CWD msg=audit(1430701212.736:555):  cwd="/etc/audit"

type=PATH msg=audit(1430701212.736:555): item=0 name="/var/log/audit/" inode=1444910

dev=08:01 mode=040750 ouid=0 ogid=0 rdev=00:00 nametype=NORMAL

type=SYSCALL msg=audit(1430701213.444:556): arch=c000003e syscall=2 success=yes

exit=3 a0=7ffff0b10911 a1=0 a2=1fffffffffff0000 a3=7ffff0b0f000 items=1 ppid=24114

pid=26665 auid=4294967295 uid=0 gid=0 euid=0 suid=0 fsuid=0 egid=0 sgid=0 fsgid=0

tty=pts4 ses=4294967295 comm="cat" exe="/bin/cat" key="LOG_audit"

type=CWD msg=audit(1430701213.444:556):  cwd="/etc/audit"

type=PATH msg=audit(1430701213.444:556): item=0 name="/var/log/audit/audit.log"

inode=1442125 dev=08:01 mode=0100600 ouid=0 ogid=0 rdev=00:00 nametype=NORMAL
```

This can be a lot to take in, of course. This is the output from the raw audit.log, which was stored in /var/log/audit on the system it was taken from. However, auditd comes with a number of reporting utilities that can be helpful to narrow things down. One of them is ausearch, which can be used to search for audit event identifiers, commands, users, groups, or a variety of other categories. You can also generate a report using aureport. You can end up with a summary report as seen below, if you just run it without any command line parameters.

```
Summary Report

Range of time in logs: 05/03/2015 20:48:31.732 - 05/03/2015 21:03:45.596

Selected time for report: 05/03/2015 20:48:31 - 05/03/2015 21:03:45.596

Number of changes in configuration: 242

Number of changes to accounts, groups, or roles: 0

Number of logins: 0

Number of failed logins: 0

Number of authentications: 1

Number of failed authentications: 0

Number of users: 2

Number of terminals: 4

Number of host names: 1

Number of executables: 13

Number of files: 22

Number of AVC's: 0

Number of MAC events: 0

Number of failed syscalls: 6

Number of anomaly events: 0

Number of responses to anomaly events: 0

Number of crypto events: 0

Number of keys: 42

Number of process IDs: 46

Number of events: 399
```

You can also create reports based on specific parameters. You might want a list of hosts, commands, events, configuration changes, or a number of other settings that aureport can provide information on. Rather than trying to sort through the entire log file, which as you can see from above, can contain a substantial number of entries (to give you an idea, the report above says 399 and this was only running auditd for several minutes before the report was generated), you should use some of the available tools to aggregate some of the data for you, so you can then narrow your search to specific information you are looking for.

SUMMARY

Log files can be very powerful tools for gathering information. Of course, there are a large number of log files and the ones covered here have really only skimmed the surface of what is available. However, there are certainly some strategies that can be used no matter what log file you are looking at. Windows Event Logs can be very good sources of information but you have to be able to extract the information from the event logs, unless you just want to look through the Event Viewer to find the information. Fortunately, the Microsoft utility Log Parser will allow you to query the log files using the Structure Query Language. While SQL can be challenging to learn if you do not have much database experience, there are some very simple queries like SELECT * that can be used to just pull all the information out into a different format like a comma separated values file.

Security logs can be very useful sources of information. Firewalls will generate a lot of entries that you will not find as easily with other tools like packet capture programs. Some of this relies on appropriate configuration of the firewall so that it can create good log entries. With Linux, you would use iptables to create firewall logs. This requires custom configuration of the firewall. Under Windows, there is a firewall that is installed and configured by default. In order to get log files that can be reviewed, however, there is some configuration that needs to happen. Since log files can take up disk space, enabling the logging is something that needs to be decided on by the system owner or manager.

One big advantage to log files is that they are generally plain text and often written in a way that people can understand. These people may need to be skilled administrators but often, the log files are written in English that can be interpreted from the context of the log and the program that generated the entry.

EXERCISES

1. Use the LogParser utility to create a comma separated value file from a Windows event log.
2. Enable auditing in your Local Security Policy and view the resulting entries in the event logs.
3. Enable Windows firewall logging and investigate the results.
4. Configure logging on a Linux system and view the resulting log file.

CHAPTER

9

Executable Programs

INFORMATION INCLUDED IN THIS CHAPTER:

- Windows Portable Executable
- Linux Executable and Linkable Format
- Mac OS X Application Bundles
- NET Common Language Runtime
- Debugging/Disassembly
- System Calls and Tracing

INTRODUCTION

At the core of any computer system is the programs that run on it. It might normally go without saying, but I am going to say it anyway. Those programs are what make computers useful but more importantly, provide us with artifacts, which make sure that forensic practitioners have evidence to look at. A program is a file on your disk that includes executable code but the program has to be put together in such a way that the operating system knows where all of the individual components of the program are. The program also has to know how to interact with the operating system. There is a lot involved in making sure that the executable code is specific to the processor as well as the program knowing, how to make use of the interface to the operating system. All of this is handled by the software that is used to take human-readable source code and convert it into machine language that can be used by the processor. That software is called a compiler and talking about the compilation process is way beyond the scope of what we are talking about here.

However, it is useful to know that there are different types of executables or programs. The reason for that is based on the CPU architecture (Intel, Motorola, 32-bit, 64-bit, etc.) and the operating system in use. The reason it is useful to know that is because we will be looking at several different types of programs.

Why do we need to know any of this? Well, there are a number of different reasons. The first is that each program maintains its own set of data. This might be file names, usernames, URLs, or a number of other pieces of data related to the functionality of the program. In order to figure out where the information is stored, you need to know the structure of the program so you can find the memory location associated with data. On top of that, if you want to work with malware, you need to know how programs are put together. There are also various tools and tricks that programmers may use that you can also use to follow a program, while it is executing and also investigate the data from the program while the program is running.

Of course, there are also programs that are not compiled directly into machine language. Some languages like Java compile to something called byte code, which can be executed on any system regardless of the processor. This requires a piece of software that will execute the byte code. Java is not the only language that uses byte code. Microsoft has languages that make use of byte code as well. Any program written using their .NET framework generates byte code that will then be run by an intermediate program. This is theoretically also machine independent but Microsoft only creates the development environment and intermediate program for Windows. There is, though, an open source software package called Mono that will run .NET programs on other operating systems like, Linux.

STACKS AND HEAPS

Before we get going, there are a couple of concepts that are important to cover up front because you will find them to be true, no matter what type of executable and what operating system we are talking about. When programs are developed, programmers generally break them up into smaller pieces, called functions. You may also hear procedure, method, or subroutine to express the same concept. One reason for doing this is to make it easier to develop the program. It is easier to break it up into chunks. You think about tasks you want to achieve then you write the code for those tasks. Once you have these tasks written, you can use them over and over again without having to write the same code over again. Once the program is compiled, the same concept applies. The program that is used to convert the source code into object or machine code, typically a compiler, will want the resulting program to be as small and efficient as possible. This means that the compiler will also try to create small pockets of code that act as procedures or subroutines. When the program executes, the execution will bounce around in memory as one procedure is called and then completed.

Each time a procedure is called, the running program has to keep track of where it last was, so it can maintain all of the data that was associated with the previous procedures. In order to do this, there is a data structure called a stack that is used. Think of a stack as a pile of plates in your kitchen cabinet. You can keep taking them off the pile, one at a time and when you put plates back on, you cannot use the ones that were previously there, until you remove the ones that you put on. The same concept applies, when it comes to running a program. Every time a procedure gets called, something called a stack frame gets put onto the stack. You can see a visual representation of the stack in Figure 9.1. Procedures A and B are both still on the stack but you can see that procedure C has been called and released from the stack. Of course, there is no natural progression of procedures as shown here. You do not guarantee that there are procedures easily marked A, B, C, and so on, so you can determine the calling order.

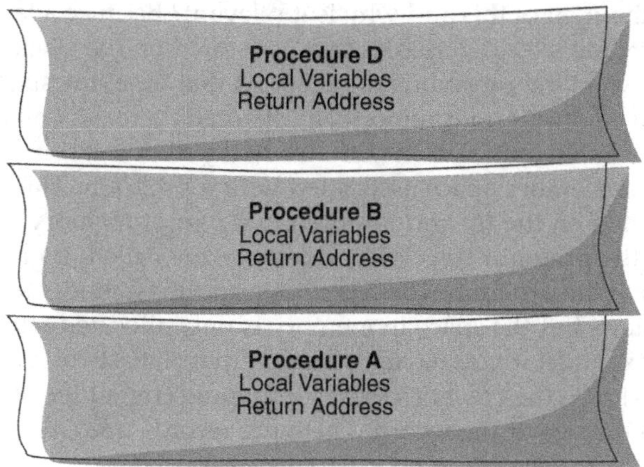

FIGURE 9.1

In reality, you will see what may even appear to be random names. In fact, taking a look at a the list of procedures called by a program called EXE Explorer, when it first starts up, we can see a list of some named procedures, but several that have either random looking names or no names at all. The debugger Ollydbg was used to create this list, called a call stack. The call stack is the list of called procedures. You can see the list in Figure 9.2. The ones in this list that have clear names are procedures from external libraries. These procedures should have identifiable names, so they can be easily called. When a compiler generates an executable, there is no need to add a name to the procedure. The machine code used to run the program would not be looking for a name. In fact, names would take small amounts of code to decipher the name and turn it into something that the computer can deal with. The computer wants an address. These addresses are also shown in the call stack in Figure 9.2. This is what the program is really looking for. In some cases, there has to be a lookup because external libraries would not have known addresses when the program initially starts. They have to be looked up.

Stack	Data	Procedure	Called from	Frame
08DBF648	76C25C93	kernel32.RaiseException	RPCRT4.RpcRaiseException+3C	08DBF644
08DBF664	76C27D61	RPCRT4.RpcRaiseException	RPCRT4.76C27D5C	08DBF660
08DBF674	76CB011D	???	RPCRT4.NdrClientCall2+112	08DBF670
08DBFA94	699E226A	RPCRT4.NdrClientCall2	davclnt.699E2265	08DBFA90
08DBFAAC	699E2211	davclnt.699E2251	davclnt.699E220C	08DBFAA8
08DBFAEC	699E26BA	davclnt.699E21E8	davclnt.NPOpenEnum+4D	08DBFAE8
08DBFB1C	737C2D41	davclnt.NPOpenEnum	MPR.737C2D3E	08DBFB18
08DBFB60	737C2F9F	MPR.737C2C36	MPR.WNetOpenEnumW+94	08DBFB5C
08DBFBE4	75A060AB	MPR.WNetOpenEnumW	shell32.75A060A6	08DBFBE0
08DBFC18	75A06031	shell32.75A06082	shell32.75A0602C	08DBFC14
08DBFC38	75B12C2D	shell32.75A05FE1	shell32.75B12C28	08DBFC34
08DBFC50	75AC0288	shell32.75ABD93E	shell32.75AC0283	08DBFC4C
08DBFC5C	75AC022D	shell32.75AC025D	shell32.75AC0228	08DBFC58
08DBFC74	759B1DB4	shell32.75AC01FA	shell32.759B1DB1	08DBFC70
08DBFCA4	6C9503A0	shell32.759B1D76	explorerframe.6C95039D	08DBFCA0
08DBFD1C	6C9308F6	explorerframe.6C9502B2	explorerframe.6C9308F3	08DBFD18
08DBFD3C	759E62FB	explorerframe.6C930856	shell32.759E62F8	08DBFD38
08DBFD58	759E8B8B	shell32.759E62A0	shell32.759E8B86	08DBFD54
08DBFDA0	759E8CBF	shell32.759E8AF2	shell32.759E8CBA	08DBFD9C
08DBFDA8	74F1B2B1	???	SHLWAPI.74F1B2AF	08DBFDA4
08DBFDB8	7720672F	SHLWAPI.74F1B2A5	ntdll.7720672C	08DBFDB4
08DBFE2C	771F2D89	???	ntdll.771F2D87	08DBFE28
08DBFF8C	753C336A	???	kernel32.BaseThreadInitThun	08DBFF88
08DBFF98	771D92B2	???	ntdll.771D92B0	08DBFF94
08DBFFD8	771D9285	ntdll.771D928B	ntdll.771D9280	08DBFFD4

FIGURE 9.2

Why do we care about all of this and why is it relevant? Because a large amount of data is kept within the procedure's local variables that are stored on the stack. The only time some of that data exists is when the procedure is called. At that time, the space is allocated on the stack as part of the procedure's information that is stored there. Not all information is stored on the stack, however. Some information is stored on the stack but some information is stored somewhere else in the memory space associated with a program. This data associated with the program is allocated on the fly and is stored in a part of memory called the heap. Since a stack is created as the program runs and procedures are called, it grows and shrinks over the course of the run of the program. The heap has a specific memory space carved out for it, when the program starts but the space in memory is only allocated when the program actually needs it. As an example, if you have a program that consists of a number of defined records like an address book, the creation of a record would trigger the allocation a new chunk of memory based on the size of the record. The more records used, the more memory would need to be allocated.

Both the heap and the stack are places where the information associated with a program is stored. In some cases, the heap and stack essentially abut one another in the memory space of the program. The stack commonly grows down, which means that it starts at the highest point of this address space and allocates space moving toward lower addresses. The heap grows up from the lowest address space. So, the heap and the stack grow towards one another in memory. If they eventually meet and one has to allocate into space occupied by the other, the program has run out of memory and will likely crash.

As we go through and talk about the program structure on the different operating systems and architectures, keeping in mind both the stack and the heap and how they operate. These are the places where you will be focused on getting useful information from.

Memory Space

So far, we have been talking about memory space. It is helpful to quickly talk about memory addresses. An address assigned to a memory space is based on the size of the bus, or you can think of it as the number of lines coming out of the CPU. In the case of a 32-bit CPU, there are 32 lines coming out of the CPU and each of them carries a bit. Together, those 32 bits refer to a memory address. Since we have 32 bits for an address, we can have a total of 2^32 memory locations, or roughly 4 billion locations. Each of these locations will store one byte. This storage size is common across the vast majority of modern computer systems. On a 64-bit system, you will have 2^64 memory locations. This is an extraordinarily large number. Your system today will have nowhere near the amount of memory that can be addressed directly.

When a program runs, it is provided a block of addresses. This is called the address space of the program. It is a set of memory that can be used by the program as it needs it. This is not to say that the entire address space is allocated in physical memory when the program runs. The amount of memory that is actually allocated depends on the program and the operating system. Each operating system and different program types will handle memory allocation and address space provided to the program differently. In each of the cases we are talking about in this book, though, the operating systems will not be handing out real memory addresses to the programs. All of the operating systems use virtual memory so virtual addresses are provided to each of the programs. This allows for the chunks of memory, called pages, to be relocated in physical memory as necessary, without impacting the running of the program at all by having to relabel all of the memory addresses referenced.

PORTABLE EXECUTABLES

Microsoft Windows uses the portable executable (PE) format for their programs. When Windows NT 3.1 was released, Microsoft adopted a variation of the common object file format (COFF) structure for their program layouts. COFF originally derived from a Unix executable object format. The PE format was originally designed as a 32-bit structure. This means that it was meant to handle 32-bit memory addresses. As processors capable of handling 64-bit memory addresses became more predominant, the address space associated with programs has changed. Now the PE format supports 64-bit memory addresses.

The PE format conveys some important information. First, it specifies the starting address for the program. The operating system needs to know, where the very first instruction is located within the executable address space. This brings us to addresses. The executable also includes a preferred address space. When the program loads into memory, it will be placed into real memory by the operating system at an address that is available. The program is not aware of the real memory address, though. The only addresses it is aware of are the virtual addresses it refers to, when it wants to move around within its own address space. The PE format does not have the capability to support position independent code, which means that it has a specific set of addresses it wants to use. When you open a PE file, you will see a clearly defined memory space.

There are two ways to specify an address. The first one is assuming you have an actual address in hand. You have a range of addresses, let us say from 0x3200 to 0x9A00. Every memory reference refers to the specific address out of that address range. If the program attempts to read from memory location 0x4864, it is reading from that actual location within the program's address space. In reality, that virtual address could refer to any address in real memory but from the program's perspective, that is a real address. This is called absolute addressing. The address referred to is the actual address in use.

Another way to refer to addresses is relative. When we are talking about relative addresses, all addresses are relative to a base address. If you use relative addressing, it does not matter where the program is located in real memory because the addressing is all relative from, say, the top of the memory space. If I were to refer to 0x1600, it would be 0x1600 bytes from the beginning of the memory space. If the memory space started at 0xA000, the address that 0x1600 refers to would be 0xB600. In order to get the actual address, I add the relative address to the base address. You can see the base address in Figure 9.3 at the top of the memory space. When you add the relative address to the base address, you get the actual address shown in the middle of the address space.

The PE format uses absolute addressing, rather than relative addressing. If two programs running and both have the same preferred base address, one of them needs to be relocated. When an access to a memory location is made, there is a lookup from a virtual address to a real address. That typically happens in a piece of hardware called a translation lookaside buffer. The operating system would look up the real address based on a particular virtual address. If I were to look up 0x1664, for example, the translation lookaside buffer needs to only

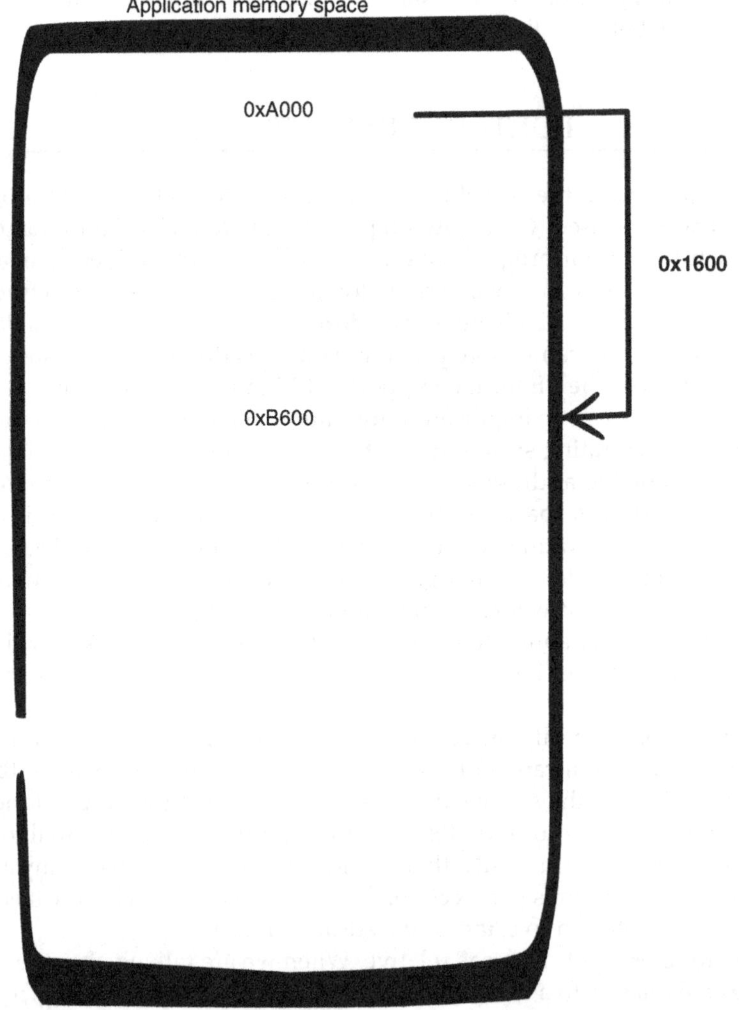

FIGURE 9.3

have one reference to 0x1664 or else it may get the wrong real address back. If two memory spaces conflict, one of the programs will need to be relocated to avoid this sort of conflict. Since all addresses in a program are absolute addresses, if a program is relocated, every absolute address reference in the program has to be recalculated and written into the program.

Finally, the PE format specifies all of the segments in the program. When the program is put into memory, there are different sections that get placed into different locations in memory. This is a way of breaking the program up into collections of like information. The following are common sections, you would find in a Windows.exe file:

.text: The text section is where all of the executable code resides. This is machine code, meaning operation codes (opcodes) and the operands that the opcodes act on.

.bss: The bss section includes all of the variables (changeable data) that are known about when the program is compiled but do not have any value when the program is compiled. This section takes up no space on disk but will be expanded into memory based on the specified size in the PE file.

.data: The data section has all of the variables (changeable data) that have values when the program is compiled.

.rdata: The rdata section contains data that is initialized but is considered constant, which means it will not change through the run of the program.

In Figure 9.4, you can see the different segments, which come with one particular program that has been opened in EXE Explorer from the company MiTEC. Each section has a size associated with it. These sizes are important. In most cases, the text section will be the largest. This is the program itself and so, unless the program does almost nothing, it will comprise the bulk of the contents in memory. The next section that would commonly be large is the data section. This is the section that carries all of the data, the program knows about. Different programs will, of course, have sections that are larger than others based on what their purpose is.

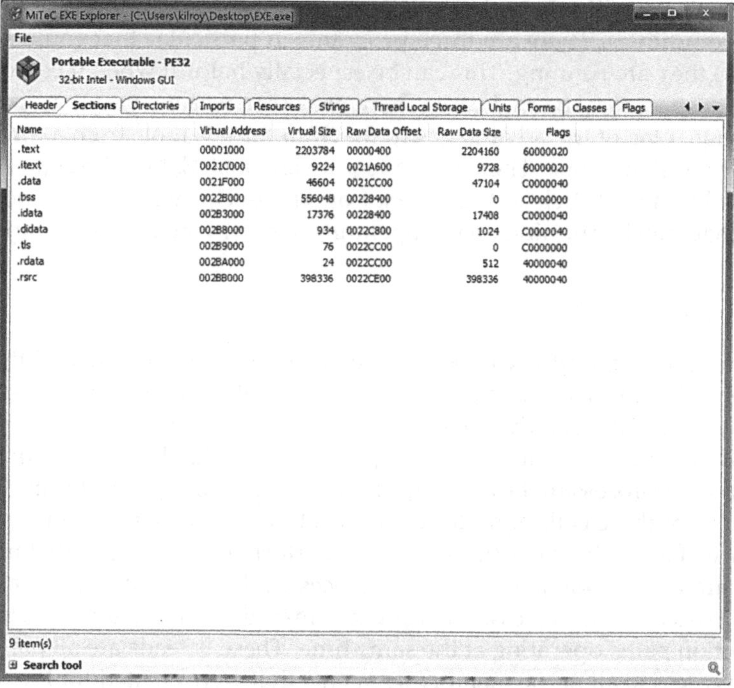

FIGURE 9.4

One reason why this is important is, when you are dealing with malicious software. While malware is not the only type of software that will utilize these techniques, they are techniques that are commonly used by malware. The first is packing. Packed software uses compression to do a couple of things. The first is to hide the actual executable from anti-virus and intrusion detection scanners. Since, the executable itself is what these systems build their signatures on, if you compress the executable portion, you change what the program looks like. If the signature gets updated to match this particular executable, all it takes is to change the compression to get a file that has a different signature without changing the functionality of the software at all. The fact that the software is packed would reflect in the section sizes. Software that is packed would have a small stub program that does actually execute. This would have a small text section because the program does not do much. The real program would be compressed and stuffed into the data section. The stub program would extract the data section into memory and hand control over to it, once it was extracted.

This can also be the case with encrypting the program contents. In order to obscure the actual program, you can encrypt it and stuff it into the data section. Again, you need a stub program, which would be in the text section. This encryption can be easily used to obscure the real program and make it harder for antivirus programs to keep up. An attacker would not have to do anything other than change the key used for encryption in order to completely change, what the data section ends up looking like. Again, keep in mind that antivirus programs rely on signatures, which are really byte patterns to look for within the executable file.

There are a number of ways of peering into a program, of course. You could make use of a debugger, which we will take a closer look at later. You could also use the Windows Sys-Internals suite of utilities. There are three programs in particular that could help us look at programs while they are running. This can be especially helpful when it comes to looking at programs you suspect may be malware. There are other reasons you may want to monitor programs, though. One of the advantages to the SysInternals tools from a forensics perspective is that they are standalone. They do not require any installation. You can store them on a portable device like a USB stick and run them from there. This way they are not corrupted by any malware that may be running on the operating system you are investigating.

ProcMon

ProcMon, or process monitor, can be used to observe the actions that all the processes on a system take. This can mean loading additional modules like libraries, it can be opening and reading of a file. This is a dynamic monitor, meaning that once you start it up, it pays attention to all system calls that the running processes make. Every time there is a system call, no matter what process makes it, it shows up in the running list of calls. Once you see a process in the list of these calls and you want to get more information, you can right-click it and get a choice of a handful of actions, you can perform on the thread that made the call. A thread is a separate execution path through a process. When you run a program and it enters into memory, it becomes a process. Each process may then create separate threads to have multiple execution paths operating at the same time. These threads are all part of the process and they have access to all of the memory segments that were created for the process. It is an important distinction, though, when we start looking at the execution path. In Figure 9.5, you can see the different options you can run on the process or thread.

One very nice feature of ProcMon is the ability to send the process to VirusTotal. VirusTotal is a website that will scan a program against a number of anti-virus signature engines. While you are investigating an application, you can directly submit the executable files and dynamic link libraries (DLLs) to VirusTotal and get a score. The score you receive is the number of engines that have a match between the file and known malware from their signature databases. Looking at the properties of the thread will show you the VirusTotal score.

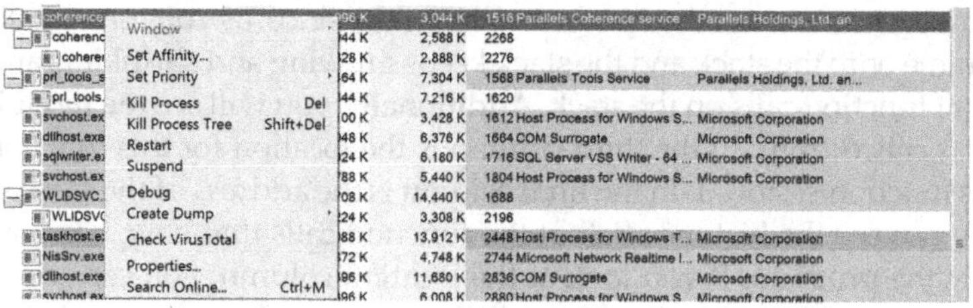

FIGURE 9.5

Another feature of ProcMon is being able to look at the stack trace. The stack trace is the listing of the functions that have been called recently. In cases where you are looking at local functions, meaning functions that are inside the executable itself, you will not see anything that makes sense. The reason for that is that your computer only cares about addresses. Having to maintain the actual function name within an executable is just space consuming for no good reason. When it comes to external libraries that a program might call, there does need to be a way of looking up the location from a name. Those external libraries will have functions that have names associated with them. When you look at a stack trace, as in Figure 9.6, you will see all of the function names from the external libraries.

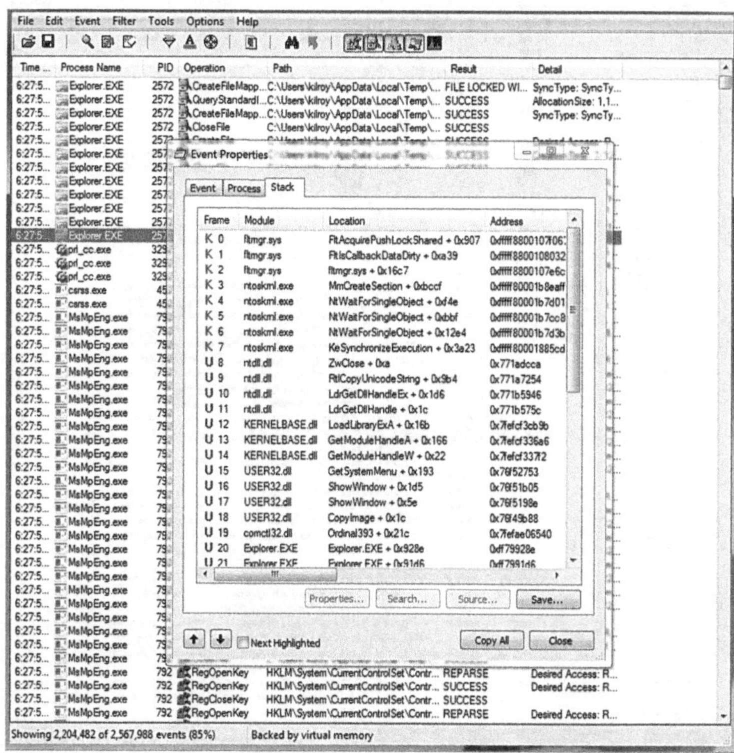

FIGURE 9.6

In the stack trace, you can see the number of the frame since, as you may recall, every function called adds a frame onto the stack and the stack keeps growing and shrinking, and there will generally be a pile of function calls on the stack. Additionally, you will see the module or library that the function was called from. In the third column is the location for this function. This is where in memory this function is stored. In the final column is the address of the stack frame. From this stack trace, you can see the history of all of the function calls that have been made throughout the execution of the program. If you look at the location column, you can see the names of the functions in the external libraries. For example, in frame 15, the function GetSystemMenu was called. According to the documentation at the Microsoft Developer Network (MSDN) website, that function is used to get a reference to the menu for the window the application is in.

ProcExp

Where Process Monitor gives you a list of all the individual system calls from all of the processes, Process Explorer gives you a list of all of the running processes on a system. It provides this list of processes in a tree view. Almost every process running on your system has a parent. There are some top level processes. One of them is the system idle process, which is a process that sits in the CPU doing nothing, if there are no other processes that need scheduling. There are other top level processes on a Windows system, which you can see in Figure 9.7, but the

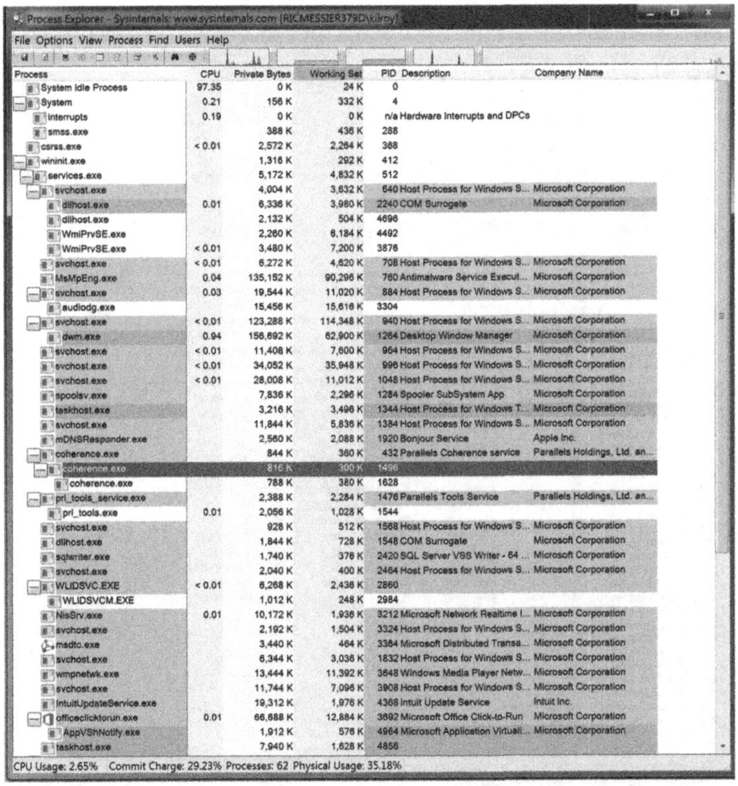

FIGURE 9.7

process that is the parent to all of the user processes is wininit. This is a system-level process that handles all of the processes that have user interaction components.

Process Monitor includes not only a list of processes that are running but also all of the threads that are associated with the processes. A process is an instance of a program once it is running. Within each process, there may be multiple individual execution paths that may appear to be separate programs from the standpoint of the scheduling process but in fact share the same memory space as the parent process. These individual execution paths are called threads. In the list of processes, you can see the details including the process identification number (pid), a description as well as the name of the software manufacturer. These last two categories require that the information is available within the executable. Without that information stored within the executable package, there is no way to obtain it. For this reason, you will see some of the entries in the process list without any information. If the developer does not bother entering information into the metadata for the executable when the program is built, it will not be available to procmon.

When you look at the process list, you can see several categories of information. This is not all that you can get from procmon, however. In addition, you can get a list of all of the user readable strings within the process. If you right click on each process entry, you will get a context menu. You can then bring up the process properties dialog. In this dialog box, you will see a number of tabs, as you can see in Figure 9.8. One of those tabs will give you a list of the strings. These strings are resources that are available to the program. A string is a set of

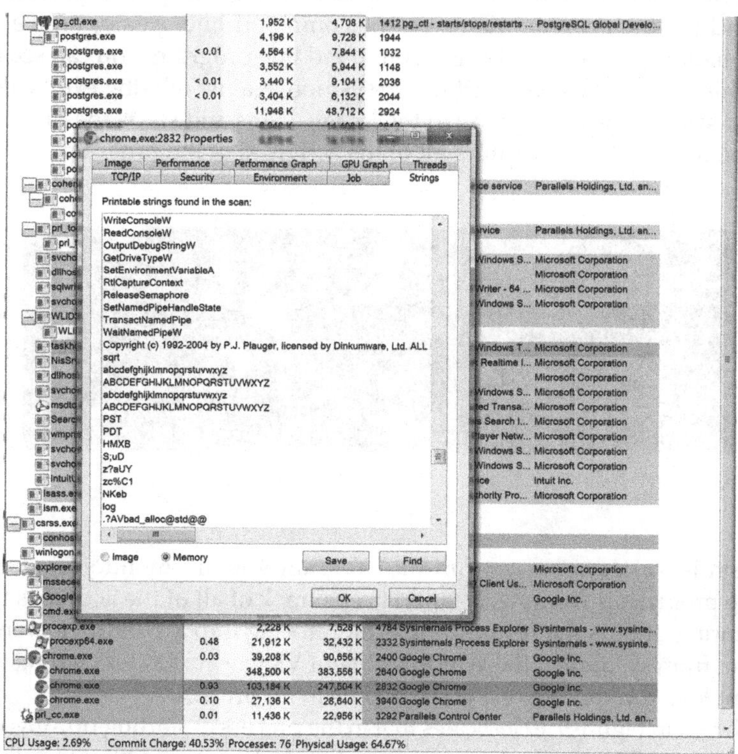

FIGURE 9.8

printable characters (e.g., a–z, A–Z, 0–9, etc) that can be easily read by someone. These values may just show up anywhere in a program, and not actually be a character string meant to be used as string of characters, but instead, what we may have is just a set of values that appear to be characters. Because of that, we have other requirements. In addition to being within the range of printable values, meaning something that can be displayed visually, when the value is converted to an ASCII character, the series of values would end in a 0. This does not mean the character 0, which has a numeric value of 48, we are talking about an actual value of 0.

In addition to the strings, you can get information about the threads that are associated with the process. You can also get the network information to see, what network communication is happening related to this program. There are a number of other characteristics related to the processes that you can look into from the other tabs in this property sheet.

Sysmon

The system monitor is another program from the SysInternals suite that is worth taking a look at. The problem with procmon and procexp is that they follow all of the processes on a system. If you want to look individually at a particular process, you can use the system monitor (sysmon) program. Where the previous two programs have a graphical user interface, sysmon runs quietly in the background. It installs a device driver that allows the program to collect system information about the programs that are running, and their activities. You can target specific processes with sysmon. In order to target a specific process, you start up sysmon and include the program name on the command line. Again, unlike the other two programs highlighted previously, this is a command line program. You can see the start up in Figure 9.9. In this example, we are starting up sysmon against ollydbg.exe, which is a debugger. Starting up sysmon, as you can see in the image, loads and starts the driver that is necessary for sysmon to operate and capture all of the activities of the program.

```
C:\Users\kilroy\Desktop\SysInternals>sysmon -i -l ollydbg.exe

Sysinternals Sysmon v3.00 - System activity monitor
Copyright (C) 2014-2015 Mark Russinovich and Thomas Garnier
Sysinternals - www.sysinternals.com

Sysmon installed.
SysmonDrv installed.
Starting SysmonDrv.
SysmonDrv started.
Starting Sysmon..
Sysmon started.

C:\Users\kilroy\Desktop\SysInternals>
```

FIGURE 9.9

Once sysmon is started, you can run the program you are monitoring. Once sysmon is loaded and the program is running, sysmon keeps track of all of the activities for the process you are monitoring. It puts the results of that monitoring into a Windows event log. You can view the output from sysmon in the Windows Event Viewer, just as you would with any other Windows event log. You can see one of the events in Figure 9.10.

The event shown in Figure 9.10 indicates that in the process of starting up, ollydbg.exe needed a dynamic link library. This particular image is out of the Microsoft Office installation directory.

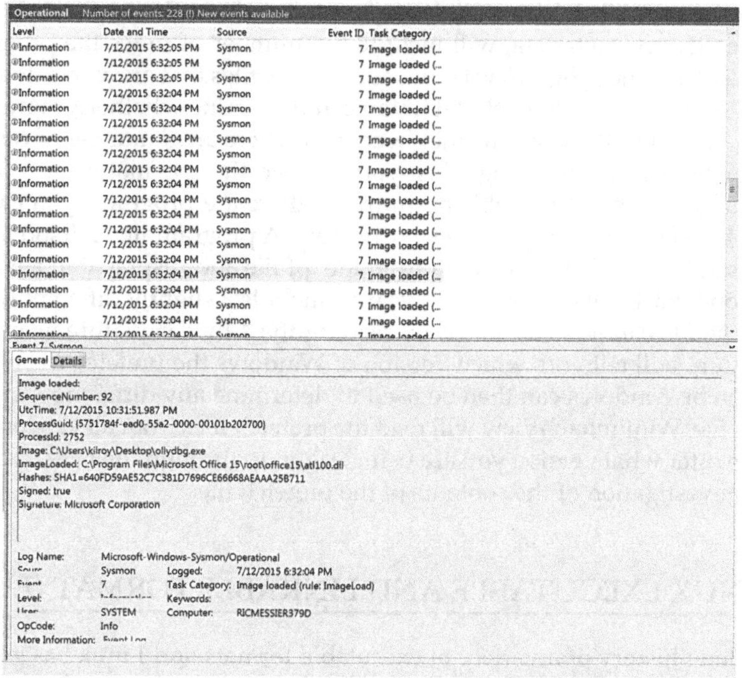

FIGURE 9.10

Sysmon took a cryptographic hash of the library as it was loaded. This allows you to easily check the validity of the library image, as long as, you have hash values of the known good libraries. The one thing sysmon does not do during this is to verify that the library that was loaded was not manipulated in some way. If the library gets replaced by a malicious process, sysmon has no way of verifying that. This is why it generates the hash and presents it for you.

Prefetch

One artifact of the programs running on Windows systems is maintained by the operating system itself for the purpose of speeding the system up. When you execute programs, the system will keep track of little tidbits of information about the program. The reason for this is so that the operating system will be able to run that program faster, the next time it is called for. For each program that has been executed recently, there will be an entry in the C:\Windows\Prefetch folder. The prefetcher was a feature that was introduced in Windows XP and was designed, in part, to speed up the boot process. If you go back far enough, you may recall how much faster XP was to start up over older versions of the Windows operating system.

The use of the prefetch files is governed by the key EnablePrefetcher key, located in HKEY_LOCAL_MACHINE\SYSTEM\CurrentControlSet\Control\Session Manager\Memory Management\PrefetchParameters. Prefetch is enabled by default, but it can be disabled by setting that key to 0.

Each file in the Prefetch folder includes information about the application the file refers to. This information, or metadata, will include the number of times the program has been executed, the last time the program was run, and a list of files that are associated with the program starting up. Using the Prefetch data, you can determine whether programs have been executed, how often and the last time they were run. There are a number of cases where this information can be critical, including when you are investigating malware.

While the metadata is not readable by humans, there are programs you can use to read through the .pf files that are in the Prefetch directory. A program like Nirsoft's WinPrefetchView can be used to extract the metadata from the .pf file and display it in a way that can be easily understood. Each version of Windows may include a slightly different format, though the format of the file can be determined by reading the 4-byte signature near the top of the file. This signature will tell you, which version of Windows the prefetch file was created using. The version of Windows can then be used to determine any differences in the format or contents of the file. WinPrefetchView will read the prefetch files from all versions of Windows so it does not matter what version you are using, right up through the latest, you will be able to perform an investigation of the contents of the prefetch file.

LINUX EXECUTABLE AND LINKABLE FORMAT (ELF)

Unix has a long history of a variety of executable formats and Linux has generally inherited the ability to support these different formats. The current standard executable format, though, is the Executable and Linkable Format (ELF). Linux is not the only operating system to use this particular format and it is also not the only format that is supported by Linux. As an example, the older a.out format is still generally supported on modern Linux systems. However, since the current standard is ELF, that is, what we will be investigating here. In some ways, this executable format will resemble the Portable Executable format discussed earlier. The reason for this is that when it comes down to it, you have code and you have data. How these are put together is part of what defines the executable format. Every executable file format is primarily a wrapper around these different components with ways of getting to the different components.

In an ELF program, you have a.text segment, which contains the executable part. All of the operation codes that the processor is going to handle and run will be in this segment. While you may think that that a program is really just a set of executable statements, it is much more than that. A program is not much of a program without some data for those executable pieces to act on. In addition to the .text segment, there are data segments, just as with a Windows program. An ELF file has a file header that provides information about the executable, as well as a pointer to the section headers. The section headers describe the different sections in the program.

On a Windows system, we have EXE Explorer and PEiD to examine the contents of the program header and display the values from those headers. On a Linux system, we can use readelf, as you can see below, to display the values from the file header. This example is for VIM, which is a file editor. It is a 64-bit executable and you can see that the program headers, which there are 9 of, start 64 bytes into the file. We can also see the address of the entry point. The entry point is the very first operation code that the program will start execution from.

There is no universally defined entry point across all programs. It varies from one to another. This is one of the important reasons for these headers to exist. They have to define these important locations in the executable.

```
root@quiche:~# readelf -h /usr/bin/vim
ELF Header:
  Magic:   7f 45 4c 46 02 01 01 00 00 00 00 00 00 00 00 00
  Class:                             ELF64
  Data:                              2's complement, little endian
  Version:                           1 (current)
  OS/ABI:                            UNIX - System V
  ABI Version:                       0
  Type:                              EXEC (Executable file)
  Machine:                           Advanced Micro Devices X86-64
  Version:                           0x1
  Entry point address:               0x43d7c4
  Start of program headers:          64 (bytes into file)
  Start of section headers:         2409832 (bytes into file)
  Flags:                             0x0
  Size of this header:               64 (bytes)
  Size of program headers:           56 (bytes)
  Number of program headers:         9
  Size of section headers:           64 (bytes)
  Number of section headers:         29
  Section header string table index: 28
```

Larger programs may not include all the program components they need. They may need to import functions from libraries. In order for programs to be able to make use of these external functions, the libraries have to have a way of both naming the functions and then a way to provide access to the functions. As a result, you have a symbol table. The symbol table in a library maps the name of the exported function to an address within the library. The most common library in use is the common C library. It contains all the common functions that are considered standard to the C language. This includes input and output functions such as printf and scanf for starters. Numeric functions are also implemented in libraries because the implementation will vary based on the type of system you are working with. Linux systems commonly use the GNU C compiler (gcc) to convert source code written in the C programming language into executable code. The GNU compiler has a GCC library to go along with the C compiler and it implements many of these numeric functions. In order to get the symbol table from a library, we use the nm utility. You can see a portion of the output from nm against the libgcc library below.

```
[root@snorklewhacker ~]# nm /usr/lib/gcc/x86_64-redhat-linux/4.8.2/libgcc.a


_muldi3.o:

0000000000000000 T __multi3


_negdi2.o:

0000000000000000 T __negti2


_lshrdi3.o:

0000000000000000 T __lshrti3


_ashldi3.o:

0000000000000000 T __ashlti3


_ashrdi3.o:

0000000000000000 T __ashrti3


_cmpdi2.o:

0000000000000000 T __cmpti2


_ucmpdi2.o:

0000000000000000 T __ucmpti2
```

On Linux systems, a library commonly has a name that starts with lib. After that comes the name of the library. So, the GCC library would have the name libgcc. The complete file name may include a version number as well, followed by the file extension. The extension is based on the type of library that it is. Some libraries have executable components that will be extracted and compiled directly into the program that is being compiled, though the process of importing those functions is called linking. These libraries are stored in library archives and have a file extension of .a. You can also have a shared object library, which is a dynamically linked library. The shared object library has the file extension .so and it is referenced, while the program is running. In order for the program to function, you need to have the library file close at hand, where the program knows where to find it. When the program needs to refer to a particular function from that library, it makes sure the library is loaded into memory and then just calls the memory location where the particular function is.

Linux programs, just like Windows programs, will also commonly have character strings that can be human readable. Rather than relying on a third-party program to extract those strings, Linux typically comes with a standard program named strings that will extract the strings from the program. With larger programs, many of the strings may be the names of the libraries it relies on, as well as the library functions the program uses. However, there are a number of other details, you can get from the strings that can provide you with insights into what the program does or how it works, without ever needing to run the program. A collection of strings, again from /usr/bin/vim, shows a number of error messages.

```
E45: 'readonly' option is set (add ! to override)
E44: Corrupted regexp program
E43: Damaged match string
E776: No location list
E42: No Errors
E459: Cannot go back to previous directory
E487: Argument must be positive
E486: Pattern not found: %s
Pattern not found
E41: Out of memory!
E233: cannot open display
E40: Can't open errorfile %s
E39: Number expected
E38: Null argument
E37: No write since last change (add ! to override)
E485: Can't read file %s
E484: Can't open file %s
E483: Can't get temp file name
E482: Can't create file %s
E247: no registered server named "%s"
E36: Not enough room
E481: No range allowed
E35: No previous regular expression
E34: No previous command
E33: No previous substitute regular expression
E32: No file name
E480: No match: %s
E479: No match
```

From this collection of error messages alone, we can see that vim can read and create files. We can also see that you can search for patterns using regular expressions. This is just from a small number of the strings available in this particular program. At the time of this writing, there were a total of 24,459 strings within the /usr/bin/vim binary. Taking a look at the rest of them, which can take a considerable amount of time considering the volume, you may be able to determine a lot more. Given the executable in question, we do not need to do a lot of investigation of the application itself, since vim is a well-known program. However, what if the binary (or executable) in question was thought to be questionable? You may want to poke around a little to see, what you think it may do before simply running it. Being able to do a little basic investigation can be important.

APPLE OS X APPLICATION BUNDLES

Mac OS X is built on a Unix foundation. Specifically, Mac OS X was built on top of a version of the Berkeley Systems Distribution (BSD) implementation of Unix. This is a result of the acquisition by Apple of the second company Steve Jobs built: NeXT. The operating system created for the NeXT system was built with a Mach BSD kernel with a graphical user interface named NEXTStep. When Apple was experiencing problems getting their operating system to one that was more modern, they acquired NeXT and used the underlying operating system beneath a merger of Apple's previous user interface and NEXTStep. As a result of all of this, the applications designed for Apple appear like a merger of the two operating systems.

Where Windows and Linux applications are generally a combination of multiple files that may be scattered around the filesystem, an Apple application is a bundle, where everything is self-contained. While it appears to be a single file when you look at it in the Apple Finder, Apple's file browser, in fact it is a directory. The operating system knows how to take the directory, locate the actual executable and run it. Additionally, there may be resources that are associated with the application like libraries, icons, or images. In order to view the bundle as a directory, you can open it up in the Finder by right or control clicking and selecting Show Package Contents, as seen in Figure 9.10. Once you have the contents of the package open, you will see a common directory structure. Common directories and files are listed in Table 9.1.

The core of an application bundle is the Mach-O executable. Just as with the other applications we have looked at, this is a collection of segments, including a .text segment and data segments. The Mach-O headers can be read using the otool utility.

```
kilroy@opus:/Applications/iMovie.app/Contents/MacOS$ otool -h iMovie

iMovie:

Mach header

      magic cputype cpusubtype  caps    filetype ncmds sizeofcmds      flags

 0xfeedfacf 16777223          3  0x80          2    43       5416 0x00200085
```

The otool utility can provide a lot more information, in addition to simply providing the Mach-O header information. Later, we will see, how it can be used to disassemble the .text

TABLE 9.1 Contents of Application Bundle

Name	Purpose
Contents	Top level directory inside the .app directory
Info.plist	This is a property list that contains information about the application, including some configuration information as well as build information about the program itself.
Resources	This directory may include a number of files associated with the program including icons, images, sound files, and any localization files that may be necessary for the program to be useful in other languages.
Frameworks	A number of libraries that may be necessary for the program to function. These libraries are also in a bundle structure, which means they are directories that follow a well-defined format.
MacOS	This is where the actual Mach-O executable resides.
Plugins	The Plugins directory contains bundles that may be loaded in order to extend functionality of the program.
SharedSupport	This is where the resources that are not absolutely necessary for the functionality of the application are. This may include document templates or tutorials, as examples.

segment, meaning it can generate assembly language from the operation codes that are in binary form in the Mach-O executable. Other platforms might require additional tools in order to see the assembly language version but on Mac OS X, if you have the set of developer tools that otool comes with, you can just generate a disassembly using the same utility that will show you the header information and display data about the different segments within the executable file.

Just as with the others executables, a Mach-O binary contains resources that are used during the course of execution, including human readable strings. Since Mac OS X is a variation on a Unix operating system, it has a considerable number of programs and utilities available that you would just as commonly find on a Linux system. One of these is strings, which can be used to get the strings that were defined in the source code and compiled into the program. This is just a recompiled version of the same strings that is running on Linux, so it works the same way. Run strings with your executable as a parameter and you will get all of the human readable collections of ASCII characters that are built into the program. In the case of an Apple application bundle, however, you should also be checking the Resources directory since there may be resources that also contain defined strings that the program can use as it needs to.

.NET COMMON LANGUAGE RUNTIME (CLR) / JAVA

There are two types of executables that are also worth mentioning here. One, since it is older, is Java. The other is not related to a specific programming language and is called the Common Language Runtime (CLR). Both use a type of execution which is different from what we have been talking about so far. The executables we have been talking about for Windows, Linux, and Mac OS X are files that contain operation codes that the CPU can make direct use of. I had a specific operation code, which is a numeric value, and the CPU knows how to execute that particular operation code. This typically means that the CPU knows which part of its circuitry to go, in order to run through the logic circuits that will execute that particular function. This may be add, subtract, move, or some other low level function that the CPU can perform. The important point here is that a compiled and linked executable, as we have been talking about them, will contain operations that the CPU can handle directly.

This is not the case with CLR or Java programs. First, CLR is the particular technology used by Microsoft's .NET foundation libraries and languages. Just as in the case of Java, CLR implements a very small virtual machine and inside that virtual machine, there is a small piece of software that converts pseudocode (a made up set of operation codes that do not directly relate to any particular CPU family) into the real operations that the processor can handle. This process of converting from one set of instructions to another is sometimes called interpreting. Traditionally, any interpretation would increase the execution time of the program by a small amount, since the program is not running directly on the bare metal (using the native operation codes for the CPU). Java and CLR programs claim to avoid this performance impact. In fact, there is some evidence that these programs may be faster.

The advantage to this is that every program runs in its own virtual machine, isolating its execution from other programs. From the standpoint of the program, the virtual machine provided to it is really the physical system. It does not know any better. This isolation, in theory, is a great way of protecting the operating system as well as any other programs that are running. Theoretically, one program cannot impact another. If something goes wrong with the program running inside the virtual machine and if the program starts to impact the operation of the virtual machine, the virtual machine can simply be halted without impacting any other program. The overall system remains operational. Of course, as has been seen, the theory does not always translate into practice, here as, there have been a number of vulnerabilities with Java, where one application can in fact have influence over the real running operating system or other running programs. While these issues are fixed when they are caught, we are left with the fact that Java virtual machines are not as airtight as they should be.

The advantage to Java in particular and CLR to a lesser degree is that the Java virtual machine has implementations for the major operating systems. It will run on Windows, Linux, and Mac OS X. This means that any Java program you write should run on every operating system without having to alter or re-compile or even be developed against a different set of libraries, which would be the case in most other programming languages. The standard set of Java libraries are implemented across all platforms, and as long as the libraries you are using in your Java program are from the standard set, your program will run on all three operating systems without having to spend time re-developing. This is a major advantage to application developers. Theoretically, this should also be a major advantage to malware developers as well, but you cannot always guarantee that the correct Java interpreter is installed on any given system. Not everyone has a need to run Java programs, after all. Java programs are generally easily identified because they have a .jar extension. It is called a JAR file because it is a Java archive, meaning that the program and everything else associated with running it is bundled up into a single file.

While it is less the case now, it was once the case that there were significant discrepancies between versions of Java, which made it harder to ensure that you could develop programs that would run more or less universally on a program, if it had a Java interpreter on it. This may be one of the reasons that malware developers have never completely taken to Java as a delivery language. Malware, after all, is probably the primary reason for any forensic investigator to want to better understand how programs operate, how they are put together, and how they interact with the operating system. A malware developer is generally wants to make sure that s/he is developing a program that would run on as many systems as possible. Malware is no longer just an annoyance, as it may have been at one time. Malware is often a money making venture and you make the most money by getting your program onto the most number of systems. Because of this, even though Java is cross-platform, meaning it can run on multiple operating systems, it is easier to focus on other languages. Java also does not allow the same sorts of shenanigans that a language like C does, meaning that the programmer is constrained to the rules of the language. In C language, the programmer is expected to know the rules and follow them without having anyone patrolling to make sure the rules are followed. This opens the door to a lot of bad programming behavior, which a malware developer may want to make use of. Java does not allow these bad behaviors, for the most part.

Common Language Runtime (CLR) programs are a slightly different story from that of Java. There is a virtual machine that isolates each program into its own virtual machine execution space. There are similar versioning issues as Java once had, though, they have mostly settled in the last few years. The difference with CLR is that it was developed by Microsoft to run on Windows systems and Microsoft has never spent time trying to make it work on other systems. This does not mean that others have not done that work, though. There have been a couple of development projects aimed at allowing .NET programs (programs designed to be run in a CLR virtual machine) to run on other operating systems. One of these, the Mono project, has become the predominant method of running a .NET program written for Windows to run on other operating systems like Linux.

Another significant difference between .NET programs and Java programs is that with a Java program, the file extension is .jar and is easily identified as a Java program. With a program written in C#, for example, the result of creating the program (compiling the source code into pseudocode) is a .exe file. This on its face is indistinguishable from a normal portable executable file. The headers in the .exe file will tell the operating system that it is a CLR file. In order to tell the difference, you would need to look at the properties on the file or use a utility like dumpbin to extract the headers correctly and tell you that it is a CLR file, meant to be run inside of a virtual machine.

Note, though, that when we talk about virtual machine here, we are not talking about a full blown instance of a real operating system as you might run across, when you run a virtual machine in VMWare or Parallels. Instead, we are just talking about a logical representation of a system that can be presented to the application. It is a very small-scale implementation of a system, which is possible because there are no users making use of this particular virtual machine. It is just the application, so there only need to be a very small subset of a complete system presented to the application.

Along with a .exe from a CLR program, you get a.config file that specifies the version of the .NET Framework that is needed for the program. The following is an example of one of these configuration files. This particular configuration file comes from a C# program.

```
<?xml version="1.0"?>

<configuration>

       <startup>

              <supportedRuntime version="v4.0" sku=".NETFramework,Version=v4.0"/>

       </startup>

       <runtime>

              <loadFromRemoteSources enabled="true"/>

       </runtime>

</configuration>
```

The file, as you can see, is in XML. This makes it nicely self-documenting for the most part. The parameter supportedRuntime is fairly straightforward. The one that is less immediately obvious is loadFromRemoteSources. This determines whether this particular program will load resources from external assemblies. Other libraries, outside of the executable, will only be available if this parameter is set to true. This is one way of preventing external libraries from being compromised and affecting the execution of the program.

DEBUGGING/DISASSEMBLY

Debugging is a process that every programmer will do at some point. When you run a program and it does not work the way you expect it to, you have discovered at least one bug. In order to track down the source of that bug, you go through a process of debugging. While sometimes this can be done with the source code, you can also debug an existing process. You might do this to observe the behavior of a program, you have no access to the source code for. Even if you have control of the source code, you may want to work inside the running program. In order to do this, you need a program called a debugger. Depending on the operating system you are using, there may be a number of debuggers you can make use of. This is especially true under Windows. With a debugger, you can step through the executable one operation at a time, take a look at memory segments and pause the execution as see fit.

Using these practices, you can get a better perspective on what a program is doing. Of course, these are not the sorts of things that anyone is likely to pick up overnight. This is not nearly the same as running something like the SysInternals tools, as an example, to see memory usage or the number of threads in use by a process. And here, again, it is worth reiterating that a process is the instance of a program as it exists in memory. Each process may have a number of simultaneous execution paths, which are called threads. As you are debugging, you will follow a single execution path through the program. Debugging multi-threaded processes can be challenging. Rather than digging into all of the complexities that are possible with debugging, we will just focus on some of the basics. Entire books are written about debugging and the various tools that are used for debugging, but we can cover some essentials on some of the different platforms.

There are different debuggers/disassemblers available for each platform but there is one that runs across multiple platforms. IDA Pro is commercial software that is very popular for people who need this functionality. While OllyDbg emulates a lot of the features of IDA Pro, there are a lot of features, including support of multiple platforms that IDA Pro has that other software like OllyDbg does not offer.

There are a few concepts to cover before we go over the use of a debugger. There are two areas, we will be covering. The first is the executable parts of the program. A program is composed of operation codes, often called instructions. When a program is loaded into memory, each operation code will have an address. The address of the very first operation to be executed is the entry point. In order to control the flow of execution, you need to know the entry point. You can set a breakpoint that can stop the execution. Once the program stops, you can step through running the program by moving on to successive instructions. While the program is running, you can observe the instructions and the address, where the instruction is located. The processor keeps track of where in memory the current instruction is through the use of a very special piece of memory called the instruction pointer. The instruction pointer is a small piece of memory located within the processor called a register.

In addition to instructions, you will be wanting to look at memory. Keep in mind that programs are often broken up into functions or procedures. This helps to keep programs smaller and more organized. As the execution of a program moves from one function to another, it will generate a stack frame. Each stack frame contains variables that are associated with the function. When you are debugging, you may want to keep an eye on the contents of each stack frame, since it will contain data that may be important. As additional functions are called, more frames get added to the stack. As a function terminates, the frame comes off the stack.

gdb/ddd

With that all in mind, let us talk about the GNU debugger (gdb), which is the primary debugger for both Linux and Mac OS X. gdb is a command line debugger but there are graphical interfaces for both Linux and Mac OS X that sit on top of the command line gdb. We can approach debugging from two perspectives. The first is starting a program through the debugger. The second is attaching to a running process. By starting a program from the debugger, you can control the flow of the program from the beginning. If you attach to a running process, you can see what is going on with the program and maybe investigate data within the running process but since it is in process, you will not have it from the beginning.

In order to start a program through the debugger, you would just run the debugger and pass the program name as a parameter. Ideally, the program will have debugging symbols, which will give the debugger information about where in the program it is. This is not always possible, of course. Production versions of programs will generally have all of the symbols removed but if you have control of the source code, you can build it with the debugging symbols enabled.

While you can have gdb load up the program from the command line, you can also load the program from within gdb. Below, you can see using file to indicate the program file, so gdb can load it. Once the file has been loaded, you can get information about the different sections that are in the program. On top of that, and more important, you will have the entry point for the program. This is the first address that the program runs from.

```
(gdb) file foo
Reading symbols from foo...done.
(gdb) info file
Symbols from "/home/kilroy/foo".
Local exec file:
      `/home/kilroy/foo', file type elf64-x86-64.
      Entry point: 0x400520
      0x0000000000400238 - 0x0000000000400254 is .interp
      0x0000000000400254 - 0x0000000000400274 is .note.ABI-tag
      0x0000000000400274 - 0x0000000000400298 is .note.gnu.build-id
      0x0000000000400298 - 0x00000000004002b4 is .gnu.hash
      0x00000000004002b8 - 0x0000000000400348 is .dynsym
      0x0000000000400348 - 0x00000000004003bb is .dynstr
      0x00000000004003bc - 0x00000000004003c8 is .gnu.version
      0x00000000004003c8 - 0x0000000000400408 is .gnu.version_r
      0x0000000000400408 - 0x0000000000400420 is .rela.dyn
      0x0000000000400420 - 0x0000000000400498 is .rela.plt
      0x0000000000400498 - 0x00000000004004b2 is .init
      0x00000000004004c0 - 0x0000000000400520 is .plt
      0x0000000000400520 - 0x0000000000400742 is .text
      0x0000000000400744 - 0x000000000040074d is .fini
      0x0000000000400750 - 0x0000000000400783 is .rodata
      0x0000000000400784 - 0x00000000004007c0 is .eh_frame_hdr
      0x00000000004007c0 - 0x00000000004008d4 is .eh_frame
      0x0000000000600e10 - 0x0000000000600e18 is .init_array
      0x0000000000600e18 - 0x0000000000600e20 is .fini_array
      0x0000000000600e20 - 0x0000000000600e28 is .jcr
      0x0000000000600e28 - 0x0000000000600ff8 is .dynamic
      0x0000000000600ff8 - 0x0000000000601000 is .got
```

```
0x0000000000601000 - 0x0000000000601040 is .got.plt

0x0000000000601040 - 0x0000000000601050 is .data

0x0000000000601050 - 0x0000000000601058 is .bss
```

Each program segment has beginning and ending address. As one example, the .text segment, where the program operations are stored begins at 0x400520 (leading 0s have been dropped for simplicity). You will note that the start of the .text segment is also the entry point for the program. The very first operation in the .text segment is the entry point. If we want to control the flow of the program execution, we want to set a breakpoint at the entry point. Below, you can see setting the breakpoint for the program then starting the execution. The program immediately stops because of the breakpoint we start.

```
(gdb) b *0x400520

Breakpoint 1 at 0x400520

(gdb) run

Starting program: /home/kilroy/foo


Breakpoint 1, 0x0000000000400520 in _start ()
```

As we run the the program, we may want to take a look at the stack flow. Just as we got information about the file, we can also get information about the stack. The stack frames for the program are below, retrieved by using info stack.

```
(gdb) info stack

#0  0x00000000004004c0 in ?? ()

#1  0x0000000000400549 in _start ()
```

We can also get a disassembly of the program. The following is a disassembly of a very small program that we have been using so far. This is, of course, in assembly language. Assembly language, as you will see below, is shown as a mnemonic for the actual operation code. The operation xor is not stored as an xor on disk or in memory. Instead, it is stored as a binary value. Since we, as humans, have fewer issues with words or letters, a disassembly shows the mnemonic for the operation code rather than the operation code itself. The xor operation is a mnemonic for an exclusive or. Similarly, mov is a three-letter shorthand for move. This means, the contents of one memory address or register is being moved to either another memory location or to a register.

```
(gdb) disassemble
Dump of assembler code for function _start:
=> 0x0000000000400520 <+0>:   xor    %ebp,%ebp
   0x0000000000400522 <+2>:   mov    %rdx,%r9
   0x0000000000400525 <+5>:   pop    %rsi
   0x0000000000400526 <+6>:   mov    %rsp,%rdx
   0x0000000000400529 <+9>:   and    $0xfffffffffffffff0,%rsp
   0x000000000040052d <+13>:  push   %rax
   0x000000000040052e <+14>:  push   %rsp
   0x000000000040052f <+15>:  mov    $0x400740,%r8
   0x0000000000400536 <+22>:  mov    $0x4006d0,%rcx
   0x000000000040053d <+29>:  mov    $0x40063c,%rdi
   0x0000000000400544 <+36>:  callq  0x4004f0 <__libc_start_main@plt>
   0x0000000000400549 <+41>:  hlt
End of assembler dump.
```

As noted earlier, you can also use the frontend for gdb, ddd. This is a graphical interface that provides a set of menus to drive the debugging of the program rather than having to remember all of the commands, you would use by just doing the command line version of gdb. However, it is important to note that the command line is still there. In fact, it shows up as one of the panes within the interface. But you do not have to type directly into it. You can use the menus instead.

Ollydbg

On a Windows system, we have several options to choose from. The most common professional debugger is IDA Pro, which also runs on Linux and Mac OS X. It is feature rich and a commercial piece of software. If you have the budget and need a really powerful debugger, you can get a copy of IDA Pro. If you have no budget, you can also find free debuggers. One popular free debugger is OllyDbg, which implements a lot of very powerful features. In Figure 9.11, you can see the OllyDbg window showing the executable code, or the .text segment, in the upper left pane. The registers are in the upper right. The memory dump for the program is in the lower left and the dump of the stack is in the lower right. Both of these is a hex dump, which means that you can see both the hexadecimal of the actual contents of memory, as well as, a conversion of the binary into an ASCII value for cases where there may be a character stored in memory.

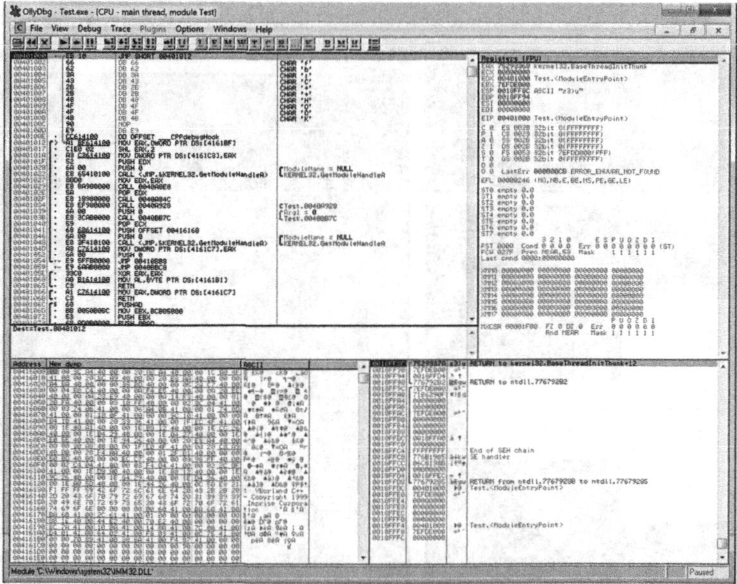

FIGURE 9.11

Just as with gdb, you can create breakpoints and start and stop the flow of execution of the program. The advantage of OllyDbg is that with the entire program in front of you, it is easier to look ahead in the code and set breakpoints visually. Plus, you can see the operations that are coming up as you step through the code. If you are not much interested in typing to step to the next instruction, there are also buttons in the interface that allow you to more easily and quickly control the application flow. The button clicking to step, start and stop is a nice feature for those who are more inclined to use mice rather than keyboards, but the ability to see the memory layout and more of the disassembled code all at once can be very helpful, as you step through a program to see what it is doing.

Immunity Debugger

Another free debugger is the Immunity Debugger, provided by Immunity, the company that is responsible for Canvas, an exploitation framework. One of the important uses of a debugger is reverse engineering. Using reverse engineering, someone who is skilled can use a debugger to find software vulnerabilities and exploits. As a result, there is a strong connection between a debugger and software exploits. In the end, the Immunity Debugger is very much like OllyDbg. It has a slightly different interface but the interface is not vastly different. You can see the Immunity Debugger interface in Figure 9.12. The layout of the disassembled code, registers, memory, and stack are the same. You also have the icons for managing the flow of the program in the toolbar at the top, just as in OllyDbg.

Figure 9.12 shows a context menu with different options in the memory pane. Each of the different panes in the window have different context menus, offering features that are specific

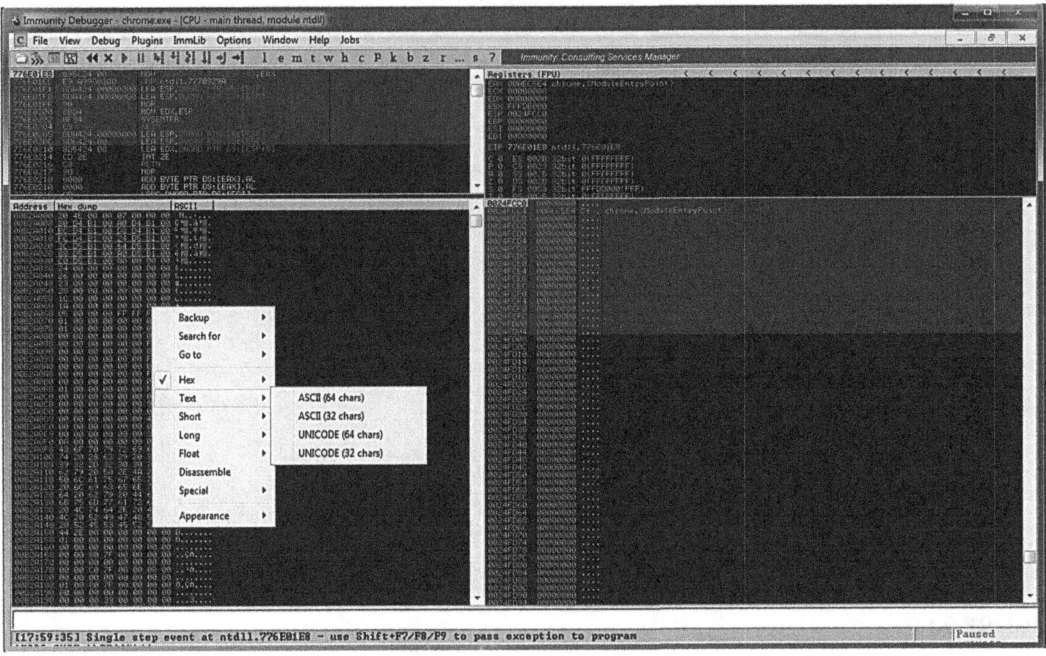

FIGURE 9.12

to the contents of the pane you are in. The program that is captured in this figure is actually one that was already running. The Immunity Debugger, like Ollydbg, gdb, and other debuggers, can attach to an existing process. This particular process is an instance of Chrome, the Web browser from Google.

Decompilers

While debuggers are capable of displaying the assembly language version of a program and, if debugging symbols are included, can be used to refer to the source code of a program, they are not capable of generating source code from the executable. There are a number of challenges with trying to recreate source code from a set of operation codes in the executable. A single op code does not translate directly backwards to a particular statement in a programming language. There are a lot of variables to take into consideration. One of them is variables. When a program has been compiled, variables get translated into address references. However, constants are also likely to be translated into address references as well. In a program, there is a difference between variables and constants.

Another major factor is the programming language. While C and C + + are two of the predominant compiled languages in use, they are not the only ones. Even if we knew, what the programming language was used to generate the compiled program, we may not know the actual compiler that was in use. Each compiler may create an executable in a different way, meaning that a single statement like for (i = 1; i + +; i < = 10) may be converted to a set of assembly language instructions in one way by one compiler but in a different way by a different compiler. Just as there are usually a number of ways to write a program, there are many different ways to convert a programming language into something that the machine itself can understand. There are no hard rules defined by the language itself.

If you could get to a point where you could actually generate source code language statements from a set of machine operations, there is no way to get back to the original source code. Everyone writes code differently. The best that you could get would be something in a programming language that would compile back to the program you have. This does not mean that it would be much more readable than the assembly language you get from the disassembler in the debugger, you are using. Certainly, it would lack all of the idiomatic nuances of the original programmer. You may get a completely different set of functions back and certainly function names would not be meaningful, since all of the function names and variable names are lost in the process of compiling a program.

While it may be nice to be able to gaze at a C program rather than a disassembly listing, decompilers are hard to come by. There are two languages where you can actually get decompilers. One of them is Java. You can get a Java decompiler, which will generate Java source code for you from the pseudocode generated by a Java compiler. Additionally, there are .NET decompilers. You can take a CLR program and decompile it to source code. Considering the large number of Java and .NET programs, this may be useful but again, most malware is not written in these languages. While you can take a number of programs and reverse the process of compiling, malware will be the most common interest for forensic practitioners. As a result, a forensic practitioner interested in analyzing malware will need to get used to debuggers to investigate programs.

SYSTEM CALLS AND TRACING

When a program runs, it executes the code that is built into the executable. This probably goes without saying again but, as mentioned before, not all execution necessarily takes place within the actual executable. Any time your program needs to access functions from the operating system, the program needs to make a system call. This may be reading input from the user or writing out to a file. It may be other hardware-related functions as well. On a Windows system, getting access to the operating system is done by making calls to the application programming interfaces (APIs), available for Windows. These not only provide hardware-level access for things like input but also provide access to the graphical interface for output. You may also want access to a number of other operating system features for monitoring or application logging. Any of these features require calls to the Windows APIs. In order to monitor those calls, you need a piece of software. One program that can be used under Windows is API Monitor. You can see a sample of the monitoring in Figure 9.13.

The APIs are what are used to gain access to kernel functions, so if there is anything a programmer needs to do to interface with any sort of hardware or gain access to memory, it is done through the API. Anything to do with processes also requires a call to an

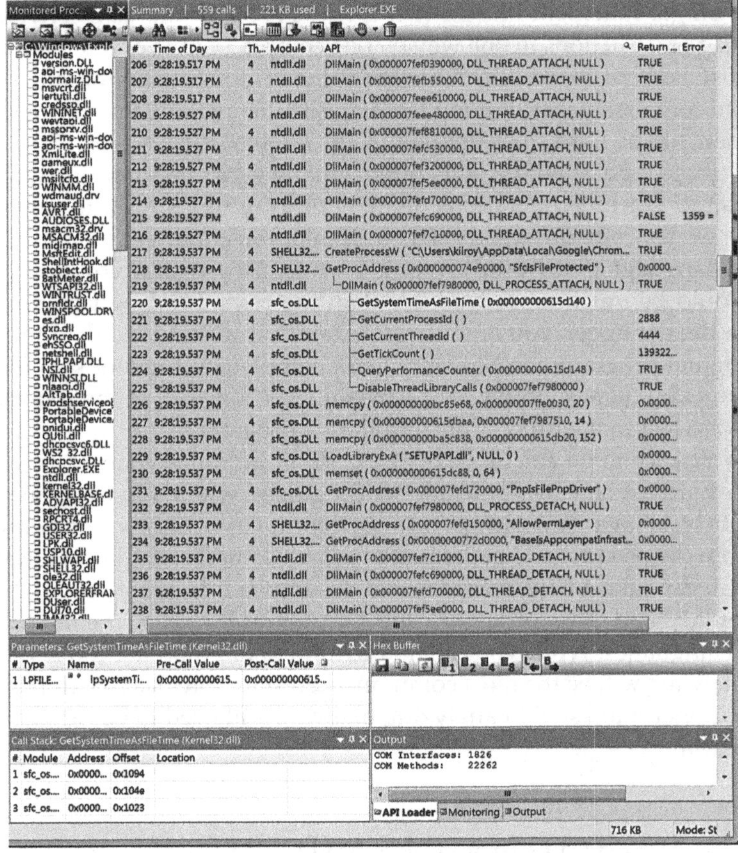

FIGURE 9.13

API. When a program begins execution, there is a function called CreateProcess that gets called. In Figure 9.13, this is called from the Shell32.dll module. While, it is normally the shell that creates new processes, any program can start up a new process. This is commonly called forking because the execution of the process suddenly has the potential to go in two separate directions, just as with a fork in a road. Up until that point, you had a single path of execution. Once the fork happens, there are two paths that exist. This means that there is a parent process and a child process. In order for the parent to gain access to the child process, it would require going through the kernel and making use of one of the APIs to do it.

Why is any of this useful to know? Because if you can follow all of the calls that are made to any function external to any program, whether it is a system API or some other external library, you may be able to get an idea, what the program is doing. This can be essential information, especially, if you are trying to track the behaviors of a rogue program. In the case of the API Monitor, and other similar utilities, you are not limited to only watching the behavior of a program you have started. This means that you do not have to start up a program that you think may be suspicious, just to see how it operates. If one is running, you can attach to it and watch it that way. This is certainly true with the API Monitor, which you choose from a list of running processes that you want to observe. Once you have done that, you will also have to select, which APIs you want to monitor, so you are not immediately overwhelmed with a lot of function calls that you may not be especially interested in or concerned by.

If you are strictly interested in the behavior of a program as it interacts with files and the registry, you could use one of the SysInternals programs that monitors that behavior across processes on a system. Process Monitor (ProcMon) looks at these behaviors of a program but also gives you a lot of additional functionality as well, including the ability to generate filters, so you are only looking at what you want to see. If you are looking for malware, you will probably want to be observing the interaction of programs with files and registry. After all, malware is not going to just sit there and spin in the processor, never interacting with the system. It is going to read from and write to files and also make registry calls. As a result, a program like ProcMon is good not only just for generally observing your system for performance problems or other types of troubleshooting, it is also good for hunting malware on your system. If you wanted to observe the behavior of a particular application to perhaps see it stuck in a particular function, you can set a filter on that application. In Figure 9.14, you can see the functions of the Windows Explorer.

Time ...	Process Name	PID	Operation	Path	Result	Detail
9:30:1...	Explorer.EXE	2888	RegQueryKey	HKCU\Software\Classes	SUCCESS	Query: Name
9:30:1...	Explorer.EXE	2888	RegQueryKey	HKCU\Software\Classes	SUCCESS	Query: HandleTags, HandleTags: 0x0
9:30:1...	Explorer.EXE	2888	RegQueryKey	HKCU\Software\Classes	SUCCESS	Query: HandleTags, HandleTags: 0x0
9:30:1...	Explorer.EXE	2888	RegOpenKey	HKCU\Software\Classes\Applications\...	NAME NOT FOUND	Desired Access: Read
9:30:1...	Explorer.EXE	2888	RegOpenKey	HKCR\Applications\Procmon64.exe	NAME NOT FOUND	Desired Access: Read
9:30:1...	Explorer.EXE	2888	RegQueryKey	HKCU\Software\Classes	SUCCESS	Query: Name
9:30:1...	Explorer.EXE	2888	RegQueryKey	HKCU\Software\Classes	SUCCESS	Query: HandleTags, HandleTags: 0x0
9:30:1...	Explorer.EXE	2888	RegOpenKey	HKCU\Software\Classes\Applications\...	NAME NOT FOUND	Desired Access: Read
9:30:19.8235405 PM	...XE	2888	RegOpenKey	HKCR\Applications\Procmon64.exe	NAME NOT FOUND	Desired Access: Read
9:30:1...	Explorer.EXE	2888	CreateFile	C:\Users\kilroy\AppData\Local\Temp\...	SUCCESS	Desired Access: Read Attributes, Disposition: Open, Options: Open Reparse Point, Attributes: n/a, ShareMode: Read, Write, Delete, AllocationSize: n/a, OpenRe...
9:30:1...	Explorer.EXE	2888	QueryBasicInfor...	C:\Users\kilroy\AppData\Local\Temp\...	SUCCESS	CreationTime: 8/7/2015 9:30:17 PM, LastAccessTime: 8/7/2015 9:30:17 PM, LastWriteTime: 8/7/2015 9:30:18 PM, ChangeTime: 8/7/2015 9:30:18 PM, FileAtt...
9:30:1...	Explorer.EXE	2888	CloseFile	C:\Users\kilroy\AppData\Local\Temp\...	SUCCESS	
9:30:1...	Explorer.EXE	2888	CreateFile	C:\Users\kilroy\AppData\Local\Temp\...	SUCCESS	Desired Access: Read Attributes, Disposition: Open, Options: Open Reparse Point, Attributes: n/a, ShareMode: Read, Write, Delete, AllocationSize: n/a, OpenRe...
9:30:1...	Explorer.EXE	2888	QueryBasicInfor...	C:\Users\kilroy\AppData\Local\Temp\...	SUCCESS	CreationTime: 8/7/2015 9:30:17 PM, LastAccessTime: 8/7/2015 9:30:17 PM, LastWriteTime: 8/7/2015 9:30:18 PM, ChangeTime: 8/7/2015 9:30:18 PM, FileAtt...
9:30:1...	Explorer.EXE	2888	CloseFile	C:\Users\kilroy\AppData\Local\Temp\...	SUCCESS	
9:30:1...	Explorer.EXE	2888	CreateFile	C:\Users\kilroy\AppData\Local\Temp\...	SUCCESS	Desired Access: Read Data/List Directory, Synchronize, Disposition: Open, Options: Synchronous IO Non-Alert, Non-Directory File, Attributes: n/a, ShareMode: R...
9:30:1...	Explorer.EXE	2888	CreateFileMapp...	C:\Users\kilroy\AppData\Local\Temp\...	FILE LOCKED WI...	SyncType: SyncTypeCreateSection, PageProtection:
9:30:1...	Explorer.EXE	2888	QueryStandardI...	C:\Users\kilroy\AppData\Local\Temp\...	SUCCESS	AllocationSize: 1,130,496, EndOfFile: 1,127,056, NumberOfLinks: 1, DeletePending: False, Directory: False
9:30:1...	Explorer.EXE	2888	CreateFileMapp...	C:\Users\kilroy\AppData\Local\Temp\...	SUCCESS	SyncType: SyncTypeOther
9:30:1...	Explorer.EXE	2888	CloseFile	C:\Users\kilroy\AppData\Local\Temp\...	SUCCESS	
9:30:1...	Explorer.EXE	2888	CreateFile	C:\Users\kilroy\AppData\Local\Temp\...	SUCCESS	Desired Access: Read Attributes, Disposition: Open, Options: Open Reparse Point, Attributes: n/a, ShareMode: Read, Write, Delete, AllocationSize: n/a, OpenRe...
9:30:1...	Explorer.EXE	2888	QueryBasicInfor...	C:\Users\kilroy\AppData\Local\Temp\...	SUCCESS	CreationTime: 8/7/2015 9:30:17 PM, LastAccessTime: 8/7/2015 9:30:17 PM, LastWriteTime: 8/7/2015 9:30:18 PM, ChangeTime: 8/7/2015 9:30:18 PM, FileAtt...
9:30:1...	Explorer.EXE	2888	CloseFile	C:\Users\kilroy\AppData\Local\Temp\...	SUCCESS	
9:30:1...	Explorer.EXE	2888	CreateFile	C:\Users\kilroy\AppData\Local\Temp\...	SUCCESS	Desired Access: Read Data/List Directory, Synchronize, Disposition: Open, Options: Synchronous IO Non-Alert, Non-Directory File, Attributes: n/a, ShareMode: R...
9:30:1...	Explorer.EXE	2888	CreateFileMapp...	C:\Users\kilroy\AppData\Local\Temp\...	FILE LOCKED WI...	SyncType: SyncTypeCreateSection, PageProtection:
9:30:1...	Explorer.EXE	2888	QueryStandardI...	C:\Users\kilroy\AppData\Local\Temp\...	SUCCESS	AllocationSize: 1,130,496, EndOfFile: 1,127,056, NumberOfLinks: 1, DeletePending: False, Directory: False
9:30:1...	Explorer.EXE	2888	CreateFileMapp...	C:\Users\kilroy\AppData\Local\Temp\...	SUCCESS	SyncType: SyncTypeOther
9:30:1...	Explorer.EXE	2888	CloseFile	C:\Users\kilroy\AppData\Local\Temp\...	SUCCESS	
9:30:1...	Explorer.EXE	2888	CreateFile	C:\Users\kilroy\AppData\Local\Temp\...	SUCCESS	Desired Access: Read Attributes, Disposition: Open, Options: Open Reparse Point, Attributes: n/a, ShareMode: Read, Write, Delete, AllocationSize: n/a, OpenRe...
9:30:1...	Explorer.EXE	2888	QueryBasicInfor...	C:\Users\kilroy\AppData\Local\Temp\...	SUCCESS	CreationTime: 8/7/2015 9:30:17 PM, LastAccessTime: 8/7/2015 9:30:17 PM, LastWriteTime: 8/7/2015 9:30:18 PM, ChangeTime: 8/7/2015 9:30:18 PM, FileAtt...
9:30:1...	Explorer.EXE	2888	CloseFile	C:\Users\kilroy\AppData\Local\Temp\...	SUCCESS	
9:30:1...	Explorer.EXE	2888	CreateFile	C:\Users\kilroy\AppData\Local\Temp\...	SUCCESS	Desired Access: Read Data/List Directory, Synchronize, Disposition: Open, Options: Synchronous IO Non-Alert, Non-Directory File, Attributes: n/a, ShareMode: R...
9:30:1...	Explorer.EXE	2888	CreateFileMapp...	C:\Users\kilroy\AppData\Local\Temp\...	FILE LOCKED WI...	SyncType: SyncTypeCreateSection, PageProtection:
9:30:1...	Explorer.EXE	2888	QueryStandardI...	C:\Users\kilroy\AppData\Local\Temp\...	SUCCESS	AllocationSize: 1,130,496, EndOfFile: 1,127,056, NumberOfLinks: 1, DeletePending: False, Directory: False
9:30:1...	Explorer.EXE	2888	CreateFileMapp...	C:\Users\kilroy\AppData\Local\Temp\...	SUCCESS	SyncType: SyncTypeOther
9:30:1...	Explorer.EXE	2888	CloseFile	C:\Users\kilroy\AppData\Local\Temp\...	SUCCESS	
9:30:1...	Explorer.EXE	2888	CreateFile	C:\Users\kilroy\AppData\Local\Temp\...	SUCCESS	Desired Access: Read Attributes, Disposition: Open, Options: Open Reparse Point, Attributes: n/a, ShareMode: Read, Write, Delete, AllocationSize: n/a, OpenRe...
9:30:1...	Explorer.EXE	2888	QueryBasicInfor...	C:\Users\kilroy\AppData\Local\Temp\...	SUCCESS	CreationTime: 8/7/2015 9:30:17 PM, LastAccessTime: 8/7/2015 9:30:17 PM, LastWriteTime: 8/7/2015 9:30:18 PM, ChangeTime: 8/7/2015 9:30:18 PM, FileAtt...
9:30:1...	Explorer.EXE	2888	CloseFile	C:\Users\kilroy\AppData\Local\Temp\...	SUCCESS	
9:30:1...	Explorer.EXE	2888	CreateFile	C:\Users\kilroy\AppData\Local\Temp\...	SUCCESS	Desired Access: Read Data/List Directory, Synchronize, Disposition: Open, Options: Synchronous IO Non-Alert, Non-Directory File, Attributes: n/a, ShareMode: R...

FIGURE 9.14

On the Linux side, there are a number of utilities that you can make use of to observe the behavior of programs. This includes library function, calls and system. There are two common utilities that would be used on a Linux system. The first is ltrace and it is used to watch library calls for a particular program. You can call the program through ltrace, meaning that if you provide the program as a parameter on the command line, ltrace will run the program and then provide the list of the library functions that are called as the program runs. You can also simply attach to a running process and you will get a list of the library functions, as it continues to run. You can see an example of that using the strace utility, which provides the list of system calls used by a program. Below you can see a list of system calls made by the terminal program that was open while strace was running.

```
read(12, "\"\\\"\\\\\\\"\\\\\\\\\\\\\\\"\\\\\\\\\\\\\\\\\\\\\\\\\\\\\\\"\\"..., 87) = 87

write(4, "\1\0\0\0\0\0\0\0", 8)          = 8

poll([{fd=3, events=POLLIN|POLLOUT}], 1, 4294967295) = 1 ([{fd=3, revents=POLLOUT}])

writev(3, [{"(\30\4\0%\0\200\3K\0\0\0)\0\270\32", 16}, {NULL, 0}, {"", 0}], 3) = 16

poll([{fd=3, events=POLLIN}], 1, 4294967295) = 1 ([{fd=3, revents=POLLIN}])

recvmsg(3, {msg_name(0)=NULL,

msg_iov(1)=[{"\1\1\304\256\0\0\0\0\0\0\0\0e\0018\33\0\0\0\0\0\0\0\0\0\0\0\0\0\0\0\0\0", 4096}],

msg_controllen=0, msg_flags=0}, 0) = 32

recvmsg(3, 0x7ffe1cf6cd70, 0)           = -1 EAGAIN (Resource temporarily unavailable)

recvmsg(3, 0x7ffe1cf6cd70, 0)           = -1 EAGAIN (Resource temporarily unavailable)

write(8, "\1\0\0\0\0\0\0\0", 8)          = 8

futex(0x7f9fa4014e60, FUTEX_WAKE_PRIVATE, 1) = 1

futex(0x7f9faf5b0c00, FUTEX_WAKE_PRIVATE, 1) = 1

poll([{fd=3, events=POLLIN|POLLOUT}], 1, 4294967295) = 1 ([{fd=3,

revents=POLLIN|POLLOUT}])
```

The purpose of the terminal program is to provide command line access to the user. You can see that the system calls are reading and writing and also polling for events. The terminal window, after all, waits for keys to be pressed so it can respond based on the key press. Most key presses are going to be regular characters that will be stored in a buffer until the entire line is done, so the terminal has to pay attention for special characters like control-C and the Return key, so it can act immediately. If there were system calls other than the ones I see earlier, I may get suspicious and want to investigate further.

Mac OS X also has facilities for monitoring application behavior. You may recall that Mac OS X has its foundations in Unix by way of its acquisition of NeXT. It is this lineage that gets some UNIX-like programs installed on Mac OS X by default. Other implementations of Unix have used a program called truss in order to monitor application behaviors. Mac

OS X has a program called dtruss, which can monitor system calls made from a program. Figure 9.15 shows the output from dtruss, as it shows system calls that are made, while the Python interpreter program is run. Just as with Linux, access to services that may interact with hardware make use of system calls on a Mac OS X system. Where Windows use shared system libraries, implementing APIs, Unix-like systems make use of system calls. Mac OS X is a Unix-like operating system, so in order to pay attention to all these system calls, we use utilities like dtruss.

```
kilroy@opus:~$ sudo dtruss python
SYSCALL(args)          = return
thread_selfid(0x0, 0x0, 0x0)          = 4489754 0
csops(0x0, 0x0, 0x7FFF5DA11268)          = 0 0
issetugid(0x0, 0x0, 0x7FFF5DA11268)          = 0 0
shared_region_check_np(0x7FFF5DA0F1A8, 0x0, 0x7FFF5DA11268)          = 0 0
stat64("/usr/lib/dtrace/libdtrace_dyld.dylib\0", 0x7FFF5DA10338, 0x7FFF5DA11268)
= 0 0
open("/usr/lib/dtrace/libdtrace_dyld.dylib\0", 0x0, 0x0)          = 3 0
pread(0x3, "\312\376\272\276\0", 0x1000, 0x0)          = 4096 0
pread(0x3, "\317\372\355\376\a\0", 0x1000, 0x6000)          = 4096 0
fcntl(0x3, 0x3D, 0x7FFF5DA0E6A0)          = 0 0
mmap(0x1021FB000, 0x2000, 0x5, 0x12, 0x3, 0x6000)          = 0x1021FB000 0
mmap(0x1021FD000, 0x1000, 0x3, 0x12, 0x3, 0x8000)          = 0x1021FD000 0
mmap(0x1021FE000, 0x1FC0, 0x1, 0x12, 0x3, 0x9000)          = 0x1021FE000 0
close(0x3)          = 0 0
stat64("/usr/lib/dtrace/libdtrace_dyld.dylib\0", 0x7FFF5DA10CB8, 0x1)          = 0 0
stat64("/System/Library/Frameworks/CoreFoundation.framework/Versions/A/CoreFoundation\0",
0x7FFF5DA10158, 0x1)          = 0 0
stat64("/usr/lib/libSystem.B.dylib\0", 0x7FFF5DA10158, 0x1)          = 0 0
stat64("/usr/lib/libauto.dylib\0", 0x7FFF5DA10008, 0x1)          = 0 0
stat64("/usr/lib/libDiagnosticMessagesClient.dylib\0", 0x7FFF5DA10008, 0x1)          =
 0 0
stat64("/usr/lib/libicucore.A.dylib\0", 0x7FFF5DA10008, 0x1)          = 0 0
stat64("/usr/lib/libobjc.A.dylib\0", 0x7FFF5DA10008, 0x1)          = 0 0
stat64("/usr/lib/libz.1.dylib\0", 0x7FFF5DA10008, 0x1)          = 0 0
stat64("/usr/lib/libc++.1.dylib\0", 0x7FFF5DA0FEF8, 0x1)          = 0 0
stat64("/usr/lib/libc++abi.dylib\0", 0x7FFF5DA0FE08, 0x1)          = 0 0
stat64("/usr/lib/system/libcache.dylib\0", 0x7FFF5DA0F918, 0x1)          = 0 0
stat64("/usr/lib/system/libcommonCrypto.dylib\0", 0x7FFF5DA0F918, 0x1)          = 0 0
stat64("/usr/lib/system/libcompiler_rt.dylib\0", 0x7FFF5DA0F918, 0x1)          = 0 0
stat64("/usr/lib/system/libcopyfile.dylib\0", 0x7FFF5DA0F918, 0x1)          = 0 0
stat64("/usr/lib/system/libcorecrypto.dylib\0", 0x7FFF5DA0F918, 0x1)          = 0 0
stat64("/usr/lib/system/libdispatch.dylib\0", 0x7FFF5DA0F918, 0x1)          = 0 0
stat64("/usr/lib/system/libdyld.dylib\0", 0x7FFF5DA0F918, 0x1)          = 0 0
stat64("/usr/lib/system/libkeymgr.dylib\0", 0x7FFF5DA0F918, 0x1)          = 0 0
stat64("/usr/lib/system/liblaunch.dylib\0", 0x7FFF5DA0F918, 0x1)          = 0 0
stat64("/usr/lib/system/libmacho.dylib\0", 0x7FFF5DA0F918, 0x1)          = 0 0
stat64("/usr/lib/system/libquarantine.dylib\0", 0x7FFF5DA0F918, 0x1)          = 0 0
stat64("/usr/lib/system/libremovefile.dylib\0", 0x7FFF5DA0F918, 0x1)          = 0 0
stat64("/usr/lib/system/libsystem_asl.dylib\0", 0x7FFF5DA0F918, 0x1)          = 0 0
stat64("/usr/lib/system/libsystem_blocks.dylib\0", 0x7FFF5DA0F918, 0x1)          = 0 0
stat64("/usr/lib/system/libsystem_c.dylib\0", 0x7FFF5DA0F918, 0x1)          = 0 0
stat64("/usr/lib/system/libsystem_configuration.dylib\0", 0x7FFF5DA0F918, 0x1)          =
 0 0
```

FIGURE 9.15

This is not the only utility that is available for Mac OS X to monitor application behavior, however. You can also use a utility like execsnoop. The execsnoop utility monitors the system for process creation. You will want to use this program to keep an eye on any new processes to watch for a process that you do not expect. If you are actively using this system, you will see a lot of processes as you run new programs. There is also a program named iosnoop that is used to monitor all input/output (I/O) functions that take place on the system. Of course, you can use iosnoop to watch all input/output across the system, which means that you are looking at all of the I/O devices. A device, no matter whether it is a mouse, keyboard, disk drive, or a network interface, is required to communicate with. I cannot get any input or send any output, if there is not a device on the system. With iosnoop, you can specify the device you want to watch.

Both iosnoop and execsnoop make use of DTrace, which is a way to dynamically watch system behavior. DTrace, or Dynamic Trace, was originally designed by Sun Microsystems for Solaris and it was introduced to Mac OS X for 10.5 (Leopard). The DTrace facility allows other programs to connect to DTrace to be able to look directly into the running operating system, which allows for very deep monitoring of system behavior. In addition to specific utilities like iosnoop and execspoof, there is also a dtrace utility available on Mac OS X that is just a front-end for the DTrace facility. The dtrace utility can be used to monitor different parts of the operating system, since it connects to DTrace on the backend.

FINDING THE PROGRAM IMPACT

Anytime you install a program, you make changes to the different aspects of the system. On a Windows system, for example, you are writing new files out to the fileysystem. You are likely adding new keys to the Windows Registry. You may be adding new services that get started up, when the system boots. You may also be adding network listeners. On Linux and Mac OS X systems, you will certainly get filesystem changes and you may also get network listeners and other changes. In general, it is a good idea to know what happens to your system when you install a piece of software, but also over time. This, again, is especially true when you are talking about malware. If you are doing malware analysis, it is useful to know what changes to the operating system are made when you are infected by a piece of malware. At a minimum, this helps to know what to undo in order to get rid of the malware, after it has infected a system. There are some tools that you can use to do some analysis of software installations or malware infestations.

Microsoft offers the Attack Surface Analyzer (ASA) as a free utility for download and use. This particular program has a number of uses and not just for malware analysis. Its expected primary usage is to understand the security impact a piece of software will have, once it has been installed. This includes understanding new services, weak access controls, and any changes that may allow for an easier attack from malicious users or other adversaries. From a forensic standpoint, you may be able to use it to see some of the changes that have happened on the system, when you introduce a piece of malware. You will not get a comprehensive list of changes but you may be able to see some changes that may be significant for you. Before you install a piece of software, you would run the ASA in order to get a baseline. The baseline will be necessary to compare a changed system against.

Once you have a baseline, you can install your software and then get another capture of the system. The two captures can then be compared. The ASA stores its result from the scans in .CAB files. When you have the two .CAB files, you run the ASA, indicates that you want to perform the analysis and select the two .CAB files. It will take some time to analyze the differences between the two, providing a list of steps, as you can see in Figure 9.16.

Once the analysis is complete, you will be presented with an HTML report. You can see an example of part of one of these reports in Figure 9.17. This report was generated based on installing Ruby. Ruby is an object-oriented scripting language that should not install

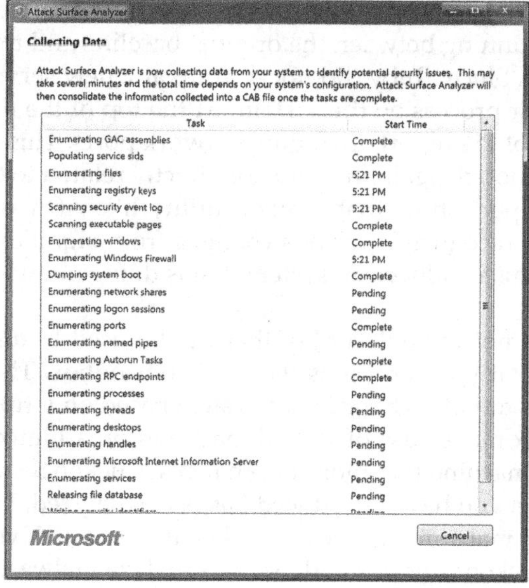

FIGURE 9.16

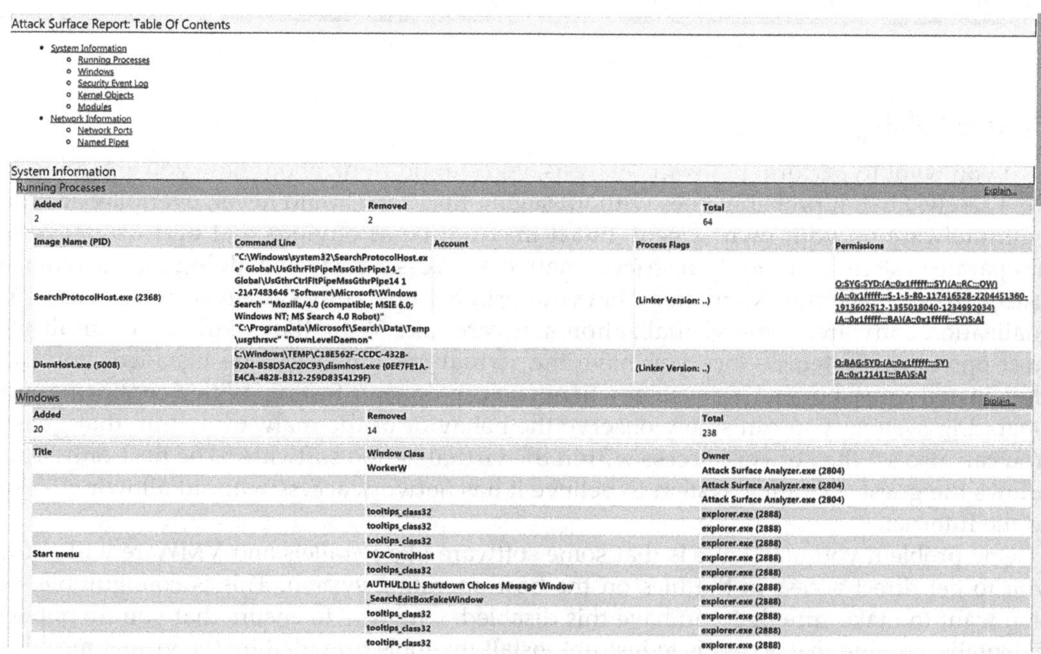

FIGURE 9.17

any services or network listeners on a Windows system. This particular report shows, there are two new processes running between the original baseline and the system capture taken after Ruby was installed. Since, Ruby did not start up any new services, these new services are a result of some other process on the system. At the top of the report, you can see links to the different sections of the report, including network ports. This report does show some changes on the system, though again they are not directly related to the installation of Ruby. The results from this report show that while a utility like ASA is very powerful, it still requires some ability to recognize spurious changes from significant changes. Of course, making sure you are using a really clean system that is doing nothing else, will help you get a cleaner result.

The Microsoft ASA is not the only utility that can be used to discover system changes, however. Another tool that you can use is the Cuckoo Sandbox. The Cuckoo Sandbox was developed specifically to monitor changes to a system based on introducing malware to that system. Cuckoo Sandbox makes use of virtual machines on a Linux system, along with an agent inside the virtual machine that monitors changes. Cuckoo Sandbox will generate a report, once the application you have introduced has been analyzed. From the report, you can determine the impact the malware sample has had on the system. If you have a Linux system, you can get a copy of Cuckoo Sandbox and use it to analyze malware samples.

There is a utility you can use on a Mac OS X system that will allow you to observe what happens when you install software. This is not exactly the same as the ASA but since Mac OS X does not have the Registry like Windows does, it will be very similar. This program is fseventer and it watches the file system on a Mac OS X system to determine changes.

Playing Safely

If you want to perform malware analysis, you should think about how you are going to do it safely. First, it probably goes without saying that you should never, ever play around with malware on your own system, but it may not be as obvious that even if you have a separate system, you should restrict its network access. One way of doing that is to make use of virtual machines. No matter what your primary operating system is, you can use virtualization software. Some virtualization software, like VirtualBox, will run on multiple host operating systems. Once you have the virtual machine software installed, you can then install a guest operating system where you can do your testing. With a confined guest operating system, you can safely observe the behavior of the malware within that guest. You can also set the network access within the virtualization software to be host-only. This allows the guest operating system to believe it has network access without allowing it out to the Internet.

One problem you may have is that some software like Parallels and VMWare will allow you to get direct access to the files on the host operating system. This is configurable, so you want to make sure that you have this disabled. One way to ensure that you do not accidentally provide that access is to just not install the tools provided by the virtual machine software. These tools are drivers that get installed in the guest operating system, enabling features like dynamic resizing of the display and access to the host filesystem. If you do not have those drivers, the guest operating system will not get direct access to the host. This does not completely remove the risk. It may be possible to escape the virtualization and gain access to the host operating system. This is a threat to be aware of, particularly considering you are working with malware.

You should always have some type of malware solution running on your system. This may be antivirus, antispyware, antiadware, or some combination of those features. When you are looking at malware samples, you need to disable that software or else your sample will disappear before you have had a chance to look at it at all. This is another advantage to using virtual machines. You can leave antivirus software off in the guest operating system, while leaving it on in the host, further protecting you from the malware leaking out of the guest into your own system.

A hypervisor, the name commonly given to the software used to manage virtual machines and enable them to run, will generally have the ability to take snapshots of the guest. This is a copy of a particular point in time within the life of that operating system. If you are using malware on a system, you may want to make regular use of snapshots. If you take a snapshot of a clean system before you infect it with malware, it is easy to restore your guest operating system back to a clean state by simply reverting back to the snapshot. This wipes away all the changes by essentially going back in time, as though the introduction of the malware never happened. On a Parallels virtual machine, you can see the Manage Snapshots screen in Figure 9.18. You may have several snapshots that you want to maintain. You could introduce malware and take a snapshot, revert to a clean image, introduce another sample then take another snapshot, and so on. You could then have multiple infected snapshots that you could refer to by just restoring to that snapshot.

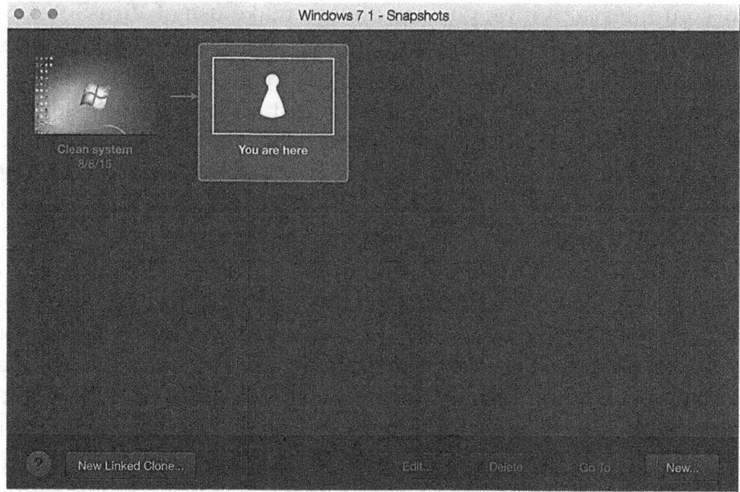

FIGURE 9.18

While you can certainly go trolling through your junk e-mail folder for malware samples and you will likely run across several, there are other places you can acquire legitimate malware samples for research purposes. Lenny Zeltser has a list of repositories of malware that can be used for research purposes. Some are going to be better than others, of course, depending on how well used and maintained they are. Zeltser also suggests the use of a honeypot to acquire malware samples. If you are technically inclined, you may make use of a honeypot, which is a system that appears to be insecure. The purpose of this system is to attract attackers. These attackers will attempt to infect the system, leading to the malware being available within the honeypot for collection. The name honeypot comes from the stories of Winnie the Pooh. In order to attract Winnie the Pooh, you left a honeypot out. This allowed you to entice Pooh to you, so you could safely capture him. The same is true in the technology world. You want to attract people to your honeypot, so you can collect information about what they are doing. As a result, you leave a system out that looks very enticing. It may appear to be very vulnerable and exposed to attack or it may simply appear to have a lot of really important information on it.

There are a few repositories that may be good places to start. One of them is Contagio Malware Dump. It is free to get access to but you will be required to register. This is a fairly common restriction. They do not want just anyone to get access to this malware, since it can be used, obviously, for malicious purposes. Another decent repository is Malwr.com. Offensive Computing, also has a repository that had a lot of good malware but at the time of this writing, is down. They plan to be back up at some point, so you may keep an eye out for them. Of course, you can search for repositories but you want to be a little careful, which ones you register with. Try to use repositories that have been identified by known malware researchers or by people you know and trust. Any time you are working with malware, it is important to be very cautious. Not only is the malware dangerous but sometimes the people who have access to it can be dangerous as well.

One final note on playing with malware. If you happen to find a sample on your own, either with a honeypot or through e-mail or just because you got unlucky in the course of your day to day computer activities, you can always make use of VirusTotal, to do the identification for you. VirusTotal is a website that allows you to submit malware samples to be compared against antivirus engines from most of the major antivirus vendors. This is a way to quickly run a number of antivirus programs against a single sample, all at once. In some cases, you may have found an obscure piece of malware that only a couple of the antivirus vendors have identified or run across themselves. Being able to have a site like VirusTotal is essential to someone who is investigating malware, either because they are interested in it or simply because they have to, as a result of being infected themselves.

On a Mac OS X system, you can use the utilities Knock Knock, TaskExplorer and Dynamic Hijack Scanner to observe what is happening on the operating system. These tools offer similar features to those offered by some of the SysInternals tools. Knock Knock is used to locate items that have installed in a way to ensure persistence. This includes showing items that have been set up to launch automatically. TaskExplorer monitors open files, network connections and dynamic libraries used by running applications. You can see an example of TaskExplorer running in Figure 9.19. Finally, Dynamic Hijack Scanner searches for programs that may be susceptible to dynamic library hijacking. Mac OS X uses dynamic libraries that are similar to Dynamic Linked Libraries (DLLs) but are called DyLibs for dynamic libraries. This means that they can be loaded at runtime by an application.

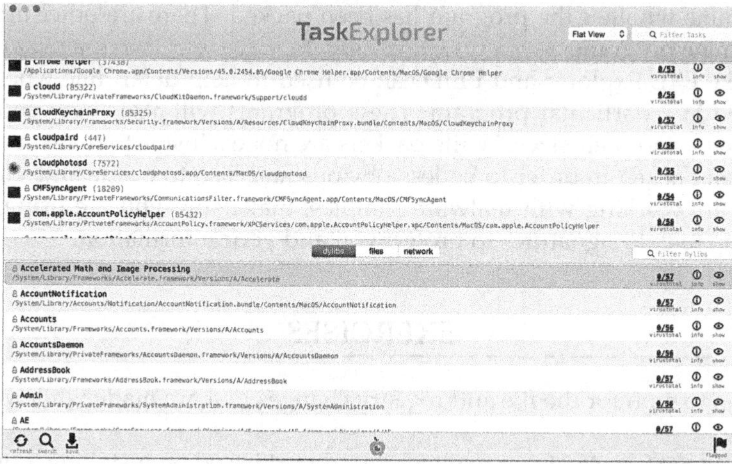

FIGURE 9.19

CONCLUSIONS

Understanding how programs run and how they interact with the operating system is essential for a number of reasons. One very common reason is because of the amount of malware in the world. At some point, most users will have to deal with malware, even if it is second hand because someone they know has been infected. If you are very technically inclined, you may be the person who gets called when their system has been infected. While Windows systems are most commonly infected for a number of reasons that have very little to do with the operating system itself, other operating systems such as Mac OS X and Linux are not invulnerable to malware attacks and outbreaks. Just understanding how to deal with malware on a Windows system – how to observe and monitor the behavior of programs – may not be enough.

In order to get exposure to other operating systems, making use of virtualization software is helpful. Virtualization software is also essential if you are doing any sort of malware investigation to help protect your own system, as well as others on the network from the effects of the malware. A virtual machine will help contain it, while still providing you the ability to examine what it does and how it interacts with the operating system. This will help you to better determine what it is doing, so you can understand the impact it will have on systems it infects, including what data, including credentials, and other personal information, may be stolen.

Once you have the malware, or any other program you want to look at, you can use tools like debuggers to better observe what the program is doing. Using a debugger, you can stop the flow of execution of the program in order to analyze the data the program stores. With a debugger, you may also be better able to see the behavior of stub programs like packers. A debugger will allow you to see how the packer unpacks and loads the real program into memory, so that execution can be passed from the initial stub program into the malware itself. Of course, you do not necessarily have to load the program into a debugger and execute it in order to determine whether the program has been packed. There are other utilities that can be used to examine programs.

Programs like EXE Explorer and PEiD can be used to help determine whether there is a packer involved in a particular program. These programs will also show you the different program segments and their sizes. While packers are not exclusive to malware, it is true that malware is often packed in order to be less obvious and also to evade anti-virus programs. Any time you are working with malware samples, make sure you are using an anti-virus solution with up to date signatures to protect you and your information.

EXERCISES

1. Use ProcMon to monitor the file and registry changes that are made while you perform a Web search.
2. Use the Attack Surface Analyzer to generate a report based on installing a piece of software.
3. Use one of the debuggers outlined in the chapter. Load a program and observe the disassembly of the code.
4. Download a malware sample and test it for packers using PEiD.
5. Get access to a Linux system and execute a common program like ls using both ltrace and strace.
6. Use Dynamic Hijack Scanner to scan a Mac OS X system for applications that may be prone to hijacking.

Bibliography

Hooked on DTrace, 2013. Part 1: Big Nerd Ranch. (accessed 09.08.2015.).

Matloff, N., Salzman, P., 2008. The Art of Debugging with GDB, DDD, and Eclipse. No Starch Press, San Francisco.

Russinovich, M., Margosis, A., 2011. Windows Sysinternals Administrator's Reference. Microsoft Press, Redmond, Washington.

CHAPTER

10

Malware

INFORMATION INCLUDED IN THIS CHAPTER:

- Malware Categories
- Using Malware Researchers
- Persistence
- Infection Vectors
- Malware Artifacts

INTRODUCTION

It is difficult to start this without using some hackneyed, clichéd expression that dramatically understates the challenge or does not put it into some useful perspective. The short version is that malware is a problem. There are millions of new types of malware developed each year. This may be an existing piece of malware that is just different enough to require a new signature, means that the way of recognizing it has changed, so any piece of software looking for it has to look for something different. Imagine that you have a criminal who has been breaking into houses, stealing valuables. The report says that the criminal has long blonde hair, is wearing a baseball cap and a Colorado Rockies jersey over a t-shirt, and jeans. The next night, another house in your neighborhood is broken into but the one who is seen leaving this time, he has dark hair, is wearing a watch cap, shorts, and a mock turtleneck. Is this the same person? More than likely, all things considered, but the description does not match. If you are looking for someone who is an exact match for the description, you will fail to find this criminal.

While antivirus software is valuable and important to have in order to protect your systems, it is not perfect. It still relies on these descriptions that are provided to it. What is even worse is the increasing number of descriptions that are necessary in order to detect all malware that is known. These descriptions are commonly called signatures and they are sets of patterns that the anti-virus programs are trying to match on. The more malware that is known about, the larger the signature databases. This increases the processing power, when the antivirus software is trying to check files that are accessed. The Independent IT Security Institute is one organization that keeps track of malware statistics. According to them, there has been exponential growth in malware development since 2011. You can see a graph of this shown in Figure 10.1. According to them, the year 2014 had more than 140 million new instances of malware. While the last line in the graph is not as long, it is only because the year is not completed.

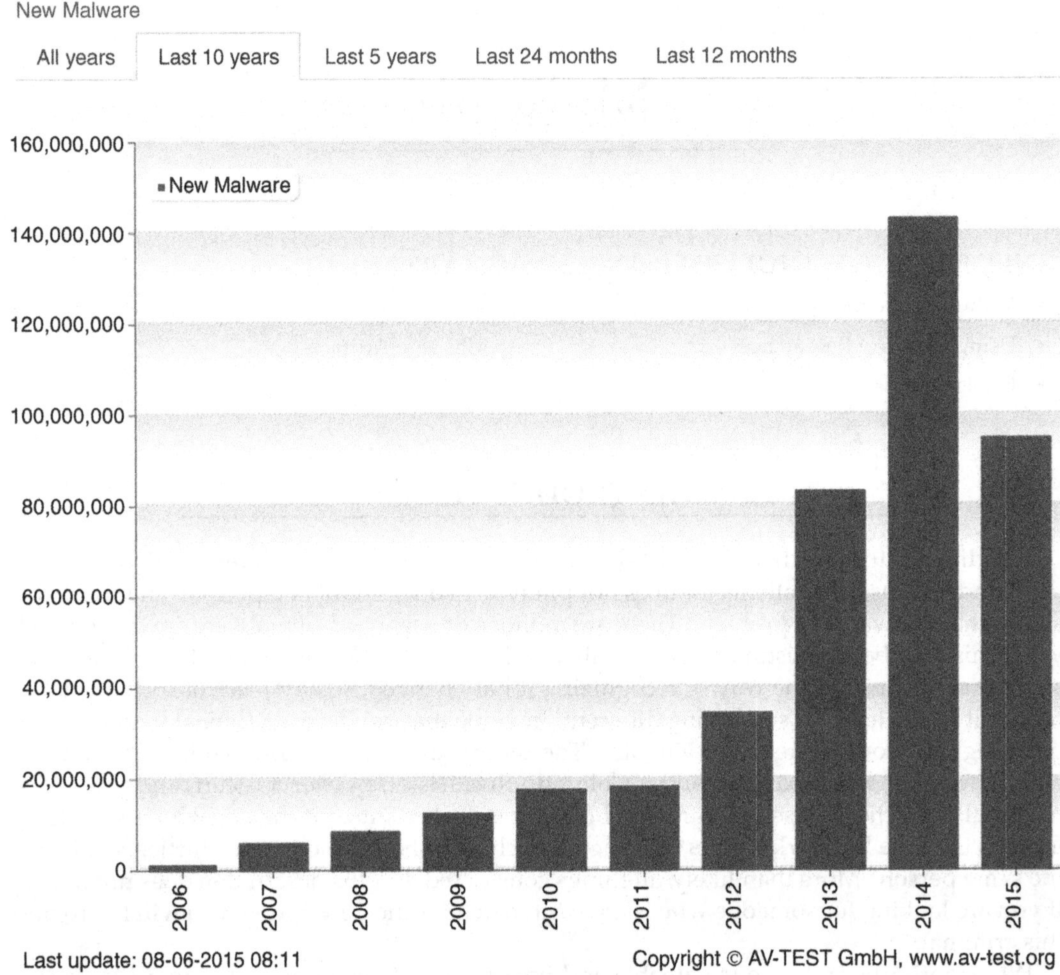

FIGURE 10.1

This graph and the numbers behind it do not take into account any malware that has yet to be detected. While anti-malware programs are generally good, they are not perfect. Signature databases need to be refreshed. Those databases need to be updated with new signatures as new malware is detected. New malware needs to be detected. Anti-malware programs, just as with any other piece of software, may interact poorly with other installed software. There are a lot of variables that need to be factored in. This is all to say that malware is not a confined problem with a well-defined solution. As a result, forensic practitioners need to be aware, at least generally, how to identify malware. This can include not only the type and family but also the infection vector, behaviors, and persistence mechanisms.

Skilled malware researchers will make use of debuggers and a number of other tools to investigate the malware. There is a lot of need for people who can really dig into the actual executable to understand what it does. We do not necessarily have to do that. There are a number of ways, you can learn more about malware and what it does. This may simply be using the research that someone else has done, except that you need to locate the malware on your system first. As a result, you need to be able to chase artifacts, including evidence that the malware exists. Once you have located the malware, you can use someone else's work to figure out what it is, and then determine what the impact to the system is. You can also use artifacts on an operating system to determine when the malware first arrived.

Maybe it goes without saying but the history is important. Often these days, you would not find a single piece of malware on your system. History and an associated timeline marking the relevant points in time will help you determine how you got infected, which can help you better protect yourself and your operating system.

MALWARE CATEGORIES

There are a number of ways to think about malware. You may categorize it because of the way it behaves. You may want to think about how it transmits from one system to another. While you may end up juggling them around a little, there are some well-known categories that are commonly used to describe malware. We will be going through other categories or other ways of thinking about malware but just as a starting point, we should get some of the basics out of the way. So, we will be going over viruses, worms, rootkits, spyware, adware, Trojans, macro viruses, and construction kits. One piece of malware may actually fall into multiple categories here but these are some very common terms and we should start here with a common dictionary.

Virus

Virus is really a generic term but it is significant in a way. The word virus, of course, comes from the world of infectious disease in the animal world (primarily human). A virus is a disease that can move from one person to another, if those two people come in contact with one another. While some people may think of the word virus as being synonymous with the word malware, we are going to make a distinction to separate the word virus from another word, worm. A virus is a malicious piece of software that requires some sort of intervention to get from one system to another. This may require that you insert a USB stick that you were given or found somewhere. It may require that you open up an e-mail attachment. There are a number of ways you can get infected with a virus that will come from normal use of a computer system. Some of them may result from you doing something while others may occur without being aware that something is going on.

Interestingly, the very first computer virus discovered "in the wild," meaning it was found outside of a lab environment on a live, in-use system, was on an Apple II in 1982. The virus, called Elk Cloner, infected disks that were inserted into the Apple II. Fortunately, it was an innocuous virus. There was no damage done aside from the process of infecting other disks in order to hopefully infect other systems. It displayed a short poem on the screen but beyond that, it was very innocuous. It was four more years before a virus infected an IBM PC system. If you are unfamiliar with the terminology, an IBM PC system was any system designed with an Intel processor that had the same architecture as an IBM PC and could run PC-DOS or MS-DOS. They were sometimes called PC-compatibles.

Both of these viruses were boot sector viruses, meaning they infected the boot sector of a disk. At the time, floppy disks were the predominant form of mass storage, though it is hard to call something that could store 360 kilobytes mass storage in today's terabyte era. Infecting the boot sector was a way to make sure that the virus remained active. In order to get the system up and running, you had to insert a bootable disk and you could turn any disk into a bootable disk. If the boot sector got infected, you ensured that the virus got loaded when the computer started up. This helped to make sure that it spread. In order to spread, the virus needed someone to insert additional disks that were not infected and the virus would then infect those. In the days before the Internet, it was pretty common to share floppy disks. You had something and your friend wanted it, you copied it off to a floppy disk and then gave the floppy disk to the friend. Your friend boots off that disk and then their system is infected.

Of course, this particular type of virus required that the boot sector of the boot floppy get infected because there was no persistence on a hard drive. You may have a dozen different floppy disks (or more) that you could boot off. If the boot sectors on all those disks were not infected, you could boot the system clean, without any infection. This is one reason why the virus would just keep writing out to boot sectors as it got access to them. It was the only way to ensure that you could not boot a clean system. The thing about the boot sector virus is that you could boot clean, then insert a disk that had been infected and because the virus was actually in the boot sector, you would not get infected. There was no way to get infected without the virus code actually running and the only way for that to happen was to boot off an infected disk.

The fact that you cannot get infected without running the virus remains true today. Just putting a virus on a disk on my system will not infect me. The virus has to execute in some fashion in order to get the program in memory and running. Viruses will use a lot of different techniques in order to make sure they get executed. Perhaps it is more accurate to say that virus writers will use a number of techniques to ensure the virus is executed. One way is to use social engineering techniques. One common technique today is to send an "invoice" to someone via e-mail. The filename looks like it may be a Portable Document Format (PDF) document when in fact, it is an executable but the file has a long name and the extension is often hidden. All you see is something that looks like invoice.pdf without recognizing that there are a lot of spaces or maybe other characters before the actual file extension which is a .exe. All you have to do is attempt to look at the invoice that you were sent and you have run the virus, infecting your system.

Viruses may also use Web sites to infect you. One particular type of attack is called a watering hole attack. With a watering hole attack, someone may recognize that a particular group of users regularly visit a particular Web site. Maybe this is a fantasy sports Web site that the sales guys at your company visit every day. The adversary will work to compromise that Web site in order to insert malicious software that will eventually infect the systems of your sales team. It may do this using a variety of techniques including a rogue Java applet, infected Flash or the adversary may make use of a browser vulnerability that will allow for code to be executed without the user being aware.

Slightly related to this is a drive-by attack. This also uses a Web site but it is more opportunistic and less targeted. An attacker infects a Web site, causing malware to be automatically downloaded and executed simply by someone visiting the site. The attacker may do this to a well-known site or they may simply create a site of their own then send out e-mail to potential victims luring them to the site. They may also populate discussion forums or comment areas on various sites to include a link to the site.

The virus does not need to have capabilities of automatically infecting other systems on its own. There are plenty of ways for adversaries to infect a number of systems. A program that is capable of propagating on its own is commonly called a worm. A worm is self-propagating. A virus requires intervention from a user to propagate. Malware is the term used to describe both.

Worm

Interestingly, the idea of a worm goes back to some of the early days of electronic, digital computers. In 1949, John von Neumann proposed the idea of self-replicating software. As a result, worms were proposed decades before viruses. Of course, you can have self-propagating software without it being malicious, which is a pretty significant difference. The very first worm to be implemented across a network was in 1971, as an experiment in self-replication. The network was the Advanced Research Projects Network (ARPANET), a forerunner to what is now the Internet. It was written by Bob Thomas, who worked at Bolt, Baranek and Newman (BBN), the company that built the ARPANET for the Department of Defense. Thomas wrote a program called Creeper, that copied itself from one system to another across the ARPANET displaying the message "I'm the creeper, catch me if you can!" on systems after they had been infected (Chen, 2005).

The first significant worm was released in November, 1988 by Cornell University student Robert T. Morris. Morris, whose middle initial is commonly used to differentiate him from his father, who is also named Robert Morris, was a graduate student who says the worm was designed to determine the size of the Internet, as it was at that time. Morris's software took advantage of several known vulnerabilities in order to infect systems across the network. While Morris was a graduate student at Cornell, the worm was released from a system at the Massachusetts Institute of Technology. Morris was the first person convicted under the 1986 Computer Fraud and Abuse Act. While the worm itself did not have any deliberately malicious capabilities, it still caused significant damages, forcing some nodes on the network to unplug, until they could get the worm under control.

The Morris worm was released during a time when the vast majority of systems attached to the network were multi-user mainframes or mini computers. The problem with the Morris worm was that once it had infected a system, it remained resident trying to infect other systems it could reach. There was no check to make sure the system it was on, was not already infected. As a result, these systems very quickly got overwhelmed with multiple copies of the worm consuming resources as it continued trying to compromise other systems on the network. One advantage from this worm was that it spawned the creation of the Computer Emergency Response Team (CERT) that remains in place in the United States today.

By this point, you may have determined that a worm is any piece of software that can create copies of itself from one system to another. Beyond that, since copying does not guarantee an infection, the worm is able to execute itself on another system. This typically requires that the worm take advantage of a vulnerability on the target system that can be exploited to run the attacker's code. If the worm cannot execute itself and just copies itself to, say, the target's filesystem, it could just sit there quietly on disk, causing absolutely no harm.

Not all worms are malicious. Just because a piece of software is capable of moving without assistance from one system to another does not mean that it is bad, or at least intentionally bad. Sometimes worms get released in order to clean up other worms. The first worm to do this was the Reaper worm, which was released to remove the Creeper worm. When the Blaster worm launched in 2003, attacking the Remote Procedure Call (RPC) service on Windows systems, it was two years after the Code Red and Nimda worms that were so devastating. Blaster was targeted at a service that was very common across Windows systems, and it was at a time when far too many people were not keeping their systems up to date. As a result, it was a serious problem. In order to get the infection of the Blaster worm under control, someone wrote and released the Nachia/Welchia worm. The purpose of this piece of software was to remove Blaster and also apply the Microsoft patch that would have prevented both Blaster and Nachia from infecting the system again. Nachia used the same vulnerabilities to infect systems.

While the intention of Nachia was to be beneficial by getting another worm under control, the reality was that it was infecting systems and running code on those infected systems. Even though the Nachia worm was doing a favor for the owners of those systems, it was still making use of the systems in an unauthorized manner. Had the Nachia worm not been tested fully, it could have easily gotten out of control, consuming resources in a way that would slow systems down, just as the Morris worm did. As a result, the Nachia worm was flagged as malware by anti-virus vendors.

Rootkit

A rootkit is a piece of malware that has a couple of purposes. It may also be considered a virus itself. It may also accompany another virus or piece of malware. One of the purposes of a rootkit is to alter system software in order to obscure the presence of both, itself and also of an accompanying virus. A virus, after all, will generally want to maintain the infection of a system. In order to do that, it has to be stealthy. This can be handled by a rootkit. On a Windows system, a rootkit may prevent directory listings from showing files associated with the malware. It may also prevent the running virus from showing up in the Task Manager. On Unix systems, rootkits have been around, since 1990. Since source code for the Unix system utilities is available, it is always been much easier to write a rootkit for a Unix system, including Linux. A rootkit author would want to alter system utilities like ls, top, and ps as starting points to prevent any system administrator from noticing that there is anything unusual about the system.

The use of rootkits led to the creation of file integrity software like Tripwire. In order to best protect your system from having system-level programs replaced by compromised software, one approach is to get cryptographic hashes of the system files and periodically check those files to ensure that the hashes have not changed. If a file's hash changes, it is an indicator that your operating system may have been compromised. This does require that you have protected the database of all of the hashes, so they cannot be updated by the attacker. If the attacker can modify the database of hashes, you will have no awareness of the change because when your file integrity checker runs, it will be checking against a compromised hash and of course it will match the compromised program's hash.

Another reason for implementing a rootkit is to obtain and maintain root level access on a system. On a Unix-like system, the administrative user is named root. This is similar to the Administrator user on a Windows system. The root user has the highest level of privileges on a Unix-like system, which includes Linux. The root user account is sometimes called the superuser. If an attacker can obtain root privileges, he or she could add users, replace system programs, start up privileged network listeners, change passwords, and also view or delete any file on the system. A rootkit may install a backdoor, which may be a listener that the attacker can always get access to, even if other remote access services are shut down or removed. While the rootkit has its origins in the Unix world, predating even Linux, both Linux and Windows rootkits are available and in use. Mac OS X is based on Unix so, of course, rootkits for Mac OS X are also available.

---

www.objective-see.com has a number of utilities you can use to help detect the existence of malware on your system, as discussed in Chapter 9. These include Knock Knock, used to locate programs that have been installed in a way that allows them to run across reboots.

Macro Virus

A number of document types, particularly word processing documents, spreadsheets, or similar document types used in an office setting, allow for users to attach small programs to the document to accomplish tasks. These small programs are called macros and they have been in office productivity software for years. The problem with macros is that the programming language the macro is written in, can sometimes have too much access to the operating system. This can allow malware authors to distribute malicious documents to unsuspecting users. If you get a word processing document, it may not occur to you that you are being attacked by a virus when you open it. It is not an executable program after all. Opening the word processing document will trigger the macro to run, though, and the macro will then compromise your system.

In 1999, the Melissa virus took over 20% of the computers around the world by some estimates. Melissa was a macro virus that used the e-mail program on a victim's computer to spread itself. The macro, written in an implementation of Visual Basic, was able to make use of the address book in order to send itself to friends of the victim. While it infected a large number of systems around the world, the intention was not to cause damage but simply to infect systems. This was long before some people figured out how to make money through the use of these types of programs. Many viruses were not nearly as dangerous or as destructive as they could have been, especially at the time of Melissa, when many users were not very sophisticated, when it came to understanding the risks of opening e-mail attachments or having up to date anti-virus programs installed.

As a result of Melissa and other macro viruses, Microsoft and other vendors began to alter the behavior of their office programs. Macros were no longer given free reign to access address books or other aspects of the system. They were no longer allowed to just run without user approval. As a result of this clamp down, macro viruses are no longer the threat they once were, but they are still a possibility and as a result, the capabilities of macros within productivity documents remain somewhat constrained.

Trojan

A Trojan is a type of virus rather than being something separate. The difference with the Trojan is that it hides itself. The term is taken from the story of the war between Troy and the Greeks. After a ten-year siege of the city of Troy, the Greeks made a final ploy, leaving a large horse outside the city, making it appear as though the soldiers had left. Instead, the soldiers were inside the horse so when it was brought into the city, the soldiers were inside the city walls that they had been unable to penetrate from the outside for a decade. Once night fell, the soldiers came out of the horse and were able to defeat the city from the inside. Similarly, a Trojan horse in the computing world is a piece of software that purports or appears to be one thing, while in fact being something completely different. This is a form of social engineering, in fact, since the objective is to get someone to do something they would not otherwise do by getting them to believe something that is not true.

One common modern approach to the Trojan horse is tricking users to install anti-virus software or other system checking programs. In fact, what they are running or installing is malicious software that may install a botnet client or software that may steal personal information, including usernames or credit card numbers, from the user. In the late 1990s and into the early 2000s, before there was much in the way of user or attacker sophistication, programs like Sub7 and BackOrifice were used as Trojans. Both of these programs are remote access tools, allowing an attacker to gain remote control of the targeted system. This was a far more direct approach than you would see used today. Using BackOrifice or Sub7, a remote attacker had direct control of the system. Additionally, there were tools that were included. You can see the administration program in Figure 10.2.

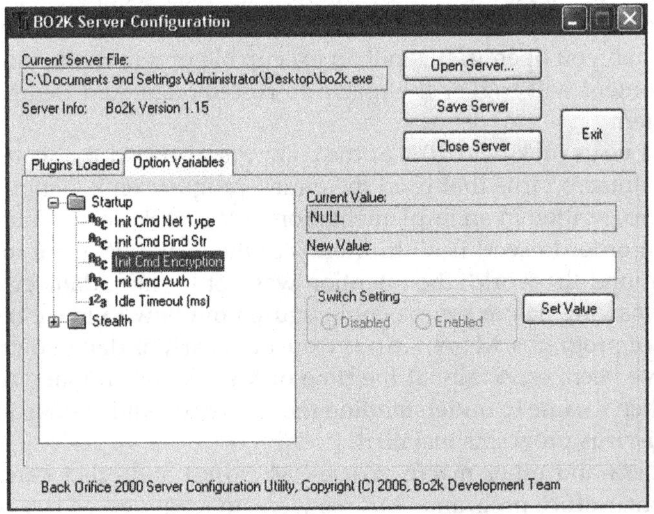

FIGURE 10.2

The original BackOrifice (BO) was replaced with a newer and better version in BackOrifice 2K (BO2K), which is what you see in Figure 10.2. Interestingly, BO2K was so feature-rich that it could function just as effectively for system administrators as remotely possible, PC/anywhere and the Microsoft remote administration programs. However, since BO and BO2K were both used as a Trojan, it was flagged as being malicious software and identified by anti-virus programs.

Botnet

While viruses can be used to infect systems, modern viruses will often download and install other software. Sometimes, the software that gets installed will turn the computer system into a slave of a larger network, controlled by malicious users. Once all of the compromised systems are collected together under a unified control infrastructure, the result is called a botnet. The software that joins a system to a botnet is called a botnet client. The botnet client software may not itself infect the host system. Instead, it may be downloaded after the fact and set up to run automatically when the system boots up. The botnet client will take its orders from a Command and Control (C&C) infrastructure. This could be a multi-tiered configuration, with some number of tiers of servers, themselves compromised computers, passing commands down to the botnet clients from a single controlling computer at the top of the pyramid. That single computer would be controlled by anyone but itself would not be compromised.

There are a number of ways that botnet clients may receive control messages from the chain of command. One of them is through the use of Internet Relay Chat (IRC) servers. A botnet client may connect to a pre-established IRC server and join a specific channel within that server. There, the control servers can place messages that the clients can pick up and act on. The actions of the botnet can be to act like HTTP servers to take orders for various products, including pharmaceuticals. Using a dynamic Domain Name System (DNS) address, a number of systems in the botnet could act as a Web server. Even simultaneously, to reduce the amount of traffic arriving at the compromised system, which may slow down network access making the compromise easier to discover.

While HTTP and IRC communications may be common, many other mechanisms can be used for communicating with the botnet clients. One example is a piece of malware that has been called HAMMERTOSS that uses Twitter as a way to communicate between the command and control servers and the clients. Twitter would be a good way to hide in the noise using an existing and well-known social networking site. HAMMERTOSS is a piece of malware attributed to a Russian threat group.

A botnet can also participate in various attacks on other systems around the world, including and perhaps especially, distributed denial of service attacks. This may not be a common use of botnets but it is certainly a highly publicized use. Every time a company comes under multiple gigabit attacks, including SYN floods, ping floods, and other types of network attacks, it is quite often, the result of a large number of botnet clients ganging together to send enormous volumes of network traffic that a single system would be unable to send. Modern operating systems and computer hardware are capable of withstanding a large amount of traffic without going down. Certainly a single system would be unable to take down a single other system at the network or transport layers.

A botnet is also often used to send unsolicited commercial e-mail (UCE), more commonly known as spam. When you spread the source of your spam out across a large number of systems, it becomes quite a bit harder to protect against that spam. One approach to suppressing spam is to create lists of IP addresses known to generate spam and then block those IP addresses. This is called a blacklist. When the IP addresses are so many, varied and changing, it becomes a lot harder to keep your lists up to date. As soon as one IP address makes its way onto the blacklist, hundreds of additional servers have been added to the botnet.

Unlike other malware, the purpose of a botnet client is not to infect other systems. Instead, the botnet itself may rely on other malware to do the infection. The purpose of a botnet is to make money for the person managing the botnet. This may be through renting out the botnet, selling various products like pharmaceuticals or even stealing information from the infected system.

Construction Kits

Malware is a business. It certainly did not start this way but the reality is that it is often used now, as a way for criminals to make money. The fastest way to make that happen is for one person to create a way to generate malware and then distribute that construction kit to others, generally for a price. There have been a number of construction kits that can be used to create a unique executable whose signature is specific to your particular implementation, based on the way you have configured it. This allows you to avoid detection by anti-virus, potentially, because it is harder to develop a signature for a number of unique executables. ZeuS was one of the early construction kits. You can see the configuration builder program in Figure 10.3. ZeuS was first identified in 2007 and was implemented as a Trojan horse that infected systems through drive-by download and phishing attacks.

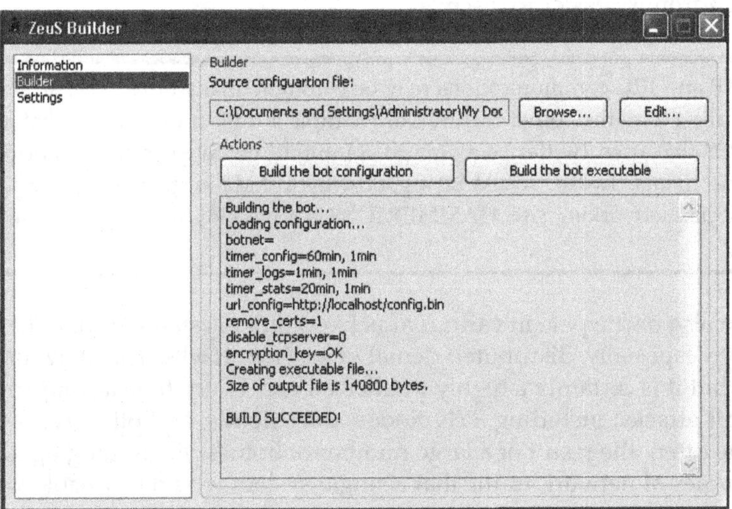

FIGURE 10.3

ZeuS was used to gather personal information from users. This includes gathering usernames and passwords from Web forms and file transfer protocol (FTP) accounts. ZeuS included the capability to capture keystrokes from a target system as one way of gathering the information that the botnet stole. While ZeuS was discovered in 2007, it appeared to have been retired in 2010, when the source code for the botnet was released. By that point, however, it had been succeeded by at least one other botnet. The SpyEye botnet appears to have succeeded ZeuS and possibly with the help of the author of ZeuS. SpyEye is known to have been sold across the Internet to those, who were interested in creating their own botnets. Botnets are often not managed by the people who wrote the software, but instead, by the people who have purchased the malicious software and configured it in a way that would allow these people to create their own botnet.

While knowing about construction kits will not necessarily help you to locate malware on an infected system, it is worth knowing that these construction kits allow for a number of variants to be created. The number of criminals who have purchased SpyEye and other, similar botnet kits, may determine the number of variants of the botnet software.

USING RESEARCH

You are not alone when it comes to addressing malicious software, though it may feel like it. Many have come before you in most cases and you can make use of their work to help yourself out. Major antivirus vendors do a lot of research on newly discovered pieces of malware. These researchers are capable of determining the path the infection generally takes as well as file artifacts that will be left behind on an infected system. You can go to these Web sites to learn more about the particular virus, you have on your hands to get advice on how best to remove the malware, and what the malware may have done while the system was infected. This can include stealing information, dropping additional malware onto the system, acting as a botnet client, being a source of spam, or acting like a rootkit among other potential actions. This does, though, raise the challenge of identifying the malware to begin with in order to start your research.

One way to identify the malware is simply to get a cryptographic hash of the executable. While the Message Digest 5 (MD5) hash is still in common use, it has been superseded in use for encryption and high security purposes by the Secure Hash Algorithm 1 (SHA1), which itself has recently been superseded by the Secure Hash Algorithm 2 (SHA2). For the purposes of file identification, MD5 is as good as anything else and there are a number of tools available on all operating systems that are capable of generating an MD5 hash. Operating systems like Linux and Mac OS X have tools for both MD5 and SHA1 either already installed or at least readily installable. While these tools are very common, it is hard to say for certain that all of the hundreds of Linux distributions will definitely have utilities installed that can generate these hash values. Certainly Mac OS X has both an MD5 and a SHA hashing program. You can see the results from both md5sum and shasum in Figure 10.4. The hash values were generated on a collection of binary files related to the Conficker worm. You will notice that the values provided are all in hexadecimal. Hexadecimal is often used as a shorter way to provide a long value that has no meaning except in the complete value. In this case, an MD5 sum is 128 bits long or 16 bytes. This would be represented as 32 hexadecimal digits.

```
kilroy@opus:~/Downloads/Conficker binaries$ md5 *
MD5 (1DB5476C766555C9995B25D19F97B9BC.EXE) = 1db5476c766555c9995b25d19f97b9bc
MD5 (223D8089F8EE82F8B05266BAECAAC61E.DLL) = 223d8089f8ee82f8b05266baecaac61e
MD5 (BD35D4D98FCBB1EC0E090FD2C631BAA5.DLL) = bd35d4d98fcbb1ec0e090fd2c631baa5
MD5 (CC7EDB2E4300AC539259F3FFDE0F1AB6.DLL) = cc7edb2e4300ac539259f3ffde0f1ab6
MD5 (CC7EDB2E4300AC539259F3FFDE0F1AB6.EXE) = cc7edb2e4300ac539259f3ffde0f1ab6
MD5 (CE18A72735FEB7A315B947DC0986009D.DLL) = ce18a72735feb7a315b947dc0986009d
MD5 (D9CB288F317124A0E63E3405ED290765.DLL) = d9cb288f317124a0e63e3405ed290765
MD5 (autorun.inf) = 7d9542ef7c46ed5e80c23153dd5319f2
MD5 (bd35d4d98fcbb1ec0e090fd2c631baa5.EXE) = bd35d4d98fcbb1ec0e090fd2c631baa5
MD5 (jwgkvsq.vmx) = c3852074ee50da92c2857d24471747d9
MD5 (jwgkvsq4.vmx) = 8c9367b7dc43dadaa3ec9da767c586cf
kilroy@opus:~/Downloads/Conficker binaries$ shasum *
f509f352e4ee0f8d8ee2902721ae3a15799baba1  1DB5476C766555C9995B25D19F97B9BC.EXE
6ede5f34e8717b470de10e56c99adc7c47307842  223D8089F8EE82F8B05266BAECAAC61E.DLL
e48b2fcb09ada376895fc838a9c3c9e233c2ffba  BD35D4D98FCBB1EC0E090FD2C631BAA5.DLL
692caa0d6fd13028bec25cdca15f13522d1b3a7d  CC7EDB2E4300AC539259F3FFDE0F1AB6.DLL
692caa0d6fd13028bec25cdca15f13522d1b3a7d  CC7EDB2E4300AC539259F3FFDE0F1AB6.EXE
6d2ffc85bf7618d4327bfefdbd3bccffcae96902  CE18A72735FEB7A315B947DC0986009D.DLL
5815b13044fc9248bf7c2dba771f0e6496d9e536  D9CB288F317124A0E63E3405ED290765.DLL
f49fa573a973500d37df219d6055fd4a50f7931f  autorun.inf
e48b2fcb09ada376895fc838a9c3c9e233c2ffba  bd35d4d98fcbb1ec0e090fd2c631baa5.EXE
7910076ec1e60326409408fc042c89e96aefefa1  jwgkvsq.vmx
5fd0af3aac0c54d4858a50f0e62d6b5a2035d97a  jwgkvsq4.vmx
```

FIGURE 10.4

Once you have the value, you can just run it through a search engine. Searching on the MD5 hash value 1db5476c766555c9995b25d19f97b9bc, yields several results. One of the first results is managed by Google and we will get into that shortly. Selecting another at random from Payload Security at www.hybrid-analysis.com yields analysis about the file, just based on the MD5 hash value. According to Payload Security, this particular virus has a threat score of 95/100 and is named W32/Downadup. You can see additional information in Figure 10.5, including additional hash values related to this particular executable. Payload Security identifies a number of files that it knows about as being related to W32/Downadup.

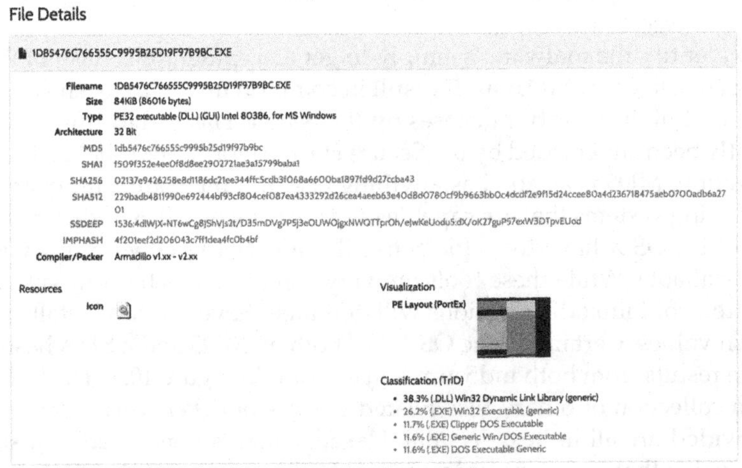

FIGURE 10.5

This brings up one of the challenges associated with malware research. Different researchers and organizations will have different nomenclatures for the malware it finds. There is no consistency about naming malware. Different research organizations will name the same malware something different. While Conficker is the most common name for this particular piece of malware, it is certainly not the only one. This brings us to the Google subsidiary known as VirusTotal. VirusTotal makes use of anti-virus engines from a large number, if not all, of the anti-virus products that are available across different platforms. If you have a particular sample you need to examine and you need to know what it is, you can submit it to VirusTotal and you will get the results from all of the engines that VirusTotal knows about. If we submit the sample to VirusTotal, we get the results, once the sample has been uploaded. The fast results are summarized in the dialog box seen in Figure 10.6. The results show us that out of the 55 anti-virus engines that VirusTotal checks against, 47 of them have the sample flagged as malware.

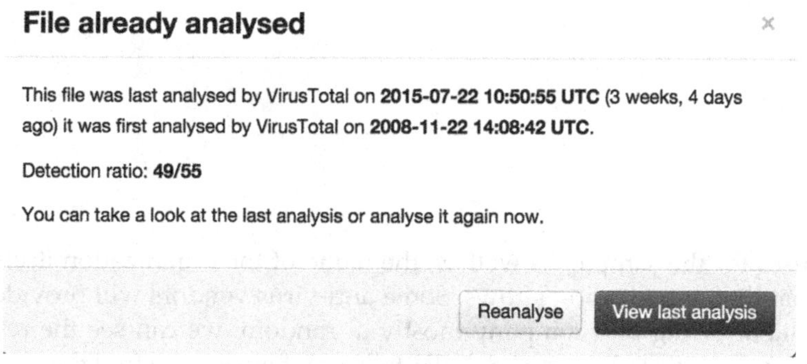

FIGURE 10.6

For more detail, we can look at the results of the last analysis. You can see some of the different anti-virus engines and the name they have given to the malware in Figure 10.7. You will notice that several of them use the same name, whether it is Conficker or Downadup or some other name. Some anti-virus will give it a completely unique name that is only used by the particular antivirus software company that developed the engine. Of course, the name given to the malware is mostly irrelevant, except as a way to identify it using a name rather than a hash value. If I were to tell you that I was analyzing 1db5476c766555c9995b25d19f97b9bc, you would likely have absolutely no idea what I was talking about, unless you are particularly good at memorizing long hexadecimal values. Personally, it is not a facility I happen to have, though you might. For me, Conficker is quite a bit easier to remember. If I were to tell you, I had a Conficker sample, it would probably mean a lot more to you.

If you have the malware name and the name of the organization that has identified it with that name, you can make use of the research that organization has done on the malware to determine how you should handle it. Select one anti-virus vendor and search on the name the

Antivirus	Result	Update
ALYac	Worm.Conficker	20150722
AVG	Crypt.BEL	20150721
AVware	Trojan.Win32.Generic!BT	20150722
Ad-Aware	Win32.Worm.Downadup.Gen	20150722
Agnitum	Trojan.Conficker.Gen!Pac	20150721
AhnLab-V3	Win32/Conficker.worm.86016	20150722
Antiy-AVL	Worm[Net]/Win32.Kido	20150722
Arcabit	Win32.Worm.Downadup.Gen	20150722
Avast	Win32:Confi [Wrm]	20150722
Avira	TR/ATRAPS.Gen2	20150722
Baidu-International	Worm.Win32.Kido.ih	20150722
BitDefender	Win32.Worm.Downadup.Gen	20150722
CAT-QuickHeal	I-Worm.Kido.I.n4	20150722
ClamAV	Worm.Kido-123	20150721
Comodo	NetWorm.Win32.Kido.ih3	20150722
Cyren	W32/Downadup.FJTN-7328	20150722
DrWeb	Trojan.DownLoad.16849	20150722
ESET-NOD32	Win32/Conficker.A	20150722
Emsisoft	Win32.Worm.Downadup.Gen (B)	20150722
F-Prot	W32/Downadup.A	20150722
F-Secure	Worm:W32/Downadup.A	20150722
Fortinet	W32/Conficker.A!worm	20150722

FIGURE 10.7

organization uses for the sample, as well as, the name of the organization itself and you can read up on what that organization knows. Some anti-virus vendors will provide more details than others will. Selecting one company mostly at random, we can see the results from the ESET Threat Encyclopedia in Figure 10.8. ESET tells us where we can find the files that Conficker leaves behind. They also provide a short explanation of what Conficker is and what it does.

Of course, ESET is just one anti-virus solution. Figure 10.8 only shows a small sample of the information that ESET provides. You may want to follow up with other companies and put together all of the information that you can get on the sample, you are chasing down.

Short description

Win32/Conficker.AA is a worm that spreads via shared folders and on removable media. It connects to remote machines in attempt to exploit the Server Service vulnerability.

Installation

When executed, the worm copies itself in some of the the following locations:

- %system%\%variable%.dll
- %program files%\Internet Explorer\%variable%.dll
- %program files%\Movie Maker\%variable%.dll
- %appdata%\%variable%.dll
- %temp%\%variable%.dll

A string with variable content is used instead of %variable% .

The worm loads and injects the %variable%.dll library into the following processes:

- explorer.exe
- services.exe
- svchost.exe

FIGURE 10.8

There are enough variants that you probably want to do as much research as you can, before you start digging into the disk image, you are working with. Ideally, you are working on a dead box when you start looking at viruses. There is too much risk of infecting other systems, if you are attempting to work on a live system, even if it is within a virtual machine. As you are looking at the disk image where the virus lives, keep in mind that some of these viruses use variable names for files and directories that are created. You can see that noted in the results from ESET. You will also note that ESET identified it as Conficker.A, which suggests that it is one variant of the Conficker worm. Make sure when you are searching that you are looking for the variant you have. Dropping the .A will yield different results for you and these results may have nothing at all to do with the virus you have.

GETTING INFECTED

There are a number of ways that you may get infected. There are also a lot of aspects of operating systems to infect. The first place to get infected, potentially, is during the boot process. Once you are booted up, there are a number of other ways you can get infected. Understanding some of the places of infection, as well as some of the infection vectors that may be used to gain access to the system. Getting infected is not only about how you might acquire the infection but also the pathway, the malware uses to get lodged into the system. You might get the malware file onto your system, for example, which may be downloaded or acquired as an attachment but what they do when they run in order to actually have an impact on your system is different. They are tied together in some ways. As a result, we are going to look at different ways that you can both get the executable file onto your system but also the sorts of things that may happen once it is there.

Drive-by Attacks and Watering Holes

One of the most common attack methods today is through the Web browser. This is because a Web browser may be the most commonly used application on your entire system. You may use it to read news, purchase goods, read e-mail, look up information, or any of countless other reasons. Because of its multiple purposes, you probably use your browser a lot during the course of any given day. As a result, it makes sense that the best place to attack someone is to through the Web browser. There are different paths that an infection can take. The first is simply for someone to download an infected executable and run it. This may take the form of a Trojan horse, where the executable looks like something else. This is probably the easiest way to get someone to run an executable that has been downloaded, since we are all encouraged to avoid running applications that are untrusted. In order to overcome that training, there has to be something highly enticing.

Another way to infect your system is to take advantage of a vulnerability. Not all pathways into your system have to be through an executable, after all. Or at least, not directly through an executable. Browsers are not impervious to bugs after all. A Web page may be able to trigger a vulnerability within the browser and compromise the system by executing code in the context of the browser. This means that the attacker would insert or inject a small set of operation codes into the memory space of the browser and then get the processor to execute that set of operation codes. In doing that, the attacker gets to control what the program does and typically the result would be the attacker getting remote access into the system. There are a few ways of accomplishing this. One way is to trigger, what is called a buffer overflow.

A buffer is a small section of memory where data is stored. This buffer would generally be stored on the stack. The thing about the stack is that it will always include an address within the text segment referring to where the program should return execution when the current function is done. Every time a function is called, the current instruction pointer, the value that indicates the memory address in the program that is the current instruction. Once the function is over, the stored instruction pointer value is taken off the stack and the value is placed back into the register that the processor uses. If an attacker can send too much data for the buffer to handle, since the buffer is a fixed size, they can overwrite the return address and get the processor to start executing the code that has been inserted into the stack. Buffer overflows are one of the most common ways to attack a running program and get it to execute code that you want, as an attacker. A representation of a stack is shown in Figure 10.9.

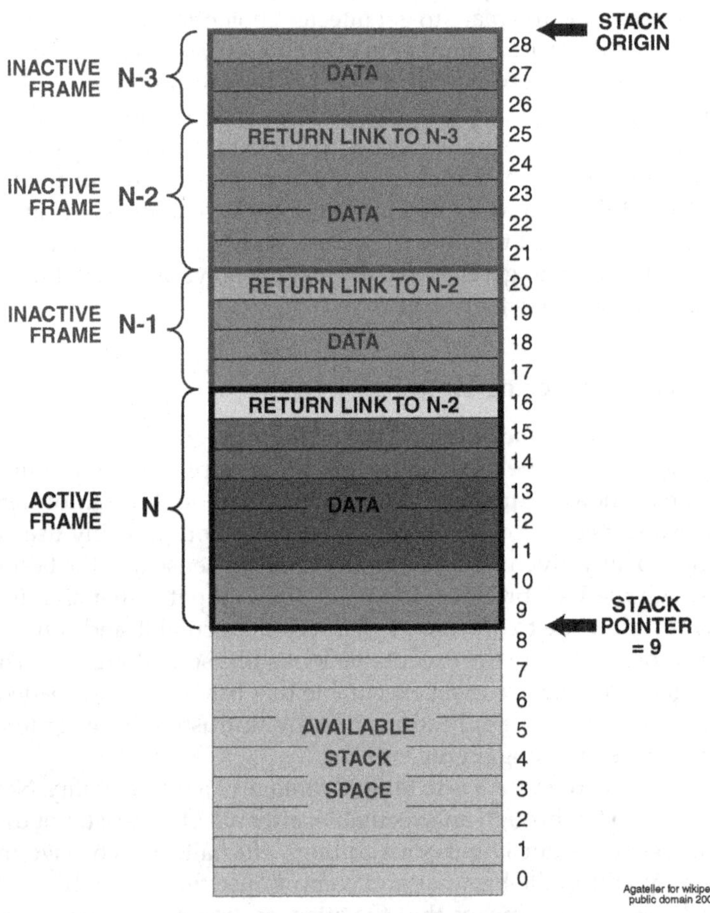

FIGURE 10.9

The illustration shows the return address in each of the stack frames and each of those stack frames. Sending too much data into an application that is not expecting it, will flood that stack frame and eventually, will overwrite the area where the return address is stored. Once the function completes, it will attempt to look up that return address and replace the instruction pointer with it. If the attacker is good, they will make sure that return address is somewhere they control or at least somewhere they know about. Once they do that, they have control of the program.

Buffer overflows are not the only ways to control a program, of course, but they have been common for more than 25 years. The Morris worm made use of some well-known buffer overflows. These days, there are other paths that an attacker can take, especially if they are trying to get control over someone's desktop. Two popular pathways currently are Java and Flash. Java is a programming language that was long thought to be a secure way to write programs. There were no buffers in Java that could be overrun because Java had tighter controls over how buffers are handled. In general, Java took control on the part of the programmer off the table and, instead, gave a lot of control to the virtual machine that ran the Java programs. This, in theory, should have resolved many of the problems that have plagued software security. However, this turns out not to have been the case, as the Java implementation in recent years has been under attack and shown that it can be vulnerable. These vulnerabilities have led to Java being another avenue to take control of a system.

Flash is a platform for providing media-rich content for Web pages. Some Web sites use Flash as a way of implementing an actual user interface within the Web site. This can include menu systems and other interactions. Flash, though, has also proven to be a means of attacking users. Both Flash and Java vulnerabilities have been used as means of attacking systems. These attacks are accomplished by luring users to Web sites, where Java applets and Flash content is stored. This content is designed to trigger a vulnerability, which will give the attacker access to the target system.

This may be a site that the target was specifically lured to where the attack code, whether it is Java, Flash, or another type of attack on a browser, for example, is waiting. This is called a drive-by attack. The user drives by the Web site, which means that all they have to do is visit the page without spending any time there at all and they have been compromised. A watering hole attack is similar in nature to a drive-by attack in that it takes place through a Web site. The difference with a watering hole attack is that it is commonly a Web site, where a lot of users are prone to visit. Where you might need to lure someone into a drive-by attack, a watering hole attack results from people visiting a known site that has been compromised.

Code Injection and File Replacement

In the case, where a piece of malware is capable of copying itself to another system without executing, it may be able to replace files that will later get executed. While this is less common today, since Windows systems have been locked down with fewer open network shares, it is still possible. Windows has also locked down sensitive directories to help protect against this sort of attack. Let us say that you were able to overwrite a commonly used file such as Notepad, Wordpad, Word, or even a system program like Explorer.exe. Every time a user went to run one of these programs, their system would be infected. If you are replacing a file that is commonly used, you need to make sure that what the user sees is what they expect to see. If someone tries to run Word and they do not get Word started, they will start to wonder what is happening. This may cause them to start looking for problems and this may end up causing them to locate the malware and remove it before it can do anything at all.

A malware author can ensure the program that is expected actually runs by using a technique called code injection. Remember that an executable has a segment where the actual operation codes that the processor runs are. When you load up an executable file, no matter what platform you are on, there is an entry point. Code injection is where you insert the malware into the existing executable file then make the change to the entry point in the executable's header. The new entry point will point to the location of the malware, so the malware becomes a wrapper for the real program. When the malware component completes, it will need to jump back to the real program in order to mask the fact that the original program has been infected.

You might say that the original program has been Trojaned through this process because you have turned your original program into a Trojan, since it is no longer what you expect it to be. There are ways to protect against this, including making sure that you cannot alter the existing files in known locations without some sort of authentication. Auditing your alterations to your filesystem can also help you know, when a program has been infected.

Droppers

While this is not a way of infecting a system, necessarily, it is worth making note of this behavior. Sometimes what happens is a small executable will perform the initial infection. What it does then is immediately goes off to download a number of additional pieces of software and other files. Later on, we will look at some automated analysis tools that can be used to perform some investigation of malware. Using one of these tools against a piece of malware that was sent via e-mail, shows a number of files that were downloaded and installed on the victim system. You can see a partial list of those files in Figure 10.10 that was generated by an

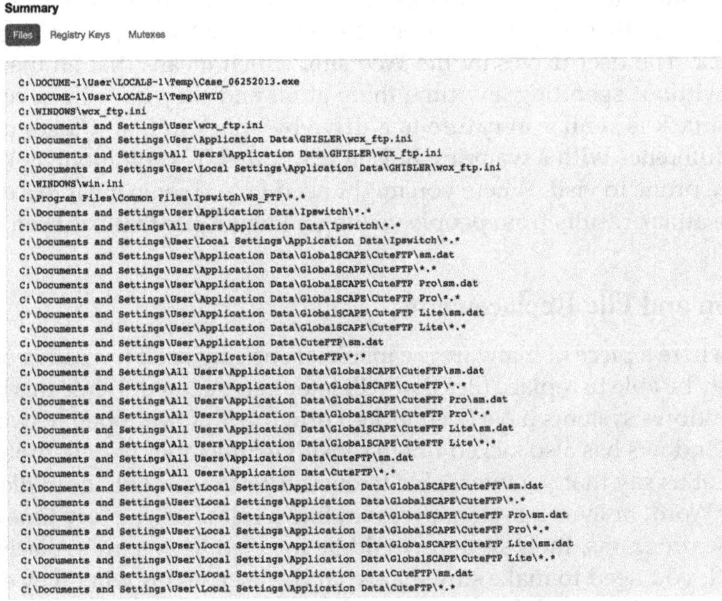

FIGURE 10.10

online malware analysis service. The total number of files that were added to the file system within a small number of minutes was over 250.

What you can see in Figure 10.10 is a number of files that were installed apparently as part of a CuteFTP installation. CuteFTP is a piece of software that can be used to transfer files from one system to another. This was one of several pieces of software that appears to have been installed from this particular infection. Without further analysis, it is hard to say, whether this was really CuteFTP or an installation of malware that was named CuteFTP to make it seem as though it is legitimate software. This is one of the challenges of file droppers. There are a number of pieces of software that a file dropper may download or install to a system. It may be software that generates ads that can be used as income for the owner of the malware. It may be legitimate software that could be used later on for some purpose related to the overall needs of the installed malware. It could also be more malware. The original infection software may be small in order to be less noticeable and the purpose of this small executable is to download a botnet client to attach to the botnet, and then additional malware to steal your credit card information and passwords.

Boot Infections

The master boot record is the first place to start, simply because it is the second place that gets touched when a system boots up. The first is the Basic Input/Output Sytem (BIOS) or Unified Extensible Firmware Interface (UEFI), depending on the particular system. Both are sets of firmware that the kernel or operating system talks to, in order to control the whole system. Once the power-on self-test is completed, the hardware and firmware attempt to pass control off to the operating system. This requires using a boot loader, which is a small piece of software used to locate and load the operating system kernel into memory. Once the kernel is in memory, control passes to it. At this point, you may see the value in hijacking that process. Most anti-virus solutions will not scan the locations, where the boot loader is stored to see if it is going to be loading the kernel.

The boot loader may be located either in the 440 bytes allocated for that in the master boot record, or it may be in a small boot partition. If a system is using a BIOS rather than UEFI, it will look at the master boot record to locate the boot loader. A system using UEFI will look for the boot partition on the hard drive and use the boot loader there, to load either the primary operating system or present a list of choices to boot other operating systems that may be stored on, whatever storage media is present in the system.

A boot loader virus makes sure that the virus is always loaded. The best way to do this is to load the virus before any piece of software that may scan for viruses is loaded. If you are booting into the virus, the virus can be certain that the system is always infected. In theory, it is always in memory and may evade notice by anti-virus solutions. If you store the bulk of the virus in either unused space on a hard drive or in a hidden partition, it can evade anti-virus solutions that are focused on scanning hard drives and downloaded files. The reason is that the hard drive being scanned is partitioned and mounted space. If a part of the disk has not been mounted, the antivirus software would not "detect" the virus. Imagine, if you are playing hide and seek with a child and you tell the child that the bathroom is out of bounds. You are looking everywhere in the house, other than the bathroom. If the child is hiding in the shower, you are not going to find that child. That is the same with the virus. If it stores itself into a space on the hard drive that is not partitioned, it is like having a place identified as being out of bounds. Viruses are not going to follow the rules.

DLL Injection and API Hooking

Two mechanisms that malware may use to get into the same space as a process are DLL injection and API hooking. A DLL is a dynamic link library, which is a way of collecting procedures into one place in a way that multiple processes can make use of these procedures. While the process is running, it can load the DLL and get access to the additional functions of the procedures. DLL injection creates a new thread in a running process and then injects the DLL into that new running thread. Malware will make use of system calls to make all of this happen. If you are monitoring system calls, some you may see are CreateRemoteThread, VirtualAllocEx, and WriteProcessMemory. CreateRemoteThread gets a running process to fork off a new thread to handle a new path of execution. When you create a new thread, you have to specify a starting point. You specify the starting point to be the LoadLibrary method, which will be in the address space of any moderately complex software, since it is a system method. Since this method is shared across multiple programs, the address for it is well-known.

LoadLibrary requires a parameter, which would be the name of the malicious DLL. WriteProcessMemory and VirtualAllocEx are used to create memory space that the malicious DLL will use. Every DLL has a DLLMain function. It is part of the way DLLs are created. The DLLMain function is called when a DLL is loaded. It allows the DLL to initialize itself. In the case of malicious software, the DLLMain is where the malicious code is. The injection is just a way to get the DLL loaded in order to run the actual malware within the space of an existing process. This is important because the malicious software will then run with all of the privileges of the process, the malware has been injected into.

Malware can also use a technique called API hooking. Complex software such as multiuser and multiprocessing systems use messages to communicate. The interface software will send messages to processes that are listening. Processes can register to listen for specific messages. An event happens and a process within the interface system passes a message to the right places. If malware registers itself to get messages like WH_KEYBOARD and WH_KEYBOARD_LL, which are messages associated with keyboard events, it can get the system processes to pass along those messages. Registering for the two keyboard messages can allow any software to receive keyboard events, which means that you can write a keystroke logger. Every key pressed on the keyboard can be sent to the software that registers for these events. Software will use the SetWindowsHookEx function in order to register for these events.

One process cannot insert hooks directly into the process space of another process, however using DLL injection, though, gives malware the ability to capture events across multiple processes. You have a small piece of software that launches the complete attack by introducing a malicious DLL into the address space of multiple existing processes. The DLL then inserts hooks to capture events across all of these different processes.

Crypto Lockers and Ransomware

A crypto locker is a piece of malware that infests a system and encrypts the contents of the file system. This encryption could be whole disk or it could just be important parts of the filesystem, like the user's documents folder. Presumably, this is where files the user considers to be important are. The malware encrypts the folder, then issues a warning to the user that the files on the system have been encrypted and they should pay a ransom in order to get the key that could be used to decrypt the files. Paying the ransom does not necessarily get you the key, however. This sort of ransomware really highlights the importance of a regular backup schedule. If you had a regular backup of your files, you might simply wipe your disk and restore your data with minimal loss. Without your backups, you cannot guarantee that the data on your disk will ever be restored.

Microsoft has included Volume Shadow Copy functionality as a way of retaining multiple copies of files. This is especially important when you are installing new software and the installation process creates a system restore point. These restore points and shadow copies could be used to restore a system that has been compromised in this way. Some of the ransomware may actually disable the restore points and shadow copies, when it installs itself. This would prevent you from getting around the ransomware using backups already managed by the operating system.

STAYING RESIDENT (PERSISTENCE)

Malware will generally want to stick around. It is hard to keep score if you leave the party too soon, for those who are just looking for large body counts, means that they are just looking to get a lot of infections. If you are in it for the money, as is more and more the case, you definitely want to stick around. You can steal a lot of information from a system when you first infect it, but more information may be coming any day so you want to hang around to get your hands on it, then send it along to the collection point where it can be of some use. Different operating systems will, of course, have different persistence mechanisms, meaning they will have different means of ensuring that they are not only sitting on the system but they remain running, keeping it infected.

Not surprisingly, each operating system has different mechanisms to persist on a system. This means more than simply sitting on the disk. It means finding ways to keep running. Sometimes, this is done through social engineering as in the case of I Love You, which replaced all media files on the infected system with a Visual Basic Script file (.vbs) with the same name as the original media file. This took advantage of a default setting in the Windows Explorer that hid the file extension, so the user would not see the .vbs extension. When someone went to look at a picture of their kids or their dog, they would be reinfecting the system all over again. Of course, this is just one way and it relies on users. There are more effective ways for malware to stay resident on a system. In order to completely remove an infection, you need to understand these different mechanisms so you can undo them.

Windows Persistence

My favorite malware persistence process, because it seemed so ingenious at the time, has to be hijacking a file handler. Windows allows you to open a document directly by simply double clicking or opening the file. Windows will automatically open the correct program and the file will be open. It uses file associations to manage this and those file associations are stored in the registry. Several years ago, I ran across a piece of malware that had infected a system and created a file association, so that all .exe files were to be handled by the malware. This is actually pretty easy to do, though it seems like it should not be possible, since you can easily cripple a system in this way. There are two registry keys that can be altered to adjust the behavior of the system. The first one can be seen in Figure 10.11. Each of the file extensions has a key under HKEY_CLASSES_ROOT, with other keys underneath keeping track of all of the possible handlers for each extension as well as a persistent handler, meaning the program that will always open that particular file extension. The PersistentHandler key in Figure 10.10 is for a GUID that refers to a program on the system. The second registry key is under

HKEY_CURRENT_USER\Software\Microsoft\Windows\CurrentVersion\Explorer\FileExts. As with HKEY_CLASSES_ROOT, each file extension has a key.

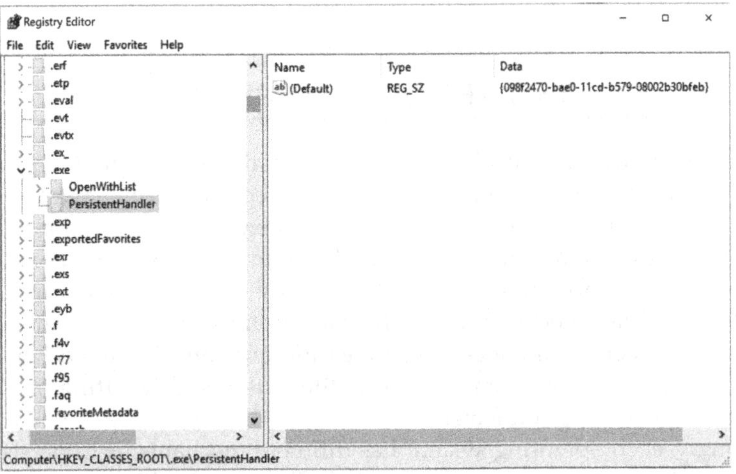

FIGURE 10.11

Malware will often want to startup when the system starts, or maybe when a particular user logs into the system. There are two registry keys to control that, one for the system and one for the user. The first key, for the system, is HKEY_LOCAL_MACHINE\Software\Microsoft\Windows\CurrentVersion\Run. The second one, specific to the user, can be seen in Figure 10.12. It is the same as for the system except it is in HKEY_CURRENT_USER rather than in HKEY_LOCAL_MACHINE. Programs with values in each of these keys, and you can see that the value has the entire path to the executable, will be executed. The values under HKEY_LOCAL_MACHINE will be executed when the system boots up. The values under HKEY_CURRENT_USER get run when a user logs in. These programs will not be seen by the user unless they have an interface. If there is not an interface, there will be no window that is created and the program will run quietly in the background.

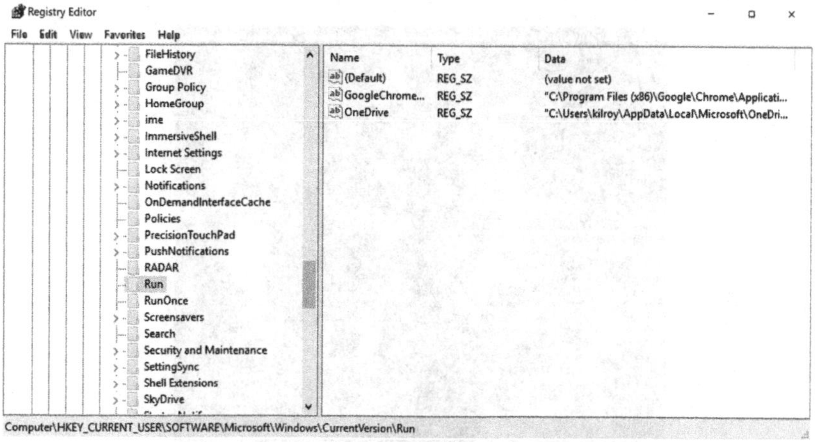

FIGURE 10.12

There are, of course, more pedestrian means for malware to remain resident on a system and ensure that the system remain infected. This may be done by either infecting a trusted executable or by simply replacing the executable altogether. The problem with this approach is that this does not keep the malware running. If malware is interested in acquiring information from the user, such as keystrokes, credit cards, or user credentials, it will need to remain running all the time, or at least be run periodically to search for information on the system, in order to transmit it in some fashion to a system somewhere on the Internet, used to collect all of this information. One way to accomplish this is to schedule a task using schtasks.exe. This program will allow a user to add a task to the list of tasks, the Task Scheduler service is responsible for running. Tasks can be scheduled to run at specific times and can be set to run every day, once a week, once a month, or even just once, if that is what you want to do. Setting malware to run as a task, where the actual executable can be anywhere, is a good way of hiding it, since checking for the entire list of tasks is not that common. In order to see the entire list of tasks on your system, you can just run schtasks.exe as seen in Figure 10.13.

This is just a portion of the tasks that are scheduled on this particular system. You can see that some of the tasks are disabled and others are simply not scheduled to run. They are, however, available to run at anytime. One of the tasks, the Microsoft Compatibility Appraiser, does have a run scheduled. Considering the length of this list, it may be easy for malware to hide in it. The best evidence of the existence of the malware would be the executable stored somewhere on the filesystem.

Services are another means for a program to run and stay running, just as in the case of programs that are started from the Run registry key. The difference with a service is that it has to be written in a particular way so that the service handler can install it and interact with it. The service program needs to be able to respond to commands to start and stop. Writing a service is not that complicated, but it does have to be done in a particular way for the service to run successfully. While there are plenty of resources to guide the creation of services and source code templates that may be used, it may simply be easier to write a normal executable

FIGURE 10.13

that can be placed on the system and run in a number of ways. Writing a service limits you to being able to install your malware as a service and that requires administrative access. If you were able to either trick a user into running the program that would install your service for you, potentially downloading it from a network location, the user would be prompted for privilege elevation. This is another reason why malware would not commonly run as a service, though it is possible. A portion of the list of services is show in Figure 10.14.

Services (Local)

Select an item to view its description.

Name	Description	Status	Startup Type	Log On As
Task Scheduler	Enables a us...	Running	Automatic	Local Syste...
TCP/IP NetBIOS Helper	Provides su...	Running	Manual (Trig...	Local Service
Telephony	Provides Tel...		Manual	Network S...
Themes	Provides us...	Running	Automatic	Local Syste...
Tile Data model server	Tile Server f...	Running	Automatic	Local Syste...
Time Broker	Coordinates...	Running	Manual (Trig...	Local Service
Touch Keyboard and Hand...	Enables Tou...		Manual (Trig...	Local Syste...
Update Orchestrator Service	UsoSvc		Manual	Local Syste...
UPnP Device Host	Allows UPn...		Manual	Local Service
User Manager	User Manag...	Running	Automatic (T...	Local Syste...
User Profile Service	This service ...	Running	Automatic	Local Syste...
Virtual Disk	Provides m...		Manual	Local Syste...
VMware USB Arbitration Ser...	Arbitration ...	Running	Automatic	Local Syste...
Volume Shadow Copy	Manages an...		Manual	Local Syste...
WalletService	Hosts objec...		Manual	Local Syste...
WebClient	Enables Win...		Manual (Trig...	Local Service
Windows Audio	Manages au...	Running	Automatic	Local Service
Windows Audio Endpoint B...	Manages au...	Running	Automatic	Local Syste...
Windows Backup	Provides Wi...		Manual	Local Syste...
Windows Biometric Service	The Windo...		Manual (Trig...	Local Syste...
Windows Color System	The WcsPlu...		Manual	Local Service
Windows Connect Now - C...	WCNCSVC ...		Manual	Local Service
Windows Connection Mana...	Makes auto...	Running	Automatic (T...	Local Service
Windows Defender Networ...	Helps guard...		Manual	Local Service

Extended Standard

FIGURE 10.14

The list of services can be seen from the Computer Management utility, where it runs as a snap-in to the Microsoft Management Console, or it can run standalone. It is still running within the Microsoft Management Console, it is just running all by itself rather than with a collection of other snap-ins, as in the case of Computer Management. The Computer Management utility also provides a means to manage your disks and view your event logs. Having all of these snap-ins available in a single console view can be very helpful.

Mac OS X Persistence

While Windows malware is more prevalent, Mac OS X viruses and worms are not only possible but there are a number of them in the wild. The means for persistence on a Mac OS X system are similar in nature to those on the Windows side. The one thing you cannot do, however, is hijack the handling of an executable as you can on Windows because executables are handled differently. Rather than using a file extension to indicate whether something is a program that is to be run, Mac OS X uses bundles, which are specific directory structures that include all of the resources a program needs, including the program itself. Just as with other Unix-like operating systems, the actual executable stored in the bundle has a specific file permission indicating that it can be run. If you were to use Terminal and enter the directory structure of the application bundle, you would be able to see that the program has the execute bit set, telling the operating system that it can be run.

Similar to the Run registry key in Windows, though, Mac OS X has two directories that you would look in, to locate programs that were scheduled to run automatically. This could be run when the system starts or it could be that they are specific to the user. Some of this comes down to permissions. In order to install a program to run when the system boots up, the program would have to run as the root user, meaning a user with administrative privileges. While users on Mac OS X systems will commonly have the ability to escalate their privileges to root, they do not run with root privileges all the time. The system would prompt for a password, if there was a task needed to be run as root that was attempting to run. This prompt would alert the user to the fact that something was happening and it may be a flag to them that they should be careful, if they did not expect that what they were doing would prompt them for a password.

Mac OS X uses daemons and agents to run quietly. A daemon is one that runs on a persistent basis. Once it starts, it does not stop. An agent is an on-demand program that would typically be used, when a user logs in. The first location to check is /Library/LaunchDaemons. This will contain plist files with details about daemons that will be launched by the system launchd process when the system boots up. As one example, the properly list file for a daemon used to keep Google software up to date is shown in Figure 10.15. This property list is in XML syntax. It includes the path to the actual executable to be run by launchd in the ProgramArguments key. Underneath that key entry is a string that has a path to an executable that will check for updates to Google software. There is another directory under / Library to look at and, that is, /Library/LaunchAgents. Unlike daemons that are always running, agents are on demand but are still available in the background, and will be launched as needed by launchd.

Of course, the /Library directory is where system launch agents and daemons are located. There is also a pair of directories for launch agents and daemons that are specific to each user.

```
kilroy@opus:/Library/LaunchDaemons$ cat com.google.keystone.daemon.plist
<?xml version="1.0" encoding="UTF-8"?>
<!DOCTYPE plist PUBLIC "-//Apple//DTD PLIST 1.0//EN" "http://www.apple.com/DTDs/
PropertyList-1.0.dtd">
<plist version="1.0">
<dict>
        <key>Label</key>
        <string>com.google.keystone.daemon</string>
        <key>ProgramArguments</key>
        <array>
          <string>/Library/Google/GoogleSoftwareUpdate/GoogleSoftwareUpdate.bund
le/Contents/MacOS/GoogleSoftwareUpdateDaemon</string>
        </array>
        <key>KeepAlive</key>
        <false/>
        <key>RunAtLoad</key>
        <false/>
        <key>MachServices</key>
        <dict>
                <key>com.google.Keystone.Daemon.UpdateEngine</key>
                <true/>
                <key>com.google.Keystone.Daemon.Administration</key>
                <true/>
        </dict>
        <key>UserName</key>
        <string>root</string>
        <key>StandardErrorPath</key>
        <string>/dev/null</string>
        <key>StandardOutPath</key>
        <string>/dev/null</string>
</dict>
</plist>
```

FIGURE 10.15

This is in the ~/Library/LaunchAgents and ~/Library/LaunchDaemons directories. The ~ refers to the home directory for the user. If the username was wubble, the home directory for that user would be /Users/Wubble. Any program referenced in either of these launch directories would only run, while the user was logged in. Most Mac OS X systems are single user so this would be very similar to being in the /Library directory. As with the system directories mentioned earlier, the entries are property lists and the programs are managed by the launchd service.

Since Mac OS X can make use of kernel extensions to add additional system-level functionality, those kernel extensions could be used as a persistence mechanism for malware. If the malware were able to install itself as a kernel extension, when the system rebooted, the kernel would load and that could force the malware to be loaded. This would also ensure that the malware would run with kernel-level privileges, which would be higher than those of a regular user. Of course, in order to install a kernel extension, you have to have administrative privileges and the operating system would prompt a user for those. This prompt should clue the user in that something they do not want, is happening.

Since Mac OS X is based on Unix, it will share some of the same persistence mechanisms as Linux. This would include job scheduling capabilities like cron.

Linux Persistence

Unix inherits the idea of daemons from Unix. A daemon is a program that runs quietly in the background, being of service to users. This may be a network service like a Web server, or it may be a local service that does things like running programs or jobs on a schedule. Different distributions may handle services in a different way but one common way is for services to be managed through shell scripts. These are small programs written in a shell programming language. Commonly, these scripts are stored in /etc/init.d/, while there are probably links in other directories like /etc/rc3.d/ back to those scripts. These links will make sure that the programs that the scripts call will run at the appropriate time. Malware can create these services scripts in order to make sure the malicious program that needs to stay resident will run when the system starts up.

Malware may also hijack existing programs in order to stay resident on the system. It may install backdoors or maybe create services and the programs that got hijacked would be used to hide the existence of the malware. These rootkits can be detected. There is a software package called rkhunter, as a start that can be used to scan the existing programs on a system. When you run rkhunter, it scans the system for rootkits. You can see some of the output in Figure 10.16.

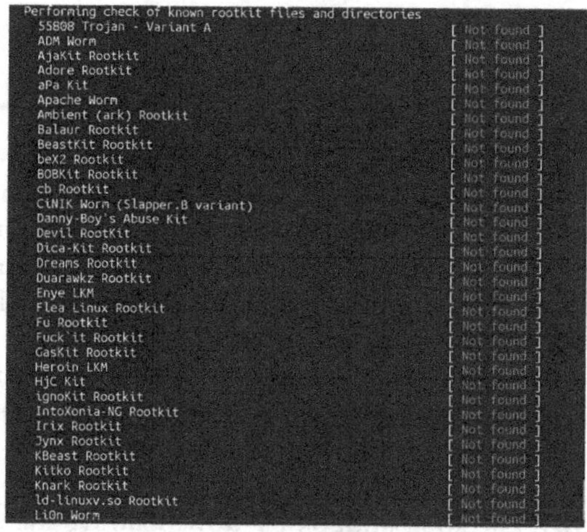

FIGURE 10.16

Apart from placing service scripts to make sure that services run at boot time and infecting existing system binaries (programs), malware may simply infect a particular user. There are ways for programs to automatically run when a user logs in, though, the most common way that is not bound to a particular user interface is using the profile scripts. Profile scripts are short programs, again written in a shell programming language, which are run when a user logs in. These scripts are only run when a user logs into a shell, meaning they launch a terminal or log into the console without a graphical interface. However, the files in the user's home directory, usually named .bashrc and .bash_profile, can have commands that set variables and also run programs automatically. A piece of malware could insert a line into a user's profile script in order to have it run when the user logs in.

ARTIFACTS

Of course, artifacts will vary based on the operating system. They will also depend on how the system is configured. For example, if a system is configured to audit events like file access, you will have logs, you can look at to determine what was done on the system and who did it. Having a detailed audit trail can be very beneficial, when you are trying to determine what happened after you detect a malware outbreak. However, everything comes with a price and audit logs are no different. While it is less meaningful in the days of multi-terabyte hard drives, audit logs do take up disk space. Of course, they are simple text but if you have a very active system with a lot of users logging in and out and making a lot of changes to the file system, you can end up with very large audit logs. If you happen to have the storage space for them, these logs can be absolutely essential and should provide you with a lot of detail about the behaviors on the system, including any aberrations from normal user behavior.

Barring audit logs, you can check registry settings on a Windows system. Often, there are trails within the registry that malware may exist on a system.

AUTOMATED ANALYSIS

There are a number of ways that you can perform analysis of malware without impacting your own system. There are software packages such as Cuckoo Sandbox that make use of virtual machines to perform an analysis of the behavior of the malware. By using snapshots of the virtual machines, you can compare the state of a system prior to the introduction of the malware with the state after the malware has been introduced. Most of these automated systems use Windows virtual machines since a large percentage of malware is targeted at Windows systems. Primarily, this is because of the large user base for Windows but also because of the ease of developing Windows applications from the substantial Windows APIs that allow malware developers to gain access to the Windows registry and Windows services, which make it easier for malware to remain installed on the system.

You can create your own Cuckoo Sandbox by downloading the software and installing it yourself. Cuckoo Sandbox is designed to run on a Linux system and can make use of the different virtualization software that runs under Linux. Cuckoo Sandbox is written in the programming language Python and uses an agent script inside the guest virtual machine, while the rest of Cuckoo Sandbox runs in the host operating system. Once you have Cuckoo Sandbox running in the host operating system and the agent running in the guest virtual machine, you use a submit script to send the malware into the guest. Once the malware has been submitted, Cuckoo runs the malware and manages the snapshots to see the impact on the system. Figure 10.17 shows Cuckoo Sandbox running with a new instance of a malware executable submitted. Cuckoo looks at not only the system behavior but will also monitor the network activity. The last line in Figure 10.17 shows that Cuckoo started up a sniffer to observe the behavior of the malware on the network.

```
Cuckoo Sandbox 1.2
www.cuckoosandbox.org
Copyright (c) 2010-2015

Checking for updates...
Good! You have the latest version available.

2015-08-19 20:20:55,586 [root] INFO: Updated running task ID 4 status to failed_
analysis
2015-08-19 20:20:55,588 [lib.cuckoo.core.scheduler] INFO: Using "kvm" machine ma
nager
2015-08-19 20:20:55,961 [lib.cuckoo.core.scheduler] INFO: Loaded 1 machine/s
2015-08-19 20:20:55,973 [lib.cuckoo.core.scheduler] INFO: Waiting for analysis t
asks.
2015-08-19 20:20:59,128 [lib.cuckoo.core.scheduler] INFO: Starting analysis of F
ILE "/home/kilroy/1DB5476C766555C9995B25D19F97B9BC.EXE" (task=5)
2015-08-19 20:20:59,139 [lib.cuckoo.core.scheduler] INFO: File already exists at
 "/home/kilroy/Downloads/cuckoo/storage/binaries/02137e9426258e8d1186dc21ee344ff
c5cdb3f068a6600ba1897fd9d27ccba43"
2015-08-19 20:20:59,250 [lib.cuckoo.core.scheduler] INFO: Task #5: acquired mach
ine win7 (label=win7)
2015-08-19 20:20:59,261 [modules.auxiliary.sniffer] INFO: Started sniffer with P
ID 2588 (interface=vboxnet0, host=192.168.122.44, dump path=/home/kilroy/Downloa
ds/cuckoo/storage/analyses/5/dump.pcap)
```

FIGURE 10.17

If you do not want to go through the process of installing Cuckoo Sandbox yourself, you can make use of the Web site malwr.com to submit malware samples and get a complete analysis of the behavior of the malware. The site will not only provide you with the raw information of registry changes, network connections, and new files on the system but it will suggest specific behaviors. The report shown in Figure 10.18, lists different behaviors like making use of command and control (C&C) infrastructure and stealing credentials. Cuckoo Sandbox, using this Web interface, has a very comprehensive report that shows a screen capture of the Windows desktop, the list of registry changes and files added as well as IP addresses, the malware is contacting.

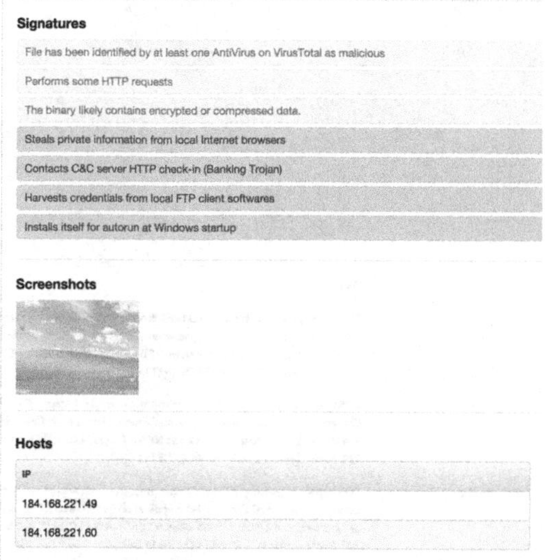

Signatures

File has been identified by at least one AntiVirus on VirusTotal as malicious

Performs some HTTP requests

The binary likely contains encrypted or compressed data.

Steals private information from local Internet browsers

Contacts C&C server HTTP check-in (Banking Trojan)

Harvests credentials from local FTP client softwares

Installs itself for autorun at Windows startup

Screenshots

Hosts

IP
184.168.221.49
184.168.221.60

FIGURE 10.18

Cuckoo Sandbox is not the only automated analysis software, though. There are several Web sites that can be used to perform automated malware analysis without impacting your own systems or having to manage virtual machines yourself. You could use ThreatExpert, ThreatTrack, Comodo Automated Analysis System, or Anubis as some examples of sites that will perform analysis for you. The different sites behave differently. Comodo will perform a static analysis of the executable without actually running it. You will get a report of hostnames that the executable will attempt to make network connections to, as well as an indication of how it will try to stay persistent on the system.

While there are a few Web sites that perform analysis for you on malware, they do not all work the same way or pay attention to the same things. This does not necessarily mean that one is better than another, though one may be better than another for your specific purposes. Additionally, the different tools will report in different ways. And they also will use different virtual machines. Cuckoo Sandbox, as implemented at malwr.com, uses a Windows XP virtual machine. Another factor on top is simply the version of Windows is the CPU. A tool like the one at www.hybrid-analysis.com, managed by Payload Security, has a number of options for virtual machine. This includes different languages as well as both 32-bit and 64-bit operating systems. A lot of malware will be 32-bit because it is a common denominator. Malware that has been compiled as 32-bit will run on a 64-bit operating system but the same is not true in the other direction.

In addition to the different selections in default language, OS version, and 32-bit vs 64-bit, the Payload Security tool provides some additional visualization in its reporting. While tools that perform this analysis will generally give you a list of hostnames or IP addresses, Payload Security will generate a map for you, as seen in Figure 10.19. It does this by looking up the IP

Contacted Countries

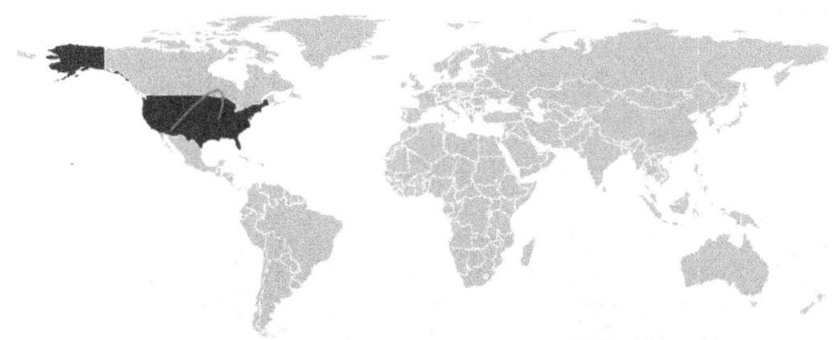

HTTP Requests

Destination	Method	URL	Data
184.168.221.49:80 (jtmccarter.com)	POST	/ponyb/gate.php	POST /ponyb/gate.php HTTP/1.0 Host: jtmccarter.com Accept: */* Accept-Encoding: identity, *;q=0 Accept-Language: en-US Content-Length: 200 Content-Type: application/octet-stream Connection: close Content-Encoding: binary User-Agent: Mozilla/4.0 (compatible; MSIE 7.0; Windows NT 6.1; Trident/4.0; SLCC2; .NET CLR 2.0.50727; .NET CLR 3.5.30729; .NET CLR 3.0.30729; Media Center PC 6.0; .NET4.0C; .NET4.0E)
184.168.221.49:80 (jtmccarter.com)	POST	/ponyb/gate.php	POST /ponyb/gate.php HTTP/1.0 Host: jtmccarter.com Accept: */* Accept-Encoding: identity, *;q=0 Accept-Language: en-US Content-Length: 200 Content-Type: application/octet-stream Connection: close Content-Encoding: binary User-Agent: Mozilla/4.0 (compatible; MSIE 7.0; Windows NT 6.1; Trident/4.0; SLCC2; .NET CLR 2.0.50727; .NET CLR 3.5.30729; .NET CLR 3.0.30729; Media Center PC 6.0; .NET4.0C; .NET4.0E)
184.168.221.49:80 (jtmccarter.com)	POST	/ponyb/gate.php	POST /ponyb/gate.php HTTP/1.0 Host: jtmccarter.com Accept: */* Accept-Encoding: identity, *;q=0 Accept-Language: en-US Content-Length: 200 Content-Type: application/octet-stream Connection: close Content-Encoding: binary User-Agent: Mozilla/4.0 (compatible; MSIE 7.0; Windows NT 6.1; Trident/4.0; SLCC2; .NET CLR 2.0.50727; .NET CLR 3.5.30729; .NET CLR 3.0.30729; Media Center PC 6.0; .NET4.0C; .NET4.0E)

FIGURE 10.19

addresses from a GeoIP database. This will provide at least a rough location that can be plotted on a map. Once the tool has done the IP lookups and generated the map, you can more easily see where in the world your malware is trying to send the messages. This may or may not be particularly interesting but the graphics are easier to parse quickly than just a list of addresses or even a list of addresses and associated countries.

One thing to be careful about, though, is knowing how each of the tools behaves. The Cuckoo Sandbox at malwr.com has complete Internet access, while the malware is running. This allows it to actually communicate with the rest of the world. Other analysis engines may only provide the appearance of network connectivity. This may affect the behavior of the malware. A connection out to a C&C server may trigger additional behavior, once the commands have been passed to the client. Additionally, if the malware gets successful responses from the network, it may do more than just trying to establish a connection. This became obvious in comparing the various Web sites against one another. The Cuckoo Sandbox that had Internet access showed considerably more file activity than other tools. A lot of software was installed to the guest, including several FTP clients. This behavior was not seen on other automated tools, likely because they had controlled network access rather than complete network access. Because of that, you may want to follow up by performing your own detailed analysis, once you have the rough overview from one of the Web-based analysis engines.

MANUAL ANALYSIS

The most important thing to point out here is the danger of playing with malware. This is why, some of the analysis engines try to control the behavior of the virtual machine. You can, of course, perform your analysis on a completely disconnected machine that you can investigate without any impact to other systems in your environment, assuming you leave the malware on your analysis system. The safest way to perform your own analysis is using a system whose sole purpose is to be an analysis system. You have an image of the operating system that you can restore once you are finished. There are several software packages that can be used to restore an operating system image to a clean state. Ghost is a classic and, of course, you can always use the Linux utility dd to completely restore a disk partition byte for byte.

A second option, slightly less safe, would be to use virtual machines. There are a couple of risks associated with this. The first is that programs can determine whether they are running in a virtual machine. There are a few different ways to do that, including checking a handful of registry values. If malware is able to determine that it is running inside a virtual machine, it may behave differently, suspecting that it is being investigated. Another problem is that if there are vulnerabilities in the virtualization software, programs can escape the virtual machine into the host operating system. This means that the host could be at risk, potentially. This does not mean that you should not perform this analysis on your own system, but it does mean that you should be careful and take necessary precautions. Isolating the system and using anti-virus is just a start.

Once you have a safe system, or at least a reasonably safe system, you can begin your analysis. There are a few places, you want to gather information. The first is the file table; whether it is the master file table, the file allocation table, or the inode tables. You should acquire the file table before you introduce the malware then after and compare the differences to get the list of new files that are on the system. The second place on a Windows system is the registry. You can use a utility like RegShot to acquire a snapshot of the registry before you introduce the malware, then after that RegShot will compare the differences. You can see an example of RegShot in use in Figure 10.20.

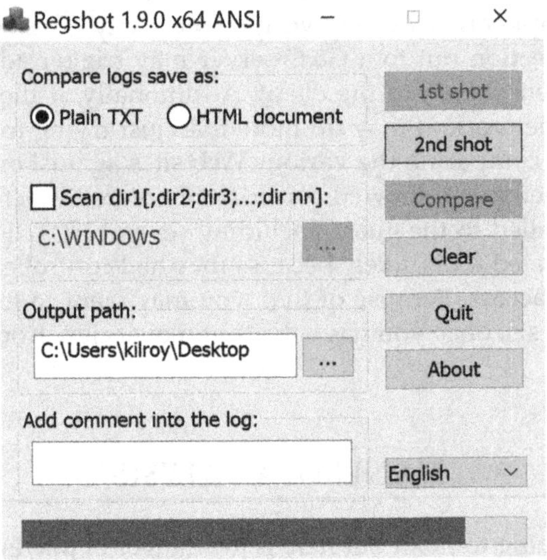

FIGURE 10.20

As you can see from the figure, you take a first snapshot then perform the action that you need to perform, like installing a software package or running malware on the system. Once you have done that, you take a second snapshot. Once you have your two snapshots, RegShot will compare the two and provide a report of the differences. You can see an excerpt from the report in Figure 10.21 after the program Memoryze was installed on the system. You can see the registry entries that were added by the installation. RegShot is capable of taking a snapshot from a running system using the standard locations for the registry files but it is also capable of making use of registry hives that have been acquired from a dead box, which means they were copied off the file system while the operating system was down. Once you acquire the registry hive files and store them in separate locations to distinguish the first capture from the second, you can run RegShot and point it at these different locations.

You can use FS Eventer to monitor changes in the file system on your Mac OS X system. This may allow you to notice when something has changed that you do not expect on your system. Once you have detected this, you can use additional tools to determine whether you have been infected with malware.

```
Values added: 160
HKLM\SOFTWARE\Classes\Installer\Features\0CCE729D31D7B294A88DD7E518938919\Complete: ""
HKLM\SOFTWARE\Classes\Installer\Features\0CCE729D31D7B294A88DD7E518938919\Dummy: ""
HKLM\SOFTWARE\Classes\Installer\Products\0CCE729D31D7B294A88DD7E518938919\ProductName: "Memoryze"
HKLM\SOFTWARE\Classes\Installer\Products\0CCE729D31D7B294A88DD7E518938919\PackageCode: "C18D67A4F05416741B247F2D1955A10B"
HKLM\SOFTWARE\Classes\Installer\Products\0CCE729D31D7B294A88DD7E518938919\Language: 0x00000409
HKLM\SOFTWARE\Classes\Installer\Products\0CCE729D31D7B294A88DD7E518938919\Version: 0x03000000
HKLM\SOFTWARE\Classes\Installer\Products\0CCE729D31D7B294A88DD7E518938919\Assignment: 0x00000001
HKLM\SOFTWARE\Classes\Installer\Products\0CCE729D31D7B294A88DD7E518938919\AdvertiseFlags: 0x00000184
HKLM\SOFTWARE\Classes\Installer\Products\0CCE729D31D7B294A88DD7E518938919\InstanceType: 0x00000000
HKLM\SOFTWARE\Classes\Installer\Products\0CCE729D31D7B294A88DD7E518938919\AuthorizedLUAApp: 0x00000000
HKLM\SOFTWARE\Classes\Installer\Products\0CCE729D31D7B294A88DD7E518938919\DeploymentFlags: 0x00000002
HKLM\SOFTWARE\Classes\Installer\Products\0CCE729D31D7B294A88DD7E518938919\Clients: 3A 00 00
HKLM\SOFTWARE\Classes\Installer\Products\0CCE729D31D7B294A88DD7E518938919\SourceList\PackageName: "MemoryzeSetup3.0.msi"
HKLM\SOFTWARE\Classes\Installer\Products\0CCE729D31D7B294A88DD7E518938919\SourceList\LastUsedSource: "n;1;C:\Users\kilroy\Download
HKLM\SOFTWARE\Classes\Installer\Products\0CCE729D31D7B294A88DD7E518938919\SourceList\Media\1: ";"
HKLM\SOFTWARE\Classes\Installer\Products\0CCE729D31D7B294A88DD7E518938919\SourceList\Net\1: "C:\Users\kilroy\Downloads\"
HKLM\SOFTWARE\Classes\Installer\UpgradeCodes\70DFF1780AECC8E408F842665B5BA8A7\0CCE729D31D7B294A88DD7E518938919: ""
HKLM\SOFTWARE\Microsoft\SystemCertificates\AuthRoot\Certificates\132D0D45534B6997CDB2D5C339E25576609B5CC6\Blob: 19 00 00 00 01 00
30 82 03 02 02 11 00 9B 7E 06 49 A3 3E 62 B9 D5 EE 90 48 71 29 EF 57 30 0D 06 09 2A 86 48 86 F7 0D 01 01 05 05 00 30 81 CA 31 0B 30 09 06
67 6E 20 54 72 75 73 74 20 4E 65 74 77 6F 72 6B 31 3A 30 38 06 03 55 04 0B 13 31 28 63 29 20 31 39 39 39 20 56 65 72 69 53 69 67 6E 2C 20
0 66 08 2F 95 93 BF AA 47 2F A8 46 97 F0 12 E2 FE C2 0A 2B 51 E6 76 E6 B7 46 B7 E2 0D A6 CC A8 C3 4C 59 55 89 E6 E8 53 5C 1C EA 9D F0 62
F1 B3 31 AD 4F 1C E1 4F 9C AF 0F 0C 9D F7 78 0D D8 F4 35 56 80 DA B7 6D 17 8F 9D 1E 81 64 E1 FE C5 45 BA AD 6B B9 0A 7A 4E 4F 4B 84 EE
```

FIGURE 10.21

The file system and registry are good places to look but they are not the only places. You will also probably want to take a look at the network connections, the malware has created. This could be done by simply capturing packets outside of the system, you are analyzing. If you had a physical system, you can capture off a network hub that the target system is connected to. If you are running inside a virtual machine, your host operating system should be able to see all of the network traffic that is coming out of the virtual guest. Using this network activity, you can get an idea of what the malware is doing. You may also want to make use of the snapshot capability of your virtual machine. If you capture a snapshot of the clean virtual machine and then get a second snapshot of the system with the malware installed on it, you can analyze the memory snapshots using a tool like Volatility and then compare your network connections before and after to get the differences.

Many of these actions are the very actions that the automated software will perform for you. The difference is that using manual techniques, you can make adjustments as necessary. An automated tool will do exactly the same thing every time you run it. Using manual techniques, you can wait a longer period of time before you gather your snapshots to see, if there are additional behaviors that occur over time. One example would be the malware that is also a file dropper. If you capture too early, the malware will not have the time to download and install everything. If you wait, you will see additional software packages that would not have been there, if you took the snapshot right away. You can still capture a quick snapshot and then compare the early snapshot with one taken later. This is not to say that you could not similarly automate this staged capture but manual investigation gives you a lot more control, which you may want, once you get some analysis under your belt.

CONCLUSIONS

Malware can strike anywhere and on any operating system. Knowing how to locate the signs of a malware infection is essential to someone, who may be responsible for responding to incidents within an enterprise. Even outside of an enterprise environment, forensic investigators may need to locate malware on a desktop system in order to weed out what is malware behavior and what is user behavior. It is probably a cliché but you may see behaviors on a system, like child pornography files as a very basic example, that are actually a result of malware, since some malware can be used to host files for other people to download. Years ago, systems used to be compromised in order to create Warez servers. Warez began as a way to serve up commercial software packages that did not need to be paid for, but you could also easily find pirated music in addition to pirated software. You may also get pornography. Since child pornography is illegal, it is not like you can just go to a regular hosting provider to get access to it if, that is, what you are looking for. Networks of compromised systems hosting this pornography is safer for the people who are making money from providing access to it, since it cannot generally be directly tied to them. This means, though, that just because you find child pornography on a system does not necessarily mean that it belongs to the system owner. Malware infestations can introduce a lot of files to a system without the user's knowledge. As a result, it is important to be able to distinguish which is the result of a user's actions and which is because of the malware.

Since that is true, forensic investigators skilled in malware analysis are important. While there are definitely packages like Cuckoo Sandbox that can perform the analysis in an automated fashion, you can also perform some manual analysis using a variety of tools like RegShot. You may also use virtual machines to do your analysis, which will give you the ability to capture snapshots of the state of the system at a given moment in time and then analyze that snapshot without needing the system to be running, while you are doing the analysis.

Because any image you are working with may include malware that could potentially escape as you are performing an analysis, it is good practice to scan any image you have for the existence of malware before you do any analysis on it. Even using virtual machines to perform your analysis, may not be enough to keep you protected.

Since you are working with malware, you definitely need to be careful. This means isolating your test system as much as possible. You may do this with a physical system or you may make use of virtual machines to perform your testing. No matter which approach you take, you should always be doing external monitoring to ensure the malware does not escape the cage you should be looking at it in. Network monitoring, as well as system monitoring like anti-virus and intrusion detection systems on your hosts that surround your test system will be an important way to make sure, the beast is not trying to poke its way out of your cage.

EXERCISES

1. Locate a piece of malware from the Junk folder, being very careful not to run it on your system. You may find an attachment with a zip file or a plain old executable. Check it against malwr.com to see how it behaves.
2. Investigate the Prefetch folder on a Windows system to see what programs are there.

3. Compare the analysis from two separate analysis engines.
4. Use RegShot to compare the Windows registry before and after installing a software package.

Bibliography

Chen, W.W.S, 2005. The Evolution of Viruses and Worms. Statistical Methods in Computer Security. Marcel Dekker, New York, Print.

Mills, E., 2009. Melissa virus turns 10 – CNET. (accessed 16.08.2015.).

Sikorski, M., Honig, A., 2012. Practical Malware Analysis the Hands-on Guide to Dissecting Malicious Software. No Starch Press, San Francisco.

CHAPTER

11

Mobile Operating Systems

INFORMATION INCLUDED IN THIS CHAPTER:

- Encryption and Remote Control
- Rooting/Jailbreaking
- Android
- Blackberry
- iOS
- Windows Phone

INTRODUCTION

Mobile devices are mainstream. When you look around at people carrying around cell phones, how many of them are so-called smartphones? It may be difficult for you to think of anyone who has a mobile device that is not a smartphone. Even more importantly, the devices that are not so-called smartphones, can still be connected to a desktop operating system, more often then not, in order to synchronize contacts, e-mail messages, pictures, and other media. Just because a phone is not capable of running complicated applications does not mean that it is not worth taking a look at. This is especially true, perhaps, when it comes to investigating mobile devices and the artifacts they leave behind if they are ever plugged into a desktop system. You can generally see information about the phone and in some cases, you may not even need the phone in order to acquire the data that is stored on it.

Phones are not the only devices to be aware of, however. More and more, people are using various tablets to replace their larger desktop systems. If you are generally using your computer system for e-mail, simple Web browsing, and social networking access, you may not need a large desktop or laptop system. You may simply need a tablet. This means that you should have at least some basic understanding of the way these mobile devices operate and the different artifacts that you can acquire from them. Over the course of this chapter, we will take a look at the predominant operating systems available for mobile devices. Additionally, we will look at the artifacts that may be left behind when a mobile device is connected to a desktop operating system.

The predominant operating systems in the mobile space are Android and iOS. These two are followed by the Blackberry, one of the first smartphones ever created, and Windows

Mobile devices. Looking at a mobile device requires many of the same skills and techniques we have been talking about to this point. A smartphone or a tablet is, after all, a general-purpose computer. It has a file system, memory, operating system, and programs that it runs. The operating system is also vulnerable to malware. Some platforms are more vulnerable than others but ultimately, every platform can be subject to malware attacks. The difference between a mobile device and a laptop or desktop system is the inputs and the interface, which are controlled. This makes it harder to get access to the data that is on the device. Fortunately, there are ways to acquire that information.

While we are going to talk about the different mobile operating systems, the objective here is not to cover them in great detail. Entire books are written about them, so we certainly are not going to get deep in a single chapter. We will be talking about what these mobile operating systems are, how they are constructed, and some ways you can extract data from them. More importantly, though, how do these systems interact with nonmobile system. While vendors are moving more toward wireless forms of communication, it is still possible for mobile devices to be plugged into desktops or laptops, where they may leave artifacts. Even if they are not plugged into the desktop or laptop, there may still be artifacts left with the operating system that could either indicate what the phone is or perhaps even include some of the contents of the phone.

When it comes to artifacts on a traditional computer like a desktop or a laptop from the use of mobile devices, you can use the same techniques we have talked about in the past. If you are connecting your mobile device to extract photos, copy files, add media, you will get USB artifacts, just as you would with other USB devices.

All smartphones have memory and storage. Memory is volatile, which means that the contents of it will disappear as soon as the system is powered off. This is the same as with desktop or laptop systems. Smartphones also have more permanent storage. This storage is flash memory, which can retain the contents after the device has lost power but does not rely on anything mechanical like a traditional disk drive. Solid state hard drives used in larger systems also make use of flash storage. This allows for a much smaller form factor. Flash storage does make use of wear leveling, though, because it has a limited lifetime for writes. This wear leveling puts storage into use and removes it from use, which means that some part of the total storage for the device will be held out of use to increase the overall life of the storage.

From a forensics perspective, both the memory and the storage are of value. Memory may be extracted, if you can get access while the phone is running. Once the phone is powered off, the volatile memory is lost but applications do retain state so they can be quickly restored to where it was, when the application was last running. Of course, not all applications retain their state but some do. If the application does retain state information, it can be retrieved from the flash storage.

Fortunately, there are a number of books and websites available for specific details related to mobile forensics, especially, when it comes to Android and IOS. As a result, we are not going to be focused on all of the aspects of evidence that can be recovered from these devices. Instead, we will be looking at basics of the three dominant operating systems and focusing on the different artifacts that are left behind, if you connect your mobile device to a desktop or laptop. The three mobile operating systems, we will cover can be backed up to a nonmobile device like a desktop or laptop. These backups can be opened without needing the mobile device at all. As a result, it is useful to have an understanding of the fundamentals of the different operating systems, but also, an idea of where to look on a traditional computing device to locate information.

We have previously covered the use of Sqlite as structured storage for application data in the context of browser information. When it comes to mobile devices, applications that need structured storage on both IOS and Android will commonly use Sqlite databases. Once you have located the data store, that will be kept in the relevant location based on the device, you just need a Sqlite database browser and some basic SQL statements to be able to extract the information that you are looking for.

ENCRYPTION AND REMOTE CONTROL

One of the biggest challenges with mobile devices is that encryption is becoming more common. Apple introduced encryption by default on the iPhone 3S, which included the processing power to be able to support real-time encryption and decryption without crippling the use of the phone. While Android has long had encryption capabilities, most Android devices do not enable encryption by default, though that is starting to change. Generally, mobile devices use the Advanced Encryption Standard (AES), to perform the encryption. When you encrypt data, you need a key. AES is symmetric encryption, which means that the same key is used to both encrypt and decrypt. Because you are using the same key in both directions, keeping the key safe is essential. Key storage and management is a critical component to any encryption scheme. Each device will use different means to protect the key, but it would be unusual to use encryption without requiring a user to have a password. If you did not need to authenticate to use the device, there would not be much point in encrypting the data on the device, since anyone could get to it any time by simply picking up the phone and making use of it. Figure 11.1 shows the settings page from a Samsung Galaxy Tab S2 tablet running Android Lollipop, which indicates that encryption cannot be enabled, unless there is a password set on the device.

This is one of the things about encrypting entire devices, as in the case of smartphones. You will need a password to get into them. Once you have the password and can get into the phone, it is like the device is not encrypted at all. The point of encrypting one of these devices, or even encrypting an entire disk on a laptop, is to prevent the information from falling into the wrong hands. If I come across a device that is just sitting there, waiting to be taken because no one is around, encryption will keep me from pulling the drive out of the laptop, plugging it into an external case and just reading the data off it. The reason for pulling the disk out is that I assume the laptop is password protected and this is a faster way of getting to the data. The same is true of a mobile device. I can plug the device in and extract the data unless it is encrypted.

If you set a password on the device and enable encryption, it does not do much good to set a long timeout on the screen lock. If you set a long timeout and leave your device behind

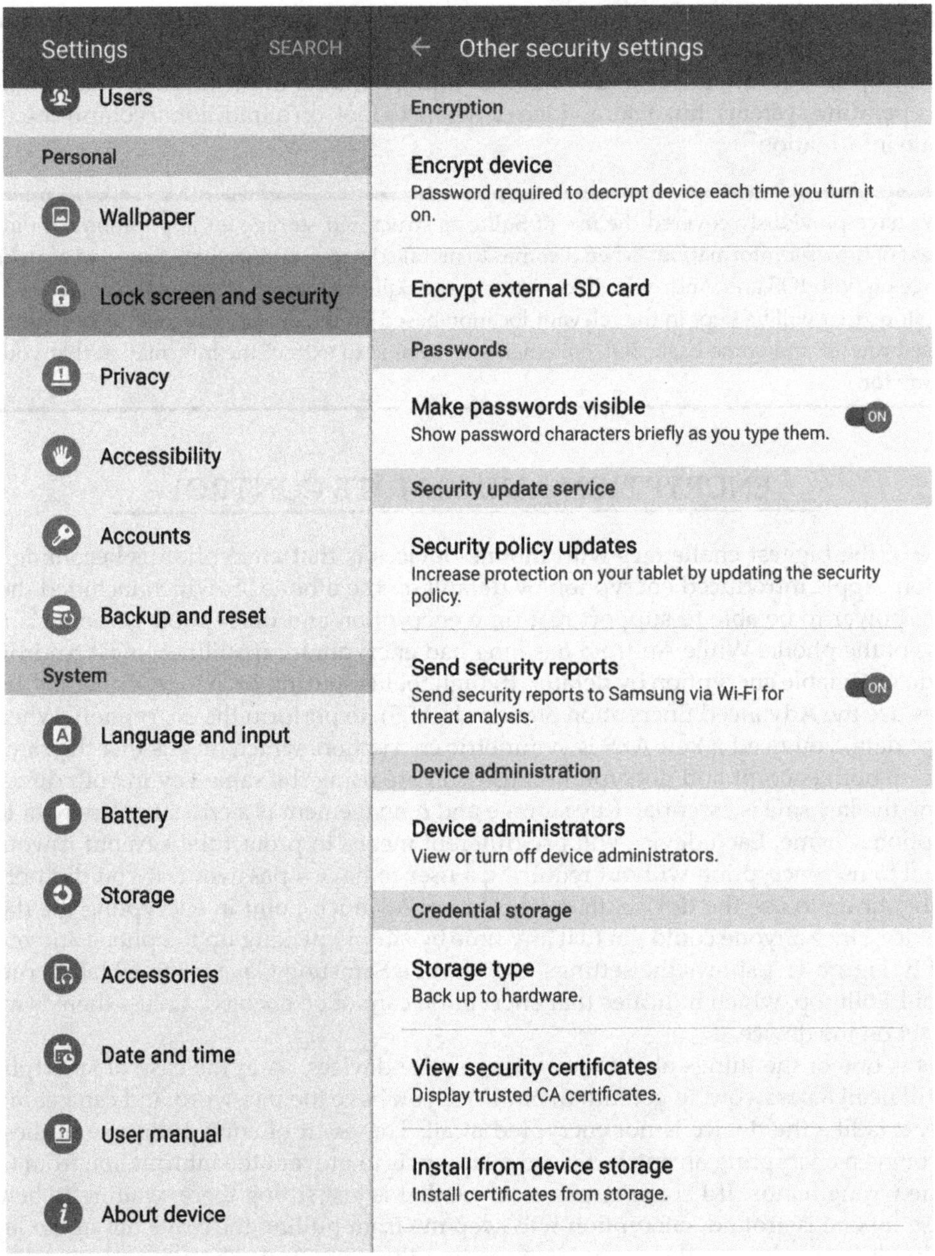

Settings SEARCH
Users
Personal
Wallpaper
Lock screen and security
Privacy
Accessibility
Accounts
Backup and reset
System
Language and input
Battery
Storage
Accessories
Date and time
User manual
About device

Other security settings
Encryption
Encrypt device
Password required to decrypt device each time you turn it on.
Encrypt external SD card
Passwords
Make passwords visible
Show password characters briefly as you type them. ON
Security update service
Security policy updates
Increase protection on your tablet by updating the security policy.
Send security reports
Send security reports to Samsung via Wi-Fi for threat analysis. ON
Device administration
Device administrators
View or turn off device administrators.
Credential storage
Storage type
Back up to hardware.
View security certificates
Display trusted CA certificates.
Install from device storage
Install certificates from storage.

FIGURE 11.1

somewhere, whether accidentally or just because you always leave it at your desk when you run to the bathroom, someone can get the device unlocked and get access to the information on it. If the device is unlocked, the data is accessible. In order to make the encryption mean something, you need to make sure that the device is locked at all times unless you are using it.

The key size is important when it comes to encryption, though you cannot compare key sizes across encryption ciphers. AES can make use of multiple key sizes. The most common key size at the moment is 128 bits, so using that as a reference point, we can figure out how many possible keys there could be. Since each bit has two possible values, we can figure out how many potential keys by multiplying 2 by itself 128 times – once for each position in the key. This leaves us with 340,282,366,920,938,463,463,374,607,431,768,211,456 potential keys. Attempting to try every one of these keys would take an extraordinary amount of time, which means that simple brute forcing is not going to be a very productive way to locate the key that will decrypt the data.

Another thing to make note of is that Apple ties the passcode to the UUID of the system. You have to actually make brute force attempts on the device itself, and this requirement will significantly hamper efforts to attempt to brute force crack the PIN or passphrase, if you wanted to try that route instead of the key.

Having said that, encrypting the device will make it impossible to extract data by force. This makes investigating an encrypted mobile device a serious challenge. Up to IOS 8, Apple was still able to remove information from the device, if it was sent to them. With IOS 8, that is no longer true. The loophole that allowed Apple to remove data if provided a device and an appropriate legal document has been closed. AES is one of the best encryption ciphers available. It is almost impossible to break AES encryption without some knowledge of the key or the password that protects the key. Your best hope when it comes to any sort of encryption, whether it is a laptop, a desktop, or a mobile device like a smartphone or tablet, is to get consent to investigate the device. Once you have consent, have the user unlock the device so you can extract the data from it.

The user does not always have control over whether their device will have storage encrypted or not. If the user connects to a mail server controlled by an enterprise policy, that policy may be set for the user. They will be notified when they connect to the mail server that the mobile device will be configured based on the policies set on the server. One of the common methods for setting mobile policy is Microsoft's ActiveSync, which typically runs on Microsoft's Exchange Server. The Exchange Server is used for enterprise communication including e-mail and calendaring. Microsoft is not the only company that will push policy settings down to a device. Google offers e-mail and calendaring services to businesses as well as many other services. As an enterprise, Google offers extensive settings that can be pushed out to the device. You can see some of the settings in Figure 11.2. This includes forcing all devices to use encryption and strong passwords, if they are going to connect to the mail server to retrieve messages.

One of the other features you will commonly find in these device management policies, which can be seen in Figure 11.2, is the ability to remote wipe the device. This means that an administrator can send a signal to the phone that will force the device to erase itself. This is not the only way that a device can be remotely wiped but this particular method is out of the control of the user. At a business or corporate level, system administrators can send a remote wipe order to devices to remove not only all corporate data but also all other data as well. It is also worth noting that these policies can prevent users from making use of the camera in the device. Some businesses do this knowing that there is sensitive or confidential information they do not want photos being taken of, so they issue business-owned mobile devices and disable the cameras remotely so when they are carried in the business space, they cannot be used to steal information through photography. This would be especially important in cases where, say, a mobile manufacturer was working on the next generation model and did not want photos of the prototypes leaking out.

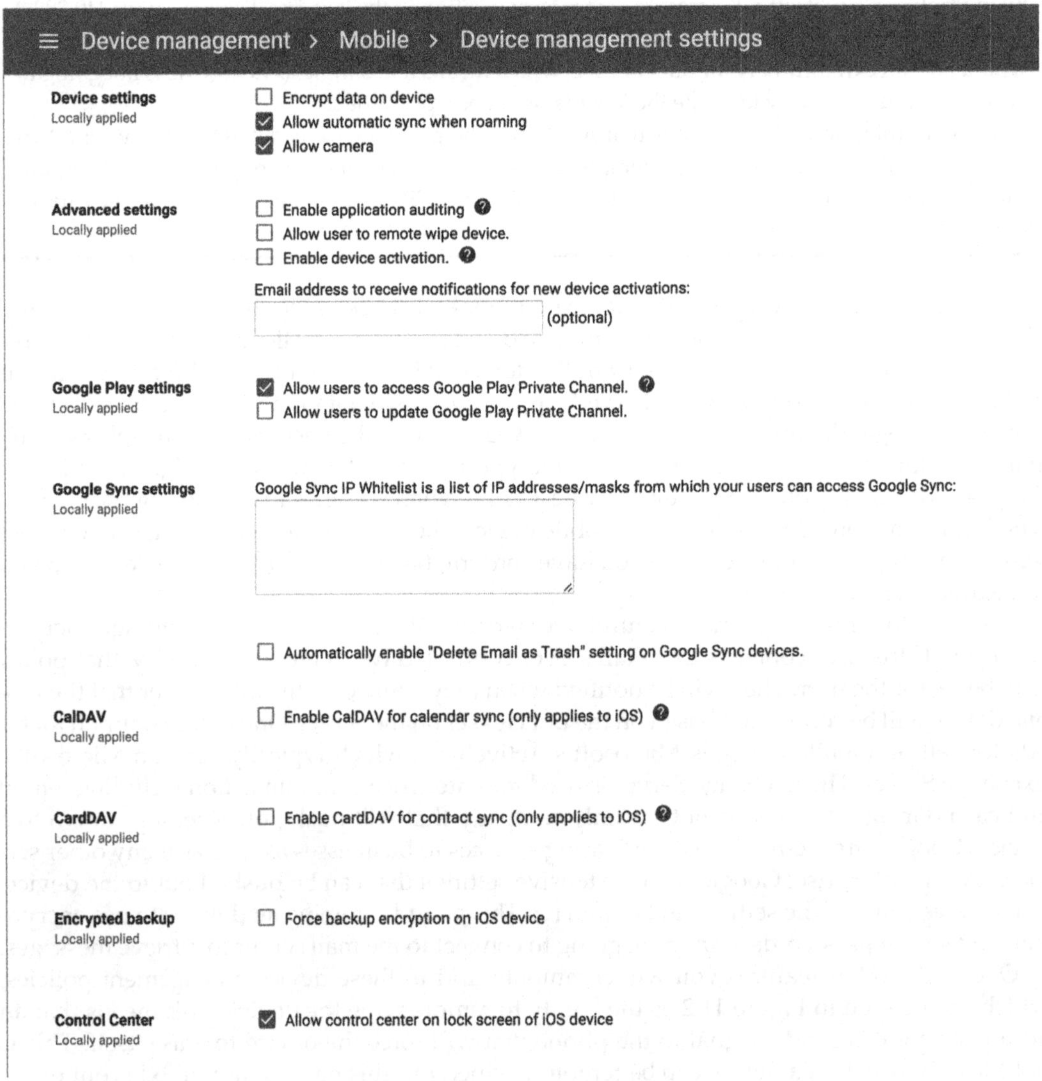

Device management > Mobile > Device management settings

Device settings
Locally applied
- [ ] Encrypt data on device
- [x] Allow automatic sync when roaming
- [x] Allow camera

Advanced settings
Locally applied
- [ ] Enable application auditing
- [ ] Allow user to remote wipe device.
- [ ] Enable device activation.

Email address to receive notifications for new device activations:
(optional)

Google Play settings
Locally applied
- [x] Allow users to access Google Play Private Channel.
- [ ] Allow users to update Google Play Private Channel.

Google Sync settings
Locally applied
Google Sync IP Whitelist is a list of IP addresses/masks from which your users can access Google Sync:
- [ ] Automatically enable "Delete Email as Trash" setting on Google Sync devices.

CalDAV
Locally applied
- [ ] Enable CalDAV for calendar sync (only applies to iOS)

CardDAV
Locally applied
- [ ] Enable CardDAV for contact sync (only applies to iOS)

Encrypted backup
Locally applied
- [ ] Force backup encryption on iOS device

Control Center
Locally applied
- [x] Allow control center on lock screen of iOS device

FIGURE 11.2

ROOTING/JAILBREAKING

Companies that create operating system software like to control the user experience, though, often in different ways. Apple generally likes to control the entire experience, without providing a lot of ability for users to make substantive changes to their experience with the device and the operating system. Google provides a lot of places where users can really customize their experience. In spite of that, Google still locks down administrative access for users. This access could be used to enable certain application types. Because of that, a user may want to get more privileges to their device. In the case of Android devices, users are looking to root it, which means gain root level access. This root level access gives them capabilities they would not otherwise have. In the case of Apple, users may want to jailbreak the phone. This loosens the restrictions that Apple has, giving the user more control over their device – breaking them out of the jail, they were in.

Google actually provides an easy way for users to get even deeper access to their systems by enabling developer access. This is really easy for a user to enable on their device. In the Settings app, if you go to About Device and tap the Build Version seven times, you enable developer options. You can see, a set of those options in Figure 11.3. While most of the developer options are not especially useful for a non-developer, one that will help us is the USB Debugging setting. The USB Debugging setting gives us more access to the system through the USB port by giving us the ability to copy files to and from the device. This could allow you to install programs without warnings or it could allow you to copy custom ROMs, which are different Android implementations created from the Android source code by different development teams.

While Google provides the facilities to copy files to your device, actually rooting it may not be possible. Some device manufacturers lock their bootloader, which is a small piece of code that actually starts up the operating system. If the bootloader is locked, it is quite a bit harder to inject software that can give you root access. Replacing the operating system implementation is one thing you can do with an Android device and many users may want to root their device to be able to perform tasks that require administrative access. On the Apple side, IOS is not open source, so there are not groups of developers creating custom implementations of IOS. The best they can do is, unlock the operating system to allow other sources to install applications from. Once you have a jailbroken phone, you can also perform a number of other customization functions with different sounds, icons, screen layouts, and more. Apple does not allow developer access to the device to perform special tasks like copying files directly to and from the file system. Instead, developers who work on jailbreaking the devices that run IOS are looking for vulnerabilities, they can exploit to get into the OS and replace code on the device. This means they are actually breaking the software in order to install their own custom software that reduces the restrictions that Apple provides.

One advantage to either rooting or jailbreaking a device is that you can install software that may make it easier to copy files to and from the device. While you can do this without installing software on the mobile device running Android, it is necessary on an Apple device. One piece of software, you can install is a Secure Shell server (SSH), which will allow you to directly access the mobile device over the network. Once SSH has been installed, you can connect to the phone from any PC that has an SSH client on it. As soon as you have connected to

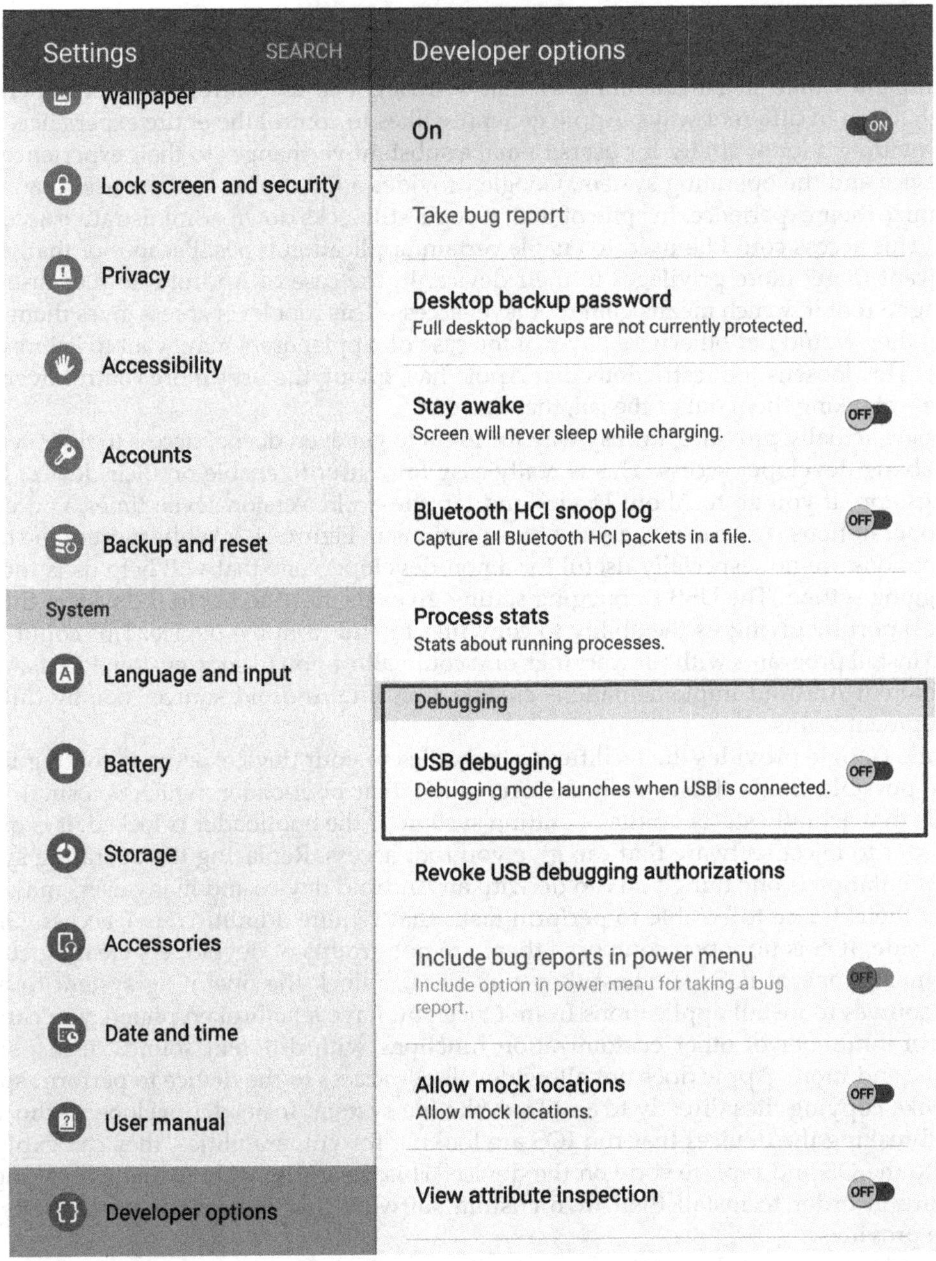

Settings
SEARCH
Wallpaper
Lock screen and security
Privacy
Accessibility
Accounts
Backup and reset
System
Language and input
Battery
Storage
Accessories
Date and time
User manual
Developer options
Developer options
On
ON
Take bug report
Desktop backup password
Full desktop backups are not currently protected.
Stay awake
Screen will never sleep while charging.
OFF
Bluetooth HCI snoop log
Capture all Bluetooth HCI packets in a file.
OFF
Process stats
Stats about running processes.
Debugging
USB debugging
Debugging mode launches when USB is connected.
OFF
Revoke USB debugging authorizations
Include bug reports in power menu
Include option in power menu for taking a bug report.
OFF
Allow mock locations
Allow mock locations.
OFF
View attribute inspection
OFF

FIGURE 11.3

the phone, you have command line access to the system and the entire file system. Of course, going down this road does mean that you have altered the software on the device and there may be implications as to the trustworthiness of what you get, depending on who your audience is. Some people will suggest that jailbreaking or rooting your phone will corrupt data on the device. As a result, it is something to keep in mind if you are working with devices that are either jailbroken or rooted.

ANDROID

Android is a mobile operating platform owned by Google. It was originally developed in 2003 by the company Android, which was purchased by Google two years later. The goal of Android was to make mobile devices smarter, more personalized, and more location-aware. Android is based on a custom Linux kernel designed to interface with all of the hardware used in the device. Mobile devices have a limited number of devices associated with them. When you run Linux on a desktop or a laptop, the user may plug in any number of extension cards or USB devices. This requires drivers and Linux typically has those drivers built in, either directly to the kernel or as a module. Because a mobile device has a small number of devices that are built into the device itself, the vendor can make the kernel very small and customized to the specific device. Each vendor, though, may have different devices. This may include different vendors for the display device or the modem that communicates with the cellular network. These are just two of the devices that would be built into the hardware, where drivers would be necessary.

Remember that Linux is just the kernel. On top of the kernel, you still need to have the entire operating environment and there are pieces of what you might consider to be a Unix-like operating environment. However, not all of the pieces are in place. This is a lightweight device from an operating system perspective, since, generally there is not as much memory in a mobile device as there is in a desktop. Certainly, the processors are not the same. Mobile processors are not the same as desktop processors. Applications are also different. On Android devices, applications are run in protected spaces. Often the programs are written in Java. Java, as you may recall, is not compiled down to machine code that can be run directly in the processor. It runs within a virtual machine that is designed specifically for an individual application. Up until Android 4.4 (KitKat), Google used the Dalvik software for its virtual machines. Dalvik uses something called just in time compilation, which means the Dalvik software converts the byte code to machine code, when it needs to.

With more recent versions of Android like Lollipop and Marshmallow, Google has moved to a virtual machine that uses pre-compiled executables. This means that when the application is installed, the operating system does the conversion to machine code, so it is ready to execute as soon as the application is launched. There would be no lag as the byte code is converted to machine code while the application is running. Not that the lag is even noticeable on new processors because they are so fast and efficient.

With Android in particular, you can get access to the underlying operating system. This is done using the Android Debug Bridge (adb), which allows you direct access to the file system in order to copy files to and from the device.adb will also perform other tasks, so it is a utility that you may want to know more about.

A challenge with Android is that it is open to a lot of people. Google does not have the same restrictions that Apple does, so some vendors can introduce their own application stores. Users can also opt to allow third party sources for applications. This can be a challenge for the reliability and security of the device, since these other sources can be a way for malware to be introduced on the system.

Filesystem Layout

While the kernel in use for Android is one customized from the Linux kernel, the rest of the environment is not the same as Linux. One place you can see this is in the filesystem layout. A typical Linux installation will have a filesystem layout that looks like Unix has always looked. You will have /etc, /usr, /var, /lib and so on. If you were to look at the root filesystem on an Android system, you would see something very different from that. This can make it harder to investigate an Android system, if you have the complete filesystem since you may not know, where everything is kept. The following are the directories you will commonly see on an Android system. Remember that not all of these are actual directories. They may be mount points, which means that the directory exists as a place to attach a partition from another location. This could be an external storage device or it could be a pseudo filesystem.

acct: The acct directory is where accounting information is stored. This accounting data keeps track of CPU usage, for a start.

cache: The cache directory stores frequently used data as well as recovered data that may have been lost because of a system failure. This directory may include a number of relevant forensic artifacts from regular device usage.

d: This directory is used for kernel debugging.

data: The data directory is where user data is stored, including application data such as contacts and text messages.

default.prop: This is a file that includes the default properties.

dev: This is the same as the /dev directory on a Linux system. It includes all of the special files that refer to hardware devices on the phone or tablet.

etc: The etc directory stores configuration files, just as it does on a Linux system.

init: The init program is the master process used to start up all of the other services and programs when the phone or tablet boots. The init program is stored in this directory.

mnt: Just as with a Linux system, this is a mount point for external devices.

proc: The proc directory is a pseudo filesystem that contains directories and files related to the processes running.

root: This is the home directory for the root user

sdcard: The sdcard directory is the mount point for the SD card where data may be stored.

sys: This is the mount point for the sysfs pseudo filesystem, which contains information related to the kernel's internal structures.

system: The system directory stores all of the common directories you would see on a Unix or Linux system. This includes the /bin, /sbin, /usr, and the /lib directories.

uventd.rc: This is the configuration file for the entries in the /dev directory.

vendor: This is a link to the /system/vendor directory.

This is the layout from the *system* partition. An Android device will have multiple partitions. The *system* partition includes the Android framework, libraries, applications that come installed by default and the system binaries. The *boot loader* partition carries the low level initialization programs. The boot loader carries the code responsible for initializing the hardware and then loading the kernel. The kernel and associated files are located in the *boot* partition. If you need to perform maintenance on your device, you would make use of the *recovery* partition, which includes a smaller operating system image. This image could be used to make necessary changes to an Android device that was not operational. A device that was updating might make use of the recovery partition and boot image. The *userdata* partition is where all of the user data is stored. This includes images, music, video, and any application data that the user may be keeping. As a result, this partition is very important.

The final partition to cover is the *cache* partition. This partition is where regularly used data is kept. Recovery data and any update packages that are downloaded over the air, meaning over the cellular network, are stored there. Because this may be used to store commonly used data, it may contain a lot of forensic artifacts that may have come from Web browsing activities. Some of these partitions are actually mounted in the live filesystem, as mentioned earlier.

Malware

Google has the Play Store it uses to distribute applications to users. Apps that are submitted have to undergo a vetting process before they can be added to the Play Store and sold. However, this vetting process is not perfect. Sometimes malware can be introduced to devices through the Play Store. Google has been getting better about their vetting processes but it is always possible for malware to make it through. Additionally, of course, users can disable any checking of applications installed from third party sources. In fact, while Android has become a significant target for mobile malware, the reality is that the vast majority of this malware comes from third party app stores that are primarily located in Asia and the Middle East (Forbes, 2014).

This is not to say that malware on Android is not a problem. However, it is such a known problem that Google is spending a lot of time and effort to make sure that the applications which are being submitted to their Play Store are checked vigorously for malicious intent. Because mobile devices are being used more and more regularly and often in place of more traditional computing devices, malware attacks against mobile devices will be more common. Because of that, some vendors of Android devices actually install antimalware software on their devices. This way, users will not need to go find antimalware software for themselves and install it. Even in cases where users may find ways to install software from third-party sources, the anti-malware will catch it. In the Settings app on some Android devices, like a Samsung Galaxy Tab S2 running Lollipop, you will find Device Security under Lock Screen and Security. Using this, you can scan your device for threats. You can see the different options under Device Security on a Samsung tablet in Figure 11.4. This particular tablet has been scanned. By default, the software does not schedule scans to check for malware. It requires users to actually go to this setting and start the scan manually. You can, though, see some additional capabilities that Samsung offers to provide additional protection. This is not common on all Android devices, of course, since Knox is a Samsung security feature.

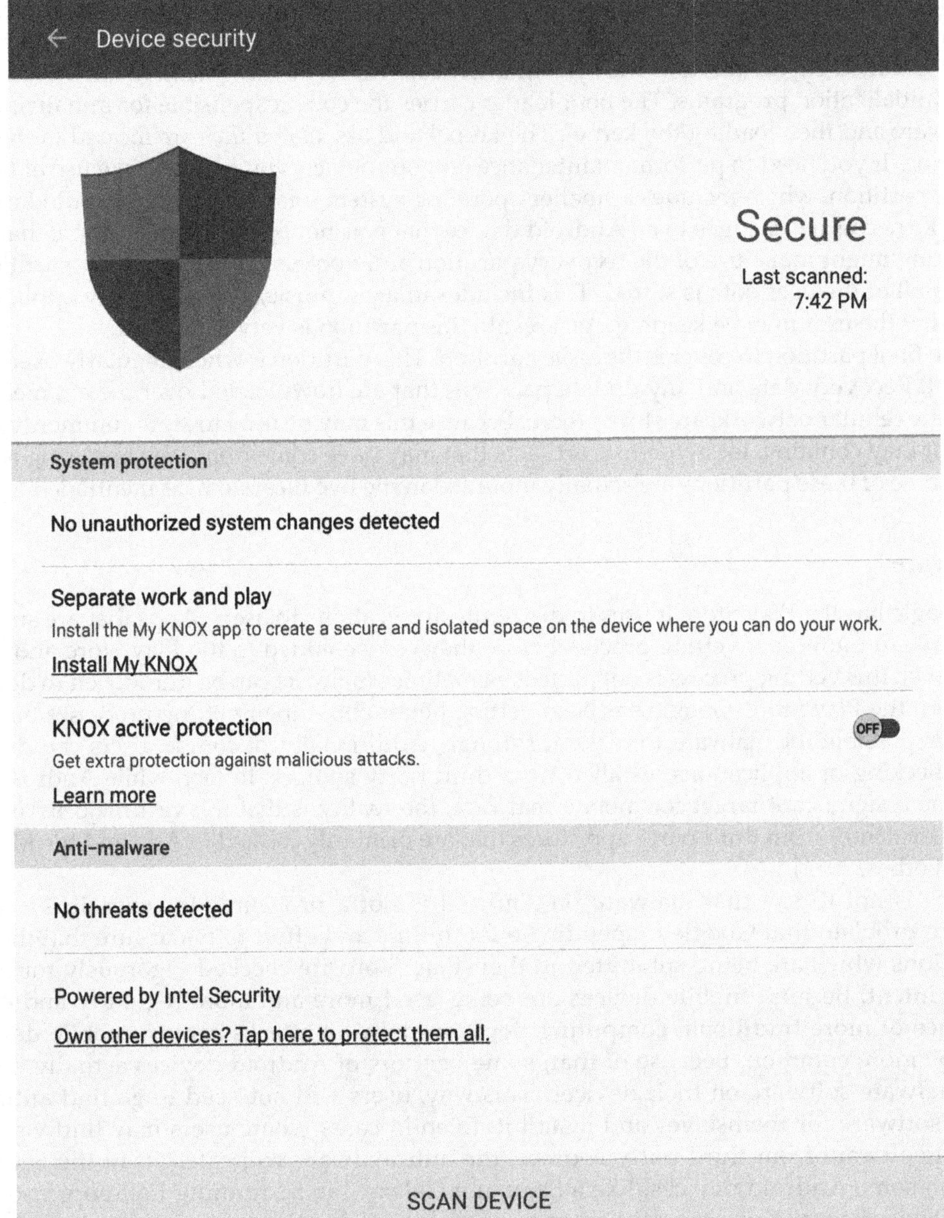
Device security
Secure
Last scanned:
7:42 PM
System protection
No unauthorized system changes detected
Separate work and play
Install the My KNOX app to create a secure and isolated space on the device where you can do your work.
Install My KNOX
KNOX active protection
OFF
Get extra protection against malicious attacks.
Learn more
Anti-malware
No threats detected
Powered by Intel Security
Own other devices? Tap here to protect them all.
SCAN DEVICE

FIGURE 11.4

Using the Android Debug Bridge (adb)

adb is used by developers to interact with Android devices. It can be installed as part of the software development kit provided by Google, used to develop Android applications, or it can be installed standalone if you just want to use it to interact with the mobile devices. adb has many capabilities but there are a couple that are more interesting from a forensics standpoint. The first is the pull function. If you call adb with pull as the parameter and then specify what you want to pull, you can extract data directly off the device. This can be done while the device is running but adb can also be run on a device that has been booted into recovery mode. Fortunately, booting into recovery mode just requires knowing the button press combination, when the system powers up. This is commonly something like holding the power button and the volume down button at the same time with the device powered off. The device will boot into recovery mode at which point you can use adb to connect to the system. Figure 11.5 shows the process of pulling the entire contents of the sdcard/ directory from a Google Nexus tablet back to the computer, I was running adb from. While this was done on a Mac OS X system, adb will run on Linux, Windows, and Mac OS X, so you can perform the same function regardless of which Android device you are trying to remove data from, and which operating system you are using to extract the data.

```
kilroy@binkley:~/Documents/ADT/sdk/platform-tools/sdcard$ ../adb pull sdcard/
pull: building file list...
pull: sdcard/Ringtones/hangouts_incoming_call.ogg -> ./Ringtones/hangouts_incomi
ng_call.ogg
pull: sdcard/Ringtones/hangouts_message.ogg -> ./Ringtones/hangouts_message.ogg
pull: sdcard/Android/data/com.google.android.music/files/._playmusicid -> ./Andr
oid/data/com.google.android.music/files/._playmusicid
pull: sdcard/Android/data/com.google.android.apps.maps/testdata/voice/en_US.i.af
afd9e3/voice_instructions_imperial.zip -> ./Android/data/com.google.android.apps
.maps/testdata/voice/en_US.i.afafd9e3/voice_instructions_imperial.zip
pull: sdcard/Android/data/.nomedia -> ./Android/data/.nomedia
pull: sdcard/Android/obb/.nomedia -> ./Android/obb/.nomedia
pull: sdcard/clockworkmod/.recovery_version -> ./clockworkmod/.recovery_version
pull: sdcard/clockworkmod/.last_install_path -> ./clockworkmod/.last_install_pat
h
pull: sdcard/UPDATE-SuperSU-v1.99r3.zip -> ./UPDATE-SuperSU-v1.99r3.zip
pull: sdcard/openrecovery-twrp-2.8.2.0-grouper.img -> ./openrecovery-twrp-2.8.2.
0-grouper.img
pull: sdcard/kali_linux_nethunter_nexus7_2013.zip -> ./kali_linux_nethunter_nexu
s7_2013.zip
11 files pulled. 0 files skipped.
4027 KB/s (1075680320 bytes in 260.817s)
```

FIGURE 11.5

Using adb, you can also explore the system using the command line. The command adb shell will give you shell access onto the system. Remember that Android is based on a Linux kernel and many of the common Unix/Linux utilities are available on the device. Using adb shell, you can get straight into the system without going through the process of installing an SSH server as suggested earlier. This just requires the device, a USB cable, and a connection to a system that has adb installed. There are other functions you can perform as well using adb including rebooting the device and specifying how to boot it up. You can boot it into recovery mode or you can put it into fastboot mode. Fastboot is another mode that can be used by developers to make changes to the running operating system, including changing out the running operating system image. You may want to do this if you were looking to install one of the custom ROMs that run Android but have additional features or settings enabled that you would not find in either the stock, unmodified Android, or in a vendor-modified version of Android.

Backups

Google will generally perform backups of devices back to the Google account that you are required to have in order to make use of your Android device. Google uses this to identify you but also to give you storage space with them for backups and photo storage. They will also automatically create you a Gmail account with your Google account. This means that you get an e-mail account when you create your Google account with your Android device. Google will store backups from as many devices as you have. This means that if you get a new Android device, Google will automatically restore the configuration and applications from an existing or previous Android device, if you tell it that you want to do that. You can check with Google at any time if you want to see the applications and other data that are being backed up for you. You can see in Figure 11.6 that I have a few Android devices that have been backed up using the same Google account. Google will show you when the device was last seen as well as the model information for the device.

While Google will typically take care of your backups for you, this is generally limited to system configurations, though Google does have applications that you can use, which will store all of your photos and other images with them and provide you a local representation. You do not have to use that application, of course, which means that photos you take will only be stored on your device. However, the new Photos App is generally superseding the older Gallery App and the Photos App keeps your photos at Google for you. Any time you take a picture with your phone or tablet, it will be uploaded to Google for you, if you are using the Photos App for your default imaging program.

Android Marshmallow includes new backup capabilities. Applications can use an auto backup feature, which will use an Android service to automatically place application data into the Google Drive for the application.

Having said that, vendors like Samsung also have desktop applications that you can use to backup everything on your mobile device. Device vendors are not the only ones to

Applications with backup on servers	Android Wallpaper Backup date: Sep 12, 2015 6:21 PM Backup size: 218.98 KB
	Android System Settings Backup date: Sep 12, 2015 6:21 PM Backup size: 4.01 KB
	Android Dictionary Backup date: Apr 5, 2015 11:01 PM Backup size: 76 B
	Android Market Backup date: Sep 12, 2015 6:21 PM Backup size: 17 B
	Google Backup date: Sep 12, 2015 6:21 PM Backup size: 431.48 KB
htc Nexus 9 No carrier	Model Name: Nexus 9 Manufacturer: htc Carrier: No carrier Last activity seen on: Sep 13, 2015 Registered date: Jun 12, 2015
Applications with backup on servers	Android Wallpaper Backup date: Aug 30, 2015 7:07 PM Backup size: 1.49 MB
	Android System Settings Backup date: Aug 30, 2015 7:07 PM Backup size: 2.77 KB
	Android Dictionary Backup date: Aug 13, 2015 10:15 AM Backup size: 45 B
	Android Market Backup date: Aug 20, 2015 10:42 PM Backup size: 17 B
	Google Backup date: Sep 5, 2015 3:43 AM Backup size: 602.84 KB
samsung SM-T810 No carrier	Model Name: SM-T810 Manufacturer: samsung Carrier: No carrier Last activity seen on: Sep 10, 2015 Registered date: Sep 7, 2015

FIGURE 11.6

offer backup solutions, of course, but Samsung in particular is following the path created by Apple to have a media manager on the computer that manages backups, music, photos, and videos. The Samsung solution is called Kies and it behaves much like iTunes does for the iPhone, iPod, and iPad. Once Kies is installed, all you need to do is connect your device to it and you can perform backups using it. You can see Kies performing a backup in Figure 11.7.

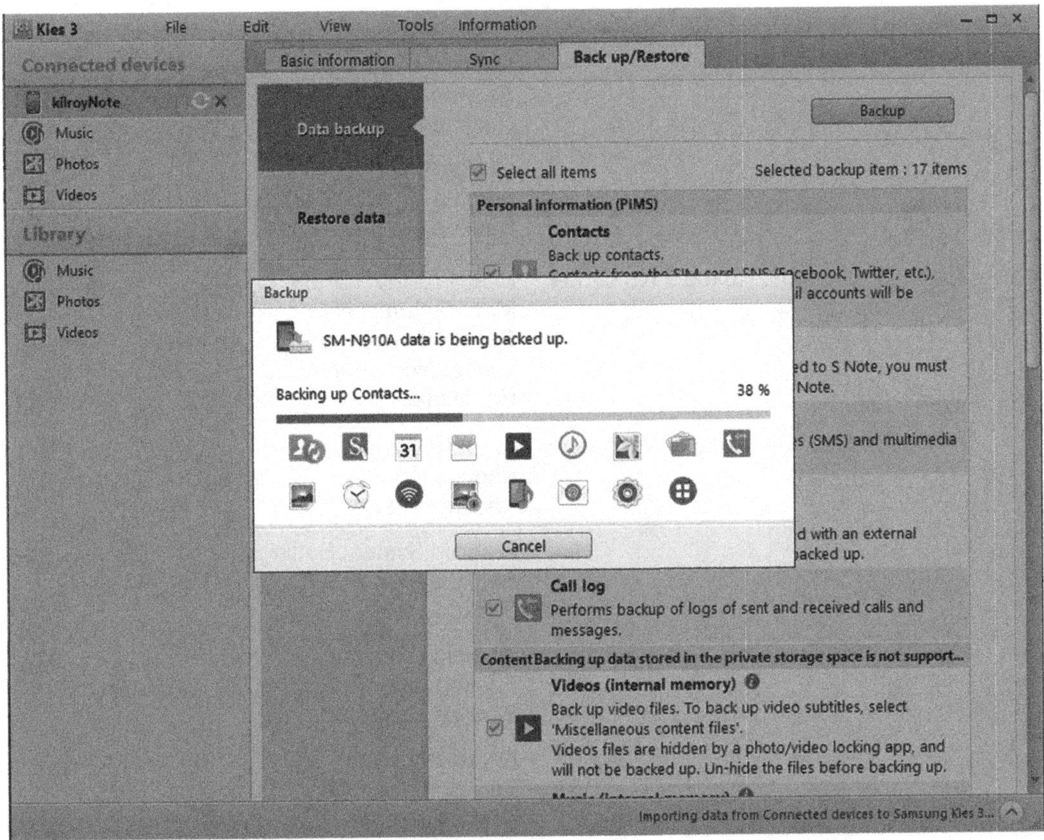

FIGURE 11.7

Once Kies has performed backups, it maintains a list of the backups in an XML document called BackupHistory.xml located in %userdir%/AppData/Roaming/Samsung/Kies3.0/BackupHistory. A sample of this XML document is below. Using this XML file, you can determine the location of the backup, the time it was performed, the name of the device, the name of the model, the version of Android it is running, the serial number, and a number of other pieces of information that will clearly associate the data found on the disk of the backup system with the device that the backup came from.

```
<BundleInfo xsi:type="BatchServiceBuldleInformation">
  <BNRInformation />
  <AppInfoList />
  <Mode>Basic</Mode>
  <FullBackupMode>True</FullBackupMode>
  <FolderPath>C:\Users\Ric\Documents\Samsung\Kies3\backup\SM-N910A\SM-
N910A_18023243021\SM-N910A_20150912211536</FolderPath>
  <Type>None</Type>
  <ItemsCount>6746</ItemsCount>
  <FileSize>3654749808</FileSize>
  <UserInputName>kilroyNote</UserInputName>
  <ModelName>SM-N910A</ModelName>
  <PlatformVersion>5.0.1</PlatformVersion>
  <SerialNumber>CECDA04C422DC3B6B8DC2BBF5A1034F6</SerialNumber>
  <BnRIMEI>C5079961633C6282D81588EA1379BB45</BnRIMEI>
  <EIMEI />
  <SavedTime>2015-09-12T21:15:36</SavedTime>
  <PhoneNumber>18003344021</PhoneNumber>
  <KiesVersion>3.2.15072_2</KiesVersion>
</BundleInfo>
```


The backup is stored as a collection of directories and files. The directories are clearly named so you can determine the contents by simply looking at the name of the directory. You can see an example of a backup structure in Figure 11.8. The figure shows directories named Application, Configuration, Music, Photo, Email, and Video among others.

The one challenge with these backups is that they are just plain files in a directory structure. While this is great in that it does not require additional tools in order to extract useful information from the backup, what it does mean is that there is no verifying information to indicate that the backup data has not been tampered with. The data is not bundled and verified in any way. There are no hash values that you can compare against. If this is just a set of backups that a user has performed, you need to know that the user could have added or removed or even edited any of the information.

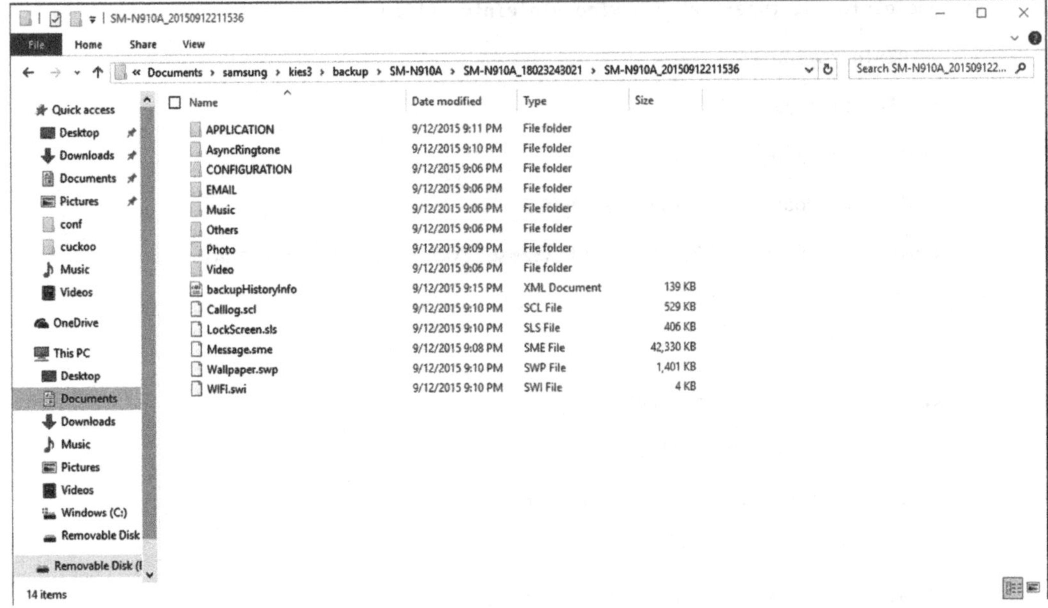

FIGURE 11.8

BLACKBERRY

BlackBerry had been around for a few years as a paging/e-mail device before they released their first smartphone in 2003. At the time, it was not called a smartphone but BlackBerry established many of the functions that were later picked up by Apple and Google. This includes adding e-mail capabilities and a direct messaging system that featured delivery and read receipts. Initially, the BlackBerry required the use of the BlackBerry Enterprise Server (BES). The BES interfaced with the corporate messaging server, pulling e-mail off the messaging server and then pushing it out to the device using the device's identification number. Other BlackBerry users could message directly using the device identification number. This was through the BlackBerry Messenger (BBM) application. This is different from text messages, which use a different set of protocols to transmit messages. Text messages or short message service (SMS) is restricted to 160 characters in transmission. This is not a limitation that exists with the BBM application.

While the BlackBerry was fairly unique when it first came out, it has fallen toward the back of the pack when it comes to other smartphones. It was one of the early devices, which added a phone to a personal data assistant (PDA) that was capable of not only keeping a calendar and contact information but could also receive e-mail. Most other similar devices would gather e-mail by syncing with the computer. The BlackBerry found a way to securely deliver e-mail to a mobile device. This meant that there was e-mail that was stored on the device as well as other messages.

While BlackBerry can operate as entirely untethered device, acquiring and sending data wirelessly exclusively, just as other smartphones, it can also be plugged into a computer to exchange data. Once the BlackBerry is plugged in, it can be backed up. BlackBerry uses a piece of software called the BlackBerry Desktop Manager that is used to interact with the BlackBerry. When you perform a backup, you get a .ipd file that stores all of the backup data. Unlike the plain file structure from the Kies backup, the BlackBerry .ipd backup is created in a database-like format. In order to read the BlackBerry backup, you would need another piece of software. There are pieces of software that can be used to read and extract data from the .ipd file. One of them is MagicBerry, developed by Mena Step Innovative Solutions. MagicBerry is capable of extracting SMS messages, e-mail, calendar data, call logs, and contact lists.

Filesystem Layout

While getting access to the filesystem on a BlackBerry can be challenging, BlackBerry does publish documents explaining what the filesystem layout looks like to the application. Just as with other mobile devices, BlackBerry applications run inside a controlled environment. The only thing that the application sees is the file system that is presented to it by the operating system. From the perspective of the application, the following is what the application sees of the filesystem.

app: The app directory contains all of the files that are installed with the application.

data: The data directory is the home directory for the application. All of the application's private data is stored here.

db: This is the database directory for the application.

logs: The application logs to this directory. Anything the application sends to standard output or standard error (well-defined input output channels commonly used by C and C-related languages) will be sent here.

shared: Data associated with the application is stored here but in directories that are named by the type of data. Documents, downloads, Dropbox, camera, music, photos, and books are some of the categories that you can find in this directory.

tmp: This is the temporary working directory for the application.

IOS

Perhaps interestingly, the Blackberry is the only smartphone that we are talking about here that is not built on a foundation of another operating system. IOS is no different from Android and Windows Mobile in this regard. IOS is built on the foundation of Mac OS X. The first iPhone was released in 2007. Since that time, Apple has released an iPad, which is a tablet that uses IOS. It also took the iPhone and made hardware adjustments in order to release a new model iPod that would not only play music like the original generation iPods but it also runs the same applications as the iPhone. The underlying software components from all of these devices are modified to fit onto a smaller device with different hardware but it is still essentially the same Darwin kernel that powers other Apple devices. Also, since no other Apple device includes touch screen capabilities, Apple had to create a new framework to support these touch screen but some of the user interface frameworks remain the same across both Mac OS X and IOS. On top of the kernel and many of the frameworks, the Apple devices use the same filesystem and basically the same layout as Mac OS X.

The Apple devices have three different boot modes. The common one is just booting into the regular operating mode. Apple devices also have a Recovery mode. The Recovery mode is used to install an operating system update in case the device gets stuck and has problems updating or booting correctly. You can see an iPhone in Figure 11.9 that has been put into the Recovery mode. Apple devices also have a Device Firmware Upgrade (DFU) mode. The DFU mode is often used when users are jailbreaking their devices. The device may go into DFU mode if there is a failure that leaves the device appearing to not have an operating system. You can, of course, also force the device into DFU mode. In order to enter DFU mode, you would hold down the power and home buttons as you turn the device on. After 10 s, release the power button but keep holding the home button down. After several more seconds, you will be notified that your device is ready. It is then in DFU mode.

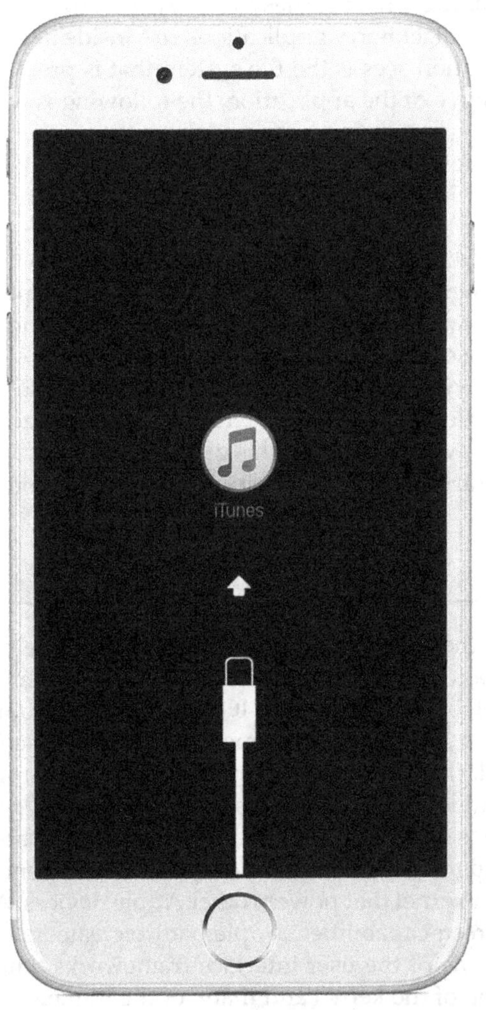

FIGURE 11.9

Filesystem Layout

IOS devices use the same HFS+ filesystem as a Mac OS X system. The fewer changes from the source operating system, the easier it is to create the new device. If you are using essentially the same operating system, you can focus your time on the hardware and worry less about the operating system and software components. In addition to the HFS+ filesystem, the directory layout is essentially the same between a Mac OS X system and an IOS device. If you were able to get into the device and examine the directories you would find in the root directory, you would see the following.

Applications: This is where the applications are stored, just as in the case of Mac OS X. Applications on an IOS device are bundles, just as they are on Mac OS X. The directory structure within the bundle on IOS is different. One directory to be aware of within an IOS app bundle is Documents. The Documents directory may include user-created data that could be useful. This would be related to the specific application you are looking at.

bin: This is where system-level binaries are stored. This is related to the Unix foundation of both Mac OS X and IOS. Common Unix utilities and programs would be in this directory.

boot: This may include over the air (OTA) updates but is generally empty.

dev: Just as with Linux, Android, and Mac OS X, this stores files that refer specifically to hardware devices available on the system.

Developer: This is unused unless the device has been enabled as a development device. If you opt to use the device for development, there will be software installed in here.

etc: Where this is commonly used for storing configuration data on Unix systems, on an IOS device, it is actually linked to /private/etc. The configuration files are actually stored there.

Library: Application support files, launch agents and daemons, logs, and preferences are all stored here. This is essentially the same as on a Mac OS X system.

lib: Libraries that are necessary for application functionality are stored here.

mnt: This is commonly where external filesystems are mounted but there are no external filesystems in use with IOS so this is really unused.

private: The var and etc directories are stored here. Symbolic links to these directories are created in the root directory.

Sbin: System binaries are stored here. This would include the different mount utilities as well as other utilities related to the file system.

System: Frameworks necessary for the operation of the system are stored here.

tmp: This is where temporary data is stored. On IOS, this directory links to /private/tmp.

User: All data stored for the user mobile, which is the nonroot user on IOS devices. This links to /private/var/mobile where all of the data is actually stored.

usr: This is a common directory on Unix-like operating systems. It includes lib, bin, sbin, and other common directories.

var: This is also common to Unix-like operating systems. This includes variable sized data like logs. In reality, this is a link to the /private/var directory.

You can see the strong similarities between Mac OS X and IOS, when we look at the directories that you can find on a mobile device. When you look into the contents of many of these directories, you will see how stripped down IOS is as compared to Mac OS X. The structure and components are the same but there are far fewer programs and libraries needed by an IOS device. If you were able to get into an IOS device at the command line or terminal, you would find many of the utilities, you may commonly use at the command line on a Mac OS X system are just not there. The structure of the filesystem on an IOS device is closely aligned with the Filesystem Hierarchy Standard (FHS), which is the standard layout for Unix and Unix-like operating systems.

Different tools may present data in different ways. Using the BlackLight forensics program from BlackBag Techologies looking at data from an iPhone running IOS 8.4, we get the results shown in Figure 11.10.

▼ /		
▶ db	2015-08-30 (EDT)	2015-09-22 (EDT)
▶ HealthDomain	2015-08-30 (EDT)	2015-09-14 (EDT)
▶ KeyboardDomain	2015-08-30 (EDT)	2015-09-12 (EDT)
▶ Keychains	2015-05-29 (EDT)	2015-09-22 (EDT)
▶ Managed Preferences	2015-08-30 (EDT)	2015-08-30 (EDT)
▼ mobile		
▶ ApplicationPlugins		
▶ Applications		
▶ Library	2015-08-30 (EDT)	2015-09-14 (EDT)
▶ Media	2015-08-30 (EDT)	2015-09-22 (EDT)
▶ MobileDevice	2015-08-30 (EDT)	2015-08-30 (EDT)
▼ preferences	2015-05-29 (EDT)	2015-09-22 (EDT)
com.apple.networkextension.plist	2015-09-22 (EDT)	2015-09-22 (EDT)
▶ SystemConfiguration	2015-08-30 (EDT)	2015-09-22 (EDT)
▶ root	2015-08-30 (EDT)	2015-08-30 (EDT)
▶ UnknownDomain	2015-08-30 (EDT)	2015-08-30 (EDT)
▼ wireless	2015-08-30 (EDT)	2015-08-30 (EDT)
▼ Library	2015-05-29 (EDT)	2015-08-30 (EDT)
▶ CallHistory	2015-08-30 (EDT)	2015-08-30 (EDT)
▶ Databases	2015-08-30 (EDT)	2015-09-22 (EDT)
▶ Preferences	2015-08-30 (EDT)	2015-09-22 (EDT)

FIGURE 11.10

Backups and iTunes

The easiest way to get backups from an IOS device is to plug your device into a computer running iTunes. iTunes was developed as a media manager for Mac OS X. It will also run on Windows systems. iTunes can also be used to manage IOS devices. When you plug your IOS device in, iTunes will probably launch. This gives you the ability to get a backup of the device in addition to copying media to your device. You can also sync media between your desktop and your mobile device. If you are doing anything with your mobile device from your desktop system, it will be done through iTunes. When you are backing up your IOS device through iTunes, you have the ability to encrypt your backup. This feature is not checked by default as you can see in Figure 11.11. When the backup is not encrypted, it can be opened by anyone. The assumption for not forcing encryption by default is that the system you are backing up to is under your control. Since it is under your control, there is less need to protect it. Physical protection is often considered to trump other types of protection.

When you connect an IOS device to a computer, you will be prompted on the device asking whether you trust the connection or not. If you do not indicate that you trust the connection, the computer will not be able to get any information from the device.

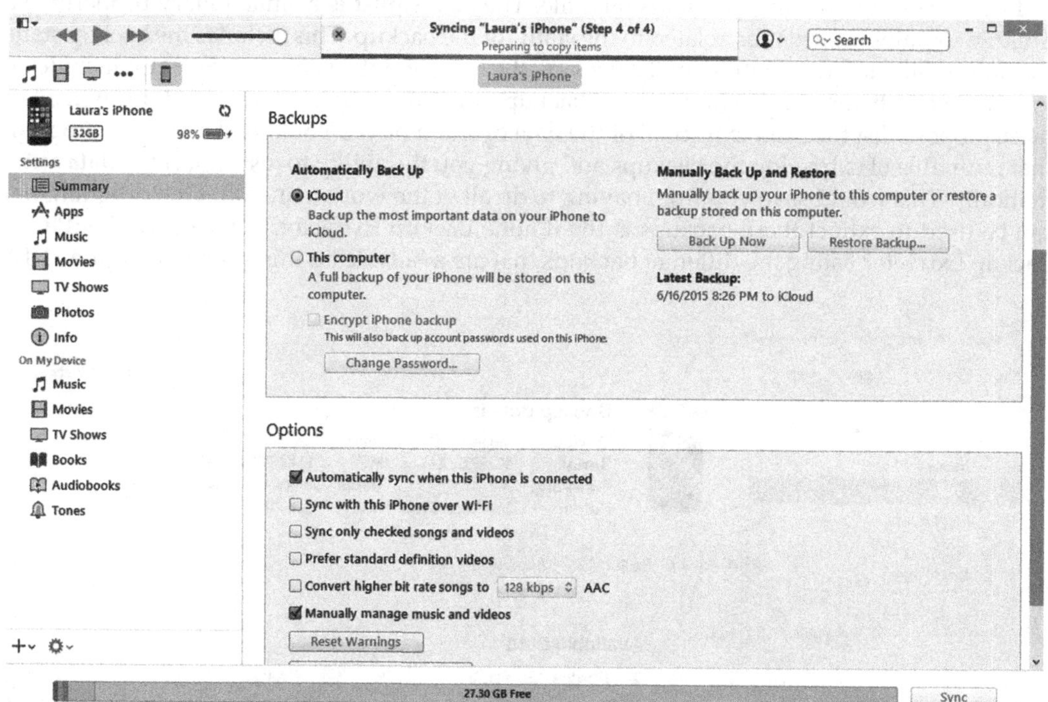

FIGURE 11.11

Local backups are stored based on the users that are logged into the system, when the backups happen. On a Windows system older than Windows Vista, you will be able to locate the backup files in the directory \Users\username\AppData\Roaming\Apple Computer\MobileSync\Backup. On a Mac OS X system, you will locate the backups in /Users/username/Library/Application Support/MobileSync/Backup. Each backup gets a folder that is named with the universal device identifier and may also include dates and times as part of the name of the directory. A differential backup, meaning a backup that only includes changes to the device since the last complete backup, will be stored with a name that includes the date and time that the backup took place.

The backup will include four files that you should pay the most attention to, since they will provide you with all the information you need related to the backup. The first is the info.plist file. This file includes all of the information related to the device. This includes the IMEI, the device name, the serial number, the phone name, the display name, and all other identifying information related to the phone. This is a property list file that is stored in XML format but in plaintext rather than binary. The manifest.mdbd is a database that includes all of the files that are included in the backup, including the path to the file as well as the type of data that is stored in the backup file. The manifest.plist is a binary property list that includes additional data related to the backup. This includes information about encryption, what Apple components are backed up and whether the backup is complete or not.

Finally, you will see the the status.plist file. The status.plist is a small binary property list. This file contains information related to the status of the backup. This includes the backup state, the universally unique identifier of the backup, the date, and the version. It will also include an indication of whether the backup is a full backup or a differential. You can read through all of these property list files and extract all of the data by hand or you could make use of a program that is capable of extracting the backups and giving you the ability to just export the data automatically. This would save you from having to do all of the work manually. One program that can be used to extract these backups is the iPhone Backup Extractor. You can see the iPhone Backup Extractor listing the different backups that are available on this system in Figure 11.12.

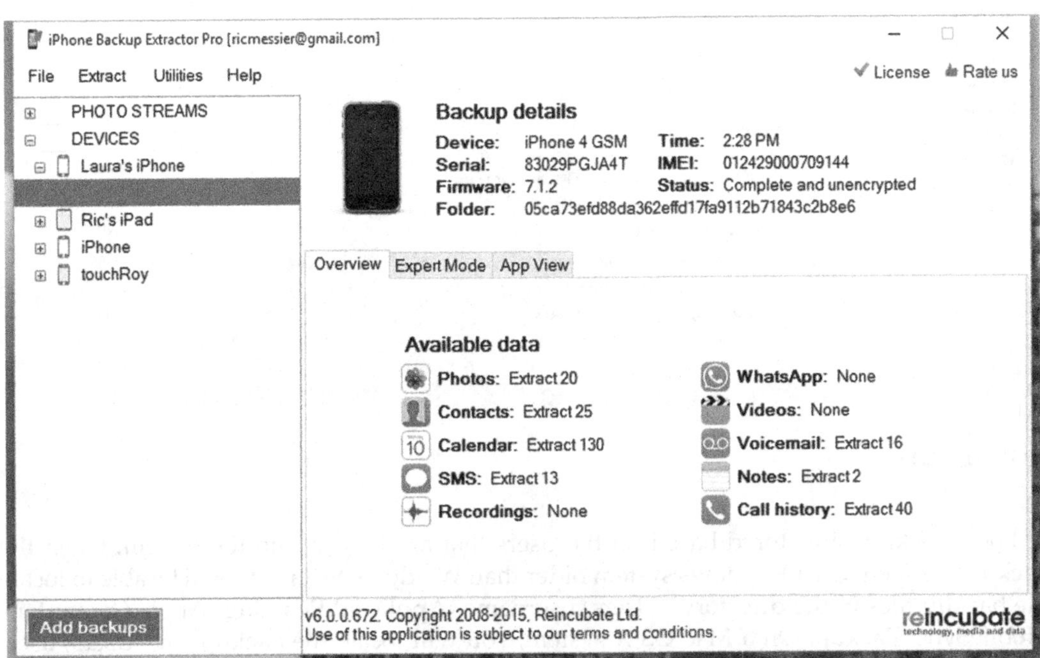

FIGURE 11.12

Once you have selected which backup you want to use, all you need to do is select which artifacts you want to extract. As an example, if you were to select the images, iPhone Backup Extractor would ask you where you wanted to store them and then extract the data for you onto your disk. Images will be extracted as images. In the case of voicemail, you will get a comma separated values file with call detail records for the voicemail messages. In this case, you will not get the audio files because the audio files associated with the voicemail are stored with the cell phone provider. They are not stored locally on the phone. However, the metadata related to the voicemail is stored because in the visual voicemail application, you can get the data about the voicemail so that data has to be stored locally on the phone. In order to listen to the voicemail, you have to connect to the cell phone provider to get the audio related to the message.

There is some data that may exist on an IOS device that may not show up in a backup. If the backup is not encrypted, any data created using the HealthKit API, which would be health data, will not be backed up.

iTunes is not only used for backups from the devices. Another feature that iTunes offers that may be of interest is the capability to automatically download applications and other media that you can purchase from the iTunes Store. While you can backup applications to your local computer, this particular feature means that you do not even need to sync your IOS device with your computer, if you have the automatic downloads feature on. This means that just by looking at the computer, you can determine what applications have been installed on the mobile device. This can give you some indication, without ever having looked at the mobile device, of other areas you may want to extend your investigation to. You may see social networking applications or dating applications or maybe even a note taking application like Evernote. Any one of these applications could provide you hints of other sources of information for your investigation.

Malware and Jailbreaking

Since, introducing the iTunes Store to allow third party applications to be installed on the device, Apple has tightly controlled access to the store. In order to submit an application, you have to register with Apple and have paid to be a developer. Paying Apple not only gets you early access to the software development kits and the operating systems, it also gives you the rights to submit applications to Apple. This does not automatically mean that your application will be added to the app store. Apple reviews application submissions to make sure that the application does what it purports to do, that it is not offensive and that it does not do anything malicious. Once it passes that review, Apple will add it to the App Store. That review process can be time consuming but one thing it does is provides a barrier for malicious developers to just get malicious applications into the App Store. This does not stop them from trying but it does provide a barrier that makes it harder and it does provide a gatekeeper in Apple. This is much like what Google does in protecting its Play Store.

At the moment of this writing, Apple's iTunes Store was recently hit with a number of applications that had been infected with malware. These applications managed to get through the review process, into the store and out to the users. Rather than introducing the malicious components directly into the software, they infected Xcode, which is the development environment Apple provides to develop applications for both Mac OS X and also IOS. Infecting the development environment meant that anyone using the malicious version of Xcode, which was not provided through an Apple source but instead was hosted by an external source in Asia, would have their application infected without their knowledge. While the barrier for malware on an IOS is fairly high, it is not impossible to get malware through. This particular example is not the only time it has happened. This just happened to have used a different entrance vector and several applications managed to get by Apple as a result. It is unlikely that this will be the last time malicious software gets through Apple's vetting process, so it is always useful to know about the potential for malicious software, no matter which device you are using.

Similarly, developers and researchers have been finding ways to break through Apple's protections, enabling the devices to be jailbroken. A lot of people like the Apple devices but wish that they had more control over their phones to do more and unlock more of its potential. Apple, of course, continuously fights against this, both by trying to make their software as impenetrable as possible and also by using legal means. When you jailbreak an IOS device, you will generally get an additional application store called Cydia. Cydia provides a large number of applications that you can install to extend the functionality of the device, as well as, allowing you to customize it more to your liking than Apple allows.

Apple has previously tried to suggest that anyone who attempts to jailbreak one of their phones is doing something illegal. The courts to date have not sided with Apple. At this point, it is still considered legal to find ways to jailbreak a device.

The challenge with performing a jailbreak on an IOS device is that you can add software that has not been vetted by Apple or, frankly, anyone else. You may have no idea what the software you are introducing actually does. Service providers have long complained about phones that have been jailbroken. They claim that a phone that has been jailbroken has the potential to harm their network. This has never been demonstrated. However, it is true that the applications in Cydia have provided a lot of capabilities to do things like spoof caller ID. This means that you can appear to be an entirely different caller, when you place a call. This behavior is now illegal in the United States, according to the Federal Communications Commission. Most of the applications that allowed for this to happen were removed. However, if you have a phone that has been jailbroken, it allows for the potential to install an illicit and illegal application that would let you do that.

Using iCloud

Typically, you may be most familiar with iCloud as a place to store your files. You can have multiple devices that can get access to the same files using iCloud. This is a storage capability like Google Drive or Microsoft SkyDrive. One thing about iCloud, though, that relates very specifically to mobile devices is that it can be used to store backups of IOS devices. Fortunately, you can use the same iPhone Backup Extractor that we discussed earlier to get access to the iCloud backups from all of your IOS devices. If you configured iCloud on your IOS device for backups, you can get to those backups using iPhone Backup Extractor. In Figure 11.13, you can see a collection of both local and iCloud backups on the left hand side and in the main frame of the application, you can see the details of one of the iCloud backups.

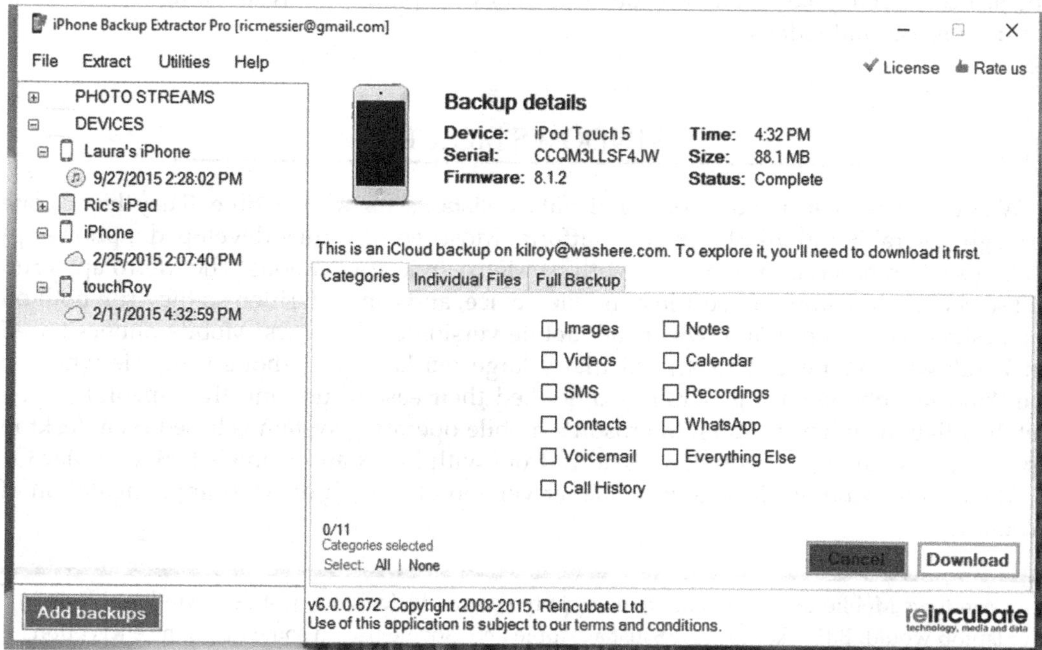

FIGURE 11.13

While it is very convenient to have a single application, which runs on both Windows and Mac OS X, that can extract IOS backups wherever they are, you need to provide credentials in order to get to iCloud backups. This may not be as helpful to an investigator unless you can get consent from the target of your investigation. If you can get consent, you can have them log into iCloud through iPhone Backup Extractor and you can grab the backups of their device. Unlike Google Drive or Microsoft's SkyDrive, you cannot just get a Web-based view to everything in your iCloud storage. iCloud relies on the specific applications. If I were to use iCloud on a Mac OS X device, I might be able to see my documents in the Finder. My contacts would also be stored in iCloud but I would not see the contacts in Finder. Similarly, I would not be able to find the backups. I need to use a program that is capable of interfacing with the iCloud APIs to get the backup data. Even if you cannot get consent, knowing that you can get to the mobile backup through Apple is helpful. It is also much harder to get to iCloud backups to delete them, even if you recognize that the backup is there. Local backups can be easily deleted if the user is aware that their device is being backed up. Apple has put all of the management of iCloud storage under their control, which can be beneficial for forensic investigators.

Just as with Google and its Photos application, Apple is using iCloud as a way to more permanently store photos for the user. This means that when photos are taken, they can be automatically uploaded to iCloud. This allows users to quickly and easily upgrade their phones to newer models, since they do not have to worry as much about backing up data on their phones because the backups are all handled automatically and when you get a new device, you just connect to your iCloud account and all of your photos are available again. The same is true of music and videos.

WINDOWS MOBILE

Windows has been making personal data assistants for a long time. They have gone through several iterations of a phone platform. Most recently, they developed a phone operating system based on Windows 8 with its Metro-style applications. The Metro apps run full screen, as you would expect in a mobile device, and can be written so they run both on the desktop version of Windows or the mobile version of Windows. Mobile phones based on Windows have never had a particularly large market share, though, people who use the Windows phone have generally really liked their ease of use and the capabilities you get. Just like the other vendors, Microsoft's mobile operating system is based on a desktop operating system. Just as with Google's Android with Linux and Apple's IOS with Mac OS X, Microsoft's Windows Mobile is a smaller version of the full desktop implementation of Windows.

Windows Mobile used BitLocker to encrypt the entire device store, just as a Windows desktop or laptop would. BitLocker uses AES just as Apple and Google use. In some cases, the encryption/decryption key may be escrowed (held safely) within an enterprise ActiveDirectory store.

Having said that, the file system in use on the phone is the same as that used on the desktop. Older versions of Microsoft's mobile operating system have used an implementation of the File Allocation Table (FAT), while the more recent Windows Mobile has used the New Technology File System (NTFS) just as the desktop version of the operating system has used. This makes it much easier to acquire data from the device and also locate data once you have an image of the system.

Just as with Android and IOS, Windows Mobile has a single user with a defined username. On Windows Mobile devices, the username is WPCOMMSSERVICES. If you were looking for contacts or SMS stores, as examples, you would need to look in \Users\WPCOMMSSERVICES\APPDATA\Local. \Users\WPCOMMSSERVICES is the home directory for the mobile user.

Similar to Google allowing phone backups to their online storage and Apple using iCloud, Microsoft will do backups of phones to your Microsoft online account. This means that your phone is storing your data with a service provider and the data can be acquired by requesting it of the service provider without even needing to touch the phone itself.

CONCLUSIONS

While it is possible to use any of the commercial tools such as Cellebrite, BlackLight, or Paraben to extract data from mobile devices, you can also use the interaction between a mobile device and a traditional computing device like a desktop or a laptop. Windows, Linux, and Mac OS X can all be used in different ways to gather data from the mobile devices. Since some of these devices have corresponding software on the desktop that can be used to interact with the mobile device, that software may leave behind artifacts like backups. If there is a backup left behind on the desktop, that backup could be used to view the data from the mobile device without needing to use the mobile device itself.

In many cases, your mobile device will be communicating with a cloud-based service. This could be the operating system itself by transmitting configuration information to Apple, Google, or Microsoft. It could be applications like Evernote storing notes and lists with the service provider. It could also be media files like photos that may be automatically uploaded to the cloud storage. This means that it is harder for users to get rid of photos, especially if they have multiple devices that are syncing with their iCloud account. Local caches of cloud storage data may be possible both on mobile devices but also on desktops, where the user is also connecting to the cloud storage providers.

The use of cloud storage for mobile devices is allowing for smaller storage sizes on the mobile devices. It is allowing for a lot of convenience on the part of the user. It is also providing a different way for forensic investigators to get access to data that they may not otherwise get access to. Even in cases where you do not have access to a mobile device, you may still be able to get data from the mobile device on a desktop because of backups and synchronization with a cloud storage account.

EXERCISES

1. Create an iPhone or iPad backup by plugging it into iTunes and starting a backup. Use iPhoneBackupExtractor to view the backed up data.
2. Use adb to extract the data from an Android device. Compress the result and obtain a hash of the resulting compressed file.

Bibliography

Epifani, M., Stirparo, P., 2015. Learning iOS Forensics: A Practical Hands-on Guide to Acquire and Analyze iOS Devices with the Latest Forensic Techniques and Tools. Packt Publishing, Birmingham, UK.

File system access, 2015. (accessed 27.09.2015.).

IOS Security, 2015. (accessed 27.09.2015.).

Kelly, G., 2014. Report: 97% of Mobile Malware is on Android. This is the Easy Way You Stay Safe. (accessed 26.09.2015.).

Report: 97% Of Mobile Malware Is On Android. This Is The Easy Way You Stay Safe. (2014, March 24). Retrieved October 18, 2015, from http://www.forbes.com/sites/gordonkelly/2014/03/24/report-97-of-mobile-malware-is-on-android-this-is-the-easy-way-you-stay-safe/.

Tamma, R., Tindall, D., 2015. Learning Android Forensics a Hands-on Guide to Android Forensics, From Setting up the Forensic Workstation to Analyzing Key Forensic Artifacts. Packt Publishing, Birmingham, England.

CHAPTER

12

Newer Technologies

INFORMATION INCLUDED IN THIS CHAPTER:

- Virtualization
- Cloud Computing
- Wearable Computing
- Drones

INTRODUCTION

The world of technology continues to march on, and on and on and on. This chapter represents a taste of things that your computers will interact with that may be new and interesting from a forensics perspective. This is by no means a comprehensive list and there is no suggestion here that there will not be something new tomorrow, next week, month, or year. Technology is always changing and companies are always looking for new devices that may be interesting. This means that there will always be new devices, operating systems, and toys to learn and get a handle on. The longer you are in the technology business, the more you will recognize opposing ends of a pendulum swing when it comes to technology. Mobile devices started off big because components had not been miniaturized yet. Then there was a move to really small and now, smartphones are swinging back the other way back to bigger. Every new mobile device that comes out seems to be just a little larger than the one from last year. That is just one example of a pendulum.

When the first computers were built they were, by necessity, very large. Additionally, they were very expensive. As a result, a lot of companies could not afford them. Certainly, no people were buying computers in the early days. Because of that, people had to go to the computer since it was centrally located. This continued for decades until smaller computers were created. The microcomputer, also called a personal computer, allowed individuals to have their own computers and more importantly, store their own information. Rather than relying on someone else to keep information safe, people could store their own information on floppy disks. Of course, this was not large volumes of data. If you had large volumes of data, you still needed a larger computer, commonly called a mainframe. The pendulum, though, was starting to swing toward decentralized computing and storage. There were, though, still a lot of computing and storage needs that could not be addressed by personal computers, so in the late 1980s and into the early 1990s, there was a swing back to centralized storage and computing using the personal computer as the access mechanism.

A swing back to decentralization with faster processors and bigger disks followed, and now we are swinging back to centralized computing and storage with a lot of companies moving toward using services that are "in the cloud" rather than ones that are local. As more data begins to be stored with service providers in the cloud, it has an impact on forensic investigators. Evidence that was previously easy to locate on local devices may not be local anymore. There may be hints of it, potentially, but it may be entirely stored with a service provider. That changes how you would perform the investigation. In most cases, these provider-computing services are operated through the use of virtual machines. This means that you can have what appear to be several computers running on a single piece of physical hardware. Each of these systems would be virtual, rather than physical. They exist only within the virtualization software and have no physical constructs themselves. Virtual machines can be run on everyday systems like you may have on your desktop or laptop. Knowing that these virtual machines exist on a system can be useful, since it would be a completely different set of locations that a user can store potential evidence in.

Another driver of "the cloud" is the increasing use of smartphones. Some device manufacturers, like Apple and Samsung, are eschewing larger storage devices in their devices in favor of streaming services or cloud storage. The less storage we get in our commonly used devices, the more we have to search off-device for places to store or music, pictures, video, and documents. Both Apple and Google are happy to have you offload your data onto their systems.

Of course, there are other computing devices that are starting to gain a lot of traction. Mobile processors are considerable faster and more capable than they have been previously, which means that you can put a computing device into your shoe or on your wrist. Of course, the computing device in the shoe, a la Maxwell Smart and his "Smart phone," is not a current product reality but devices on the wrist, like those used by Dick Tracy in the comic strips decades ago, are absolutely real. While they commonly use a mobile device like a smartphone or tablet for their storage and computing power. This means more information that is being pushed out to cloud storage, since some of these smart watches may include a camera, and pictures taken on these camera watches will get pushed out to the phone by default, since there is not a lot of storage in the watch itself and most of that is taken up by the watch operating system.

You do not even need a computing device to have something wearable that is capable of generating data. This data may get pushed to a smartphone or it may just get pushed up to a cloud storage solution. Pedometers, for example, are getting considerably smarter than they have been in the past. They have become activity monitors more than just a traditional pedometer. Additionally, there are a number of other devices like heart monitors and sleep monitors that you may strap on that are capable of monitoring your activities and behaviors. Even pets are getting wearable computing devices these days, including collars that will send out tweets or updates to Facebook. The point is that more and more, we will be generating information regarding our whereabouts and activities, as computing devices get smaller and more powerful. In all likelihood, this trend is something that a forensic practitioner should be aware of.

VIRTUALIZATION

As virtual machines are the underpinnings for at least some cloud computing services, it seems fitting to start with them. We already have a bit of a head start here, since we had talked about virtual memory earlier. Virtual memory is where you appear to have more memory than you really do. Since this may mean that you are oversubscribed in the memory department, it means that you have to have a place to offload memory contents when those contents are not in active use. The same is essentially true when we are talking about virtual machines. If you are using virtual machines, you are using hardware that does not exist, the same as you may have been using memory that did not really exist with virtual memory. In order to make that work, though, you need a piece of software that can take care of all requests to make use of hardware. That piece of software is called a hypervisor.

There are two types of hypervisors. The first type, Type I, runs on what is called the bare metal. This means that when the computer boots, it is the hypervisor that the system boots to. Some of the earliest virtual machine hypervisors were Type I hypervisors. IBM's VM/CMS operating system as well as its OS/360 operating system were examples of Type I hypervisors. The computer booted to the hypervisor and within the hypervisor, you constructed virtual machines that would then be booted within the hypervisor. The hypervisor would handle all hardware requests and either fulfill them directly or pass them off to the physical hardware, depending on the hardware request. A disk request, for example, may get handled by the hypervisor itself, since the "disk" may actually simply be a file in the physical filesystem. As a result, the hardware request to get access to the disk would be handled by the hypervisor and translated into a file request to the physical disk. VMWare's ESX server line is another example of a Type I hypervisor.

The second type of hypervisor, a Type II hypervisor, is one you may be more commonly used to. VMWare Player and Workstation, as well as Parallels Desktop and VirtualBox are all examples of a Type II hypervisor. This means that there is a host operating system that the hypervisor runs on top of. The hypervisor still handles requests (which may be called interrupts in the case of hardware requests) from the guest operating system and then makes requests of the host operating system as necessary. This means that the hypervisor is acting like a proxy for the guest operating system, since it cannot directly handle requests on its own as in the case of a Type I hypervisor.

There are probably many ways to visualize these two types of hypervisor. One way of looking at it is in Figure 12.1. If you think of it like a stack, the hardware is always on the bottom. In a Type I hypervisor, the hypervisor sits right on top of the hardware. In a Type II hypervisor, there is an operating system like Windows, Linux, or Mac OS X that sits directly on the hardware. No matter which type of hypervisor you have, the guest operating systems will always run on top of the hypervisor. You could also think about it as a series of concentric circles as well. The hypervisor on a Type I hypervisor runs inside of the physical hardware then the guest operating systems would run inside of the hypervisor. Each inside layer is contained within the layer just outside. However you want to think about it, all of the different pieces are interrelated.

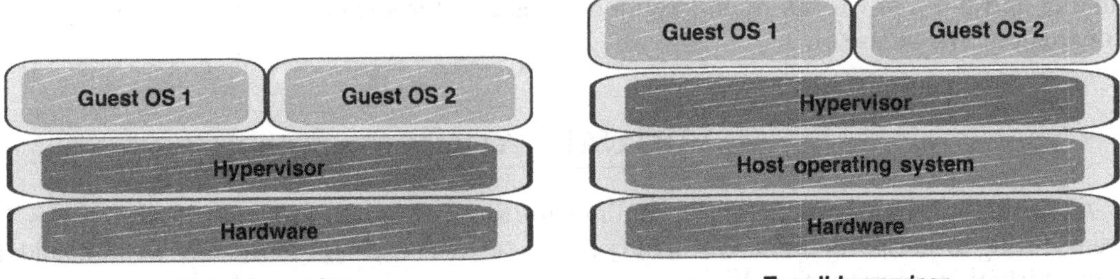

FIGURE 12.1

From the standpoint of the user, there would be no difference in terms of the functionality of the guest operating systems. Windows would still be Windows and Linux would still be Linux. The one place where it may make a difference is for Mac OS X, but the same restriction exists, no matter whether you are running inside of a virtual machine or not. Mac OS X will not install or run on non-Apple hardware without modification. If you are running a Mac OS X virtual machine, you are either running it inside of a hypervisor that is running on a Macintosh of some sort or else the operating system has been altered in order to run on non-Apple hardware. This includes creating special kernel extensions that are capable of tricking the operating system to start and operate correctly. Even then, as long as the modifications have been made correctly, the user would not have any particular idea that they were in a virtual machine.

This does not mean that you cannot determine that you are running inside of a virtual machine, though. The quickest and easiest way is generally to look at your network interfaces. Your media access control (MAC) address will be one that belongs to the vendor of your hypervisor. The first three octets (bytes) of the MAC address are the organizationally unique identifier (OUI). You can look up this OUI to determine the vendor of the interface. This OUI should resolve to VMWare, Parallels or Oracle, if you are using one of the common hypervisors for personal computers. Most hypervisors will also have a set of tools that get installed within the guest operating system. This enables functionality like copying files to and from the guest from inside the host, dragging and dropping into and out of the guest operating system and other features. The virtual machine will still operate perfectly without these tools, so the lack of these tools installed is not a good indication that you are not running inside of a virtual machine.

On a Windows system, you can check registry settings from inside of your virtual machine to determine that you are in a virtual machine. One of the easiest places you will find evidence of the use of a virtual machine is in the drivers. Searching for the word Parallels in a Windows virtual machine that is inside of Parallels Desktop turned up a number of locations. The first locations and most predominant were in the driver database. One of the drivers that was found is shown in Figure 12.2. Most of the hardware devices that are in use on the system are provided by the hypervisor so it makes sense that the drivers for those devices would have some sort of reference to the hypervisor itself.

Generally, the only reason you as a forensic investigator should need to know whether this is a virtual machine or not is if you are simply provided with a disk image without additional information. In most cases, this will not be the case. You will have access to the system where

Name	Type	Data
(Default)	REG_SZ	oem27.inf
ImportDate	REG_BINARY	70 bc cc 30 33 f3 d0 01
InfName	REG_SZ	prl_dd.inf
OemPath	REG_SZ	C:\Program Files (x86)\Parallels\Parallels Too...
Provider	REG_SZ	Parallels
SignerName	REG_SZ	Parallels, Inc.
SignerScore	REG_DWORD	0x0f000000 (251658240)
StatusFlags	REG_DWORD	0x0000001a (26)
Version	REG_BINARY	00 ff 09 00 00 00 00 00 68 e9 36 4d 25 e3 ce...

FIGURE 12.2

the virtual machine is installed. However, if you are provided just a disk image, it can be useful to know whether it is a physical system or whether it is a virtual machine.

Recognizing a system that has a hypervisor installed should be an easy task. You would see not only the hypervisor as software that was installed but you should also see the virtual machines, which are typically stored in the home directory of the user. This is different on a Linux system, where the actual virtual machines may be stored in a directory underneath the /var directory. Each virtual machine will commonly be a collection of files. You will generally be interested in the virtual disk file or files. In a VMWare installation, the disk files will have a file name that has a .vmdk extension. This extension is the same regardless of the platform you are running VMWare on. You may also be interested in the.vmem file as well as the .vss file, when you are looking at a virtual machine.

If you are looking at a Mac OS X system, you may run across Parallels Desktop as the hypervisor. On a Mac OS X system, you will find that the Parallels virtual machine looks like a single file with a .pvm extension. In fact, this is a bundle just as an application on a Mac OS X system is. If you open up the .pvm bundle by either control clicking or right-clicking and selecting Show Package Contents, you will see all of the files that are associated with the virtual machine. Inside the package, you will find the hard drive with the extension .hdd. In fact, this is also a bundle rather than being a regular file. Inside that bundle, there is a collection of files that describe the hard drive and also have the contents of the hard drive. The .hds file will be the file you are looking for that contains the actual data contents of the virtual hard disk.

One advantage to using VMWare as your hypervisor is that many forensic tools are natively able to handle the .vmdk format. You can import it into tools like EnCase ,as an example. Other tools and utilities are similarly able to handle.vmdk files, as though they were normal disk images that you had acquired using traditional disk acquisition tools like dd or the other acquisition tools available in commercial tools like FTK Imager.

Malware, as noted, can detect the existence of a virtual machine. Once it has detected that it has been installed inside a virtual machine, it may alter its behavior. It may choose to go dormant and not do anything. It may also decide to attack the host system, which may allow it to gain control over multiple virtual machines.

CLOUD COMPUTING

Cloud computing is a fairly vague term. The idea of something being "in the cloud" is a reference to network diagrams. If you are drawing a network using a diagramming tool like Microsoft Visio, you will invariably come to a place, where you want to convey the idea that there is something without getting into the specifics. Commonly, this is anytime an Internet connection is needed. There are cloud images that are used. You cannot really see into a cloud but you know there are edges to it and you can sometimes clearly see where the edges are. Something that enters the cloud essentially disappears from the perspective of someone looking from the outside. Eventually, it appears on the other side just as it entered, though perhaps slightly damper than when it went in. The same is true if you are developing a network diagram. You need to have something to designate an object where data passes through without being impacted, so it can then come out the other side. It is this amorphous, squishiness that we are referring to when we make use of a cloud as an analogy.

In fact, when we are talking about "in the cloud" in reference to data or computing services, we are really talking about the services that are offered by a service provider. "In the cloud" really means that it is stored with a service provider somewhere (we do not really care and may not even know) and not on our premises at all. Cloud services will almost always be offered using Web technologies. This means that one of these cloud services will be offered and accessed just the way you would any other Web page that you went to. Administration, management, billing, configuration, and consumption of the service will all be handled through a Web interface. This is part of what has allowed these services to become so popular. Web technologies are well-understood, are allowed through security infrastructure like firewalls and mature enough that complex functions can be performed both in the browser and also in the interaction with the server at the service provider.

There are a number of different types of cloud services. You can rent computing time from a service provider, giving you virtual infrastructure with a few clicks of your mouse. You can make use of an application through a Web interface, using the storage and infrastructure of the providing company. You can also just use raw storage for very little money. In fact, in some cases, the lower end options are free, making them very enticing to many users. Once you really start using their service, they start charging money for more usage of course. The convenience, speed, and reliability of these services, assuming you have selected reliable providers, is very enticing to a lot of people.

One of the challenges with service providers is that they are generally located in a different jurisdiction from the suspect. The location of the data may be in an entirely different jurisdiction. This means that you may run into jurisdictional issues that you should be aware of. When you obtain the data from the provider, you need to be aware of both the chain of custody and also how you can verify what you get.

Infrastructure as a Service

Infrastructure as a Service (IaaS) is where you are purchasing computing power for very little cost. This service is typically provided using virtual machines on the service provider side. IaaS allows you to very quickly acquire, provision, and enable a computer with an operating system that you choose installed on it. The advantage to doing this with a service provider is that if you were to do it yourself, you may need to buy the computer, wait for it to arrive, install the operating system you want (even if there is an operating system on it, you should have an image that you prefer to use with specific features enabled and others disabled), get it racked' and stacked in your data center, powered on … Well, you get the idea. It could be a very long time. Even if you have a physical system in place, it will still take time. Okay, we are talking about physical systems here and it is not really a fair comparison, since the service providers are using virtual machines. Faster provisioning, right? Well, yes. Faster than a physical system but even if you have a snapshot or copy of a virtual machine you want to use to start from, you still need to copy it into place and configure it the way you want with a new name, new MAC address, and memory settings if you want something different and anything else that may be specific to what you are doing with the new virtual machine.

In the case of a service provider, you have a Web interface, you can select the operating system you want, as you can see in Figure 12.3 from the creation of a new Amazon EC2 instance, and very quickly get the system up and running. It is all automated. Unless you are doing a lot of virtual machine creation, you probably have not spent the time to automate your provisioning process. On top of that, you probably do not have the choice of multiple geographic locations, multiple system sizes, and also the infrastructure, a company like Amazon or Google has in place. These are companies that have built their businesses around a lot of computing devices so they have power redundancy, network redundancy, network failovers, backups, redundant hardware, and a lot of other very expensive protections. Make use of the money someone else has spent to make your service more reliable.

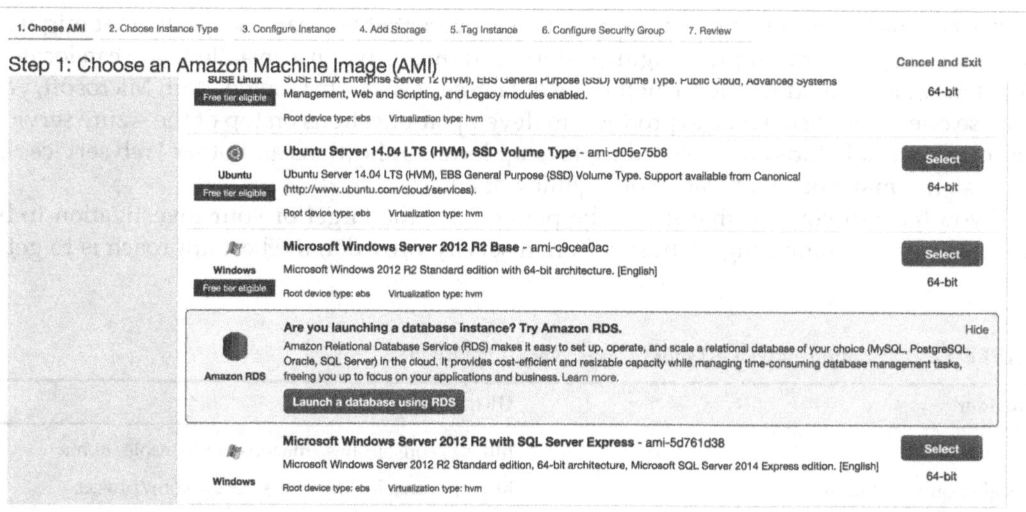

FIGURE 12.3

This is the internal discussion someone may have, especially, if they are working at a business and want to save some money. It can be quite a bit cheaper over the long run to make use of a service provider for your computing services simply because they are sharing the costs of some very pricey data center real estate, once you have factored in network, floor space, power, failovers, redundancies, etc. Businesses are not the only ones using this model, though. It is so cheap, in fact free in some cases, that anyone can make use of the service to launch pretty much anything they want. Once they have a system, they could establish a Web server to serve up whatever content they wanted to. They also have a lot of really cheap computing cycles. Some enterprising folks have used these computing platforms to sell password-cracking services. You pay someone money, they use really cheap computing cycles on some very fast machines in someone else's data center, and you end up with cracked passwords from a file of password hashes. Since there are a number of pieces of software that will perform these cracks and that software is very easy to get your hands on, this is a very easy business model, especially if you can write a Web interface that will allow someone to feed you a file and take payment for processing the file. You barely have to be involved.

These sorts of activities are easy to accomplish using the Amazon EC2 engine, Google Compute Engine, Microsoft Azure, or a number of other lesser-known services. And, as pointed out previously, cheap and easy to get up and running quickly. Since the activity takes place with a service provider, it is a little harder to immediately attach it to a specific user. The evidence located on the users desktop or laptop will not be the actual content like images, videos, payment systems, or other types of similar content that could be considered illegal. The evidence you will find locally will be subtler but still there. You will be looking at their browsing habits. There will be references to access to the various URLs associated with the consoles for each of the services. Table 12.1 will show you the different URLs, you may look for in browsing history to show that the user has been accessing IaaS providers and may have computing infrastructure with one of these providers.

The Google Compute Engine also provides software that you can use locally that might be used to manage your Compute Engine instances. If this software is installed, you can locate it and it may also provide evidence of the use of IaaS services from Google. With Microsoft, you can use one of the Visual Studio products to develop applications on top of the Azure service. Of course, Visual Studio is also used to develop local applications and other Web services so its existence may not be indicative of anything at all.

If you have discovered that it may be possible for the target of your investigation to be using one of the computing platforms from a service provider, the best approach is to get a

TABLE 12.1 Administrative URLs for Cloud Computing Providers

Provider	URL
Amazon EC2	https://console.aws.amazon.com/console/home
Google Compute Engine	https://console.developers.google.com/project
Microsoft Azure	https://manage.windowsazure.com

subpoena. With the right justification, these companies will provide you the evidence you are asking for. They are all used to getting these legal instruments on a regular basis and they will have a team of people who handled these sorts of requests. Providers of the size of Google, Amazon, and Microsoft get a lot of these sorts of requests. If you are ever concerned about how to handle interactions with them, you can look it up. Locating the transparency report from these service providers will generally take you to a page, where you can not only get statistics, as you can see in Figure 12.4, but also you can generally get their standard processes and procedures.

FIGURE 12.4

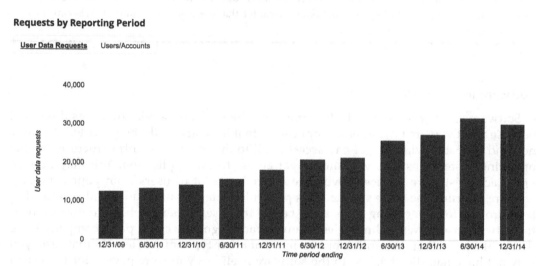

More and more providers are providing these transparency reports, primarily so users know, how many requests are being processed by the provider each month. We are looking at service providers for computing services specifically now but the requests they receive span the range of all of their user-focused services. Other services, like Facebook, also provide transparency reports. There are variations in what the data looks like, of course. Microsoft, for example, breaks out their information by country while Google primarily just provides aggregated data. You will notice from the graph in Figure 12.4 that the requests have been going up, since they started tracking this information. The last bar is not as long only because it was acquired partway through the reporting period.

Related to IaaS, but slightly different, is Platform as a Service (PaaS). For the purposes of what we are talking about here, they are essentially the same thing. Instead of a raw operating system image, the PaaS system will have an entire Web development stack on it including, potentially, a database server, Web server, application server, and any necessary languages that may be used. This may include scripting languages or it may be runtime platforms for Microsoft's .NET or Oracle's Java. Ultimately, they will look very similar if not identical from the perspective of the user's system and anything you may need to do from a forensic investigation, so there is not much reason to go into great detail about what PaaS is and how it specifically differs from IaaS.

One advantage to browsers and applications storing passwords is that if you get access to the computer system these cloud services are accessed from, you should be able to just connect to the cloud service. This, of course, requires that the scope of your warrant or subpoena allows you to get access. You may not necessarily need to issue a subpoena or warrant to a service provider, if you can just connect to the service from the suspect's computer. This is an area to be careful of, though. You may run into issues of data alteration and proof that the data has not been altered. If you obtain the data from the service provider, you can better guarantee that there is no data alteration because you are getting it directly from the source.

Software as a Service

Software as a Service (SaaS) is different from the previous service offerings discussed because what you are buying is an application that is hosted with the provider. You may not, and probably will not, get any access at all to the underlying infrastructure like the operating system. Instead, you simply get access to the application. You may be provided administrative services if you are managing a lot of users from your company, who are all using the same service. This particular category of cloud-based services has been around for a very long time. Long before these services were being delivered over the network using Web technologies. Many decades ago, you could pay a company to do things like payroll or accounting or a number of other types of services. In that case, you may not have had direct access to the software itself but you were paying for the use of the software and the outcome from the use of the software. You may have used one of these companies, sometimes called service bureaus, for very specific, infrequent functions like sorting and purging mailing lists in order to print labels for catalogs that the service bureau may also do.

Now, of course, the software on offer is varied. Often, you will find business-related software offered as a service. Customer Relations Management (CRM) software can be difficult for companies to install and offer themselves so this is a common offering. You may run into Salesforce.com as SaaS offering that is used a lot. Almost anything that you can get as a piece of software to run locally can be run remotely now with both the application and the associated data stored on a system in a data center at a service provider. In fact, Google offers companies the ability to use their services for mail, calendar, and storage. In addition, Google offers an App Marketplace for SaaS offerings that are integrated with Google. If you have a Google for Business account, you can go to the App Marketplace and add these applications onto your account, so all you need to do is go to your Google account to get access to everything. There are hundreds of applications that are available. You can see some of the categories as well as some of the applications in Figure 12.5. While Google has made it easier through the use of application programming interfaces (APIs) and, more importantly, authentication services, these are services that were generally available outside of what Google was doing.

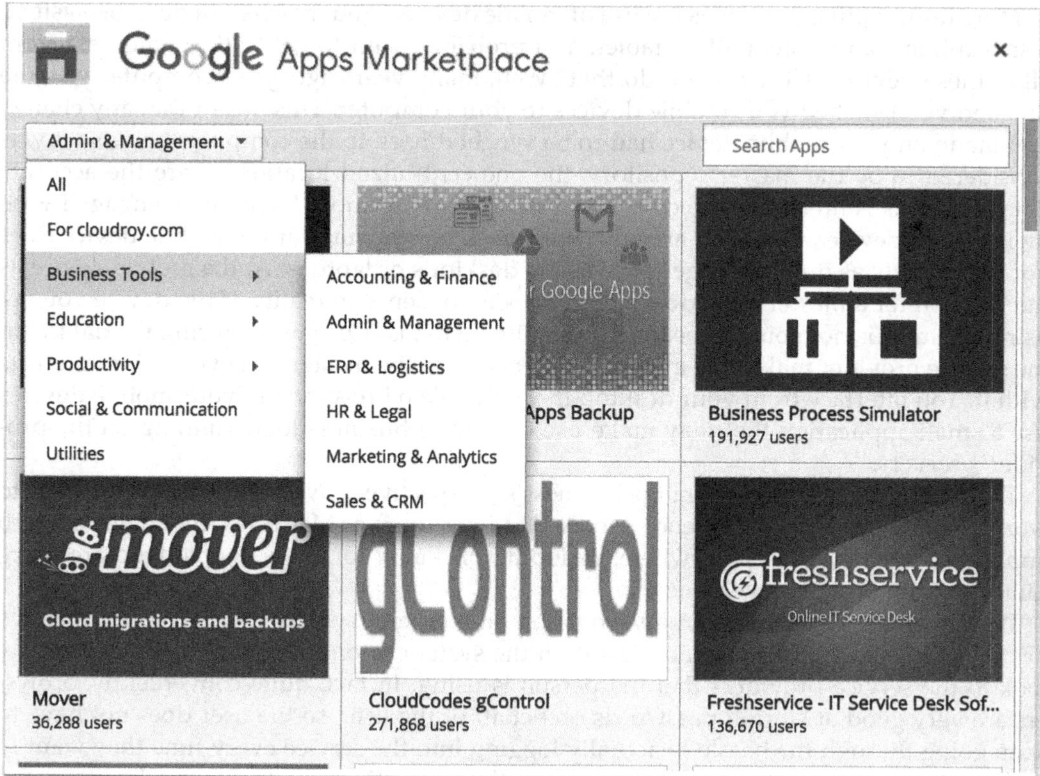

FIGURE 12.5

Why does SaaS matter to a forensic investigator? For a start, you should recognize that economic crimes may not have evidence on the perpetrator's system. They may be doing all of their accounting using a service provider. This means that all of their business data may be stored only with the service provider and nothing will be stored locally. Intuit, for instance, offers their various accounting and bookkeeping software through a Web interface, where the data is stored with them. The same can be true for individuals as well as businesses. Intuit owns Mint, which is a business that used their storage and infrastructure to keep track of personal finances.

Why is software as a service such a big thing now? For a start, it is a lot more convenient and doable now than it ever was in the past. Large chunks of the population now have reasonably fast Internet connections. They are using browsers that can handle complex applications being developed and run inside of them. Storage has become cheap, so it is easier for these service providers to go and get a large amount of storage and then use that storage to keep their customer's information. On top of that, there is very little risk to the business if they are breached and the customer information is lost. A lot of upside with very little downside in terms of liability for the provider.

More importantly, though, is the use of mobile devices. You may have a desktop system, a smartphone, and potentially a tablet. You probably want to get to the same data from all of these devices. How do you do that? Well, many years ago, your computer was the hub and you synched your mobile devices to your computer. This meant that any change you made on your mobile device had to be synched back to the computer because it was considered to be the master repository, the one centralized location where the accurate data was. This is no longer the case. Some people are far more likely to be engaged with their mobile devices than they are with their desktop system. But the mobile device does not have nearly as much storage space as the desktops or laptops. And a mobile device as the location for a master copy does not make a lot of sense in reality. If the device you are using the most is not going to be the master, then what is? Of course, storing the data with the service provider makes the most sense. It becomes the master and everything interacts with it. You interface from your desktop through a Web browser and your mobile devices use a small application that may make use of a lot of business logic running on the provider's servers.

This makes a lot of sense from the business's perspective as well. They no longer have to worry about limiting their audience to only Windows users or Mac users. If you write a Web application, you can run everywhere, including on Linux for those people who are using Linux for their desktop. Everyone wins.

When you are performing an investigation on a system and looking for some sensitive or critical information and do not find it on the system or on the mobile device, you may look to the service providers that the person is using. In fact, quite conveniently, browsers are very good at storing passwords on behalf of the user, so the user does not have to keep going through the hassle of actually logging into the service every time they want to make use of it. Instead, browser will populate the credentials into the page when the page is presented and all the user has to do is click the Login button. Simple, right? Except that this means that you may be able to recover passwords in cleartext from the user's system in order to gain access to their cloud services. Apple makes this particularly easy using their Keychain Access utility that is always installed on a Mac OS system. You can see Keychain Access in Figure 12.6. If you know the user's password, you can quickly and easily retrieve Web passwords, application passwords, and wireless passwords using Keychain Access. If you open up one of the individual items you see in the list in Keychain Access then enter the user's password, Keychain Access will show you the cleartext password that has been stored.

In addition to looking for passwords, you should also be doing the usual browser-based investigation of looking through history and bookmarks to see where the user has been or where they are going. Once you have evidence that your suspect is making use of a service provider for some critical function, you can issue a subpoena or a warrant to the service provider and they will be expected to produce the evidence you are requesting. As always, you have to have a reasonable basis for requesting the information. If what you are asking makes sense, the service provider will have what you need and will provide it to you. Larger companies should be used to these sorts of requests, while smaller providers may take longer or be less aware of their obligations in this regard.

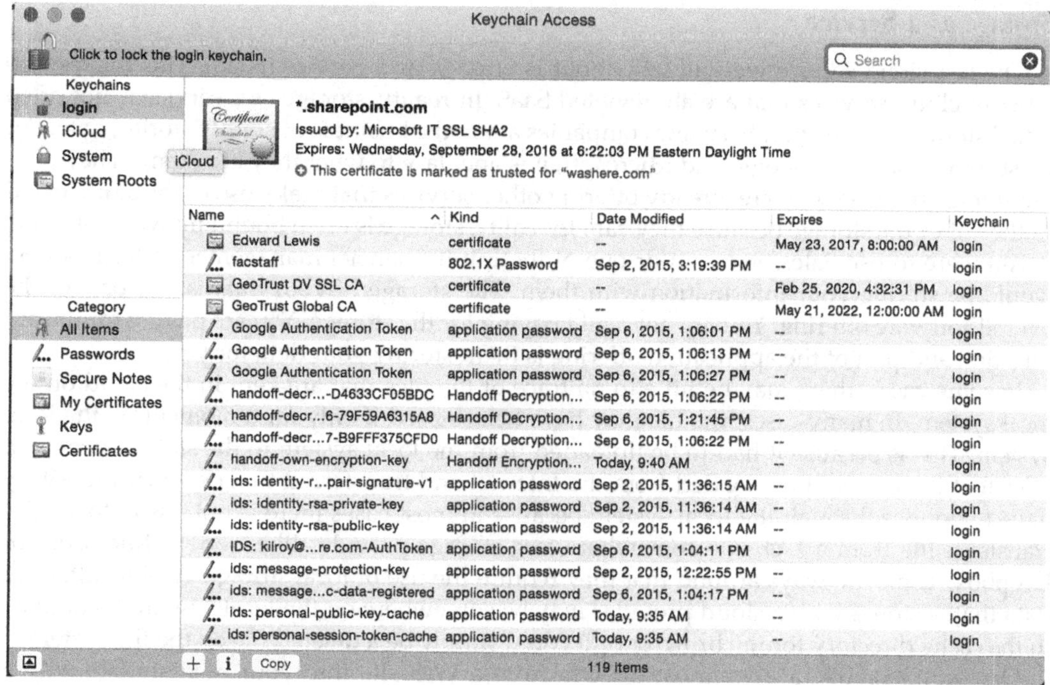

FIGURE 12.6

You may find that you cannot find evidence of the use of these services on the computer, in spite of a suspicion that they are using a cloud-based service. Browsers can be configured to clear history and caches, making it much harder to determine where the user has been going. They may also be using The Onion Router (TOR), which is a private browsing service. No evidence is stored locally as to what the user has been doing and all requests and responses to Web sites are routed out through the TOR network, meaning that they are routed through different systems of users who are also using the TOR network. This can make it much harder to determine what they are up to. One place you can still resort to is their mobile device. They may have an application loaded that gives them access to their accounts or information. If you are obtaining a warrant or subpoena for service provider data, you should also make sure the request covers mobile data as well.

One product that happens to be very good about locating information about these services is Internet Evidence Finder (IEF). IEF is a commercial product but they will do a good job of categorizing their findings for you, which makes it a lot easier to quickly locate what you are searching for. Rather than getting a long list of Web sites someone has visited, IEF will give you categories of data that you can look through to get to the actual evidence faster.

Storage as a Service

The last cloud service we will talk about is Storage as a Service (SaaS). This makes two types of cloud services that are abbreviated SaaS. In reality, storage as a service is not often called storage as a service. Very few companies are in the business of simply storing data. For most companies, like Google and Microsoft, it is ancillary to what they are doing. They offer the storage because they are already offering other services that make use of the storage and so they offer the storage because they can. In reality, storage is often bound up with software. If you were to use Salesforce.com or one of the Intuit financial management offerings, you would be storing your information with them. The storage of your data is just part of the overall software offering. You are not really paying for the storage. You are paying for the application and part of the application offering is them storing your data for you.

In some cases, there may be little to no trace of the files that are kept in the cloud on the local system. In many cases, the file may have been stored if only for a moment on the local system. This is because it had to be uploaded from the local system to the storage provider. Files that have been downloaded from the Internet and transferred to a personal repository have to bounce through the local system because in most cases there is not a way to simply transfer a file from a Web site somewhere to a storage provider like Google, Microsoft, or Dropbox. There are ways around that they require the use of local storage. As a result, even data that is stored with a cloud provider may be somewhere on the local system. It could be in the cache directory for the browser or it could simply be a deleted file on the file system.

One way to move a file almost directly from a Web site into your own storage with a service provider is to use a local application. In Figure 12.7, you can see the Apple Finder on a Mac OS X system. Along the left-hand side, you can see both iCloud Drive and Google Drive. These are folders on the local system that are used as drop boxes for files that you want to be sent to the respective service provider. If I were to download a file into the Google Drive folder on my system, there is an application that is running, watching changes to that folder in order to make the same changes within the storage at the service provider. Above the Finder window, you can see a section of the top menu bar. The icon that is third from the left that looks a bit like a triangle is the Google Drive application running, performing a sync of the files on Google Drive with those on my local system and vice versa. Any file that gets dropped into that folder will simultaneously exist both on my local hard drive and in my Google Drive account. If a user has these applications installed in order to keep their data synchronized, the files will always be kept on the local file system. If the Google Drive app is running, it will be monitoring both the Google Drive storage as well as the local storage to make sure they are in sync.

Google and Apple are not the only service providers who have these sorts of applications, of course. There are a lot of storage providers and some of them have applications for the different operating systems that will keep local storage and cloud storage in sync. Dropbox and Microsoft both have their own applications, for instance. Microsoft has OneDrive, formerly SkyDrive that it offers to users. Interestingly, Microsoft makes a distinction between their OneDrive for Business and their OneDrive that they just offer to regular users. They use two different applications for their business and consumer OneDrive offerings, meaning that you cannot connect to a non-business account from their OneDrive for Business application and vice versa.

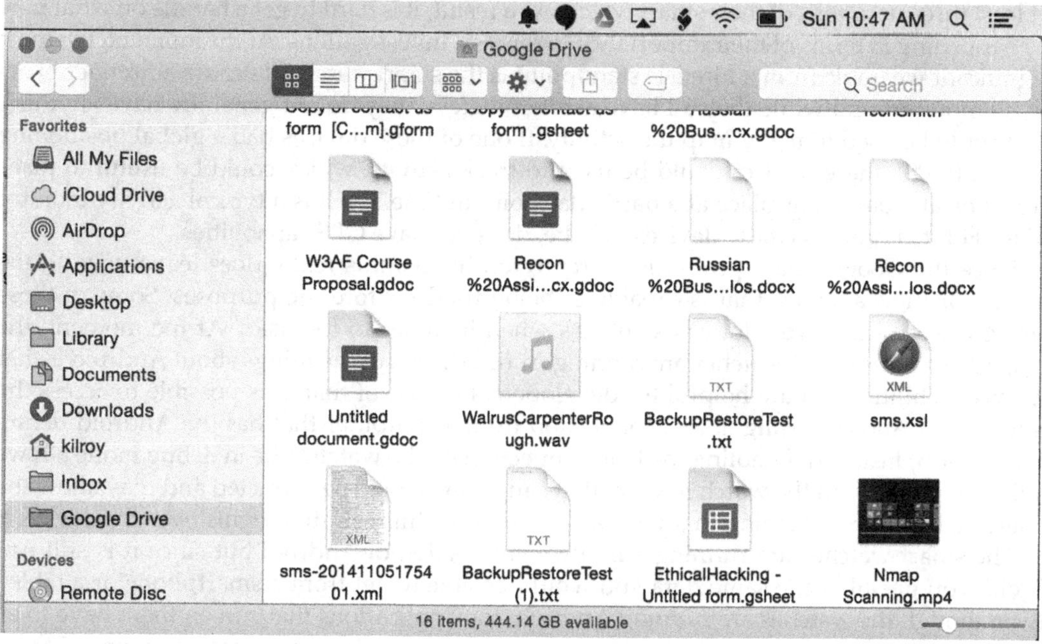

FIGURE 12.7

When you are performing an investigation on a system that has used cloud services, it is important to remove the system from the network. If the system is connected to the network, changes in the storage at the service provider may alter the local storage. Programs like Evernote, for example, will create a local cache of data from the service provider but that cache will change as information is changed with the service provider.

Users do not have to make use of these special client programs in order to keep their data synchronized. All of them have traditional Web interfaces and it is perfectly reasonable to expect that users will only use the Web interface to interact with their files. Some of the storage providers will have file viewers, so you do not ever have to download the file to look at it. This may be especially useful for image or video files that you will not be altering, so there is no particular reason to have a copy locally. If you can view the file through the Web interface to the storage provider, that may be all that you need.

WEARABLES

This particular category is in a state of considerable flux. You may have noticed this with the introduction and subsequent dropping of Google Glass, as well as the rapid introduction of new watches on the Android side. Samsung, at the time of this writing, has gone through at least three iterations of their smart watch. As a result, it is hard to get a handle on what may be happening in terms of their importance to forensic investigations. At the moment, the most significant wearable from a forensic standpoint is the smart watch. There are a number of activity monitors and while they all have accelerometers, they do not generally have anything that could be used to really map the activity. If one of these devices had a global positioning system (GPS), these devices could be used to track activity, which could be useful to place someone at a particular place at a particular point in time. As, it is a typical activity monitor like a Fitbit, as good as these devices may be, does not have GPS capabilities.

Since the Google Glass project is currently on hiatus, this really does leave us with the smart watch as a device that is capable of being used for forensic purposes. Some of these smart watches do have a lot of usefulness when it comes to forensics. At the moment, the majority of these smart watches are running Android. One of the things about Android is that it has capabilities that are helpful for developers. Because of that, it is possible to access the internals of Android using a USB connection from a computer that has the Android debug bridge (adb) installed. Enabling the USB connection on the watch to be in debug mode allows adb to interface with the watch in ways that can allow data to be extracted and may allow the watch to be rooted, meaning that you can obtain full administrative rights over the device.

The smart watches are running a lightweight version of Android but since it is still Android, you get all of the same data you would be able to get from a smartphone or a tablet. Even though the watches are running Android, the applications that run on them have to be custom designed for the watch. You cannot run just any Android application on one of these smart watches. While Samsung may have been first, they are not the only one and while the first watch was running Android, it was not using Android Wear, which is software from Google designed specifically for wearables. Android Wear is still essentially Android, but it offers some additional APIs as well as introducing the Google Now notification cards. As a result, you end up with a watch that will offer you quick hints about weather, meetings, sports scores, and other useful pieces of information. Generally, the Android watches rely on the phone in order to get information. The watch does not do much on its own, though it is capable of storing information.

Samsung has its own operating system that they have also deployed to smart phones called Tizen. Tizen watches behave a lot like the Android watches, though it is a different operating system. One of the big differences with the Tizen watches is that there are applications that will run directly on the watch rather than relying as much on the phone for all of the information. Samsung actually offers a watch that can function as a phone all by itself. It is capable of connecting to the cellular network without relying on the phone at all. It can also connect to wireless networks, so it really is capable of standing on its own. The advantage here, from a forensics standpoint, is that the watch itself may actually have its own call logs that are different from those that the phone has.

Android devices are not the only smart watches out there, even if you count the Tizen watches that communicate with Android devices. Apple also has their own watch, based on iOS and at this point they are already on a second generation of the watch software within a handful of months of the initial watch being available. The Apple watch is capable of most of the same types of functionality that the Android watches are capable of. This means that you will get notifications about phone calls, messages, and other communications. The one thing that is different about these watches is that you would not connect a watch to a computer and get backups as you might with a smartphone. This is primarily because while they are capable of storing information and maintaining some amount of data, they are not designed to be storage devices. Any data that is on the watch would be temporary.

DRONES

A drone is really just a remote control flying device. Where remote control devices have been around for decades, it has become popular to introduce intelligence into the device allowing them to be controlled with smartphones or other mobile devices. More and more, these devices are getting high-resolution cameras or at least are capable of supporting a high-resolution camera as a carry-along device. While a remote control flying device may simply be an annoyance if not used responsibly, when you add cameras, it becomes an entirely different situation altogether and a potential for illegal activities. This is not to suggest that drones themselves are or even should be illegal. However, like a lot of other new technologies, it opens doors for bad people to be doing bad things. A drone could easily be used to spy on people or companies. It can look into windows that you would not otherwise be able to look into. This is a challenge and there is a very good chance that there will be cases of these drones being used for illegal activities, which means that the drones themselves will need to be investigated as evidence.

There are a wide variety of drones with a lot of different capabilities. Some of them may simply stream video back to the controller, which may mean there is nothing on the device itself. A drone like the Parrot BeBop, though, has 8 gigabytes of storage on board and the device itself actually runs Android. Additionally, it has a USB connector, allowing you to plug your drone into your computer to extract data that is being stored on the drone. The BeBop has high-resolution video that is stored locally on the device. It is also capable of snapping photos that are also stored on the device. Fortunately, extracting this data is really easy, since it acts just like an Android device. You can plug it into a Windows system and it will show up as though it were a USB drive. Plugging it into a Mac OS X system requires the Android File Transfer program to extract files from it. However, they are sitting there as video and image files. There is nothing secret or fancy about any of it.

The one thing that is really interesting about a drone like the BeBop is that it has GPS built into it. This means that it is capable of storing flight data. In addition to the video, you will also get location information as an artifact from these drones. The GPS data is not always stored, since it is up to the operator to enable and disable the GPS capability but the fact that the drone is capable of storing this flight data makes it forensically significant.

Video cameras are everywhere. Closed circuit cameras are not only used for police work to keep streets safe but are used in homes as well. At the time of this writing, I am looking at Samsung Smartcam across the room. Because home Internet connections are protected behind network address translation, which makes it harder for remote users to get direct access to devices on the inside of the network, these cameras by Samsung, Withings, Nest, and a number of other manufacturers, will generally use a facility like cloud storage that will allow people to get access to the video from wherever they are in the world. Home security cameras are really an extension of the Web cameras (webcams) that have been used for years. These cameras have long been available online and often they do not require passwords.

Video forensics is a whole subset of forensics, which requires knowledge of the codecs that are used to encode the video into a digital format. In addition to codecs, you have multiple containers. A container is a way of organizing the structure of the video and connecting the video to the audio. The container is the file format, put another way. Just as with many other forensics problems, you have to be worried about alteration of the video. This attention to the challenges of video is relevant to home security cameras, drones and anywhere else you are looking at video evidence. This is similar to the problems with alteration of photos or other graphic images. The difference with video is that there is audio associated and the audio has to be synced to the video. Additionally, where you may have one image or even a handful to worry about with photos, when we talk about video, you are talking about dozens of images every second, all in the correct order. These are some serious challenges with video forensics that you should be aware of.

CONCLUSIONS

Technology is constantly changing. Where forensics has been focused on locating information on physical systems and in some cases has found challenges there, technology is starting to shift so that evidence may no longer be located on the local device. More and more, important information is being stored with service providers. This may simply be files that the user wants to be able to access no matter where they are, but it could also be a way to offload potentially incriminating information, hoping that there would be no way to associate the data with its actual owner.

Our computers are becoming so powerful and fast that we are not coming anywhere near to taxing their processing power. As a result, you can run multiple virtual machines on a single physical machine and still not push the system to its limits very often. It also gives you a way to run multiple operating systems on a single machine. As an example, I primarily use Mac OS X systems because I like having UNIX at my fingertips. However, I use Parallels Desktop to give me quick access to both Windows and Linux. I may have all three operating systems running on my system at any given point in time and my system barely knows the difference.

One area that will be worth keeping a close eye on is the progress of wearables. For the moment, it seems as though development of them has stagnated. This may suggest that most people do not see the immediate utility of these smart watches. While Google Glass has effectively died as a project, Google has suggested that they are not done with the idea. This may mean more wearable computing devices on the head. Other companies are moving into headwear that is capable of computing. This currently includes Microsoft, though it is unclear, if this is primarily about an interface to existing systems or if the device could be used in a more standalone model.

Finally, drones are not going anywhere. They are popular and many of them are cheap. They can be a lot of fun and can also be very useful for a variety of purposes. You can get high quality video and pictures that would otherwise be very difficult to get. Most users will be casual users who just think it is fun to have a remote control flying device with video capabilities. Flying devices are not the only remote control devices that are being developed. They may not get the publicity that the drones are but they may also be worth keeping an eye on. Smaller devices on wheels may also be sources of evidence in some cases. You never can tell where a camera and GPS capability may provide you with something really useful.

EXERCISES

1. Search the Windows registry in a virtual machine guest for drivers associated with the hypervisor you are using.
2. Locate the use of a cloud storage service by searching browser history.
3. Locate the use of software as a service by searching browser history.
4. Locate the transparency information for Google and determine where you would send any legal request.

CHAPTER

13

Reporting

INFORMATION INCLUDED IN THIS CHAPTER:

- Writing Style
- Artifacts
- Reporting Considerations
- Reporting Requirements
- Report Samples
- Testifying

INTRODUCTION

Once you have completed your investigation, no matter what type of investigation it is, you will probably have to generate a report. In other words, you want to convey your findings in a way that can be easily understood. You will probably have acquired a fair amount of data and you will not want to simply hand it all over. One of your tasks as a forensic investigator or incident responder is performing some analysis on the information. What you should end up with is a way for someone who may not easily understand the process or the raw results to understand what you ended up with. This may include documenting your process clearly and certainly should include all of the efforts to make sure that you are working from an exact copy as the original. Your process and how you do the reporting may vary depending on what your objective and role is.

Your organization may have specific needs or requirements when it comes to reporting and there will definitely be a different set of needs if you are doing a corporate investigation as compared with a legal investigation. There are a number of important considerations, some of which will be the same no matter what you are working on. Others will vary from one circumstance to another. There will be some essentials, though, like how you write and convey the information you have. There will also be a set of artifacts you end up with that you need to document in some manner. Different circumstances will require different reports so you should always understand what the requirements are for your report before you begin. Before you start pulling your report together, there are a number of things you should consider, not least of which who you will be presenting to.

Once you have all of these things in mind, we can talk about some report samples. This will encompass different aspects of reports since you may not simply have a single narrative report to write. You may end up having a series of documents that present facts extracted from your efforts. We will look at possible ways of presenting that information since the presentation can be just as important as the actual information. You always want the information you have to present to be clearly understandable. This can mean that it should be something easy to parse visually. You want the person reading the report to know exactly where to locate the information they are looking for as well as being able to understand what that information means. This is where the report format and structure can be important.

WRITING STYLE

It was a dark and stormy night. A classic, courtesy of Snoopy from Peanuts. Not exactly considered good writing, though. The good news here is that you will not be expected to be able to write the great American novel when you are generating your report. This means you will not need to be incredibly expressive or evoke great images when you write. Long, complicated sentences will generally be considered to get in the way of communicating your points. Consider writing short and simple sentences. In fact, when you are writing up a lot of your evidence, you may want to stick with simple, declarative sentences. A declarative sentence is where you make a statement of fact like "I am writing this sentence." That is a very simple declarative sentence that is factually correct as well as being clear and understandable.

This brings up the question of how you are writing, though you probably do not want to write in first person. First person is where you become part of the process, using the word I a lot. You spend your time describing what you did and what you found. While this is accurate and you can easily write short declarative sentences in first person, what happens is that the focus turns to you as the investigator rather than on the evidence where it should be. No matter what the circumstance is, you should always strive to write professional reports and first person is generally not considered to be professional. A professional report will be impartial, conveying information in an impersonal manner. Using a first person approach will place a person into the situation, which makes it harder to present your findings in an impartial manner. Once a person is in the middle, the reader can imagine that person tampering with the evidence or manipulating findings. It is just better overall to take anyone involved completely out of the process when you write up your findings.

As an example, you will probably have to image a hard drive at some point. You certainly could write "I took an image of the source hard drive," but it is better to take yourself out of the situation altogether. A better way of saying that removes the investigator altogether. "The image used to perform the investigation on was created from the source disk using dd, a utility that generates a bit for bit copy." This conveys the method as well as the fact that you are working from a bit for bit copy. You would then go on to make it clear what a bit for bit copy was and how you know that it is identical to the source. Again, this can be easily accomplished without introducing yourself into the process. "A bit for bit copy is identical in every way to the source. This was verified by generating a cryptographic hash from both the source and the copy then comparing them." You could potentially break this up into shorter sentences but it is still clear what was done and hopefully what it means.

One area to be aware of is making sure to provide attribution where appropriate. This commonly will not be necessary. If you are relating your actions and the specific findings, you are responsible for your own output. In some cases, you may need to explain something, though. As an example, earlier there was a reference to cryptographic hashes. It will not be immediately obvious what these are to most people. You will need to explain what it is and why it is used. Using a resource to help you better understand them so you can explain them is something you definitely should do. You want to make sure that you are providing accurate information, after all, and most people will not be able to easily explain these off the top of their head. If you are using a book as your reference source, make sure that you are not copying verbatim from your source unless you are quoting and attributing the book as your source. While this is not likely to get you into trouble if you do not do this, it is really bad form to use someone else's work as though it were your own. Using someone else's words that have been printed somewhere is a violation of copyright. You will not land in prison or anything for making use of those words but it is not very respectful to the author for you to use their work without letting people know that it is your work.

You may actually be expected to write a complete report, particularly if you are working for a business and doing investigation on a corporate incident. In that case, the writing is more important. Rather than a series of basic, factual statements, you will need to provide more narrative and the report should be readable. It will likely be several pages long, depending on the investigation and how much information you have looked at. This is not at all to say that a corporate investigation is more important. Instead, the audience is different and the purpose for the report may be different. We will go over more about the different components of a report later on but it is worth mentioning here that your writing style and the expectations for your writing skill will be different from one situation to another. No matter what your situation, though, you should be sure you are working on your ability to easily convey information. Write clearly and make sure you are saying exactly what you mean to say.

ARTIFACTS

Different situations will, of course, generate a different set of artifacts. No matter what the situation you are reporting on, you will have evidence you have looked at. You want to make sure you have clearly documented all of the evidence you have looked at. This should not only include a list of the evidence but also your chain of custody, a chronology of your investigation and verification evidence that everything you did had no impact on what you were investigating. Also, perhaps most critically, include any legal paperwork like the authorization you were provided that allowed the evidence to be gathered in the first place. This may be a warrant or subpoena but it could also be corporate approval from the relevant management level. You may also simply get consent of the owner. This should be documented. If you are performing a corporate investigation, make sure to include your own version of authorization for your investigation.

It really cannot be overstated that one thing you should always do is make sure you get cryptographic hashes of all of your evidence. It does not take that long and takes very little storage space. It will always allow you, though, to demonstrate that the evidence has not been altered. Both Linux and Mac OS X come with utilities that will generate a cryptographic hash, whether you are doing a Message Digest 5 (MD5) or a Secure Hash Algorithm (SHA-1) hash. On the Windows side, there is nothing that is available within the operating system itself, but there are a number of utilities that will perform cryptographic hashes on Windows. One of them is from the people at Nirsoft, who have a number of other forensics-focused utilities. In Figure 13.1, you can see a number of hashes generated by HashMyFiles, the utility from Nirsoft. You will notice that it will generate an MD5, SHA-1, and a Cyclic Redundancy Check as well as SHA-256 hash. This is SHA hash using 256 bits instead of the 128 bits that is used for a SHA-1 hash. What you cannot see because it is outside of the viewable window to the right, is that it will also generate a hash with larger values, including 385 bits and 512 bits.

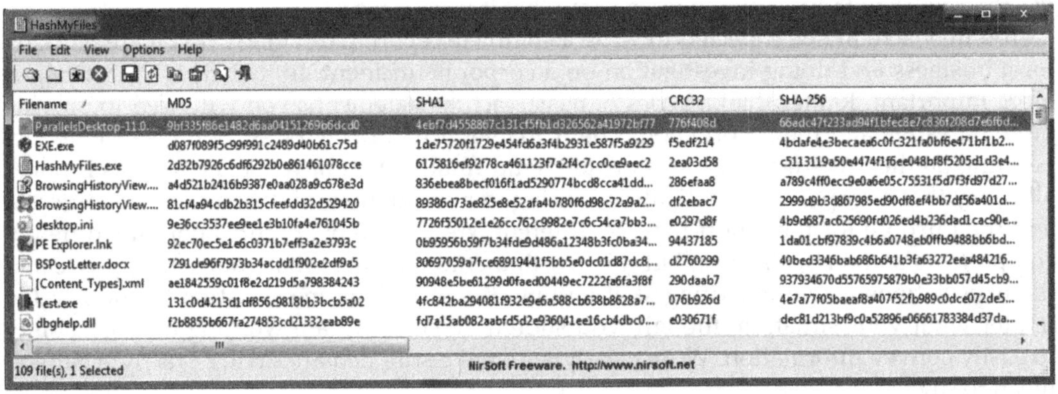

FIGURE 13.1

One thing you will need to generate as you go through your reporting stage of your investigation is a list of all of your evidences. This should include the original source and its disposition as well as any copies you have created. If you have a cell phone, for instance, you should mention the phone including its model number and serial number or international mobile station equipment identifier (IMEI). The same is true no matter what you have acquired for physical evidence. Computer systems including hard drive and any other hardware, should be identified specifically with serial numbers or any other identifying information that may be available. The list of evidence and its disposition is important. Disposition means you need to indicate what happened to it, including any copies of digital media and the associated hash values of the original and the copies. If you were able to get memory captures, you need to make a list of the images you acquired and include hash values of that, though you will not be able to get a hash of the original physical memory. This complete list of all of the evidences will be an important artifact resulting from your investigation.

> You may also need to include photographic evidence as part of your investigation and also the documentation you provide. This may include documenting the location of the evidence you acquire. As you are taking photographs, you should have a way to indicate what case you are taking the photograph for. A quick and easy approach, which makes sure that if you develop or just offload the photos, is to write the case number and evidence number on a piece of paper and include that piece of paper in the photograph you are taking.

One very important artifact, probably regardless of the type of investigation, is the chain of custody. The chain of custody, as mentioned earlier, is the evidence indicating how all of the evidence was handled. If the copy you are working from is stored in a digital locker and you check it out to perform analysis, that act needs to be documented. This is especially true when you are dealing with physical artifacts such as cell phones and disk drives or external drives like USB sticks. The list should clearly indicate when you took possession of the evidence and for what purpose. It should then indicate when you checked it back in. Ideally, so you have a clear indicator of what happened, you would be performing a hash when you check the evidence back in so you clearly indicate that it did not change in your possession. If the evidence has been handled a dozen times, or maybe even less, over the course of the entire investigation and you get to the end of the investigation and check your hash only to discover that it is changed, you have no idea when it changed.

Once you have a piece of evidence that has been compromised and you do not know when it was compromised, your investigation becomes suspect because you have no idea where it changed. A cryptographic hash itself also cannot tell you how it changed. A single bit may have become unreadable and that will throw off an entire hash value. Any change at all, even by a single bit, will create a completely different hash value. This new hash value tells you nothing at all except that there has been a change and it is no longer bit for bit identical.

If you provide a hash value at every step, you can know where it changed and then perform an investigation to determine why. It will also allow you to go back and create a new copy to work from. It cannot be overstated that if you end up with a mismatched hash value at the end but you cannot determine where it happened, your entire investigation will become suspect. You should, of course, never have a mismatch in hash values anywhere along the line but checking every step along the path will make sure that your entire investigation is not corrupted but also that the last investigatory step has not been corrupted. It guarantees that you can show a very clear chain of custody that has not corrupted the evidence at all. This should actually be included in your report.

> You start with a piece of evidence. Your chain of custody demonstrates that the evidence has always been in the control of someone known for purposes that are known. The hash value you take allows you to demonstrate that the evidence you end up with is unaltered and authentic. Exactly as it was provided to you to begin with.

A chronology of investigation will also be very useful even if it may not always be essential. It is better to have a document you do not need than to discover down the road that you really did need something documented and you did not create it. This chronology will be a list of all of the steps you took during the course of the investigation. Having this chronology will allow you to recreate the steps if it comes to need to present your findings. This may be at a trial or it may be to an after action review board or it may be an executive committee. Keeping a list of all of your actions will store your memory for you so you are not relying on it entirely when it is really important.

You may also keep a list of actual artifacts, by which I mean the actual pieces of digital evidence. This may be the master file table, it may be the Windows registry, it may be a collection of plists or Sqlite databases. In addition to the actual list of artifacts, you should maintain a collection of the raw data. Again, you may not actually include all of this in the report you generate but it should be available as necessary to provide substantiation if you are ever questioned about your findings. This raw data may be difficult to keep track of easily. Of course, if you had access to a commercial tool, it can store case notes as well as all of the evidence in one convenient location. Not all investigators will have the budget for these sort of tools, and there may be some situations where you do not have access to these sort of tools so getting into the habit of keeping track of them is not really a bad idea. If you have two separate locations where you are storing them, you can always be sure you have the evidence you need.

REPORTING REQUIREMENTS

Your situation is going to be what drives your report. Always keep in mind what your audience is and what the reason for writing your report is. This will give you a good understanding of what the requirements for your report are. Writing a report for an executive board after a security breach at your company will follow a completely different set of requirements than a report generated for someone being investigated for storing and viewing child pornography on their laptop. The audience is completely different, of course. One report will likely get far more use than the other and there will likely be more narrative in the breach investigation report than in the child pornography case. This is not to say that one is more important than the other but just that the scope and depth of the breach investigation is likely to be considerably different from the child pornography case.

Having said all that, it is good to get the requirements clear before you start to write the report. You will need to understand who your audience is for the final report. Are you expected to convey analysis of the evidence you find or are you supposed to simply provide the specific raw data and allow the reader to draw their own conclusions? Is this for a legal case that will eventually end up in court? If so, will you be the one doing the testifying at trial? If you are not going to be testifying, adding as much detail as you can to assist the person answering to the report will be better for the case being presented.

Keep in mind that your report should always be unbiased. You are not investigating to prove a theory. You are investigating to gather evidence related to the case. This means that when you write your report, you should include all evidence that is related to the case, not simply evidence supporting a particular theory. In other words, you do not provide evidence that proves that Scott Peterson killed his wife, as one example. You provide all relevant evidence even if some of those artifacts may suggest that he did not.

If you are writing this in a business situation, having an executive summary will be helpful. There will be many people who are interested in your findings who may not have the time to read the entire report. There will also be people who may not be able to understand the technical aspects of your findings so you will have to provide a short summary highlighting the important information. This should always include anything that is actionable. If you have recommendations that result from your investigation, which would be the case from a breach or malware investigation, these need to be put into the executive summary. It is called an executive summary because the expectation is that executives are only going to read the one or two-page executive summary and not read the entire report. Providing recommendations there means they understand what needs to happen so they are aware. If it is not something they need to do themselves, then at least they are aware of what they may need to follow up on with others. Making your executive summary short will help to ensure that it gets read. This is not to sound cynical but the longer it is, the more you risk someone not reading the whole thing. Include critical information with enough substance so someone reading just the executive summary will understand at a high level what happened and what needs to be done to prevent it happening again.

Once you understand the requirements as dictated by the situation, you can get down to writing the report. The requirements may not be sufficient, though. There may also be other ideas to take into consideration as you are drafting your report.

REPORTING CONSIDERATIONS

The first thing to mention when it comes to reporting considerations is the voice that you use. This is all about tone and style. This is generally not where you want to start to develop a penchant for overly stylish or flowery language. Short and simple will generally be the best approach. This ensures that it is not only readable but clearly understandable. There will likely not be a lot of need for a lot of adjectives or adverbs as you write. Just simple, to the point language will quickly and clearly convey what you need to convey. Part of this is also the voice you use. As discussed previously, it is probably best to stay away from first person. It is too easy for the language to get fatiguing if you are writing in first person. I took the disk drive out of the machine. I placed it into an external case then I connected the case to my acquisition machine. I was careful to use a write blocker. There are simply too many I's in those sentences and it will start to wear on the reader.

It is not just adjectives that you should consider avoiding. You should absolutely avoid vagaries. Do not say a lot, large, many, excessive or anything else that is not specific. Be very specific. Do not say a large hard drive. Say a 1 terabyte hard drive. Do not say a lot of images were found. Say 1243 images were located on the hard drive. Always be precise and specific.

In addition, it will start to look as though you are the focus of the investigation, which should never be the case. Take yourself out of the equation as much as possible and just talk about the data. What data did you find? What does it mean, if that is relevant to the requirements you have? Using I in your reports is also generally not considered to be highly professional so even if you are less worried about taking the emphasis off the evidence, which may be the case in a corporate report, it still may be a turn off to use I in a report you are expected to hand in to executive management. Save the "I" for the status reports to your management where it is far more apropos.

We have talked about audience previously and that will always be a consideration as you write your report. If this is for a trial, remember that you may be presenting evidence to people with a variety of backgrounds and technical understanding. Using clear, nontechnical language so it can be easily understood will always help your case. Try to explain your findings in a way that someone not familiar with all the technical aspects of the investigation can understand.

However, if you are writing for an audience that may include technical people, you may want to put in a section on methodology so you can explain the tools you used and the methods you used to acquire and investigate. This will not only give the technical people something to sink their teeth into but it will also clearly demonstrate your process. This will, of course, potentially open you up to criticism if you are using a process or tools that may differ from those used by others. This may be especially true if you are using offbeat tools or processes. This is, though, an opportunity to learn if someone else has a different way of performing the investigation with a different set of tools. Getting feedback from professional colleagues should always be a good thing since we can all learn from one another. Having your peers review your report when it is done can also be a way to get another set of eyes on your findings in case you overlooked something or in case you found something you forgot to include in the report. A second set of eyes is a very good idea.

An important part of any investigation that we have not spent a lot of time talking about is that it must follow a process. Locating the evidence must be done using methods that are repeatable so anyone can locate the evidence. This repeatable, understandable approach is part of the scientific method that we use to make sure we can prove the truth of our findings. This is exactly the reason why the Frye and Daubert cases have become standards of evidence. If you are using unusual methods, clearly document them. This should include all steps and any processes you used so your results can be repeated. Without this, the results cannot be relied on and you end up with evidence that cannot be trusted.

When it comes to corporate investigations, you may find that you want to create an entirely separate document with the executive summary. This may also provide a way for the company to give information to outside parties without conveying the dirty details of what happened. As a result, you may need to think about sanitizing the executive summary so as not to give away corporate secrets or anything that may leak out and provide internal information to another potential attacker. If you provide the executive summary in a separate document, it should also be quite a bit shorter than the full document, which makes it easier to pass around to those who need to read it.

The need to present information to third parties is a significant consideration in corporate investigations. You may end up with two reports. One for internal consumption that can include all of the relevant details and one that can be passed around to partners, vendors or even the media as necessary. This report should have all of the internal details removed but still provide enough detail that they can be assured you got to the bottom of it. This will be particularly important to vendors and other third parties who may be worried about doing business with you going forward if it is not clear that you handled the incident appropriately.

REPORT SAMPLE FORMATS

Of course, you will have your own set of requirements based on your own situation but the following are some report structures that may work well for you. The first is the set of headers that you may use in a report for a corporate investigation. You may need to vary this depending on what you are looking to convey.

Executive Summary
Background (or Overview)
Methodology
Findings
Analysis
Conclusion
Appendices

The Executive Summary is where you provide a brief one or two-page overview for the executives or anyone who has less interest in all of the specifics. This should include any relevant information including any action items you want executives to know about.

The Background or Overview is where you provide a summary of what happened and what led to the investigation to begin with. You need to include your search authority here. This may be consent or a legal document. Include what it is and how it was obtained. This section should provide context for the remainder of the report. Include as much detail here as necessary to completely set the stage for your investigation and analysis.

The Methodology section is where you can provide an overview of what tools you used, how you used them, any acquisition details, and anything about handling evidence that is relevant to the investigation. You may have a better idea of how best to handle this section, depending on your organization. Knowing who your audience is, you may want to include more or less information here on the technical side. Of course, you may only want to provide a very high level overview of what you did. Again, this will be very dependent on your organization and audience.

Findings is where you would present the evidence you have. Just the evidence. Where you looked and what you found there. This may include your chronology just so it is clear what happened and when it happened. Avoid doing any analysis here since that is a separate section. For the moment, let the evidence you have stand on its own, entirely unadorned.

Analysis is where you apply your intelligence and expertise to what you found. Provide a narrative here that tries to explain the order of events. This will be especially important in a breach investigation as you will need to track back the breach to its source and it may take a number of systems to step back through to do this. Include how you believe the breach occurred in each case and how you know that.

Finally, you will get to the conclusion and provide a quick summary of what was covered. Again, if there are action items, cover them here. If you want to present large quantities of evidence that you only suggested in the Findings section, put them into the appendices.

If you are performing a law enforcement investigation, you will probably present a very different report than the one referenced earlier. Just as an example of some sections, you may consider in your report for a law enforcement organization, the following headings will sketch a structure for a report:

- Case Details
- Case Overview
- Chain of Custody
- Acquisition Details
- Analysis/Technical Details
- Files of Interest
- Results/Conclusion

The Case Details is where you identify the case by name and case number as well as identify yourself with your name and the agency or organization you are with. You may consider including your contact information and also the subject of the investigation if that is not identified in the case name.

In the Case Overview, provide the details of the case. This should include anything related to any warrant that was executed. If you obtained consent and did not require legal documents like a warrant or subpoena to obtain the evidence, include the details of that. Locations of evidence and the evidence that was included in the case. This should clearly set out what it is, what you are looking for, and why. What you are looking for and why is the scope of your investigation. You have to be careful to not exceed your scope as you investigate and your report must show that you did not exceed your scope. This will guide the reader as they go through the rest of the report.

The Chain of Custody speaks for itself. Include the entire chain of custody here for the evidence you have. If it is lengthy and includes many pieces of evidence, you may refer to an appendix that would contain all of the pages if it ends up being a large number of pages. This may be the case if it is a large investigation including a significant number of pieces of evidence.

In the Acquisition Details, clearly describe how you acquired the evidence. This should include any hardware used as well as the method you used to acquire the evidence. If you used external drive enclosures and write blockers, include that here. What tools did you use to get the evidence? Was it a commercial tool like FTK Imager or was it simply a Linux boot disk and dd? Include all of these details in this section.

The Analysis/Technical Details section is where you provide your analysis of what you found and how you found it. Include any narrative that may be available that can be determined from a timeline you have established.

Files of Interest should include any files you may have found. This may include the Internet history files or any documents that were located. Anything that relates to the case should be highlighted here. This should correlate very tightly with the analysis section. You should be referring to the files of interest in your analysis.

The Conclusion is self-explanatory again. Wrap up your investigation with a short summary of what you did and what you found.

Again, these are just samples. You can use them if it is helpful to you and, of course, tailor them to your specific needs based on what you have for requirements.

CONCLUSIONS

While the investigation is going to be very time consuming, you might argue that the report is the most important part because it is where you convey all of your findings. This is where you get to present everything related to the investigation in a very clear and understandable fashion. As a result, your tone and writing style is very important. This may take some time for you to fully develop. The more writing you do, the easier it will get to understand how best to convey your findings. No matter what your circumstances are, keeping it simple will generally be better. It helps to ensure that your readers will know exactly what you are saying without needing to interpret and potentially get it wrong or misunderstand.

There is no one size fits all approach to reporting, of course, even considering the potential differences in why you are performing an investigation. Different law enforcement agencies may use different reporting requirements and corporate investigations will often have requirements that may vary from situation to situation. Understanding your requirements and your audience before you begin will really help you find the right approach to draft your report and make sure that the evidence you have found is heard so it can be acted on accordingly. In the end, that is always the most important thing – making sure that what you found is understood clearly so the right action can be taken based on those findings.

Subject Index

E

J

K

L

X

Y

Z

Printed in the United States
By Bookmasters